The Epic Film in World Culture

From Ridley Scott's *Gladiator* to John Woo's *Red Cliff*, from Ang Lee's *Crouching Tiger, Hidden Dragon* to Paul Thomas Anderson's *There Will Be Blood*, the epic has reemerged as a major form in contemporary cinema. *The Epic Film in World Culture* explores new critical approaches to contemporary as well as older epic films, drawing on ideas from cultural studies, historiography, classics, and film studies. Many of the fifteen original essays in the volume are animated by the central paradox of the epic genre, the contradiction between the traditional messages embedded within epic form—the birth of a nation, the emergence of a people, the fulfillment of a heroic destiny—and the long history of the epic film as an international, global narrative apparatus not bound by nation or ethnicity. Truly international in scope, the contributors focus on issues including spectacle, imagined community, national identity, family melodrama, and masculinity that are central to epics from Hong Kong to Hollywood and beyond.

Robert Burgoyne is Professor and Chair of Film Studies at the University of St Andrews. His recent publications include *Film Nation: Hollywood Looks at U.S. History*, revised and expanded edition (2010) and *The Hollywood Historical Film* (2008).

The Epic Film in World Culture

EDITED BY

ROBERT BURGOYNE

Routledge
Taylor & Francis Group

NEW YORK AND LONDON

First published 2011
by Routledge
270 Madison Avenue, New York, NY 10016

Simultaneously published in the UK
by Routledge
2 Park Square, Milton Park, Abingdon OX14 4RN

Routledge is an imprint of the Taylor & Francis Group, an informa business

Typeset in Spectrum MT by Glyph International Ltd.
Printed and bound in the United States of America on acid-free paper by Edwards Brothers, Inc.

Library of Congress Cataloging-in-Publication Data
The epic film in world culture / edited by Robert Burgoyne.
    p. cm. – (AFI film readers)
Includes bibliographical references and index.
1. Epic films–History and criticism. 2. History in motion pictures. I. Burgoyne, Robert, 1949- II. Series.
PN1995.9.E79E76 2010
791.43'658–dc22

ISBN 13: 978-0-415-99017-2 (hbk)
ISBN 13: 978-0-415-99018-9 (pbk)
ISBN 13: 978-0-203-92747-2 (ebk)

This book is dedicated to the memory of my father-in-law, Eli Shaban; geographer, historian, and friend

contents

contents

viii

illustrations

figures

tables

boxes

acknowledgments

Like the genre itself, *The Epic Film in World Culture* originates from a wide range of interests and encompasses an array of critical motives, shifting shape as it moves into uncharted terrain and emerging, at the end, as an expression of something that could not have been predicted at the outset. The critical idea I set forth as the organizing purpose of this volume has led to a surprising and gratifying panorama of approaches, and a more compelling argument for the epic as a cross-cultural popular form than I could have imagined. The diversity of contributors to this volume mirrors the global reach of the genre. The authors come from six different continents, and the critical inflections they bring to the project have affirmed my sense that the epic is a form that is now in the forefront of new developments in world cinema. In gathering and editing these essays, I was continually surprised by the way such different voices could come together in an enterprise of ambitious scope. The wandering poets who crafted the first epic songs knew the value of adding different cultures and peoples to the stories they told, and in editing this volume I have rediscovered the value and the unpredictable pleasures of drawing on friends and colleagues from different disciplines and critical orientations.

My heartfelt thanks go to my friends and series editors, Charles Wolfe and Edward Branigan, who received my initial ideas for this volume with enthusiasm, and who encouraged and supported me in a way that was exceptionally generous. Their insights and immediate, helpful advice braced my spirits exactly when needed, and I thank them for their insight. I also wish to thank Matthew Byrnie, film and media editor at Routledge, for his keen appreciation of this project and his confidence in me. For early encouragement and opportunities to present this work, I thank Professor Rita Terazhina Schmidt of the Federal University of Rio Grande do Sul; Professor Anelise Reich Courseuil of the Federal University of Santa Catarina; and Professor Sandra Goulart Almeida of the Federal University of Minas Gerais. I also wish to thank Walter Edwards and the Humanities Center of Wayne State University for research support and an opportunity to read an early version of the essay on *Gladiator* published here. For the final and delightful opportunity to convey my ideas to a faculty steeped in transnational theory and criticism, I thank Professor Dina Iordanova, founding chair of the Department of Film Studies at the University of St Andrews. For a final proofreading, and for her good judgment and excellent taste, I thank my friend Maura Gatowski. I wish to thank my son, Alexander Burgoyne, for his splendid work on the images that adorn this volume, and that could not have been produced without him. Finally, I wish to thank Tova Shaban, and my son Brian Burgoyne for inspiration beyond what they could know.

An earlier version of Chapter 4 by Robert Burgoyne was published as "Techno-Euphoria and the World Improving Dream: *Gladiator*" in *Ilha do Desterro*, no. 51 (spring 2007); a different, earlier version was published in my book *The Hollywood Historical Film* (Malden, Mass. and London: Wiley-Blackwell, 2008) under the chapter title, "The Epic Film." An earlier version of Chapter 14 by Alison Griffiths was published as "The Revered Gaze: The Medieval Imaginary of Mel Gibson's *The Passion of the Christ,*" in *Cinema Journal* Vol. 47, No. 4 (winter 2006–07). Sections that discuss the "revered gaze" (but not Mel Gibson's *The Passion of the Christ*) also appear in her book *Shivers Down Your Spine: Cinema, Museums, and the Immersive View* (New York: Columbia University Press, 2008). Both are reproduced with permission from the publishers. Thanks to Brigham Young University for permission to use two images in Chapter 10 by Philip Wagner.

introduction

robert burgoyne

With the recent release of several spectacular films set in the ancient and medieval past, the epic has once again become a major form in contemporary cinema, providing a striking example of the resiliency of genre forms, their ability both to recall past usages and respond to the present in a new way. As Mikhail Bakhtin writes, genres serve as "organs of memory" for particular cultures; they both "remember the past and make their resources available to the present."[1] The resurgence of the epic genre in the contemporary period, a period marked by heightened and conflicting appeals to national, ethnic, and religious belonging, presents a particularly compelling subject for critical analysis and invites a broad reconsideration of the genre from a variety of perspectives. Among several questions considered here is the link between the epic and the imagined community of nation and whether this link remains the defining feature of the epic film. Traditionally framed as an expression of national emergence and national consciousness, and strongly associated with the category of national cinemas, the contemporary epic, with its complex array of nested and overlapping production and distribution arrangements, has become the very exemplar of transnational and global modes of film production and reception. The tension between the evolving global context of film production and reception and the particular provenance of the epic as an expression of national mythology and aspirations creates what Bakhtin calls a double voice, a new social accent, which changes our understanding of epics produced in the present as well as our perception of epic films from the past.

The Epic Film in World Culture explores new critical approaches to contemporary as well as older epic films, drawing on ideas from cultural studies, historiography, classics, and film studies. Many of the essays in the volume are animated by the central paradox of the epic genre, the contradiction between the traditional messages embedded within epic form—the birth of a nation, the emergence of a people, the fulfillment of a heroic destiny—and the long history of the epic film as an international, global narrative apparatus not bound by nation or ethnicity. From its earliest incarnation, the epic film traversed national boundaries, moving among different cultures, acquiring new identities and regional inflections as it crossed national and hemispheric boundaries. The influence of the epic form on the early development of international cinema culture is pervasive, extending from the Italian spectacle films *Quo Vadis?* (1912) and *Cabiria* (1914) to the American films *The Birth of a Nation* (1915) and *Intolerance* (1916), to the Afrikaaner epic *Winning a Continent* (1916) and the collectivist Soviet paeans *Battleship Potemkin* (1925) and *October* (1928). Like a holograph that displays one face from a certain angle and a completely different image from another, the genre appears to have a dual identity. Long defined as a nationcentric form, epic films have achieved extraordinary international visibility and success. As Cecil B. DeMille said in 1936:

> As a producer of spectacular films, I never lose sight of the fact that the whole world is my canvas—and that millions of people outside the United States await each new DeMille film, knowing that it was not made for the American public alone, as so many films are, but for the entertainment of the entire world. In some cases, the earnings of my pictures abroad are double what they are in America.[2]

Early international audiences evidently read these films as something other than nationalist projects. Far removed from the nation of origin and certainly unconcerned with the nationcentric messages embedded in the form, audiences were drawn to epic films, I argue, for the unprecedented experience of the cinema itself that these films provide. The features that define the epic film—tactility and immersion, spectacle and eroticism, monumentality and sensuality—suggest that the sensory excitement of the medium itself played a role in their success. Epic films, transcending cultural differences, delivered an experience of modernity in a form that could not be duplicated in other genres of the emergent mass media.

Contemporary epic films, with their multinational casts and crews, international production and distribution arrangements, global circulation and extended second lives in DVD sales and global internet discussion groups urge a new assessment of the genre. The contemporary epic represents, in its production circumstances, narrative forms, and subject matter, a transnational orientation and an appeal to cross-cultural structures of belonging and identification. This theme, visible in contemporary films such as *Gladiator* (2000), *300* (2007), and *Hero* (2002), encourages us to look at epics differently, to read them against the grain, to consider them in terms of a postnational project focusing on broad stories of affiliation and community across ethnic, religious, and geographic boundaries.

part one: spectacle

The Epic Film in World Culture is divided into five main parts. The first part focuses on spectacle—the signature trait of the epic genre and its most visible link to the earliest expressions of the form. Epic spectacle condenses the signs of the past in a singularly emphatic way, evoking both the history of the genre as well as what Deleuze calls the "immense synsigns" of past civilizations, the bazaars and palaces of Egypt, the temples and columned cities of Ancient Greece, the legions and senate of Rome—simultaneously registering as an assertion of cinematic ambition as well as a statement of cultural affinity.[3] In the epic film, the great civilizations of the past "communicate via the peaks," as Deleuze writes.[4] A genre noted for its flamboyant mise-en-scène, monumental sets, and mass choreography, the epic's expansive visual style has been interpreted in both positive and negative ways. Roland Barthes, moved and impressed by the immersive power of widescreen cinema, described the experience of epic films as akin to "standing on the balcony of history," while Vivian Sobchack has endorsed the epic film for its carnal engagement with the past, its dilation of time and space to create a sense of "eventfulness" that provides audiences with a somatic experience of being in history.[5]

More frequently, however, epic spectacle has been considered an emblem of political bad faith and cultural vulgarity, a vertiginous assault on the senses that produces a kind of adrenalized stasis in the narrative that compels either laughter or consent. Gilberto Perez, in an otherwise considered take on epic style, writes that "There is epic cinema, for example, epic not in the sense of cast of thousands—which as a rule means neither narrative nor drama but sheer spectacle."[6] More pointedly, epic spectacle has often been seen as promoting the causes of nationalism. Whether the spectacle of a Roman triumph, for example, is meant as an object-lesson in the decadent excesses of a corrupt civilization or as an anticipatory promise of an emergent world germinating within the old, films such as *Ben-Hur* (1959) and *The Sign of the Cross* (1932) have often been read as explicitly political gestures and in some cases have been grafted into overtly nationalist messages. And with the advent of CGI (computer-generated imagery), digitally enhanced or created spectacle sequences have become an even more significant aspect of epic cinema. *Gladiator*, for example, with its computer-enhanced sets of the Colosseum and the Roman Forum, introduced to a new audience the surge and splendor of epic form familiar from older films such as *Cleopatra* (1963) and *The Ten Commandments* (1956). It also allowed an extended and explicit quotation of Leni Riefenstahl's *Triumph of the Will* (1935), a reference that some writers read as auto-critique and others as a suggestive analogy.[7] As Rob Wilson argues, the spectacular special effects of recent epic films can be equated with displays of globalizing technological prowess. *Gladiator*, he writes, may signify a new global imperialism, creating, partly through special effects, a "hegemonic technology of sublime spectacle," the "techno-euphoric reign of aestheticized spectacles of empire."[8]

Several essays in this volume consider the design-intensive form of the epic as one of its central features, exploring the range of messages communicated by spectacle sequences in both older and more contemporary epic films. Essays on *300, Gladiator, Alexander* (2004), *Hero,* and others included in this part offer a nuanced reading of epic spectacle focusing on contemporary technological advances, on historical antecedents in pageantry, painting, and architecture, and on the thematic and symbolic messages embodied in scenes of spectacle. Whether considered in terms of aesthetic imagination and advanced visual technique, as a sensory assault designed to produce an extreme emotional response, or as a colonizing gesture aimed at creating a kind of techno-euphoria in its audiences, the contemporary epic, as demonstrated in this volume, conveys a range of messages that are in many ways synthesized in their most spectacular, virtuosic sequences.

The combination of ancient legend and advanced computer technology in Zack Snyder's *300* is the subject of Monica S. Cyrino's essay, "'This Is Sparta!' The Reinvention of the Epic in Zack Snyder's *300*." Cyrino explores one of the enduring and universal themes of the epic—the concept of freedom—a theme that is usually associated with the advent of a new order or the dawning of an epoch, the point when the "ferments of decadence" give way to the "germs of new life."[9] In films such as *Spartacus* (1960), *Gladiator,* and *Braveheart* (1995), freedom is something to be realized in the future, a utopian fulfillment or anticipation of the days that change the world. In *300*, however, the Spartan order is defined as the already-existing exemplar of freedom in the ancient world, both universal in its appeal and historically specific to Ancient Spartan identity. Cyrino moves among several historical sources in her analysis of the film and brings these sources into dialogue with the imagery of the graphic novel by Frank Miller on which the film is based. Characterizing the film as one that is especially rich in intertextual allusions, including imagery found on heroic friezes and in Greek ceramic pottery, Cyrino connects the outstanding digital cinematography of the film to the history of epic stylization, a form that has long been characterized by heroic idealization. The film's extraordinary international success, she maintains, is partly due to its contemporary style, its embrace of digital effects to amplify the dramatic intensity of the battle of Thermopylae. But it is also due to the explicit focus on the theme of freedom, a theme that resonates with current political aspirations throughout the world and that is both specific to Spartan identity and a completely mobile concept that resonates in many different national settings. Reading the film against a widespread critical assumption that the work emblematizes Bush-era American politics, with its martial ethos and assumed moral authority, Cyrino defines the ways in which *300* spans two affective worlds, conveying a historically accurate dramatization of Spartan law while evoking contemporary struggles for independence, communicated through the heroic self-sacrifice of Leonidas, the leader of the Spartans.

Kirsten Thompson, in "'Philip Never Saw Babylon:' 360-Degree Vision and the Historical Epic in the Digital Era" provides a detailed analysis of the digital techniques employed in current epic films. The sensory impact of "sights never before seen" is a compelling feature of epic films, part of its generic signature and a major element of the way it creates a sense of historical eventfulness. The potent association of epic with spectacle, which reaches back to the earliest films of the genre, such as *Cabiria* and *Quo Vadis,* led to its near-extinction in the early 1960s as the expense of constructing the mammoth sets and mass choreography of armies, navies, and teeming populations finally made the epic too costly to produce. Now, however, with the rise of digital-imaging techniques such as crowd-replication software, digital set extensions, 3D animation, and performance capture, epic films released in recent years have surpassed even the most impressive visual achievements of earlier films. Works such as *300, Troy* (2004), and *Alexander* have expanded the visual vocabulary of the epic in dazzling ways. Thompson provides a thorough analysis of the range of digital techniques used in these films, tracking advances in visual stylization and drawing out some of the implications of digital imaging for film production. For example, films are now produced on a twenty-four-hour cycle, with digital compositing taking place in one part of the world and live shooting in another. Shots are "built" and composed on a daily basis from images generated in several different locations and matted together. The global spread of the most sophisticated visual-effects studios has created a genuinely international community of artists and technicians. Thompson's careful, detailed breakdown of the many digital techniques used in epic films such as *Alexander* provides a helpful index of the state of the art in digital imaging, vividly illustrated by her detailed analysis of particular scenes from several important films.

Leon Hunt, in "Heroic Chivalry, Heroic Sacrifice: 'Martial Arthouse' as Epic Cinema," details the visual sumptuousness and overall tone of glamour and prestige that has elevated the Chinese martial-arts film from popular genre production to international success in recent years. With extravagant productions drawing on the talents and financial resources of several nations, films such as *House of Flying Daggers* (2004)*, Hero,* and *Crouching Tiger, Hidden Dragon* (2000) have drawn international acclaim. Departing from the usual comparisons to the western and the musical, Leon Hunt argues that "martial arthouse" is more closely tied to the emotion-laden dramaturgy of epic form, with its thematic underpinnings of sacrifice, the conflict between private passion and the demands of a higher code, and the rewriting of historical events distanced in time to suggest the concerns of the present. The complex mediation of history, myth, and the politics of the present in the case of epic films from mainland China sometimes results in competing interpretations of key historical events, as evidenced in the films *Hero* and *The Emperor and the Assassin* (1998), and in competing interpretations of the way these films engage with the contemporary political world. Further, the emergence of the female epic figure in the characters played by Ziyi Zhang, who Hunt compares to the male star Jet Li, create a hybrid emblem of freedom and sexual desire co-present in a character who seems to express Ernest Bloch's utopian "wished for transformation of the world."[10]

In "Bare Life and Sovereignty in *Gladiator,*" I explore the potential of the epic genre as a form of transnational cinema and reconsider its traditional role as a vehicle of national ideology and aspirations. I suggest that the contemporary historical epic conveys a sense of double-voicing by adapting epic themes usually associated with national narratives to collectivities that are not framed by nation. Reading the epic alongside the work of Giorgio Agamben, I draw particular attention to the ways that the contemporary epic foregrounds the potential of "bare life" as a form of historical agency, emphasizing the emergence of the multitude and the mongrel community. I also consider the particular formal characteristics of the epic film—its design-intensive mise-en-scène, its use of spectacle and its style of sensory expansiveness—as producing an affective and emotional relation to the historical past, creating a fullness of engagement and amplitude of consciousness. Drawing on the work of Ernest Bloch, a Frankfurt School theorist who writes on the utopian potential of mass cultural forms, I suggest that the epic film provides a sense of anticipatory consciousness, articulated precisely through its use of spectacle, its climaxes of color, and its panoramic camera work.

part two: center and periphery

The second part of this book considers epic cinema in terms of the relation between center and periphery. Designed for a broad international audience, epic films typically draw a significant portion of their revenue from distribution outside the traditional centers of market dominance, that is, from distribution and release outside the USA, or from outside Hong Kong. Several recent films have garnered a world audience that in many cases far eclipses the audience from the domestic box office. Enormously popular around the world, films such as *Troy, The Passion of the Christ* (2004), and *Hero* have become global cultural phenomena that reach well beyond any national or specific cultural framework. The contemporary epic brings together a global talent community on the production side with an international audience on the exhibition and reception side. In contrast to the conventional understanding of the epic as a vehicle of national prestige and a form that provides what Jacques Rancière called "the legend of the formation of the code," the epic film today evokes a different kind of imagined community, a sense of collective affiliation and powerful emotion once connected to homeland and heritage, but now largely untethered from ethnic community and national context.[11]

The powerful yet amorphous sense of collective identification that characterizes the audience response to films such as *Gladiator, 300,* and *Troy,* to mention only the most familiar cases, seems to me to be something new and to speak to a nonspecific or perhaps inchoate sense of collective desire that exists outside the bounds of nation, ethnicity, or religion. Grant Farred has given a name to this cross-cultural sense of mongrel identity and will, an emerging population of social actors he calls the "politizen," composed mainly of the marginalized youth of industrialized nations, "the foreigner among citizens," neither members "of the subaltern or the mob."[12] Perhaps the global resurgence of contemporary epic films—works that deal directly with nomadic and mongrel communities, the refugee, the slave, and the rebel, can be read as allegories of current political discontent.

Dina Iordanova, in "'Rise of the Rest:' Globalizing Epic Cinema," considers the international box-office success of films such as *Troy, Crouching Tiger, Hidden Dragon, Hero, 300,* and, to a lesser extent, *Alexander* and *House of Flying Daggers,* as evidence of a striking shift in the way the film market is presently conceived and valued. Rather than domestic earnings accounting for the major portion of revenues, many films now earn their principal profits from the international marketplace, a shift that has led to a significant rise in international coproductions, innovative distribution arrangements, and a much more acute sense of the global audience among film producers. The Asian film industry, in particular, has benefited from this increased exposure and, with its lower cost of production, has been able to compete on an equal footing with many Hollywood films. Iordanova provides an assessment by comparing the costs, domestic versus international profits, and total box-office receipts of several films to empirically demonstrate the rising stature of Asian cinema, in particular the cinemas of China and Hong Kong. With the increased significance of international markets, which are now the largest source of revenue for many films and production companies, certain film genres have attained a high degree of prominence and prestige. Iordanova argues that the "rise of the rest" in the context of the epic has led to a much greater awareness among filmmakers and audiences of the tastes, values, and interests of the global filmgoing community. However, a deeper understanding of non-Western cultures has not followed on the popularity of these films, and epic films from Thailand, India, and Kazakhstan, which display most of the ingredients of successful epic films, remain beneath the radar of Western audiences. The contradiction between the international taste for the sumptuousness of Asian epic cinema and the lack of interest in wider, more intellectually informed understandings of Asian cultures appears to limit the humanistic and political value of the globalizing movement of epic cinema.

In "Sign of the Times: The Semiotics of Time and Event in Sirk's *Sign of the Pagan*," Bettina Bildhauer considers the little-known but highly accomplished work of Douglas Sirk in the epic genre, a director best known for his melodramas of the 1950s. *Sign of the Pagan* (1954) exhibits all of the visual style, the intricate social architecture, and the signifying richness of gesture and landscape that are so prominent in his more celebrated works. Focusing on the semiotics of time in *Sign of the Pagan*, Bildhauer delineates the different concepts of temporality that structure the actions of the Roman centurion Marcian and the Barbarian king Attila as he prepares to conquer Rome. Contrasting the linear, teleological concepts of purpose and consequence that guide Marcian to the sense of temporal simultaneity that drives Attila, Bildhauer shows how temporal signs are embedded in landscape, in camera movement, in the physical movements and trajectories of the characters, and in the scenic design. Here, Roman maps are set against Barbarian mystical portents, Roman writing against Attila's gestural authority. The film, in Bildhauer's reading, communicates a dense chronotopic understanding of the saturation and abundance of time in epic form.

Tom Conley, in "*The Fall of the Roman Empire:* On Space and Allegory," describes the paradoxical temporality of the epic—its abundance of time and eventfulness combined with the imminence of a world approaching its end—by considering the maps of empire that frequently appear in epic films. Reading *The Fall of the Roman Empire* (1964) as a model of what Christian Metz calls the "mobile geography of the film," Conley analyzes the constellation of messages produced in the scene just prior to the death of Marcus Aurelius, a scene that folds together the ailing body of the emperor, the vellum map representing the empire itself, and the words Marcus Aurelius speaks, "Time is short." Understood as an emblem of the simultaneous historical compression and temporal expansiveness of epic form, the utterance conflates the failing body of the emperor, the amount of time the empire will endure, and the foreshortened time of allegorical representation.

Conley reads the "Fall" of the film's title as an allegorical reference to the contemporary moment of the film's creation, its situation at the historical precipice of the Vietnam War. Arguing that allegory is consistently evoked in epic films—and is especially evident in *The Fall of the Roman Empire*—he urges a reading of the epic as a history of the past that engages what cannot be said directly in the here and now. In *The Fall of the Roman Empire,* the film "becomes a matter of meshing historical speeds," using diegetic temporality to join together distant historical periods. The geography evoked by Marcus Aurelius on his last campaign, a geography dominated by the peripheral outposts of empire, comes to redefine and overtake the center, a perspective that will soon be rehearsed in the American experience of Vietnam.

Mark Jancovich, in "'An Italianmade Spectacle Film Dubbed in English:' Cultural Distinctions, National Cinema and the Critical Reception of the Postwar Historical Epic," explores the critical reception of Hollywood epic films produced during the 1950s and the remarkably ambivalent response of American critics toward "foreign" epic productions of the same period. The Hollywood epic film in the 1950s was both celebrated and vilified for its scale, its sumptuousness, and its sacrifice of historical accuracy for dramatic effects. No critic was more troubled by the success of the epic in this period than the writer Dwight Macdonald, who engaged in a long-lasting polemic against what he saw as its aspirations to cultural authority. Blurring the line between legitimate culture and popular forms, the epic embodied the worst excesses of middlebrow culture for Macdonald, becoming the very symbol of the erosion of cultural distinction created by the rise of mainstream culture. Jancovich finds that another set of anxieties also played into the mainstream press's troubled response to the epic: the presence of "foreign" elements in films made in Hollywood and the success of foreign filmmakers in making spectacular epics that rivaled American products. Highlighting the critical response in the USA to the rise of the epic film, Jancovich details the cultural value associated with American epic films that made use of non-US locations, actors, and writers, and the scorn heaped on European directors and producers who employed the same transnational orientation. The work of Dino De Laurentiis, in particular, aroused the ire of critics for its inauthenticity, its seeming betrayal of European high-art traditions. Films such as *El Cid* (1961) and *Cleopatra,* by contrast, were happily embraced for their willingness to utilize European artistic talent and traditions. Jancovich suggests the critics' interest in preserving the "authenticity" of European artistic traditions while endorsing the transnational approach of the American epic captures the combination of ethnocentrism and global ambition of American culture in the 1950s and early 1960s.

In "*Red Cliff:* The Chinese-language Epic and Diasporic Chinese Spectators," Ruby Cheung considers the Chinese epic *Red Cliff* (2008) as a paradoxical work that attempts to instill a sense of social cohesion among widely disparate Chinese populations, scattered in diaspora across Southeast Asia and throughout the world. Cheung notes that the release dates of the two installments of the film were timed to immediately precede and follow the Beijing Olympics in 2008 and can be seen as part of a broader effort to project a sense of national unity and purpose. John Woo, the film's director, worked for many years in Hong Kong and then in Hollywood, and was able to capitalize on his status as an "interstitial" director who worked between and within two different centers of cultural influence and power. Populating the cast of the film with Chinese and Japanese actors of mixed heritage and national provenance, Woo brought a transnational range of talent into the production of a film whose avowed aim was to create a potent sense of belonging to the motherland, China. However, despite the film's massive box-office success, the messages that viewers took from the film were anything but uniform or consistent. Analyzing the diasporic communities' response to the film by way of social media such as blogs, fansites, Facebook, MySpace, Twitter, and others, Cheung distinguishes the responses to the film of Chinese people from Taiwan, Japan, Malaysia, America, and mainland China, and marks how strikingly different their interpretations of the film seemed to be. Rather than identifying with a greater China or exhibiting nostalgia for a heroic past, the diasporic community found points of connection to the historical past that are surprising, contemporary, and distinctive depending on their location, their generation, and their own particular emotional connection to certain stars of the film. Cheung concludes that the historical epic, rather than unifying the population around heroic achievements of the past or producing a nostalgic longing for an ancient golden age, provides a medium for individuals to create their own sense of agency in relation to the past, a productive negotiation that can take the form of fan identification with the stars of the film, with the larger values expressed in the film, or with the undercurrents of eroticism that are frequently present in epic films.

part three: remembering the nation

The third part of the book considers the epic of national emergence, the most familiar form of the epic film and a mode that imprints all subsequent variations. Centering on motifs crucial to the formation of national identity—legendary heroes, an ancestral homeland, hallowed landscapes, and sacred sites—and employing a narrative voice that Gilberto Perez describes as "telling a national story that everyone knows and that the narrator, speaking for everyone, relates from a stance of sure knowledge," the epic of national emergence remains a potent form of collective expression.[13] Analyzing the basic genetic code of epic film, the essays collected here also consider the apparatus of mythmaking in the twentieth century. Epic films are products of their contemporary culture. Although they rehearse and recall a broad range of inherited cultural discourses, they also weave contemporary issues concerning race, ethnicity, and politics into the drama. Never static, the epic genre is shaped by past events and past versions of the form, but it also responds to the present in a new way, an insight that is concretely demonstrated in these works.

The elaborate discursive machinery used to construct a successful epic film is the subject of Phil Wagner's "Passing through Nightmares: Cecil B. DeMille's *The Plainsman* and the Epic Discourse in New Deal America." An epic western, little-known today but celebrated in the Depression period in which it was made, *The Plainsman* (1936) provides a case study in the slippages between authenticity and invention that characterize epic discourse. Wagner's study of the production, marketing, and exhibition history of Cecil B. DeMille's story of Wild Bill Hickok, Calamity Jane, and Buffalo Bill details the powerful cultural impact of DeMille's film, which derives from the producer's keen appreciation of reenactment and analogy. DeMille went to extraordinary lengths to bolster the historical legitimacy of this work, employing Native Americans and cavalrymen who had actually participated in the events depicted, modeling his compositions after those of Frederick Remington, and eliciting dramatic testimony from veterans of the period who verified its authenticity. But the main impact of the film came from the analogies DeMille constructed between the heroic portrayal he gave of the settling of the West and the struggles of ordinary people in the Depression. DeMille cannily reinforced parallels between his film, the radio Fireside Chats of President Roosevelt, and the mythology of the American pioneer to stage a celebratory work that evoked the emotions of collective identity. The participatory reenactments that DeMille staged as the film was released, including Boy Scout pageants, costumed premieres, and essay contests, made use of public reenactments to create the quality of eventfulness that Sobchack defines as characteristic of epic cinema. Wagner's analysis, richly supported by research, delineates the large-scale cultural apparatus that epic films call upon and build into their mode of address, defining the specific ways epic discourse is created in a particular historical moment.

Bruce Babington, in "Epos Indigenized: The New Zealand Wars Films from Rudall Hayward to Vincent Ward," describes the shifting treatment in epic films of one of the foundational stories of New Zealand, the war between the Imperial British Army and the Maori in the 1860s, which has received five major cinematic treatments over an eighty-year period. Although the events these films depict are clearly epic in their significance and fully embody an "origin of nation" symbolic weight, the slim resources of the New Zealand film industry prevent the films from displaying the devices of spectacle, immersive cinematography, and monumentality that are typical of epic treatments. Nevertheless, the four films—*The Te Kooti Trail* (1927), *Rewi's Last Stand* (1940), *Utu* (1983), and *River Queen* (2005)—convey a powerful, fully realized sense of what György Lukács defines as one of the strengths of the historical novel: "the split of the nation into warring parties always runs through the center of the closest human relationships." The racial and cultural divide between Maori and settler is the subject of each of these films, and the shifting relations between race and national identity is marked in both subtle and obvious ways in these works. Illuminating the political message of these films through careful analysis of narrative and visual form, Babington offers a persuasive reading of these films as both products of their time and as texts that allow a comparatively progressive racial message to emerge. The cultural shifts that have defined race relations in New Zealand in terms of assimilation, integration, biculturalism and multiculturalism are reflected in these works, each of which emphasizes that the conflict at the heart of New Zealand identity was a civil war rather than a war against outsiders.

part four: the family epic

A fourth subject to be considered in this volume is the family melodrama or family saga as a mode of epic expression. Films such as Bernardo Bertolucci's *1900* (1976), Zhang Yimou's *To Live* (1994), and Marco Tullio Giordana's film, *The Best of Youth* (2003), to name three films that exemplify this strand, share certain aspects of epic cinema as it is ordinarily understood. In other respects, however, these films constitute a distinct subgenre. Set in the recent as opposed to the ancient past and defined by generational conflict and fraternal struggle rather than the conflict of historical collectivities, the epic melodrama depicts another face of the world dramas that now imbue the epic form. The impact of modernity on family solidarity, the failed promises of nationalism and its effects on youth, and the desperate and wrenching gap between cosmopolitan dreams and straitened familial circumstances provide powerful themes for a narrative form shaped by the ambitious striving of individuals pulled toward a global future on the one hand and bound by family loyalties and pathologies on the other. The essays gathered in this part of the book consider a wide geographic array of films, including the work of Bengali director Ritwik Ghatak (*The Cloud-Capped Star*, 1960), the Mexican director Arturo Ripstein's *The Beginning and the End* (1993), as well as Paul Thomas Anderson's *There Will Be Blood* (2007). This part focuses on the particular combination of mythic and historical elements that imbues the family saga with an epic sweep and proportion.

Bhaskar Sarkar, in "Epic Melodrama, or Cine-Maps of the Global South," joins together two distinct traditions in his innovative analysis of melodrama as an epic form. Describing the way the melodramas of the "global

South" articulate a vision of nation under duress from the competing pressures of traditional family expectations and the demands of a modern, market economy, Sarkar reads the work of the Mexican filmmaker Arturo Ripstein and the Bengali filmmaker Ritwik Ghatak as a form of epic cinema that conveys the limits of the nation from the perspective of the intimate dramaturgy of family life. Sarkar proposes that these melodramas, articulating the story of nation through the familial lens, constitute a new subgenre of films coming primarily from the global South, a subgenre that he names the "epic melodrama." Drawing from Bertolt Brecht, Walter Benjamin, and Fredric Jameson, Sarkar argues that the family epics typical of what Antonio Gramsci calls the "South," which include Visconti's *Rocco and His Brothers* (1960), Ripstein's *The Beginning and the End,* and Ghatak's *The Cloud-Capped Star,* foreground tensions in the politics of personal life to "map an entire material and intimate geography" that links films that are widely disparate in national origin. Emerging from a "geophysical configuration that . . . derives from embodied experiences of comparable material conditions in far-flung locations such as Egypt, Italy, India and Mexico," Sarkar finds that epic melodrama provides a new aesthetic approach to large scale historic issues without relying on suspect categories of nation, heroic destiny, or the totality of a people. The structures of feeling elicited by the powerful melodramatic films of Ghatak and Ripstein can be read as articulating a story of emergent nationhood as a fracturing, and ultimately disabling global reality, one that deforms the traditional familial structures that sustained collective life in earlier periods.

Anne Gjelsvik, in "'Black Blood': *There Will Be Blood,"* reads *There Will Be Blood* as a dark reversal of the usual epic themes, simultaneously a story of emergence and of familial exploitation and degradation, the founding of empire and the destruction of community. The myriad meanings of "blood" conveyed in the film's title—the blood of sacrifice, the blood of kinship, the blood of collective purpose and the blood of destruction—all coalesce around the potent metaphoric connection Paul Thomas Anderson makes between blood and oil, a connection that is made manifest in numerous scenes in which blood and oil are visually indistinguishable. The quotation from Exodus that provides the film's title—a reference to the plagues of Egypt and the turning of the rivers, ponds, streams, and wells of Egypt to blood, urges us to see the film as a kind of Old Testament allegory, a theme that Gjelsvik develops by noting the prevalence of biblical motifs in Anderson's films and by connecting the film to the tradition of the jeremiad.

part five: the body in the epic

The fifth part of the volume considers the depiction of the male body in epic films. Usually dismissed as an obvious excuse for prurient display, the male body in film has recently received a good deal of nuanced and imaginative critical analysis. Much of this work has made use of psycho-analytic approaches, emphasizing domination and subordination, fetish-ism and masochism, although some essays have discussed a wider range of contexts, including ancient constructions of masculinity, artistic conven-tions of male display, the emotional cross-currents, and the tension between duty and passionate feeling that express themselves in male ges-tural codes. Perhaps the most common trope of epic films, the heightened display of the male body in scenes of virtuoso athletic performance or in abject defeat evokes a range of art-historical and cultural traditions and emphatically registers the eroticized violence that pervades the genre. Nearly all of the essays written for this volume consider the subject of the male body in epic cinema. The two essays that comprise this part open new perspectives on the topic, foregrounding subjects that have been widely noticed but little discussed: the body of Christ and the portrayal of the black male body.

Among the many fine essays written on the subject of the male body in epic films, few have focused on what must rank as the most exemplary subject of male display: the body of Jesus. From the early medieval period onwards, the display of the suffering and crucified Christ has dominated Christian iconography as well as classical painting and sculpture. The depiction of Jesus's Passion has also created intense controversy from the medieval period to the present day. Alison Griffiths, in "The Monstrous Epic: Deciphering Mel Gibson's *The Passion of the Christ*," offers a rich analysis of a film usually dismissed as an example of torture porn masquerading as a devotional work of Christian uplift. Gibson's *The Passion of the Christ* became a box-office phenomenon, helped by its aggressive promotion in Christian churches in the USA. Polarizing audiences—who saw it alternately as a cathartic reawakening of Christian religious fervor or as an anti-Semitic rehearsal of ancient stereotypes—the film was received in dramatically dif-ferent ways, a reception that resumes much older debates concerning the representation of Jesus's punishment and death. Typically centering on the depiction of the male body and the violent spectacle of the flogging and crucifixion, these debates focused on issues of sexuality, embodiment, and verisimilitude, subjects that were intensively considered in the medieval period when reenactments of the Passion were elaborately staged with an abundance of special effects, including skin-colored suits, which could be peeled off layer by layer as the reenactment of the flogging continued, and hydraulic systems for squirting fake blood. Griffiths details the long his-tory of the Passion play and its peculiar mode of spectatorship, drawing comparisons to the biblical epic film and its traditions of immersion, spectacle, and the agony of the male body in extreme states of physical distress.

In "Diegetic Masculinities: Reading the Black Body in Epic Cinema," Saër Maty Bâ explores the alternative histories embodied in the black male characters of *Gladiator, Spartacus, Amistad,* and in earlier epic films, *Winning a Continent* and *The Birth of a Nation.* Introducing a new vocabulary to epic discourse, Bâ reads the black male characters of epic films as an instantiation of cross-currents of different concepts of time, belonging, and destiny that Paul Gilroy calls Planetarity and Conviviality, considering the marginal, nomadic status of the black epic hero as making visible the importance of the "contact zone" in epic discourse. The wide geographies and intersecting domains of ethnicities and empires in epic films find their crossing point in characters such as Juba, Draba, and Cinque. Defining these characters as counterweights to the tragic figures of Maximus, Spartacus, and the larger society of slave-holding America, Bâ points out the value of Gilroy's concepts of planetarity and conviviality for conceiving the utopian, forward-looking register of the epic text. He also considers Andrei Tarkovsky's ideas concerning temporality—the sense that a cinematic moment can suggest time moving in multiple directions, penetrated by past, future, and present—as a way of grasping the multiple relations to history that the characters of Juba, Cinque, and others bring into view.

The essays gathered in this volume represent a starting point for further work on several fronts. The emergence of global genre forms, the interplay of broadly transnational production, distribution, and exhibition practices in creating new artistic and audience affiliations, the complex reading practices of audiences who find in epic films an alternative way of being in history, the changing role and nature of spectacle in the digital environment, and the role of racial otherness in epic films: each of the essays collected here marks a new departure for a genre that, despite its importance, has only recently received serious critical attention. The range of critical ideas set forth in *The Epic Film in World Culture* suggests the rich potential of the epic as a form of contemporary cultural expression. And the powerful inventiveness displayed in these essays offers a striking example of the many different ways of conceiving a genre that now links much of the world.

notes

1. For a discussion of the concept of "genre memory," see Gary Saul Morson and Caryl Emerson, *Mikhail Bakhtin: Creation of a Prosaics* (Palo Alto, Calif.: Stanford University Press), pp. 278–297. See also Robert Burgoyne, *Film Nation: Hollywood Looks at US History* (Minneapolis, Minn.: University of Minnesota Press, 2010).

2. Cecil B. DeMille, "Address to Havana Convention," delivered August 30, 1936, Box 528/Folder 5 Cecil B. DeMille Collection, Brigham Young University. The remainder of the quote reads as follows: "In some cases, the earnings of my pictures abroad are double what they are in America, so it is

to keep faith with you gentlemen and with the picture-goers of the globe who have been so faithful to me, that I endeavor to make pictures of world-wide appeal."

3. Gilles Deleuze, *Cinema 1: The Movement-Image* (Minneapolis, Minn.: University of Minnesota Press, 1986), pp. 148–149.

4. Gilles Deleuze, *Cinema 1*, p. 149.

5. Roland Barthes, "On CinemaScope," trans. Jonathan Rosenbaum, available online at http://english.chass.ncsu.edu/jouvert/v3i3/barth.htm (accessed March 13, 2010). First published 1954. Vivian Sobchack, "Surge and Splendor: A Phenomenology of the Historical Epic," *Representations*, 29 (winter 1990): 24–49.

6. Gilberto Perez, *The Material Ghost* (Baltimore, Md.: Johns Hopkins University Press, 1998), p. 79.

7. See Martin M. Winkler, "Gladiator and the Colosseum: Ambiguities of Spectacle," in Martin M. Winkler (ed.), *Gladiator: Film and History* (Malden, Mass.: Blackwell Publishing, 2004), pp. 87–110; and Arthur J. Pomeroy, "The Vision of a Fascist Rome in *Gladiator*," in Winkler, *Gladiator: Film and History*, pp. 110–123.

8. Rob Wilson, "Ridley Scott's Empire and the Spectacle of Empire: Global/Local Rumblings Inside the Pax Americana," *European Journal of American Culture*, 21 (2): 64.

9. Gilles Deleuze, *Cinema 1*, p. 151.

10. Ernest Bloch, *The Principle of Hope*, trans. Neville Plaice, Steven Plaice, and Paul Knight, (Boston, Mass.: MIT Press, 1986), vol. I, p. 409.

11. Jacques Rancière, "Interview: The Image of Brotherhood," trans. Kari Hanet, Edinburgh '77 Magazine, 2 (1977): 26–31.

12. Grant Farred, 'Foreigners among Citizens', *Cultural Critique*, 67 (fall 2007): 141–159.

13. Gilberto Perez, *The Material Ghost*, p. 79.

spectacle

part one

"this is sparta!"

the reinvention of epic in

zack snyder's *300*

one

monica silveira cyrino

"Experience history at swordpoint . . . and moviemaking with a cutting edge."[1] The DVD cover of the Warner Bros. film *300,* directed by Zack Snyder (2007), delivers its seductive selling points with uncommon accuracy, as well as a refreshing lack of irony, for no epic film promises a more compelling alliance of gripping historical narrative content with arresting and ground-breaking visual form. With a budget of just under $65 million, much of it spent on technological innovations in cinematic computer graphics, Snyder's *300* is an unapologetically brawny and surprisingly zesty take on the recently reborn genre of "ancient" epic films, offering a rousing and spectacular-looking recreation of one of the most universally significant and heroic events in world history: the story of the battle of Thermopylae.[2]

a new epic

The film *300* derives its title from the number of Spartan warriors who, led by their indomitable king, Leonidas, held the narrow pass at Thermopylae on the northern coast of Greece against the massive forces of the Persian Army assembled by King Xerxes.[3] This small but elite band of Spartans held the Persian invaders at the "Hot Gates" for three brutal days in the late summer of 480 bc, just long enough for the cantankerous city-states of Ancient Greece to join together and mobilize their forces to repel the overwhelming enemy assault from the East. Likewise, the film premiered in heroic form, conquering all early estimations and instantly garnering legendary status. Released on March 9, 2007, Snyder's *300* reaped an astonishing and record-breaking $71 million on its opening weekend, with the largest-ever box-office total in March history and the third-highest for any R-rated film, leading one film critic to note: "The industry was stunned by the magnitude of the Spartan victory."[4] The film went on to earn an amazing domestic box-office total of $211 million and soon proved its global popularity with a worldwide total gross of $456 million, nearly matching the $458 million worldwide gross of the sword-and-sandal genre's undisputed champion, Ridley Scott's *Gladiator* (2000).[5] After the relative disappointments of Wolfgang Petersen's *Troy* (2004), which posted only $133 million in domestic gross (far less than the $175 million production budget), and Oliver Stone's critically lambasted *Alexander* (2004), earning less than $35 million at home (barely making a dent toward the $155 million production costs), the staggering commercial success of Snyder's *300* provides strong leather-clad support for any filmmaker who wishes to reach back to hallowed antiquity for story inspiration.[6]

The film is based on *300*, the vivid graphic novel written and illustrated by artist Frank Miller.[7] While enjoying a cult following as the creator of several popular graphic novels going back to the 1980s, Miller had recently made his mark on the cinema world when he co-directed with Robert Rodriguez a successful film version of his graphic novel *Sin City* (2005).[8] Notably, the graphic novel *300* had a cinematic pedigree before it even became a film: Miller says he was inspired by the earlier epic film, *The 300 Spartans* (1962), directed by Rudolph Maté and starring Richard Egan as King Leonidas.[9] When he first saw the film as a young boy, Miller was captivated by the powerful story of the fearless Spartan unit and their Alamo-like last stand against the imperial Persian invasion. Miller recalls how his view of what it means to be a hero evolved after watching Maté's film: "I stopped thinking of heroes as being the people who got medals at the end or the key to the city and started thinking of them more as the people who did the right thing and damn the consequences."[10] The historical battle of Thermopylae, one of the most glorious and influential moments in Greek history, is recounted with lively narratives and snappy dialogue by the great Greek historian, Herodotus (c. 484–425 bc) in his work *The Histories;* and the Spartans' ultimate sacrifice is commemorated in the famous epigram by the contemporary Greek poet, Simonides of Ceos (556–469 bc): "Go tell the Spartans, passerby: that here, by Spartan law, we lie."[11] Miller borrows this and many other memorable lines directly from the Ancient Greek sources and uses them liberally throughout his graphic novel. For example, when ordered by the Persians to hand over their weapons, the Spartan king Leonidas yells back the tart rejoinder, "Come and get them," a line lifted precisely from the Greek biographer, Plutarch (c. ad 45–125).[12] Or when a Persian emissary warns that their flying mass of arrows will blot out the sunlight, a Spartan officer gives the terse reply, "Then we will fight in the shade."[13] By using the Ancient Greek sources in this realistic way, Miller injects an evocative sense of history and epic grandeur into his graphic novel.

Just as Miller drew on the Greek sources, so director and co-screenwriter Snyder respects Miller's original artistic imagination in creating his film version. Snyder, who had made his feature film debut directing a brilliant remake of George Romero's zombie classic *Dawn of the Dead* (2004), saw himself more as a "steward of another person's vision" rather than the architect of his own, such that whenever he had to make a creative decision, he asked himself, "What would Frank do?"[14] Snyder meticulously follows Miller's stirring narrative, images, and dialogue as he recreates the graphic novel's austere aesthetic vision in his high-concept film. The film was shot almost entirely in a warehouse in Montreal, using bare, simple stages and minimalist sets. To add a third dimension to Miller's page, Snyder skillfully employs blue-screen technology in filming the actors; then computer technicians fill in the background imagery, digitally shading every frame in intense hues of storm, smoke and metal. "For Snyder it was simply the only way to get the look of Miller's *300* off the page and onto the big screen," as one critic explains.[15] With more carnage and gore than *Gladiator* and *Troy* combined, *300* comes by its R rating honestly, if not discreetly. The film is spectacularly violent, but the violence reveals a heavy dose of post-*Matrix* cinematic stylization: the battle scenes are edited in the now familiar slow-to-fast-motion photographic technique known as "bullet time," where the frame slows down to capture a warrior lunging to hurl his spear and then speeds up again to show computer-generated blood gushing artfully from impaled torsos and severed heads. As an added benefit to its eye-popping visual impact, the computer-generated bloodshed from all the skewered bodies and decapitations would also prove to be easier to calibrate digitally if the *Motion Picture Association of America*'s ratings board became too squeamish. The overall choreographic effect, as described by the director's wife and producing partner, Deborah Snyder, was like "a ballet of death."[16] And the end result is a stunning virtual recreation of this authentic yet highly idealized moment in history when a band of Spartan warriors refused to surrender their freedom and so saved the Greek-speaking world.

With so much visual artifice, the only "real" thing in the film is the well-toned physical presence of the actors. Snyder decided to cast non-Hollywood types in the principal roles, since less-well-known actors would keep initial costs down and a more international cast would make the film easier to market later during overseas distribution. As the noble King Leonidas, Scottish actor Gerard Butler is leonine and somber as he growls his famous battlefield one-liners through the bronze face-mask of his helmet. When Butler roars in his thick highland brogue, "Spahhhrrr-TANZ, prepare for glohhhrrry!," the viewer half expects the cast of warrior clansmen from *Braveheart* (1995) to appear on the scene wearing tartan sashes and blue war paint. Butler, a relative unknown except as the Phantom in the recent film version of *The Phantom of the Opera* (2004), was generally praised by critics in his star-making role as the Spartan king: "Butler's turn as the impossibly muscled Leonidas may be the most ferocious performance since Russell Crowe's Maximus."[17] Vincent Regan, who played Achilles' loyal lieutenant Eudorus in *Troy*, fixes his intense blue-eyed stare on the special Spartan forces as Leonidas' experienced right-hand man, known only as the Captain. His eldest son, Astinos, played by Tom Wisdom, joins the fateful band of warriors to add a measure of familial pathos to the storyline.[18] David Wenham, familiar to movie fans as Faramir in *The Lord of the Rings: The Return of the King* (2003), is the trusted warrior Dilios, who, on Leonidas' orders, takes the thrilling tale of the battle back home to Sparta. As in the graphic novel, Dilios serves as the narrator of the story, and his voice-over narration frames the film while allowing the director to unfold the story more imaginatively from one Spartan warrior's subjective perspective.

The actors were put through a grueling, eight-week training and diet regimen to make them look and fight like Spartans: those bulging muscles are thoroughly real, accentuated only by tan make-up and body oil. Indeed, the exceptionally healthy-looking cast led one irreverent critic to dub the film a "Spartan workout video."[19] With little to go on from the historical record about Spartan combat techniques, fight choreographer Damon Caro, who also choreographed the stunts in *Fight Club* (1999), devised a blend of mainly Asian styles of martial arts for the warriors to use in Snyder's film. While the Spartans most likely did not go to battle wearing just long red capes and leather briefs, their bare abdominal muscles rippling with every sword thrust, the filmmakers chose to stay true to Miller's pictorial vision as laid out on the page. Snyder also wanted to create a film that would attract an audience beyond the young male fan base of the graphic novel: "The buff, largely unclad Spartans are also the producers' main hope of getting anyone other than straight men to see *300*."[20] With so many strikingly fit, half-naked male bodies on display, not surprisingly the film attained a degree of celebrity in popular culture for having a somewhat homoerotic sensibility. At the 2007 MTV Movie Awards, comedian and host Sarah Silverman quipped, "They got the name *300* by measuring how gay it was on a scale from 1 to 10."[21] Such notoriety as an object of satire and even parody is a sure sign of the film's pervasive influence on popular culture.[22] Yet the director claims he was only following Miller's artistic vision in portraying the universal ideal of the athletic male form as it was drawn on Ancient Greek vases, and most viewers would confirm that the actors admirably realize this goal on screen.

In fact, the film had much broader appeal than even the filmmakers imagined. After a pair of test screenings, the producers were astonished to discover that the film engaged female audiences to an extraordinary level: "We got, like, a 100 percent recommend from women under 25," according to the director.[23] Possibly, women viewers responded to the film with such enthusiasm because *300* overturns the typical male-focused visual and narrative conventions of earlier epic films by showcasing a strong female-lead character.[24] Queen Gorgo, wife of Leonidas, played by British actress Lena Headey, gets a much more prominent role in the film than in the graphic novel, where she is barely seen. Over Miller's initial objection—"this is a boys' movie," he grumbled—Snyder and his producing-partner wife Deborah decided to elevate the queen's role from cameo to royal colleague, believing that "Leonidas needed something specific to fight for and female ticket-buyers needed someone to identify with."[25] Snyder's *300* introduces Gorgo as the political and sexual equal to Leonidas: her prominence in the film accords well with the fact that Herodotus mentions the historical Gorgo by name in two anecdotes that firmly emphasize her bold intelligence, candor, and morality.[26] Early in the film, Gorgo joins her husband to meet the Persian envoy, who insults her as he demands Spartan "submission," then the Queen nods her stern approval before Leonidas kicks the insolent trespasser into a pit. That night in bed together, Gorgo encourages her husband to take on the suicidal task of holding off the Persian invaders and afterward shares an extended erotic sequence with him that is atypical of the Hollywood epic-film genre for its length and explicitness. Actress Headey notes of her role as the strong-minded Gorgo: "I love that she manages to be feminine alongside being really secure."[27] The film also enlarges the family with historical accuracy to include the royal couple's young son, Pleistarchos (played by Giovani Cimmino), thereby giving both Gorgo and Leonidas "something to fight for," since the boy symbolizes the enduring continuity of the Spartan people. While she stands in a shoulder-high field of wheat, an emotionally charged epic film site ever since Maximus ran his fingers through the golden stalks in *Gladiator,* Gorgo speaks the famous line—"Come home with your shield or on it"—to the departing Leonidas, whom she will never see again (see Figure 1.1).[28] Later in the same wheat field, Gorgo embraces their son after telling him of his father's sacrifice for their freedom.

Snyder's film also adds a new subplot for the Queen: after Leonidas leaves to confront the Persians, Gorgo must deal with the corrupt, stay-at-home politician Theron, played by British actor Dominic West, best

Figure 1.1

300: Gorgo, queen of Sparta, stands with her son in a field of wheat as her husband departs for battle.

known for his performance as Detective Jimmy McNulty in the critically acclaimed HBO television series, *The Wire* (2002–2008). Theron, an invented character, is depicted in the film as a slimy bureaucrat, who is always shown fully clothed, as if trying to conceal his treachery under his robes, in contrast to the heroically bare bodies of the Spartan warriors: indeed, the viewer wonders how such a craven specimen as Theron could have ever survived the *agoge,* the rigorous Spartan early childhood education system.[29] Calling himself a political "realist," Theron is in fact a traitor, secretly taking Persian bribes to promote Spartan capitulation. Early in the film he is seen paying off the crooked old Spartan priests, the *ephors,* so they will use trumped-up religious reasons to forbid Leonidas from taking the Spartan Army to war with Persia. When Gorgo seeks Theron's help in persuading the Spartan Council to send military reinforcements to Leonidas and his men, Theron viciously extorts sex from the Queen in exchange for his insincere promise to support the war. Later, in the council hall, the double-crossing Theron accuses her of trying to bribe him with sex, to the shock and dismay of the assembled elders. But Gorgo's moment of revenge is what one critic calls "the signature applause moment in the film": she seizes a guardsman's sword and runs Theron clean through, as gold coins stamped with Xerxes' face spill from the voluminous folds of his robe and clatter upon the marble floor, gleaming proof of Theron's treason and betrayal of Spartan integrity.[30]

One of the film's more controversial representations is that of the Persian Emperor, Xerxes. Although he is not physically described in the Greek historical sources, from ancient relief images scholars can surmise that the Emperor probably wore a long, thick beard and sat on his throne far away from the front lines of battle. Yet Miller portrays Xerxes as a hairless giant who gets in Leonidas' face and demands submission, and Snyder's film again follows suit. The figure of Xerxes, played by Brazilian actor Rodrigo Santoro, is digitally enlarged and his voice deepened to intensify the Persian's corporal threat and to infuse it with distinctly sexual undertones. The director confirms his intention to make the young males in the audience feel uncomfortable: "What's more scary to a 20-year-old boy than a giant god-king who wants to have his way with you?"[31] In the film, Santoro plays Xerxes as a sexually ambiguous figure, covered in abundant pieces of gold jewelry, with dark eyeliner and long, pointed fingernails (see Figure 1.2). As Santoro describes Xerxes: "He's this giant . . . who believes he's a god. He's very manly, but at the same time has a feminine side."[32] By showing multiple piercings on his body, following the depiction of the Emperor in the graphic novel, the film offers a clear visual signal of his physical and moral corruption that would have been familiar to the Ancients, since the definition of a Greek citizen male was the impenetrability of his body.[33] The Spartans, on the other hand, exhibit unpainted skin that is perfectly smooth but for chiseled battle scars, the obvious badges of their invincible warrior masculinity.

To be sure, the film and the graphic novel on which it is based engage in the kind of politics of representation that would have been familiar to Ancient Greeks in the early fifth century. Almost immediately after the events of 480 bc, the battle of Thermopylae was mythologized in Ancient Greek art and literature as an epic showdown between manly, freedom-loving Greeks and the enslaved hordes of effete Asian tyrants.[34] The disparate physical images highlighted in the film are reminiscent of the distinct visual contrast presented in contemporary Greek vase paintings, where there is a marked opposition between the depictions of Persians wearing their elaborate clothing, with highly patterned leggings and caps with long ear-coverings, and the representations of Greek warriors with their well-muscled arms, chests and legs stripped bare in what art historians call "heroic nudity." One prominent ancient historian concurs that "the Greeks themselves often embraced such impressionistic adaptation" in their vase paintings and dramatic plays.[35] So, the use of such contrasting imagery in the film could conceivably have resonated with an Ancient Greek audience

Figure 1.2

300: Xerxes, king of Persia, presents himself to the Spartans.

just as it does with modern moviegoers. Indeed, it is a common strategy of the modern epic film to use this kind of polarizing "us vs. them" imagery to encourage the viewing audience to identify with the chief hero figure(s), in this case, the Spartan warrior-protagonists, while rooting against the villains, here unmistakably the Persian raiders.[36] Yet it is important to note that the most sinister character in the film is not the gold-pierced, kinky-looking Xerxes, nor the sad, misshapen Spartan defector, Ephialtes, but rather Theron, the smug, heavily draped Spartan traitor who justifies himself as an opportunist. It is Theron who represents the true outrage in this beautiful, surrealistic world where a few hundred near-legendary warriors made a valiant last stand for the concepts of duty, sacrifice, loyalty, but especially for freedom.

Even so, Snyder's *300* was severely lambasted by antagonistic critics, whose main argument against the film was that it is insufficiently ironic, that is, the film takes its themes—the aforementioned duty, sacrifice and loyalty, as well as "the preservation of Western civilization against enormous odds"—way too seriously.[37] Apparently, some critics thought the filmmakers were obliged to exhibit a certain smug awareness of the fact that they were producing a campy, self-conscious parody of an ancient battle that shaped global history. A few touchy commentators also condemned the film for simplistically dividing the "white" good guys and the "brown" bad guys along ethnic lines, somehow neglecting to acknowledge that the nature of the historical event in question pitted two distinct peoples against each other in a fierce, seismic clash. Moreover, the film drew attention from both sides of the ideological spectrum for the way it seems to tap into current debates about the American role in the Middle East, whether that role is seen as uninvited aggression (by the progressives) or a crucial intervention on behalf of democracy (to the conservatives). On the left side of the aisle, *300* was labeled "a pro-Iraq-invasion war whoop," while the right-wingers, who might have been expected to praise the film for its celebration of old-fashioned martial virtues, were instead nervous that "Emperor Xerxes of Persia, not the freedom-loving Leonidas, might be George Bush."[38] Even the modern Greeks and Iranians, the heirs of the Ancient Greeks and Persians, chimed in with their reactions to the film. The Iranian government decried *300* as "insulting" to its civilization, calling it "psychological warfare" against its people, and banned it from its theaters.[39] Some Greek commentators as well were troubled by the film's presentation of "pompous interpretations and one-dimensional characters," though one Greek film critic offered a voice of reason: "This is not a university lecture, it's a movie."[40] Yet pundits, journalists, and academics always seem to find much more political content in films than most filmmakers will admit to inserting therein: in fact, Snyder has unequivocally and consistently disavowed any political subtext to the film.

Although professional classicists and historians delight in comparing films about the ancient world to the "real" historical record, most mainstream moviegoers will readily acknowledge that Snyder's *300* is not a documentary: it is a technologically advanced film experience based on a popular graphic novel inspired by an old-school epic film from the 1960s which was largely derived from an historical account of a celebrated battle that was swiftly mythologized in its own time.[41] Snyder's film is simply one more stratum in the process of a reception that is hundreds of years in the making. Furthermore, what matters is not just the scholarly application of source criticism to the film or an exploration of how the film evokes or participates in archetypal epic cinematic genre conventions, but the recognition that *300* is a blockbuster movie event. As this writer notes in another context, "New meanings are conceived, generated and transmitted to current audiences every time the ancient world is represented on the modern page, stage, or screen."[42] So it is not only important but compulsory for scholars and critics to ask why is *300* so engaging to modern sensibilities? The film's massive popular appeal exploded around two major dynamics: first, the filmmakers' brilliant reinvention of an engaging narrative content in a way that emphasizes the universally gratifying theme of "freedom," and second, their ground-breaking use of an innovative and arresting visual style. The filmmakers skillfully exploit the form to deliver the subject matter in a broadly convincing and extremely successful transmission of cinematic message.

a new "freedom"

The persuasive power of the historical epic film to project a compelling mythology onscreen, and its consequent commercial success in doing so, has long been observed by critics.[43] Such projection of an appealing historical or mythic past is intended both to entertain the audience with rousing tales of a hero's fateful journey and glorious destiny and at the same time to inculcate viewers with ideologies of nationhood and the emergence of national identity. With the revival of the epic genre in the recent period, modern filmmakers are presenting new and more expansively conceived versions of these traditional epic narratives. Spurred on by financial incentives and creative aspirations to express a more enlightened, global outlook, contemporary historical epics, such as Scott's *Gladiator* and Petersen's *Troy,* seek to reach the widest possible international audiences. So contemporary filmmakers are now crafting their narrative strategies to engage with and promote broad cross-cultural and even universal structures of identification, affinity, and inclusivity. For example, the hero of *Gladiator,* Maximus, exemplifies the ideals of personal honor, spirituality, and sacrifice as he seeks to restore the collective Roman soul; in *Troy,*

Achilles' individual quest for undying fame is romanticized into an expression of the shared human aspiration to achieve immortality.[44] In the case of *300*, the film highlights as its main theme the unanimously aspirational ideal of "freedom," both of the individual and the society at large, and Snyder invests this theme with an updated, global spin to appeal to transnational audiences.

The "freedom" motif is utilized liberally throughout *300*, in spoken (and shouted) dialogue as well as in visual iconography contrasting the liberty-loving Spartans with the enslaved Persians. Among the many distinct city-states of a free Greece, Spartan society is portrayed in the film as representing the epitome of human freedom and the willingness to fight for its defense. When Leonidas confers with his wife on his options for saving Sparta—and so save all of Greece—from the Persian invasion, Gorgo instructs him to think of himself not as a king or a husband, but rather ask: "What should a *free* man do?" Her emphasis on the word "*free*" indicates that is the supreme title to which any Spartan can aspire. Indeed, the Spartans' last stand at Thermopylae is represented as the moment where they put their ideologies into action, as the Spartan warrior Stelios links these values together in his promise never to surrender: "For Sparta, for freedom, to the death!" The film skillfully conveys how the notion of "freedom" embraces both individual and communal concerns, when the narrator, Dilios, claims: "We march for our lands, for our families, for our freedoms. We march." Moreover, Gorgo connects the idea of collective liberty with personal sacrifice, when she decides to ask the Spartan Council to send reinforcements to Leonidas, telling her friend, the Loyalist: "Freedom isn't free at all. It comes with the highest of costs—the cost of blood." Later, when she faces the Council, claiming that she speaks "on behalf of three hundred families that bleed for our rights," Gorgo demands: "Send the army for the preservation of liberty!" By connecting the notion of defending one's own family with that of defending the unique national identity of a free Sparta, and by conflating both with the universal ideal that "freedom" is necessary and desirable, *300* invites the eager mainstream audience to identify with the Spartan cause. As one critic noted about his experience in the theater, "the distinctly non-Greek viewers at my showing seemed to have no trouble placing themselves in the sandals of the ancient Spartans."[45] Far from being a politicized "wedge issue," the battle of Thermopylae projected onscreen is intended as a unifying entertainment.

As the warriors arrive at Thermopylae, joined by a band of Arcadian Greeks, the image of the Spartan family is further enlarged to encompass all of Greek society, as Dilios continues his incantatory voice-over: "Into the Hot Gates we march. Spartans, citizen soldiers, freed slaves, brave Greeks all—brothers, fathers, sons—we march. For honor's sake, for duty's sake, for glory's sake, we march."[46] The enslaved hordes of Persians, on the contrary, are described as "motherless dogs": their freedom deficit and lack of family bonds render them nonhuman. The contrast between the Spartan and Greek warriors, on the one side, united by their free will and desire to fight, and the Persian slaves forced to do their king's bidding on the other, is again emphasized when Stelios, amid the sound of whips lashing Persian soldiers, orders a Persian envoy: "Go now and tell your Xerxes he faces *free* men here, not slaves." After the first decisive conflict, Leonidas himself tells a grimacing Xerxes: "The world will know that *free* men stood against a tyrant, that few stood against many, and before this battle was over, that even a god king could bleed." The final words of *300* belong to Dilios, as the film brings his narration up to the present moment on the battlefield of Plataea, where "ten thousand Spartans commanding thirty thousand free Greeks" finally ejected the Persians from Greece.[47] Here, Dilios declares that the telling and retelling of the story of Spartan courage in defense of freedom will ensure the continuation of freedom itself: "For from free Greek to free Greek the word was spread that bold Leonidas and his three hundred so far from home laid down their lives not just for Sparta but for all Greece and the promise that this country holds." In portraying the Spartans at the head of a familial coalition of free Greeks yearning for and dying to preserve their freedom for all Western human-ity, the film deftly converts the Spartan experience into a universal one. While the traditional epic narrative articulates the unique national mythol-ogy of a free Sparta, the new epic translates that cinematic mythology into a more global conception of human freedom.

That *300* represents the Spartans in the film as the embodiment of the ideal of "freedom" as well as the incontestable heroes of the battle of Thermopylae is consistent both with the historical record and with the Spartans' legendary reputation as fearless warriors with a take-no-prisoners style of combat.[48] More importantly, it accords well with modern popular receptions of the Spartans as a distinctive, exclusive culture that was radically different from all the other city-states of Ancient Greece. As a military society comprised of expertly trained male citizen warriors, the Spartans are seen in the popular imagination as more warlike, disciplined, and duty-bound, and thus more closely linked to the concepts of martial glory and personal honor, almost as if they were proto-Romans.[49] In the opening scenes of the film *300,* the narrator elucidates the uncompromising resolve and self-control drilled into Spartan youth during the *agoge:* "Taught never to retreat, never to surrender, taught that death on the battlefield in service to Sparta was the greatest glory he could achieve in his life." Unburdened by the complexities that marked other, more intellectually nuanced Greek tribes—with their drama, philosophy, and mathematics—the warrior lifestyle of Ancient Spartan society, dedicated to the clear-cut ideals of glory and freedom, comes across as more straightforward and uncomplicated and thus more directly and affectively appealing to wider audiences.

This affective, emotional appeal is most pronounced in the character of Leonidas, the King of Sparta, champion of Thermopylae, and hero of *300* (see Figure 1.3). "Heroic affect" denotes the emotions aroused when a cinematic hero does what the audience expects, values, and desires in a crisis situation.[50] Leonidas in *300* fulfills the role of an affective hero in two ways. First, as the narrative personification of the Spartan ideologies of duty, glory, and self sacrifice, the figure of Leonidas responds to the modern popular conception of the ultimate Spartan warrior. Actor Butler sums up the ultimate trial Leonidas faced:

> The king realizes that he has to take his best men and go and make a stand to save his nation to fight the most massive army ever assembled, and they have to go and do what is their dream essentially . . . which is to die in the perfect battle.[51]

Second, Leonidas is also the designated hero protagonist of *300,* and thus the filmmakers unabashedly make him the vessel for the moral point of the story to ensure that viewers will identify with him and make him the object of their emotional allegiance. Because he occupies this most powerful level of imaginative engagement, Leonidas becomes the agent of the audience's expectations "by proxy, carrying out acts that vindicate the problem or conflict that sits at the center of the story."[52] Ingeniously counting on the constancy of the fan base for the modern epic film, *300* even seeks to remind viewers of their recent previous affinity with Maximus, the hero of the wildly successful *Gladiator:* at the very beginning of the film, Leonidas encourages his young son to remember the Spartan combat lessons of "Respect and Honor," an unambiguous echo of Maximus' exhortation of his Roman troops to fight with "Strength and Honor."

30

Figure 1.3

300: Leonidas, king of Sparta, prepares to battle the Persian invaders at Thermopylae.

Moreover, to guarantee the broadest popular appeal, Leonidas in *300* embodies the quintessential elements of modern heroic affect inside the character of an ancient hero. Like the rest of the Spartan tribe to which he belongs, Leonidas epitomizes the ideal of "freedom" that contemporary audiences anticipate and admire. This popular model of "freedom" is frequently interpreted in film through the prism of heroic independence and individual free will. By modern cinematic convention—whether in westerns, cop movies, or comic-book fantasies—the hero-protagonists are fiercely autonomous, often isolated from society; they tend to work outside the system, usually with violence, even breaking the law if necessary to achieve their goals and to reinstate social order. But ancient heroes are more inclined to try to respect and abide by society's rules, since defying established norms or separating themselves from the community can be disastrous.[53] For example, when an alienated Achilles drops out of the war at Troy and thus violates the warrior code in Homer's *Iliad,* he starts a catastrophic downward spiral leading to personal and collective tragedy that is only resolved when he restores himself to society. One scholar explains how ancient and modern heroic affect differs in terms of autonomy: "hence Shane rides into the sunset, but Oedipus cannot."[54] Even the historical epitaph for the Spartans who died at Thermopylae celebrates the warriors' obedience "to Spartan law" in going to meet their glorious deaths on the battlefield. But the film *300* succeeds in having it both ways, by conflating the modern viewers' predilection for heroic autonomy with the historical fact of Spartan duty, deference, and devotion to community.

In the film, Leonidas must consult the corrupt priests and their intoxicated young oracle, but he shrewdly circumvents their edict forbidding him to lead the Spartan Army to meet the Persian invaders; instead, he decides to take with him only an elite band of 300 warriors, as the Captain assures him, "All with born sons to carry on their names."[55] When confronted by Theron and the council elders, who enjoin him not to "break the law," Leonidas tells them he is merely "out for a stroll with his personal bodyguard," and adds coyly, "I think I'll head north." This strategic act of disobedience, exercised within the Spartan system, is an expression of Leonidas' personal autonomy that stirs heroic affect inside the modern audience, since it will also set up the entire narrative of his virtuous self-sacrifice in the name of "freedom." In this way, the film *300* combines two heroic traditions, ancient and modern, to provoke the most passionate level of viewer engagement: "Identification as allegiance is a powerful form of attraction."[56] On the night before the final battle, when the hunchback traitor Ephialtes has given them up, and even the Arcadians retreat from the passageway in fear, Leonidas calls to his men and, as dawn rises behind him, rouses them to battle: "By Spartan law, we will stand and fight and die! A new age has begun—an Age of Freedom! And all will know that 300 Spartans gave their last breath to defend it!" Again the audience hears an echo of a recent popular epic film, as actor Butler's brogue-tinged call for "Freedom" recalls the brawny battle cry for Scottish independence shouted by Mel Gibson in his portrayal of the quasi-mythic late-thirteenth-century freedom fighter and guerrilla warrior, William Wallace, in 1995's *Braveheart*.[57] Both films, *Braveheart* and *300*, seek to rouse audience affect with stirring narratives of "freedom" amid gritty but highly romanticized warrior settings, while proposing modern paradigms of national identity set against the backdrop of the historical past. Both films focus on the costly triumphs incurred by their charismatic hero-leaders, who dedicate themselves to the larger ideals of "freedom" and community. But *300* goes one step further by allowing Leonidas to span two affective worlds, as he looks back to the authentic laws of Ancient Sparta and forward to the contemporary popular partiality for heroic independence.

The film *300* uses another narrative strategy to evoke contemporary heroic affect in the figure of Leonidas, during the climactic scene of his death among his band of Spartan warriors. The historical Spartans' stated desire for a "beautiful death" on the battlefield accords well with the epic cinematic tradition, where true heroes always die at the end of the last reel. As one critic notes, "An extended and painful demise was the prerogative of a hero."[58] In the modern epic film, the hero must be sacrificed not just to protect his family and friends but also to liberate his entire society and to restore his people's endangered freedom. For the modern audience, "fully heroic affect does not occur unless a hero fights both for a good cause and to avenge a personal outrage."[59] The epic film invites the audience to engage intimately in the pathos of the scene of the hero's death, which often involves apocalyptic levels of violence, so that the viewers also experience the violent redemption of society at large. Prominent examples of the hero's "death as salvation" axis appear in two recent epic films notable for their commercial and critical success: in *Braveheart*, national hero Wallace suffers excruciating torture and capital punishment by the order of the evil King Edward in a protracted scene at the end of the film, but his gruesome death rallies his fellow Scotsmen to wage war to avenge their leader's murder and to liberate their country from English rule; and in *Gladiator*, the people's champion Maximus, fatally weakened by a poisoned blade, fights his long, last battle in the Colosseum against the evil Emperor Commodus, but before he dies he slits the Emperor's throat, avenges the wrongs done to his family and restores the Roman Republic. Thus, the two epic film heroes arouse emotional affect in their audiences through prolonged, violent death scenes that validate their righteous actions.

In *300*, Leonidas' death scene is also an extended panorama of hyperrealistic violence and mayhem, evoking the bloody cinematic deaths of both Maximus and Wallace in its use of imagery and editing. As he faces Xerxes for the last time, Leonidas refuses to surrender to the Persian's bribes and threats. The narrator's voice-over informs the viewers that the King feels only "a heightened sense of things." The phrase initiates an aural and visual flashback to the opening of the film, where the adolescent Leonidas felt the same "heightened sense" before slaying an enormous wolf in a narrow rocky passage: this earlier scene provides a proleptic image for the fight against the bestial Persians wedged between the Hot Gates. Acutely aware of his men behind him, who are all "ready to die" for freedom, Leonidas slowly removes his helmet, in a gesture as old as Homeric epic, to signal his imminent demise.[60] Just as the Spartan desire for a "beautiful death" is the pinnacle of heroism, wanting to survive is absolutely antiheroic. So now, before the final battle, Leonidas curses Ephialtes, the enemy appeaser: "May you live for ever." This is a sure sign of Ephialtes' monstrous immorality, as much as his twisted, deformed body is a visual cue for the traitor's defective loyalties. In the moments before his death, Leonidas has a vision of his wife through the waving fronds of a wheat field, just as Maximus does in *Gladiator*, and reaches out to her in his reverie. The King calls for one last charge, but the Spartans are slaughtered to a man: the audience watches as the great bare chest of Leonidas is pierced full of Persian arrows. He turns south to face Sparta, and with his last dying breath calls on his queen, as more missiles rain down on him, knocking him to the ground. The camera pans slowly upward from his corpse, surrounded by his slain brothers-at-arms, to reveal his arms spread wide and his head fallen to one side in a pose reminiscent of artistic depictions of the crucifixion of Christ: here *300* intensifies the redemptive affect with a clear visual echo of the Christ-like death tableau of the executed Wallace at the end of *Braveheart* (see Figure 1.4). Like the two earlier epic film heroes, Maximus and Wallace, Leonidas is brutally yet heroically sacrificed to preserve his closest friends and family and to underscore his personal honor, but most importantly, his violent death delivers and liberates his entire people.

The stunning, stylized violence of Leonidas' death scene brings up a final consideration about how *300* employs technological innovation

Figure 1.4

300: Leonidas after his heroic death at Thermopylae.

to enhance the epic cinematic experience and to reach out to a wider, global audience of viewers. Ever since the lavish historical movie spectacles were produced in the 1950s and 1960s, the film industry has always used the epic film as a showcase for the display of new cinematic technologies, as they sought to lure bigger audiences to the movie theater by promising "the pleasures of the look" in all their widescreen CinemaScope and Technicolor glory.[61] With the recent advent of computer-generated imagery (CGI), blue-screen and other modern technological advances, extravagant digital special effects have become, and continue to be, an intrinsic part of the production of contemporary epic cinema. The Hollywood studios that cut distribution, satellite, and internet deals on the international market are now banking on technological novelty in movies as a precondition of transnational exchange and globalization. For example, CGI was brilliantly used by Ridley Scott in the blockbuster *Gladiator* to reinvent the ancient epic landscape when the director digitally recreated the upper tiers of the Roman Colosseum atop the lower two tiers of a bricks-and-mortar model built to full scale.[62] Similarly, Snyder recombines and reprocesses earlier images of the ancient world in *300* by taking many of his visual cues from the graphic novel: for example, the director follows the cartooning convention by which exterior physical appearances reveal interior states (beautiful = good, ugly = bad), and he sustains a recurrent "lambda" motif as a visual code throughout the film.[63] But the film's most impressive artistic originality remains in its application of striking digital technologies. As described above, *300* was mostly shot on a soundstage; then computer technicians added CGI effects and backgrounds and boosted up the colors to produce the movie's sharply stylized, high-contrast look. Since such sophisticated special effects offer the viewing audience a powerful, sensual, almost kinesthetic experience of history, they generate a new visual language for the epic film to attract more ticket buyers and to convey its message to an ever broader audience of spectators. The film *300* uses technological innovation and spectacular special effects not so much to engage with contemporary moral questions and problems of war and politics but rather to communicate a stylized portrayal of the Spartan warriors as the unquestioning defenders of the universally desirable paradigm of "freedom." As Snyder promised when he set out to make this film, "The genre is ripe for reinventing . . . so let's reinvent it."[64]

notes

1. The quote is from the back cover of the *300* DVD, Warner Bros. Entertainment Inc. (2007).
2. Jon Solomon coined the term "ancients," modeled on the designation for the film genre of "westerns," to refer to films and television productions set in antiquity, in his book *The Ancient World in the Cinema,* 2nd edn (New Haven, Conn.: Yale University Press, 2001).

3. The tale of the historical battle of Thermopylae is recounted by the Ancient Greek historian Herodotus in *The Histories* 7.176–239. On the history of the battle, see Paul Cartledge, *Thermopylae: The Battle that Changed the World* (Woodstock, NY: Overlook Press, 2006); for the historical Spartans, see Paul Cartledge, *The Spartans: The World of the Warrior-Heroes of Ancient Greece* (New York: Vintage Books, 2004), and *Sparta and Lakonia: A Regional History 1300–362 bc,* 2nd edition (London and New York: Routledge, 2002).

4. Josh Rottenberg, "The Conquering Heroes," *Entertainment Weekly* (March 23, 2007), p. 27.

5. The production budget for *Gladiator* was $103 million. See www.boxofficemojo.com for all figures.

6. But note that both films grossed about three times as much overseas as domestically: *Troy* earned $364 million overseas, for a worldwide total of $497 million (nearly half a billion dollars!), and even *Alexander* made $133 million overseas, for a worldwide total of $167 million. See Steve Daly, "Double-Edged Sword," *Entertainment Weekly* (March 16, 2007), p. 37.

7. The graphic novel *300* was published in 1998 by Dark Horse Comics, with colors painted by Lynn Varley.

8. On the rising enthusiasm in Hollywood for film adaptations of comic books, see Rebecca Winters Keegan, "Batman's Half Brothers: Graphic Novels Are Hollywood's Newest Gold Mine," *Time* (June 30, 2008), pp. 57–59.

9. For more on this film, see Solomon, *The Ancient World in the Cinema,* pp. 39–40.

10. Quoted by Lev Grossman, "The Art of War," *Time* (March 12, 2007), p. 60.

11. Miller uses this succinct translation of the epigram in the graphic novel *300.* Simonides' epigram is recorded in a number of ancient sources, including Herodotus, *The Histories,* 7.228.2; *The Palatine Anthology,* 7.249; and Diodorus Siculus, *The Library of History* 11.33.2. The epigram was engraved as an epitaph on a commemorative stone marker set atop the burial mound of the Spartans at Thermopylae, upon the hill where the last of them died. Since the original was lost, a new stone epitaph was erected in 1955 and can still be seen today, covered with flowers.

12. Plutarch, *Spartan Sayings,* 225c.11; the line is also engraved on a plaque beneath a bronze statue of the Spartan king at the modern "Leonidas Monument" that stands near Thermopylae today.

13. Herodotus, *The Histories,* 7.226.

14. Keegan, "Batman's Half Brothers," p. 58.

15. Grossman, "The Art of War," p. 60.

16. Quoted by Daly, "Double-Edged Sword," p. 38.

17. Chris Nashawaty, "Most Buzzed About: Gerard Butler," *Entertainment Weekly* (November 30, 2007), p. 47.

18. The character does not appear in the graphic novel but was added by Snyder and named for his car, an Aston Martin, as the director cheekily confesses on the DVD commentary track.

19. Richard Corliss, "Why Can't a Woman . . . Be a Man?" *Time* (April 16, 2007), p. 67.

20. Grossman, "The Art of War," p. 61.

21. The MTV Movie Awards were held June 3, 2007. Note that the film has been accused of being both homophobic as well as homoerotic, charges the filmmakers simply shrug off: see Daly, "Double-Edged Sword," p. 38.

22. The film has spawned innumerable web spoofs and YouTube mash-ups. Film parodies include the short film, *United 300* (2007) and the feature film, *Meet the Spartans* (2008).

23. Daly, "Double-Edged Sword," p. 38.

24. On the visual and narrative prominence of male-centered relationships in epic films of the 1950s and 1960s, see William Fitzgerald, "Oppositions, Anxieties and Ambiguities in the Toga Movie," in Sandra R. Joshel, Margaret Malamud, and Donald T. McGuire, Jr. (eds), *Imperial Projections: Ancient Rome in Modern Popular Culture* (Baltimore, Md.: Johns Hopkins University Press, 2001), pp. 23–49.

25. Daly, "Double-Edged Sword," p. 38.

26. Herodotus, *The Histories* 5.51 and 7.239.

27. Quoted by Tim Stack, "Having a Moment: Lena Headey of *300*," *Entertainment Weekly* (March 30, 2007), p. 21.

28. For the use of the wheat field in *Gladiator* as a symbol of eternity and the possibility of reunion with loved ones in the afterlife, see Monica S. Cyrino, *Big Screen Rome* (Malden, Mass.: Blackwell, 2005), pp. 253–254. The line is from Plutarch's *The Sayings of Spartan Women* (*Moralia*, 241).

29. The name recalls that of the historical Theron of Acragas, a bellicose tyrant in Greek Sicily in the early fifth century bc, and is perhaps intended to suggest the movie character's political power. Compare the use of the name "Gracchus" in films about Ancient Rome, such as *Spartacus* (1960) and *Gladiator*: in these cases, the name is used to evoke the reform-minded populism of the famous Gracchi brothers during the second century bc in the Roman Republic. On the *agoge*, see Nigel M. Kennell, *The Gymnasium of Virtue: Education and Culture in Ancient Sparta* (Chapel Hill, NC: University of North Carolina Press, 1995).

30. Richard Roeper, "Go over the Top Spartans," *Universal Press Syndicate* (March 9, 2007).

31. Quoted by Daly, "Double-Edged Sword," p. 38.

32. Quoted by Daly, "Double-Edged Sword," p. 38.

33. On the inviolability of the citizen male body in Ancient Greece, see most recently Marilyn B. Skinner, *Sexuality in Greek and Roman Culture* (Malden, Mass., Blackwell, 2005), p. 7.

34. Near-contemporary literature that offers critical depictions of the Eastern invaders includes Aeschylus' tragic play, *The Persians* (first performed in 472 bc), and *The Histories* of Herodotus (written c. 430 bc).

35. Victor Davis Hanson, "Viewers Still Get the Right Message in Dramatized *300*," syndicated column (March 25, 2007).

36. On the way modern films intentionally arouse audience allegiance with the hero figure(s) to augment popular appeal, and thus box-office receipts, see Gary C. Woodward, *The Idea of Identification* (Albany, NY: State University of New York Press, 2003), pp. 45–69.

37. For a summary of the hostile criticism of the film, see Neal Stephenson, "It's All Geek to Me," *The New York Times* online (March 18, 2007).

38. Steve Daly, "Message Movies?" *Entertainment Weekly* (August 1, 2008), p. 23. Stephenson "It's All Geek to Me."

39. "Iran Condemns Hollywood War Epic," *BBC News* online (March 3, 2007).

40. "Greek Critics Lash Hollywood's Ancient Epic *300*," *International Herald Tribune* online (March 8, 2007).

41. A particularly joyless example of the academic "tsk-tsk" mode of criticism, scolding the film both for historical inaccuracies and political

incorrectness, is Subho Basu, Craige Champion, and Elisabeth Lasch-Quinn, "*300:* The Use and Abuse of History," *The Classical Outlook,* 85 (1) (2007): 28–32.

42. Monica S. Cyrino, "Introduction," in Monica S. Cyrino (ed.), *Rome, Season One: History Makes Television* (Malden, Mass.: Blackwell, 2008), pp. 1–10; p. 7.

43. Still the most thorough analysis of the genre is Derek Elley, *The Epic Film: Myth and History* (London: Routledge & Kegan Paul, 1984). See also Robert Burgoyne, *The Hollywood Historical Film* (Malden, Mass.: Blackwell, 2007), pp. 74–99.

44. On *Gladiator,* see Martin M. Winkler (ed.), *Gladiator: Film and History* (Malden, Mass.: Blackwell, 2004); and on *Troy,* see Martin M. Winkler (ed.) *Troy: From Homer's Iliad to Hollywood Epic* (Malden, Mass.: Blackwell, 2007).

45. Stephenson, "It's All Geek to Me."

46. According to Herodotus (*The Histories* 7.202), the Spartans were joined by a handful of troops from other city-states in the Peloponnesus, including Arcadians, for a total of about 4,000 auxiliaries.

47. The battle of Plataea, fought in the summer of 479 bc in southern Greece, was the last major conflict of the Greco-Persian Wars, where an alliance of Greek city-states finally defeated the Persian invaders.

48. For the tradition of romanticizing Ancient Sparta, see Elizabeth Rawson, *The Spartan Tradition in European Thought,* 2nd edn (Oxford: Oxford University Press, 1991).

49. On the problems of "selling" Ancient Greece to cinema audiences, compared with the more accessible Roman culture, see Gideon Nisbet, *Ancient Greece in Film and Popular Culture* (Exeter: Bristol Phoenix Press, 2006), pp. 1–44.

50. This argument draws on the analysis of reception psychology of contemporary film heroes by Sally MacEwen, *Superheroes and Greek Tragedy: Comparing Cultural Icons* (Lewiston, NY: Edwin Mellen Press, 2006), pp. 133–261.

51. The quote is from "The Making of *300*" in the Special Features of the DVD (2007).

52. Woodward, *The Idea of Identification,* p. 52. For a description of progressively involving levels of identification in film, see also Murray Smith, "Altered States: Character and Emotional Response in Cinema," *Cinema Journal,* 33 (4) (1994): 39–41.

53. On the differences between ancient and modern notions of heroic autonomy, see MacEwen, *Superheroes and Greek Tragedy,* pp. 178–194.

54. MacEwen, *Superheroes and Greek Tragedy,* p. 185.

55. This criterion is another expression of Spartan dedication to community, since men with sons would be more likely to stand firm and fight and die for their society to ensure their sons' future place in it.

56. Woodward, *The Idea of Identification,* p. 53.

57. For the so-called "*Braveheart* effect," i.e. the way the film affected the modern nationalist movement for Scottish independence in the late 1990s, see Graeme Morton, *William Wallace: Man and Myth* (Thrupp: Sutton Publishing, 2001), especially pp. 137–154.

58. Woodward, *The Idea of Identification,* p. 52.

59. MacEwen, *Superheroes and Greek Tragedy,* p. 213.

60. On the change of heroic status indicated by the removal of headgear in the Homeric epic, see Seth L. Schein, *The Mortal Hero: An Introduction to Homer's Iliad* (Berkeley, Calif.: University of California Press, 1984), pp. 174–177.

61. As a result of the growing competition with television during this period, Hollywood studios invested heavily in technological innovations and big-budget productions to enhance "the pleasures of the look": see Maria Wyke, *Projecting the Past: Ancient Rome, Cinema and History* (London and New York: Routledge, 1997), 24–32; p. 24.

62. See Cyrino, *Big Screen Rome,* pp. 226–227.

63. The lambda, or Greek "L," stands for Leonidas, Lakedaimonia (the Ancient Greek word for Sparta), and perhaps *lykos,* or "wolf," the King's family totem. The lambda motif, an inverted "V," occurs in numerous visual iterations: as the insignia on the Spartan shields and the clasps of their capes; in the shape of their spearheads, in Leonidas' beard, in the Spartan phalanx and in the pipes of the Spartan musician. Snyder adopts the lambda motif directly from the graphic novel and then often applies a match cut to move from the image in one frame of film to the next.

64. Quoted by Daly, "Double-Edged Sword," p. 37.

"philip never saw

babylon"

360-degree vision and the

historical epic in the digital era

kirsten moana thompson

Roland Barthes described CinemaScope, the exciting new widescreen technology of the 1950s with its "stretched-out frontality" as akin to putting the spectator on the Balcony of History, at arm's length to the widescreen image.[1] Oliver Stone's *Alexander* (2004) literalizes this spatialization of history in Ptolemy's prologue.[2] Following an opening flashback to Alexander's death, the film begins with Ptolemy (Anthony Hopkins), as an old man, standing on his balcony and gazing out over the city of Alexandria, as he dictates the story of Alexander the Great. Like the film itself, Ptolemy's balcony offers panoramic vistas, as we gaze with him out onto the Alexandrine harbor, with its *theamata* or "spectacular sight," the famous Lighthouse of Pharos.[3] As Ptolemy reflects on Alexander, he refers to him as a "Colossus," thus linking the great general with another *theamata*, the Colossus of Rhodes, and, by extension, suggesting that the subject and form of *Alexander* will also be a wondrous spectacle.

Not only does Ptolemy's balcony offer us the spectacle of monumental architecture and landscape—the city and its colossal lighthouse—which, along with crowds, battles, and sartorial and set extravagance are key attractions in the historical epic, but the balcony is also a pivot point for 360-degree vision, which spatially inserts us into the narrative. We look over Ptolemy's shoulder as he begins his story, gesturing, first to his right "To the East, the vast Persian Empire ruled almost all the known world," and then to his left "to the West, the once great city-states, Thebes, Athens, Sparta, had fallen from pride" (see Figure 2.1). As Ptolemy muses and wanders through the balcony, the Steadicam dollies and swoops, as we follow his meandering and circular path past lush Egyptian papyrus plants, statuary and exotic birds. The camera's movements and the image itself subtly trace the dynamic and far-flung vision which the modern historical epic offers us. With the words "it was Philip, the one-eyed," Ptolemy and camera take us into the famous Alexandrine library. There, with its circular shape, monumental stacks of scrolls and prominent map, this "theater of documents" exemplifies and puns on Alexander's global and stereoscopic vision, a vision that vastly expanded his monocular father's reach.[4] Like Barthes, it suggests that History is theater: it surrounds and beckons us.

How have digital special effects transformed the aesthetics of the historical epic? I begin with an industrial survey ("the state of the business") which shows how computer-generated imagery (CGI) has reshaped all genres in a Hollywood film industry in which (digital) special effects now play a dominant role and in which the special-effects industry is a transnational, round-the-clock and round-the-world enterprise that shapes not only film production but also pre- and post-production. "State of the art" then discusses important technical and aesthetic innovations of the digital-effects era through three recurrent elements of the historical epic: spectacular action, spectacular architecture, and spectacular detail. We will look at how new digital technologies such as crowd-replication software, digital set extensions, 3D animation, and performance-capture films create spectatorial experiences in *300* (2006), *Gladiator* (2000), *Troy* (2004), and

Figure 2.1

Alexander: To the West: Ptolemy looks over the harbor of Alexandria with the Lighthouse of Pharos in the distance.

Alexander, which offer both the observational distance and scope of Ptolemy's balcony *and* a sense of immersion, of "history in the round."

industrial context and economic factors: the state of the business[5]

cgi is widespread spectacle and invisible effect

Special effects are traditionally used to create images or environments which are too dangerous, costly or simply impossible to photograph in reality. Shilo McClean's recent study of digital special effects suggests that digital effects function in a number of different ways. They can extend scenes or images of violence, exaggerating the illusion and proximity of danger. They can expand temporal or spatial manipulations (such as speed ramping in *300*), intensify kinetic thrills, and heighten verisimilitude. Finally, and especially in the historical film, special effects can create exotic creatures, sets, and locations and offer imaginary or impossible points of view of events, such as large-scale battles.[6]

With the release of *Gladiator* in 2000, CGI enabled the revitalization of a vanished genre because it obviated the need for the large casts and expensive sets that had been the death knell of the historical epic in costly failures such as *Cleopatra* (1963) and *The Fall of the Roman Empire* (1964) nearly forty years before. *Gladiator's* enormous financial and critical success led to a new cycle of the genre, with entries such as *Alexander, Troy, Kingdom of Heaven* (2005), and more recently, *300*. Special effects in the historical epic cannot be considered separately from the now extensive role of digital effects in many other Hollywood genres and, most especially, in the fantasy film (*The Lord of the Rings Trilogy* [2001–3], the *Harry Potter* series [2001–], *The Chronicles of Narnia* [2005, 2008], *The Golden Compass* [2007], *Stardust* [2007]), the action thriller (*Die Hard With a Vengeance* [1995], *The Bourne Supremacy* [2004]), the comic-book or graphic-novel adaptation (*Batman* [1999–2008], *X-Men* [2000], *Hellboy* [2004], *Sin City* [2005], *The Spirit* [2008], *Watchmen* [2009]), the science-fiction genre (*AI* [2001], *Minority Report* [2002], *I, Robot* [2004], *Cloverfield* [2008], *The Incredible Hulk* [2008]), and the 3-D animated film (*Shrek* [2001], *Ratatouille* [2007], *Wall-E* [2008]). The top twenty domestic and worldwide grossing films are effects films, and (adjusted for inflation), eight of the top twenty grossing films of all time are digital-effects films.[7] Especially in the science-fiction and fantasy genres, digital effects invite spectatorial attention to the visual surface of the film. This representation and self-reflexive deployment of technology can sometimes halt the narrative, prompting spectatorial awe in the face of the technologically sublime.[8] As Tom Conley has suggested, digital effects have become the symbolic coin of the realm, the attraction that sells.[9]

But it is the "invisible effect shot," or one designed not to be noticed by the spectator that forms a far larger role onscreen than the CGI cinema of spectacle. Indeed, from small dramas to big-budget films, invisible effects such as wire and dust removal, face replacement, color timing, and the addition of atmospheric elements such as smoke, fire and water, as well as other touch-ups and adjustments form up to 80 percent of the work of the visual-effects industry.[10] For example, the special effects for the pioneering film of the contemporary cycle, *Gladiator,* were deliberately designed to enhance verisimilitude and spectatorial immersion in the scenes in the Colosseum and Forum and to be functionally seamless, if not invisible.[11]

cgi is film

Lev Manovich suggests that in the digital era cinema is closer to both painting (no longer Kino eye but Kino brush) and to animation in that live-action footage is but one of its many elements.[12] Instead of an optical or chemical process, image creation and manipulation are now digital. The image can be generated in one of three ways—on location, on a soundstage, or in a digital studio—and, increasingly, the image combines all three sources.[13] Added to the fragmentation of *image capture* is the fragmentation of *image manipulation,* for CGI works in depth by compositing or combining image layers, working from background to foreground or vice versa; as Gray Marshal suggests, "visual effects artists are deconstructionists— Give us the pieces and we'll build it for you."[14] The boundary or distinction between analogue and digital, between production and post-production, no longer applies. Once live-action footage is digitized, it is indistinguishable from a 2D image that is created in a paint program, or a 3D image that is modeled and animated, for whatever the source, they all become pixels of information that can be composited, morphed or otherwise manipulated. Consequently, digital effects increasingly blur the boundary between the ontology of pro-filmic reality and the final CGI image, and, in some cases, the number of effects shots increasingly approaches the *total shot count of a film,* such as the 1,472 shots of *300.*[15]

Necessitated by the sheer volume of work, studios now hire multiple effects houses for a contracted number of effects shots, in an assembly-line system that echoes the division and specialization of labor of the Classical Hollywood studio system but which is largely out-sourced rather than in-house.[16]

For example, *300* used twelve different effects houses in Los Angeles, Montreal, and Sydney to create more than 1,400 CGI shots for a film whose global cast of Scottish, Bermudan, and Brazilian actors paralleled the global makeup of its effects technicians. Like the Classical Hollywood assembly system, many of these effects houses specialize in particular types of digital illusion; for example, German company Scanline was hired to create the CGI shots of the Persian armada collapsing in the storm in *300,* because of the company's proprietary software and water-effects work for *Poseidon* (2006).

cgi is part of a global twenty-four-hour production system

Digital effects work enables an artist to experiment in ways that would have been inadvisable or impossible in an optical compositing era.[17] Production time has been revolutionized; previously, where compositing a single shot would take weeks in the optical era, it now takes hours, and, in addition, a shot can now be worked on simultaneously by multiple artists.[18] With outsourcing of CGI production now global rather than national, secure digital pipeline systems have transformed the production of film into a twenty-four-hour cycle, with effects houses from France (BUF) to New Zealand (Weta) submitting shots for approval in Los Angeles, while production and postproduction go on simultaneously elsewhere in Malta, Mexico or Morocco.[19] The historical epic continues to be global in its production scope. Fort Ricasoli in Malta (*Gladiator, Troy*), Mexico (*Troy*), Morocco (*Gladiator, Alexander*), and Thailand (*Alexander*) are favored for their spectacular and varied scenery, and Shepperton and Pinewood Studios in England and Cinecittà in Rome remain in demand for their large-scale soundstages. The prevalence of British, Irish, and Australasian actors in contemporary historical epics such as *Alexander* and *300* continues a long Hollywood tradition of importing international talent.[20] Foreign extras cost much less than domestic extras (thus *Troy* used Mexicans and Bulgarians, and *Alexander* Moroccans, Spaniards, and Thais). Moreover, the emergence of Canada, England, New Zealand, Australia, and France as key players in the effects industry means that special-effects production is also now a transnational phenomenon. Production dollars follow cheaper offshore labor, and, in future, non-Western effects specialists will be significant competitors to US effects companies. For a twenty-fifth-anniversary survey of the industry, the editors of *Cinefex* suggested that

> Effects shops have had a diversity of surnames and accents for a long time. But at some point, the cream of the crop will stay home and start their own companies in their own countries. And that company in India or Latin America where they can get technologically trained people for next to nothing is going to be a very appealing option for producers and studios.[21]

cgi shapes preproduction and production

No longer just a "postproduction" component, digital techniques shape the planning of camera angles and movements, equipment requirements, location shooting, and cinematography, and blur the traditional boundaries between set and production design, cinematography and editing, especially given that many of these departments already plan and create their shots with digital tools. First, in the transition from treatment to screenplay to storyboard, "Previz" or previsualization software and animatics storyboard the film as an animated map of shot types, camera angles, and movement; in effect, *a microcosm of the film itself.* But while previz was initially designed with such technical functions in mind, it is increasingly used as a conceptual aesthetic tool, as Colin Green of Pixel Liberation Front observed: "the technical questions aren't even asked until the very end. It's there purely to define the visual approach."[22] For example, "previz" software helped plan Oliver Stone's idea to show the epic sweep of the battle of Gaugamela in *Alexander* from a digital eagle's point of view, flying over 300,000 Macedonian and Persian soldiers. It also helped plan the stunning aerial shot of the landing of the vast Greek armada in *Troy,* with its composite of aerial photographic plates captured on location at Golden Beach, Malta, combined with 400 extras. As Visual Effects Supervisor Nick Davis described it, "The armada landing was one of the first shots Wolfgang [Petersen] described in our initial meeting . . . He wanted a helicopter shot flying over the beach, looking down on all the ships as they hit the beach, tilting up to reveal thousands of men jumping off the boats. It was his vision for the movie."[23] Previz software helped plan where people would be placed on the beach. Framestore CFC used synthetic crowd replication and other digital tools to "paint in the crowd," creating 6,000 characters and forty landing boats from 1,000 motion-capture (mocap) clips. Previz also helped imagine possible camera angles and movement and plan camera equipment necessary to photograph *Troy*'s "Battle of the Arrows" sequence, a major set piece in which 50,000 Greeks are massed outside the gates of Troy, where they engage in battle with 25,000 Trojans.[24] Previz planned a high-speed camera movement that swoops down from 60 to 12 feet over the heads of the Greeks charging into the Trojans. As Petersen said, "it's exciting to create these worlds, first in computers, and then you see it more and more realized, and [then] you see the final product."[25]

As a marketing tool, animatics can even help greenlight a movie and is increasingly used as a "proof of concept" visualization device to demonstrate the spectacular set pieces or novelty attractions of a film in pitches to studio heads and investors. Warner Bros. commissioned such a test from Australian effects Animal Logic for *300* to illustrate the film's distinctive graphic design. They photographed stills of a live-action performer in a cape and helmet and then manipulated the image in Adobe Photoshop to emulate the source novel's stylized color palette.[26] Planning blocking, lighting or camera movement requires a precise knowledge of what the final composited shot looks like. With the increasing use of greenscreen in Hollywood film (which can be 80 percent of a shot), previz is also used to show directors, actors, and cinematographers what they *cannot* see by looking through the camera lens; in other words, it compensates for the temporally and visually fragmented nature of digital assemblage. For example, in *Alexander,* the shot of Ptolemy standing on the balcony looking out at the harbor was a composite of photography on the Shepperton studio sound-stage (Hopkins and the balcony set), combined with digital plates of Alexandria's city and harbor, created in 3D animation, while scenes with Alexander and his men gazing out at Babylon combined Pinewood sound-stages with a "digital backlot" created by French effects house BUF. Not only is previz a production tool, it is also a postproduction tool. Sometimes called "postviz," animatics fill in the greenscreen parts of the image so that editors have all the necessary elements to help them design and time the cutting of the film.

Today, a personal computer with off-the-shelf software (Maya, Shake) or in-house proprietary software can create special effects, instead of the capital-intensive hardware of first-generation Cray Supercomputers or second-generation Silicon Graphics workstations that once were used by pioneering effects companies such as Industrial Light and Magic and Digital Domain. As a result of cheaper hardware, in around 1995 the number of boutique special-effects companies exploded, competing for niche work, while in this same period midsize facilities largely disappeared and studios began closing their in-house special-effects companies.[27] While the industry went through an expansionist period in the early to mid-1990s, which Michelle Pierson termed its "wonder years," today the marketplace is also a place of increased competition and price underbidding, in which effects houses struggle to survive or make a profit.[28] In the wake of Hollywood studios' transformation into adjuncts of global media companies, new corporate oversight in the last decade has led to the slashing of effects budgets and pre- and postproduction timetables. Ironically, given the aesthetic dominance of CGI shots, effects artists feel they are "the ugly stepchild of production."[29] As Ian Hunter of New Deal Studios bemoans, "they cut pre-production and postproduction because in the corporate world, they don't understand what preproduction and postproduction mean in a movie. They just want production because production equals product. So they go right to shooting without a finished script."[30]

key elements of cgi in the historical epic: the state of the art

Given the radical transformation of the film industry by the digital era and in light of the all-pervasive role of CGI as both spectacle *and* invisible effect, how has the historical epic been transformed? What does the new digital age of special effects enable that has not been seen before?

Digital innovations in special effects have enabled the intensification of the historical epic's distinctive generic attributes of *spectacularity, monumentality, and immersiveness.* As Bordwell, Staiger, and Thompson have suggested, the adoption of a new technology has three principal functions: it leads to greater efficiency; it offers product differentiation; and it allows the product to meet prevailing quality standards.[31] Meeting the first criteria of greater efficiency, the shift from the optical to the digital era has led to a rapid increase in the production and number of effects shots and, in some cases (such as crowd replication and performance capture), allows for completely new types of shots. Offering product differentiation, tools such as artificial-intelligence software, digital camera movements, and environmental extensions create a novel and immersive spectatorial experience while advancing the predominant Hollywood aesthetics of photorealism and historical verisimilitude (thereby fulfilling the prevailing quality standard). And although the reimagination and reinvention of the past would not be physically or financially possible without these new tools, CGI nonetheless operates in combination with more traditional effects techniques of the pre-digital era, such as miniatures, prosthetics, or forced perspective—indeed, certain techniques such as compositing and 3D animation are simply the digital equivalent of earlier effects like the matte, traveling matte, and glass shot.

Digital effects are most closely tied to the following key narrative conventions in the historical epic: *spectacular action (both individual and crowd-based), spectacular architecture,* and *spectacular detail.* While these three are also elements in other genres from fantasy to science fiction, they are consistent elements in the historical epic, and, as I will go on to suggest, new digital tools enable a visualization that exceeds the scale and spectacle of earlier eras.

spectacular action: the hero and the mass

the hero: alexander

>*Conquer your fear and I promise you will conquer death.*[32]

Historical epics celebrate the heroic male body, a figure of physical prowess who must prove his courage and skill. Like Achilles, he may be initially intransigent or, like Maximus, humbly reluctant, but eventually his leadership is in service to the army, tribe or proto-nation, and, by extension, to his own immortality. As with the heroic deaths of Maximus in *Gladiator* and Leonidas in *300,* the historical epic often suggests that the male body is a figure of redemptive sacrifice.[33]

Star casting in the historical epic brings together the heroic body of the character with the star body of the actor, without which the film cannot be made.[34] In reality it is Brad Pitt's face, not that of Helen of Troy, who launches a thousand (digital) ships, and it is his star body, which stands in for a second celebrity body, that of the heroic warrior, Achilles, and which in turn allegorically represents all Greek warriors. The film literalizes this metonymic function when Patroclus deliberately dresses as Achilles and, as a result, is mistakenly killed by Hector. In other words, whether it be

Achilles' Myrmidons or Leonidas' brave 300, the leader's body is coextensive with those of his men.

The spectacle of the hero engaged in solitary battle against an adversary is a generic characteristic of the historical epic, where battle functions to reveal character. Through the combatants' skill, strategy, and bravery in the course of the fight, we learn that Achilles and Hector are well-matched adversaries, but we also see that Achilles' rage at Patroclus' death gives him a swift fury that will lead to his victory against Hector. By contrast, Paris is a lover, not a fighter, and his cowardly failure in combat with Menelaus brings him a dishonor that he will only assuage by later killing Achilles. Single combat offers up the spectacle of brutality and violence through the choreography of movement and, whether by sword, shield or spear, offers narrative set pieces in which the viewer may identify with the hero's struggle for survival. *Gladiator*'s narration of individual and group-based combat in the gladiatorial arena takes this generic set piece and self-reflexively foregrounds it as fundamental to our spectatorial experience of the epic, demanding, as Maximus does of the crowd, "Are you not entertained?" The narrative formula of solo combat figures extensively in *Troy*, through the battles of Achilles and Hector and their respective adversaries: Achilles vs. Boagrius (the champion of Thessaly), or Hector vs. Ajax, and Hector vs. Patroclus (disguised as Achilles), culminating, finally, in what Wolfgang Petersen calls the "monumental fight," the battle of Achilles vs. Hector.[35] Its other common variant is the hero fighting an exoticized or mythical animal or monstrous human; in *300* (the young Leonidas vs. the wolf), in *Gladiator* (Maximus vs. Tigris of Gaul, Maximus vs. Bengal tigers); in *Alexander* (Alexander vs. a wild horse, Alexander vs. an armed warrior on an elephant); and in *Beowulf* (1999) (Beowulf vs. Grendel, Beowulf vs. Grendel's mother, and Beowulf vs. dragon). Sometimes the hero fights another human, made monstrously intimidating through their physical appearance or height, with the disparity in size and scale of the protagonist and their adversary underscoring the skill and bravery of the hero, as we see when Achilles fights the tall Boagrius in *Troy* or Leonidas, the Über Immortal in *300*.[36]

Historically, special effects (both practical and digital) are necessary because real weapons are too dangerous to be used in proximity to actors. Accordingly, special effects play an instrumental role by intensifying the verisimilitude of violence and the proximity of danger. For combat scenes, digital effects are usually combined with practical effects (prosthetics, makeup, animatronics, foreshortened or collapsible rubber swords, paper arrows), which in postproduction are digitally manipulated to add in weapon extensions, rotoscoped arrows, sparks flying from clashing swords, and weapons penetrating bodies. To show Maximus fighting the Bengal tigers in *Gladiator,* the tigers were photographed separately in front of blue-screen, and then composited in the final shot, along with atmospheric dust details. To show combat scenes in which limbs are sliced off by swords, amputee actors, dressed as Romans or Goths wore prosthetic limbs, which were "amputated" in battle by electrical charges in combination with blood-bag effects. While this latter instance is an example of a practical effect, for which Neil Corbould, Special Effects Supervisor, used similar strategies in the battle sequences of *Saving Private Ryan* (1998), digital extensions of swords and other weaponry (in conjunction with sound effects) help complete the illusion. In other words, special effects are always *hybrid,* combining digital and predigital techniques.

Vast numbers of arrows, often created by particle or other 3D animation, increasingly appear in the historical epic (as well as action film) as a spectacular new generic attraction. Prominently featured in Zhang Yimou's *Hero* (2002), innumerable arrows visually express the scale of battle or the immensity of an army. In *300,* the Persians are so numerous that their arrows blot out the sun, and, although the Spartans vow to "fight in the shade," it is these arrows which finally kill Leonidas and his men.[37] Because real arrows don't tend to "read on camera," and given their danger for actors and crew, Framestore CFC and Cinesite added up to 1,000 digital arrows for the "Battle of the Arrows" in *Troy* through 3D computer animation and modeling programs Maya and Houdini. Like Shake, an image-compositing program, software plug-ins can tackle specialized tasks such as the animation of fire, water, cloth, and smoke effects. In *Troy,* paper arrows propelled by cannons were photographed and then digitally amplified with arrows detailed with flames and smoke trails, while in *Gladiator,* Mill Film extended the trajectories of the arrows and pitch pots of flame in the opening battle of the Romans against the Germanic tribes.

the mass

> *I am leading an ocean!*
> Xerxes

The second dimension of spectacular action is the exponential multiplication of heroic bodies into a mass or crowd. Through their leadership and courage, the hero (Achilles, Alexander, Maximus, Leonidas, Beowulf) prompts the phalanx, tribe or army to follow in battle, as Alexander's heroic charge at Darius or Leonidas' defiant spear that wounds Xerxes exemplify. The spectacle of the crowd can also emphasize the scale of a city such as Babylon or Rome or can enhance a spectacular event or ritual such as Commodus' triumphant entry into Rome or the crowds assembled to watch the games in the Colosseum in *Gladiator.*

Huge battles involving hundreds of thousands of warriors are an important new element of spectacle in the historical and fantasy epic. As I have written elsewhere, the battles of Helm's Deep, Pelennor Fields, and Minas

Tirith in Peter Jackson's *The Lord of the Rings* trilogy were created by MASSIVE (Multiple Agent Simulation System In Virtual Environment) software, the first crowd-replication artificial-intelligence program and now widely used in the industry.[38] Artificial intelligence programs such as MASSIVE, Alice (developed by Moving Picture Company [MPC] for *Troy*) and Sheep (developed by Scanline VFX for *300*) are 3D-animation systems that generate crowd scenes based upon individual characters, called agents, who are capable of independent, autonomous action. Physical movements (walking, running, throwing spears, shooting arrows, etc.) are entered into a database through mocap technology, which involves the digital recording of an actor's *movements* rather than appearance. Live-action performers wear special bodysuits with white markers attached to them, which enable the rotoscoping or tracing of their physical movement and which in turn are used to create 3D-animated models. *Beowulf* and *The Polar Express* (2004) are two recent examples of this important new genre, or what is increasingly called the *performance-capture film*.[39] 3D agents are then generated from this database of mocap performances. Randomly assigned variables enable the production of thousands of "unique" copies of these master agents through a process called "instancing," which creates the vast numbers of warriors needed for epic battle scenes.

Crowd-replication software programs such as MASSIVE, Alice, and Sheep are virtuoso tools in the digital era of the historical epic because they enable the creation of crowd or battle scenes on a scale that was not possible even in the halcyon days of *Spartacus* (1960) and other earlier generation epics, in which thousands of real extras were used. Animal Logic used MASSIVE to generate up to 50,000 characters for the Persian Army as it poured onto the battlefield in *300*, while Scanline's Sheep created hundreds of tiny sailors on the Persian armada as it is shipwrecked in a storm. Indeed, the use of crowd-replication software and bluescreen is so widespread and well known to the public that a film such as *Meet the Spartans* (2008), a spoof of *300*, uses several bluescreen jokes.[40]

To create the crowd of 300,000 soldiers at the battle of Gaugamela in *Alexander,* in which 250,000 Persians battle 50,000 Macedonians, effects house BUF established a motion-capture studio on location in Morocco with four video cameras and photographed every element from multiple angles—all soldiers, chariots, camels, weapons, banners, and other props and sets in order to build a database from which effects artists could create 3D character animation. No bluescreen was used on location (as it would have constrained movement), and dust was a particular problem for the insertion and rotoscoping of digital extras (as it blurred the lines between foreground and background). Similarly, MPC created fifty effects shots for sequences relating to Alexander's conquest of India. Using a mocap database which they had originally created for *Troy,* MPC used Alice crowd-simulation software to multiply fifty actors photographed on location in

Thailand into 400 members of Alexander's cavalry, and to double thirty elephants to sixty.[41]

The spectacle of the crowd, indeed the crowd as collective character, is central to *Gladiator*'s narrative and themes. The digital amplification of the Colosseum's crowds and architecture was a key visual strategy to suggest the colossal scale of the Roman Empire. As scholars have noted, the striking aerial shots of the Colosseum echoed both Leni Riefenstahl and contemporary sports-arena photography and are an early example of the ways in which digital effects offer a spectacle of sights that have never been seen before.[42] Mill Film digitally extended the arena by two-thirds and with AudioMotion used crowd-replication software to turn 2,000 extras into 33,000 spectators. Because 90 percent of the aerial shots of the Colosseum were digital, the sailors working the velarium and extras walking outside the arena were performance captured and inserted into the digital environment. Similarly, thirty extras (photographed three times, straight on, or at 45 degrees from the side, or above) and also photographed in three different lighting setups (shade, partial shade, full sun) formed a database of individual crowd members, and later these could be placed anywhere they were needed in the Colosseum arena shots. Each extra was dressed in a toga and photographed in front of a greenscreen, so that Mill Film could later digitally replace the togas with any range of colors and multiply the extras into thousands of spectators (with richer spectators wearing white seated in the lowest seats, and poorer plebs wearing brown togas in the upper ranks).

spectacular architecture: the digital backlot

"Size matters!"[43]

The second category of spectacle in which digital effects plays an instrumental role is in the digital creation or extension of exotic and often monumental architecture, cities, landscapes, and bodies of water. The construction of environments which are entirely digital (*300*) or partially digital (*Alexander*) reconstruct lands like Sparta or cities like Babylon through a combination of large soundstages or location sets photographed with green or bluescreen. These green or bluescreen backgrounds are then replaced by digital vistas composited into the final image to create a seamless digital environment.[44] For example, in *Troy,* when Hector and Paris first return to the city with Helen, we see a location set (Fort Ricasoli in Malta) composited with a CGI background of the city of Troy created by MPC. In a similar way, *Gladiator's* famous shot of Commodus' triumph, with thousands of assembled Praetorian Guards and the Colosseum in the distance, was a photographic plate of the Senators on a practical set in Fort Ricasoli in Malta with a bluescreen background. Mill Film composited these practical elements with a digital image of the city and guards to create the final spectacular image of Rome.

Production-design decisions in both *Troy* and *Alexander* deliberately magnified the historical scale of the cities. Jan Roelfs, Production Designer for *Alexander,* conceived of Babylon as a giant metropolis, which we see from a balcony where Alexander and his soldiers gaze out in wonder, upon their initial arrival in the city (see Figure 2.2).[45]

BUF increased the Tower of Babel from its historical size of 300 feet to 1,000 feet, and the Babylonian gates of the city were also doubled in height. Together with concept artist Adam Brockbank, Roelfs created drawings of the city in perspective, which BUF scanned and from which it created 3D architectural models. These models were texture mapped or painted, dressed (largely in an alternating blue and brown color scheme for the façades) and lit. For Alexander's triumphal entrance into Babylon, partial practical sets of the famous gates of Babylon were constructed and patterned with cuneiform script, fluted columns, and statues of bulls on capitals. The gates featured a pearlescent blue-paint finish to retain its luminous mosaic finish in the harsh sun of the location in Marrakech, Morocco. These partial sets were photographed and later digitally amplified to enhance the scale of the city. The immensity of Alexander's conquest is further exaggerated by Stone's subjective editing and cinematography, which create a dreamlike spectatorial experience that simulates Alexander's awe as he is welcomed into the city. A spectacle of color, sound, and texture, Stone uses extreme low-angle and canted camera angles, slow motion and shallow depth of field to show Alexander's point of view as he crosses a bridge and enters through the Babylonian gates, to a crowd that cheers and showers him with rose petals. Finally, a crane shot moves from an over-the-shoulder shot of Alexander on horseback moving through the welcoming Babylonian crowd into a panoramic vertical shot of the city.

Figure 2.2

Alexander: "Philip never saw Babylon." Gazing with Alexander upon the city of Babylon, with the city gates and Tower of Babel.

Blended with a digital camera movement that continues the crane's vertical direction, the shot becomes a spectacular aerial shot of an entirely digital environment, with a long shot of the main thoroughfare of Babylon and the Tower of Babel prominently framed on the left.

Troy also integrated partial practical sets with vast digital extensions. A 40-foot-tall, 500-foot-long section of the walls of Troy was built on location in Cabo San Lucas, Mexico, with 60-foot center gates. Like the gates of Babylon, the Trojan gates were a key aspect of the mise-en-scène because they suggested both the majestic and besieged nature of the city. The gates dominate the shots in the Battle of the Arrows, in which the Trojans initially triumph over the invading Greeks. Successfully protective, the gates prompt the Greeks to adopt the stratagem of a 40-foot-tall Trojan horse as a means to enter the city. As Nigel Phelps, *Troy*'s Production Designer recognizes, the film's epic scale fused hybrid design elements: "What I've done is mix up several different cultures of the period, the scale of the Egyptians, [with] some of the forms that the Mycenaeans created."[46] Like *Alexander,* the historical size and scale of the city is exaggerated. Phelps populated the practical and digital back lots with 115 columns that ranged in size from 15 to 40 feet, and Trojan statues that were 40 feet high (rather than the historically accurate size of 10 feet). MPC used Maya plug-ins like City Builder to construct virtual 3D environments, beginning with ten generic buildings, which appeared completely different from all four angles. These then were multiplied to between fifty and eighty new buildings and dressed with set elements (tables, pots, plants, etc.), using textures from 5,000 digital stills photographed in Malta. MPC placed these computer-generated buildings on a terrain with architectural software that used overlapping aerial photographs to create an illusion of stereoscopic depth. This computer-generated cityscape was then combined with one full-scale street built on location in Malta.[47] In these ways, through a combination of practical sets and digital amplifications, films such as *Alexander* and *Troy* create a key attraction of the contemporary historical epic: the illusion of a monumental architectural world. As if we are eyewitnesses to history, we stand there on the balcony with Alexander, sharing his view of a city his father could never have imagined.

tiling of backgrounds

Digital tools can also suggest or enhance an immersive three-dimensional environment by tiling together wide-angle plates of landscapes or actors. Tiling is the combination of individual photographic plates, which are then combined to create a much larger widescreen or mosaic image. For example, by photographing individual plates of mountains or other landscapes as backgrounds and then combining them, one can simulate the original 360-degree environment or create an entirely new immersive space which may not exist in reality. The latter strategy was used extensively in *The Lord of the Rings* trilogy, where the fictitious mountains of Isengard and Mordor and the Rivendell location were composites of photographic plates taken by second-unit aerial cameras in different locations in the South Island, New Zealand.[48] In Norman Klein's recent study of special effects he suggests that nineteenth-century European panoramas or American cycloramas created immersive spaces that were founded upon a baroque aesthetic, "When a movie set is prepared for a shot, the space tends to look Baroque. The seams left by trompe l'oeil artifice and mixed media stand out."[49] Klein goes on to suggest that this baroque construct produces verisimilitude, because "once the camera records the shot, what winds up on film may well look panoramic, a long shot ten miles deep. Certainly, artifice disappears."[50] This is exactly what tiling does. By linking Vistavision plates of extras in *Gladiator*'s opening battle between the Romans and Germanic tribes (shot on location in Bourne Woods in the UK), Mill Film used tiling to create a fictitious environment, combining individual plates of 1,500 extras, alternately dressed and photographed as either Roman or Germanic soldiers, and which, when combined, multiplied them into 10,000 warriors. Unified by a digital-camera movement in postproduction, tiling of individual plates was a cost-effective solution to budget constraints. With a kinetic scene of fire and blood, tiling transformed the forest into an immersive and chaotic combat space and was a dynamic way to begin Maximus' story.

camera movement

Digital sets also make possible digital-camera movements, which intensify the spectatorial experience of a panoramic digital environment. Digital back lots enable digital fly-through and 360 rotation around the actors, and this vertiginous camera movement was also used extensively by Peter Jackson in his trilogy. Given the extensive number of aerial digital shots of the Colosseum in *Gladiator*, Mill Film Visual Effects Supervisor John Nelson suggested that Ridley Scott should also consider digital camera moves. Accordingly, Scott chose a 360-degree digital Steadicam shot, whose movement echoed the circular shape of the Colosseum. Scott's digital-camera movement around Maximus and the gladiators helps suggest something of their amazement (and by extension our own) as they gaze upon the most spectacular arena they have ever seen: the Roman Colosseum. The intensely dizzying effect of the digital camera's point of view as it moves through an imaginary mise-en-scène is another way in which this technique transforms the affective experience of the viewer, moving us from a static and more contemplative position, like Ptolemy or Alexander's balcony viewer, into a more active and immersive spectatorship.

Certainly a panoramic effect can also be achieved by a physical camera movement on location (such as the track, dolly or Steadicam), in combination with CGI background plates, as we see in the sequence that opens *Alexander's* Battle of Gaugamela. As we hear Ptolemy's ominous voice-over, "It was mad. Forty thousand of us against hundreds of thousands of barbarian races," we open with a long shot of vast, apparently empty desert terrain, and the caption "Gaugamela, Persia, 331 bc—45 years earlier." As the camera pans right, Alexander appears, sitting on his horse, facing frame left, and, as the camera continues to pan, he wheels his horse around to face right. We are on a hill overlooking the plains of Gaugamela, and, as the camera pans away from Alexander to his point of view, we see a CGI valley filled with thousands of Persians, suggested by vast clouds of dust suspended in the air. Shot on location in Morocco (whose Atlas mountains stood in for the Hindu Kush), the desert locations were composited with CGI crowds of Persian and Macedonian warriors. The viewer is offered an immense vista of landscape and men girding for battle, and these immensities of natural and human form metonymically suggest the epic scale and historic significance of the battle itself.

Stone first introduces a soaring eagle in the battle of Gaugamela, whose reappearance throughout the film establishes a thematic and symbolic association between Alexander and bird, and one that also subtly suggests Alexander's Promethean ambition.[51] This eagle is the narrative pretext for a stunning series of CGI shots in which digital-camera movement simulates the swoop of the eagle over the battle, allowing the viewer to step back from the details of ground-level combat and to see the tremendous scale of the battle (see Figure 2.3).

Aided by consistent screen direction and helpful onscreen labels (Macedonian center, left, and right flanks), we understand the broader tactical strategies which Alexander and his men adopt. The final sequences combined computer-generated camera movement, physical Akela crane shots, and second-unit helicopter shots, as well as two real eagles.[52]

Figure 2.3

Alexander: Eagle's Point of View: An eagle flies over the vast battle of Gaugamela in which the Macedonian Army battled the Persians.

The digital blending of real and simulated aerial photography offers a vision of battle that might remind us of films such as *Apocalypse Now* (1979) and the contemporary war genre, or of news footage in documentaries or television. In this way, digital effects offer new spectacle, deploying the technology and cinematography of the twenty-first century to photograph the ancient world in a way that seems to transport us back into the past.

the spectacle of detail

Vivian Sobchack has suggested that the historical epic produces History from "a transcendence of accuracy and specificity enabled by a general and excessive parade and accumulation of detail and event."[53] The spectacle of detail invites our attention to *surfaces.* Through costumes, makeup, props, sets, and other signifiers of historical period, the fetishism of color, texture, design, object, and environment offer some of the genre's compelling attractions. And while many of the elements of the spectacle of detail are not rooted in special effects, I want to conclude with one element which is: the digital manipulation of color.

color

In production, narrative color schemes can be shaped by careful selection of costumes, set and production-design elements, and cinematographic choices, and in postproduction through color timing. Whether it is the mass Bactrian wedding scene in *Alexander,* whose red, brown, and dark purple Asian textiles were intensified by chocolate filters or the harsh contrasting whites and blues of the Macedonia sequences, or the greens, oranges, and pinks of India, Stone and Director of Photography Rodrigo Prieto chose a distinctive color scheme for each narrative section of Alexander's life. This included a radically innovative choice of infrared film stock to express Alexander's near-death experience, in which greens turned magenta and skin white. And while these color manipulations are cinematographic ones bound by choices of film stock, lighting schemes, and costume tonal ranges, since its first extensive use in *O Brother, Where Art Thou?* (2000), the digital scanning and grading of film is an important new tool which can supplement, or in some cases replace, analogue or practical color effects. In *300,* a stylized color and design scheme developed by Montreal Meteor Studios called "The Crush" opted for a graphic aesthetic that increased light and dark contrasts in a predominantly sepia color scheme, punctuated by red and black visual accents which digitally emulated Lynn Varley's color design in Frank Miller's graphic novel *300.* Animal Logic's Art Director Grant Freckleton suggested that the Crush "gave the audience a visual cue that they were looking at stylized imagery, rather than something that was striving to be realistic."[54] Animal Logic adapted techniques that they had previously created for a television commercial and which mimicked the look of coffee stains. Freckleton continues, "I started integrating some of these old coffee stains, ink-splats and blobs of watercolors that had soaked into the paper, creating fractal effects, like clouds. . . . [to come up with] a look that was obviously not a photograph, but not quite a painting; it was something in-between."[55]

The digital era of special effects offers this "something in-between," moving between contemplative vistas and the novelty of full immersion. Motion-capture and artificial-intelligence software offer epic battle and crowd scenes on a scale that have never been seen before. Three-dimensional animation and rotoscoping enhance our sense of immersion in a battle with realistic details and a heightened sense of the proximity of violence. Digital back lots create a spectacularly exoticized environment, reimagining cities such as Troy or Rome, which are textured, detailed and intensely colorful, while digital tiling and camera movement can take us into panoramic environments, rotating our point of view and intensifying our sense of awe. Where the panoramas of the historical epic of the 1950s proffered contemplative but relatively static vistas from the Balcony of History, the new era of digital effects enables an affectively exciting and intensely embodied spectatorship. Like the eagle at the battle of Gaugamela, which periodically swoops down and through the action, so too do we. And while Philip may not have seen Babylon, digital technology takes us a little closer to Alexander's experience: not only have we *seen* Babylon, we have *felt* it a little too.

notes

1. See Roland Barthes, "On CinemaScope," trans. Jonathan Rosenbaum, available online at http://english.chass.ncsu.edu/jouvert/v3i3/barth.htm (accessed March 13, 2010). First published in *Les lettres nouvelles,* February 1954 (1999), pp. 1–2. See also James Morrison's "On Barthes on Cinemascope," *Jouvert,* 3 (3) (1999): 3–7.
   ]] Available online at http://social.chass.ncsu.edu/jouvert/v313/barth.html (accessed July 30, 2008).
2. Ptolemy's prologue acts as a bracket to the film, although there are changes in the content and sequencing of events in the three versions of the film: the theatrical release (2004), the first DVD version, *Alexander, Special Edition* (2005), and the final DVD, *Alexander Revisited: The Final Cut* (2007).
3. *Theamata* is sometimes inaccurately translated as "Wonder of the World," rather than the more precise "things to be seen" which embeds within it the supposition that the object to be seen is a spectacular one. The Seven Ancient Wonders of the World were first attested in the second century bc in the *Laterculi Alexandrini* (Berlin Papyri, 13044v, col. 8–9) and in Antipater of Sidon (*Anthologia Palatina,* 9.58). Besides the Lighthouse of Pharos, there were the Pyramids of Egypt, the Hanging Gardens of Babylon, the Temple of Artemis at Ephesus, the Statue of Zeus at Olympia, the Mausoleum of Halicarnassus, and the Colossus of Rhodes. Sometimes the city gates of Babylon are listed instead of the Lighthouse, and later lists, such as Pliny the Elder's, included different structures such as the Temple of Zeus at Cyzicus

and the Labyrinth of King Minos of Crete: "Seven Wonders of the Ancient World," in Simon Hornblower and Antony Spawnforth (eds), *The Oxford Companion to Classical Civilization* (Oxford: Oxford University Press, 1998).

4. The "theater of documents" was conceived by Production Designer Jan Roelfs and reminds us of Barthes' notion of CinemaScope as the "ideal space of the great dramaturgies," (On CinemaScope," p. 2). According to historical consultant and classicist Robin Lane Fox, the roundness of the library's shape would have been considered avant-garde for the period. See Robin Lane Fox, *The Making of Alexander* (Oxford: R & L, 2004), p. 83.

5. To mark its twenty-fifth anniversary, industry journal *Cinefex* conducted fifty interviews with key personnel in dozens of effects houses and condensed eighty hours of taped interviews into two articles: "State of the Business" and "State of the Art." I draw many of my observations and conclusions from these extensive interviews. See Jody Duncan (ed.) "State of the Art: A *Cinefex* 25th Anniversary Forum," interviews by Don Shay and Joe Fordham, *Cinefex*, 100 (January 2005), pp. 17–112 and Jody Duncan (ed.) "State of the Business," interviews by Don Shay, Joe Fordham, and Jody Duncan, *Cinefex*, 101 (April 2005): 12–49.

6. Shilo T. McClean, *Digital Storytelling: The Narrative Power of Visual Effects in Film* (Cambridge, Mass.: MIT Press, 2007), pp. 160–161.

7. A number of others on the all-time box-office hits (adjusted for inflation) feature innovative pre-digital effects sequences (including *Gone with the Wind, Ben-Hur, The Ten Commandments, Jaws, The Exorcist*). Available online at www. boxofficemojo.com/alltime (accessed July 30, 2008).

8. See Scott Bukatman, *Matters of Gravity: Special Effects and Supermen in the 20th Century* (Durham, NC: Duke University Press), pp. 115–116; cited in McClean, *Digital Storytelling*, p. 166.

9. In an essay on cartography and *The Lord of the Rings* trilogy, Tom Conley suggests that cartography shapes our perception and cognition of space in the film and is closely connected to the power of the camera to produce special effects. Tom Conley, "*The Lord of the Rings* and the Fellowship of the Map," in Ernest Mathijs and Murray Pomerance (eds.), *From Hobbits to Hollywood: Essays on Peter Jackson's Lord of the Rings* (Amsterdam and New York: Rodopi, 2006), pp. 215–230. "In *The Fellowship of the Rings* the symbolic money of the film is fantasy. And fantasy is shown to be the product less of Tolkien than of special effects" (p. 227). By extension, we might consider whether the historical epic (in which cartography too is central) is less the product of historical sources (archeology, classics) than it is the product of special effects.

10. In a *Cinefex* interview, Van Ling, Visual Effects Supervisor, noted, "Those kinds of utility shots [like wire removal], as opposed to the hero stuff, are probably a good eighty to ninety percent of the business." (Duncan, "State of the Art," p. 25). See also Paula Parisi, "The New Hollywood Silicon Stars," *Wired*, December 1995, pp. 142–145, 202–210.

11. Shilo T. McClean makes a distinction between invisible and seamless effects, where "the seamless use of effects is continuous with invisible usage, but seamless effects are discernible if subjected to consideration and scrutiny" (*Digital Storytelling*, p. 78). She gives the example of a digital matte painting of destroyed Warsaw as a background plate in Roman Polanski's *The Pianist* (2002) as an example of a seamless effect. For Ridley Scott's desire for special effects to enhance verisimilitude, see Kevin Martin. "A Cut Above," *Cinefex*, 82 (July 2000): 13–31; p. 31.

57

12. Lev Manovich, *The Language of New Media* (Cambridge, Mass.: MIT Press, 2001), pp. 302, 307.

13. McClean, *Digital Storytelling,* p. 8.

14. Duncan, "State of the Art," p. 34.

15. There were 746 effects shots in *Troy,* 350 in *Alexander,* and ninety in *Gladiator.*

16. The film *300* featured the work of Warner Bros Inhouse Unit (158 shots), Animal Logic (191), Hybride (560), Hydraulx (48), Pixel Magic (107), Scanline VFX (7), Meteor Studios (111), Buzz Images (106), Screaming Death Monkey (96), Lola Visual Effects (66), Technicolor Digital (21), and Amalgamated Pixels (1). For special-effects techniques in the film, see Joe Fordham, "A Beautiful Death," *Cinefex,* 109 (April 2007): 64–86. For *Troy,* 746 CGI shots were created by four effects houses: MPC (430 shots), Framestore CFC (130), Cinesite Europe (116), and Lola Postproduction (70). See Joe Fordham, "Bronze Age Ballistics," *Cinefex,* 98 (July 2004): 38–98. For *Alexander,* French Company BUF created more than 200 shots, while fifty shots were created by MPC. For special effects in the film, see supplementaries on the DVD special edition of *Alexander Revisited: The Final Cut* (2007) and production information in Fox, *The Making of Alexander,* as well as Alan Bielik, "*Alexander:* Digitally Pushing the Sword and Sandal Genre," *VFX World,* November 24, 2004, available online at http://vfxworld.com/?atype=articles&id=2303 (accessed August 2, 2008). For *Gladiator,* British effects house Mill Film created CGI "blimp" or aerial shots of the Colosseum, digitally extended two-thirds of the Colosseum, added 33,000 to the 2,000 extras through crowd-replication software, inserted backdrop shots to Commodus' triumphal parade, enhanced the opening Roman battle against the tribes in Germania and the combat sequences in the gladiatorial-training school in Morocco, and composited Oliver Reed's face onto a body double after his untimely death. See Martin, "A Cut Above."

17. Rob Legato points out that "digital allows you to do things over and over again—an opportunity you would never get on film—you get better at it. It's like editing on the Avid. I can make ten mistakes and finally get it on the eleventh try" (Duncan, "State of the Art," p. 24).

18. This improvement in productivity has led to a new problem: that digital techniques are increasingly used (but at great expense) to fix problems which originated in production, such as errors in lighting, sets or camera angles. See issue discussed in Duncan, "State of the Art," pp. 25 and 32.

19. For *Gladiator,* London-based effects house Mill Film communicated with the Los Angeles head office over a WAMINET, which enables speedy transfer of large media files. Visual-Effects Supervisor John Nelson worked with Ridley Scott and editor Pietro Scalia, sending production notes via email to Mill Film in London at night (LA time). At 4 p.m. London time the British visual-effects team would send back their completed shots just as the Los Angeles staff were starting their workday. As Nelson observed, "So the sun never set on the visual effects for *Gladiator*" (quoted in Martin, "A Cut Above," p. 31).

20. *Gladiator* also featured an international cast from New Zealand/Australia (Crowe), Ireland (Richard Harris), England (Hemmings, Jacobi), Benin (Hounsou), and Denmark (Nielsen), as well as the USA (Phoenix). Similarly, *Troy* also featured a predominance of English (Bloom), Scottish (Cox), Irish (Gleeson, O'Toole), and German (Kruger) actors, while *300*

included a cast from England (Dominic West), Australia (David Wenham), Scotland (Gerard Butler), and Bermuda (Headey).

21. Duncan, "State of the Business," p. 118. The historical epic also depends for its success on a global box office. For example, with its budget of $155 million, *Alexander* was a box-office failure in the USA, grossing $34 million domestically, but did much better in overseas markets, securing $133 million. Similarly, *Troy,* with its $175 million budget, grossed $133 million in the USA but garnered an additional $364 million in overseas box office. The most successful historical epic has been *300* with its relatively moderate budget of $65 million and profit of $456 million worldwide. See www.boxofficemojo.com/movies/?id=alexander.htm (accessed July 30, 2008).

22. Duncan, "State of the Art," pp. 42–44.

23. Fordham, "Bronze Age Ballistics," pp. 57–59.

24. "An Effects Odyssey," featurette Disk 2, *Troy.*

25. "An Effects Odyssey." See also Fordham, "Bronze Age Ballistics," pp. 59–60 on use of previz and wire-flown camera rig.

26. Later tests added circular camera movement, and shooting at 150 frames per second, the film's characteristic speed-ramping technique (where the sequence snap-zooms from one frame speed to another). Animal Logic added 3D environment extensions, digital sword hits, blood effects, crowd replication, and a 2D sepia sky. See Fordham, "A Beautiful Death," p. 66.

27. Three at Disney and three at Warner Bros. have closed in the past ten years. Duncan, "State of the Art," p. 48.

28. Michelle Pierson, *Special Effects: Still in Search of Wonder* (New York: Columbia University Press, 2002), p. 93.

29. Cinefex editors, quoted in Jody Duncan, "State of the Art," p. 33.

30. Effects companies struggle with the cyclical nature of the production calendar, with late winter production for summer releases of effects-heavy films remaining the busiest time. Unpredictable work at other times of the year leads many effects houses to work in television, advertising, music videos, and gaming. Average budgets for large-scale Hollywood productions run between $150 million and $185 million, with effects budgets that can run from $35 million to $60 million. Duncan, "State of the Art," p. 33.

31. Cited in McClean, *Digital Storytelling,* p. 13.

32. *Alexander,* script by Oliver Stone, Christopher Kyle and Laeta Kalogridis.

33. The final shot of *300* uses hagiographic imagery, zooming back from a shot of Leonidas embedded with dozens of Persian arrows, arms flung out in a crucifixion pose, which figures him as a St. Sebastian or Christ-like figure. See Leon Hunt, "What Are Big Boys Made Of? *Spartacus, El Cid,* and the Male Epic," in Pat Kirkham and Janet Thumin (eds), *You Tarzan: Masculinity, Movies and Men* (New York: St. Martin's Press, 1993), pp. 65–83, and Robert Burgoyne "The Epic Film: *Gladiator* and *Spartacus,*" in Robert Burgoyne, *The Hollywood Historical Film* (New York: Blackwell, 2008), pp. 74–99.

34. Hence the importance of Kirk Douglas for *Spartacus* and Richard Burton for *Cleopatra,* and more recent examples include the star casting of Colin Farrell and Angelina Jolie for *Alexander.* Brad Pitt's face and body were emphasized in the editing of the trailer for *Troy* (as were those of Eric Bana and Orlando Bloom). See also Vivian Sobchack's discussion of conceptual mimesis in which, as she suggests, "the very presence of stars in the historical epic mimetically represents not real historical figures but rather the *real significance* of historical figures." Vivian Sobchack, "Surge and Splendor:

A Phenomenology of the Hollywood Historical Epic," in Barry Keith Grant (ed.), *Film Genre Reader II* (Austin, Tex.: University of Texas, 1995), pp. 280–307; p. 294.

35. "In the Thick of Battle," the first featurette on *Troy*'s DVD, suggests the importance of combat in the ancillary marketing of the film.

36. These height differences are created through a combination of tall extras. The Über Immortal was played by 7-foot-tall Robert Maillet with makeup prosthetics, while the illusion of the 7½-foot Xerxes (Rodrigo Santoro) was created through body doubles, cheated perspective, and bluescreen shots.

37. The Orphanage used particle animation for the arrows effects in *Hero*. See Estelle Shay, "Hero's Welcome," *Cinefex* Weekly Update, 34, September 7, 2007. Available online at www.cinefex.com/weeklyupdate/mailings/ 34_09072004/web.html (accessed July 8, 2008). Animal Logic used particle animation to create a dense 120 arrows per square foot in the Spartan battle with the Persian Army, in *300*. See Fordham, "A Beautiful Death," pp. 82 and 118. Particle Physics were an earlier form of artificial-intelligence software used in *Star Wars Episode II: Attack of the Clones* (2002) and *Star Wars Episode III: Revenge of the Sith* (2005).

38. See my article, Kirsten Moana Thompson, "Scale, Spectacle and Movement: Massive Software and Digital Special Effects in *The Lord of the Rings*," in Ernest Mathijs and Murray Pomerance (eds.), *From Hobbits to Hollywood: Essays on Peter Jackson's Lord of the Rings* (Amsterdam and New York: Rodopi, 2006), pp. 283–299. Originally created by Stephen Regelous for Peter Jackson's Weta and *The Fellowship of the Ring*, MASSIVE has become the leading artificial-intelligence software package. It won a Scientific and Engineering Academy Award in 2004 and was officially adopted by Digital Domain in 2005. It has been used to create effects for dozens of films, from comedies to fantasy and war films, including *King Kong*, *The Chronicles of Narnia*, *Happy Feet*, *Blades of Glory*, and *Flags of our Fathers*. See www.massivesoftware.com/company.

39. As the character of Gollum in *The Lord of the Rings* trilogy suggests, performance-capture films allow artists to design not only imaginary characters but also what Tom Gunning describes as "variations that hybridize or relate the human form to animal and mineral forms" such as the design of the dragon in *Beowulf*, a composite of human (Ray Winstone's eyes) and animal (dolphin's tail and batwings) features. See Tom Gunning, "Gollum and Golem: Special Effects and the Technology of Artificial Bodies," in Ernest Mathijs and Murray Pomerance (eds.), *From Hobbits to Hollywood: Essays on Peter Jackson's Lord of the Rings* (Amsterdam and New York: Rodopi, 2006), pp. 319–350; p. 348. Performance capture's separation of voice and movement from physical appearance enables a cinematic idealization of the male body. Instead of the 5 feet 6 inches rotund actor played by Ray Winstone, *Beowulf*'s eponymous hero becomes a 6-foot blonde, muscular warrior with abs. At the same time, star persona also shapes performance capture, especially given the dominance of photorealism in Hollywood. The design of Grendel's mother is informed by the sexual dimensions of Angelina Jolie's star persona, whose translation through mocap into a perpetually metamorphosing archetype of female sexuality (Circe crossed with Medusa) is marked by both its familiarity (it offers a recognizable Jolie face) and difference (the serpentine tail and skin), and also recalls these elements in her previous live-action role as Olympias, the hero's snake-handling mother in *Alexander*. Performance-capture films offer the director

absolute control. Jerome Chen, Visual Effects Supervisor (and co-supervisor on *Polar Express*) suggests it "enable[s] a filmmaker to isolate and record actor performance without the distractions and potential misfires of camera, lighting, sets and costumes . . . once he has the performance captured, he can begin to create the film cinematically." See Jody Duncan, "All the Way," *Cinefex,* 112 (January 2008): 44–59, 46.

40. Xerxes points to his army, and we see several men holding up a bluescreen image which contains multiplied men inside it. Xerxes explains to Leonidas that his soldiers will be digitally added in postproduction.

41. MPC was the first effects company to insert animation into live action that was shot on infrared film stock.

42. "The crowd was a major character in this story," said John Nelson, Visual Effects Supervisor for *Gladiator,* quoted in Martin, "A Cut Above," p. 28 (on blimp shot). For Riefenstahl intertext, see Arthur J. Pomeroy, "The Vision of a Fascist Rome in *Gladiator,*" in Martin Winkler (ed.), *Gladiator: Film and History* (Malden, Mass.,: Blackwell, 2004), pp. 111–123, and for the sports-arena analogy see Monica Cyrino, "*Gladiator* and Contemporary American Society," in Winkler, *Gladiator: Film and History,* pp. 124–149; p. 138.

43. Arthur Max, Production Designer of *Gladiator,* quoted in Ron Magid, "Rebuilding Ancient Rome," *American Cinematographer,* 81 (5) (2000): 54–59; p. 54.

44. There are certain problems connected to bluescreen, as it is expensive and extremely difficult to light. It also can constrain a director's freedom to use camera movement because of the need to "lock down the set." For this reason, Oliver Stone chose not to use bluescreen on the battle of Gaugamela set. See Duncan, "State of the Art," p. 63.

45. The idea of a vista of Babylon came to Stone when he visited composer Vangelis Papathanassiou and spent time on his apartment's balcony in modern Athens; see Fox, *The Making of Alexander,* p. 84.

46. "From Ruins to Reality," *Troy* DVD featurette.

47. Digital Domain has developed a proprietary software package called Terragen, which can generate terrain procedurally and is the latest word in virtual-set technology. Joel Hynek suggests that plate photography will end up being a "design guide for the Terragen guys" and that the viewer will not be able to tell the difference between computer-generated and "real" terrain. See Duncan, "State of the Art," p. 58.

48. See Thompson, "Scale, Spectacle and Movement," p. 289.

49. Norman M. Klein, *The Vatican to Vegas: A History of Special Effects* (New York: New Press, 2004), p. 46.

50. Klein, *The Vatican to Vegas,* p. 46.

51. Alexander's ambition is established in the Pella cave sequence in which Philip shows his son many paintings of famous mythological figures such as Achilles and Medea, and where Alexander vows that "one day I'll be on walls like these." One of these paintings shows Prometheus chained to a rock (with an eagle feasting on his liver). Eagle imagery is a leitmotif throughout the film and suggests that Alexander's talent and ambition are as soaring and regal as the eagle but at the same time can incur a Promethean punishment. This latter threat—that Alexander may go too far—is underscored by a sequence of shots which cut from a vulture feasting on one of the dead at the battle of Gaugamela to an extreme close-up (ECU) of Alexander's eye, followed by a graphic match of an ECU of the eagle's eye and a final match cut of Alexander's eye.

52. Two eagles flapping their bodies in front of air currents in England were photographed by Aurélia Abate and Sebastien Drouin of BUF. As the wing movement of the two flapping birds was too exaggerated, the final screen eagle was a hybrid of a computer-generated eagle's body and wings and the photographic plates of the real two eagles' heads. See Fox, *The Making of Alexander,* p. 155, and Rachel K. Bosley, "Warrior King," *American Cinematographer,* November 2004, available online at www.theasc.com/magazine/nov04/alexander/page1.html (accessed July 20, 2008).
53. Sobchack, "Surge and Splendor," p. 285.
54. Fordham, "A Beautiful Death," p. 67.
55. Fordham, "A Beautiful Death," p. 67.

heroic chivalry,

heroic sacrifice

"martial arthouse" as epic cinema

t h r e e

l e o n   h u n t

"Epic" cinema has largely been defined in relation to the film industries of Hollywood and Europe. Gilles Deleuze, for example, associates "the large form" with the cinemas of Hollywood (Griffith, DeMille, and their grandiose successors) and Soviet Russia, and their contrasting narrations of "the birth of a nation-civilisation."[1] However, the Chinese *wuxia pian* (martial-arts chivalry film) can also be seen as a type of epic cinema, in Derek Elley's sense of a genre that "transfigures the accomplishments of the past into an inspirational entertainment for the present, trading on received ideas of a continuing national or cultural consciousness."[2] Elley even includes a brief discussion of the genre in his Afterword on "Epic Aftertastes," films that fall outside of his main remit but which "contain elements from the epic legacy.[3] Historical martial-arts films take place in a liminal space between "history" and myth; tales of knight-errants (*xia*) or the patriotic mythology of the Shaolin Temple. They have a literary connection to an epic tradition of sorts: historical and quasi-historical texts, prose romances, mythological patchworks like *The Water Margin,* and elaborate serialized narratives. They offer a cinema of spectacle, with particular emphasis on the body (athletic, superhuman or graphically mutilated). They also share with key Hollywood epics a model of heroism often bound up with sacrifice (with the significant difference that the *wuxia pian* also encompasses *female* heroism).

Chinese martial arts cinema has in the past been compared to other Western popular genres, most notably the Musical and the western. However, there are reasons for thinking that comparison with the epic might be more productive. First, historical spectacle has played an important role in the transnationalization of East Asian cinema, with the Japanese *jidaigeki* (historical film) and particularly director Kurosawa Akira important antecedents. Second, while it might be hard to establish that it is more than a coincidence, it is interesting that the current cycle of prestigious pan-Chinese *wuxia pian* (what some critics have termed "martial arthouse") has roughly paralleled the return of the Hollywood epic (*Gladiator* [2000], *Troy* [2004], *The Passion of the Christ* [2004], *Alexander* [2004], *Kingdom of Heaven* [2005], *300* [2006]). The label "martial arthouse" refers most directly to *wuxia pian* directed by arthouse auteurs: *Crouching Tiger, Hidden Dragon* (2000), *Hero* (2002), *House of Flying Daggers* (2004), *The Promise* (2005), *The Curse of the Golden Flower* (2006) and *The Banquet* (2006). A slightly earlier film needs to be included here, too. *The Emperor and the Assassin* (1998) is a historical epic (by a mainland auteur) that has an obvious connection to *Hero* insofar as they both deal with the attempted assassination of Ying Zheng (Qin Shi Huang) during the Warring States era that preceded the "unification" of China; they offer contrasting versions of the "birth of the nation-civilisation."[4] It shares a common theme with a number of films in the martial arthouse cycle, namely heroic sacrifice, and several English-language reviews likened *The Emperor and the Assassin* to the epic.[5] I also want to extend the category of martial arthouse to include similarly large-scale films by more populist Hong Kong directors: *Seven Swords* (2005), *Fearless* (2006) and *The Warlords* (2007).

The aim of this essay is to explore martial arthouse as a form of epic cinema. In doing so, it focuses on three particular aspects associated with the epic as a cinematic mode. First, it considers martial arthouse's transfiguration of "history" into national myth, paying particularly close attention to *The Emperor and the Assassin* and *Hero* as contrasting representations of the same historical events. Second, it considers the epic and martial arthouse as cinemas of spectacle, a spectacle both spatial and kinetic. Finally, I will examine how heroism and particularly heroic sacrifice are shared by the Western epic film, the traditional Chinese martial-arts film and the recent cycle of martial-arthouse variants. Epic heroism often maps onto particular star personae; Charlton Heston comes most immediately to mind. Two key Chinese stars—Jet Li and Zhang Ziyi—have particular prominence in martial arthouse, each representing very different incarnations of the tensions between individual desire and dutiful self-sacrifice, heroic, and romantic destiny.

"when he had removed the map, the dagger appeared": history and myth

With his emphasis on "the romantic possibilities of past civilisations," Derek Elley seems to imply that incomplete historiography is a prerequisite for the all-important mythic dimension of the epic, something that promises a separation from the banality of the present, even though the narrative might invite us to find resonance in the present (or recent past).[6] It is the "mythic" that raises the form above "mere reportage," creating a space for "the irrational, the inexplicable or magical."[7] Similarly, James J. Y. Liu locates Chinese chivalrous tales in an "intermediate position between the popularization of history on the one hand and tales of the miraculous on the other."[8]

The traditional *wuxia pian* is generally reticent about specific historical events, apart from those of doubtful veracity such as the burning of the Shaolin Temple during the Qing Dynasty. While it incorporates "Great Masters" from Chinese history, it delineates historical periods in broad strokes as a backdrop to narratives of transcendent heroism and martial excellence. The Ming Dynasty (1368–1644) is full of intrigue and corruption, rife with internal divisions. The Qing Dynasty (1644–1912), on the other hand, is the genre's rough equivalent to "Rome"; an occupying, decadent power (from Manchuria) that bears the seeds of its own destruction. The treatment of Chinese history in martial-arthouse cinema varies in emphasis and relative gravity. Consider, for example, the very different representations of the Qing Dynasty in *Crouching Tiger, Hidden Dragon, Fearless* and *The Warlords;* respectively, a *wuxia* romance about a stolen sword with uncanny power, an anticolonial kung-fu film about a historical master, and a brutal military epic that encompasses trench warfare as well as swordplay. *Crouching Tiger, Hidden Dragon* betrays little interest in tensions between the Hans and the ruling Manchus, even though its impulsive heroine (Zhang Ziyi) is of Manchurian birth; it largely confines itself to the abstract martial-arts underworld, *jianghu,* a world of wandering masters, androgynous swordswomen, rival clans, bandits, security guards, and itinerant performers. *Fearless* and *The Warlords* both set male heroism against epochal national upheavals. In *Fearless,* the declining Qing era is further weakened by imperialist forces that necessitate a symbolic national strengthening. Its villains constitute a kind of transnational trading cabal rather than any nation in particular. *The Warlords'* backdrop is the Taiping Rebellion (1850–1865), an anti-Qing uprising that spread through southern China. In the latter film, the Empress Dowager is a shadowy but malign presence, figurehead of a decaying, venal regime. Like *Fearless,* the film's sense of tragedy is predicated on Chinese turned against one another, but this time the bad guys are closer to home.

The Emperor and the Assassin and *Hero* share a very specific "historiographical referent."[9] Sima Qian's *Shi Ji* [*The Records of the Grand Historian*] (c. 90 bc) has been likened to Herodotus and Thucydides, offering the earliest surviving attempt at a complete history of China up to the time of its author during the Han Dynasty. For our purposes, its most significant sections deal with the transition from the Warring States era (403–221 bc) to the brief reign of the Qin Dynasty (221–206 bc), initially under the first "August Emperor" Zheng, former King of Qin. In 219 bc, the Emperor had stone tablets inscribed with eulogies to the Qin Empire and including the following words:

> All under heaven are of one mind, single in will.
> Weights and measures have a single, standard, words are written in
> a uniform way . . .
> He erases doubt and establishes laws, so all will know what
> to shun.[10]

The totalitarian tone is central to the Emperor's contested reputation: tyrant (book-burner, mass-murderer) or visionary (the Great Wall, China as powerful nation-state). *Shi Ji* leaves us in little doubt about Sima Qian's view of the Emperor:

> the First Emperor was greedy and short-sighted, confident in his own wisdom, never trusting his meritorious officials, never getting to know his own people. He cast aside the kingly Way and relied on private procedures, outlawing books and writings, making the laws and penalties much harsher, putting deceit and force foremost and humanity and righteousness last, leading the whole world in violence and cruelty.
>
> Qin put an end to the Warring States period and made itself ruler of the empire, but it did not change its ways or reform its system of government, which shows that the means employed to seize an empire differ from those needed to guard it.[11]

This is, conspicuously (and controversially), not the King Zheng of *Hero* (or at least not if we take the film at face value), but this account clearly informs the representation of the charismatic but paranoid dictator of *The Emperor and the Assassin*. Two further chapters in *Shi Ji* are significant here, "The Biographies of the Wandering Knight-Errant" and "The Biographies of the Assassin-Retainers." The account of the "Knights-Errant" (the historical basis for the *wuxia* hero) offers the following description of those:

> whose deeds are outside the path of righteousness, but whose words are always trustworthy; who are relentless until the goal is reached; whose promises are sincere, who rescue others without minding injuries to themselves;

who do not fear their own death; who do not abuse their skills, nor fear that meanness would diminish their virtue.[12]

This is somewhat at odds with his account of Jing Ke, the would-be assassin of the King of Qin, in "The Biographies of the Assassin-Retainers." Jing is described as a swordsman of modest skill at best—we learn that he made strategic retreats from two confrontations with rival swordsmen—employed by the Crown Prince of Yin, one of the rival kingdoms to Qin during the Warring States era, to threaten, and if necessary, kill Zheng.[13] Jing Ke was made Chief Minister, given expensive quarters and gifts, but was initially reluctant to set out on the mission.[14] When he finally visited the King of Qin, he carried with him the head of disgraced General Fan (who willingly gave up his head to allow Jing to get near enough to Zheng) and a dagger concealed in a rolled map. What followed emerges as something of a mess. Jing Ke was accompanied by a supposedly "brave man of Yan," Qin Wuyang, "so fierce that no one dared to even look at him crossly," but who quaked with fear once in the King's chamber.[15] Jing was unable to stab the King and chased him around the palace. Attendants in the upper throne room were not permitted to carry weapons, although the King's physician struck Jing with his medicine bag. The King was unable to remove his sword from its scabbard as it hung at an awkward angle, and armed attendants outside the chamber were forbidden to enter without a specific command. Finally, the King managed to unsheathe his sword and stab Jing Ke.[16]

The Emperor and the Assassin is fairly faithful to this episode, with one important narrative twist. The "Assassin" is initially part of the King's plan to conquer Yan; Lady Zhao (Gong Li) is sent to find someone who will stage a failed assassination and legitimize Qin's attack on the rival kingdom. Instead, a disillusioned Zhao persuades Jing Ke (Zhang Fengyi) to make a genuine attempt on Zheng's life. On the film's DVD commentary track, director Chen Kaige describes Jing Ke as a "hero," and even in *Shi Ji* he receives an epitaph from one of the swordsmen who had intimidated him—while acknowledging that he "never properly mastered the art of swordsmanship," he concedes, "how blind I was to his real worth."[17] The Jing Ke of *Shi Ji* is a human-scale hero—flawed, but brave enough to give his life up on a mission he wasn't entirely equal to. Given that this undignified scuffle isn't the stuff of chivalrous legends, Jing is given a more romantic back story in *The Emperor and the Assassin*. He's a penitent assassin, who lives as a peddler after slaughtering the family of a blind girl, shocked out of his ruthlessness by her suicide. He's also a more formidable swordsman, whose "failure" is partly attributed to the guards having broken his sword before allowing him into the King's palace (see Figure 3.1). His heroism lies in his willing sacrifice and the suspension of his pacifism for a higher cause—even if he succeeds, he is not going to return. As in *Shi Ji* he sets out on his mission to the words "Brave men once gone, never come back again."

Figure 3.1

The Emperor and the Assassin: Jing Ke's attempted assassination of the King of Qin.

The film's King Zheng (Li Xuejian), meanwhile, embodies the "burden of empire"; Chen Kaige has likened the film to the Roman epic.[18] The King's visionary ideals are compromised by duty to his ancestors; he inherits the "all under heaven" mandate as something that must be lived up to, often in conflict with his personal desires. Just as *Hero* invents its noble knights (including its anonymous assassin), *The Emperor and the Assassin* fabricates Lady Zhao, who represents the King's alienated conscience, articulating the idealized version of "all under Heaven" (benevolent, protective, peaceful—effectively the same sentiments articulated by Nameless and Broken Sword in *Hero*). Both films frame their narratives through distancing devices: the self-contained chapters in *The Emperor and the Assassin,* the *Rashomon*-like multiple-narratives of *Hero.* Both offer "history" as allegory for the present: *Hero's* assertion of unification, *The Emperor and the Assassin's* equation of the King with Mao Zedong and more recent Chinese leaders.[19] *The Emperor and the Assassin* stages history as tragic epic, *Hero* as *wuxia* fantasy. While *Hero's* King (Chen Daoming) shows glimpses of the legalist tyranny of the future emperor (the standardization of written Chinese, amongst other things), he is redeemed by the essence of his antagonists' heroism, which will miraculously transform him into a benevolent ruler. But the climax shares with *The Emperor and the Assassin* (albeit more subtly) the sense that imperial violence can operate independently of the corporeal king. In *The Emperor and the Assassin,* the eunuchs remind Zheng of his duty whenever he wavers, and it is the King's archers who demand Nameless's death in *Hero.* Jet Li's enigmatic face, as Nameless willingly sacrifices himself, begs the question: What is he expressing? Benign resignation? Contempt that the "enlightened" King has already authorized another death? As Robert Eng, one of the few critics to challenge *Hero's* "authoritarian" reputation observes: "the Qin king himself is helpless to make an independent judgment to save the assassin Nameless despite his own personal feelings and supposed supreme power, since the impersonal and relentless Qin bureaucratic-legal machinery demands the execution of Nameless."[20] Hero underlines the fact that a "Chinese epic" brings a certain amount of baggage with it, complicating Elley's notion of "inspirational cinema for the present" (inspirational for who?) and a "continuing national or cultural consciousness."[21]

Wuxia epics regularly face the accusation of Orientalizing Chinese history for a Western gaze, even though, as Kenneth Chan suggests, anti-Orientalist critiques run the risk of denying the wuxia pian any contemporary presence, given that it is "by its very nature traditionally 'ethnic' and exotic in its appeal."[22] Hero is doubly contentious as it faces charges of misrepresenting Chinese history at best or constituting aestheticized propaganda at worst. According to Eng, "there is not a single concrete indication that Qin unification will bring about peace, justice and benevolent rule . . . What we actually see of the Qin state is its relentless war machine and pitiless and faceless bureaucrats."[23] There is some truth to this, and yet The Emperor and the Assassin and Hero each use "history" as closure, in the form of end titles. Hero ends with a shot of the Great Wall and tells us only that "the First Emperor" ceased his expeditions and sought to "protect his subjects." The Emperor and the Assassin reminds us that the Qin Dynasty only lasted fifteen years and that the King's victory was "short-lived." Given that such lavish, transnational films seek a global audience not necessarily conversant with Chinese history, such inclusions and omissions cannot be underestimated.

immersed in the peony pavilion: spectacle and the embellishment of space

While spectacle (however extravagant) is not in itself the defining feature of the epic, it is often seen as "the genre's most characteristic trademark."[24] Mark Jancovich observes that epics were frequently "sold with the promise that these spectacles not only represented history but themselves were historically momentous achievements," not just the spectacle of history, but spectacle as history.[25] They are most commonly seen as "colossal or spectacle films, genres named for décor."[26] When Chinese martial-arts films were compared to epics by English-language reviewers prior to their current prestige incarnation, it was more likely to be with the low-rent Italian variant, the peplum or "Sword and Sandal" film: cheap, fanciful, formulaic, inauthentic. Martial arthouse, on the other hand, has proven more than capable of equaling the spectacle of the Hollywood epic and even surpassing it in some respects. Crouching Tiger, Hidden Dragon, Hero and House of Flying Daggers come with a prestige bestowed by size and scale, celebrated directors and to-die-for casts. Each in their way trade on the notion of "sights never seen before."[27] *Hero* is often referred to as "the first Chinese Blockbuster."

The epic offers spectacle both kinetic and spatial: the genre luxuriates in space with scenes designed to foreground monumental production design and huge crowds. Increasingly, both have become the province of digital effects—one of *The Emperor and the Assassin*'s distinguishing points was its CGI-free battle scenes involving vast numbers of extras recruited from the Chinese military. As a cinema of spectacle, the martial-arts film is generally seen as a kinetic body-centered cinema—graceful, athletic bodies performing seemingly impossible stunts. The martial-arthouse films have no shortage of the "spectacle of movement," but several (particularly those directed by Zhang Yimou) are also marked by a high degree of what Charles and Mirella Jona Affron call "design intensity."[28] *Hero*'s colors may be semiotically banal but seem to have possessed an aesthetic and emotional intensity for many viewers. *The Guardian*'s film reviewer was particularly enraptured by the Peony Pavilion in *House of Flying Daggers*:

> The Peony Palace is one of the most remarkable movie sets I've ever seen: Massive in scale, attended by hundreds of supporting artists in full costume, and sumptuously and intricately designed with ostentation that goes beyond vulgarity or absurdity. I just wanted to step through the screen and wander around this incredible, dream-like place.[29]

At one level, this does little to assuage accusations of Orientalism—the film set as exotic virtual tour. But it is also suggestive of the pleasures inherent in a certain type of "historical" cinema; the way, according to Michele Pierson, that design-intensive films set in the past "make history an important site of subjective investment for audiences."[30] While the Peony Pavilion is the site of one of the film's most spectacular action sequences, the Echo Game, it becomes an immersive space rather than simply one in which action takes place.

The Affrons offer four levels of design intensity, classified according to "relative transparency or opacity:"

> from denotation, in which the set functions as a conventional signpost of genre, ambience, and character; to punctuation, where the set has a specifically emphatic narrative function; to embellishment, where the verisimilitudinous set calls attention to itself within the narrative; to artifice, where the set is a fantastic theatrical image that commands the centre of narrative attention.[31]

Generally speaking, the traditional martial-arts film offers set design (the term itself seems derisory in some films) at the ground level of *denotation* and *punctuation*. The former would include the minimalist settings of low-budget 1970s kung-fu films or the recycled sets that are recognizable from one Shaw Brothers film to the next. But environments can be kinetically *punctuative*—the narrow streets that fighters have to adapt to in the climaxes of *The Martial Club* (1981) and *Once Upon a Time in China II* (1992) or the "House of Traps" in the climax of *The Magic Blade* (1976). Budgets rarely run to *embellishment*, let alone *artifice*, where "the viewer exits the theatre whistling the sets."[32] This is one of the distinguishing features of martial arthouse; *The Guardian*'s reviewer isn't just whistling the Peony Pavilion, he appears to have learned some of the words, too. *House of Flying Daggers'* opulent pleasure house blurs the line between embellishment and artifice. Embellishment exhibits "an elevated level of rhetoric, of style . . . verisimilitudinous yet unfamiliar, and intentionally striking."[33] The epic is an embellishing genre par excellence, inclining toward the monumental and the calligraphic, "the reconstruction of an environment whose authenticity is not validated through the filmgoer's direct observation but refracted through his or her experience of art and architecture."[34] On the *House of Flying Daggers* DVD commentary, Zhang Yimou explains that the colors used in the Pavilion were based on the paintings in the Dunhuang Grottoes in Gansu Province, where monks carved the caves into the cliffs as a site for Buddhist art over a 600-year period. This has the effect of rendering the huge set as simultaneously "authentic" and arresting. The notion of embellishment is very similar to the second of the three aspects of "history" in the "large form" that Deleuze adapts from Nietzsche, *antiquarian* history.[35] The antiquarian emphasizes "action and intimate customs, vast tapestries, clothes, finery, machines, weapons or tools, jewels, private objects . . . the sign of the actualisation of the epoch."[36] Deleuze could easily be speaking of *House of Flying Daggers* when he identifies fabrics as "the fundamental element of the historical film, especially with the colour-image."[37] The Peony Pavilion immerses the viewer in silks, beaded curtains that surround sunken baths, painted paper screens that reflect the movement of water in a semi-darkened room, a floor patterned with butterflies and a floral design at the centre. It offers "action and intimate customs"; a game in which a bowl of tea is passed along a rope, Mei's performance of the song *Jia Ren Qu,* her slow dance based on movements of her hips and waist.[38] For the Affrons, artifice is distinguished from embellishment by "the fiction effect," the "invention of the patently unreal."[39] Its genres are the fantastic (*The Cabinet of Dr Caligari* [1920], *La Belle et la bête* [1946], *Blade Runner* [1982]) and the performative (the "unreal" sets of the musical). It is the performative that partly places the Peony Pavilion in the realm of artifice, as a highly theatrical space (see Figure 3.2).[40] The scene, which lasts for over sixteen minutes, breaks down into a series of performances; the initial "flirtation" between Jin and Mei, her performance of *Jia Ren Qu,* the Echo Game, and the fight with Captain Leo that begins in this performance space (surrounded by the drums that accompanied the Echo Game) and continues in the adjacent baths.

Figure 3.2

House of Flying Daggers: Mei performs in the Peony Pavilion.

The performances range from song and dance to fighting, from duplicitous "double agents" to the rhetoric of seduction, from the more-or-less "authentic" to the heavily stylized.

This design intensity is particularly evident in the films that trade on an auteur figure—the "arthouse" dimension of the *wuxia* blockbuster—but stars (and their bodies) play a central role in this spectacular cycle, too. The final section examines the intersection of heroic star presence with a particular thematic preoccupation.

heroism and sacrifice (or, jet li is an axiom)

The most compelling thematic link between the epic and the *wuxia pian* is the emphasis on transcendent heroism, whether it be the chivalry of the traditional knight-errant or the macho individualism of the "new style" *wuxia* novels of the 1950s and 1960s, which carried over into the historical swordplay films produced by Shaw Brothers and others. A subsection of the epic (what I have called the "male epic") deals with the transfiguration of a heroic male through death—El Cid's corpse riding into battle strapped to his horse, the crucified body of Spartacus.[41] According to Stephen Teo, "We may define 'the essence of heroism' [in the *wuxia pian*] as the drama of mortal men who fight and die for a worthwhile cause, attaining epiphany in death."[42] But the nature of this epiphany runs the gamut from the homosocial melodrama of John Woo's *Last Hurrah for Chivalry* (1979) (sacrifice in the name of friendship) to patriotic sacrifice (countless Shaolin heroes, Bruce Lee in *Fist of Fury* [1972], Nameless in *Hero*) to the nihilistic death drive displayed in Zhang Che's films. The sacrificial deaths of Spartacus and the Cid are fraught with the anxieties of only being able to live up to a transcendent name in death (the "Cid," the myth of "Spartacus" that is inevitably bigger than a human subject can be). In Zhang Che's films, death represents "ultimate transcendence . . . an act of self-affirmation," and there is sometimes a sense that the heroes of these films orchestrate their own demise as a spectacle.[43] Wang Yu's Silver Roc, in *Golden Swallow* (1968), dies with the words "I am still the supreme swordsman"—he is mortally wounded due to a misunderstanding (the tragic dimension), but still undefeated. What death offers him is the preservation of his "name," which he has preserved thus far through his consummate skill, and the opportunity to choose the time and manner of his demise—he recovers long enough to wipe out another gang of bandits. He dies standing up, his arms outstretched to his sides, a monument to himself.

I emphasize this perverse quality (which is well documented in writings about Zhang Che) to underline the fact that neither heroism or sacrifice are static qualities in a genre which does, admittedly, often seem to have a limited dramatic repertoire. And yet heroism and sacrifice are among the most contested features in the martial-arthouse films. The question seems to be: do these films "fail" to depict *wuxia* heroism or do they redefine or critique it in a genuinely self-reflexive way? Stephen Teo, for example, suggests that Ang Lee "has not grasped the quality of heroism" in *Crouching Tiger, Hidden Dragon,* so that while Li Mubai's (Chow Yun-Fat) death is tragic, there is no epiphany because of "the lack of a heroic gesture."[44] Li is killed by accident—the fatal needle from villain Jade Fox is intended for Jen (Zhang Ziyi)—but Teo's concerns are the "ambiguity" of his sacrificial cause, the modest scale of his death and the fact that he is killed by a woman.[45] Jen's leap from Wudang Mountain is dismissed as "the kind of open, ambiguous ending that ultimately plays to the Western sensibility of an arthouse movie rather than to the Chinese sense of a satisfying action movie finale."[46] While Felicia Chan agrees that "Li Mubai fails as a traditional *wuxia* hero," she suggests that *Crouching Tiger, Hidden Dragon* can be seen as exhibiting a degree of self-reflexivity about the genre's conventions.[47] While it may lack *Crouching Tiger, Hidden Dragon*'s dramatic weight, *House of Flying Daggers* offers a more revisionist break from sacrifice defined by Confucian self-denial and loyalty to the *jianghu* underworld. Mei, the third of Zhang Ziyi's very modern *nuxia* (female knights), sacrifices herself for love rather than the greater cause of rebellion against the decadent Tang government. The film's "epic" confrontation—between government troops and the Flying Daggers group—happens offstage, with the film's climactic action favoring the intense triangle between Mei and her two rival lovers. This move from the large to the intimate, the sacrificial to the willfully "selfish," makes *House of Flying Daggers* the least like an epic of the films discussed here. *Hero* has been found by some critics to be doubly inauthentic, as "history" and as "heroic" narrative. On the latter point, Yu Sen-lun observes that Zhang Yimou "violates many of the fundamental principles of the chivalric hero character—apolitical, self-interested, carefree—in order to achieve a grander vision, which unfortunately pulls the carpet out from under the feet of his 'heroes,' leaving them looking merely foolish."[48]

Two stars have loomed particularly largely in martial arthouse, both positioned in different ways to at least the possibility of sacrifice. Zhang Ziyi brought the figure of the *nuxia* to an international audience and in some ways is martial arthouse's central icon. The female knight sets the *wuxia pian* apart from the Western epic, where, apart from *Joan of Arc* movies and a few other exceptions, women do not participate in active heroism. In *El Cid* (1961), for example, Jimena (Sophia Loren) is prevented from avenging her father "as a son would"; romantic love (for her father's killer) overtakes revenge and honor, which is established as the exclusive province of chivalrous men. In the traditional epic, the central female character desires but does not fight. For the traditional *nuxia,* the opposite is true: entry into *jianghu* is conditional on the absence of sexual desire. She is dutiful, stoic, and chaste, often powerful but never posing a threat to the heroic male. In contrast, Zhang's martial-arthouse heroines are willful, romantic, capricious and fully sexualized. In *Crouching Tiger, Hidden Dragon,* her rebellious antiheroine Jen threatens to disrupt the patrilineal structures of martial learning, while Mei in *House of Flying Daggers* is a fighter, but her fight is explicitly linked to desire—both sexual desire and a longing for "freedom" that goes beyond even the idealized mobility of the *jianghu* underworld. In this respect, she is also connected to modernity, destabilizing traditions, rules, and authority. In *House of Flying Daggers,* the *nuxia* also doubles as a kind of *femme fatale* (or even a Chinese Helen of Troy); *Jia Ren Qu* (the song she performs while posing as a blind dancer in a brothel that is a cover for underground female fighters) characterizes her as destroying cities at a glance:

> A rare beauty from the North
> She's the finest lady on earth
> A glance from her, the whole city goes down
> A second glance leaves the nation in ruins
> There has been no city or nation
> That has been more cherished than a beauty like this.

Zhang's characters sacrifice themselves (or at least appear to) in both *Crouching Tiger, Hidden Dragon* and *House of Flying Daggers,* but in neither case is it unequivocally a heroic sacrifice. As I have argued elsewhere, it isn't clear that Jen is sacrificing herself at the end of *Crouching Tiger, Hidden Dragon* when she leaps from Wudang Mountain.[49] As Teo observes, the film's arthouse trappings invite an "open" reading, although viewers might choose to interpret it as restoring Li Mu-bai to life in accord with the tale she has a heard of a young man who performed a similar leap to have his wish granted—such a reading reintegrates Jen into a heroic trajectory. On the other hand, they might interpret her wish as returning to the desert with her bandit lover Luo, an ending that would bring the film closer to *House of Flying Daggers.* The latter is defiantly revisionist in having its heroine turn her back on the struggle for justice and die instead for romantic love. Zhang, then, represents a transgressive figure within the genre.[50] Martial arthouse's other star icon, however, brings male heroic sacrifice back to the centre of the epic.

Derek Elley describes Charlton Heston as "*the* epic presence," manifesting a "particular brand of heroic intensity,"[51] while Michael Mourlet famously characterized the actor as an "axiom" whose very presence onscreen constitutes both tragedy and physical beauty.[52] Martial arthouse has its own axiom in Jet Li, embodying a stoic sacrificial masculinity that runs counter to Zhang Ziyi's personification of romantic self-gratification. Li came with a clearly defined persona (and transnational marquee value) from his Hong Kong films, associated particularly with historical martial-arts heroes such as the Confucian patriarch Wong Fei-Hung. Li is not a sacrificial figure in his Hong Kong movies, even when playing characters associated with early deaths such as Fong Sai-yuk or Chen Zhen, the character played by Bruce Lee in *Fist of Fury*. But *Hero*, *Fearless* and *The Warlords* all climax with deaths in which he in some way willingly participates. In *Hero*, he impassively faces those Qin arrows (see Figure 3.3). In *Fearless*, poisoned during a challenge match, he insists on continuing with the fight at the cost of his life—he "wins" by withholding the killing blow, distilling the progressive chivalry of his hard-won philosophy as well as demonstrating that China is both morally and martially strong. *The Warlords* builds to the most ambiguous of these sacrifices, given that Li's character is a morally questionable figure—he demands that his former friend deliver the killing strike in accordance with their blood oath, "whoever harms another brother shall die." He faces an undistinguished death, assassinated by the regime that no longer has any use for him, but is able to recuperate his demise as something more heroic by choosing his ultimate assassin.

If the connection I made earlier between the Hollywood neo-epic and pan-Chinese martial arthouse is largely speculative, *Fearless* makes some

Figure 3.3
Hero: Nameless faces the arrows of the Qin army.

rather more explicit references to *Gladiator*. An aerial computer-generated shot of the French Concession Theatre in Shanghai, where Huo Yuanjia (Li) fights a series of non-Chinese challengers, resembles similar footage of the Colosseum in Ridley Scott's film. As Huo dies at the end of the film, he is granted an elegiac reunion with the blind village girl from the film's middle section, echoing the "Elysian Fields" coda of *Gladiator*.[53] While Huo and Maximus are very different heroes, both undergo a fall and rebirth, and both will die to "heal" a nation that will shortly become an enlightened republic. The Rome of *Gladiator* is corrupt and decadent—the "Ancient Rome" in which the epic revels—while the China of *Fearless* is the "Sick Man of Asia," weakened by imperialism and the decaying Manchu government. For Huo, there is more to this "sickness" than colonial bullying, there is a cultural self-hatred that needs to be cured, too: "Only the weak need to prove their power through force, but what force leads to is endless hatred." Huo has earlier embodied some of these weaknesses: suffering from asthma, his father a martial-arts master who refuses to teach him, he grows up into a braggart and a brawler who brings about his own downfall.[54] When he kills a rival master in a challenge match, the retaliation of a disciple destroys his family and sends Huo into grief-stricken exile. He undergoes a rebirth, reconceptualizing martial arts as a nonviolent form of self-improvement, shunning death matches, and seeking to befriend his opponents. His sacrificial death, then, is also the culmination of a self-healing process. The "weak" Huo falls short of his father and his family name (the name, also, of the fighting style that he inherits). As a child, Huo witnesses his father "lose" a match rather than deliver a lethal blow or make his opponent lose face, misreading it as a humiliating defeat.[55] His own tragedy brings about an epiphany in which he recognizes his father as the moral and martial victor; such victories, he learns, need not be public ones, even though his own will be. Huo dies in the process of achieving similar transcendence as he fights the noble Japanese master, Tanaka. Weakened by poison (an imperialist plot), Huo withholds the final blow before collapsing, but Tanaka refuses the victory, knowing "in my heart" that Huo was the victor.

The Warlords is based on the Qing-era story "The Assassination of Ma," a historical incident that has been adapted several times. The most famous version is the Shaw Brothers' *Blood Brothers* (1973), in which Di Long plays Ma Xinyi, an ambitious general who befriends two bandits, Zhang Wenxiang (David Chiang) and Huang Zhong (Chen Guantai), the three of them drawn into suppressing the Taiping uprising. In *Blood Brothers*, Ma is explicitly villainous, corrupted by power and by his desire for Huang's wife Mi Lan (Jing Li). When Ma arranges to have Huang killed, Zhang avenges the murder at the cost of his own life. Zhang is the chivalrous hero, narrating the main story in flashback and prepared to undergo torture and execution—the film climaxes with the public mutilation of his body, his heart removed while he is still alive. *The Warlords* places a greater emphasis on the historical background and politics of the period but changes the names of its leading characters. Ma becomes Pang Qin-yun (Li), Zhang becomes Jiang Wu-yang (Kaneshiro Takeshi), and Huang turns into Zhao Er-hu (Andy Lau.) The scale and spectacle are larger than a Shaw Brothers budget could have dreamed of, but, like *House of Flying Daggers* (and *Blood Brothers*), the dramatic emphasis is on a triangle, or rather two overlapping triangles: the three "Blood Brothers," two of whom desire the same woman (Lian, played by Xu Jinglei). Pang is a more complex figure than *Blood Brothers'* Ma—darker than Jet Li's usual roles (sufficiently so to win an acting award in Hong Kong), but conflicted enough to be a compromised hero rather than outright villain. His filmic entrance is an inglorious one, climbing from beneath the corpses of his comrades, where he has hidden during the massacre of his men. In a subsequent scene, he sobs with a mixture of grief and shame. In place of naked ambition, he is driven by a dream in which "everyone, men and women alike, should be free from oppression." This involves making "difficult" decisions that bring the ruthless military strategist in him to the fore—sending cannon fodder to their deaths, executing two sobbing young soldiers after they rape women in a captured town, executing prisoners of war who might use up food provisions desperately needed by his men. The latter drives a wedge between Pang and the more emotionally instinctive Zhao, a conflict that leads to the latter's murder. The casting of Li lends weight to Pang's vision of justice being sincere, if flawed, but the military/political machine has a momentum of its own; as the war continues, he appears to be literally swallowed up by his armor, glowering and remote. Only once does the film make Pang look as villainous as Ma in the earlier film, when Jiang glimpses him on a boat with Lian, looking darkly at the "brother" who is starting to see him in a different light. When Pang has Zhao killed, it isn't clear whether he is eliminating a romantic rival, whether he sees him as an obstacle to his dream of a better nation (another of his "hard" decisions) or is simply ingratiating himself with the Qing court. He weeps as he drinks a toast to his friend—simultaneously shot down by arrows in an intercut sequence—insisting that his fallen friend will eventually recognize that he was right. In the latter section of the film, the focus shifts to Jiang, but he is never as central a figure as Zhang in *Blood Brothers,* in spite of periodic voice-overs that comment on Pang's trajectory. When he assassinates Pang to avenge Zhao, Jiang doesn't see enough of the bigger picture to be the film's sacrificial hero (he is executed offscreen)—a cannon salute drowns the Qing rifles that fatally wound Pang and enable his former friend to finish him off.[56] Pang's "dream" has been misguided because history has placed him on the "wrong side," fighting for an oppressive regime that has him killed on the Empress Dowager's orders—he "doesn't know how things work," as an observer comments. What enables Pang to achieve some kind of heroic epiphany is the *wuxia pian*'s prioritization of homosocial bonds: "There's nothing more important than the love between brothers," as Zhao puts it. The three male leads are bound by a blood oath—"a brother who harms another brother must die"—and Zhao is led to his death when he is tricked into thinking Pang himself is in danger. When Jiang hesitates in finishing off Pang, the latter insists that he "honor our pledge now!" The nation cannot be healed, but the film can't quite give up on having its charismatic heroes die for *something*, even if it's only each other.[57]

Like the epic (both "old" and "new"), martial arthouse's signifiers of prestige—scale, spectacle, history, myth—don't always translate into their critical reception. While *Crouching Tiger, Hidden Dragon, Hero,* and *House of Flying Daggers* were international successes, the cycle has been met with growing weariness by some critics, dismissed as Orientalist kitsch. Mark Jancovich identifies in the epic a "condition of being neither one thing nor the other," referring to a middlebrow quality that seems to antagonize their detractors—films that want to be taken more seriously than they have any right to be.[58] The martial arthouse film's neither/nor quality is also bound up with the complex cultural politics of crossover that the genre must negotiate as a culturally specific form with international ambitions. According to Christina Klein, a film such as *Crouching Tiger, Hidden Dragon* "is materially grounded in multiple geographic locations, has multiple aesthetic affiliations, and fails to map neatly onto a single nation-state or cultural tradition. Awareness of this multiplicity enables us to step beyond the sterile binaries of domination and resistance, corruption and authenticity."[59] This doesn't stop the films being accused of inauthenticity, however (just as the Western epic often was)—neither the sort of serious films that should be representing "prestige" Chinese cinema internationally nor "proper" martial-arts films (lowbrow, but at least "authentic"). Perhaps the final thing these films have in common with the epic is of both culturally and geographically not knowing their place.

notes

1. Gilles Deleuze, *Cinema 1: The Movement-Image* (London: Athlone Press 1986), p. 148.
2. Derek Elley, *The Epic Film: Myth and History* (London: Routledge & Kegan Paul, 1984), p. 13.
3. Elley, *The Epic Film,* p. 160. Interestingly, Elley later joined the chorus of voices that linked *Crouching Tiger, Hidden Dragon*'s comparative failure in East Asia to its cultural inauthenticity. "For many Asians—and Western Asiaphiles," he claimed in *Variety,* "*Tiger* is cleverly packaged chop suey . . . an expertly served meal designed primarily to appeal to a general Western clientele"; see Derek Elley, "Asia to 'Tiger': Kung-Fooey," *Variety,* February 7, 2001, available online at www.variety.com/article/VR1117793240?categoryid =1019&cs=1&query=kung%2Dfooey&display=kung%2Dfooey (accessed June 2, 2006). Elley certainly knows his *wuxia pian,* but the sincerity of his concerns probably aren't helped by the Orientalist puns that litter the article.

4. Several earlier films might retrospectively be considered "martial art-house." King Hu's *Touch of Zen* (1971) was the first *wuxia pian* to be screened as an "art" film in the West, including a Cannes screening, and *Ashes of Time* (1994) transports Wong Kar-Wai's elliptical storytelling and introspective characters to the world of Jin Yong's *wuxia* novel *The Eagle Shooting Heroes*. Neither, however, achieved the global success of *Crouching Tiger, Hidden Tiger* and its successors.

5. See, for example, Richard Falcon "*The Emperor and the Assassin,*" *Sight and Sound*, 10 (8) (2000): 43–44; p. 44.

6. Elley, *The Epic Film*, p. 12.

7. Elley, *The Epic Film*, p. 10.

8. James J. Y. Liu, *The Chinese Knight Errant* (London: Routledge & Kegan Paul, 1967), p. 82.

9. Michel Lagny, "Popular Taste: The Peplum," in Richard Dyer and Ginette Vincendeau (eds), *Popular European Cinema* (London and New York: Routledge, 1992), pp. 163–180; p. 174.

10. Sima Qian, *Records of the Grand Historian: Qin Dynasty*, trans. Burton Watson (Hong Kong and New York: Renditions and Columbia University Press, 1993), p. 47.

11. Qian, *Records of the Grand Historian*, p. 81.

12. Sima Qian, quoted by Koo Siu-Fung, "Philosophy and Tradition in the Swordplay Film," in Lau Shing-On (ed.), *A Study of the Hong Kong Swordplay Film, 1945–1980* (Hong Kong: Hong Kong Urban Council, 1981/1986), pp. 25–32; p. 27.

13. Sima Qian, *Records of the Grand Historian*, p. 167.

14. Sima Qian, *Records of the Grand Historian*, p. 172.

15. Sima Qian, *Records of the Grand Historian*, p. 173.

16. Sima Qian, *Records of the Grand Historian*, pp. 175–176.

17. Sima Qian, *Records of the Grand Historian*, p. 177.

18. Sima Quoted in Wade Major, "Wisdom of the Ages: Portrait of a Warrior," *Kungfu Qigong*, April 2000, p. 26.

19. "I tried to disclose the similarities between the current regime and the first emperor of China . . . I think someone like him is just like Mao Zedong," Chen Kaige, interviewed by Major, "Wisdom of the Ages," p. 27. Mao was known to be an admirer of the "August Emperor."

20. Robert Y. Eng, "Is *Hero* a Paean to Authoritarianism?," *Asia Pacific Media Network*, July 9, 2004, available online at www.asiamedia.ucla.edu/article. asp?parentid=14371 (accessed June 29, 2005).

21. Elley, *The Epic Film*, p. 13.

22. Kenneth Chan, "The Global Return of the *Wu Xia Pian* (Chinese Sword-Fighting Movie): Ang Lee's *Crouching Tiger, Hidden Dragon*," *Cinema Journal*, 43 (2004): 3–17; p. 7.

23. Eng, "Is *Hero* a Paean to Authoritarianism?"

24. Elley, *The Epic Film*, p. 1.

25. Mark Jancovich, "'The Purest Knight of All': Nation, History and Representation in *El Cid*," *Cinema Journal*, 40 (2000): 79–103; p. 79.

26. Charles Affron and Mirella Jona Affron, *Sets in Motion: Art Direction and Film Narrative* (New Brunswick, NJ: Rutger University Press, 1995), p. 39.

27. Jancovich, "The Purest Knight of All," p. 79.

28. Affron and Affron, *Sets in Motion*.

29. Peter Bradshaw, "*House of Flying Daggers,*" *The Guardian*, December 24, 2004, available online at www.film.guardian.co.uk/News_Story/Critic_Reviews/ Guardian_review/0,4267,1379290,00.html (accessed 7 March 2005).

30. Michele Pierson, "A Production Designer's Cinema: Historical Authenticity in Popular Films Set in the Past," in Geoff King (ed.), *The Spectacle of the Real: From Hollywood to Reality TV and Beyond* (Bristol and Portland, Oreg.: Intellect Press, 2005), pp. 139–149; p. 143.

31. Affron and Affron, *Sets in Motion*, pp. 36–37.

32. Affron and Affron, *Sets in Motion*, p. 39.

33. Affron and Affron, *Sets in Motion*, p. 38.

34. Affron and Affron, *Sets in Motion*, p. 39.

35. The other two are *monumental*, "the physical and human encompasser, the natural and architectural milieu" (Deleuze, *Cinema 1*, p. 149) and *critical* or *ethical*, where the "ancient or recent past must submit to trial" (Deleuze, *Cinema 1*, p. 151). The latter pertains especially to *The Emperor and the Assassin*, which enlists the past in a judgment of more recent history.

36. Deleuze, *Cinema 1*, p. 150.

37. Deleuze, *Cinema 1*, p. 150.

38. Deleuze, *Cinema 1*, p. 150.

39. Affron and Affron, *Sets in Motion*, p. 39.

40. It offers an interesting point of comparison with another immersive set designed to facilitate combat and musical performance, the House of Blue Leaves in *Kill Bill Volume 1* (2003), a mixture of nightclub, dojo, and gangster hideout. Without *House of Flying Daggers'* "authenticating" referents, the House of Blue Leaves is a much more abstract design.

41. Leon Hunt, "What are Big Boys Made Of? *Spartacus, El Cid* and the Male Epic," in Pat Kirkham and Janet Thumin (eds), *You Tarzan: Masculinity, Movies and Men* (London: Lawrence & Wishart, 1993), pp. 65–83.

42. Stephen Teo, "Love and Swords: The Dialectics of Martial Arts Romance," *Senses of Cinema*, 11 (2001), available online at www.sensesofcinema.com/contents/00/11/crouching. html (accessed July 10, 2001).

43. Jerry Liu, "Chang Cheh: Aesthetics = Ideology?" in Lau Shing-On (ed.), *A Study of the Hong Kong Swordplay Film, 1945–1980* (Hong Kong: Hong Kong Urban Council, 1986), pp. 159–162; p. 162.

44. Teo, "Love and Swords."

45. Stephen Teo, "*Crouching Tiger, Hidden Dragon:* Passing Fad or Global Phenomenon?" in David Chute and Cheng-Sim Lim (eds), *Heroic Grace: The Chinese Martial Arts Film* (Los Angeles, Calif.: UCLA, 2003), pp. 23–26; p. 26.

46. Teo, "Passing Fad or Global Phenomenon?" p. 26.

47. Felicia Chan, "*Crouching Tiger, Hidden Dragon:* Cultural Migrancy and Translatability," in Chris Berry (ed.), *Chinese Films in Focus: 25 New Takes* (London: British Film Institute, 2003), pp. 56–64; p. 62.

48. Yu Sen-Lun, "Heroes Who Fail to Amount to Much," *Taipei Times*, January 17, 2003, available online at www.taipeitimes.com/News/feat/archives/2003/01/17/191384 (accessed 29 June 2005).

49. Leon Hunt, *Kung Fu Cult Masters: From Bruce Lee to Crouching Tiger* (London: Wallflower Press, 2003), pp. 138–139.

50. For a more detailed account of Zhang's *wuxia* films, see Leon Hunt "Zhang Ziyi, 'Martial Arthouse' and the Transnational *Nuxia*," in Silke Andris and Ursula Frederick (eds), *Women Willing to Fight: The Fighting Woman in Film* (Newcastle: Cambridge Scholars Press, 2007), pp. 144–160.

51. Elley, *The Epic Film*, p. 158. Quoted in Richard Dyer, *Stars* (London: BFI, 1979), pp. 148–149.

52. Michael Mourlet, quoted in Richard Dyer, *Stars* (London: BFI, 1979), pp. 148–149.

53. One could make some slightly more tenuous connections between *The Warlords* and *300* (its "800 against 5,000" battle scenes and desaturated palette) although it otherwise owes little to the literal comic-book aesthetic of the much-derided Hollywood film (which looks like the most expensive *peplum* ever made, it's certainly homoerotic enough to make Steve Reeves blush).

54. Huo Yuanjia (1860–1910) was a real martial-arts master famous for defeating Western and Japanese fighters in challenge matches. A number of films and television series have told different versions of his life, but in the most famous, *Fist of Fury* (1972), his death is used as a pretext for Bruce Lee's war on the Japanese presence in Shanghai.

55. The principle of competitive matches that avoid injuring or shaming an opponent (*dian dao ji zhi*) has precedents amongst the historical *xia* (chivalrous martial artists). As Sinkwan Cheng explains, "The point of matches was supposed to be a friendly exchange of ideas about *gongfu* [kung-fu] techniques. It was meant to be a learning experience for both sides, and not an occasion for acquiring domination over . . . the other party." Sinkwan Cheng, "The Chinese *Xia* versus the European Knight: Social, Cultural and Political Perspectives," *EnterText,* 6 (1) (2006), pp. 57, 71, endnote 56. In the director's cut of *Fearless,* a framing device links the idea to a plea for *wushu* (martial arts) to be recognized as an Olympic sport.

56. Or at least he is in the Hong Kong version of the film, according to end titles. In the international print, we are told that Pang's killer was never caught.

57. In contrast with the more austere *Hero,* the other two Li films embrace the melodramatic dimensions of male sacrifice—one trailer for *The Warlords* emphatically foregrounds the tears of its three leads.

58. Mark Jancovich, "Dwight McDonald and the Historical Epic," in Yvonne Tasker (ed.), *Action and Adventure Cinema* (London and New York: Routledge, 2004), pp. 84–99; p. 88.

59. Christina Klein, "*Crouching Tiger, Hidden Dragon:* A Diasporic Reading," *Cinema Journal,* 43 (4) (2004): 18–42; p. 21.

bare life and sovereignty

in *gladiator*

four

robert burgoyne

In this chapter, I wish to explore the potential of the epic genre as a form of transnational cinema and to reconsider its traditional role as a vehicle of national ideology and aspirations. Placing special emphasis on the film *Gladiator* (2000), I argue that the contemporary historical epic provides a striking example of what Mikhail Bakhtin calls "double-voicing"—the adaptation of an older genre to a new context—revising themes and motifs customarily associated with narratives of nation in order to provide a narrative form that is transnational or postnational in its appeal.[1] Departing from the conventional, nationcentric motifs of epic form—the legend of a people, the battles and treaties that define a sacred landscape, and the emergence of particular heroic and sainted figures—contemporary epic films place a different accent on the legendary past, emphasizing the multiethnic community, the nomadic passage across the boundaries of empire, and the unknown or anonymous hero. Much of this can be traced, I think, to the economic dimension of epic films, which make international coproductions and multinational distribution and exhibition arrangements a necessity, a subject that has been considered in several essays included in this volume.[2] Epic films need to appeal to an international audience in order to recoup their investment. But on another plane, this new focus of the epic also seems to echo the contemporary political importance of social groups operating outside the bounds of national entities. Reading the epic alongside the work of Giorgio Agamben, I draw particular attention to the ways that the contemporary epic—and older epics as well—foreground the potential of "bare life," of the slave community, of the refugee and the dispossessed, as a form of historical agency, emphasizing the emergence of the multitude as a collective force in history.[3]

Traditionally, epic films have been understood as particularly vivid expressions of the myth-making impulse at the core of national identity. The combination of myth and history in the epic film, the layering of "what might have been" over "what actually occurred" produces a narrative structure that derives from real events but transmutes the elements of the historical past into an inspirational form, "trading on received ideas of a continuing national or cultural consciousness."[4] One writer has said that "true film epics can only be made at a time when a country's national myths are still believed—or when a nation feels itself slipping into decline, which produces a spate of nostalgic evocations of those myths."[5] This is especially evident in critical discussion of the American historical epic. As Gilles Deleuze writes, "the American cinema constantly shoots and reshoots a single fundamental film, which is the birth of a nation-civilization . . . it and it alone is the whole of history, the germinating stock from which each nation-civilization detaches itself as an organism, each prefiguring America."[6] In his reading, the Hollywood epic communicates "via the peaks" with the great civilizations of the past, discovering in them a prefiguration of America, an anticipation of the nation to come.[7]

Moreover, Rome was often taken as a metaphor for the grandeur of Hollywood itself, its glamour and aesthetic innovation, with Ancient Rome in many films serving as a privileged subject for the spectacular display of the technological superiority of Hollywood cinema. As Michael Wood writes, Hollywood's histories of Rome are "a huge, many-faceted metaphor for Hollywood itself."[8] And as Maria Wyke further comments,

> The projection of ancient Rome on screen has functioned not only as a mechanism for the display or interrogation of national identities but also, and often in contradiction, as a mechanism for the display of cinema itself—its technical capacities and its cultural value . . . Ancient Rome has been constantly reinvented to suit new technologies for its cinematic narration and new historical contexts for the interpretation of the Roman past in the present.[9]

On this model, *Gladiator* seems to exemplify the continuing importance of Ancient Rome as a mechanism for the display of national identities and cinematic technique. Its extraordinary Colosseum and battle sequences, its dramatic narrative arc depicting the progress of the title character from general, to slave-leader of a mongrel population of gladiators, to "protector of Rome" in his final moments, and its dualistic projection of both punitive authority and humanitarian beneficence, all rendered with spectacular technological virtuosity, seem designed to evoke an emerging national mythology that communicates "via the peaks" with the past. Many critics have seen the film as an especially persuasive demonstration of American technological superiority: the film's reinvention of the Roman past, for Rob Wilson and others, can be seen as a particularly striking instance of the "legitimation of the imperial machine," achieved through contemporary media forms—a "neo-epic mode of global enchantment, spectacular violence, and mass circulation." Wilson asks if *Gladiator* was not, implicitly, "so much a representation of the Roman Empire but a blasted allegorization of the Pax Americana itself in its neo-liberal mode of moral innocence, global ratification, and soft hegemony."[10] For many critical theorists, the film vividly expresses the workings of the current regime of postmodern US globalization, a regime characterized, according to Michael Hardt and Antonio Negri, not by the old state form of land-bound imperialism but rather by a fundamentally new form of rule, in which the proliferation of difference, hybridity, and the decentered aspects of contemporary life are encouraged, captured, and managed through the mass media and the Internet.[11]

The initial images of the film offer what seems to be a crystallized expression of these themes, as if the text were directing us to read the narrative in terms of the constellation of Rome, Hollywood, global enchantment, and new forms of imperial power. Beginning with its production logos, the film unfolds its imperial history under the signs of reverie, enchantment, and global reach, communicated explicitly by the DreamWorks logo that initiates the film and by the spinning globe of the Universal Studios that follows. The DreamWorks logo and the Universal globe are colored in tones of antique gold and black, evoking the past through color and cueing the emotions of the spectator. An emphatic change from the primary colors that both studios traditionally employ, the logo sequences that introduce *Gladiator* convey to us a past that has a kind of heirloom prestige about it, as if the past were being presented in black felt and precious metal.[12] The Universal ribbon that circles out from behind the globe is also colored in antique gold. Following the logo sequence, the film begins with a fade-in to a misty, dull-red background, the sound of a female voice singing a song of mourning, and an inscription:

> At the height of its power, the Roman Empire was vast, stretching from the deserts of Africa to the borders of Northern England. Over one quarter of the world's population lived and died under the rule of the Caesars . . .

84

Just one final stronghold stands in the way of Roman victory and the promise of peace throughout the empire.

Here, the logo sequence followed by the historical epigraph form a striking parallel construction: the Rome of the past and the Hollywood of the present both encircle the world, one empire standing in for another, Rome and Hollywood communicating "via the peaks."

Following *Gladiator's* opening epigraph, a tracking shot follows a man in close-up walking through a golden wheat field with his hand held out grazing the tops of the stalks. The song from the opening epigraph, which sounds like a dirge or lament, continues over these images, as the distant sound of children's laughter and the sound of wind carries the shot along. Suddenly, we cut to a frontal shot of Maximus, the main character of the film, standing quietly in a burnt-out field, a shot that has a cold, blue look and that creates a sharp contrast with the warm hues of the wheat field in the earlier tracking shot. A Spanish guitar is heard on the soundtrack. Maximus, "the Spaniard," is dressed for battle, and his face is grimy, unshaven, and resolute.

The opening sequence associates Maximus with the natural world of wheat fields and children's voices, with the earth that he rubs into his hands before battle and the bird that lands near him. But he is also associated with the imagery of war, the smoke and ash and the song of mourning that we hear on the soundtrack. It thus condenses in an exemplary way the tones of "moral innocence" and punitive authority, the innocence of the natural order and the implicit violence of empire. Seeming to evoke what one writer calls the "imperial humanitarianism" of the new global order, the sequence describes Maximus with contradictory connotations.[13] In this version of the Roman epic, the empire is identified not as it usually is with decadence, sickness, and death, but with the promise of peace; far from the "fatally stricken," diseased Rome of *Spartacus* (1960), poisoned at its core ("And even at the zenith of her pride and power, the republic lay fatally stricken with a disease called human slavery")—Rome is here one victory away from attaining "peace throughout the empire." And from the opening moments of the film, Maximus is defined as the agent of this historical process. Although he is portrayed in a static portraiture shot, with a troubled expression on his face, the residue of tradition clings to his figure: the epic past is crystallized in his powerful build, in his contemplative gaze, and in his evident stature in the narrative world, signified by the framing, cutting, and camera movement with which he is introduced (see Figure 4.1).

From the perspective described above, *Gladiator* could be seen to crystallize the cultural tone of what Hardt and Negri describe as a "fundamentally new form of rule."[14] Its teleology is not the usual endpoint of epic films, for, as one critic says, "Romans no longer need to turn into Christians in order to remain interesting to an American audience."[15] Rather, it speaks to

Figure 4.1

Gladiator: Maximus the General.

another kind of imperialism, a "soft hegemony" where diversity, difference, and hybridity are encouraged and cultivated and where the global
reach of the mass media solicits consent.[16]

But another message can be sensed in the opening as well, a message
that has found its way into certain cultural responses to the film, and
which I would like to highlight here as a motif that might lead to another
type of reading. What is unusual about the logo, epigraph, and opening
sequence in *Gladiator* is the somber, melancholy mood that the opening
communicates, as if the film were a collective commemoration ritual, the
recalling of an ancient past not in order to express a triumphal communication with the Roman Empire but rather to express a contemporary sense
of foreboding and crisis. Rather than conveying a new "master-narrative of
enlightened imperialism," as Wilson would have it, *Gladiator,* released in the
year 2000, seems to foreshadow the crisis of national identity and modern
social structures catalyzed by the events of 9/11.

The figure of Maximus, and the film itself, have been inscribed in
American culture in a particularly complex and resonant way. Maximus,
for example, became a popular figure in body art in the immediate aftermath of 9/11, with the figure of the gladiator assuming a particular value as
an icon of honor and mourning. The imagery associated with *Gladiator,*
integrated into the shield and battalion imagery of firefighters, became a
favored way of memorializing fallen firefighters, and the slogan, "Strength
and Honor" featured in the film became a popular inscription in tattoos.[17]
A more complete indexing of borrowed and repurposed imagery from the
film would undoubtedly reveal an extensive array of narratives and discourses in which the film has been inscribed. What I wish to emphasize
here is one of the ways in which *Gladiator* has been connected to a powerful
and particular moment of national anxiety and trauma, to a changing
concept of nation, and to surprising acts of solidarity with the past. The
relationship between commemoration, collective mourning, and body

modification, including tattooing and scarification, circulating within the cultural responses to *Gladiator*, suggests that the imagery and narrative messages of the contemporary epic are open to appropriation in ways that are not limited by nationalistic or imperialistic expressions, but rather may serve different, vernacular needs.

writing the body

The extensive literature on tattooing and scarification emphasizes its connection to liminal moments of social and historical crisis; the popularity of tattooing peaks during periods of cultural, social, and religious upheaval. In some cultures, tattoos are regarded as magical, an invocation against death and an expression of the desire for rebirth, a theme that is patently present in the imagery popular in tattoos seen after 9/11. Much of the commentary on tattoos after 9/11 describes them as a form of solace, as "medicinal," and as "a public declaration of loss, defiance, and survival," themes that link them explicitly to blood rituals of inclusion and community, to the idea of passage through ordeal, to a kind of "writing on the body by experience," and to remembrance and commemoration.[18] Here, the practice of tattooing speaks to an alternative understanding of being in history. As Kim Hewitt writes, tattoos and body scarification are "acts that asked to be witnessed."[19]

The popularity of *Gladiator* as a source of imagery for tattoos—one of the best-known ink parlors in New York is named "Maximus Tattoos"—brings into relief certain aspects of the film that have not yet been explored in the critical literature. Considered in terms of this kind of vernacular recoding, the film's narrative takes on a different coloration than that described by many critical theorists, one of blood ritual and commemoration, of identities constructed outside the dominant discourse. The vernacular response to the film, with its emphasis on the physical, somatic re-experiencing of loss and remembrance, suggests that for some audiences its narrative patterning and imagery are deeply interwoven with a sense of the physical, corporeal body. Rather than seeing the film as a "new master narrative of enlightened imperialism," I suggest, following Vivian Sobchack, that *Gladiator* may be understood as an epic film that provides a carnal and subjective ground for historical reflection, an embodied sense of history.[20]

In a well-known essay, Paul Willeman writes about the voyeuristic pleasure involved in viewing the male figure in film and describes the way in which certain film genres typically display the male body: "The viewer's experience is predicated on the pleasure of seeing the male 'exist' (that is, walk, move, ride, fight) in or through cityscapes, landscapes, or more abstractly, history. And on the unquiet pleasure of seeing the male mutilated . . . and restored through violent brutality."[21] The spectacle of the male figure riding, fighting, or moving "through history" is of course the keystone of the epic cinema, along with the violent brutality that finds the male hero first mutilated and then symbolically restored.[22]

The complex messages that coalesce around the body in epic films are typically understood in terms of dualisms: the pleasure of seeing the body "exist," and the "unquiet pleasure" of seeing the body mutilated, the body depicted as exultant or as abject, in the case of the Roman epic, as "Roman," or as "animal."[23] I would like to extend these dualisms in another direction by reading the epic alongside the work of the contemporary theorist Giorgio Agamben, who stresses, in Ancient Roman law, the surprising dualism and mutual implication of "bare life" and "sovereignty" in the figure named as "homo sacre."[24] In Agamben's work, the value and importance of what he calls "bare life"—creaturely life, a life that exists outside the established juridical or religious order—emerges in its close relation to "sovereignty:" the two terms are intertwined and mutually defining, like "animal" and "Roman" in *Spartacus.* Although his argument for bare life serving as the ground of sovereignty in Roman law is too complex to detail here, his example of a contemporary instance of bare life and its implications for sovereignty is relevant. The refugee, he writes, represents a contemporary form of "homo sacre," or bare life, a figure that exists without the protections of citizenship, religion, or national membership or obligation. The rights of the refugee have value only in the form of "basic human rights," and as such the refugee brings the sovereign nature of human life to the fore. He is "homo sacre," set apart, outside the national political or religious order, excluded from juridical or religious authority, and thus, paradoxically, survives and exists only as "the man of rights."[25]

In the epic film, the value of bare life is foregrounded in the physical, creaturely body that is such a key part of the epic form, in the masses of slaves and subalterns, in the great crowds of the marginal and excluded. The ethical and moral message of the epic film seems to be centered in the depiction of bare life, seen as the repository of collective identity, moral gravity, and historical change. Typically, the epic hero gains the authority, the mandate to complete his quest only after becoming one with the multitude, falling into slavery, becoming a nomad, drawing from the multitude a heightened sense of purpose and nobility. What I would like to argue here is the extent to which *Gladiator,* and other epic films as well, render the value and the rights of bare life, and create from bare life the position of sovereign authority that would seem to be its opposite. In *Gladiator,* this passage is literalized, as Maximus begins the narrative as a near sovereign, descends to the underworld of the community of slave-gladiators and reemerges as the embodiment of sovereign power. But the general cultural resonance of the dualism of bare life and sovereignty is powerfully present in the vernacular responses to the film as well, for the value of life in its most naked and vulnerable form reappears in acts of performative identification such as the writing on the body described above.

It is in this light that we can read the relationship of Maximus and Juba, the African gladiator who heals Maximus' wounded arm. Terribly wounded in his struggle with the Roman execution squad, Maximus follows Juba's instruction to let maggots eat away the infected flesh; Juba then embeds the wound with healing paste. Soon afterward, Maximus performs self-surgery on his own tattoo, the insignia that binds him to Rome, erasing his identification with the legions of Rome. From this point forward, the film weaves together the stories of Maximus and Juba, a device that is reflected in the interweaving of musical styles in the film's soundtrack which increasingly features African and Asian motifs. Chained together in the ring in one early scene, Maximus and Juba must fight as one in order to survive. Shadowing each other's movements, the two gladiators are virtuosos, performing a spectacular, choreographic duet in which they devastate their opponents, devise a new weapon from the chain that binds them, and arouse the crowd to frenzy (see Figure 4.2).

In the black–white pairing of Juba and Maximus, the motif of bare life takes on a specifically contemporary accent; the traditional epic themes—the emergence of a people, the birth of a nation, the fulfillment of a heroic destiny—are here rewritten to express a story of emergence in which black and white are connected by a central thread. The scenes among the gladiators emphasize the cross-cultural, multiethnic composition of the school of gladiators, a population drawn from the radial points of the Empire: Africa, Spain, Gaul, and Germania. The gladiator-slaves here might be seen as a kind of counter-empire, a mongrel mixture of nomads and remnants, a focus that "pushes through empire to come out the other side," naming and dramatizing a force of resistance in the ancient, and by extension, in the contemporary world.[26]

In contrast to the conventional reading of the epic as a nation-centered text, I suggest that the hybrid composition of the multitude here, its emphasis on cross-cultural connection, can be read as a force of resistance,

Figure 4.2
Gladiator: "Spaniard" and Juba.

and that the epic film might be read against the grain as a counter-imperial genre. Rather than an expression of national triumphalism, the epic may be considered as a focused dramatization of social and historical crisis that foregrounds the prospect of bare life as an agent of change. In the case of *Gladiator,* the film powerfully responds to what Ernesto Laclau describes as a current, if inchoate, political sensibility characterized by a plurality of identities and points of rupture.[27] It captures the contemporary drama of empire and the difficulty of resistance. And while for many critics it seems to be at one with the very type of imperial order I maintain it is directed against, the film also offers a scenario of political recognition in scenes that "ask to be witnessed."[28]

This idea is exemplified in *Gladiator* in the striking reversal of sovereign power that takes place in the arena. Here, bare life and sovereignty are portrayed as interconnected and mutually defining, emblematically expressed in the proximity of the Emperor Commodus and Maximus. Physically linked in the arena, the interconnection of the two main characters in the film defines sovereignty in a way that clarifies its basis and enacts its reversal. The complex reversal or, better, the deconstruction of sovereignty described by Agamben is expressed in a direct way in their relationship. Here, Maximus emblematizes the condition of bare, naked life: he erases his identity, becomes wholly incorporated into the raw, creaturely life of the gladiators—a point made manifest as blood from slaughtered animals is dripped onto his body on his way to his first gladiatorial contest—and becomes known simply as "Spaniard." From a position of near-sovereignty at the beginning of the film—the favorite of Marcus Aurelius and the designated "protector of Rome"—Maximus has now become the embodiment of what Agamben calls "homo sacre," a man without an identity, stripped of status, occupying the margins of Roman life. Paradoxically, through this lack of identity, he gains access to the equalizing power of spectacle, similar to the way Agamben describes refugees in the contemporary period gaining "rights" through media visibility, a turn that puts a very different complexion on the usual association of mass spectacle and political manipulation. Now the favorite of the Roman populace, Maximus can no longer be executed, he is not subject to religious sacrifice, and, as Commodus says, he "simply will not die!"

Maximus frustrates the sovereign power of Commodus, which is exercised primarily in the power over life and death. After defeating the celebrated gladiator, "the Tiger of Gaul," in an especially sensationalized event, Maximus also defeats Commodus in the visible exercise of his sovereign authority. Despite Commodus' command of "thumbs down," Maximus appropriates the sovereign gesture by sparing the life of his abject opponent. Here, he extends the sovereign gesture of sparing life, recalling to the Roman citizens in the Colosseum the basis of sovereignty, the power to grant an exception to bare life. The Roman audience immediately starts chanting, "Maximus the Merciful," a phrase that effectively shifts the sovereign power of exception from Commodus to Maximus, as if bare life and mongrel community has here pushed through to take up the position of sovereignty (see Figure 4.3).

techno-euphoria and the world-improving dream

The reversal of sovereignty and bare life, which forms what Deleuze would call the film's ethical-critical core, is a deeply resonant theme in epic cinema, a variation on the theme of collective emergence that privileges bare life as a source of renewal. Yet this powerful message in *Gladiator,* which I take as an expression of possibility for what Hardt and Negri call a "new social body beyond Empire," is mitigated and obscured for many critics by its overpowering sonic intensity, kinesthetic action, and choreographic camera work.[29] Many contemporary critics understand the climactic scenes of spectacle in *Gladiator* in terms of a direct projection of dominant political values. Characterizing the film in terms of the "hegemonic technology of sublime spectacle" or as the "techno-euphoric reign of aestheticized spectacles of empire," writers such as Wilson and White equate *Gladiator* with the strategies and values of the dominant political culture, specifically the projection of US cultural and military hegemony across the globe. Emphasizing parallels between its portrait of imperial Rome and the imperial globalization of the American political, cultural, and military orders, Wilson characterizes *Gladiator* as the "legitimation of the imperial machine."[30] The message communicated by the film, in this reading, is a message concerning the new forms of imperialism characterized as "soft hegemony," expressed through Maximus' identification with subaltern groups and the incorporation of the peripheries and mongrel populations into the new global order. But these "soft" messages, in his view, are contained within an overarching discourse of domination and imperialism, as the technological

Figure 4.3

Gladiator: Commodus about to determine his own fate.

and cultural superiority of the dominant culture is happily reaffirmed in sublime orchestrations of unprecedented visual spectacle.

Equating spectacular form with displays of globalizing technological prowess, Wilson and White recognize the visceral appeal of the epic, its sense of "surge and splendor," as Sobchack describes it, but they understand its aesthetic and affective potential only in negative terms. From another perspective, however, the emotional appeal of spectacular form in *Gladiator* suggests a particularly vivid example of what Jane Gaines calls the "utopianizing effect" of cinematic aesthetics.[31] Here, I would like to consider the design-intensive form of the epic in a different, more positive light, arguing that the magnifications of scale, the virtuosity of special effects, the detonations of violence and the climaxes of color so characteristic of the form create what Gaines calls a utopianizing effect and what Sobchack has called "a carnal experience of history" in film.[32] The concept of epic film as a carnal embodiment of history, accessed here through potent kinesthetic imagery and scenes of spectacle, provides a way of understanding *Gladiator* that complicates the reading of the film as "imperial nostalgia . . . Empire as spectacle and simulacrum."[33]

Gaines develops an extended argument concerning the utopian messages of certain cinematic forms and techniques, referring specifically to the panorama, the magnification of scale, the widescreen proportions and the epic magnificence of classic cinema. Drawing on the dialectical approach to mass-culture forms associated with Fredric Jameson and Stuart Hall, she emphasizes how the products of the entertainment industry have been understood dialectically in cultural studies and in film studies, displaying a productive tension between the ideological and the utopian, "the forces of containment and the forces that cannot be contained."[34] For most theorists, the balance of the argument falls on the side of the ideological. But in the pioneering work of the Frankfurt School theorist Ernst Bloch, the power of mass cultural forms to create a "hope landscape," or a "world-improving dream" are endorsed as strategic, a way to pull "the world improving aspirations out of the society itself and play them back to us."[35] In Bloch's work, the film can be a "mirror of hope [that portrays] the mime of the days which change the world," a point that is very much in keeping with the epic form's concentration on what might have occurred, rather than on what actually did occur.[36]

In an argument that echoes and extends Bloch's and Gaines's ideas, Sobchack considers the epic film's extended length, monumentality of scale, and accumulation of detail as creating a phenomenological impression of "being in history," an impression of being immersed in the flow of historical time and space: "our sense of historicality . . . begins in our reflexive existence as *embodied subjects*. It is as carnal as well as cultural beings that we presently sit in a movie theater to see a representation of past events and somehow get caught up in a comprehension of time."[37]

Where Barthes poetically describes the experience of watching the wide-screen epic as like "standing on the balcony of history," Sobchack makes a larger point.[38] The Hollywood historical epic, she writes, "can be considered as the form best able to represent the subjectively lived time of its particular cultural moment as objectively 'historical' [by] constructing a particular and contingent sense of 'being-in-History'."[39] Rather than an emblem of technical and cultural dominance and the aesthetic ratification of a new empire, the sublime spectacle offered by epic cinema becomes, in this reading, a way of accessing the somatic, physical apprehension of being in history, the burning in of experiences in a way that links us to other times and other places. Gaines and Sobchack both offer a critically sophisticated defense of the role of spectacle in film, one that I think is useful for reminding us of the "utopianizing dream" that is often forgotten in contemporary accounts.

Implicit in all of this is the sense that spectacle is crucial to the affective sense of history that is produced in the epic; the physicality of the genre, its imposing sets and accumulations of detail create a phenomenological impression of "being in history"—a quality that is very much in evidence in critical discussions of *Gladiator*. Characterizing this affective dimension in negative terms, Wilson says: "*Gladiator* helps to make this amorphous Empire palpable as a global structure of feeling. The movie . . . secures consent to its military machine not so much via domination and plunder as via aesthetic ratification, mediated trauma, and modes of civilian awe."[40] The scene of Commodus' entry into the Forum seems to validate his point. Drawing explicitly from Leni Riefenstahl's *Triumph of the Will* (1935), the camera descends from the clouds to reveal Commodus riding a chariot through a massed, excited crowd. Commodus arrives at the steps of the Senate to be greeted by children with flower bouquets, and a population gathered below—another direct quote from Riefenstahl's film. Moreover, the film's depiction of the Roman Forum, as Arthur Pomeroy points out, with its Senate at one end and the Colosseum at the other, flanked by massive buildings and columns that dwarf the human population, is visually similar to the planned architecture of "Germania," Hitler's grandiose vision for a new Berlin.[41] Here, the massive set, the crowds of extras, the camera's sweeping movement accomplished through the use of computer-generated imagery evoke the Roman past in a way that echoes the imagery and the use of spectacle associated with the Third Reich, a point reinforced by other elements of the film's iconography, such as the eagle standards, the black uniforms of the Praetorian Guard, and even the motto of the legions, "Strength and Honor," which bears an uncomfortable similarity to the Nazi slogan "Blood and Honor."

The film's use of spectacle, however, can also be seen in terms of Bloch's "mirror of hope," and "world-improving dream."[42] It dramatizes the replacing of a pathogenic historical structure with an exemplary one.

Rome is depicted here as a society made in the image of its crimes, an empire whose excesses and pathologies have been concentrated in the spectacle of the Colosseum. The spectacle of the Colosseum, however, is also depicted as the source of its renewal, the place from which it is issued a pardon. In the intensive focus on the action of the duel between Commodus and Maximus, it is as if the spectacle itself actualizes the possibility of regeneration. Spiraling down to this one moment of action, the film defines the space of the Colosseum, the action of the duel, and the gaze of the Roman spectators as the essence of an epoch, the concentrated and distilled point of Roman history. Spiraling out, it also suggests a new milieu, a new situation: the film uses the spectacle of the Colosseum to create an "originary world," to use Deleuze's expression, one that places the senators, the gladiators, the Praetorian Guard, the nobility, the slaves, and the citizens of Rome all on the same level platform, a world that departs from the historical setting of the ancient past and confers on Rome a different future (see Figure 4.4).

These scenes can clearly be read as examples of sublime spectacle, designed to solicit a kind of voyeuristic consent from its cinematic audience. But with the perspective opened up by Bloch, it seems that a different reading is equally available as an interpretive response. This duality is expressed succinctly in the film's closing shots, which depict Juba burying Maximus' family figurines in the sand of the Colosseum. Here the film both recalls Riefenstahl's *Olympia* (1938) with its close-up shot of Jesse Owens digging a sprinter's toehold in the dirt, as well as suggesting what Deleuze calls the "germinating stock, the germs of new life," a condensed expression of Bloch's wishful action or wishful landscape.[43] *Gladiator* stands as a particularly vivid example of the mixture of hegemonic fantasy and its counterforce in popular films, specifically, the dualism of imperial nostalgia and anticipatory consciousness that defines the epic film. In the contemporary period, in which global cultural narratives are being rewritten

Figure 4.4

Gladiator: The Rome of the Future.

from various directions, the epic film can again be seen as a key form of symbolic expression.

notes

1. For discussion of the concept of "genre memory," see Gary Saul Morson and Caryl Emerson, *Mikhail Bakhtin: Creation of a Prosaics* (Palo Alto, Calif.: Stanford University Press, 1990), pp. 278–297.
2. The production of *Gladiator*, for example, involved location shooting on two continents and four countries: Morocco, Italy, the United Kingdom, and Malta. The cast of the film provides perhaps the most vivid example of the transnational character of epic film production: the main actors come from Denmark (Connie Nielsen), Benin (Djimon Hounsou), the United Kingdom (Richard Harris and Oliver Reed), the USA (Joaquin Phoenix), and New Zealand (the part-Maori Russell Crowe).
3. Giorgio Agamben, *Homo Sacre: Sovereign Power and Bare Life,* trans. Daniel Heller-Roazen (Stanford, Calif: Stanford University Press, 1998).
4. Derek Elley, *The Epic Film* (London: Routledge & Kegan Paul, 1984), p. 13. Elley quotes Aristotle who remarks, in the essay *On the Art of Poetry,* that the epic poet's job is "not to say what *has* happened but what *could* happen."
5. Allan Barra quotes the British critic Paul Coates in "The Incredible Shrinking Epic," *American Film,* 14 (5) (March 1989): 40–45.
6. Gilles Deleuze, "The Action-Image: The Large Form," in *Cinema 1: The Movement-Image,* pp. 141–159.
7. Deleuze, "The Action-Image," pp. 141–159. Deleuze is eloquent in his description of the epic film, defending the historical conception underpinning the genre. Finding that the epic film sets forth a "strong and coherent conception of universal history," he analyzes the structure of the epic as consisting of three interlocking aspects, the monumental, the antiquarian, and the ethical.
8. Michael Wood, *America in the Movies; or, "Santa Maria It Had Slipped My Mind"* (London: Secker & Warburg, 1975), pp. 173 and 166–177.
9. Maria Wyke, *Projecting the Past: Ancient Rome, Cinema, and History* (London and New York: Routledge, 1997), p. 338. Wyke writes that Hollywood's Roman history films are an extension of a long tradition of borrowing from the Roman past in order to crystallize and critique aspects of the nation-state, a tradition exemplified by the architecture of Washington, DC, which is modeled on the Roman Forum, and the numerous depictions of George Washington in a toga, holding a Roman-style scroll. The decadence and opulence of Ancient Rome, however, were also emphasized by early writers, who warned that the social inequalities in the fledgling nation-state could lead to a fate similar to Rome's. Hollywood films set in Rome typically exploit these contradictions, depicting Ancient Rome as a site of both ideal civic virtue as well as of decadent excess and imperial domination.
10. See Rob Wilson, "Ridley Scott's *Gladiator* and the Spectacle of Empire: Global/Local Rumblings Inside the Pax Americana," *European Journal of American Culture,* 21 (2) (2002): 62–73. See also Brian J. White, "*American Beauty, Gladiator,* and the New Imperial Humanitarianism," *Global Media Journal,* 1 (1) (2002): 1–36.
11. Michael Hardt and Antonio Negri, *Empire* (Cambridge, Mass.: Harvard University Press, 2000).

12. See Paul Grainge on history and logo sequences in "Branding Hollywood: Studio Logos and the Aesthetics of Memory and Hype," *Screen*, 45 (4) (2004): 344–362.

13. White, "*American Beauty, Gladiator*, and the New Imperial Humanitarianism."

14. Hardt and Negri, *Empire*, p. 146.

15. White, "*American Beauty, Gladiator*, and the New Imperial Humanitarianism," p. 24.

16. Wilson, "Ridley Scott's *Gladiator* and the Spectacle of Empire," p. 63.

17. Coco McPherson, "That Was Then, This is Now," *Rolling Stone*, September 19, 2002, pp. 90–96.

18. Tara Godvin, "Tattoos Become Personal Memorials to Sept. 11 and Most Loved Ones," www.Boston.com, accessed September 15, 2006.

19. Kim Hewitt, *Mutilating the Body* (Bowling Green, Ohio: Bowling Green State University Popular Press, 1997).

20. Vivian Sobchack, "Surge and Splendor: A Phenomenology of the Hollywood Historical Epic," *Representations*, 29 (winter 1990): 24–49. See also Vivian Sobchack, *Carnal Thoughts: Embodiment and Moving Image Culture* (Berkeley, Calif.: University of California Press, 2004).

21. Paul Willeman, "Anthony Mann: Looking at the Male," *Framework*, 15–17, (summer 1981): 18.

22. Friedrich Nietzsche found a similar appeal in epic literature as well. Writing about the "will to power" displayed in the Greco-Roman fascination with agonistic battle, he stresses "the visual stimulation of seeing muscular bodies in vigorous exertion, defying death and injury." See Ekhart Koehne, Cornelia Egwigleben, and Ralph Jackson (eds), *Gladiators and Caesars: The Power of Spectacle in Ancient Rome* (London: British Museum Press, 2000), p. 47.

23. Ina Rae Hark, "Animals or Romans: Looking at Masculinity in *Spartacus*," in Steven Cohan and Ina Rae Hark (eds), *Screening the Male* (London and New York: Routledge, 1993), pp. 151–172.

24. Agamben, *Homo Sacre*.

25. The authority of the sovereign, based on the division between his citizen-subjects and the excluded other, outside the law, is challenged by the refugee, who represents the "bare life" within. In Agamben's formulation, the refugee, or "homo sacre" in the ancient formulation, cannot be executed or sacrificed. Not "worthy" of religious sacrifice, and not a "citizen" who can be tried by law, he can be killed but not executed by the state or sacrificed by religion. In fact, his "basic human rights," his bare life, requires—obliges—an exception on the part of the sovereign.

26. Hardt and Negri, *Empire*, p. 206.

27. Ernesto Laclau, "Can Immanence Explain Social Struggles?" in Paul Passavant and Jodi Dean (eds), *The Empire's New Clothes: Reading Hardt and Negri* (New York: Routledge, 2004), pp. 21–31.

28. Hewitt, *Mutilating the Body*.

29. Hardt and Negri, *Empire*, p. 206.

30. Wilson, "Ridley Scott's *Gladiator* and the Spectacle of Empire," p. 71.

31. Jane M. Gaines, "Dream/Factory," in Christine Gledhill and Linda Williams (eds), *Reinventing Film Studies* (London: Arnold, 2000), pp. 100–113.

32. Sobchack, "Surge and Splendor," p. 38.

33. Wilson, "Ridley Scott's *Gladiator* and the Spectacle of Empire," p. 70.

34. Gaines, "Dream/Factory," p. 107.

35. Gaines, "Dream/Factory," p. 108.

36. Gaines, "Dream/Factory," p. 108. For the original formulation of these ideas, see Ernst Bloch, *The Principle of Hope,* vol. I, trans. by Neville Plaice, Stephen Plaice, and Paul Knight (Cambridge, Mass.: MIT Press, 1986), especially pp. 406–412.

37. Sobchack, "Surge and Splendor," p. 37.

38. See Roland Barthes, "On CinemaScope," trans. by Jonathon Rosenbaum, available online at http://english.chass.ncsu.edu/jouvert/v3i3/barth.htm (accessed March 16, 2010). First published 1954. James Morrison's illuminating analysis of Barthes's very short essay is particularly interesting. Barthes writes that "the balcony of History is ready. What remains to be seen is what we'll be shown there."

39. Sobchack, "Surge and Splendor," p. 38.

40. Wilson, "Ridley Scott's *Gladiator* and the Spectacle of Empire," p. 71.

41. Arthur J. Pomeroy, "The Vision of a Fascist Rome in *Gladiator,*" in Martin M. Winkler (ed.), *Gladiator: Film and History* (Malden, Mass.: Blackwell, 2004), pp. 111–123.

42. Gaines, "Dream/Factory," p. 107.

43. Deleuze, "The Action-Image: The Large Form," p. 148.

center and

periphery

part two

"rise of the rest"

globalizing epic cinema

f i v e

d i n a   i o r d a n o v a

Learning from the rest is no longer a matter of morality or politics. Increasingly, it is about competitiveness.[1]

In recent years, international epic cinema has been gaining increased visibility on a global scale. Developing in a way that might be compared to the increased presence and importance of "the rest" in all areas of economic and society, a rising tide of non-Western epic super-productions has gained international distribution and attention, acquiring significant competitive advantage. In this essay I would like to weigh the commercial advances in the circulation of non-Western epic films against the still limited interest in and appreciation of non-Western history and civilization.

Historically, most international epics have been critically esteemed but have not found a popular audience. Films such as Sergei Eisenstein's *Alexandr Nevsky* (1938), Sergei Bondarchuk's *War and Peace* (1968) or Akira Kurosawa's *Ran* (1985) are textbook examples of critically important films that few have actually seen, whereas epic masterpieces such as K. Asif's *The Great*

Mughal (1960) or Abdullah Shadaan's *Rabia Balkhi* (1965) have never been properly acknowledged. Others still, like the historical epics produced in Poland or Romania, will probably remain in the realm of specialist film historiography.[2] More recently, international epic "auteurs" rivaling in reputation epic masters such as David Lean or Anthony Mann, have come to the stage, including directors such as Chinese Zhang Yimou[3] and Chen Kaige[4], Indian Ashutosh Gowariker[5] and Santosh Sivan[6], or Russian Sergei Bodrov[7], as well as the Thai Prince Chatrichalerm Yukol,[8] and others. Their films tell epic stories of greed, ambition, and intrigue, display panoramas of majestic battles and intricate plots, and focus on the lives of influential rulers and commoners, who lived in a range of historical epochs from the third century bc to the eighteenth century, in a range of countries (China, India, Kazakhstan, Thailand, Mongolia, and more). Each one of these films—their plots briefly described in Box 5.1—qualifies as an epic in that it evolves around a tragic protagonist whose historical mission puts him at odds with the limitations of the era. They are all lavishly staged monumental spectacles, the stories of which build around anxieties of contested identity

---

Box 5.1 Internatonal epic super productions (selection)

Films are listed chronologically. They all enjoyed international distribution and attention over the last decade. Each one qualifies as an epic, on the basis of key features identified by Burgoyne (2008) such as

- spectacle, monumentality and lavish *mise-en-scène*
- distilled expression of ideas, anxieties, and conflicts in national self-definition
- technological prowess of the production
- heroic protagonist compelled to make choices that affect the course of history.

Destiny (*Al-Massir*, Egypt/France, 1997, Youssef Chahine). Set in the twelfth century in Arab-ruled Andalusia at a time of rising Islamic fanaticism. Philosopher Averroes and Caliph Al Mansour are forced into difficult political manoeuvring in the face of historical change.

The Emperor and the Assassin (*Jing ke ci qin wang*, France/Japan/China, 1998). Epic tale set in third century BC and featuring court intrigues of the rule of Ying Zheng, heir to the Kingdom of Qin, an influential emperor whose ambition is to expand his power. The film is directed by acclaimed Chinese émigré director Chen Kaige of *Farewell My Concubine* fame.

Jinnah (Pakistan/UK, 1998, Jamil Dehlavi). Epic biopic of the life of Pakistan's founder Mohammed Ali Jinnah. Made for an estimated $6 million, the

---

film focuses on Jinnah's fateful decisions related to the partition of India along religious lines and on the relationship of Islam and Hinduism. Told in a flashback, the film includes a scene of an imaginary "trial of history" in the context of which former Western colonial rulers are challenged in court.

Asoka (India, 2001). The story of the eponymous emperor from the third century BC, a warrior king from the Mauryan dynasty who was committed to spreading Buddhism, and in the course of this endeavor united various groups and secured the prosperity of his kingdom in India. The film was produced by megastar Shah Rukh Khan, who plays the role of Asoka, and is directed by acclaimed cinematographer Santosh Sivan.

Lagaan: Once Upon a Time in India (India, 2001). Epic tale of the glorious resistance put up by a bunch of villagers, led by Bhuvan (Aamir Khan), against the local British rulers. Set in the late nineteenth century, it all plays out in a challenging game of cricket. A brainchild of director Ashutosh Gowariker and produced by lead star Khan, the film was the most expensive Indian production at the time and earned a nomination for foreign-language Oscar.

The Legend of Suriyothai (Thailand, 2001). The sprawling tale of sixteenth-century Queen Suriyothai and the Kingdom of Ayutthaya, involving court intrigue, treacherous erotic subplots, a foreign invasion and a civil war, and featuring majestic elephant battles. Made with the direct endorsement and financial support of Thailand's royal family by director Prince Chatrichalerm Yukol and having premiered for the Queen's birthday in 2001, the film at the time of its release was said to have been the most expensive Thai production.

Hero (*Ying xiong*, Hong Kong/China, 2002). A stunning spectacle of colours by Chinese master Zhang Yimou, the film is set in the third century BC, during the rule of First Emperor Qin when China is still split into a number of warring feudal kingdoms. Jet Li, the nameless 'Hero', a man of extraordinary fighting skill, has protected the Emperor against three of his assailants. As his story, told in color-coded flashbacks, reveals him as the ruler's worst enemy, he is destroyed in a valiant sacrifice under a hail of arrows (a memorable scene replicated in the digital epic *300*).

House of Flying Daggers (*Shi mian mai fu*, Hong Kong/China, 2004). Epic extravaganza by Zhang Yimou, set in the time of Tang Dynasty in the ninth century AD. The film, which stars famous transnational Asian stars, evolves around intricate stories of betrayal, romance, and honor, and features spectacular and impeccably choreographed swordfight routines.

Nomad (Kazakhstan/France, Ivan Passer/Sergei Bodrov, 2005). Epic tale of the glorious beginnings of the Kazakh nation in the eighteenth century,

Continued

Box 5.1 (*Continued*)

made on the initiative of president Nazarbaev. Conceived and executed by a transnational crew as a product clearly geared toward international markets.

The Curse of the Golden Flower (*Man cheng jin dai huang jin jia*, Hong Kong/China, 2006). Set around the end of the Tang Dynasty in the tenth century AD, this is the most lavish of Zhang Yimou's costume epics, featuring more than 1,000 extras along with the world's most bankable Chinese-speaking stars (Chow Yun-Fat and Gong Li), extensive battle scenes and superbly elaborate sets and costumes. Out of the three historical films made by Yimou, this one comes closest to the Western concept of an epic film in that it places large-scale historical movements in direct dependency to the intrigues and the complex relations of the Royal court, linking personal and social history and foregrounding moral dilemmas.

Mongol (Germany/Kazakhstan/Russia/Mongolia, 2007). Internationally produced epic tale of the early years of Genghis Khan and his rise to power in the twelfth century. It is the brainchild of Sergei Bodrov who embarked on this project immediately after completing *Nomad*; the director has said that he is planning a trilogy about Genghis Khan, of which *Mongol* is supposed to be the first instalment.

Jodhaa Akbar (India, 2008). This impressive example of filmmaking on an epic scale, enjoyed the widest international release given to an Indian film ever. Promoting religious tolerance, this fictional account of the love between Mughal emperor Akbar (Bollywood heartthrob Hrithik Roshan), who is a Muslim, and his wife, Rajput princess Jodhaa (Aishwarya Rai), a Hindu, is set in sixteenth-century India, during the rule of the Mughals. It is produced, written and directed by Ashutosh Gowariker, a high profile Indian *auteur* who also counts the monumental *Lagaan* (2001) among his credits.

and moral standards and are usually linked to matters of homeland and belonging; their technological proficiency is so remarkable that it is often emulated by Hollywood.[9]

The improved circulation and appeal of these films, however, does not appear to have created a greater-than-before urge to understanding the past of non-Western civilizations and nations. The sumptuous spectacle is seen and appreciated, but the particular ethnic or national history that gives shape and purpose to the spectacle has not been conveyed. In spite of the commercial advances these films have enjoyed, the narratives that these works set forth are still not included in our thinking on the epic genre. There seems to be an unspoken premise that constrains the epic genre exclusively to the doctrines and the foundations of Western civilization.

My investigation is focused on two key areas. On the one hand, I explore distribution patterns behind the increased circulation of international epic super-productions. Evidence related to market share, distribution and transnationalizaton of production consistently reveals that mass markets are changing and that epic entertainment coming from non-Western production centers is of much greater notice than just a decade ago. On the other hand, the investigation of reception reveals that difficulties in discourse and genre-related interpretative framework persist and no noticeable progress in the intracultural dialogue that these films purport to trigger, is taking place. Be it because of limitations of national interests, misguided tuning in to Western conventions, or narrow-mindedness in the use of the concept of "epic genre," in spite the increased competitiveness of this cinematic material, "learning from the rest" remains "a matter of morality or politics," to use Fareed Zakaria's apposite expression.

international epic cinema: matters of circulation

International epics released over the past decade, especially those made in Asia, have enjoyed a better circulation in the West than similar films have had in the past. There is a significant increase in the market share of these films, and new patterns of successful international distribution have emerged. There is also an increased direct involvement of transnational professionals in the process of production.

Even if it is difficult to assess its precise impact, the triumph of Ang Lee and James Shamus's brainchild *Crouching Tiger, Hidden Dragon* (2000) served as a great impetus for the incursion of international epics-cum-martial scenes into the international arena. The acclaim given to *Crouching Tiger, Hidden Dragon* served as a definitive confidence booster for many of the international production companies and directors that entered the market for epic entertainment since 2000, such as Zhang Yimou and Sergei Bodrov, as they and other professionals have regularly credited the film (and its commercial success in particular) as an important formative influence. Even though some more recent international epics may have surpassed its commercial results, *Crouching Tiger, Hidden Dragon* is still remembered as a runaway box office hit.

Even in the context of limited data, Table 5.1 reveals that lavish epics from Asia are turning into a lucrative market that capitalizes on the interest in stories that take place in distant lands. Unlike foreign films that generally receive limited exposure, the new Asian epics are being sought out in the new global image marketplace and are claiming a more significant share of the international market; sometimes they even prove more commercially successful then their expensive Hollywood counterparts. The increased visibility of these films is part of the intensive processes of global integration and transnationalization in international epic cinema. It plays

Table 5.1 Budget and revenues of some recent international epics

Film	Budget	North American box office	International box office	Total box office
Emperor and the Assassin	not known	$1,328,435*	not known	not known
Crouching Tiger, Hidden Dragon	c. $15 million	$61,231,307	$40,000,000	$101,23,307
Asoka	c. $2.5 million	$731,277	c. $1 million (UK)c. $1,700,000 (India)	c. $3,400,000
Suriyothai	c. $9 million*	$454,736	not known	not known
Lagaan	c. $5 million*	$909,043	c. $10,200,000*	c. $11,000,000
Hero	c. $31 million	$53,710,019	$123,684,413	$177,394,432
House of Flying Daggers	$15 million*	$11,050,094	$81,813,851	$92,863,945
Nomad	c. $40 million*	$79,123	$2,760,998	$2,840,121
Curse of the Golden Flower	c. $45 million*	$6,566,773	$72,002,204	$78,568,977
Mongol	c. $18 million	$ 5,705,761	$ 21,024,813	$26,730,574
Jodhaa Akbar	c. $7.5 million*	$3,440,718	$11,467,231	$14,907,949*

Source: Box Office Mojo listings, unless differently indicated. Data taken from IMDb listings and Wikipedia entries on concrete films are marked by *. As in April 2009.

out at various levels: in the movement of creative personnel (actors, directors, cameramen, composers, and editors) and below-the-line skilled labor (special effects, stunts), in the emergence of new distribution patterns, as well as in the increased role of new reception patterns enabled by the growing diversity of (and interaction within) viewer communities.

market share

Writing on the relationship between Hollywood and East Asian cinema in *The Contemporary Hollywood Film Industry,* Asian film industry specialist John Lent claims there is "a slight improvement in Americans' awareness of Asian film."[10] The change, however, seems to be even more significant than Lent is prepared to concede. Available data suggest that the international epics enter the marketplace and claim a share that is higher than the average of 1 percent usually attributed to foreign film revenues within the North American market. What we know about the market performance of these films is not comprehensive, but even on the basis of limited data one can see that international productions are taking a fair share of both the global and the domestic North American market.[11]

Data provided in John Trumpbour's evocatively titled text on recent Hollywood exports, "Export or Die," reveal clearly that only the most successful Hollywood films bring in significant international revenues.[12] For Trumpbour "today [. . .] the foreign box office is significantly greater than the domestic US market."[13] What is particularly important in this context is that while for a Hollywood production exporting is often a matter of breaking even, for international epics, usually made for significantly lower budgets, recouping can take place domestically, and revenues realized internationally account for sheer profit. The revenue configuration for many of the international epics has North American box-office account for about one-fifth or even less of worldwide returns.[14]

A suitable example of a year that illustrated the changing market share and profitability pattern of international epic film was 2004, as one can see from the box-office data presented in Table 5.2. Three films that would qualify as epic blockbusters premiered in that year and were circulated in a similar pattern: *Alexander* (2004), *Troy* (2004), and *Hero* (2002) (which was made earlier but only released in the USA late in 2004). Taken together, the three films cost about $360 million to make and returned a total of $840 million, of which about $220 million within the North American market and about $620 million from international distribution, a domestic: international ratio of roughly one to three.

Alexander was not particularly successful in commercial terms as its total returns were only about 8 percent above the budget. Made for $155 million, it grossed $34 million domestically and $167,298,192 worldwide: clearly, the film was heavily reliant on international revenues in order to break even, it only recouped 20 percent of its budget from the domestic North American market. The ratio of domestic to international for *Alexander* was roughly one to five.

Troy, made for $175 million, recouped most of its budget domestically ($133,378,256) and, with a worldwide gross of $497,409,852, got the status of a quasi "threebagger" (to use investor Peter Lynch's famous term referring to the number of times an investment increases in value by 100 percent).[15] The film confirmed the trade reputation of its director, Wolfgang Petersen, as a blockbuster expert and consolidated Brad Pitt's reputation as one of the most bankable Hollywood actors. The ratio of domestic to international for *Troy* was roughly one to three.

Hero, which cost only $31 million to make, made over $53 million in the USA and amassed an extra $123,684,413 internationally, for a worldwide gross of $177,394,432, thus bringing in profits of about 600 percent and becoming a "sixbagger."[16] The ratio of North American to international for *Hero* was roughly one to two and a half. Thus, speaking in commercial times, not only is a "sixbagger" like *Hero* the most successful of the three films, even though its distribution history, discussed in Box 5.2, was particularly convoluted. It also claimed a share of about 25 percent from the domestic North American market ($53 million out of $220 million), dina iordanova

Table 5.2 Box-office performance of three major epic films in 2004

Film	Budget	US Release	Domestic	International	Total	Return (Revenues/Budget) %
Troy	$175 million	May 2004	$133,378,256	$364,031,596	$497,409,852	c. 300%
Hero (China)	$31 million	August 2004	$53,710,019	$123,684,413	$177,394,432	c. 600%
Alexander	$155 million	October 2004	$34,297,191	$133,001,001	$167,298,192	c. 8%
Total	$361 million	2004	$221,386,466	$620,717,010	$842,102,476	c. 233%

Source: Box Office Mojo. Data derived in August 2008.

Box 5.2 US distribution of *Hero* (2002)

Zhang Yimou's *Hero,* which was made for about $30 million and earned its budget six times over, is by far the most commercially successful film in the context of this discussion. Its distribution history in the US reveals patterns that may be of particular significance. The film was made in 2002 and released across Asia where it soon became a blockbuster hit; it was on the short list for a foreign Oscar but it did not win. Miramax secured US and some international distribution rights in 2002 but, similar to the way they are known to have handled other acquisitions, they took a long time in deliberating when and if a US release should take place. (Critic Jonathan Rosenbaum [2002] has claimed that keeping films away from the market by acquiring distribution rights and then not releasing the product has been a standard practice for Miramax.)

Meanwhile, the film, which had entered clandestine circulation in the USA through copies of the DVD imported from other countries (a commercial practice which, given the absence of a US-labeled product, fell in a gray zone in terms of legitimacy), gained sizable cult following across North America. It took a personal intervention from director Quentin Tarantino to persuade Disney and Miramax as to the commercial potential of the material and make them finally release the film (Hoberman 2004). Because of the delay, by the time of *Hero's* theatrical release, members of the sizable Chinese community in the USA had already seen the film on DVD, either pirated or imported from HK. Nonetheless, even with the delayed release, *Hero* quickly ended up among the highest-grossing foreign films.

For more on the distribution and reception of *Hero* see my discussion at http://www.DinaView.com/?p=144 (17 July 2008).

as well as about a fifth of the total revenues for the three films ($177 million out of $842 million). The Chinese film, however, cost less than 10 percent of the cumulative budget of the three films.

This is, of course, a general and tentative calculation. It would take many more market details and fine-tuning to attempt to see what the real picture is, and I do not think we are properly equipped to provide robust and reliable calculations yet. The picture would change substantially, for example, if one included here Mel Gibson's "twentybagger" *The Passion of the Christ,* which was also released in 2004. Made for $30 million, the film returned over $370 million domestically and made over $600 million worldwide. If *The Passion of the Christ* was included, the total size of the domestic "epic" market would go up to $590 million, of which *Hero's* revenues of $53 million would still stand at a healthy 9 percent.

109

Figuring out the precise strength of internationally produced epics in the global marketplace is inevitably a somewhat speculative undertaking. For the sake of consistency, I am using market data available through the Box Office Mojo consultancy (also the main source used for distribution information by the Internet Movie Database [IMDb]). Box Office Mojo's data-gathering, however, is limited to theatrical distribution; they draw their information only from a selection of US-based companies that readily report revenues, and where they provide data on worldwide revenues these only reflect the revenues realized by internationally operating US distributorships and their subsidiaries. Thus, the complete (but missing) picture of the worldwide circulation of Asian epics is likely to be even more favorable because the auxiliary income that is not monitored is of particular importance for the revenue structure of foreign film and because these films are also distributed by an array of smaller international companies that do not report to a central agency and are thus not included in the numbers with which I am working.

The dynamically shifting context, where foreign-produced films' performance often rivals the revenues of Hollywood productions, turns timing the market into an increasingly challenging endeavor. Hollywood distributors now have to reckon with a much more complex domestic market, further complicated by the clandestine media-consumption practices of various diasporic groups. They cannot always get a grip on the international terrain either, where new highly competitive products originating from all over are made available on almost a weekly basis, a context that necessitates realistic understanding of the rapidly changing power dynamics.

distribution

There is growing diversity in patterns of international dissemination, marked by the entry of new players and alternative distribution set-ups. Foreign epics are distributed differently from the established Hollywood model where studio films receive global exposure in more than thirty territories through an internationally positioned major and a further lease of life through a network of international subsidiaries that takes them to another twenty or thirty territories, often coming to a total of fifty to sixty territories worldwide. But even if differently distributed, the international epics, which in most cases reach out to a more modest spread of up to thirty countries, are increasingly dependent on international revenues and are progressively more successful in tapping international markets. Reaching out to global audiences and ensuring distribution deals for multiple territories is a matter of pressing importance that leads to the formation of new circulation patterns.

Films that have become a visible part of the international circuit clearly benefit from the general international boom in Asian cinema that has lasted for the past decade; some of these Asian epics even come to rival the market performance of their Hollywood counterparts. There are differences, however, in the ways Asian films are marketed. The Chinese, with their newly found brotherhood with Hong Kong, command serious clout in Hollywood and come across as the shrewdest operators when it comes to distribution. The Indians are holding on to their own Bollywood distribution networks and still primarily market to the diaspora. Others, such as the truly supranational operation of migrant Bodrov are targeting global markets by using an idiosyncratic recipe of Asian-flavored (and financed) fare made by European and other migrant professionals.

The most successful model seems to be the one used in connection with Zhang Yimou's three Chinese super-productions where worldwide distribution was achieved by using Hollywood's global marketing machine in combination with about fifteen other international dissemination operators from various Asian, European, and Latin American countries, with one major Hollywood-linked partner (Miramax for *Hero* and Sony Pictures Classics for *House of Flying Daggers* [2004] and *Curse of the Golden Flower* [2006]) and a parallel host of special arrangements with the international outposts of other Hollywood players (Warner Bros., United International Pictures, Buena Vista International, etc.), thus ensuring that the widest possible range of countries is covered. This model resembles the set-up used in the distribution of Hollywood epics, such as *Troy* or *Alexander,* which also use a combination of international distributors wherever needed in order to cover territories to which Hollywood may not have direct access. A similar model is being tried out in the context of supranational operator Sergei Bodrov's recent *Mongol* (2007).

The distribution model for large-scale Indian productions differs: they are traditionally handled by diaspora-orientated Indian companies, such as Eros International, Yash Raj Films, or UTV, all of which now routinely make simultaneous releases to about fifteen territories worldwide. On more recent occasions, however, their releases have been wider, involving up to thirty countries and over 1,000 screens worldwide. For example, UTV's release of epic superproduction *Jodhaa Akbar* (2008) in February 2008 secured simultaneous opening for the film across twenty-six territories and over 1,500 screens, a launch that is fully compatible with high-profile Hollywood releases. However, even if ensuring global exposure, this set-up still limits the exposure mainly to countries with significant Indian diasporic presence.

Auxiliary distribution (DVDs in particular, mostly found on DVD rental sites and sold in ethnic grocery stores) is another important channel through which these films travel and reach out to audiences. More and more international epics are now available in subtitled versions on DVD, be it for domestic or classroom use. Circulation through the festival network also provides dissemination of sorts. *Mongol,* for example, played at over forty festivals internationally, a promotional strategy that asserts the view that festival showings give wonderful exposure to a film. Such an extended play across festival venues, however, also raises the question if the festival circuit forms an added "window of distribution" that almost certainly cuts into revenues. International epics may be faced with a situation where theatrical distribution potential is exhausted by festival exposure.

Like Hollywood product, internationally made epic films are also affected by piracy. Over the years, various reports commissioned by the *Motion Picture Association of America* have been estimating the annual losses Hollywood suffers globally in different territories; countries such as China or Russia have been identified as priority areas for combating piracy. No comparable exercise, however, is carried out for international films and no estimates exist on the losses that international blockbusters may be suffering. However, one can easily come across instances where one would encounter the rampant piracy affecting international films. For example, the discussion of *Mongol* on IMDb includes postings from people based in countries where the film has not played yet; one can only make educated guesses as to how they could have watched it. And while the release of India's *Jodhaa Akbar* on DVD in the West was postponed several times in the course of 2008, thus making it impossible to acquire a copy of the film by legal means, a Google search for this title made in 2008 would immediately produce several invitations to view it online for free and readily direct to BitTorrent sites from where it is available. *The Emperor and the Assassin* (1998) is also available for pirate downloads online. Other films can be found in their entirety cut into ten-minute-long segments and posted on You Tube. It is only as of recently that distributors of non-Hollywood product have begun raising issues of losses and protection.[17]

international epic cinema: matters of reception

So far this investigation established the increased presence of foreign epic entertainment on Western screens. But does this mean that, along with the evidence that these epics are now claiming a bigger market share and more robust presence, viewers in Europe and North America are becoming more receptive to the diversity of narrative conventions and styles that these films bring along?

Over the past decade there have been several types of non-Western epic films—projects of national glory, heroic pictures that explore the dialogue between East and West, and ambitious Asian tales that adopt Western narrative conventions—that would rightfully claim a place in the annals of epic filmmaking while simultaneously challenging established views on civilization and colonial history and attempting to introduce alternative narratives into the public sphere. In this part of the discussion, I will try to assess what factors stand in the way of an improved dialogue and diminish the influence of these narratives in the Western discursive space, and identify patterns of reception suggesting that traditional and rigid concepts of film criticism and film genre may hinder a more open-minded reception of international texts.

Circulation data reveal that non-Western films are claiming a significant commercial share of the market for this type of cinema. As soon as the focus of investigation moves to assessing the influence of these foreign epics, however, it becomes difficult to maintain that alternative narratives of history and civilization have come into meaningful circulation in the West. Even if the new epics are more widely available, they have not yet become part of the curriculum in history, nor have they triggered public discourse of a size or type that would necessitate a supple and enhanced understanding of other civilizations. The international epics are out there, but their impact is sporadic. The very project of multicultural education itself does not seem to have advanced significantly since the time it was developed evocatively on the example of cinema in Ella Shohat and Robert Stam's *Unthinking Eurocentrism.*[18]

epics of national pride

These epics are usually produced and publicized with the ambition to showcase glorious national history; such projects remain of utmost significance within the context of the producing nation and are mostly suited for internal usage. Sometimes, however, their producers seek international exposure, even if the film is likely to be only of niche interest. Domestically, such instances of export are given disproportionate media coverage that evolves around a concocted narrative according to which the national saga has been truly embraced and admired abroad. In reality, these national sagas go largely unnoticed. Nonetheless, it is handy to have such films in circulation even where this is vernacular distribution as they are occasionally used in the teaching of the culture and the history of the given nation.

One such recent epic project is *Nomad* (2005), a technically proficient tale of the glorious beginnings of the nation in the eighteenth century filmed on the initiative of Kazakhstan's president Nursultan Nazarbaev. Made for $40 million, the project was given public-relations importance as it aimed to emancipate the Kazakh identity from the shadow of the Soviet past. Conceived and executed as a product clearly geared toward international markets, the film relied on the directorial involvement of well-known diasporic US-based Europeans. It was nominated for a Golden Globe and distributed by the Weinstein Company who secured an international and a North American release; later on it was published on DVD, in dubbed English and French versions. Nonetheless, the returns of the film's worldwide distribution came to only about 10 percent of the budget.

Similarly, the US distribution of *Suriyothai* (2001), a lavish sixteenth-century spectacle of national pride from Thailand, featuring majestic war scenes and elephant battles that are said to have directly influenced Oliver Stone *Alexander*'s Asian representation, was treated as a project of utmost national importance. There was a sustained (but unsuccessful) campaign aimed at getting the film an Oscar nomination in the foreign-language category. The carefully orchestrated US release took place with assistance from Francis Ford Coppola, a personal friend of the director, who edited a version of the film for the North American market. Theatrical distribution was handled by Sony Picture Classics (which placed a total of twenty two prints in circulation) and the DVD release by Columbia TriStar Home Entertainment.

Thus, even though distributed internationally, *Suriyothai* never reached the popularity that had been planned for it. In her analysis of the domestic discourse on the film, anthropologist Amporn Jirattikorn argues that, in spite the massive campaign for international exposure, the film's construction of "Thai-ness" effectively promotes a narrative of self-sufficiency and positive isolationism, thus furthering the ideology of Thailand's ability to remain intact by colonizing flows and to maintain its sovereignty today like it has been able to do in the past.[19] And, indeed, Thais do not seem to have made further efforts to distribute internationally the subsequent epic dramas made by *Suriyothai*'s director, thus confirming Jirattikorn's commentary on the ideological underpinnings of self-sufficiency, conscious distancing from the West and focusing on cultivating discourse on Thailand's history exclusively within the country.[20]

Could this be seen as a confirmation that producers have realized that epics of national glory do not seem to stand much chance at the international marketplace?

dialogue of cultures

Other international epics are conceived in much more dialogic fashion; the aim of the producers here is to make points related to subtleties of the encounter of the West with other civilizations. These films are often concerned with reassessing colonial history and are addressed to imaginary Western spectators. The fact they do not really seem to be properly noticed speaks of the self-content attitude of their target audiences. Besides being works of "technological prowess" and "monumental" persuasive power, these films clearly fit Robert Burgoyne's definition of the epic in that they bring a definitive "ethical-critical vision" and "transformative power" which, if allowed into mainstream discourse, would certainly have "the ability to transfigure the accomplishments of the past."[21] But even though enjoying acclaim among diasporic viewers, they remain below the radar of Western public attention.

Some recent films from India could have successfully raised important issues of reassessing colonial legacies and improving the dialogue between the West and the Subcontinent if only they had been noticed beyond the diaspora. Indeed, some of these films openly sought to correct the record on matters of post-colonial emancipation, offered new takes to India's colonial history and attempted to reassess the past as it shapes the lives and attitudes of India's younger generation. These included Aamir Khan's Oscar-nominated *Lagaan: Once Upon a Time in India* (2001), the acclaimed *Paint It Yellow* (2006), and, to some extent, Aamir Khan's other vehicle, *The Rising: Ballad of Mangal Pandey* (2005), but also films such as Deepa Mehta's *Earth 1947* (1998) and Rajkumar Santoshi's *Legend of Bhagad Singh* (2002).[22] All these films are sui-generis epics, often taking a highly original approach to historical material in problematizing issues of colonial dependency, following the evolution of self-assertion, and tackling emancipation and representation in connection with present-day identity. As soon as the matter comes to challenging established accounts on colonial history, however, the films are treated as promoting subterranean narratives and rarely manage to reach out beyond their immediate diasporic spectatorship. They have been extensively discussed by scholars involved with the study of India but have barely had public presence in the West beyond these circles.

The English-language production of *Jinnah* (1998), a modern biopic of the life of the founder of Pakistan, Muhammad Jinnah, is an equally bold narrative of epic proportions that raises issues of historical responsibility and Islamic liberation in the context of colonial dominance and minority discourse. The concluding scenes of the film feature an imaginary historical trial, where British Dominion officials such as Lord Mountbatten and Sir Cyril Radcliffe are called to the court of history to answer queries about their role in the traumatic events of India's partition. *Jinnah* had a limited theatrical run in the UK and played at a handful of festivals; it remains unknown in the West.[23]

Other international films have tried to address issues of dialogue between civilizations and religious tolerance. The recent Indian blockbuster *Jodhaa Akbar,* a Mughal Empire period epic, explored issues of dialogue and tolerance between religions; it went unnoticed by Western mainstream media.[24] Egyptian master Youssef Chahine's *Destiny* (1997), an epic drama set in twelfth-century Andalusia of the Arab Caliphate and focusing on philosopher Averroes' life, was critically praised in France for the original way in which it tackled awkward aspects of the relations between Islam and Christianity. It received awards at Cannes but was never distributed in other countries. The highly original Turkish fairy tale *Who Killed Shadows?* (2006), set in thirteenth-century Bursa, offered sophisticated historical reassessments on matters of religious tolerance and gave a fresh take on Islam, Christianity, Judaism, and Greek classical culture within the early period of the Ottoman Empire. The film only had a limited run in a few European countries where it was reviewed as a period comedy; its important message on religious dialogue fell through the cracks of critical attention.

One would think that in the context of today's heightened sensitivities on the matter of religious and civilizational discord particular attention would be paid to works of art that come from different parts of the world as they may have something important to say, on the subject matter of Islam in particular. This does not seem to be the case, however, as foreign films that address such key issues remain largely ignored. Ridley Scott's *Kingdom of Heaven* (2005) is still seen as one of the few epic films that critically explore the relationship of Christianity and Islam.

adjustment to western conventions

A tactic that some international epics have adopted as part of their endeavor to break into the mainstream discursive space of the West has been to adjust narrative structure and moral message in line with established Western ethical and aesthetic conventions and to follow the supposedly universal Aristotelian principles of dramatic construction. However, such attempts, aimed at bringing Oriental wisdom and Western mindset closer together, have not been particularly successful.

An example is found in Zhang Yimou's *Curse of the Golden Flower*, the narrative of which comes close to fulfilling all Western criteria of an epic in that it provides a Bakhtinian type of "layered record" and places monumental historical shifts in direct dependency to the moves of the protagonists that move within the closely knit royal family's universe amidst deception and deplorable ploys. Its plot is most directly reminiscent of classical-style tragedies and could be compared to the density of emotion found in Ancient Greek tragedies or to classical Shakespearean plots. And, indeed, actors involved in the film have made references to *Hamlet* or *King Lear*. Yet, while coming the closest to Western standards of plot and style, *Curse of the Golden Flower* is also the film that was least commercially successful of the three Zhang Yimou epics. It appears that its Euripidean or Shakespearean dramatic quality only limit its prospects in the West.

Zhang Yimou's earlier *Hero*, the story of the moral ascent of an unnamed fighter whose body, at the culminating point of the film, serves as sublime intersection of providence and history, is a fully fledged epic that can compare to *Gladiator* (2000) in more than one respect: concepts such as "duty," "destiny," "masculinity," and "symbolic message" apply equally successfully to both films. No such interpretative framework, however, was ever offered to *Hero*. Instead, the film has mostly been assessed as propaganda and exposed as Chinese Communist ploy.[25] One could have easily interpreted *Hero* through the concept of *jianghu* ("world of knightly chivalry"), used by Felicia Chan in her analysis of *Crouching Tiger, Hidden Dragon*, but I am

116

not aware of any such attempts; other possible interpretations have simply not been given.[26]

genre matters

Can a Chinese film with sword-fighting be an epic film at all? Why would *Gladiator* or *Spartacus* (1960) be epics while *Asoka* (2001), *Mongol* or *Hero* would not? Can we think of the "epic" without intrinsically linking it to the roots of Western civilization and system of values? Or, to continue with questions that Felicia Chan, drawing on Stephen Neale's work, asks along the same lines: "Are genres dependent upon a particular culture? Can a genre sufficiently translate from one culture to another? [. . .] Do genres themselves create a culture of reading?"[27] She concludes that while "genres depend on a spectator's familiarity with its conventions, built upon from knowledge gained from other films of the same genre" it all appears to be an "inherently circular process," which, at the end, impacts audience expectations and modifies them, conditioning a possible widening of the boundaries of a genre.[28]

Most definitions of the epic do not limit the concept to specific civilizational or religious boundaries; therefore Eastern and Southern, Confucian and Muslim societies, as well as Christian and Western cultures ought to be able to equally successfully produce epics that display the vital mimetic and cathartic qualities needed for a work of art to qualify as epics if scrutinized in the context of Aristotelian canon of epic poetry. Most films mentioned in the course of this investigation would qualify as epics also in the terms of Hegelian aesthetics, in particular keeping in mind Hegel's view of the epic protagonist as a "situated individual," a free human being who is faced with adverse circumstances and overwhelmed by the larger context in which one finds himself. What the protagonists of films such as *Hero, Jinnah, Lagaan, Asoka* or *Mongol* are is determined as much by the state of affairs in which the heroic characters find themselves as by their own will; the consequences of their actions dialectically rise beyond their control.

In addition, these films qualify as epics in that they are all technically accomplished lavish spectacles, all deal with heroic historical or mythic protagonists, all build on the dialectics of social and personal duties and conflicts, and all look at the relationship between individual action driven by ideas of moral duty and the political repercussions of such action on society and history at large. Yet, when it comes down to critical reception and film historiography, they are not likely to be listed in the annals of the epic genre.

Andrew Tudor, who sees genre as contextually defined, has insisted that generic definitions should span beyond mere textual characteristics to also include the circumstances of a film's production and reception.[29] If we are to apply his three-prong criterion (comprising of text, production

117

background, and reception milieu), the Asian blockbusters are most likely to qualify as epics only in regard to their textual and production premises. But they would not be recognized as epics, as they are clearly not received as such. This shortage of "epic" quality, however, would then not be an immanent feature of the films but a shortcoming of a reception context that proves incapable of flexible and dialectical understanding of heroic matters.

shifting patterns of reception

Even when commercially successful, international epics are not widely debated by mainstream critics, who usually find the epic narratives put forward in Asian films distant or far-flung. Asian directors who build reputations through such epics are not really recognized as "auteurs" in the pantheon of the epic genre the same way their Western counterparts would be. Ashutosh Gowariker, for example, may be responsible for films of epic proportions and ambition—*Lagaan* and *Jodhaa Akbar*—but his name is barely known in the West.[30] A host of patronizing comments have been made about Cannes-winning Chinese master's Zhang Yimou's multimillion-earning blockbuster epics.[31] The work of Thai director Yukol is familiar only to a narrow circle of connoisseurs and, when covered, is treated with a certain level of lofty derision. Double standards in assessment are widespread, with critics seen to renounce features found in foreign films while turning a blind eye on the same traits in Western product. There is always something that is not quite right in these Asian epics. Critical narrow-mindedness is displayed most often in regard to length (excessive), characterization (one-dimensional), subplots (too intricate); there are frequent accusations that international epics are short in suspense or that the dramatic build-up is schematic, even naive. A choir of critics tirelessly voice their aversion to drawn-out Indian sagas in a context where recent Western epics have been getting longer and longer.[32] Bollywood epics still get haughtily downgraded by critics who deplore the "ambling, uneconomical nature of popular Indian storytelling" while admitting that Indians surely know how to stage battles "with bold assurance," and all in all agreeing that "Bollywood is poised for wider commercial impact beyond its already substantial established niche."[33]

However, there are some signs that the reception context may be changing. With the progress of new technologies that radically shift the position of traditional film criticism and enable new forms for dissemination of film review and appraisal, as well as with the unprecedented proliferation of global discussion forums, the reception of international films increasingly takes place in a context of heightened consciousness of the multiple possible interpretations of a film. One of the most influential sites where film reputations are made or broken nowadays is the diverse group of "users"

118

posting directly to IMDb. The transnational crowd posting on the IMDb user forums consists of Westerners and diasporic individuals based in the West, as well as of people based in the countries from where the films originate, or even elsewhere. Contrary to mainstream critical opinions that often express reservations when covering international epics, these viewers share overwhelmingly positive reactions in most instances. Reading the IMDb exchanges confirms that many of the foreign epics have, in fact, gained dedicated followers and enjoy notable cult standing. Even more, the exchanges that are taking place in these and other online forums (such as Twitch, dedicated to Asian film specifically) create durable and evolving dialogues that bring together the views of people based in North America, Europe, Central, East, and Southeast Asia, and elsewhere, all of whom can engage in a unified discussion and highlight to one another the multiplicity of transnational contexts, considerations, and possible interpretations. These new cinephiles are becoming ever more active on forums that bring them together and allow them not only to meet others of similar awareness and knowledge but to also supply their views with previously unattainable visibility that equals or even supersedes the authority of officially sanctioned film criticism.

conclusion

In the 1990s, Samuel Huntington proclaimed that the world consisted of encapsulated discrete civilizations that interacted with each other mostly when engaging in conflict; he prophesized that future interactions between civilizations could only take the shape of a "clash." He insisted that the West should work to protect its uniqueness against the ever-more assertive invasion of "the rest." In order "to survive as vibrant and powerful civilization," the West was to "abandon the pretence of universality" and "close ranks."[34] Huntington's view soon became a widely embraced and influential interpretative framework that still defines policies and media coverage and informs education.

There is no use in seeing the "rise of the rest" as an ill-omened threat, however. Some evidence in support of a more sanguine worldview—one where a certain "unthinking" of Eurocentrism is effectively taking place, instigated by the influx of films from abroad that enter the market and move closer to the mainstream than ever before; one that uncovers signs of civilizations entering productive, meaningful and creative interactions with each other—was presented here. By witnessing the spread of internationally produced epic cinema which has already made significant inroads in the West, we are widening our understanding of the diversity and multifaceted nature of history, even if in order to do this we still need to expand and adjust our generic interpretative framework. It is largely a matter of choice to see the "rise of the rest" as intimidating invasion of potentially parochial alien forces that endanger the uniqueness and the achievements of the West or to decide to operate with a more inclusive and tolerant mindset, to deprovincialize, and to broaden our horizons.

acknowledgment

Research for this chapter was generously supported by the Leverhulme Trust, the Carnegie Trust for the Universities of Scotland, and the Caledonian Research Foundation/Royal Society of Edinburgh.

notes

1. Fareed Zakaria, *The Post-American World and the Rise of the Rest* (New York: Allen Lane, 2008), p. 3.
2. See my discussion on the importance of historical epics in East Central European cinema and Poland in particular in Dina Iordanova, "Heritage Epics," *Cinema of the Other Europe: The Industry and Artistry of East Central European Film* (London: Wallflower Press, 2003), pp. 49–53. See also Anne Jaeckel's essay on Sergiu Nicolaescu's *Michael the Brave* (1970) and other Romanian epics from the 1970s, 'Michael the Brave', in Dina Iordanova (ed.), *Cinema of the Balkans* (London: Wallflower Press, 2006), pp. 101–112.
3. *Hero* (2002), *House of Flying Daggers* (2004), *The Curse of the Golden Flower* (2006).
4. *The Emperor and the Assassin* (1998).
5. *Lagaan* (2001), *Jodhaa Akbar* (2008).
6. *Asoka* (2001).
7. *Nomad* (2005) *Mongol* (2007).
8. *The Legend of Suriyothai* (2001), *Legend of King Naresuan: Hostage of Hongsawadi* (2006); *The Legend of Naresuan: Part 2* (2007).
9. Whereas I do not engage in in-depth examinations of individual cases, I have discussed aspects of the concrete production, distribution, and reception of these films in shorter pieces that can be viewed independently. These can be accessed in the section "Epic Cinema" at my blog, DinaView (www.DinaView.com).
10. John Lent, "East Asia: For Better or Worse," in Paul McDonald and Janet Wasko (eds), *The Contemporary Hollywood Film Industry* (Oxford: Blackwell, 2008), pp. 277–285; p. 283.
11. For a more detailed discussion on the limitations of data and the changing picture in our awareness on market penetration of non-Hollywood product, see Dina Iordanova, "Rise of the Fringe: Global Cinema's Long Tail," in Dina Iordanova, David Martin-Jones, and Belen Vidal (eds), *Cinema at the Periphery* (Detroit, Mich.: Wayne State University Press, 2010), pp. 23–46.
12. John Trumpbour, "Hollywood and the World: Export or Die," in Paul McDonald and Janet Wasko (eds), *The Contemporary Hollywood Film Industry* (Oxford: Blackwell, 2008), pp. 209–220; pp. 215–216.
13. Trumpbour, "Hollywood and the World," p. 213.
14. *Mongol,* released in the USA on June 6, 2008, in the context of much bigger studio releases, nearly recouped its $6 million budget just from North American distribution (taking $5,705,761 in revenues by September 2008). Having taken about $21 million from international markets, the film was a "fourbagger" even before being released on DVD, forming a one-to-three

pattern of North American vs. international revenues. *House of Flying Daggers* was made for an estimated 100 million Chinese yuan (c. $15 million) and within China it made about 55 million Chinese yuan on theatrical release (c. $8.1 million). Clearly, the film could only make successful business on the realization of international revenues. Distributed by Sony within the USA, by Focus Films internationally, and by about another fifteen companies regionally, the film made a total of $92,863,945 worldwide during the eighteen weeks that the Box Office Mojo has monitored the release in 2005, of which about 88 percent came from international revenues ($81,813,851) and only 12 percent was domestic US ($11,050,094 at 1,189 screens), setting the ratio of revenues to about one to eight. According to the (incomplete) data made available at Box Office Mojo, *The Curse of the Golden Flower*'s worldwide gross was $78,568,977. US domestic revenues were about 8.4 percent ($6,566,773) while the international ones accounted for an even bigger proportion of 91.6 percent ($72,002,204), a ratio of about one to nine. Handled by Sony Classics, the film had a run of about fourteen weeks, between January and March 2007, reaching its widest US release at 1,234 screens. It played in theatrical distribution across thirty-five or so territories, in North and South America, Asia and Europe. About a dozen or so companies were involved in the film's international distribution, half of which were overseas arms of Hollywood players such as Buena Vista International (Singapore) or Columbia TriStar (Argentina).

15. Peter Lynch, *One Up on Wall Street: How to Use What You Already Know to Make Money in the Market* (New York: Penguin, 1990).

16. *Hero*'s revenues model roughly displays a ratio of one to two and a half, of which the domestic US market accounts for 30.3 percent ($53,710,019) and the international box office for 69.7 percent ($123,684,413). Thus, the $53 million North American revenues not only recouped the film's $31 million budget but also brought in 75 percent extra in profits. According to Box Office Mojo, *Hero*'s worldwide gross came to $177,394,432, a profit of roughly $147 million. By way of comparison, again according to Box Office Mojo, *Crouching Tiger, Hidden Dragon*, which was made for an estimated $15 million, made about 60 percent of its revenues from the domestic US market ($61,231,307) and only about 40 percent from international territories (c. $40 million), totaling slightly over $100 million in 2001.

17. According to a *France Presse* report ("Bollywood Piracy Fighters"), India's entertainment industry loses $4 billion and 800,000 jobs yearly because of piracy. In April 2008, a group of Indian distributors sought the protection of the US Government against what they described as a "rampant piracy" which they alleged plagues the fate of their product in North America. They took their case to the US Congress, lobbying for anti-piracy protection similar to the one granted to Hollywood product. "Bollywood Piracy Fighters Take Battle to US Congress," *Agence France-Presse*, April 21, 2008, available online at http://afp.google.com/article/ALeqM5i5u8wX6GL_QtBpBoDg9FCnGZSvaw (accessed August 8, 2008).

18. Ella Shohat and Robert Stam, *Unthinking Eurcentrism: Multiculturalism and the Media* (London and New York: Routledge, 1994).

19. Amporn Jirattikorn, "Suriyothai: Hybridizing Thai National Identity through Film," *Journal of Inter-Asian Cultural Studies*, 4 (2) (2003): 296–308.

20. Since *Suriyothai*, director Yukol has continued working in the epic genre, releasing in 2006 and 2007 two even more ambitious and more generously

funded lavish productions (*Naresuan* and *The Legend of Naresuan: Part 2*), again depicting events from the important sixteenth-century period of Ayutthaya's proud independence. For the time being these two sequels have only been released in Thailand where they have beaten all local box-office records. There is no international discussion of these films at the IMDb, only a few postings originating from viewers based in Bangkok. It appears that no international exposure whatsoever is being sought as the films have not been entered at film markets, nor made available at DVD; the only festival at which they appear to have played in single screenings is the New York Asian Film Festival, June 2008.

21. Robert Burgoyne, *The Hollywood Historical Film* (Oxford: Blackwell, 2008), p. 77.

22. *Lagaan,* the first Indian film to be nominated for a foreign-language Oscar since *Mother India* in 1958, remains largely unseen. The DVD of this 2001 film is out of print and can only be acquired second-hand.

23. Several years after the original release date of 1998, a round of fund-raising among the Pakistani diaspora in the US, UK, and the Gulf led to the subsidized release of the film on DVD; it can be found nowadays through second-hand purchase.

24. I went to see *Jodhaa Akbar* in February 2008 in Toronto; it played at the centrally located Varsity as well as at other multiplexes around town. Being distributed by Bollywood operator UTV and not by a Hollywood subsidiary, the film did not make it to the listings of Toronto's *NOW* magazine, which neither mentioned nor covered it. Other newspapers such as the *Toronto Star* and *Toronto Sun* covered it briefly as costume extravaganza. *Jodhaa Akbar* was released precisely at the time when my twelve-year-old son, a seventh grader, was studying about the empire of the Mughals as part of his history curriculum. Had *Jodhaa Akbar* been properly reviewed and covered in mainstream media, it could reach the attention of a wider community of viewers and, in particular, teachers, who could have incorporated it in their teaching of a more diversified historical curriculum.

25. Mark Harrison, "Zhang Yimou's *Hero* and the Globalisation of Propaganda," *Millennium: Journal of International Studies,* 34 (2) (2006): 569–572. Harrison dismisses *Hero*'s technical prowess as "an empty spectacle" and "an exercise in cinematic bombast." To him the film has got no plot and no character development, its dialogue is "made up of declarations of fortune-cookie clichés" that are nothing but "apologia for the contemporary dictatorship of the Chinese Communist Party" (pp. 570–571). As I cannot afford to go into detailed analysis here, I should note that Mark Harrison's piece is not the simple dismissal that it appears to be from the above quotes. It puts forward some important arguments that deserve separate investigation and that have validity in the context of his concerns related to the way Chinese culture projects its image globally. Were we to apply Harrison's critical approach to some recent Hollywood epics, however, one would most likely end up describing them in equally dismissive terms as propaganda cartoons.

26. Felicia Chan, "*Crouching Tiger, Hidden Dragon:* Cultural Migrancy and Translatabilty," in Chris Berry (ed.), *Chinese Films in Focus: 25 New Takes* (London: BFI, 2003), pp. 56–65; p. 59.

27. Chan, "Cultural Migrancy and Translatabilty," p. 61.

28. Chan, "Cultural Migrancy and Translatabilty," p. 61.

29. Andrew Tudor, "Genre," in B. K. Grant (ed.), *Film Genre Reader* (Austin, Tex.: University of Texas Press, 1986), pp. 3–11. To Tudor, genre is "best employed

in the analysis of the relation between groups of films, the cultures in which they are made, and the cultures in which they are exhibited . . . It is a term that can be usefully employed in relation to a body of knowledge and theory about the social and psychological context of film ("Genre," p. 10).

30. Gowariker's next epic project, a filmed biography of Buddha (scheduled for a 2010 release), is produced by Hollywood's David S. Ward, Michel Shane, and Anthony Romano and underwritten by Indian billionaire Bhupendra Kumar Modi. Liz Shackleton, "Gowariker to Direct Buddha Biopic," ScreenDaily.com, May 11, 2009, available online at www.screendaily.com/gowariker-to-direct-buddha-biopic/5000960.article (accessed 17 May 2009).

31. Apart from the fact that most Westerners do not know how to pronounce his name, Zhang Yimou appears to be gaining some degree of mainstream recognition in the West as "the wizard behind Beijing's opening night" after he directed the spectacular Olympic ceremony for Beijing's Olympic Games in 2008. David Barboza, "Gritty Renegade Now Directs China's Close-Up," *The New York Times,* August 7, 2008, available online at www.nytimes.com/2008/08/08/sports/olympics/08guru.html (accessed May 17, 2009).

32. The various versions of *Alexander,* for example, run between 167 and 207 minutes; *Troy* is between 163 and 201 minutes in length. By comparison, at 213 minutes *Jodhaa Akbar* is only a few minutes longer, yet is reviewed by the critics as tediously drawn out, while Indian *Asoka,* running between 155 and 180 minutes for its various versions, is, in fact, the shortest one.

33. David Rooney's review of *Asoka* in *Variety.* Available online at www.variety.com/review/VE1117798945.html?categoryid=31&cs=1&p=0 (accessed September 23, 2003).

34. Samuel Huntington, "The West: Unique, Not Universal," *Foreign Affairs,* November/December 1996, pp. 28–46. Here is how he sums it up: "As countries modernize, they may Westernize in superficial ways, but not in the most important measures of culture—language, religion, values. In fact, as countries modernize they seek refuge from the modern world in their traditional, parochial cultures and religions. Around the globe, education and democracy are leading to 'indigenization.' And as the power of the West ebbs, 'the rest' will become more and more assertive. For the West to survive as a vibrant and powerful civilization, it must abandon the pretence of universality and close ranks. Its future depends on its unity. The peoples of the West must hang together, or they will hang separately" ("The West: Unique, Not Universal," p. 45). Admittedly, I have had problems with Huntington's distrustful and gloomy view of the world for a number of years now (see Dina Iordanova, *Cinema of Flames: Balkan Film, Culture and the Media* [London: BFI, 2001]). In a crudest and militant version, these ideas were embraced on either side of the newly outlined cultural divide and dangerously brought into practice by bigoted leaders who opted to conceptualize the world along the lines of the profound rupture that Huntington had outlined.

sign of the times

the semiotics of time and

event in sirk's *sign of the pagan*

s i x

b e t t i n a   b i l d h a u e r

Analogy or its extended mode of allegory compares two similar but separate objects or points in time and has long served as the explanatory paradigm for the epic film. What Deleuze calls an analogical or parallel construction of history underpins the epic film, an imagined mirror relationship between the distant past and the nationalist concerns of the present. In this chapter, I shall argue that the genre is based not only on an analogical similarity between past and present but on a multilayered view of time that includes a linearity, simultaneity, and the pregnant moment full of future possibilities. A genre that is replete with chronotopic complexity, the epic may be said to stage a contest of temporal modes, a framework that becomes most visible in film that take the distant past as their subject. In *Sign of the Pagan* (1954), directed by Douglas Sirk, the "clash of civilizations" conveyed by the film is organized and undergirded by the different understandings of time, history, and event that form the central motifs of the plot. Part of the pleasure of watching an epic is precisely that it creates both an illusion of a linear, logical timeflow and a sense of a disordered abundance of time. I shall suggest that the premodern is where the epic finds its attitude to history, agency, and representation most closely prefigured.

flat visuality

Sign of the Pagan was produced by Universal International studios under the direction of the German émigré Douglas Sirk and first released in 1954. Despite the critical attention lavished on Sirk, this film has not been the subject of any sustained discussion in print.[1] This is probably due to its generic outsider status in an authorial body of work dominated by melodrama in combination with practical difficulties in accessing the film. Much scholarship has also been all too happy to rely on the eloquent interpretations of Sirk's works provided by the director himself and may have been discouraged by Sirk's brusque characterization of this film as "one of my worst."[2] (That he praises only the title may be a cunning way of drawing attention to the issue of signification that finds such a rich treatment in this film, starting with its title.)[3] I shall show that *Sign of the Pagan* is ripe for rediscovery in the context of postmodern debates on popular films and approaches to history. It turns out to be a highly intelligent and challenging film that reflects more deeply on time, signification, and the accessibility of the past than most academic historiography. It also betrays an affinity to an intellectual tradition that sees the premodern and especially the medieval as external to the constraints of linear time and of written historiography and that postulates film as a new medium for rethinking and representing history and signification. *Sign of the Pagan* returns to a medieval aesthetics of exploiting visual presence over the staid reliance on written and linguistic expression.

At first glance, *Sign of the Pagan* is an absolutely classical historical epic. It tells the story of Attila's failure to conquer Rome and Marcian's rise to emperor. Marcian (Jeff Chandler) is a Roman centurion who is captured by Attila, King of the Huns (Jack Palance) on his way to deliver the message to the East Roman Emperor Theodosius that West Rome is concerned about his loyalty in the face of Barbarian attacks. Marcian escapes Attila and gets to Constantinople, where he fails to win around Theodosius to West Rome but falls in love with Theodosius' beautiful sister Pulcheria. Attila also arrives at Constantinople and makes a secret pact with Theodosius for mutual protection. He then decides to attack West Rome with the support of the Barbarian kings, despite threatening portents. Marcian is imprisoned by Theodosius but manages to escape and depose Theodosius with the help of Pulcheria and loyal General Paulinus. Attila's seer warns him against an attack on Rome because of his visions, but the King reinterprets them as predicting the fall of Rome. Marcian travels back to Rome to support it against Attila's anticipated assault, while the West Roman emperor Valentinian flees, leaving Marcian in charge of the city. Attila is increasingly disturbed by the warning signs and visions and, at the last minute, turns back from Rome's gates. But Marcian fights him on his retreat, and Attila is killed, while Marcian returns to marry Pulcheria and become emperor.

The film has all the hallmarks of the historical epic: the requisite cast of thousands of humans and horses, action-laden fights, two ultramasculine heroes, marginal women, a backdrop of world-changing events, and what Michael Wood calls "the big scenes (the orgy, the ceremonial entry into the city, the great battle, the individual combat, and where possible, a miracle or two) and the big, earthshaking themes."[4] But, as is usual with Sirk, viewers are asked to look underneath the shiny surfaces that are just a bit too perfect to be realistic, to search for a different meaning. By having the plot revolve around the issue of how to interpret signs and visions, Sirk encourages the viewer to think about the way in which the film itself makes meaning at the same time as enjoying its seemingly authentic style of display.

The film's aesthetic turns out to be reliant on visual impact, achieved through setting in motion a mixture of "flat" images echoing medieval art and images of greater depth of field indebted to ancient art. As is typical of Sirk's films, there is an emphasis on the reflective surface and what lies behind, and whether one is more real than the other. In *Sign of the Pagan*, given the historical scarcity of glass and mirrors, we get shadows instead. The lattice doors' shadows do not so much *symbolize* Pulcheria's and Marcian's entrapment by Theodosius as *show* it physically (see Figure 6.1), modeling a way of film-viewing that emphasizes visual impression over narrative emplotment or symbolic interpretation.

Figure 6.1

Sign of the Pagan: Pulcheria and Marcian entrapped by shadows.

This aesthetic, based on visible flat surfaces, rejecting less "immediate" modes of communication such as language and writing, is precisely what accounts for the epic's affinity to the premodern and its attraction to premodern plots. Film is, rightly or wrongly, commonly perceived to access the past more directly than writing, because we know that the camera, unlike the pen or word processor, had been in the direct presence of what it recorded.[5] In *Sign of the Pagan,* in addition, visuality itself is staged as a return to past forms of more authentic communication, to Attila's and Marcian's superior presence over the written word. The premodern, here the Barbarian Middle Ages, is imagined as a time when immediate, physical, face-to-face communication was still widespread, before the arrival of printing made the written word the main means of human interaction.[6] Attila performs his leadership over the other Barbarian kings by physically meeting them and staging his superior strength and authority (for example, in a show fight with a Byzantine strongman). Marcian learns his technique of asserting power through physical presence and visual display to invigorate the Ancient Roman culture that had relied too heavily on writing to enact political power. This is the form of communication that the film itself also uses, showing the superior impact of visual impression. In an early article, Fred Camper sensitively observes such medieval aesthetics in Sirk's work in general: all his characters are blind in the sense that their filmed reality is all surface, no depth, too perfect to be believable: all his frames "operate in a kind of pre-Renaissance flatness."[7] In other words, this aesthetics draws attention to the filmic quality of film, to cinema's nature as a projection of light onto a two-dimensional screen, although it hints that "somewhere, in some other space, there is a physical reality."[8]

Sirk himself also claimed to have been influenced by the seminal theorist on the alleged flatness of medieval painting before the Renaissance "discovered" the representation of perspective: Erwin Panofksy. Sirk maintains that he studied under Panofsky at the University of Hamburg and wrote a seminar paper on "the relations between medieval German painting and the miracle plays."[9] If this is not true, as several other of Douglas Sirk's autobiographical statements are not, it is convincingly invented. It shows at the very least that he is aware of Panofsky's ideas about the special aesthetics of medieval art and of the way painting can be translated into performing arts. Panofsky famously argued that medieval painting was concerned with the two-dimensional surface of a painting rather than with creating an illusion of depth, of looking into a room or space, as ancient art did and modern art would again do from the Renaissance onwards. Many of Sirk's frames also foreground the two-dimensional film-icness of film, rather than imitating human perception by recreating the human eye's functioning. In *Sign of the Pagan,* there is a marked scarcity of panoramic or establishing shots, despite the pioneering use of CinemaScope.

The horizon tends to be high; the camera can rarely see into the distance. In many scenes, the action is restricted to the foreground and set in front of a plain backdrop, such as a bare wall, and many frames have little depth of field, reducing even more animated backgrounds to mere foils (Figure 6.2). In acknowledging his debt to Panofksy's view of medieval art, Sirk draws attention to the role of medieval aesthetics in his films and aligns his emphasis on the visual, the use of the physical object to focus attention and make meaning, with the premodern that underlies many of his films, and that is his explicit topic in *Sign of the Pagan*.

However, Sirk combines such "medieval" images (that nonrealistically emphasize the two-dimensional rather than imitating depth) with frames that have a greater depth of field. This happens particularly—though by no means exclusively—in scenes set in the city of Constantinople, where many frames appear to be modeled more closely on classical art as represented by Panofsky, with its interest in the human form set in a perspectivally represented space (Figure 6.3). To the action in the foreground or middle ground is added an interesting backdrop, often including ancient statues of naked humans in motion or busts of important men, as well as mosaics representing the Virgin Mary and other Christian figures and symbols. While within the diegesis Christian art is clearly shown to work in the two-dimensional medium of mosaics and ancient art in three-dimensional statues, the film's aesthetics combines both in motion. To a premodern "flat" aesthetics, *Sign of the Pagan* adds not only a more ancient perspectival aesthetics but also the vastly expanded possibilities of moving pictures. While premodern art is clearly emulated to an extent, so is ancient art, while exploring the potential of the modern art of cinema. Even the aesthetics of this film introduces a certain temporal disorientation to the attentive spectator, and this mixture of different times will turn out to be one of the film's distinctive characteristics, shared by any premodern epic.

Figure 6.2

Sign of the Pagan: Attila's ensign in a flat space.

Figure 6.3

Sign of the Pagan: Pulcheria in perspective with classical art.

The setting in historical time: orientation and disorientation

Tom Conley observes that spatial orientation provided for a viewer to make clear where a film is set—paradigmatically a map—at the same time occasions disorientation because it draws attention to the distance between the imagined place of the setting and the viewer's actual location, offering profound ontological confusion to pensive spectators.[10] The same disorientating effect, I suggest, is built into the ostensibly orienting filmic paratexts of historical *time:* advance information about the film, voice-overs, subtitles or calendars. A plot's positioning in historical time occasions the mixed pleasure of both temporal orientation and temporal disorientation: an illusionary time travel to a point in the past and bewilderment at the fact that this is even conceivable. This is close to the sublime experience as described by Kant as one where the discomfort of not being able to *imagine* a great quantity is combined with the pleasurable feeling that one is thereby encouraged to develop one's rational ability to *know* that it nevertheless can possibly exist.[11]

Sign of the Pagan relies mostly on an extradiegetic voice-over to situate its plot in historical time, but the credits already begin to introduce the setting as well as temporal confusion through their images of rustic riders that could be from the Wild West or distant past and through the last of the acting credits, which lists, as is common in earlier historical films, the names of actors together with historical characters: "Glenn Thompson, Chuck Roberson, Walter Coy, Rusty Wescoatt, Norbert Schiller and Statesmen, Citizen, Soldiers of the Armies of the Roman Empire and the Hordes of Attila." Even the viewer who has heard nothing about the content of the film in advance can glean the rough historical setting here, but the viewer is also presented with a text in which 1950s actors inhabit the same slice of historical reality as the Ancient Romans they impersonate—either a blurring of the distinction between reality and fiction or a conflation of different points in time. As the final credit fades out and we see the Hunnish hordes burning and pillaging, a voice-over by an unironically authoritative male voice continues this temporal orientation which also serves as a mode of disorientation:

> It was 1,500 years ago, shortly after Christianity had been established as the official religion of the Roman Empire, that the Empire itself had been split in two, with rival capitals, one at Constantinople and the other at Rome, and weak because of its division. Stories of the weakness had reached the barbarians who roamed Europe when suddenly there appeared from the north a fierce plague of Mongol horsemen, the Huns. They began to vanquish the Barbarian tribes, spreading terror and bloodshed under the Pagan sign, welding them into a merciless horde led by the most ruthless conqueror of all times: Attila the Hun.

This is a seemingly straightforward, even clichéd introduction of the historical backdrop to the plot. But, as is common in historical films, it is initially unclear from what point in time the narrator purports to speak because he begins with a shifting marker: "1,500 years ago." This is not a fixed point of time like, say, the year 1500, but the signified changes according to when this phrase is uttered. As the sentence continues to state that what happened 1,500 years prior also happened "shortly after Christianity had been established as the official religion of the Roman Empire," it becomes likely that the speaker is situated in the twentieth century, probably around the time of the filming.[12] Moreover, even as the point in time of the setting is established, we are asked to imagine its pre-history, related in the past-perfect tense (when Christianity was established and the Empire split). We are only finally brought into the present of the action as the voice-over ends over images of Attila. Attila had previously only been indirectly represented, though his presence is richly foreshadowed: the film opens with images of his battle ensign, filmed from below against a clear blue sky, moving toward the camera and accompanied by lively, triumphal orchestral music—in short, it is introduced as the epic hero himself may conventionally be introduced; superimposed are then the written words "Sign of the Pagan," a written representation of the sign that signifies Attila; and finally the voice-over names him. These written, spoken, and visual signs are now replaced by Attila's physical presence in one fell swoop, starting the action and making Attila himself an illusionary contemporary of the viewer for the next ninety minutes.

This temporal positioning of the film as part of broad sweeps of history, coupled with a certain vagueness about the temporal setting, is part of the epic genre's allure. Vivian Sobchack perceptively explores the pleasurable feeling induced by the epic of the sheer excess of history, of the huge weight of historical time, of all the monumental changes influencing millennia dimly remembered from school: the beginnings of Christianity, the division of the Roman Empire, the migration period—"[T]he Hollywood historical epic is not so much the narrative accounting of *specific historical events* as it is the narrative construction of *general historical eventfulness.*"[13] Sobchack argues that this feeling of an excess of eventfulness allows us to sense ourselves as historical subjects, to get a glimpse of the expanse of time of which the entire life of an individual is only a miniscule part.

Such experiences of temporal vastness are often associated with the premodern, and this is why many epics choose a premodern setting. In Tom Conley's discussion of how maps orientate as well as disorientate in *Gladiator* (2000), it is not by coincidence a *late medieval* variation of Ptolemy's maps that stands in for the ancient original so that in the very act of spatial orientation, confusion about time is introduced by recourse to medieval representation.[14] One of the reasons why the premodern past is so attractive to makers of epics is because less of it is commonly known so that the artistic license to play with chronology and to incorporate large swathes of monumental events is greater; and because the more distant past automatically opens wider vistas of time. This even allows for a blurring between reality and fantasy, because it seems more plausible to audiences that supernatural events could have happened in premodernity than in rational modernity, as Arthur Lindley and Derek Elley have observed.[15] Laura Mulvey spots such an allusion to the Middle Ages as a vague temporal setting—that is actually not so much in the past as in a vast epic excess of time—even in one of Sirk's melodramas, *Magnificent Obsession* (1954), where Switzerland is "unravaged by the Second World War and available for folksy, kitschy representations of a village lifestyle that has remained unchanged, like a movie fantasy of an ahistorical Middle Ages."[16] The Middle Ages are here not a historical period but an ahistorical one, a continued presence at least in faraway Switzerland, at least in the movies. (The achrony is taken further when Mulvey interprets the theatrical staging of a witch-burning in this village unusually not as medieval but as a haunting presence of the United States in 1952: now it is not the modern that still looks medieval but the medieval that seems modern.) Moreover, the Middle Ages are commonly believed to have a different, less linear perception of time, especially a Christian view of time as predetermined and eternally present to God.[17] Compression of time into a vague heroic past is already prefigured in premodern epics so that separate historical events such as Attila's death at the hands of his wife Ildiko or the rise of Marcian to Emperor can be told as if they were contemporary with each other.

The temporal disorientation is mirrored in the plot, as premodern characters unsuccessfully try to situate themselves in historical time. When Attila tries to convince the Barbarian kings that they should attack Rome, two seers recount two different prophesies: that Rome would last either for twelve centuries from its foundation, ending the following autumn (because twelve vultures had landed on its twelve hills when it was founded) or for fourteen centuries (because seven vultures had landed on the seven hills and then flown away again). Attila sides with the former opinion because he wants to attack that year. This plan gives the remainder of the plot a rough time frame of a few months—no more precise than "when the leaves turn brown" (whereas the time that passed between the initial episodes in the Barbarians' camps and in Constantinople had been unclear). But the estimate is 200 years out of date—the time for the fall of Rome, predicted by the right prophecy, has not yet come. Attila's premodern way of finding his position within historical time is to set himself in relation to an anticipated future rather than in a particular year calculated in a universal calendar.

linear vs. circular time

As regards the epic tradition, the emphasis is usually believed to be on narrative continuity as opposed to contingent moments. David Quint writes of the literary epic:

> To the victors belongs epic, with its linear teleology; to the losers belongs romance, with its random or circular wandering. Put another way, the victors experience history as a coherent, end-directed story told by their own power; the losers experience a contingency that they are powerless to shape to their own ends.[18]

But *Sign of the Pagan* combines what Quint sees as the linear logic of the epic and the random logic of romance in a way that is actually typical of premodern epic film (and of many written epics dating from premodernity). It shows that this genre has an equal investment in the contingent moment that carries the possibility of historical change as in a linear plot. *Sign of the Pagan* stages the conflict between those two ways of perceiving time as one between Marcian and Attila—"the Roman," as the Huns call him, versus "the Pagan" of the title.

From the perspective of the Roman, the plot could be described as following a linear trajectory: Marcian encounters Constantinople's treacherous Theodosius, falls in love with Pulcheria, defends Rome with her and Paulinus' help first against the traitor Theodosius, and then against Attila, and is crowned emperor in the end. Its narrative works chronologically without flashbacks or flashforwards, with densely packed events leading causally from one to the other. Marcian acts purposefully. He plans and then carries out these intentions: to deliver his message, to overthrow Theodosius, to travel to Rome, to ambush Attila. He tries to meet deadlines—escaping from Attila before he has to teach him Roman warfare, leaving Constantinople before Theodosius arrests him, moving his legions to Rome before Attila attacks. His linear ordering of time is expressed spatially, too, in the frequent shots where he is shown riding or walking toward a target that is visible in the frame.

But the film has a second, at least equally important plotline following Attila and the barbarians, who experience history as much more of a "random or circular wandering." Attila physically roams the indistinct dusty countryside, seemingly always ending up at the same bent tree. The camera position rarely allows us to see where the Huns are going; they usually ride toward and past the camera to an unknown aim. Little changes for Attila during his fruitless circling of Rome from the beginning to the end of the film, and he dies without having learned or developed much in its course.

Most crucially, the film as a whole could not be said to follow the epic or indeed the romance pattern as described by Quint but mixes elements of both temporal sequencing and temporal circularity in a way that cannot be described as linear. The film's favored way of cutting from one episode to the next is the lap-dissolve, by which the last image is faded out and the new one faded in without the screen ever being blank. According to David Bordwell, this is one of Hollywood's favorite techniques of creating temporal sequence, "a superb way to soften spatial, graphic or even temporal discontinuities."[19] But it also introduces temporal uncertainty, as it combines two filmed moments into one image, and in addition leaves it unclear how much time is meant to have lapsed from one scene to the next.

continuity and contingency

In any case, the conflict of linear vs. circular time turns out to mask a deeper ontological problem in both these notions of time: the conflict between a belief in the co-presence of all moments in time; a pre-set teleology which is here shared by all characters, Pagan and Christians; and a belief in genuine possibilities for change. Mary Ann Doane has explored this tension as characteristic of film's relationship to time. That film can make the moment of its recording present was celebrated by many modernist thinkers as allowing access to that "which is so dear to modernity—the possibility of the new, novelty, the continual difference and variation that constitutes the sensory basis of the modern."[20] The present moment, where change and the interference of chance happen, could be captured. But if each moment is indiscriminately repeatable and archivable, this also opens it to the danger of arbitrariness. Doane argues that cinema typically limits the contingency of the moment by editing, by splicing the arbitrary images into a narrative. Through the "narrativization of chance," the moment is made significant again by its embedding in a narrative where it forms part of a logical chain of events with beginning, middle, and end.[21] The fascinating presence of the filmic image is counterbalanced not only by encouraging distancing reflection on its workings but also by its embedding in a continuous narrative. The tension between continuity and moment echoes the general philosophical conflict between what philosophical classification calls the B-theory of time, which stresses continuity by holding that each point in time is equally real and the difference between past and future is only a psychological effect, as opposed to the A-theory, which focuses on the moment by holding that only the present exists or "is," not past or future.[22] In *Sign of the Pagan*, both concepts are represented.

On the one hand, all points in time are equally real and present insofar as time is predetermined in *Sign of the Pagan*. For both Pagans and Christians, the future already exists, as history will unfold according to a pre-existing layout, and the past is still present, too. The main difference between the two cultures appears to be to what degree they know this past and future. For Pagans, visions can access only segments that then have to be interpreted.

133

In the words of Attila's seer, "Each sees only a part of the eternal scene, a small glimpse of the greater whole." For Christians, the future is clearer as it will include Christianity's victory according to God's preordained plan. Pope Leo tells Attila, when the Hun claims that Rome will fall, "Only if God wills it so." Moreover, the past still appears to be present for Christians as well as Pagans. In Constantinople and Rome, the evidence of past activity is tangible everywhere in buildings, artifacts and statues. Most importantly for the plot, the Christian martyrs are still present as an army fighting on the side of the Romans. For Pagans, the past has again somewhat less currency, as they live in temporary campsites, but there is a sense of tradition and the "Hun way of life," including customs of polygamy, warfare, and horsemanship. Attila has an individual memory that motivates him—that of his childhood mistreatment in Rome—as well as a sense of historical perspective. His stated aim is to make his people's bards sing of him in the future by destroying Rome and restoring what the Romans destroyed. This impression of a co-presence of all points in time is also confounded by the fact that this film through its premodern setting creates what Doane calls the "spectatorial experience of the presence" (and future repeatability) of the past, merging these different times.[23]

But although time is predetermined and all points in time coexist at least on a transcendental level, *Sign of the Pagan* is also invested in allowing historical change, making the moment count. While the notion of human agency is based on a belief both in linear continuity and in change, in this film it is clearly on the side of the latter pole.[24] The heroic characters must be free to shape their lives and to influence the course of history by their actions. Again, the difference between Pagan and Christian is one of degree, and where for Marcian the coexistence of future, past, and present is more important because it is more evident, for Attila, the moment, with its possibility for human agency, is the key focus of his idea of time. This is partly the case because he cannot simply follow the epic winner's trajectory from sandal-maker to emperor, as Marcian does.

the struggle against the future

Attila's struggle against predetermined, "always already" present time happens mainly on semiotic level. His tragedy lies not so much in that his future is already present or that he cannot decipher what the signs and portents mean but that he has to undertake a heroic struggle against their obvious meaning, to escape what God has willed and the stars predicted. The only way in which this is possible is to make this a fight not over what will happen but over how we can know and who can say what will happen—about the interpretation of the signs rather than about the predetermined future revealed in them. This is what Attila tries to do in his quarrels with the other readers of the portents.

In the dispute over the predictions of Rome's downfall, for instance, just when he raises his sword above his head in a triumphant gesture and shouts "there is but one God who can lead us to victory and this is his sign," a thunderbolt hits a bent tree so that it crushes the seer who had prophesized that Rome would fall that autumn. That this is a sign and what it means is only too plain to the assembled kings who now speak. They presume the death of the seer to have a direct, causal relationship to his prophecy: this seer was wrong, and the Christian God is giving a warning. Most film spectators are likely to agree with this reading because they know of the seven (not twelve) hills of Rome and of Attila's historical failure to bring the empire down. They may also be reminded of the legends of the Christian God striking holy Germanic trees down by lightning, and indeed perhaps themselves attribute power to God. But Attila does some fancy footwork around the tree both physically and metaphorically, giving another, less plausible because more circuitous reading: the seer has been struck to make this, his greatest prophesy, his last. Attila appears not so much deluded as willfully not wanting to see the portents and instead manipulating signs to his advantage. When he later admits that he fears the Christian God's lightning, it is clear that he does not believe his own interpretation but is trying to carve out the space for him to make a historical move by claiming the authority to interpret the signs predicting the future.

His interpretations become increasingly far-fetched and desperate in trying to convince others as much as himself that he can alter the predetermined course of events. This is most clearly so when he tries to escape the obvious meaning of a vision his nurse had told him as a child of him as an adult lying on the ground, his blood soaking the earth, and the shadow of a Christian cross falling onto his body. This quite patently refers to his death, vanquished by Christians, which we later see to come to pass in exactly this image. But Attila tries to give a symbolic reading to this vision after he has killed his daughter Kubla, suggesting that she is "part of him" and his blood, so that her dead body on the ground is symbolically or metaphorically his body and blood and the prophecy has thus been fulfilled. This fails for the audience as an obviously contrived interpretation, even before the remaining seer tersely points out: "My Lord Attila, there is no shadow."

But even the King of the Huns is not able to change that which is "written," that is, predetermined: the course of history and the future. Despite his mastery of physical presence, he is not a historical agent insofar as he is unable to influence his destiny. Although there is a suggestion that he would have survived had he read the signs differently and not attacked Rome, this is given the lie by the fact that he dies after he decides not to attack and by the way in which we know history has ended. The main understanding of history underlying this film is thus a Christian and Pagan one of preordainment: the epic logic of the winners and the B-theory of

135

time as co-presence of all its moments. But much of the film, and much of our sympathy, lies in the struggle against this, in the logic of the losers and the hope for the possibility of change in the present moment. We can see in the film and we know from history that Attila will die and fail but in his dogged attempts to fight despite the fact that he himself knows that he will fail he displays precisely the heroic behavior that endears him to audiences.[25] More so than Marcian, he makes the present moment count: his power rests on his physical presence and on his strength and control of his subjects through direct face-to-face interaction.

deliberate naivety

So the one solution that the film offers to the dilemma of acting heroically in the face of inescapable fate is to *choose* not to know. Attila willfully ignores his future doom in order to fight Rome nonetheless. If he wanted to, he could "see" his future, as past, future, and present are eternally coexistent, and at least partially visible to humans in portents. But Attila *chooses* not to see the future and attempts to resist the linear flow of time, to sack Rome two centuries before it was meant to fall. Only when he is fatally stabbed does he ask his seer, "Here, that's the end?" because he is finally resuming his position in the linear time that is circumscribed by a conventional linear life from birth to death and "always already" predetermined.

In this way—of not wanting to see reality—Attila displays the paradoxical attitude of deliberate naivety. While Camper described Sirk's characters as blind and living in a world of "pre-Renaissance flatness," Jean-Luc Godard detects an element of choice in this blindness and again links this to Sirk's medievalist aesthetics. In his well-known "madly enthusiastic review" of *A Time to Love and a Time to Die* (1958), Godard says he will "talk about this film . . . as though, in other words, John Gavin and Liselotte Pulver were Aucassin and Nicolette 1959. This, anyhow, is what enchants me about Sirk: this delirious mixture of medieval and modern, sentimentality and subtlety, tame composition and frenzied CinemaScope."[26]

Godard here associates the medieval with the thirteenth-century romance *Aucassin et Nicolette* (1975) and structurally with sentimentality and tame composition; and the modern with subtlety and frenzied widescreen shots. The rest of the review makes clear that he connects something else with the medieval, too: its darkness and ignorance. To Godard, the lovers in *A Time to Love and a Time to Die* are characterized by their desire to ignore the reality around them, to shut their eyes and bury their heads in the sand like ostriches and thereby gain another kind of knowledge and authenticity and "ultimately delve deeper into themselves than any other character in a film to date."[27] By choosing not to see, by deliberately staying naive, they are able to romantically believe in their love in a way not possible to the realist. Crucially, for Godard, the film itself shares this deliberate blindness and naivety:

> Because I get the feeling that the images last twice as long as in most films, a twenty-fourth of a second instead of a forty-eighth, as if this ex-editor from UFA, through fidelity to his characters, had tried to bring into play even the lapse of time during which the shutter is closed.[28]

The voluntary blindness of the characters, the not-wanting-to-see, is incorporated into the film by its pointing toward the twenty-four times in which the cinema screen is black during an average projection. That Godard describes this as a lengthening in time of each image chimes also with the fact that the Middle Ages are often claimed to have a less rushed sense of time. The film experience for Godard here is one of time slowed down, mirroring a presumed premodern experience of time. Modernity's cherished belief in its "acceleration" of time, the greater speed of movement, information, and of progress itself in the twentieth century casts the Middle Ages as having had little sense of historical progression and change from one generation to the next. Godard seems to associate the medieval with blindness, with the dark screen, with not wanting to see, and the modern with reality and realism. But an experience of medieval slow time and deliberate blindness becomes an integral part of the film viewing and functioning here and is no longer clearly distinct from the modern in this rambling account—which is fitting, as "the only logic which concerns Sirk is delirium."[29]

By following the narrative logic of conventional cinema but allowing his protagonist *not to see* this narrative logic, Sirk has found another solution to the epic's investment in continuity and change, a solution that is appropriate to this genre: one from *within* narrative. *Sign of the Pagan* manages not to choose between narrative *or* contingency, between meaningful flow and historical agency on the one hand *or* randomness and pure and uncontrollable meaninglessness on the other. It links moments into a coherent narrative but allows the contingent moment to be reintroduced as part of the narrative.

As we have seen, it also manages to thematize this in the plot by translating it into a parallel contradiction in Pagan and Christian ideas of linear time: that between historical agency and a preordained timeline. Christianity as well as Attila's Paganism hold that the future is predetermined but simultaneously believe in the free will of each human being, making him or her an autonomous agent capable of influencing history. Through his deliberate naivety, history looks changeable to Attila, which creates an element of contingency to it for him (and to some extent for the audience) that keeps things exciting and empowers the human agents. This, then, is the main difference between Pagan and Christian time: Marcian accepts the glorious path God has preordained for him; Attila rebels against it despite sharing the belief that it is inescapable.

Attila in this way precisely models the attitude required of audiences wanting to enjoy a historical epic. Spectators are asked to forget what they know about history and to accept it as full of open-ended possibilities again, and witness what could happen, not what happened.[30] The moment is reinstituted as the carrier of change and contingency if we ignore that we know the outcome. But at the same time, in order to fully enjoy the sense of foreboding, viewers have to periodically let themselves be reminded of the tragic end that Attila is destined to meet. Sirk's technique for allowing both predetermination and open-endedness is the combination of the forward propulsion of narrative movement with an unusual emphasis on visually striking moments mentioned above that give pause for thought. Mulvey describes a similar phenomenon in Sirk's melodrama, where the "frozen moments" typical of the genre invite the audience to ponder a particular image as a "point of punctuation" that both interrupts and structures the narrative.[31] Sometimes CinemaScope's potential is used to combine visual impact and narrative progress in one widescreen frame, which can show much background detail clearly while the action can progress in the foreground.[32] On other occasions, the spectacular moments that characterize the epic are tightly integrated into the narrative rather than pausing it. As Mark Jancovich has shown to be typical of the epic genre, the physical presence of the spectacle and its service to the narrative are not mutually exclusive.[33]

For instance, the camera frequently lovingly lingers over medium close-ups of Pulcheria's face and upper body, the spectacular value enhanced by looks by flattering makeup, costumes, coiffure, jewelry, lighting, and even some soft focus in the classical Hollywood way where, in Wood's words, "too much style is just enough."[34] Marcian resists to stay and watch this spectacle: when Pulcheria flirtatiously tells him that before getting his orders from General Paulinus, "you can first spend a little time with me," he replies that "I fear I would lose all count of time in the presence of so much beauty," and leaves. But it turns out that the long takes of Pulcheria actually further the love plot at least as much as Marcian's leaving ultimately does. The camerawork and editing knows more than the characters do: that they will become a couple is mapped out in the way in which Pulcheria is introduced to him as spectacle. Viewers familiar with either genre conventions or history, or both, can let themselves be reminded of the likely outcome or assume the (deliberate) naivety of the characters and keep the suspense going, or, for maximum enjoyment, experience and reflect on the tension between the two.[35]

The relationship postulated by *Sign of the Pagan* between the fifth century and the twentieth century is likewise one of both continuity and change, long-term causal chains and contingent moments. Apart from showing that film can revive the visual, physical communication style of Attila and Marcian through the momentary "spectorial experience of presence," *Sign of the Pagan* also, through Christianity, establishes an ongoing link to the present. Despite its setting at the end of the Roman Empire, it shows not the end of the Empire, which here gains a late victory, but the continuity of Christianity. The Roman Empire is not so much *similar* to the USA as the same: Christianity is *still* the major force that it was then—as part of the always already preordained unfolding of world events. The film's functioning on the basis of its visual immediacy and continuity in combination could be interpreted as a reinvigoration of Christianity through film. Melodrama as a genre, according to Peter Brooks, guarantees a value system in a postsacral world following a "process of desacralization that was set in motion at the Renaissance."[36] This has been much applied to Sirk, but it appears that there is no such rupture between the medieval Christian world and the modern here: *Sign of the Pagan* imbues the Christian value system with new energy, new meaning through physicality rather than replacing it.[37] Attila's seer's vision of a holy man floating on a white cloud with many bleeding men and women who are both dead and alive turns out to be, despite its seemingly impossible content, quite physically true. As Attila's troops are gathered outside Rome, Pope Leo I really does arrive on a boat across the Tiber, surrounded by cloud-like mist. Likewise, the people who are dead yet alive are not a riddle, but martyrs, who in Leo's faith are physically, not just symbolically resurrected. Attila continues to misunderstand this as merely symbolic and underestimates how Christians are strengthened through their belief in resurrection and martyrdom. Film could be seen to show that, like its historical characters, martyrs are still alive. But, as always, this one-sided pro-Christian reading rings somewhat hollow: the vision of the holy man on the cloud which is meant to be the visual centrepiece of the film, showing Attila's blindness to the beauty and newfound physical power of Christianity, looks cheap and draws attention to its status as a not-very-special effect out of the fog machine. The film makes no attempt to visualize the martyrs' living yet absent presence. As well as being confronted with the visual impact of Christian presence, we are reminded that this is a twentieth-century film as well as fifth-century scene.

Some critics have denied the possibility of interpreting Sirk in the way that I have done, as both drawing on the power of illusion and encouraging reflection. These critics often describe Sirk's aesthetics as more totalitarian, ideological or fascistic in a way that connects his output in Nazi Germany with that after his emigration to the USA. Lutz Koepnick, for instance, has carefully argued that Sirk does not show such a Brechtian aesthetic of both dazzling with beauty and distancing and appealing to thought at the same time, but instead aims for a Wagnerian *Gesamtkunstwerk* that is to heal the split between popular imagination and high art.[38] Eric Rentschler warns that "aesthetic complexity is not necessarily a mark of ideological subversion."[39] But resistance, as Foucault observes, never stands outside power; ideology and its undermining go hand in hand. The fact that Sirk continues to polarize critics is an indication of the success with which he, in some viewers, stirs thought as well as aesthetic pleasure in conjunction. It also points to the levels of sophistication of classical Hollywood epics. Far from naively rewriting history as entertainment fodder, their deliberate naivety draws attention to the blind spots necessarily underlying *all* representations of history, to that which has been left out and remains unseen as well as that which is shown. If Sirk's films come under suspicion of totalitarianism, then so should all historical epics and especially the less self-reflexive *written* representations of history.

In any case, epics have emerged in my interpretation not only as having a double investment in a conservative conception of linear time, but also in the creation of a sense of presence of the past and in allowing sublime feelings of being overwhelmed by the "eventfulness" of historical time. While linear time is often staged as paradigmatically modern, the less linear view of time finds its prefiguration and intellectual soulmate in the premodern. The conflicting demands of these two aims create the endlessly productive tension at the heart of this genre.

acknowledgments

I would like to thank Anke Bernau, Axel Bohmann, Robert Burgoyne and Claire Whitehead for helpful comments on this essay. I am also grateful to my students in a course on Medieval Film at the University of Freiburg in the summer of 2008 for their stimulating discussions of some of the topics raised here, and especially to Axel Bohmann, to whose excellent coursework essay on *Sign of the Pagan* I owe many insights.

notes

1. Brief discussions of the film are included in Douglas Sirk, *Sirk on Sirk: Conversations with Jon Halliday,* edited by Jon Halliday, revised edn (London: Faber and Faber, 1997), pp. 112, 114–117, 141; Jean-Loup Bourget, *Douglas Sirk* (Paris: Edilig, 1984), pp. 74–78.
2. Sirk, *Sirk on Sirk,* p. 117.
3. Sirk, *Sirk on Sirk,* p. 141.
4. Michael Wood, *America in the Movies; or, "Santa Maria, It Had Slipped My Mind"* (London: Secker & Warburg, 1975), p. 175.
5. On this temporal dimension of film, see Mary Ann Doane, *The Emergence of Cinematic Time: Modernity, Contingency, the Archive* (Cambridge, Mass.: Harvard University Press, 2002), p. 107; Philip Rosen, *Change Mummified: Cinema, History, Theory* (Minneapolis, Minn.: University of Minnesota Press, 2001), especially pp. 3–41; Philip Rosen, "History of Image, Image of History: Subject and Ontology in Bazin," *Wide Angle,* 9 (4) (winter 1987/1988): 7–34, reprinted in

Ivone Margulies (ed.), *Rites of Realism: Essays on Corporeal Cinema* (Durham, NC: Duke University Press, 2003), pp. 42–79; Gertrud Koch, "Das Bild als Schrift der Vergangenheit," in Birgit R. Erdle and Sigrid Weigel (eds), *Mimesis, Schrift und Bild: Ähnlichkeit und Entstellung im Verhältnis der Künste* (Cologne: Böhlau, 1996), pp. 7–22.

6. See Bettina Bildhauer, "Forward into the Past," in Bettina Bildhauer and Anke Bernau (eds), *Medieval Film* (Manchester: Manchester University Press, 2009), pp. 40–59.

7. Fred Camper, "The Films of Douglas Sirk," *Screen,* 12 (2) (1971): 44–62; p. 51.

8. Camper, "The Films of Douglas Sirk," p. 50.

9. Sirk, *Sirk on Sirk,* p. 11. However, he also makes much of the subtext of Marlowe to *Sign of the Pagan,* claiming that he had wanted to shoot his *Tamburlaine* instead, as he had been impressed as a boy seeing his Dr. Faustus with the "baroque Renaissance quality of Marlowe's piece, the masks and symbols," Sirk, *Sirk on Sirk,* p. 115.

10. Tom Conley, *Cartographic Cinema* (Minneapolis, Minn.: University of Minnesota Press, 2007).

11. This is the "mathematical" sublime in Immanuel Kant, "Kritik der Urteilskraft," edited by Otto Buek, in *Immanuel Kants Werke,* edited by Ernst Cassirer, 11 vols. (Berlin: Cassirer, 1912–1923), vol. V (1914), pp. 232–568; p. 331. English translation in Kant, *Critique of Judgment,* translated by Werner S. Pluhar (Indianapolis, Ind.: Hackett, 1986), p. 117.

12. There is still some temporal imprecision, as Theodosius I had declared Christianity state religion in ad 380, which would situate the speaker in 1880. By the very end of the film, when Attila is killed, it seems most likely that the voice comes from 1953, as the historical Attila died in ad 453 (precisely 1,500 years before the start of the filming). The seer dates his fall 1,200 years after the founding of Rome, which is traditionally given as 753 bc, so that the plot would take place in ad 447 and the voice come from around 1947.

13. Vivian Sobchack, "'Surge and Splendor': A Phenomenology of the Hollywood Historical Epic," *Representations,* 29 (winter 1990): 24–49; p. 28. Sobchack here also comments on the role of the authorizing prologues and "Voice of God" narration in achieving this effect (pp. 25, 34–35); and on the way in which it is not just the films' plots that "allegorically" represent such a feeling of being part of the splendor of history but also the production that thrives on creating an impression of excess—of extras, of production costs, of stars, even of a film's length—on a historical scale (especially pp. 29–30, 35–38).

14. Conley, *Cartographic Cinema,* p. 198.

15. Derek Elley, *The Epic Film* (London: Routledge, 1984), especially pp. 12, 16; Arthur Lindley, "The Ahistoricism of Medieval Film," *Screening the Past,* III (2008, online), n.p.

16. Laura Mulvey, "Social Hieroglyphics: Reflections on Two Films by Douglas Sirk," in Laura Mulvey, *Fetishism and Curiosity* (London: BFI, 1996), pp. 29–39; p. 38.

17. This was famously formulated, for example, in Aron Gurevich, "Au Moyen Age: conscience individuelle et image de l'au-delà," *Annales (Economies, Sociétés, Civilisations),* 2 (1982): 255–275, Translated by S. C. Rowell as "Perceptions of the Individual and the Hereafter in the Middle Ages," in Aron Gurevich, *Historical Anthropology of the Middle Ages,* edited by Jana Howlett (Cambridge: Polity, 1992), pp. 65–89.

18. David Quint, *Epic and Empire: Politics and Generic from Virgil to Milton* (Princeton, NY: Princeton University Press, 1993), p. 9.

19. David Bordwell, "The Classical Hollywood Style, 1917–60," in David Bordwell, Janet Staiger, and Kristin Thompson, *The Classical Hollywood Cinema: Film Style and Mode of Production to 1960* (London: Routledge & Kegan Paul, 1985), pp. 1–84; p. 47.

20. Doane, *Emergence of Cinematic Time,* p. 100. See also Leo Charney, "In a Moment: Film and the Philosophy of Modernity," in Leo Charney and Vanessa R. Schwartz (eds), *Cinema and the Invention of Modern Life* (Berkeley, Calif.: University of California Press, 1995), pp. 279–294.

21. Doane, *Emergence of Cinematic Time,* pp. 105–107. On the tension between linearity and the copresence of all the parts of the plot in narratives see Paul Ricoeur, "Narrative Time," *Critical Inquiry,* 7 (1980): 169–190.

22. Mark Currie, *About Time: Narrative, Fiction and the Philosophy of Time* (Edinburgh: Edinburgh University Press, 2007), especially pp. 15, 17, 142.

23. Doane, *Emergence of Cinematic Time,* p. 103.

24. On historical agency as living one's life as if it *were* a narrative, and the effect on imaginations of time, see Hayden White, "The Metaphysics of Narrativity: Time and Symbol in Ricoeur's Philosophy of History," in Hayden White, *The Content of the Form: Narrative Discourse and Historical Representation* (Baltimore, Md.: Johns Hopkins University Press, 1987), pp. 169–184.

25. On Attila's rather than Marcian's role as protagonist, see Bourget, *Douglas Sirk,* pp. 74–75; Sirk, *Sirk on Sirk,* pp. 112, 115–116.

26. Jean-Luc Godard, "*A Time to Love and a Time to Die,*" *Cahiers du Cinèma,* 94 (April 1959), English translation in Jean-Luc Godard, *Godard on Godard,* edited by Jean Narboni and Tom Milne (New York: Secker & Warburg, 1972), pp. 134–139; pp. 135, 136.

27. Godard, "*A Time to Love and a Time to Die,*" p. 138.

28. Godard, "*A Time to Love and a Time to Die,*" p. 138. Godard had already associated the extension of the moment, "the world between two blinks of the eyelids," with premodern legend in a comment that *Summer Interlude* (1951), like any Bergman film, is "one twenty-fourth of a second metamorphosed and expanded over an hour and a half . . . enough to send Maj-Britt Nilsson off like Orpheus and Lancelot in quest of paradise lost and time regained," in Jean-Luc Godard, "Bergmanorama," *Cahiers du Cinéma,* 85 (July 1958), English translation in English translation in Jean-Luc Godard, *Godard on Godard,* edited by Jean Narboni and Tom Milne (New York: Secker & Warburg, 1972), pp. 75–80; p. 77.

29. Godard, "*A Time to Love and a Time to Die,*" p. 136.

30. Elley, *Epic Film,* p. 13.

31. Laura Mulvey, "Repetition and Return: Textual Analysis and Douglas Sirk in the Twenty-First Century," in John Gibbs and Douglas Pye (eds), *Style and Meaning: Studies in the Detailed Analysis of Film* (Manchester: Manchester University Press, 2005), pp. 228–243; pp. 236, 239.

32. For a discussion of the effect of CinemaScope on editing, see David Bordwell, "Film Style and Technology, 1930–60," in David Bordwell, Janet Staiger, and Kristin Thompson, *The Classical Hollywood Cinema: Film Style and Mode of Production to 1960* (London: Routledge & Kegan Paul, 1985), pp. 339–364; pp. 358–364.

33. Mark Jancovich, "'The Purest Knight of All': Nation, History, Representation in *El Cid* (1960)," *Cinema Journal,* 40 (1) (fall 2000): 79–103; especially pp. 79–81.

34. Wood, *America in the Movies,* p. 7.

35. This foreshadowing technique also shapes the film's main narrative arc to Attila's death: that this is the outcome of the film is clear at least from the point at which he recounts the vision of his lifeless body under the shadow of the cross, which itself is foreshadowed in the many crosses, both Christian crucifixes and cross-shaped objects, which are shown in the film (see, for example, Figure 6.2, a detail shot of Attila's battle standard that links death in the index of the skull to the shape of the Christian cross).

36. Peter Brooks, *The Melodramatic Imagination: Balzac, Henry James, Melodrama and the Mode of Excess* (New Haven, Conn.: Yale University Press, 1976), p. 15.

37. Lutz Koepnick, *The Dark Mirror: Germany between Hitler and Hollywood* (Berkeley, Calif.: University of California Press, 2002), pp. 201–233; Jean-Loup Bourget, "God is Dead; or, Through a Glass Darkly," *Bright Lights Film Journal,* 48 (May 2005), no pagination; originally published in *Bright Lights Film Journal,* 6 (winter 1977–1978). On Sirk's religious side see also Jan-Christopher Horak, "Sirk's Early Exile Films: *Boefje* and *Hitler's Madman*," *Film Criticism,* 23: 2–3 (winter–spring 1999): 122–135. Dave Grosz "*The First Legion:* Vision and Perception in Sirk," *Screen,* 12 (2) (1971): 99–117.

38. Koepnick, *Dark Mirror,* pp. 201–233. Gerd Gemünden summarizes the debates in his introduction to *Film Criticism*'s special issue on Sirk: Gerd Gemünden, "Introduction," *Film Criticism,* 23: 2–3 (winter–spring 1999): 1–13. See also Lutz Koepnick, "Sirk and the Culture Industry: *Zu neuen Ufern* and *The First Legion*," *Film Criticism,* 23: 2–3 (winter–spring 1999): 94–121.

39. Eric Rentschler, "Douglas Sirk Revisited: the Limits and Possibilities of Artistic Agency," *New German Critique,* 95 (spring–summer 2005): 149–161; p. 161. See also Gertrud Koch, "Detlef Sierck to Douglas Sirk," *Film Criticism,* 23: 2–3 (winter–spring 1999): 14–32.

the fall of the roman empire

on space and allegory

s e v e n

t o m   c o n l e y

Historians of cinema are quick to note that in the 1970s and 1980s many critical studies of psychoanalytical orientation were built upon a process called *reading through* film. Based on the concept of *working through*, it referred to what Freud had made famous in the name of *Durcharbeitung*, the way that a person in treatment might cope with the difficulties of being alive: how he or she would address the traumas that make life what it is.[1] It went without saying that the relation of the film to the viewer was felt to be not unlike that of the analyst and analysand. Cinema became what Félix Guattari called "the poor man's divan," the place where the images of a film prompted viewers to sort through their own memories in order to come to terms—and since by its nature analysis is interminable, never quite to term—with themselves.[2] Spectators who took soundings of their own memories by way of films could afford analysis in the *camera obscura* of the movie theater.[3]

The concept has no doubt since broadened to include in its purview that of the *lecture de regard*, that is, the comparative reading of images and words *across* works, often of different facture, for the sake of opening onto areas where conjugation of memory, sensation, and vision prompts reader and spectator alike to make vitally new and different "takes" on objects unseen or overlooked in the frame of everyday life. Viewers of cinema "work through" a given film by mixing and correlating textual evidence that allows them to obtain a compass on the psychogeographies of their lives. The concept could be extended to film studies *tout court*, at least to the degree where the analyst uses historical material to account for the constant attraction a film exerts upon the viewer. The analyst is prone to ask why a given film—usually that comes "out of the past" of childhood or adolescence—has a continually nagging presence *here and now*. More often than not a film of this sort gets mixed with the impressions a person associates with a given moment in his or her life. The film (that need not have been a feature of historical merit or worth inclusion in a pantheon of collective memory) catalyzes recall for reasons unknown or that prompt inquiry as to why they are unknown. Thus a complex *lecture de regard* begins when a film repeatedly comes forward as if to ask the viewer to wonder why and how it emerges as it does.[4]

Such is Anthony Mann's somewhat dubious classic of 1964, *The Fall of the Roman Empire*, for which, along with many others, Leslie Halliwell spared few kind words.[5] The film is said to belong to the last of the director's three "cycles" that turn from the taut and gripping B-style film noir (*T-Men, He Walked by Night* [1948], *Raw Deal* [1948], *Border Incident* [1945], etc.), the postwar western (*Winchester 73* [1950], *The Man from Laramie* [1955], *Bend of the River* [1952], etc.) to epic features that include *Cimarron* (1960) and *El Cid* (1961), two films, like *The Fall of the Roman Empire*, of vast and ample girth (of 147 and 184 minutes respectively). Seen from afar it would qualify as a *film d'auteur* insofar as it reaches into history, as Mann had done in *The Black Book* (1948), in which the French Revolution is the backdrop for photographer John Alton's ways of folding *film noir* into a costume drama. *The Fall of the Roman Empire* clearly has the panorama (and requisite panoramic shots) of the westerns that deal with foundation and conflict, such as *Bend of the River*, and it ends with reflection on the end of things, as had both *The Naked Spur* (1953) and *Man of the West* (1958). Partisans of *auteur* theory would be tempted to find in the pertinent differences the genuine stamp of the director-creator who works across genres and contexts so as to yield a signature at once bold and common, salient and faded, remarkable and given to oblivion.

To "work through" *The Fall of the Roman Empire* in search of a signature would require it to be seen in a gallery of other epics of the "peplum" variety that include *Quo Vadis* (1951), *The Robe* (1953), *Demetrius and the Gladiators* (1954), and William Wyler's version of *Ben-Hur* (1959). Or would it? For of late, along with *Spartacus* (1960), the film has surfaced in the shape of a long and direct quotation in much of *Gladiator* (2001).[6] Working with the film would require it to be seen not only in view of the flush of epics produced in the 1950s but also, as it were, through a sort of "resurrection" and oblique homage to Mann on the part of Ridley Scott. In this way, *The Fall of the Roman Empire* can be recognized as "a writing of history" by which a "history" of the past is engaged because no language of the present moment can quite convey, much less put in words, the living conflicts of here and now. Appeal is made to the imagination of another time and space in order to deal with what consciously or unconsciously cannot be said of the here and now. Where the past is honored it addresses the present and, concurrently, is "eliminated" by virtue of being displaced into the present. Certain codes that belong to the "historiographical operation" require issues pertaining to current time to be elided into the past that the epic form renders "actual." The events of the former epoch, assumed to be dead, require exhumation in order for a space of the present to be created and discerned. In this way historiographic elements of the epic film are inevitably related to allegory, to a "saying-other" of what in the present, for political or ideological cause, of needs "goes without saying."[7]

Here *The Fall of the Roman Empire* finds an appeal extending beyond its moment. The title portends a story recalling the breadth both of Gibbon's *The History of the Decline and Fall of the Roman Empire* (1776) and that of the historical works of Will Durant, adviser to the film, who then was author of *The Foundations of Civilization* (1936), *The Story of Philosophy* (1943), *Our Oriental Heritage* (1954) and—if gentle irony is allowed—other modest titles.[8] In accord with Gibbon's history, the film indeed locates in the effects of the evil Commodus, the surviving son of Marcus Aurelius, the beginning of the fall. It would be in ad 182, two years after the death (or assassination) of his father. Where many histories of the first six centuries of our millennium attest to a complex transformation of an empire shrinking over a long duration of time, the film centers on a single moment that it takes to be a first station on the downward turn of a Wheel of Fortune. Following Gibbon, Marcus Aurelius (Alec Guinness) personifies a final and afflicted hour of glory. The fortunes of Commodus (Christopher Plummer), which take up most of the film, are implied to be the causes of the depredations to follow.

Compression of duration becomes the defining trait of the epic. Collective destiny gets compacted into a family romance set in front of a grandiose world. Representing several years that define the parabola of centuries to follow, the film must be *long* and *protracted* in order have the chronology of the narrative feel as if it were both the *decline* and *fall*, in other words, as if it were working with and through what the title elides in its indirect allusion to Gibbon. To sustain its duration, the film needs to resemble a Christian *passion*, a medieval play whose well-known ending requires hours of participatory labor (and all the more in view of the success of *The Ten Commandments* of slightly earlier vintage). The wager for the director and producers entails creating a narrative that, while moving along a plane of inexorable decline, must include ups and downs,

Aristotelian peripatetics drawing a line between the historical "places" of the film—discernible *loci communes* or commonplaces in Roman history—and setting into a design a *space* of the film's own facture and signature.

Tradition (and Wikipedia) assert that Mann's epic turns real history into a "fantasia" through a concatenation of real events it links to imaginary counterparts. In Mann's epic, concatenation is taken literally: viewers recall that in the final pyre the hero and heroine are chained to their fate. After wrestling free of the manacles of their irons, riveted to the wooden stakes in the midst of a consuming blaze, they soon leave the tumult as if they were two biblical figures fleeing a universal conflagration (see Figure 7.1).

More than a display of its contents, the film *as film* becomes a matter of meshing historical "speeds." As in *Intolerance* and other epics, the *longue durée* implied by an inexorable decline and fall of a civilization requires compression of duration to convey its effects within a reasonable viewing time.

voice-over as *incipit*

Two are crucial to the epic form. The first is the voice-over that inaugurates and ends the story at the same time it implements the way the film is to be seen. Like that of a stage director or the word of God that comes from everywhere and nowhere, the voice-over is heard at two edges of the film, the beginning and the end, where it draws an implied frame about its story. In the beginning, following the credits, themselves an epic execution of fresco- and mosaic-like scenes of Roman history, a fade-out in black gives way slowly to a wintry landscape in which a foreground under a very light cover of snow thresholds a forest to the right and hillsides (although in

Figure 7.1
The expulsion from a world in conflagration.

Spain, resembling the White Mountains of New Hampshire) in the distance (see Figure 7.2).

The top of a peak in the background is shrouded under grey clouds that reveal a single patch of blue sky. After holding on the landscape for two seconds the camera pans right slowly. When, two seconds later, a stone tower—the first sign of the presence of "man"—comes into view, a learned voice (speaking in received English) intones, "Two of the greatest problems in history . . . are how to account for the rise of Rome . . . and how to account for her fall. We may come nearer to understanding the truth if we remember . . . that the fall of Rome, like her rise, had not one cause, but many . . ." As the words are spoken, the camera brings into view a walled fort on either side of a basilica (a row of fluted columns support the atrium at the center). The sober voice continues uninterrupted: "and was not an event, but a process spread over three hundred years." At the mention of chronology the camera stops and centers on the structure set against the grey horizon. "Some nations have not lasted," it utters, as the shot cuts to a view of six centurions huddled around a fire whose smoke (in the left center of the wide frame) obscures the sight of the architecture in the background. When the voice continues, "as long as Rome fell," the camera slowly pans upward.

The effect of the long span of time denoted in the title finds the moment in which the voice-over states that it is taking place. The slow and somber panoramic conflates a long elapse of time into a crepuscular landscape that extends before our eyes. Duration is shown as protracted motion across a landscape. Just seconds into the second shot, without a pause, the voice-over begins a new sentence: "In the year 180 ad, the Emperor Marcus Aurelius was leading his Roman legions against Germanic tribes [the camera while still slowly rising centers on architecture in crepuscule, light

Figure 7.2
Opening shot, of a frozen landscape.

emanating from the basilica and the tops of its five towers and torches below] along the Danube frontier." The voice-over ends there. The narrative begins when the shot cuts to medium view of two couples of standing men, spread across the width of the frame, two at a podium where one, ostensibly blind, is touching an object resting upon it while the others stand by a fire. Reference from the soundtrack that would identify Marcus Aurelius in the frame of the image is impossible to discern. Although assured that the Emperor is present, the spectator cannot find a bearing. The scene is one in which a soothsayer notes that omens are ill. The fall has begun.

time is short: a map of the roman empire

The second compression of duration, in which the film can be said to become not only an "archive" of past time but a "diagram" of the present moment, takes place when a map, a graphic complement to the voice-over in the opening shot, displays the geography of the Roman Empire.[9] It is folded into the narrative in the context of two complementary sequences, one outside by day and the other, inside and by candlelight. They both sum up the film at the same time as they bear on the narrative.

In the first, the ailing Marcus Aurelius (forcibly wise, perhaps because Alec Guinness portrays the dying hero with suave and frail grace), speaks to his armies. The regional representatives of the Empire are set in a parade. The dying leader casts a sad gaze over a review of chariots in a procession that indeed "declines" the regions of the Empire. Each vehicle carries a leader, a driver, various ensigns and heraldic paraphernalia of a province: of the twelve that pass by—three of which the King cannot quite identify— nine are reviewed in detail. The pattern of shots, a trait of Mann's cinematographic signature, displays the breadth of the scene from the Emperor's bird's-eye view on the terrace above. It is set in counterpoint by long shots from below that include in the visual field the parade in the middle ground and the leader, minuscule and barely discernible, set against the rustic fortress in the back. Of almost ten minutes in duration (10:37 to 19:05), the parade and the address require length and splendor fatiguing enough to cause concern for the monarch who seems to have barely life enough to live through the ceremony.

The sequence builds upon an unspoken geographical allegory. The political center of the title, Rome, has been displaced to a periphery where tasks that in the best of worlds require diplomacy are reduced to war. The site is a "limit" and a border in which the world seems to be thrown topsy-turvy.[10] In the hinterland, both emperor and empire are beyond their frame of control, yet it is there where a procession affirming of the force and unity of the political body is performed. The texture of the film emphasizes the point: cold, dark, and dusted with snow, the hilly world (in northern

149

Spain) that would be near the Danube strikes a vibrant contrast with the brightly lit and studio-like world of Roman splendor that will follow.

What has just been shown requires a plan or map. The crucial sequence (19:06–22:17) in which mention is first made of dynastic succession, the character of Commodus, and the challenges Livius will face—following the first and last affective encounter of Marcus Aurelius and his daughter—has at its core a map of the Roman Empire. Its expanse is shown in strong contrast to the two words, repeated at the beginning and the end of the sequence, that form one of the principal conundrums of the epic movie in general: *time is short*. Where the Empire is vast the narrative time of its fall is of the essence, and all the more in view of a historical map of the Empire.[11] To suggest (as in the voice-over, at once within and outside of the narrative) that the Empire will crumble within the duration of the film, a compression of space is required. It is here where the first of two maps is crucial to the visual design. In *The Fall of the Roman Empire*, a cartographic backdrop of three centuries of history serves as a foil to the twice-uttered remark that frames the sequence. On cursory view this segment of the plot is developed to introduce the good citizens and lovers Drucilla (Sophia Loren) and Livius (Stephen Holden) to Marcus Aurelius and to set the "fall" into motion. The ceremonial gathering of the provincial leaders and their soldiers has just taken place.

> **Shot 1 (19:06):** Dissolve from a long shot of the throng of soldiers to a close-up of the blind soothsayer (his right eye momentarily masked by a tower) to the right and, to the left, in the background, seen through a latticed doorway whose wooden tracery marks an "X," Marcus Aurelius sits alone, pondering. The sound of footsteps distracts the blind man who looks to his left. He turns and *looks* to his right at the sound cue of a door that opens.

One of the traits of the director's "signature," the staging of opposing elements in counterpoint in extreme depth of field (here, even in a dark interior scene), is evident. The solitary hero, minuscule, is juxtaposed to the figure in the foreground, who, like many of the famous blind personages in the history of cinema (such as the balloon-seller in *M*) calls attention to the division of seeing and hearing in what will be a drama of dissimulation.

150

> **Shot 2 (19:10):** Cut to interior, in a medium shot, of the study or "map room": the blind man stands to the left, by the latticed doorway in medium foreground. The camera moves right as Drucilla first, then Maximus, enter from the doorway in the background. The camera dollies forward to put them in view of the blind man who stands rigidly, as if he were a sculpted enigma. The camera moves forward to record the couple passing through the doorway behind the blind man. As it tracks

forward, following Drucilla in search of her father, it pans slightly left and right before it reaches Marcus Aurelius, seated, lost in thought.

In twenty-five seconds the mobility of the camera—its ease in traveling through the compartmentalized space it is defining—becomes as notable as the characters to whom it seems partially attracted.

> **Shot 3 (19:35):** Cut to medium close-up of Livia facing Marcus Aurelius seated, arched forward, his head bent over. She kneels before him.
>
> **Shot 4 (19:39):** Cut and counter shot, taken from the same side, now of Marcus Aurelius as Drucilla faces him. He raises his head and takes delight in seeing her. To the left stands a great metal urn and to the right, by a grey panel, the first glimpse of a set of parchment maps on a wall and a table. He kisses her hand. "Drucilla, each time I see you . . . I wonder if I fathered something so beautiful." He pulls himself back, placing his hands on his knees, and sighs, "You make it hard for me to leave this life."

Although Maximus is illuminated in the center, the background to the right displays the folded animal hides on which the map of the Empire is drawn. The element of licit *fathering* anticipates its obverse when, at the end, the plot will reveal that Commodus is the poisonous fruit of an impious union, and all the more when, in the next shot, kinship is keynote:

> **Shot 5 (19:58):** Cut to medium close-up (as in Shot 3). Drucilla: "Father, you have a long life ahead of you."
>
> **Shot 6 (20:02):** Cut and counter-shot (as in Shot 4). Marcus Aurelius responds, stretching his right hand to touch Drucilla's cheek, "Death is in the order of things." He pulls his arm back, adding, "Didn't they teach you that in school."

Allusion to "school" carries anachronism in the confusion of memory that fuels the allegory for the reason that the viewer cannot fail to recall the "primary" moments of our own classrooms in which the hard facts of life are taught.

> **Shot 7 (20:07):** Cut to medium close-up (as in Shot 3). Drucilla: "I would not let you leave me." Marcus Aurelius: "Is there a choice?"
>
> **Shot 8 (20:10):** Cut to close-up of Marcus Aurelius, now taken over Drucilla's shoulder. He looks wistfully at her and continues, "Soon this trickle of blood and these few bones, this net woven of nerves and arteries will be dust," as he nods, "no choice."
>
> **Shot 9 (20:22):** Cut to counter-shot of Drucilla listening, then responding, "Now that I am here, I will see that you take better care of yourself."

Shot 10 (20:25): Cut to close-up (as in Shot 8). Marcus Aurelius speaks, "Even so . . ." then turns left, and stands up.

Up to here, a sense of unfettered intimacy, of an ideal filial relation, no doubt thanks to the elegance of Alex Guinness's manner of speech in view of the close view of Sophia Loren, overshadows the fact that the context is one of surveillance and deceit.

Shot 11 (20:30): Cut to medium shot of Drucilla, left, holding Marcus Aurelius's right hand as he continues to turn, now toward the maps seen along the edge of the frame on the right. The camera pans right to display the maps as the Emperor, his left hand on his chest, looks at the assemblage of plans. "Time is short . . ." The camera dolly-pans in following Marcus Aurelius, who now is seen from the back, staring at the maps. "There is a decision . . . which I can no longer delay." He drops his hand, turns left, sighing, "I must sacrifice the love of my son. . . . Commodus must never be my heir. Livius . . . "

The *topos* of the epic is given in a different sense of counterpoint: the Emperor looks at the map, centrally framed within the image field, as if to contemplate a great expanse of space and time, before he turns left to gaze upon his daughter, who would be—even Sophia Loren—"a net woven of blood and arteries."

Shot 12 (20:50): Long shot in deep focus, now framing Marcus Aurelius in a small space by the maps at the right side of the frame. Drucilla stands middle-right while Livius is to the left behind her, and, in the foreground, the blind man, in close-up, stares blankly, as if to somewhere outside of the frame. The Emperor continues, without being shown addressing Livius: "Livius, it is my wish that you should succeed me."

The shot cues on the utterance "Livius" the figure of whom is barely visible in view of the face of the blind man in the foreground to the left. The sudden cut from the long to the medium shot underscores the importance of the *naming* of the would-be inheritor.

Shot 13 (20:57): Cut to medium shot of Marcus Aurelius walking forward, the maps behind him. As he moves ahead, he states, "And I intend to present you to the leaders of the Empire, openly, as my successor." As he completes his sentence, the camera dollies back to bring Livius into view, separated from Marcus Aurelius by the lattice-work window in the background while Livia stands behind, not far from the maps on the edge of the frame. "But, you said . . ." utters Livius.

Shot 14 (21:06): The shot cuts to medium close-up of Livius, seen over Marcus Aurelius's shoulder: "But . . . you said yourself, Caesar, it will need someone who will change . . . who will find new ways . . . a man of the *tenth* century of Rome . . ."

Shot 15 (21:14): Cut to medium shot as positioned in Shot 13. Livius, speaking flatfootedly at once to the Emperor and Drucilla far behind him: "but I know only the ways of war. I would not know how to make allies out of the Barbarians." Marcus responds, pulling back, "You will find new ways," then patting him on his arm, "You have the heart for it, Livius." Livius: "But Commodus already shares the throne with you." Marcus: "I had hopes that position and responsibility would make him grow up." The camera follows him until he turns about with Sophia Loren: "But he is interested only in games and gladiators."

Because he stands in shadow, obscured by the window between himself and Marcus Aurelius, the would-be hero's voice is both "in" and "off," as if detached from the body and floating in the ambient space.

Shot 16 (21:36): Cut to medium close-up of Livius: "But it was you Caesar who brought me into your family . . . Commodus and I are . . . like brothers."

Shot 17 (21:43): Medium close-up of Marcus Aurelius and Drucilla. He responds: "I love Commodus too, but . . . that's just a feeling." He turns to Drucilla and clasps her right hand with his left, "just a personal feeling." Voice-off of a messenger: "My Lord Caesar . . . "

When the "feeling" becomes "just a personal feeling," the issue of *perception* comes forward. When the Emperor avows that his affection is a perception—something that can be faulty or suspect—the very "family" is called into question. And thus the voice-off signals an impending complication of the family romance:

Shot 18 (21:47): Medium shot taken from behind Drucilla and Marcus as, in the middle ground, Livius turns right to acknowledge the arrival of a messenger adjacent to the blind man (now connoted to be a stool pigeon). The messenger (whose voice resembles that of a radio broadcaster): "Prince Commodus sends you his greetings. He is in the snow country, two days' journey from here." Livius, turning to face Marcus and Drucilla: "Perhaps I should go to meet Commodus." Marcus, moving forward: "Yes, Livius, go to meet Commodus. And think about what I have said, but remember [as he puts his right hand on Livius's left arm, Drucilla is shown looking at the two men] that my *time is short*."

Shot 19 (21:53): Medium close-up of Drucilla who registers the scene. Heraldic music intones.

Shot 20 (22:17): Cut to plan of Shot 18 to register Livius leaving before a dissolve into the scene, outdoors, of the tower of the castle of the former sequence, now set against the gray sky before the camera pans and tracks down to register a chariot charging through a portal to the castle.

153

The succession of Shots 10 and 11 (as numbered here) elegantly betrays the tension of the epic. "Time is short," the Emperor utters as he moves from the realm of pathos and "family" (he has gazed upon his stunningly beautiful daughter) to that of the future of the Empire. As he begins, "And there is a decision that has to be made," Marcus Aurelius pivots so as to have *decision* uttered paradoxically, both voice-in (because he is in frame) and voice-off (because we see him from behind as he faces the map) (see Figure 7.3).

The utterance, in what Christian Metz would have called the "mobile geography of the film" can be inferred to come both from the map and the Emperor.[12] Time is short because it is represented in graphic terms, in a history in which different epochs and places inform the *forma* or map itself. Yet the composition is designed to mesh with the Emperor's words that, because they float in the space of the frame, can refer both to his bodily condition and to the substance and the graphic representation of the map itself. In the narrative, Marcus Aurelius's Shakespearian turn, "soon this trickle of blood and these few bones, this net woven of nerves and arteries will be dust," can refer not only to the dying emperor but also to the history to be recounted in the film. But it is tied to the patchwork map, made of what appears to be nine pieces of parchment sewn together that hang from a wall. In the dissection that the film is implied to be making of history the Roman Empire is inferred also to be a "net woven of nerves and arteries" that will go the way of all flesh. The Emperor's body is conflated with those that comprise both the map and the lands it represents.

The allegorical force of the map overtakes its appearance. In the middle and lower-right panel, the representation of the Italian peninsula resembles *Italia* of Ptolemy (ad 145, a topographical map made known early in the

Figure 7.3

Marcus Aurelius, pondering the future heir of the Empire, having looked at his map.

fifteenth century) while the vast expanse of land stretches from the northern tip of the Adriatic to the west is riddled with orthogonal lines depicting roads, indeed what Roman maps had made famous. The vellum surface seems to recall the tradition of the medieval portolan chart, indicating that the creation is at once a hodge-podge and an elegant fantasy drawn to correspond with the Emperor's frail "net woven of nerves and arteries."[13]

voice-over: end

The film leads to its promised end in the Forum, where crowds take part in a great public spectacle. At the center, dozens of the monstrous emperor's captives are burned at the stake in a pyre over which Commodus had set his eyes prior to meeting his own demise in gladiatorial combat with Livius. Livius retrieves Drucilla before she is engulfed in flames. In a long tracking shot, the couple flees as if from an infernal garden of grisly delights. Refusing the emperor's crown, the hero tells the senators in his midst that were he the leader he would *crucify* them for their criminal deeds. The couple hastens away after a subaltern buys the Empire. The camera pulls back to set the pyre in view of a gigantic sculpted hand (out of which Commodus had just emerged) and to bring a sense of perspective to the events. The voice-over with which the film had begun intervenes for a second and final time, in ostensive quotation of Will Durant. "This . . . was the beginning of the fall of the Roman Empire. . . . A great civilization is not conquered from without until it has destroyed itself [the camera pans upward and outward to the sky] from within." The grandiose music accompanies the oily smoke from the pyre that billows heavenward as the shot fades to black and into an end-credit, in grisaille, where "the end" is set between a falling column to the left and to the right, a destroyed monument above a recumbent and tortured body. The fall is written into "the end" (see Figure 7.4)

Yet the end-credit that "falls" in place where fate destines it to be is conjoined with the front-credits, the title itself, perhaps the most telling single image in the entire film. At the outset we read in three tiers, in upper-case, the fall of the Roman Empire that floats (because of the slight shadow the letters cast to the right) over a background that could be at once a decrepit wall displaying flaking whitewash, a map of an empire that bears vague resemblance to the Mediterranean basin, a cave-painting recalling the stone surfaces of Altamira or Lascaux, or even a petroglyph much like the great stone carving of Bedolina over the Oglio river in northern Italy (see Figure 7.5).[14]

Below the title are the outlines of three human forms: a man in profile displaying a muscular torso and a right arm pointing to the left, the silhouette of a woman who looks in the same direction, and a full view of a

Figure 7.4
The end of ends.

woman whose body is in a slightly cruciform pose. To the right is a perched bird that clearly recalls the hunting scene in Lascaux, and below it is a monogram reminiscent of designs elsewhere in the cave. The same can be said for a horse and an elk or a bovine (drawn in the twisted perspective of Cro-Magnon art) to the left, that on the apparent palimpsest is below the frontal view of a Roman face that sports a blackened left eye. Crucial to the depiction of the title is, to the left of the Roman Empire, a graffito in upper-case roman that seems—but only seems, because it resembles the writing in our dreams that we see but cannot register—to spell "pax romana," an inscription over which is slashed a glaringly broad white line. To its right, on the other side of the credit, is drawn something like "vox poivu" that

Figure 7.5
The opening credit.

could also be—for the patient paleographer—another version of "vox romana." The mix of graffiti images and shards of Latin script clearly recall the contemporary paintings of Cy Twombly, whose immense canvases stage the drama of the writing and erasure of Roman civilization. Like the credit card in view, the paintings show, as one reader has noted, that "the essence of an object has some relation with its waste: not forcibly what remains after it has been used, but what is *tossed* out of use."[15] The title that stands over this elegant detritus of images and writing indicates that the film concerns not just Rome but the entire history of the Western world. The empire stands over the remainders of preceding civilizations that reach back to human origins. The allegory of the feature that leads to the "end" bears on the entire world.

What leads up to the end-credit is then taken to be a brief (but inexorably long) drama of three hours, felt to be at once a wisp of time but also a trophy or a "turning point" in history, a history, however, built over a patently Oedipal structure. In the last moments, the narrative reveals that in an illegitimate union a soldier had sired Commodus, who, upon learning of the identity of his real father, in a mad rage suddenly stabs his elder to death. A Freudian *deus ex machina* is required to finish what a realistic portrayal of time could never achieve.[16] The voice-over assigns a terminus to the narrative while the camera affords a dubious promise of ascension and apotheosis as it seeks to "transcend" what has just been related in the course of 182 minutes. With the gamut of incest, blackmail, torture, random murder, and intolerable crime, the viewer wonders if the words about intestinal strife are enough to summarize the epic and to project it into the greater history. Are words in deficit in respect to what they conclude? For reason of allegory the answer is probably affirmative. The words offer closure that "ends" only insofar as viewers can *work with* the allegorical structure of the film.

In 1964, the unvarnished evil that the film put on display could not go without reference to the Holocaust and to the military regime of Germany's Third Reich. Mann's epic begs the spectator to remember what the current political regime and decorum did not allow to put forward in any direct way. *The Fall* comes at the moment, the spectator also recalls, of the dubious rise of what Dwight Eisenhower had called the American "military-industrial complex." It coincided with the beginning of the war in Vietnam. The fall of the Roman Empire could not then—as now, when it is replayed to audiences willing to live through it—go without reference to what would soon cause turmoil and dissent in the USA. Where the dying Emperor's advocacy of diplomacy with the northern tribes gave way to getting and spending (that might be called "deregulation"), the film was, like a good allegory, addressing the moment of its creation. And where the film took to task the ways that media—what it shows to be the Roman entertainment industry, a summation of peplum effects that run from

Ben-Hur to the array of epics in CinemaScope—it makes clear how its material can be recycled with strong symbolic effect. Since allegory is a machinery that adapts itself to different times and places, the film can be said to apply to the economic and military policies that have spawned the crises in which we find ourselves today. The fantasized history that the film tells indeed reveals how epic and allegory not only "work" together but, in their best usage, also apply to very different moments. Some of the effects are salient where the ambient history of the years in which the feature was made are woven into the film; others, from other epochs past and future, can be drawn through its structure, if indeed structure is understood here as that which frames the tensions and contradictions of real social facts. By way of conclusion we can say that the art of working through and with an epic film, thanks to *The Fall of the Roman Empire,* is cued upon what we make of it in consort with the resilient force of allegory.

notes

1. The definition of reference is found under *perlaboration* in Jean Laplanche and Jean-Baptiste Pontalis, *Vocabulaire de la psychanalyse* (Paris: Presses Universitaire de France, 1967), pp. 305–306, in which the verb *durcharbeiten* finds its adequate English translation in "working-through." The authors note that in an article of 1914 Freud defines the concept as one that bears on resistances, follows the interpretation of a resistance in such a way that "a period of relative stagnation can recover this eminently positive labor in which Freud sees the principal factor of the effectiveness of therapy" (Laplanche and Pontalis, *Vocabulaire de la psychanalyse,* p. 305). Through repeated effort the analysand can "move from refusal or purely intellectual acceptance of repressed drives that 'nourish resistance' to a conviction based on the lived experience of them" (Laplanche and Pontalis, *Vocabulaire de la psychanalyse,* p. 305).
2. In "Le Divan du pauvre," Guattari distinguishes "working through" from "acting out" when he notes that most cinema, like psychoanalysis, is a drug that "normalizes" both spectators and patients. In the worst conditions of production, nonetheless, "good films can be produced, films that modify the workings of desire, that break stereotypes, that open the future," just as good analytic sessions can lead to "good discoveries." Félix Guattari, "Le Divan du pauvre," *Communications,* 23 (1975): 96–103; p. 103. At the same time—and it is the aim of the paragraphs above—we can say that what we "do with" a film when we "work through" it in terms that are ours, by allegorical means, we can reach similar results.
3. In this respect, a decisive work is Marc Augé, *Casablanca* (Paris: Seuil, 2007), a short account of the author's relation to the Exodus and Occupation of 1940 recalled *through* childhood memories that mix with those that Michael Curtiz's eponymous film of 1942 (appearing in France in 1947) had engendered.
4. Surely Jean-Luc Godard's *Histoire(s) du cinéma* "works through" cinema of the past in order to show how certain films obsess the author at the same time their contradictions and inner and often unknown relations with one another draw the broad lines of a history that can be charted through shards and fragments of words and images. His history is in fact an *epic* insofar as it reaches the origins of film and repeatedly goes back and over again to the same bits and pieces as it moves forward in its serial form.

5. "Would-be distinguished epic with an intellectual first hour; unfortunately the hero is a priggish bore, the villain a crashing bore, the heroine a saintly bore, and the only interesting character is killed off early. A chariot race, a javelin duel, some military clashes and a mass burning at the stake keep one watching and the production values are high indeed," Leslie Halliwell, *Halliwell's Film and Video Guide* (New York: HarperCollins 2001), p. 271.

6. Which Robert Burgoyne studies tersely in a *lecture de regard* with *Spartacus* in Robert Burgoyne, *The Hollywood Historical Film* (Malden, Mass.: Blackwell, 2008), pp. 74–99.

7. These words are in allegiance with Michel de Certeau's notion of "The Historiographical Operation" in Michel de Certeau, *The Writing of History,* trans. Tom Conley (New York: Columbia University Press, 1992), pp. 56–113, especially p. 102.

8. Edward Gibbon's *The History of the Decline and Fall of the Roman Empire*'s work (London: W. Strahan & T. Cadell, 1781) includes a frontispiece portrait and two folded maps by Thomas Kitchin. These cartographic "diagrams" that accompany the text form a crucial part of its composition. As it will be observed above, they bear strongly, too, on the epic film.

9. It is worth recalling that the third volume of the 1781 edition of Gibbon includes a map of the "western part of the empire" (by Thomas Kitchin, "hydrographer to His Majesty") that facilitates the reading of the years ad 379–582, which in the Table of Contents are set in columns in accord with the pages. The graphic design offers a stenography and reference tool to locate details within the immensity of the project: front matter (four folios) to *The History of the Decline and Fall of the Roman Empire,* Vol. III.

10. Adepts of the *auteur* Mann would quickly see how the sweeping panoramic and tracking shots, like that of the beginning of the film, are of a measure with the westerns; or even that the film begins as something of a "border incident" which recalls Mann's penchant to mesh psychic and geographical limits and frontiers.

11. What follows supplements, in the mode of a *lecture de regard,* a study of the map sequence of *Gladiator,* clearly based on Mann's film, in this author's *Cartographic Cinema* (Minneapolis, Minn.: University of Minnesota Press, 2007), pp. 195–198. Time and space (and perhaps, allegory) prohibit study of the mosaic-map later seen in *The Fall of the Roman Empire.*

12. Christian Metz, *L'énonciation impersonnelle ou le site du film* (Paris: Meridiens/ Klincksieck, 1991), p. 20. Metz discovers a "metafilmic doubling" inhering in cinema where the play of speech *off* and *in* "invites us to broaden our idea of enunciation."

13. Hodge-podge is not to be taken pejoratively. In confusing various cartographic modes and strata of time the map gains allegorical power merely because it does not belong to a single historical moment. The types of Roman maps and their functions are taken up in O. A. W. Dilke, "Itineraries and Geographical Maps in the Early and Late Roman Empires," in J. B. Harley and David Woodward (eds), *The History of Cartography,* Vol. I: *Prehistoric, Ancient, and Medieval Europe and the Mediterranean* (Chicago, Ill.: University of Chicago Press, 1987), pp. 234–257—along with O. A. W. Dilke's *Greek and Roman Maps* (London: Thames & Hudson, 1985).

14. Christian Jacob calls it "the first map" in Christian Jacob, *The Sovereign Map: Theoretical Approaches in Cartography throughout History* (Chicago, Ill.: University of Chicago Press, 2006), pp. 21–27.

15. Roland Barthes, "Cy Twombly ou *Non multa sed multum*," in Roland Barthes, *L'Obvie et l'obtus: Essais critiques III* (Paris: éditions du Seuil, 1982), p. 146.
16. It is a Freudian *deus ex machina* in the sense that the father of psychoanalysis could never bring an end to the interminable process of transference and its opposite. Already in the Dora case he uses the very formula to finish what he would rather not conclude. Sigmund Freud, *The Standard Edition of the Complete Psychological Works of Sigmund Freud*, Vol. VII: *1901–1905*, ed. James Strachey (London: The Hogarth Press, 1953), p. 114.

"an italianmade spectacle film dubbed in english"

cultural distinctions, national cinema,

and the critical reception of the

postwar historical epic

m a r k   j a n c o v i c h

In *Solomon and Sheba* (1959), Solomon is a wise king who maintains unity among the twelve tribes of Israel. However, in a bid to fragment this alliance between the tribes, and so conquer and enslave the Israelites, the Pharaoh of Egypt makes a pact with the Queen of Sheba, who plans to seduce Solomon and so alienate him from his people's affection. Although she succeeds in her mission, Sheba falls in love with Solomon and is converted to his faith. Furthermore, as she prays for Solomon's God to protect him, Solomon finds a way to reunite the tribes and defeat the Pharaoh's army. However, Sheba still represents a foreign presence in Israel, and, although she bears Solomon's only child, she does not remain in Israel to become its queen. Instead, she willingly returns to Sheba and promises that on her return her people will learn to worship Solomon's God and that she will raise Solomon's son to be Sheba's ruler—Sheba's matriarchal throne will become a patriarchal one. Not only does the film explicitly concern contamination in which a range of distinctions are threatened but the figure who represents the threat of contamination is a woman and, more specifically, an Italian sex symbol, Gina Lollobridgida: "the original

Italian overstuffed star."[1] Filmed on location in Spain and featuring an international cast, this biblical epic presents its "foreign" materials both as marketable spectacle and as problems that need to be managed and contained.

Nor were these problems simply managed by the films themselves. The critical reception of historical epics during the 1950s and 1960s also reveals a series of anxieties about cultural distinction and their erosion. As I have argued elsewhere, Dwight Macdonald developed an extensive polemic against the historical epic, in which he took issue with what he saw as its explicit overstatement, an objection that was rooted in his critique of middlebrow culture.[2] For Macdonald, the historical epic was a problem precisely because of its aspiration to cultural authority. Its use of historical materials, and of legitimate literature, theatre, and visual arts, blurred the line between high and low culture. He therefore attacked *The Greatest Story Ever Told* (1965) as "the full middlebrow, or Hallmark Hall of Fame treatment."[3]

Nor was this position unique to MacDonald. Although the *New York Times* reviewers did not universally condemn the historical epics of the period, they also demonstrated an anxiety with the middlebrow status of these films. While some films were definitely praised, either for transcending the type or for never making any pretence to quality, the *New York Times* reviewers saw many of these films as problems on the grounds that they combined supposedly incompatible materials and so blurred cultural boundaries. Furthermore, these arguments were not only mobilized in relation to distinctions between materials from different positions within cultural hierarchies but also materials from different national cultures. While certain aspects of European culture were held up as the epitome of quality to which American cinema was meant to aspire, other examples were seen as potentially corrupt and corrupting. For example, as Eric Schaefer has pointed out, since at least the 1930s, the Hollywood film industry had both promoted itself and fought competition from abroad through an explicit distinction between "clean" American films and "filthy" foreign ones.[4]

As a result, while the cycle started out in an attempt to emulate British historical films, and particularly Olivier's *Henry V* (1944), and while many of the early historical films were originally judged according to this standard, the *New York Times* critics began to display serious concerns about the historical epics by the late 1950s and early 1960s, a period in which the historical epics were not only becoming bigger and more spectacular but in which Europe was becoming more than simply a source of locations and talent. In other words, by the late 1950s, figures such as Samuel Bronston in Spain and Dino De Laurentiis in Italy were producing huge historical epics that actively sought to compete with Hollywood, while a range of smaller European productions began to inundate the American market, films such as *Hercules* (1958), which became a major hit despite its low budget and lowbrow status.

The following chapter will explore the critical reception of historical epics in the *New York Times* and the ways in which anxieties over their middlebrow status were also related to anxieties over their blurring of distinctions between different national cinemas. The first section will concentrate on the ways in which the *New York Times* reviewers demonstrated anxieties about the blurring of distinctions between supposedly incompatible materials and accused many of these films of cheapening the cultural materials on which they drew, or of simply being pretentious films that sought to pass off lowbrow materials as highbrow ones. Many historical epics were identified as heterogeneous products, and it is here that questions of national cinema play a particularly central role. The second section focuses on the ways in which the international nature of many productions was dealt with by the *New York Times* reviewers, particularly in relation to the historical epics associated with Dino De Laurentiis. While many Hollywood productions had been praised for their use of foreign locations and talent, many Italianmade epic films were accused of being inauthentic films due to the ways in which they drew on talent from different national contexts and were designed for an international audience. In the process, these films were also accused of blurring distinctions between different types of Italian cinema. The final section moves on to look at the ways in which critics responded to the low-budget Italian historical epics on the one hand and the Italian arthouse historical epics (and antiepics) on the other. The chapter will therefore demonstrate the ways in which these reviews both promoted and defended Hollywood. While Hollywood had long been an international cinema, other national cinemas were accused of inauthenticity if they challenged its status by drawing on international talent and explicitly targeting international audiences.

"a staggering combination": heterogeneity, incompatibility and the problem of the historical epic

For Macdonald, the problem with the historical epics was their supposed lack of action, which made a film such as *Ben-Hur* (1959) "bloody boring": "Watching it is like waiting at a railroad crossing while an interminable freight train lumbers past, often stopping completely for a while."[5] However, for Bosley Crowther, the leading film critic at the *New York Times*, the problem was very different, and he often objected that there was simply *too much* going on in many of the historical epics and that these elements were not properly integrated. For example, writing on *Joan of Arc* in 1948, he objected that while the filmmakers have "fashioned a stupendous film,"

> somehow, the huge combination of pageantry, legend
> and pathos—of spectacle, color, court intrigues and the

historic ordeal of a girl—while honestly intended, fails to come fully to life . . . and the main reason for this is that the real human values have been lost—or curiously dimmed—in the paramount and prolonged illumination of spectacle.[6]

In other words, the film fails to bring its disparate elements together and to make them meaningful in relation to "the real human values" that, it was argued, should have been the organizing principle of the film. Similarly, the review of *Quo Vadis* (1951) refers to the film as "a staggering combination of cinema brilliance and sheer banality, of visual excitement and verbal boredom, of historical pretentiousness and sex."[7] Again, it is maintained that the problem with the film is that it combines materials that fail to integrate and, it is suggested, should probably not be combined in the first place.

If the incompatibility of these materials is only suggested in the case of *Quo Vadis,* it is fully explicit by the time of *Knights of the Round Table* (1953), which is supposed to have replaced the "poetic eloquence and grandeur of those distinctly literary works" such as "Tennyson's 'Idylls of the King' or Mallory's 'Morte d'Arthur'" with "a sweep of dramatic action and romantic symbols which is straight Hollywood."[8] Furthermore, the film's use of CinemaScope is identified as its major problem, and the whole project is dismissed as a major violation of its literary sources. Similarly, *Helen of Troy* (1956) was claimed to have replaced the "poetic qualities" of *The Iliad* with "CinemaScope, Warner-Colored," a trade that, like *Knights of the Round Table,* was claimed to have replaced poetic literature with cinematic spectacle on the one hand and with hackneyed Hollywood conventions on the other.

Helen of Troy is therefore described as having succeeded in "reducing the 'Iliad' to slang," while *Knights of the Round Table* goes one better:

Even though all the outdoor action was shot in England and Ireland on the rolling downs and against craggy cliffs and ruins that ideally bespeak the Arthurian age, the dramatic concept and performance is on the level of "Sir Lancelot went thataway." One waits to hear instanta-neously shouted the command, "The rest of you knights, follow me!"[9]

In this way, these reviews do not simply take issue with the visual spectacle but also with the quality of the dialogue, which is seen as inappropriate to the literary sources. As has been pointed out elsewhere, many later films featuring spectacular bodies would be dismissed as "dumb films for dumb people," with stars such as Stallone and Schwarzenegger being derided for their lack of verbal skills, but even in the early 1950s many of the historical epics were accused of featuring an embarrassing contemporary idiom or for using an even more embarrassing pastiche of "olde English."[10] Nor was the *New York Times* the only paper to respond in this way: *Time* magazine even presented its entire review of *The Black Knight* as though it were written by its "Camelot correspondent" and began the review as follows: "Thynngs are tuffe here, ywis. Thre times in this dretched yere hath this our Fayr Demesne been sore aforbled of the hungrie bande that Slounketh out of the Woode called Holly."[11]

Nor was it simply the visuals or language that were seen as incompatible with the historical and literary sources on which many of these films drew. Many reviews implied that these films were little more than lowbrow efforts pretentiously disguised through the use of highbrow materials. For example, *King Richard and the Crusaders* (1954) was described as featuring a "Wild West finale," which had nothing to do with Sir Walter Scott, who wrote *The Talisman,* the novel on which the film was based: "Believers, infidel and poor Sir Walter Scott are all ridden over roughshod."[12] Nor are these references to the "Wild West finale" meant to conjure memories of a classic period of the western but rather to associate the film with the lowbrow elements of Hollywood cinema. *The Vikings* (1958) is similarly dismissed as a "Norse Opera," while *The Conqueror* (1956), which featured John Wayne as Genghis Khan, was described as an "Oriental 'Western'" in which "an illusion persists that this Genghis Khan is merely Hopalong Cassidy in Cathay."[13] Alan Ladd also finds himself the butt of a *New York Times* reviewer, who writes of his supposedly medieval adventure, *The Black Knight:* "What if the armoured nobles, stalwart hero, beauteous heroine and scheming villains behave as though they were Hopalong Cassidy, wronged ranchers and a passel of rustlers?"[14] Moreover, what distinction the film does achieve from the Hollywood westerns is not necessarily positive:

> Credit the producers with some truly imaginative touches. There is one lively scene depicting our hero dispersing the Saracens, who have captured some monks and our Lady Linet for sacrifice by pagans at Stonehenge. One wonders how Saracens happened to be in England when ritual sacrifices were being made at Stonehenge, or at Camelot, for that matter. It's a safe bet you won't find *that* in any Western.[15]

Nor is the western the only lowbrow material associated with the film, and the reviewer further ridicules the film with the claim: "King Arthur and his court occasionally . . . speak lines reminiscent of comic strips."[16]

Of course, Twentieth Century Fox's *Prince Valiant* (1954) was actually based on a comic, "Harold R. Foster's 'Prince Valiant' cartoon," and it is described as a "wide-screen conglomeration of Douglas Fairbanks and horse-opera derring-do."[17] The film is therefore multiply damned. Not only is it based on a cartoon, and "whipped up . . . in precisely the spirit and the aspect of the comic book original," but it also simply gathers together a series of unrelated materials such as the supposedly old-fashioned swash-bucklers for which Fairbanks had been famous in the 1910s and the 1920s and yet more lowbrow westerns.[18] Its use of Arthurian materials is seen as not only incompatible with these other elements but even as profoundly illegitimate.

The complaint here was less about comic books and westerns and more about pretension. For the *New York Times* reviewers, the problem was not with the lowbrow materials but with the attempt to disguise them as something else. Again, then, their concern was with films that blurred the line between legitimate culture and the lowbrow, and lowbrow films were not a problem so long as they knew their place. Consequently, if there is a hint of affectionate indulgence in the review of Alan Ladd in *The Black Knight*, the review of *The Black Shield of Falsworth* (1954) makes the point overtly. If one takes "it for comic-book romance," the "kiddies should find it fascinating" and even the "adult escorts should get a few guffaws."[19] It is therefore "hard to be vexed with this nonsense. It is so utterly innocent of guile or any sort of historical significance or dramatic artistry . . . it is simple acrobatics played in elaborate costumes."[20] It may be claimed that "the dramas of Warner's King Richard, M-G-M's Arthurian court and even Twentieth Century-Fox', Prince Valiant are made to seem, in retrospect, like works of art" when placed in comparison with this film, but it is precisely *The Black Shield of Falworth*'s lack of ambition that is its virtue: "If Twentieth Century-Fox or anybody thinks they're going to keep ahead of Universal when it comes to reducing the knighthood business to comic book terms, they have another think coming."[21]

"more like hollywood than hollywood itself": national cinemas, international ambitions and the threat to hollywood

If *The Black Shield of Falsworth* is purely lowbrow and has no pretensions to anything else, the problem with other films was their impurity. However, such impurity was not only a matter of the mixing of materials from high and low culture but was also related to issues of national cinema and the ways in which many of the historical epics were the products of interna-tional collaboration. For example, *Sodom and Gomorrah* (1962) was described as a "ridiculously gross and stilted picture," and as a "feeble imitation of 'The Ten Commandments,'" and one that was associated with the lowbrow "burlesque" through its heterogeneous mixing of incompatible elements: "This is one of those mammoth costume splurges, in color and wide screen, that has no more truth or drama in it than a burlesque show dressed in union suits."[22] Nonetheless, the hybrid character of *Sodom and Gomorrah* was not only a feature of its borrowings from DeMille or its various spectacular displays, for it is described as having been "made in Italy under the direction of Robert Aldrich, with Stewart Granger and Pier Angeli in leading roles."[23] In other words, it was produced in Italy with an American director and featured both British and Italian stars. Of course, Crowther's objection was not to its foreignness per se. As we have seen, many films were criticized for their Hollywood clichés, while the *New York Times* reviewers often championed British historical films, particularly Olivier's *Henry V,* as exemplars of quality, films that were used as the standard in relation to which other historical films were often judged. For example, *Ivanhoe* (1952) is praised for having "brought to the screen almost as fine a panorama of medievalism as Lawrence Olivier gave us in 'Henry V'."[24] Even as late as 1960, Crowther was claiming that the visual achievement of *Spartacus* (1960) was such that it "matches the Battle of Agincourt in 'Henry V.'"[25]

Nor was it seen as a problem if American films were shot overseas. On the contrary, the use of foreign locations and facilities were often seen as a positive. *Knights of the Round Table* was therefore praised for its "outdoor action [which] was shot in England and Ireland on the rolling downs and against craggy cliffs and ruins," and it is claimed that these locations "ideally bespeak the Arthurian age."[26] Similarly, *Alexander the Great* (1956) was filmed "on the plains and rocky slopes of Spain," a factor that is seen as having contributed to the film's "truly mammoth scenes."[27] The *New York Times* therefore presented the use of foreign locations as one of the major attractions on offer in many historical films so that the claim that *Helen of Troy* was "made-in-Italy" was listed alongside its use of "CinemaScope" and "Warner-Color" as one of the key reasons for seeing the film.[28] As the hyphenation of "made-in-Italy" suggests, Italy was not simply a location but a brand, and the Italians were seen as having both the locations and the production facilities necessary for the making of epic films.

While foreign locations and facilities were seen as valuable, they were not seen as sufficient in themselves, and, by the late 1950s and early 1960s, as filmmakers in Spain and Italy began to compete with Hollywood, the reviews of these historical epics became increasingly negative. For example, it is claimed of *Barabbas* (1961) that "producer, Dino De Laurentiis, who made this film in Italy, has spared no expense to match it, shock for shock, with 'Spartacus' and 'Ben-Hur,'" a position that not only implies that the film is imitative rather than original, but also that De Laurentiis has become distracted from the "personal drama [which] is lacking."[29]

If the *New York Times* reviewers repeatedly attacked De Laurentiis's historical epics, their objection was not simply to their scale but rather to their ambitions. Early in 1962, *Time* had reported on De Laurentiis's "new $11 million studio, located on a 750-acre site 13 miles south of Rome," a studio that demonstrated that "one of Italy's most vital export industries is its booming movie business, and that the biggest thing in Italy's movies is Dino De Laurentiis."[30] Furthermore, De Laurentiis is explicitly presented as a threat to Hollywood, a figure who is "pampered by the government with tax concessions and subsidies," and who was "preparing for the motion picture that will make Ben-Hur seem like a minor travelogue, the ultimate, unstoppable, millennial religious epic—a $30 million, twelve-hour adaptation of The Bible."[31] For this project, it was reported that he would require a "dozen directors" and that he was not content to simply rely on mainstream Hollywood talent but was also considering a number of arthouse directors: "De Laurentiis thinks Frederico Fellini (La Dolca Vita) might get things off to a rousing start with the Creation. He is saving Ingmar Bergman for the Apocalypse."[32] In short, De Laurentiis is seen as a major threat to Hollywood who was not only drawing divergent elements of cinema into his orbit but was also responsible for a situation in which "the Italian cinema—which in its first postwar years could barely afford a Shoeshine— now looks more like Hollywood than Hollywood itself."[33]

De Laurentiis's films were therefore accused of not only being big-budget productions with cultural pretensions but also of being an ugly amalgamation of elements from different national contexts. For example, his culturally ambitious film version of War and Peace was attacked for its "international group of producers, writers, actors, director and camera men" who were presented as another melding of incompatible materials.[34] Indeed, the word "international" sounds increasingly negative as the review progresses, particularly when one of the main complaints is that "out of these many characters, who speak in accents that range from the American drawl of Mr. Fonda to the Scottish burr of the Russian peasant, John Mills, there is realized little feeling of the national crisis and human torment of 'War and Peace.'"[35] The film's international talent prevent it from cohering and results in a production that is "ponderous . . . oddly mechanical and emotionally sterile."[36]

If this review deflects matters onto the film's international talent, the review of Attila (1954) two years later directly targeted the film's "Italian film-makers" whose "period adventure descended upon the city Saturday with 'saturation' booking at more than 100 theatres," and "clinches the fact that the formidable Italian producing combine of Lux-Ponti-DeLaurentiis has mastered the art of crowding 'thousands' of fur-clad extras in a scene that wasn't intended to mean anything in the first place."[37] Certainly the film is accused of being "an extensive rewriting of the encyclopedias," in which "the sack of Rome didn't take place" and Attila "turns his back on war in an apparent fit of religious conversion" when "confronted by an army of white-clad pilgrims at the Tiber."[38] However, its real crime is supposed to be that it is no more than a boring exercise in spectacle for spectacle's sake and that it is therefore ultimately meaningless.

In this way, Italian historical epics were increasingly presented as phony imitations of Hollywood that could only be inferior to the original. Furthermore, while the New York Times critics often praised the ways in which Hollywood cinema drew on international talent, Italian uses of international materials were presented as further evidence of its lack of authenticity—if Italian cinema was an imitation of Hollywood and therefore inferior, its attempt to imitate Hollywood was also presented as a failure to engage with its own national culture and hence to be inauthentically Italian.

This process may become clearer if we turn to contemporary debates over cosmopolitanism. According to Hannerz, the cosmopolite is one who is not defined by place but through travel as they search for new experiences, experiences that can often be converted into capital that can be traded.[39] For example, cosmopolites often present themselves as experts who mediate the strange to others. In this way, the cosmopolite "stages an 'authentic' engagement" with the cultures that they encounter through travel, an engagement that relies on an "antinomy between cosmopolitans (mobile) and locals (fixed)."[40] To put it another way: "One person's cosmopolitanism depends on the constitution of some else as local."[41] Furthermore, in their analysis of his television show, *Jamie's Great Escape,* Bell and Hollows explore the ways in which celebrity chef Jamie Oliver is positioned as a cosmopolite who legislates on the locals that he encounters on a tour of Italy, condemning some as "too fixed, too local, too traditional" and insufficiently open to new experiences, and others as not local enough.[42] For example, they note that:

> his attempts to fix Italy in a premodern or "less modern" state repeatedly come unstuck: A trip to discover the great gastronomic traditions of the Italian monastery is undermined when he discovers the monks living on a diet of badly cooked, unhealthy, processed foods. At this point, Jamie has to sell mythologies of Italian food back to the monks to restore his vision of Italianicity and to keep the Italians in place.[43]

As we can see, then, the figure of the cosmopolite depends upon that of the local, and the authority of the former is also dependent on its mythologization of the latter.

Moreover, if the cosmopolite ranges over space, appropriates from local cultures and then markets that which has been appropriated as exotic experiences for consumers across the globe, he also works hard to police the local cultures from which he appropriates. The local must stay in its place, if the cosmopolite is to operate as the mediator between the local and the global. In a similar way, the Hollywood film industry has long presented itself as a world cinema which is able to appropriate resources from across the globe and to market them to an international audience, but it has therefore also required that other cinema industries must remain in place and conform to specific mythologized images of national cinemas. They must remain authentically local or be castigated as inauthentic.

As a result, it was only by the late 1960s, once the threat of De Laurentiis was no longer an issue, that the *New York Times* reviewers became more sympathetic. Thus, while *The Bible* (1966) hardly receives a favorable review, it is not seen as representative of some larger problem but only as a film that fails to achieve its goal. By this point, De Laurentiis had seriously limited his ambition for the project, and the review complained that, rather than the twelve-hour epic involving a dozen directors, which De Laurentiis had promoted in the early 1960s, the film's covers "only the first half of the Book of Genesis."[44] In addition,

> The next surprise and disappointment is this: For all its size, for all its extravagant production, its extraordinary special effects, its stunning projection on the wide screen (D-150) and its almost three-hour length, 'The Bible' is lacking any sense of conviction of God in so much magnitude or a galvanizing feeling of connection in the stories from Genesis.[45]

It is conceded that there is some glimpse of what is missing—if "only faintly"—in "the way Mr. Huston plays Noah" and "something warm and mysterious" in "the brief dialogic scene in which Abraham is visited by the Three Angels, all played symbolically by Peter O'Toole," but the film is generally dismissed on the grounds that it "does not employ the cinema medium to create a true 20th-century iconography" and "relies on literal enactments and the sheer sonority of holy writ."[46] The film is therefore criticized, but, by this point, it was clear that De Laurentiis was no threat to Hollywood and that his ambitions had already been checked, even if his historical epics still displayed the old pretensions.

pretension, exploitation, and the art cinema

Of course, these concerns with the blurring of distinctions between different national cinemas were also related back to questions of cultural hierarchies. As a result, the problem with De Laurentiis's historical epics was largely associated with the ways in which they also threatened distinctions between different types of Italian cinema. As the *Time* article made clear, his grandiose filmmaking was a world away from Italy's "first postwar years [when it] could barely afford a Shoeshine" but when it had also managed to achieve international recognition with the neo-realist films of Rossellini, De Sica and others.[47] On the other hand, it looked very different from another type of low-budget Italian filmmaking with which American viewers were also familiar. If *Barabbas* was a big-budget production, with a prestigious screenwriter, playwright Christopher Fry, and a respected director, Richard Fleischer, it was clearly distinguished from films such as *Hercules*, low-budget Italian historical films that the *New York Times* rarely even bothered to review prior to the late 1950s but which had begun to acquire a new visibility toward the end of the decade. For example, in its review of *Hercules*, the *New York Times* reviewer even acknowledged that this "Italianmade spectacle film dubbed in English" was "the kind of picture that normally would draw little more than yawns in the film market."[48] However, the reviewer also maintained that the film was only receiving attention due to the actions of "promoter Joseph E. Levine," who had "launched the movie throughout the country with a deafening barrage of publicity" and had therefore given the film a prominence that it did not warrant.[49] As a result, not only did the review dismiss *Hercules* as an "exploitation film," but it even suggested that this phrase alone should speak for itself and that the business of actually reviewing the film was "hardly necessary."[50]

Similarly, *Colossus of Rhodes* (1961) was also seen as a fairly worthless example of the low-budget historical epic. In this case, the film was described as a "rip-roaring corn harvest," for which "Jesus Mateos, the art designer, and Francisco Assensio, art engineer, have constructed a very effective plastic giant for Rory Calhoun, the warrior hero, hordes of rebellious slaves and sadistic Rhodes royalty to clash in—complete with a fire-bearing tower and a labyrinth of torture chambers."[51] However, while this set inspires the comment, "What a place!" and while the effects are claimed to be "rather awesome," the reviewer's final judgment is that the film is "otherwise pretty terrible."[52] Again the problem is supposed to stem from its European origins, although in this case the film is an "Italian-Spanish co-production, with dubbed English, clubbed dialogue, and an absurd plot."[53] If many Italian historical epics were seen as poor imitations with no authentic relation to Italian national cinema, *Colossus of Rhodes* is condemned as an overt coproduction, a film that is implied to have an even more tenuous identity.

If De Laurentiis's films clearly aspired to greater respectability than either *Hercules* or *Colossus of Rhodes,* they were supposed to lack the artistic status of other historical films made in Italy. For example, while the *New York Times* objected to the presence of Burt Lancaster in *The Leopard* (1963) in terms that are very similar to those directed against *War and Peace*—"unfortunately Mr. Lancaster does have that blunt American voice that lacks the least suggestion of being Sicilian in the English-dialogue version shown here"—Visconti's film is seen as one of the finest examples of the historical epic.[54] The *New York Times* even drew a parallel with the preeminent historical epic in cinema history at the time: "I just wonder how much Americans will know or care about what's going on, how much we will yield to a nostalgia very similar to that in 'Gone with the Wind.'"[55] However, in its comparison between the two films, *The Leopard* is implied to be the superior film, and its outstanding feature is its "stunning visualization of a mood of melancholy and nostalgia at the passing of an age," a feature that is not simply one of surface style but central to its central theme and the dramatic interactions of its characters.[56]

However, it is Pasolini's *The Gospel According to St. Matthew* (1964) that was held up as the real masterpiece of the historical epic by the *New York Times* reviewers, precisely through its elision of epic spectacle. It was therefore noted that, while "we'd been hearing exciting information about an Italian film shown and honoured" at the Venice Film Festival, the film itself "turns out to be more exciting that even the first flash reports on it were and more rewarding in its surge of human drama and spiritual power than one had hoped it might be."[57] In this way, the film is explicitly discussed in terms of its "contrasts with the all-too-familiar type of Hollywood Biblical Film," and it is claimed to be "a strikingly unusual picturing the story of Jesus, done with a cast of nonprofessionals on locations in southern Italy and directed by a man who was an acknowledged Marxist and atheist."[58] In this version, Jesus "is no transcendent evangelist in shining white robes, performing his ministrations and miracles in awesome spectacles," and the story is "told in the simple naturalist terms of a plain, humble man of the people conducting a spiritual salvation campaign in an environment and among a population that are rough, unadorned and real."[59] It is therefore claimed that there is a "remarkable avoidance of clichés on Mr. Pasolini's part" that make for "a most uncommon film."[60]

Indeed, the article continually hints at a comparison with *The Greatest Story Ever Told*, which had been released the year earlier and was described by the *New York Times* as "the world's most conglomerate Biblical picture."[61] Again, the word "conglomerate" is hardly flattering but yet again implies the combination of supposedly incompatible materials: the story is told "against the vast topography of the American southwest" but also finds a way of "mingling the mystical countenance of Max von Sydow, the Swedish actor, with a sea of familiar faces of Hollywood stars."[62] As a result, the film features "things of supreme and solemn beauty" and "scenes in which the grandeur of nature is brilliantly used to suggest the surge of the human spirit in waves of exaltation and awe" but it also features "annoying excursions into large-screen theatricality" that "look extravagant and gross."[63] Moreover, if the film has elements that are "so drawn-out and repetitious that they become monotonous," the reviewer finds the "intrusions" of "frequent pop-ups of familiar faces" particularly "jarring," the most "shattering and distasteful" being the appearances of "Carroll Baker and John Wayne in the deeply solemn and generally fitting enactment of the scene of Jesus carrying the cross to Calvary."[64] The film's director, George Stevens, is not only condemned for "handling his familiar material hyperbolically" but also for providing "little simple realism in this massively scenic Passion play," precisely the qualities for which Pasolini's film is praised.[65]

conclusion

For the *New York Times* reviewers, then, the problem with De Laurentiis's historical epics was not only that they were placed somewhere between the supposedly authentic Italian art cinema on the one hand and the low-budget historical films on the other but also that they were supposedly caught between an authentic Italian cinema and Hollywood. They blurred the distinction not only between both high and low culture but also between supposedly different national cinemas. While Hollywood had long drawn on international talent and marketed itself to an international audience, Italian attempts to compete with it were derided as inauthentic. Not only does this reproduce a problematic notion of authentic national cinemas but it also works to promote and defend Hollywood from foreign competition in much the same way as the industry itself had been doing for many years. Hollywood could therefore operate as an international cinema that drew its personnel and inspiration from across the globe and targeted markets outside the USA, but other national cinemas were required to remain indigenous national cinemas from which elements could be borrowed but which should not have similar international ambitions.

notes

1. Bosley Crowther, "'Solomon and Sheba': Film by King Vidor Is Shown at Capitol Yul Brynner and Gina Lollobridgida Star," *New York Times,* December 26, 1959, p. 7.
2. Mark Jancovich, "Dwight Macdonald and the Historical Epic," in Yvonne Tasker (ed.), *Action and Adventure Cinema* (London: Routledge, 2004), p. 84–99.
3. Dwight Macdonald, *Dwight Macdonald on Movies* (Englewood Cliffs, NJ: Prentice-Hall, 1969), p. 431.
4. Eric Schaefer, *Bold! Daring! Shocking! True! A History of Exploitation Films, 1919–1959* (Durham, NC: Duke University Press, 1999), pp. 160–161.
5. Macdonald, *Dwight Macdonald on Movies,* p. 424.
6. Bosley Crowther, "Ingrid Bergman Plays Title Role in 'Joan of Arc' at Victoria," *New York Times,* November 12, 1948, p. 30.
7. Bosley Crowther, "The Screen: Two New Movies Shown Here: 'Darling, How Could You!' from Play by James M. Barrie, Stars Fontaine and Lund; 'Quo Vadis,' Based on Sienkiewicz Novel and Made in Rome at Two Theatres," *New York Times,* November 9, 1951, p. 22.
8. Bosley Crowther, "The Screen in Review: Music Hall Screen Resounds to 'Knights of the Round Table' in M-G-M CinemaScope," *New York Times,* January 8, 1954, p. 17.
9. Crowther, "Music Hall Screen Resounds," p. 17.
10. Yvonne Tasker, *Spectacular Bodies: Gender and Genre in the Action Movie* (London: Routledge, 1993).
11. Anon., "The New Pictures," *Time,* November 8, 1954, www.time.com.
12. H.H.T., "The Screen in Review: 'King Richard and the Crusaders Opens," *New York Times,* August 23, 1954, p. 20.
13. Bosley Crowther, "Norse Opera," *New York Times,* June 12, 1958, p. 35; A. H. Weiler, "Screen: 'The Conqueror': John Wayne Stars in Oriental 'Western,'" *New York Times,* March 31, 1956, p. 13.
14. A.W. "'The Black Knight' Wins His Spurs at the Globe," *New York Times,* October 29, 1954, p. 27.

15. A.W. "'The Black Knight' Wins His Spurs at the Globe," p. 27.

16. A.W. "'The Black Knight' Wins His Spurs at the Globe," p. 27.

17. Bosley Crowther, "The Screen in Review: 'Prince Valiant' Comes to the Roxy," *New York Times*, April 7, 1954, p. 40.

18. Crowther, "'Prince Valiant' Comes to the Roxy," p. 40.

19. Bosley Crowther, "The Screen in Review: Opening Here for 'Black Shield of Falsworth'," *New York Times*, October 7, 1954, p. 16.

20. Crowther, "Opening Here for 'Black Shield of Falsworth," p. 16.

21. Crowther, "Opening Here for 'Black Shield of Falsworth," p. 16.

22. Bosley Crowther, "Screen: '40 Pounds of Trouble': Film Is Witless Remake of a Runyon Story Blunt Promotion, Thin Humor Film Script 'Sodom and Gomorrah,'" *New York Times*, January 24, 1963, p. 5.

23. Bosley Crowther, "40 Pounds of Trouble," p. 5.

24. Bosley Crowther, "The Screen in Review: Sir Walter Scott's 'Ivanhoe' Makes Lavish Metro Film, Now at the Music Hall," *New York Times*, August 1, 1952, p. 8.

25. Bosley Crowther, "Screen: 'Spartacus' Enters the Arena: 3-Hour Production Has Premier at DeMille," *New York Times*, October 7, 1960, p. 28.

26. Crowther, "Music Hall Screen Resounds," p. 17.

27. A. H. Weiler, "Screen: A Saga of Ancient Times: 'Alexander the Great' Is Sweeping Pageant," *New York Times*, March 29, 1956, p. 23.

28. Bosley Crowther, "Screen: 'Illiad' Revisited: Helen's Face Launches Ships at Criterion," *New York Times*, January 27, 1956, p. 21.

29. Bosley Crowther, "The Screen: Story of the Thief Who Was Spared: Anthony Quinn Stars in Fry's 'Barabbas' Adaptation of Novel by Lagerkvist Opens," *New York Times*, October 11, 1962, p. 49.

30. Anon., "No, But I Saw the Picture," *Time*, January 26, 1962, www.time.com.

31. Anon., "No, But I Saw the Picture," *Time*, January 26, 1962, www.time.com.

32. Anon., "No, But I Saw the Picture," *Time*, January 26, 1962, www.time.com.

33. Anon., "No, But I Saw the Picture," *Time*, January 26, 1962, www.time.com.

34. Bosley Crowther, "Screen: 'War and Peace': The Cast," *New York Times*, August 22, 1956, p. 26.

35. Crowther, "'War and Peace': The Cast," p. 26.

36. Crowther, "'War and Peace': The Cast," p. 26.

37. Richard W. Nason, "'Attila' at Local Theatres: Anthony Quinn and Sophia Loren Star Italian Import is a Rewrite of History," *New York Times*, May 19, 1958, p. 19.

38. Nason, "'Attila' at Local Theatres, p. 19."

39. Ulf Hannerz, *Transnational Connections: Culture, People, Places* (London: Routledge, 1996).

40. David Bell and Joanne Hollows, "Mobile Homes," *Space and Culture*, 10 (1) (February 2007), p. 9.

41. Bell and Hollows, "Mobile Homes," p. 9.

42. Bell and Hollows, "Mobile Homes," p. 7.

43. Bell and Hollows, "Mobile Homes," p. 8.

44. Bosley Crowther, "The Screen: 'The Bible' According to John Huston Has Premiere: Director Plays Noah in Film at Loew's State Fry's Script is Limited to Part of Genesis," *New York Times*, September 29, 1966, p. 40.

45. Crowther, "'The Bible' According to John Huston," p. 40.

46. Crowther, "'The Bible' According to John Huston," p. 40.

47. Anon., "No, But I Saw the Picture," www.time.com.

48. Richard Nason, "Screen: Weak 'Hercules': Italian-Made Spectacle Opens at 135 Theatres," *New York Times,* July 23, 1959, p. 32.
49. Nason, "Screen: Weak 'Hercules'," p. 32. Levine had also released De Laurentiis's *Attila.*
50. Nason, "Screen: Weak 'Hercules'."
51. Howard Thompson, "Colossus of Rhodes," *New York Times,* December 14, 1961, p. 55.
52. Thompson, "Colossus of Rhodes," p. 55.
53. Thompson, "Colossus of Rhodes," p. 55.
54. Bosley Crowther, "Screen: 'The Leopard' at the Plaza: Burt Lancaster Stars in Adaptation of Novel," *New York Times,* August 13, 1963, p. 25.
55. Crowther, "'The Leopard' at the Plaza," p. 25.
56. Crowther, "'The Leopard' at the Plaza," p. 25.
57. Bosley Crowther, "Screen: 'The Life of Jesus': Pasolini's Film Opens at the Fine Arts," *New York Times,* February 18, 1966, p. 23.
58. Crowther, "The Life of Jesus," p. 23.
59. Crowther, "The Life of Jesus," p. 23.
60. Crowther, "The Life of Jesus," p. 23.
61. Bosley Crowther, "Screen: 'The Greatest Story Ever Told': Max von Sydow Stars in Biblical Film," *New York Times,* February 16, 1965, p. 40.
62. Crowther, "The Greatest Story Ever Told," p. 40.
63. Crowther, "The Greatest Story Ever Told," p. 40.
64. Crowther, "The Greatest Story Ever Told," p. 40.
65. Crowther, "The Greatest Story Ever Told," p. 40.

red cliff

the chinese-language epic and diasporic

chinese spectators

nine

r u b y   c h e u n g

> *To fight and conquer in all your battles is not supreme*
> *excellence; supreme excellence consists in breaking the enemy's*
> *resistance without fighting.*[1]
> *Time doesn't affect anything in this world if "change" is*
> *constantly factored in; in other words, we are just part of the*
> *lasting eternity while time passes.*[2]

introduction

This chapter is inspired by John Woo's Chinese diasporic status to analyze the historical effects of his first Chinese-language epic film, the four-hour-long diptych *Red Cliff* (Part I, 2008; Part II, 2009), from the perspectives of the film's production and reception.[3] Joining thousands of refugees and emigrants from China to escape political turmoil such as Chinese involvement in the Korean War and Cultural Revolution, mainland-born Woo (born May 1, 1946) moved with his family to the British colony Hong Kong at the age of five. The Woos spent a number of years in hardship living in a local slum area. Young Woo was lucky enough to be sponsored by an American family to receive his education which his family could not afford to give him. Woo gradually developed his love for cinema during his formative years while under the inspiration of Christianity from the local Catholic school he attended.

With his passion for film, in 1969 Woo was hired as a stage assistant by the now-defunct Cathay Studio. In 1971, Woo was employed by the largest local studio Shaw Brothers and became an assistant to the action-cinema guru Zhang Che, whose influence on Woo has lasted throughout the latter's directorship. By the mid-1980s, Woo, who had now become a director at Golden Harvest Studio, had made several comedies which turned out to be box-office failures in the local market. He later took up a director job in Taiwan as a gesture of self-exile to retreat from the prospering Hong Kong film industry. Before long, Woo obtained an opportunity in 1986 to direct *A Better Tomorrow*, now a Hong Kong cinematic classic, back in Hong Kong. It was from that time onwards when Woo's directorial career started to pick up momentum. Woo created his unique sense and aesthetics of making action cinema in such films as *The Killer* (1989), *Bullet in the Head* (1990), and *Once a Thief* (1991), winning the admiration not just of local audiences but also of Hollywood executives. The filmmaker got a Hollywood contract in 1993. Considering the possibly adverse socio-political effect of the reunification of Hong Kong and China on the society, Woo decided to leave Chinese soil for the USA, where he stayed until 2008 when he decided to direct *Red Cliff*.

As a typical epic film, *Red Cliff* arguably opens up a dialogue between the ancient past and the present day of China, where national unity remains one of the major concerns of its authorities.[4] Yet such an exchange is not straightforward. While mediating a historic incident through this film, Woo's diasporic sentiments have led him to magnify one facet of history but neglected the others which may be more important to his main markets in East and Southeast Asia, in particular those Chinese in the same diaspora as the filmmaker. This has gradually been proven by the online messages posted on virtual forums by *Red Cliff*'s spectators, a phenomenon contradicting the film's handsome box-office income accumulated in its regional markets.[5]

This essay addresses two principal concerns in the midst of the idea of "history" in *Red Cliff*. First, it explores the role Woo plays as a diasporic Chinese director in making this film. My reading of the film, which I will call a "diasporic reading," begins with an aesthetic analysis coupled with consideration of the film's wider socio-political contexts.[6] Prompted by the places of origin of the cast in this film, the second half of this chapter deals with the film's reception among its target audiences in Chinese diaspora, revealed by an online survey I conducted during the first year of the film's theatrical release. Hamid Naficy's concepts of diasporic filmmaking in

An Accented Cinema serves as a starting point to explore the issues that revolve around diasporic filmmakers in particular and displaced people in general.[7] Yet his underlying assumption that all diasporas are closely connected with their respective homelands may not be flexible enough to articulate and reflect the complex situations and mentality of different diasporas, such as those diasporic Chinese communities under discussion here. As a case in point, online messages dedicated to one of *Red Cliff*'s male leads, Takeshi Kaneshiro, and his role as Zhuge Liang, reveal that the national unity envisioned by Woo may not overlap with that of the film's spectators, a divergence that I attribute to differences in "historical consciousness" among distinct East and South Asian markets as well as more widely scattered diasporic communities.[8] In every case, the past which is constructed in the film provides a medium for connecting the existential present of diasporic spectators with the ancient, legendary past of one of China's most tumultuous periods.

red cliff and epic

Made for theatrical release in East and Southeast Asia at around the time of the Beijing Olympics in the summer of 2008 (first installment) and Chinese New Year 2009 (second installment), *Red Cliff* reenacts imaginatively and majestically an important battle in the distant past of China. The film is thus far the most expensively produced, mainstream Chinese-language film. Marketing efforts for the film have focused primarily on its mega-budget of $80 million, co-financed by four Asian equity investors from China, Japan, South Korea, and Taiwan respectively without recourse from outside money, and on the fact that it was coproduced by companies based in China, Hong Kong, Japan, South Korea, and Taiwan.[9] It joins the resurgence of intricately plotted and sumptuously made Chinese-language epics—a trend initiated by the international success of Ang Lee's *Crouching Tiger, Hidden Dragon* (2000).[10]

According to Robert Burgoyne, epics are a type of historical film, which has its "basis in the documentable past, and [its] shared project of making the world of the past knowable and visible."[11] Moreover, these often overtly romanticized epics are "[u]sually associated with spectacle, monumentality, and lavish *mise en scène*" and communicate "a distilled expression of ideals, anxieties, and conflicts in national self-definition."[12] *Red Cliff* in this sense certainly qualifies as an Eastern exemplar of the epic genre with its strikingly reenacted battle scenes. Moreover, the scheduling for the release of the two *Red Cliff* installments around two Chinese-related cultural celebrations with a six-month interval in between them helped evoke nationalistic feelings among ethnic Chinese. Understandably, the film's promotion and marketing plans suggested that all Chinese spectators feel strongly, if not equally, about their (imagined) motherland and ultimate roots.

The evocation of national pride and nationalistic ideals among Chinese descendants not living in China, however, is especially problematic, given the complex and manifold history of China, marked by the succession of different ruling dynasties and shaped by the direct and indirect effects of natural calamities, wars, and colonization. Robert A. Rosenstone writes in *History on Film/Film on History* about the interweaving relationship between the historic past, the restaging of that past on screen, and the interpretation of it by contemporary spectators.[13] The author argues that history in historical films gives us a unique film experience in that "[t]hey are what help to create in us the feeling that we are not just viewing history, but actually living through events in the past, experiencing (or so we think, at least momentarily) what others felt in times of war, revolution, and social, cultural, and political change."[14] In this regard, *Red Cliff* as a modern epic film helps magnify the problem of a lack of national unity in China's past and present, as much as romanticizing a historic past in which the present generation of viewers cannot live.

directing in a diasporic present

the plot

Red Cliff tells the story of two opposing factions in chaotic Ancient China. On the one side, there is the allied force made up of righteous individuals. The main characters are Zhou Yu (Tony Leung Chiu-wai) and Zhuge Liang (Takeshi Kaneshiro). On the other side, the corrupt camp is led by the arrogant antagonist Cao Cao (Zhang Fengyi), a historical hate figure due to his aggressiveness and hunger for power.[15]

The film restages the famous battle of Red Cliff (ad 208) (a.k.a. the Battle of Chi Bi), which was the last war Cao entered into with two other warlords, Liu Bei and Sun Quan, before they divided Ancient China into a tripartite territory and began the period of Three Kingdoms (ad 220–280), one of China's most infamous eras of disunity. It opens in ad 208 in Xuchang (in the north). Cao, the chancellor of the Eastern Han Dynasty who holds the real power of the state, coerces the Emperor to approve the war he will soon wage on Sun (in the south) (You Yong) and Liu (in the midwest) (Chang Chen), in the name of annihilating these enemies to unify the country. Cao and his 800,000 soldiers first seize the military advantage and defeat Liu in a war historically known as the battle of Changban.[16] Thereafter, Liu and his subordinates retreat to the southeast, bringing along with them thousands of refugees, civilians, and soldiers.

Strategist Zhuge suggests to his lord Liu to forge an alliance with Sun in order to combine their two smaller camps together and to fight off Cao's offensive attack. Agreed by Liu, Zhuge goes to persuade Sun in person and is successful. The arrogant Cao's soldiers underestimate the strengths of the allies and indulge themselves in food, women, and other pleasures that characterize the lives of the southern provinces along their southward march. They lose the initial combat on the eve of the battle of Red Cliff, ending the first installment of the film.

The second installment focuses on the gradual unfolding of the battle of Red Cliff. Zhou (viceroy on Sun's side) and Zhuge work together to undermine Cao's army with clever tricks, including counterspying and leading Cao to kill two of his most competent naval generals. Important female figures from the allied force, such as Sun's sister Shangxiang (Zhao Wei), and Xiao Qiao (Lin Chiling), the wife of Zhou, also undertake critical missions to create disturbances on Cao's side. Cao is defeated by the tactics of Zhou and Zhuge, not by superior numbers or dominant martial prowess, a point illustrated by the climactic scene of the burning of the fleet. Cao has chained all his ships together to stabilize them and thus minimize the incidence of seasickness, which had created a major problem for Cao's soldiers earlier. Once the wind turns, the allied forces initiate a major fire attack on Cao's fleet, which is unable to maneuver. At the end, all the ships of Cao's army are burnt. Cao is badly defeated and is sent back to the north.

film material and essence

As confirmed by Woo and the main actors of the film, *Red Cliff* is factually based on *The Records of Three Kingdoms,* which was written by Chen Shou in the 300s and is commonly regarded as the official history of the Three Kingdoms period.[17] This chronology provided future generations of literary works, folklore stories, myths, and even popular cultural merchandise such as video games, with invaluable background information from that era. The way Woo re-presents this well-known past and introduces his major characters with minimal written information on screen suggests that Woo relies heavily upon his target audiences' knowledge of this past. Naturally, those who are less familiar with this history may get lost at certain points in the film.

However, Woo's film also revives many of his favorite topics dating back to his filmmaking career in Hong Kong in the mid-1980s to early 1990s. Themes and allusions, such as national unification and unity, social collectivism, male bonding, courage and bravery, and peacemaking and anti-war idealization found in *Red Cliff* make the film thematically in line with the Chinese literary classic *Romance of the Three Kingdoms,* a lengthy novel based on that chaotic past written by Luo Guanzhong in the 1300s. One may argue that this is how Woo answers concerns that traditional values such as loyalty, honesty, justice, and commitment are being taken less and less seriously in contemporary life.[18] Woo talks about the importance of "friendship" and its associations with other virtues, such as honor and loyalty, as prevalent themes in his films from the 1980s: "The way I see it, it is only by bonding together and trusting each other that we will survive."[19] On another occasion, Woo maintains, "I was advised by my teacher Zhang Che to uphold the ideals of the East in film while making use of filmmaking techniques from the West. I have been following his advice diligently throughout these years."[20] Tony Williams reaffirms such qualities of Woo's cinema when the author writes about Woo's post-1986 films, arguing that the director "contrasts desolate worlds of present and future with visions of China's heroic past as a means for survival."[21] If the same holds, *Red Cliff* may be seen as another manifestation of the director's mission in filmmaking. Elements of an imaginary past are employed in this homecoming project to convey the diasporic director's yearning for cultural and national Chinese ideals that remain difficult to actualize.

This brief tracing of *Red Cliff*'s historical, thematic, and cinematic lineages helps establish the film's status as an onscreen projection of an entrenched, culturally specific Chinese history. The film reconstructs an important past for its producers and recipients, including the director, producers, cast and crew, and audiences. However, by considering the production of this film in terms of the transnational milieu evoked by its production and reception, we can view what is apparently a nationalistic epic on another horizon. Homi K. Bhabha describes the ambiguous relation between a presumed cultural origin and its relations of otherness, the area between periphery and center, as a "third space." Bhabha argues: "This third space displaces the histories that constitute it, and sets up new structures of authority, new political initiatives, which are inadequately understood through received wisdom."[22] Embedded in this notion is the cultural translation that exists due to the collision of social, cultural, and political differences and negotiations occurring in what he calls an interstitial zone. This is exemplified by the acts and consequences of human migrations across national borders.[23] Here, national cores no longer matter. Working liminally within and between dominant systems, diasporic and exilic filmmakers are productively displaced. According to Naficy, these "accented" filmmakers originating from the Middle East and now working in the West,

> do not live and work on the peripheries of society or the film and media industries. They are situated inside and work in the interstices of both . . . To be interstitial, therefore, is to operate both within and astride the cracks of the system, benefiting from its contradictions, anomalies, and heterogeneity. It also means being located at the intersection of the local and the global, mediating between the two contrary categories, which in syllogism are called "subalternity" and "superalternity." As a result, accented filmmakers are not so much marginal or subaltern as they are interstitial, partial, and multiple.[24]

Woo's filmmaking career within the mainstream systems of Hollywood and East Asia is comparable to that of the Middle Eastern "accented" filmmakers in the West described above. While Woo's existential conditions are different from his "accented" counterparts whose (dis)locations have much to do with the political climates of their homelands, Woo productively works the interstices of two mainstream cinemas, as is evident from his work. Many scholarly studies of Woo's auteurship and oeuvre have already noted the deep effects of the director's displacement from Chinese soil, his profound knowledge of China's historic past and culture, and his Christian beliefs on his cultural–nationalistic worldview.[25]

Yet accented films are and are not *auteur* films, even in the broadest definition, according to Naficy.[26] This is because accented filmmakers often inscribe themselves in the film texts in various distinctive ways, often revealing their desire for their homeland and to express their grievances over its loss as a result of their resettlement elsewhere. For Naficy, "How they [the accented filmmakers] inhabit their films . . . how they are 'personified' varies: they may inhabit them as real empirical persons, enunciating subjects, structured absences, fictive structures, or a combination of these."[27] Such a "performance of the self" on the part of the filmmakers, however, is hard to capture because different accented filmmakers have undergone diverse lives in their liminalities.[28] In the case of *Red Cliff,* two kinds of visual elements immediately stand out as revelations of Woo's own inscription in the film. One is concerned with his artistic reconstruction of two battle scenes in the film's first installment to encompass the Ancient Chinese idea of the universe. In both sequences, round objects such as a village well and an array of eight-trigram military formation convey a philosophical and historical conception specific to Ancient Chinese belief. Eight-trigram military formation is an ancient Chinese military strategy of arranging cohorts in the battlefield in such a way that the physical arrangement of the array looks like an eight trigram. The other element is the embodiment of the director's worldview in the cast. The "Chinese" look of a select cast of popular East Asian stars can be read in terms of Woo's desire to see national and regional cohesion.

the aesthetics of the past

Let me digress a little bit here to talk about Ancient Chinese cosmology as a possible underlying philosophy backing up the visuals that I am going to discuss. As early as in Zhou Dynasty (c. 1045–256 bc), the earth was conjured up as the core of the universe (which was also known as the heaven or the sky bearing a different meaning from the Christian sense). It was flat and square in shape, while the universe was round like an immensely huge vault hanging over the earth—hence the old Chinese saying "round heaven, flat land" (*tian yuan di fan*).[29] The "round heaven" was believed to link seamlessly with the "flat land" on which everything grew and prospered. The land remained calm and unmoved when the heaven (or the sky) changed cyclically. Harvests on the land depended upon the mercy of the sky/heaven.[30] This belief emphasized the harmonious relationships among every creature in Mother Nature. It also introduced such concepts as yin and yang.[31] A related concept Taiji (aka Tai Chi) was also established to encompass the principles of complementariness, governing the ideal state of existence of beings. The symbol of Taiji is perhaps one of the most recognizable Chinese philosophical signs in the world. It is a solid circle divided into equal halves by a curvy line in the middle. Half of the circle is black in color (representing yin) enwrapping a little white circle (representing yang) to signify the embrace of its opposite; the same goes with the other side in the circle except with a reverse of color.

It is not surprising to see that Woo has orchestrated this Ancient Chinese cosmic concept in Red Cliff to paint his own imagined picture of that bygone period and to connote his wish for harmony and peacemaking.[32] In particular, two objects can be identified in the mise-en-scène of Red Cliff: Part I that have specific cultural and nationalistic implications. One of them is a village well; the other is the shape of the eight-trigram military formation seen from an aerial angle. The sequences that feature these two round objects stand out from the gory details in the film. Determined by their specific appearances, each suggests a differing connotation with regard to the film as a whole. The village well comes across as exposing the bitterness of striving to achieve cultural and national unity, while the eight-trigram military formation conveys more positive messages.

village well

We can find the round village well in the sequence in Red Cliff: Part I that details the historic moment of General Zhao Yun (Hu Jun) saving his lord Liu's baby son from the hands of Cao's army in a wrecked village. In that sequence, the village well seems like a silent killer that indirectly marks Cao's illegitimate attack on the allies. It helps underscore the brutality of battles which have caused the disunity of the country.

The battle of Changban first comes on screen at around eight minutes into the film when Cao launches his major attack at Liu. Several Wooesque slow-motion shots paint a dreadful picture of the war carnage and introduce Liu's several aides such as General Zhao fighting bravely to protect the civilians. The camera then cuts to the marching troop of Cao and then back to the refugees on Liu's side. Filled with thousands of extras, the scene evokes the Exodus in the epic The Ten Commandments (1956), where Moses is leading a large group of Hebrew slaves out of Egypt. In Red Cliff, Liu has effectively assumed the Moses-like role as a selfless and humanitarian leader. A soldier reports to Liu that his two wives and the infant son are still in the village they have just left behind. The unarmed women are trapped in their broken horse-drawn cart and surrounded by enemies. From the close-up of Liu's baby, the camera cuts to Liu who does not utter a word but externalizes his worries by helping a toddler who trips nearby. Realizing his lord's personal difficulties, Zhao rides in the direction of that village. Meanwhile, one of Liu's wives is killed in the village. The surviving wife continues to run but is hit by a spear thrown at her. Startled, she almost drops the baby into a village well next to her. The well in the olden days of China was a sign of nourishing lives, but in this particular scene not only is the well unable to perform its usual function of water supply, it is there to lessen the Lady's chances of survival.

A series of rapidly paced shots follows to feature Zhao's timely arrival to save the woman and the baby. Yet both the woman and Zhao are soon badly injured. Pondering over the chances of survival for herself, her baby son, and Zhao (represented by a quick point-of-view shot of the burning houses and ruins in the village), the woman looks at the well by her side. A shot quickly zooms out and shows the round exterior of the well (Figure 9.1). It suggests that the well is probably the only exit for the injured woman. But this is an exit to death; not an exit to survival. It looks like a black hole ready to annihilate any lives that are physically close to it. At this juncture, the camera changes position by shooting from inside the dark well while the woman is jumping down the well to kill herself in order not to burden Zhao further. Yet the round shape of the well is now all the more highlighted, as the well opening is the only lit prop of the mise-en-scène. Shooting from the bottom of the well creates the impression that the well opening forms the "round sky" (or "round heaven"). It, nevertheless, also looks like the light at the end of the tunnel of life because this well-"round heaven" kills the Lady. Her self-sacrifice quiets the melancholic music (percussions and wind instruments) that has been accompanying the fight scenes early on.

Figure 9.1

Red Cliff: The round exterior of the village well.

A similar story arc in the semi-fictional East Asian epic *Three Kingdoms: Resurrection of the Dragon* (2008) depicts the same historic moment. Yet Andy Lau, who plays Zhao, becomes the focal point while the mise-en-scène is reduced to a minimum. There is only one hut in the supposed village which is now littered with corpses. No village well or similar round object is shown, indirectly underlining that Woo's film has uniquely made use of the village well to intensify the visual brutality of the war.

Woo's deployment of this well foregrounds the vulnerability of those innocent, weak, and unarmed individuals in the war and, indirectly, the hardship they have to endure before the national disunity is over. Contrarily, the round eight-trigram military formation featured in *Red Cliff: Part I* shows the concept of "round heaven, flat land" in a more benign manner.

This part of the narrative starts with Zhuge suggesting the allied army deploy the eight-trigram military formation in order to defeat Cao's troop. The eight trigrams initially represent eight basic elements in nature. They are heaven, earth, water, fire, wind, thunder, mountain, and lake. These elements are symbolically represented by eight different combinations of three lines, whether broken (representing *yin*) or solid (representing *yang*), stacking on top of each other and often surrounding the symbol of *Taiji*. Figure 9.2 shows the symbol of an eight-trigram pattern.

Chinese philosopher JeeLoo Liu notes that besides representing natural elements, eight trigrams are often applicable to other things such as interpersonal relationships, colors, and directions, among others.[33] More inspiringly, they represent the changing process in the universe. What matter here are the "change," and the flexibility that the "change" automatically gives to the things, people, and beings involved. Applied to military formation,

Figure 9.2
An eight trigram symbol.

eight trigrams certainly give the practicing troops an advantage over their opponents. Woo restages such a military formation on screen by employing thousands of extras to form arrays of human walls, which are similar to the lines in an eight-trigram pattern if viewed from the air (Figure 9.3).

The first of these aerial shots appears almost right at the beginning of the significant land combat on the eve of the battle of Red Cliff. Sun's sister Shangxiang begins it by an ambush on one of Cao's battalions. Shangxiang, accompanied by her female unit, provokes Cao's soldiers to chase after them on horses. It is too late when Cao's soldiers find themselves in a trap. Right in front of them is the well-arrayed eight-trigram military formation consisting of the Sun-Liu allied army, who shoot them with arrows and kill many of these northern invaders. The surviving ones are shocked. They dash around for an escape, only to find themselves being trapped deeply in the gutters within the formation. Resembling the outlook from a highly mounted command tower, the camera zooms out to show a high-angled aerial view of the magnificent eight-trigram military formation.

Inside, all the human-formed lines of the trigrams are moving smoothly. They collide at some points while separating at others, illustrating the fluid movements within the formation which has now become a large circle on the exterior. There is a small circle of allied soldiers in the centre of this formation but they soon join their counterparts at the periphery of the formation to fight against Cao's soldiers, who have succumbed completely to the attack of the allied force. After a series of exquisitely choreographed action scenes featuring individual generals on the allied side, the allied force defeats the enemies and gains initial victory. An ending aerial shot of this battle shows that the eight-trigram military formation has fulfilled its function and is now disassembled, leaving only the traces of circles on the ground. The roundness of this military formation is thus more positively portrayed than that of the village well from the point of view of the allied army.

Figure 9.3

Red Cliff: Aerial view of the eight trigram military formation.

Apart from the round objects in the mise-en-scène just discussed, the cast of *Red Cliff* may be read in terms of Woo's authorial inscription. Important roles in *Red Cliff* are performed by famous actors and actresses from different territories in East Asia; on the most obvious level, this is a result of transregional marketing considerations and synergies among regional filmmaking talents, reflecting the star appeal of individual actors and actresses. As Derek Elley observes, "An actor may not necessarily resemble his historical counterpart, but the charisma he brings to a role is a powerful asset."[34] The two male protagonists Zhou and Zhuge are played by Tony Leung Chiu-wai (Hong Kong) and Takeshi Kaneshiro (Taiwan), while the antagonist Cao is performed by Zhang Fenyi (mainland China). These three main actors are supported by popular actors and actresses from different East Asian territories, namely, Chang Chen (Taiwan), Zhao Wei (mainland China), Hu Jun (mainland China), and Shido Nakamura (Japan).[35] In the film they have their voices dubbed over if they are non-Mandarin speakers.

Their geographical origins, however, prompt speculations of deeper geopolitical implications and what the cast could have embodied. For instance, given the divergence of opinions between the People's Republic of China (PRC) and Taiwan over the sensitive issues of national unification, a Japanese–Taiwanese actor (Kaneshiro) playing the male lead on the allied side opposite a mainland Chinese actor (Zhang) in the leading role on the opposition side is very suggestive politically. When we consider the international relationship between contemporary China and Japan in the implications of this cast, there is another level of geopolitical complication. This is because, first, China and Japan have fought against each other in major wars such as the two Sino-Japanese wars (1894–1895; 1931–1945 as part of World War II). Second, Japan was a regional imperialist once colonizing Hong Kong, Taiwan, and Korea in different periods of time in the twentieth century. Casting an actor of half-Japanese and half-Chinese origin to play opposite other ethnic Chinese actors may remind the audiences of the traumatic war experience between the two countries. Hence, in casting these actors from different nations in East Asia to play specific roles on both sides of the battle, the filmmaker has induced the audience to think beyond what is shown on screen.

Rosenstone argues that historical films help stimulate a dialogue between the historic past and the present through the viewing experience of spectators.[36] Burgoyne also suggests that:

> In contemporary media culture, the most significant "historical" events are often transformed into spectatorial "experiences" that shape and inform the subjectivity of the individual viewer; with the media continually and

effortlessly re-presenting the past, history, once thought of as an impersonal phenomenon, has been replaced by "experiential" collective memory.[37]

Bearing in mind Woo's advocacy of Chinese national unification, however, I believe it is more important to understand how such a dialogue happens after it is initiated by the filmmaker through the film and before the spectators receive and respond to it. In Woo's case as a homecoming, diasporic director, we may want to ask how individual actors may have embodied Woo's worldview and displacement sentiments, thereby becoming Woo's diegetic alter egos?[38] Further, how have the target audiences responded to Woo's messages?

a trans-asian star, fansites, and diasporic chinese online fandom

These questions urge me to see things not just from the director's point of view but also from the receiving end of the film. I find the diasporic Chinese online fandom expressed through Kaneshiro's fansites particularly interesting and thought-provoking. Through dedicating their love for the star and openly talking about it on fansites' message boards, these diasporic Chinese fans let each other know their different opinions on *Red Cliff,* history in film, and, indirectly, their diasporic status.

In order to understand these fans and what first brings them together, we will start with Kaneshiro—a trans-Asian star who has ambiguous origins. Kaneshiro was born on October 11, 1973, to a Japanese father and Taiwanese mother in Taipei (Taiwan) and raised there, while holding Japanese citizenship. He is fluent in Taiwanese, Mandarin, Cantonese, Japanese, and English. Even though Kaneshiro considers Taiwan as his home, his Japanese citizenship led to his recent disqualification from competing in the "Outstanding Taiwanese Filmmaker of the Year" award in the 45th Golden Horse Awards (the Taiwanese equivalent to the Oscar Awards) in December 2008.[39]

On a positive note, Kaneshiro's ambiguous origins and his command of several Asian languages give him an edge to win the hearts of fans from different countries in East and Southeast Asia, who can identify with him easily as belonging to their own territories. Apart from his mainland Chinese fans, other of his East and Southeast Asian fans are mostly the descendants of the first generations of immigrants from China who had continuously resettled across Asia until the 1940s.[40] Many of these overseas Chinese in East and Southeast Asia nowadays were locally born and bred, while they are also fully aware of their diasporic and minority status in their host countries. Yet, as they are more familiar with the local cultures and lives than with things happening in mainland China, unlike other diasporic communities they may not necessarily tightly connect with their motherland, China. They serve as counterexamples for the definition of diaspora offered by Naficy: "People in diaspora . . . maintain a long-term sense of ethnic consciousness and distinctiveness, which is consolidated by the periodic hostility of either the original home or the host societies toward them."[41]

Not only is there weak psychological link between these second or third generations of overseas Chinese with their putative motherland China, many overseas Chinese cannot speak or write Chinese languages.[42] Or, they may very likely belong to different dialect groups, inherited from their immigrant ancestors. Although overseas Chinese fans of Kaneshiro originate from the same Chinese diaspora, they are far from being homogenous and may not have much in common except for their mutual interests in Kaneshiro. In this sense, Kaneshiro is literally an agent helping to reunite these disparate Chinese descendants.

Yet, in contrast to many megastars in East Asia who maintain regular connect with their fans through fan-club activities, Kaneshiro does not have an official fan club for reasons not known to the public.[43] He has an official website hosted by his agent company in Japan, but that site has not been updated since January 24, 2007.[44] Known for keeping a low profile outside his filmmaking schedule, Kaneshiro's up-to-date news is only available from local press sources. It is then picked up by his fans in various East and Southeast Asian countries to share with each other via fansites and virtual forums.

Media scholar Henry Jenkins argues that, thanks to the internet, we are now participating in a "convergence culture, where old and new media collide, where grassroots and corporate media intersect, where the power of the producer and the power of the media consumer interact in unpredictable ways."[45] The consumer's active participation and social interaction with other consumers help circulate mass-media contents.[46] Another internet researcher, Nancy Baym, also observes the impact of online fandom, members of which have become actively self-organized marketing tools and publicists of popular cultural products, such as online music. Online fan communities exist in a "complex ecosystem of sites" and on various kinds of virtual platforms, such as blogs, discussion forums, and private messages.[47]

The arguments of these two researchers hold true as far as the online fandom of Kaneshiro's diasporic Chinese fans are concerned. In addition to being Kaneshiro's virtual publicists, members of these fan communities demonstrate a distinctive sense of belonging to the given fansites and their fan-based communities. They may correspond with each other in chat rooms or leave each other thread messages, which are written in Chinese as the major communication medium if they learn of each other's Chinese ethnicity. Yet it is worth noting that these fansite participants, physically based in different East and Southeast Asian territories, are writing and speaking in distinctive Chinese dialects (Cantonese Chinese and Mandarin

Chinese most notably), each with a unique vocabulary, grammar, and syntax. In some cases, what is written may not be intelligible to ethnic Chinese not from the same dialectic groups. Despite these nuances, written Chinese has become the major tool used by Kaneshiro's diasporic Chinese-speaking fans to proactively identify with the star, the fansites, and their fellow Kaneshiro fans. Such a subcultural sharing also allows these fans to explore the films in which Kaneshiro plays major roles and to (re)interpret the messages conveyed through these films.

online survey and findings

For the purposes of exploring how diasporic Chinese audiences of *Red Cliff* come to terms with their historical awareness and self-understanding with the help of a restaged past, and how they may contemplate the future as a result, in March and August 2009 I conducted a series of random, online studies. My survey was based on observation and content analysis of the fan-authored online messages that mushroomed in the first year of *Red Cliff*'s theatrical release in East and Southeast Asia. By registering as a member on these fansites and virtual forums and being a native speaker of Chinese language, I was in a position to collect primary information from these sites. I divided my studies into two major categories. The first one revolved around the film itself, consisting of investigations of the official sites of *Red Cliff* and other virtual forums found on five of the most popular web-based social networks, namely, Facebook, MySpace, Twitter, Friendster, and Bebo. The second category made a detour to see how Kaneshiro's fans and their online fandom helped generate useful information for us to learn more about the specific opinions of diasporic Chinese audiences on the film, which would otherwise be difficult to obtain with methods such as focus groups and personal interviews due to time and the financial constraints of my research. This second category of my studies was further divided into two groups. The first subgroup focused on those fan pages and member groups of Kaneshiro found on Facebook, MySpace, Friendster, and Bebo as well as Kaneshiro-related tweets on Twitter. The second subgroup dealt with individual fansites. Underneath these studies lies the assumption that these Kaneshiro fans-cum-*Red Cliff* viewers are those who actively take part in the recent phenomenon of online "participatory culture," enabled by the internet and, in particular, the advent of Web 2.0.[48]

I hypothesized that there would be at least three types of spectatorial responses to *Red Cliff* among its diasporic Chinese viewers. First, the audiences might aspire to what Woo has intended to highlight: a clearly articulated cultural and national identity transcending their present nationalities as stipulated on their passports. This Sinocentric outlook might be embraced by those spectators, for example Korean and Japanese, who are not ethnic Chinese but who have been interacting with Chinese culture for a long time.[49] Second, for those overseas-born ethnic Chinese, I hypothesize that there might be regrets that a pure Chinese cultural and national identity as portrayed on screen is an impossible dream in real life, as these overseas Chinese may know little about Chinese culture and China's ancient past. The third response, which I argue is the most inspiring, involved a negotiation between the historical and diasporic consciousness of *Red Cliff*'s ethnic Chinese audiences now settled in various East and Southeast Asian countries. Both historical and diasporic consciousness have been abundantly considered in the critical literature. Historical consciousness has been defined by Seixas, among others, as "individual and collective understandings of the past, the cognitive and cultural factors that shape those understandings, as well as the relations of historical understandings to those of the present and the future."[50] "Diasporic consciousness" is defined by William Safran as "an intellectualization of an existential condition" of those who are in diaspora.[51] Naficy highlights the fact that "diasporic consciousness is horizontal and multisited, involving not only the homeland but also the compatriot communities elsewhere."[52] Hence, we may interpret that "historical consciousness" involves the thought of being aware of one's role in a temporality running vertically down from the past, through the present to the future. "Diasporic consciousness," in contrast, intercepts one's self-awareness in this vertically running timescale by introducing a horizontal web of connections with other members in the same diaspora.

Tables 9.1 and 9.2 summarize the findings of my online research. As far as the film is concerned (Table 9.1), there were six official sites mounted by its film marketers to appeal to the markets in the PRC, Japan, Hong Kong, Taiwan, France, and South Korea respectively. Only the one for the PRC market contained a message board that linked to posts on blogs powered by the same umbrella site sina.com.cn. There were 114 blog messages found, inclusive of seventy-three positive comments (i.e. 64 percent of the total) and forty-one explicitly negative comments (i.e. 36 percent of the total) on the film. This created a stark contrast to the cases on Facebook (thirteen fan pages or member groups) and Twitter, which recorded 392 messages related to *Red Cliff* in total by late August 2009, but only six of them were overtly negative (i.e. 1. 5 percent of the total). Such contrast was most likely attributed to the difference in demographic profile among visitors of different sites and their literacy of Chinese culture and history, with the language use being a clear indicator of such a difference. We can see that whereas most of the Facebook and Twitter visitors left messages in English (thereby also evidencing both the film's and these media's international appeal), those posts found on *Red Cliff*'s China site were written in simplified Chinese.

The above comparison draws a distinction between *Red Cliff*'s mainland Chinese audiences from its international viewers. Closer analysis of the

Social networks on *Red Cliff*'s official sites
Found only on *Red Cliff*'s China site (http://chibi.sina.com.cn) (as of August 24, 2009)
  Number of blog messages: 114 (they are from blogs linked to *Red Cliff*'s China site
    and are hosted by sina.com.cn)
  Number of positive comments: 73
  Number of negative comments: 41

Facebook
Total number of fan pages and member groups (as of August 24, 2009): 13
Total number of fans/members registered with these pages (as of August 24, 2009):
  3,738
(Note: Duplicate membership is possible from the same fans/members.)
Accumulated number of posts about *Red Cliff* (as of August 24, 2009): 239
  Number of messages in English and other languages: 233
  Number of messages in Chinese: 6
  Number of bilingual (English and Chinese) messages: 0
Accumulated number of posts about *Red Cliff* (as of March 31, 2009): 108
  Number of messages in English and other languages: 105
  Number of messages in Chinese: 3
  Number of bilingual (English and Chinese) messages: 0
Information of creators/administrators: 2 based in Singapore, 1 based in LA, 1 based
  in Missouri, 9 with unknown location. All of these identified creators/
  administrators have Chinese surnames

Twitter (August 15–24, 2009)
Total number of tweets about *Red Cliff*: 153
  Number of tweets about *Red Cliff* (in English and other languages): 125
  Number of tweets about *Red Cliff* (in simplified/traditional Chinese): 28

Bebo, MySpace and Friendster (as of August 24, 2009)
There are no messages about *Red Cliff*.

Note: No specific forum dedicated to *Red Cliff* can be found online.

blog messages on the film's China site revealed an interesting phenomenon: while all the positive comments focused on the on-screen spectacles
that Woo established for *Red Cliff*, all of the critiques censured the way in
which the film has departed from history. Messages (my translations) such
as the following abounded:

> "The quality of the film is really bad . . . many well-known historical
> scenes are badly treated . . . many lines are laughable and contemporary.
> They do not synchronize with the actual historical period."

> "*Red Cliff* has insulted the traditional culture of China. It distorts our
> history in front of the foreigners. It is a classic example of forgetting
> about the past."

> "*Red Cliff* is based on real history and adapted from the famous
> *Romance of the Three Kingdoms* and *Records of Three Kingdoms* . . . Yet many of
> the famous episodes from the two classics are either abandoned, simpli-
> fied, damaged or distorted . . . and all those household names in history
> are caricatured."

Table 9.2 Summary of online survey of interactive websites dedicated to Takeshi Kaneshiro

Facebook

Total number of fan pages and member groups (as of August 24, 2009): 14

Total number of fans/members registered with these pages (as of August 24, 2009): 52,810 (Note: Duplicate membership is possible from the same fans/members.)

Accumulated number of posts (as of August 24, 2009): 1,253

Accumulated number of posts related to *Red Cliff* (as of August 24, 2009): 42
  Number of messages in English and other languages: 40
  Number of messages in Chinese: 2
  Number of bilingual (English and Chinese) messages: 1

Accumulated number of posts related to *Red Cliff* (as of March 31, 2009): 36
  Number of messages in English and other languages: 34
  Number of messages in Chinese: 2
  Number of bilingual (English and Chinese) messages: 1

Information of creators/administrators: 4 based in Hong Kong, 1 based in Massachusetts, 1 based in Australia, 1 based in the UK, 1 based in France, 6 with unknown location. Creators/administrators are believed to be individuals of different ethnicities.

MySpace (as of August 24, 2009)
  Number of pages dedicated to Kaneshiro: 10 (all in English)
  Number of pages borrowed Kaneshiro's name but not dedicated to him: 13

Twitter (August 15–24, 2009)

Total number of tweets about Kaneshiro's role in *Red Cliff*: 4
  Number of tweets about Kaneshiro's role in *Red Cliff* (in English and other languages): 4
  Number of tweets about Kaneshiro's role in *Red Cliff* (in simplified/traditional Chinese): 0

Bebo (as of August 24, 2009)
  Number of Bebo pages dedicated to Kaneshiro: 1 (in English)
  Number of fans registered with that page: 24
  Number of posts in that page related to *Red Cliff*: 0

Friendster (as of August 24, 2009)
There are no messages about Kaneshiro's role in *Red Cliff*

Individual Fansites

Nine individual fansites are found; highlighted information is as follows:

www.fulong.jp/kaneshiro/takeshi.html (Japanese-language site; official site hosted by Kaneshiro's agent company in Japan; without forum)

www.takeshikaneshiro.net (Chinese-language site; Administrator (Derrick Tao) of Chinese origin, based in Hong Kong; one of the most systematically organized fansites dedicated to Kaneshiro, consisting of an interactive forum which carries comprehensive thread messages from fans believed to be based in different East/ Southeast Asian territories. The fansite description and fan messages are written in Chinese, implying that the ability of fans to read and write Chinese languages is a prerequisite for them to join this site.)

city.udn.com/1124 (Chinese-language site; Taiwan-based forum but not interactive; no information on administrator available. Functions as a Kaneshiro news portal.)

tkaneshiro.net/site (Chinese-language site named "TKaneshiro. net"; Administrator (Maggie) of Chinese origin and based in LA; forum inoperative.)

www.takeshikaneshirocn.com (Chinese-language site named "Takeshi China," based in mainland China; no information on administrator available; 19 news topics about *Red Cliff* found on the forum with few replies.)

193

Continued

Table 9.2 Continued

www.takeshikaneshiro.org (English-language site named "Takeshi Kaneshiro fansite"; no information on administrator available; forum not utilized by registered users which has a number of less than 50; forum posts related to *Red Cliff* are written by administrator only [all with nil reply].)

Red Cliff Movie Review (posted July 17, 2008) views: 1,523
Red Cliff movie new China box-office record (posted August 12, 2008) views: 1,570
Red Cliff Opens in Japan (posted October 25, 2008) views: 1,655
Red Cliff 2 to be Released on January 7th (posted December 30, 2008) views: 1,655
Red Cliff 2 Review (posted January 16, 2009) views: 1,022

s7. invisionfree.com/SimplyTK (English-language site with forum; hosted by a company in Virginia, USA; administrator of Japanese origin.)
www.geocities.com/Tokyo/Island/7258 (English-language site named "TK Land"; no information on administrator available; no forum.)
www.asianhunk.net/takeshi-kaneshiro (English-language site; no information on administrator available; not updated since March 22, 2008 and no comments on Kaneshiro's role in *Red Cliff* available.)

The less appreciative remarks from these mainland Chinese bloggers provide us with cases against which we can compare the viewing experience of different Chinese communities of the film so that we can deduce the impacts of localities on their perception of the film and the restaged ancient past in this film. That is, if mainland Chinese viewers embrace firmly the "real" history to evaluate the film and insist that the film should be faithful to the "history" that they are familiar with (suggested by those negative comments), how nonmainland Chinese audiences think of the film will then tell us the effect of diasporic experience on their perception of the film and the cinematically re-presented history in it. Most messages on Facebook's *Red Cliff* fan pages and member groups and on Twitter were, however, written in English by writers from around the world. It was thus difficult to tell their ethnic or cultural origins. The concise nature of these wall posts and tweets also made it hard for the writers to express deep thoughts for the film. Messages found on those Kaneshiro-related web-based social networks and his fansites then became instrumental in helping us to generate more insights.

Compared to those web-based social-networking forums that are solely on the film *Red Cliff,* fan pages and member groups on Facebook, MySpace, and Bebo—as well as *tweets* on Twitter dedicated to Kaneshiro (see Table 9.2)—showed more enthusiasm from "grassroots" participants around the world. There were fourteen fan pages and member groups found on Facebook dedicated to the star, one more page than was dedicated to *Red Cliff.* MySpace had ten pages dedicated to the star while Bebo had one page for him. The total number of fans and members registered with these pages on Facebook and Bebo was 52,834, fourteen times the number of registrants (3,738) of *Red Cliff* pages on Facebook. Although the number of messages written about Kaneshiro on both Facebook and

Twitter amounted to 1,257 in total, there were only forty-six messages written either about the star's role in *Red Cliff* or the film itself, much less than the number of messages on those *Red Cliff*-focused pages. In addition, the language use (mostly English) on these Kaneshiro-related pages and the way they were concisely written did not reveal much about what diasporic Chinese viewers thought of the film per se. That left us with Kaneshiro's fansites to carry out content analysis, a possible way to gain knowledge of how Kaneshiro fans, who were also *Red Cliff*'s audiences in the Chinese diaspora, thought of Woo's film as a historical epic.

Nine individual Kaneshiro fansites were found for this purpose. One of them was written in Japanese, four in Chinese, and four in English. However, not all of them functioned as truly interactive forums to allow Kaneshiro fans to express their views. Among them, only Chinese-language site www.takeshikaneshiro.net embedded insightful information for a better understanding of the views of diasporic Chinese on *Red Cliff*. It was one of the most systematically organized fansites revolving around different aspects of the star persona of Kaneshiro, for example, his latest news, journal, participation in mass media, and a message board for fans to leave their comments and to exchange their ideas.

The message board on this site was divided into various topics such as films, advertisements, music videos, and other mass media, all of which Kaneshiro has been heavily involved in as a trans-Asian, multimedia star. Members identified themselves as originating from mainland China, Hong Kong, Taiwan, Formosa, Malaysia, and so on. The site could roughly be divided into three layers: the first layer was the thread, second the entries in each thread, and third the number of views of each thread.

In late March 2009, after both installments of *Red Cliff* had already been theatrically released in East and Southeast Asia (except Japan where the second installment of the film was released on April 10), messages and comments about Kaneshiro and his appearance in *Red Cliff* mushroomed on the message board of this site. Under the topic of "films," there were fifty-seven threads of messages and 246 entries on Kaneshiro's role as Zhuge, with page-view number ranging from a few hundred to around 2,000 for each thread. Under the topic of "general discussion" of Kaneshiro, there were a few threads discussing the film *Red Cliff* more generally.

These figures could only tell that Kaneshiro is indeed very popular among his fans. Because of him, *Red Cliff* has also become popular among his fans-cum-*Red Cliff* spectators. Yet the sheer number could not articulate how these Kaneshiro fans-cum-*Red Cliff* spectators thought about the film, their viewing experience, their sense of self as part of the Chinese race, and what they thought about themselves in terms of Chinese history. Analyzing the content of these messages, however, showed us indirectly these historical and ideological considerations among these fans-cum-spectators amidst a sea of thousands of texts and messages that were no more than babbles showing the fans' admiration for the star. Several cases are identified and translated here for exploration. All of the messages found on this site were written in either traditional or simplified Chinese characters, depending on where the writers were from.

1. *Amy* (Hong Kong) (posted July 11, 2008, 22:31): Lin Chiling's Xiao Qiao is important in *Red Cliff*, for Cao Cao waged the whole war in order to get her as his woman.

    Jiner (Shanghai) (posted July 14, 2008, 14:08): Woo made it all up. Men wage war usually for their hunger for power and ambition. If they can become the emperor one day, they can get all the women. It just doesn't make sense in this film to start a war because of Xiao Qiao. This reason of fighting a war will just piss Cao Cao's admirers off. I believe the role of Xiao Qiao is purely for appealing to the film's foreign audiences. Otherwise, she shouldn't be there at all.

2. *Jiner* (Shanghai) (posted January 10, 2009, 19:00): The most exciting sequence is the one that portrays Zhuge using straw boats and scarecrows to snatch arrows from the Cao camp. This story is so famous in history . . . Takeshi is just great in that scene. He resembles much of the Zhuge in the minds of *Romance of the Three Kingdoms'* readers.

3. *Creamy* (mainland China) (posted February 13, 2009, 22:40): (sarcastically) *Red Cliff* has brought us a lot of "fun" with all those ridiculous scenes and babbling lines. Moviegoers (in mainland China) seemed to enjoy it as a comedy.

In Case 1, the shared affection for their idol helped bind the two female fans together. Regardless of the dialect barrier and the cultural contexts in which they wrote the messages, the two females managed to shed some light on the narrative of *Red Cliff*. Jiner's remarks were very similar to all those negative comments found on *Red Cliff*'s official China site. She demonstrated an example of mainland Chinese spectators who preferred faithful film adaptation of the classic *Romance of Three Kingdoms*—a classic literary work more well known than the historical record of the Three Kingdoms period during which the historical figure Xiao Qiao did not have a prominent place. Jiner furthered this thought in Case 2 here by associating Kaneshiro with her (and other *Romance of Three Kingdoms* readers') imagined Zhuge. This explains why Creamy in Case 3 commented sarcastically on the "inauthenticity" of the film and its likely awkwardness from the viewpoint of mainland Chinese audiences.

Obviously with a different socio-cultural upbringing in Hong Kong, Amy did not agree with Jiner in Case 1 here, as she saw the events and personalities with regard to the film's diegesis only. She might not have been fully aware of the importance or unimportance that the role Xiao Qiao played in history, most likely because her different experience in Hong Kong has allowed her to have some other analysis of the film texts and the history itself. In this conversation, both fans showed their own interventions and interpretations of a historic past of which they would not have first-hand experience. What they could do was to make reference to the experience and lives with which they were most familiar. However, how they did it might not necessarily be in the same way that Woo might have expected when he directed the film.

4. *Pui* (Malaysia) (posted July 18, 2008, 03:00): Why is there censorship here? Why can't we watch the scene where Zhuge helps the cow [sic: horse] to deliver a baby? Why can't we watch the scene where Lin Chiling practices calligraphy and names her future baby? The Malaysian government just censors whatever there is of importance in the film. DVD released here will also be like this. I am angry. I want to get the DVD version from Taiwan.

5. *Sara* (Hong Kong) (posted November 3, 2008, 17:25): A poll in Japan shows that Takeshi's Zhuge Liang is the most popular role in *Red Cliff*. Takeshi wins the heart of Japanese easily because he has a Japanese background. He is also attached to Taiwan but he is disqualified from competing in the Golden Horse Awards . . . Boo . . . Taiwan has hurt Takeshi's heart.

   Kwun (Hong Kong) (posted November 3, 2008, 17:52): Mind you! Golden Horse Awards is different from the place Taiwan. I believe Mr. Kaneshiro still loves Taiwan very much as Taiwan is his home . . . but I really don't understand why he is not there in the award.

Cases 4 and 5 directed our attention toward what it means to be diasporic Chinese in the minds of different individuals who are in the same Chinese diaspora, and how closely connected these displaced people are with China. In Case 4, it was unclear why this Malaysian fan specified wanting to have a Taiwanese version of the film's DVD release, as the film was also released in DVD format in regions such as Hong Kong and Japan. Unconsciously, this fan was engaging herself in a distribution channel that is typical of diasporic communities to gain access to the films produced in their ancestral land. In this case, China, as the country of production of *Red Cliff*, was not mentioned. Taiwan, on the other hand, seemed to be better known for its insistence on maintaining Chinese cultural heritage among different Chinese diasporic communities. The fan assumed Taiwan but not China as the last resort for buying *Red Cliff*'s DVD. This cast doubt on the closeness between diasporic Chinese and their supposed motherland.

Similar viewpoints backed up the conversations between two Hong Kongers in Case 5 when they talked about how Kaneshiro's ambiguous origins had caused his disqualification from an important film award in Taiwan. Instead of reaffirming Kaneshiro's (half-)ethnic Chinese background,

Kwun in Case 5 only said that Taiwan was the star's home. There was no mention about China or the star's Chinese roots. The posts in Cases 4 and 5 here thus contradicts Naficy's opinion on people in diaspora who, according to him, would forge close affinities with their motherlands as much as with their fellow diasporic communities elsewhere in maintaining their ethnic consciousness.

6. *Kwun* (Hong Kong) (posted July 21, 2008, 13:34): There are many people who don't like Takeshi's Zhuge Liang, claiming that Takeshi doesn't match with the image of this historical figure traditionally known and portrayed. But I quite like Woo's re-presentation of the historical figure of Zhuge. From what I know in history, the real Zhuge at the time of the battle of Red Cliff was in his late twenties . . . so I think the casting of this role is appropriate . . . Moreover, if Woo relies too much on tradition and history to design this role, it will not bring fresh viewing experience to the audiences . . . We as spectators should approve this kind of cinematic creativeness . . . Who can really tell what real history is? Everyone of us should have our own interpretation of history.

    Xue B (Taiwan) (posted July 22, 2008, 12:29): Thanks for sharing this. I totally agree!!!

7. *Sara* (Hong Kong) (posted July 29, 2008, 16:44): It depends on what you expect to see in *Red Cliff*. If you anticipate watching a real history on screen, you will be disappointed . . . Although the lines in *Red Cliff* are contemporary, I didn't find them laughable. I watched the film at around noon on a Tuesday on Hong Kong Island. The cinema was 90 percent full that day. All spectators took the film very seriously and didn't laugh at its historical inaccuracies . . . I really don't understand why the spectators on the Mainland complain so much about this film.

    Cloud (unidentified location, writing style close to that of Taiwan Chinese) (posted July 30, 2008, 02:22): I agree with Sara . . . On the sources of this film, director Woo said many times in media interviews that he has collected information from legitimate, historical texts as well as anecdotes and fictions to recreate a group of personalities from the period of Three Kingdoms. Woo is very creative to reinterpret the stories in that historical period. Now we see all good guys from the angle of Liu and regard the others, such as Cao, as bad guys. How about if we stand in the position of Cao, will it make any difference to our understanding of these historical figures?

    Bububei (unidentified location, writing style close to that of Taiwan Chinese) (posted October 22, 2008, 23:27): I am happy to see that so many of us are coming here to write some feelings after watching the film . . . I don't like wars but enjoy what is shown on screen in *Red Cliff* . . . in the scene where Zhuge and Zhou play the instruments, I can even smell some unnamed attraction between the two men.

The conversations in Cases 6 and 7 were particularly interesting in showing the spectators' responses in a context where written history itself was not particularly important. What was more significant was the spectators' realization of their roles in reinterpreting the historical messages that were mediated through the medium of film by the filmmaker. During this process, they automatically reinvented themselves into agents for mediating the historic past, raising questions to each other in the hope of furthering their own understanding. For example, the way in which Bububei in Case 7 reinterpreted a scene from the film as an understated homoerotic episode showed an obvious deviation from not just the known history but also from what Woo might have intended to bring to his audiences. Such an interpretation showed a reference to the general acceptance of gay culture worldwide today. In this fan's case, history as portrayed in *Red Cliff* allowed her to reevaluate some known historical facts and to reaffirm her agreement with the convention in the present time. Interestingly, these fans in Cases 6 and 7 are nonmainland Chinese. The fact that they were not living in mainland China could have given them some distinctiveness in terms of ideological upbringings, leading them to see history differently from their mainland counterparts who disliked the film due to its unfaithfulness to "history."

It is worth noting that certain methodological constraints could have influenced my interpretations of these web-based messages. For instance, the fact that I conducted the online survey in random months (March and August 2009) in the first year of the film's theatrical release means that I would not be able to see any future responses to these threads, which are likely to extend in time. These messages only reflected the active participation of some fans and might not represent the views of those much less active online.[53] How these others, for example the elderly or financially disadvantaged ethnic Chinese settled in different East and Southeast Asian territories might react to *Red Cliff* remains uncertain. This problem of representativeness would pose further methodological difficulties if I were to examine fansites of not just Kaneshiro but other trans-Asian stars featured in this film, such as Tony Leung Chiu-wai and Chang Chen.

On the whole, my research did not confirm my first hypothesized, spectatorial response made earlier about diasporic viewers' complete agreement with the director on the issues of cultural and national unification. For my second hypothesized, spectatorial response, which considered a pure Chinese cultural and national identity being an impossible dream, there was not much evidence displaying the fans-cum-spectators' negative views on their own diasporic status vis-à-vis the Sinocentric, cultural and national identity as mediated in the film. There was also no particular enthusiasm about Chinese culture. The "imagined" homeland of China simply hadn't weighed much with these ethnic Chinese spectators of *Red Cliff* in their daily lives. Hence, my findings in this online survey could not comfortably support or refute my second hypothesized, spectatorial response.

Confirming my third hypothesis about the negotiation between the historical and diasporic consciousnesses of *Red Cliff*'s diasporic Chinese audiences, online messages showed that these Kaneshiro fans-cum-*Red Cliff* spectators had unconsciously positioned themselves at a historical "crossroads." They were empowered by watching this film to participate in a collective rethinking of a historic past; yet different spectators might see it differently when they looked inward into their own subjectivities. Moreover, their status of being fans of Kaneshiro and becoming members of his fansites had granted them online, border-crossing opportunities to exchange with each other. Their awareness of their diasporic status (as shown in Cases 4 and 7 here) had given them the impetus to look at their Chinese cultural heritage from both an insider's and an outsider's point of view. They were thus reunited somehow in the virtual space of the internet to renegotiate and rearticulate their own Chineseness through the use of written Chinese language. In this sense, Woo's *Red Cliff* was successful in bringing together these diverse Chinese communities in East and Southeast Asian region in an online cultural sphere.[54] The downside of this reunification was that their culturally peripheral position was confirmed once again, as suggested by the difference in thoughts between them and their mainland counterparts. Yet, from the perspective of non-Chinese speakers, these Kaneshiro fans' online unity through using Chinese languages had also excluded other communities which do not speak and write Chinese or know much about the historic past of Ancient China. This socio-cultural exclusion of the Other from an ethnocentric standpoint certainly creates tensions among different viewing communities in a globalized world.

conclusion

Red Cliff is emblematic of the united East Asian efforts in transnational filmmaking practice. Such industrial practice breaks down the limitations created by the stiff national boundaries of modern nation-states. Indirectly, it also challenges the monolithic hegemony that is often related to the epic films made by Hollywood studios. I have investigated in this essay the manner in which Woo has combined his cultural and historical knowledge of China to reconstruct an on-screen spectacle of the battle of Red Cliff for his target audiences and the director's possible intent to stimulate thoughts for cultural and national unification among diasporic Chinese. Through this process, Woo has practically empowered himself and the film as historical agents, helping his spectators (that is, the viewing Other) to reevaluate a past that no one in the contemporary era could have lived in. I argued that he has made use of certain filmic devices such as the round objects in the mise-en-scène and the transnational cast to fulfill his directorial intent.

Yet, what Woo has done can only show one facet of how individuals living in the present engage in a dialogue with the past to reaccentuate what had come before our time, and in doing so, to reunderstand our present time and ourselves. In contrast, my study of Kaneshiro's online fandom has attempted to look at multifarious activities that an epic such as *Red Cliff* could have generated among its audiences.

As if prompted by the cultural and nationalistic messages of the film, the online fandom devoted to Kaneshiro did unite members from different diasporic Chinese communities now settled in various East and Southeast Asian territories. However, while these diasporic spectators of Woo's film could be reunited through this film via such off-screen channels as web-based social networks and Kaneshiro's unofficial fansites, these Kaneshiro fans-cum-*Red Cliff* spectators do not speak directly to the redefined past that Woo orchestrated for them. Their participation in the online chats created a launching pad for other kinds of possible interpretations of and engagement with this particular historical incident. Moreover, while these online activities provided Kaneshiro fans with the opportunities to forge virtual bonds with each other via their shared, double identity as the star's fans and diasporic Chinese, their very existence and their online activities also spoke vociferously of their diasporic status. It confirmed once again their culturally peripheral standing in a larger Chinese narrative without them feeling the urge to do anything about it. With the use of Chinese language to communicate with one another even though it might not be entirely comprehensible across different Chinese dialectic groups, these fans-cum-spectators might sustain yet another layer of separation of themselves from those outside their cultural-linguistic circle. In view of all these complications triggered by the diasporic experiences of the director and his target audiences, *Red Cliff* as an epic film may not only reinforce a rethinking of a lost past, it also elicits a tapestry of reevaluations of the present and reenvisioning of the future, which may or may not be directly connected to the original, historic past.

notes

1. Sun Tzu, *The Art of War* (China, c. 600 bc), Section III: Attack by Stratagem.
2. Su Shi, *Qian Chibifu (First Rhyme-prose of the Red Cliffs)* (c. ad 1080–1086); my translation.
3. A condensed version combining the two installments was released outside Asia in January 2009.
4. See Maria Wyke, *Project the Past: Ancient Rome, Cinema, and History* (London: Routledge, 1997), p. 13.
5. The target markets of *Red Cliff: Part I* in East and Southeast Asia include the PRC, Hong Kong, Taiwan, Singapore, Indonesia, South Korea, Japan, Thailand, and Malaysia. The film opened in these countries on or around

July 10, 2008 (except Japan, which had the film opened in November that same year), synergizing the marketing efforts and the anticipated word-of-mouth effects for the film across the whole region. This suggests a well-thought-out, international marketing plan on the part of the film distributors to capitalize fully on these distinguished markets. *Red Cliff: Part II* opened only in these markets (which are the same as that of *Part I*, except Thailand and Malaysia) in January 2009 (April 2009 in Japan), topping again the first weekend box-office gross chart in these individual markets (Indonesia box office data not available). Main source of the box office data is www.boxofficemojo.com.

6. See Christina Klein, "Crouching Tiger, Hidden Dragon: A Diasporic Reading," *Cinema Journal*, 43 (4) (2004): 18–42.

7. Hamid Naficy, *An Accented Cinema: Exilic and Diasporic Filmmaking* (Princeton, NJ: Princeton University Press, 2001).

8. Peter Seixas (ed.), *Theorizing Historical Consciousness* (Toronto: University of Toronto Press, 2004).

9. While the IMDb lists *Red Cliff*'s production companies as including those from these five territories plus an American company Lion Rock Productions founded by Woo and Terence Chang, trade press *Variety* confirms that *Red Cliff* has four Asian equity investors. See Anne Thompson, "H'wood in Thrall of Great Wall," *Variety*, 410 (3), March 3, 2008: 8(2); Patrick Frater, "Asia Piggy Bank Has Gobs of Gold: India, China, Japan All Show Financial Strength during Cannes," *Variety*, 411 (2) (May 26, 2008), p. 8. The second news article cited here contains a brief quotation from Woo saying that China now has the world-class production capacity to make big-budget films such as *Gladiator* or *Troy*.

10. Immediate precedents of *Red Cliff* are *The Warlords* (2007), and *Three Kingdoms: Resurrection of the Dragon* (2008).

11. Robert Burgoyne, *The Hollywood Historical Film* (Malden, Mass.: Blackwell, 2008), p. 2.

12. Burgoyne, *The Hollywood Historical Film*, p. 75.

13. Robert A. Rosenstone, *History on Film/Film on History* (Edinburgh: Pearson, 2006).

14. Rosenstone, *History on Film/Film on History*, p. 39; see also Monica Silveira Cyrino, *Big Screen Rome* (Malden, Mass.: Blackwell, 2005), pp. 2, 7, 207–256.

15. Romanization of the characters' names follows mainly the *pinyin* system with surname coming first, whereas the names of the crew and cast are presented in their most recognizable form. For example, in the case of John Woo, the surname Woo is used after the first mention of the director, while the surname Zhang will be acknowledged in the case of Zhang Fengyi.

16. The cinematic reconstruction of the battle of Changban, whose name is not mentioned in the film, suggests the director's intention to capitalize on the target spectators' knowledge of this battle. This gives evidence that the director has intended to appeal specifically to his Chinese viewing communities in East and Southeast Asia.

17. Interviews of the director and cast (in both Mandarin and Cantonese languages) are found in the Hong Kong version of the film's DVD (*Part I*); see also promotional material on www.yesasia.com—the online shopping website boasting itself as the leading shopping site for Asian entertainment products.

18. Tony Williams, "Space, Place, and Spectacle: The Crisis Cinemas of John Woo," *Cinema Journal* 36 (2) (winter 1997): 67; see also "Things I Felt Were Being Lost" (interview), *Film Comment* 29 (5) (1993): 50.

19. Stephen Teo, *Hong Kong Cinema: The Extra Dimensions* (London: BFI, 1997), p. 179.

20. Zhang Sun, "John Woo on Cao Cao and Zhou Yu" (in Chinese), posted February 8, 2007, available online at http://ent.sina.com.cn/m/c/2007–02–08/10191443070.html (accessed October 23, 2008); my translation.

21. Williams, "Space, Place, and Spectacle," p. 79.

22. Jonathan Rutherford, "Interview with Homi Bhabha," in Jonathan Rutherford (ed.), *Identity: Community, Culture, Difference* (London: Lawrence & Wishart, 1990), p. 211.

23. Rutherford, "Interview with Homi Bhabha," p. 212; see also Homi K. Bhabha, "How Newness Enters the World: Postmodern Space, Postcolonial Times and the Trials of Cultural Translation," in Homi K. Bhabha, *The Location of Culture* (London and New York: Routledge, 1994), p. 224.

24. Naficy, *An Accented Cinema*, pp. 46–47.

25. Jillian Sandell, "Reinventing Masculinity: The Spectacle of Male Intimacy in the Films of John Woo," *Film Quarterly*, 49 (4) (summer 1996): 23–34; Julian Stringer, "'Your Tender Smiles Give Me Strength': Paradigms of Masculinity in John Woo's *A Better Tomorrow* and *The Killer*," *Screen*, 38 (1) (spring 1997): 25–41; Teo, *Hong Kong Cinema*; Williams, "Space, Place, and Spectacle"; Lisa Odham Stokes and Michael Hoover, *City on Fire: Hong Kong Cinema* (London: Verso, 1999), pp. 38–63; see also John Woo, "John Woo; Filmmaker," *Film Quarterly*, 52 (1) (fall 1998): 71.

26. Naficy, *An Accented Cinema*, pp. 33–35.

27. Naficy, *An Accented Cinema*, p. 35.

28. Naficy, *An Accented Cinema*, p. 35.

29. Zhen Yao-huan, "Round Heaven Flat Land and Round Land Flat Heaven" (in Chinese), *Physics Bimonthly*, 27 (6) (December 2005): 786–791, available online at http://psroc.phys.ntu.edu.tw/bimonth/v27/786.pdf (accessed March 16, 2009); Lou Qingxi, *The Architectural Art of Ancient China*, trans. Li Zhurun (Beijing: China Intercontinental Press, 2001), p. 60.

30. Lou, *The Architectural Art of Ancient China*, pp. 54–63.

31. JeeLoo Liu, *An Introduction to Chinese Philosophy: From Ancient Philosophy to Chinese Buddhism* (Malden, Mass.: Blackwell, 2006), pp. 7–8, 32.

32. Interview with Woo (in Cantonese) in *Red Cliff: Part I*'s DVD release (Hong Kong version).

33. Liu, *An Introduction to Chinese Philosophy*.

34. Derek Elley, *The Epic Film: Myth and History* (London: Routledge & Kegan Paul, 1984), p. 16.

35. Tony Leung Chiu-wai from Hong Kong is famous for his Cannes award-winning role in Wong Kar-wai's *In the Mood for Love* (2000), and Takeshi Kaneshiro is famous for his role in *Chungking Express* (1994). Zhang Fenyi is most famous for his leading role in Chen Kaige's *Farewell My Concubine* (1993). Chang Chen was celebrated for his debut role in *A Brighter Summer Day* (1991) at the age of fifteen and later his role in Ang Lee's *Crouching Tiger, Hidden Dragon*. Zhao Wei is generally regarded as one of the four most popular mainland Chinese female stars nowadays. Hu Jun has been heavily involved in Hong Kong-based coproduction blockbusters such as *Infernal Affairs II* (2003). He is well-known across East Asia. Shido Nakamura's latest international film roles is Lieutenant Ito, the anti-hero who lies down in the open air among the corpses and waits to be killed by the American troop in *Letters from Iwo Jima* (2006).

36. Rosenstone, *History on Film/Film on History*, pp. 13, 16.
37. Robert Burgoyne, "Memory, History and Digital Imagery in Contemporary Film," in Paul Grainge (ed.), *Memory and Popular Film* (Manchester: Manchester University Press, 2003), p. 225.
38. Naficy, *An Accented Cinema*, pp. 10–17, 273.
39. Available online at http://chinanews.sina.com/ent/2008/1030/09573028915.html (accessed April 11, 2009); see also Marcus Lim, "Golden Horse Disqualifies Thesp: Takeshi Kaneshiro Nixed after Nationality Mix-up," *Variety.com*, posted October 31, 2008, available online at http://variety.com/article/VR1117995079.html?categoryid=13&cs=1 (accessed April 11, 2009).
40. Milton J. Esman, "The Chinese Diaspora in Southeast Asia," in Gabriel Sheffer (ed.), *Modern Diasporas in International Politics* (London and Sydney: Croom Helm, 1986), p. 130.
41. Naficy, *An Accented Cinema*, p. 14.
42. Ien Ang, *On Not Speaking Chinese: Living between Asia and the West* (London: Routledge, 2001).
43. Jamie Russell, "Takeshi Kaneshiro: House of Flying Daggers," BBC, c. 2004, available online at www.bbc.co.uk/films/2004/12/10/takeshi_kaneshiro_flying_daggers_interview.shtml (accessed August 6, 2008).
44. Available online at www.fulong.jp/kaneshiro/new_2006.html (accessed March 26, 2009).
45. Henry Jenkins, *Convergence Culture: Where Old and New Media Collide* (New York: New York University Press, 2006), p. 2.
46. Jenkins, *Convergence Culture*, p. 3.
47. Nancy K. Baym, "The New Shape of Online Community: The Example of Swedish Independent Music Fandom," *First Monday*, 12 (8) (August 6, 2007), available online at http://firstmonday.org/htbin/cgiwrap/bin/ojs/index.php/fm/article/view/1978/1853 (accessed March 8, 2009).
48. Henry Jenkins, *Fans, Bloggers, and Gamers: Exploring Participatory Culture* (New York and London: New York University Press, 2006).
49. See Kim Hyung-eun, "Historical China Film Lives Up to Expectations" (Film Review), *JoongAng Daily*, posted July 11, 2008, available online at http://joongangdaily.joins.com/article/view.asp?aid=2892148 (accessed October 23, 2008); Lee Hyo-won, "'Red Cliff': Megastars Bring Mega Action," *The Korean Times*, posted July 3, 2008, available online at www.koreatimes.co.kr/www/news/art/2008/07/141_26959.html (accessed October 23, 2008); Maggie Lee, "Film Review: Red Cliff," *The Hollywood Reporter*, posted July 11, 2008, available online at www.hollywoodreporter.com/hr/content_display/asia/reviews/e3i74e046bb4149b4ce3648a181c0b4fdf9 (accessed October 23, 2008); Aaron Toronto, "An Epic Return," *Thanh Nien Daily*, posted July 20, 2008, available online at www.thanhniennews.com/entertaiments/?catid=6&newsid=40393 (accessed October 23, 2008).
50. Seixas, *Theorizing Historical Consciousness*, p. 10.
51. William Safran, "Diasporas in Modern Societies: Myths of Homeland and Return," *Diaspora*, 1 (1) (spring 1991): 87.
52. Naficy, *An Accented Cinema*, p. 14.
53. See Mohan J. Dutta-Bergman, "Access to the Internet in the Context of Community Participation and Community Satisfaction," *New Media & Society*, 7 (1) (2005): 89–109.
54. Guobin Yang, "The Internet and the Rise of a Transnational Chinese Cultural Sphere," *Media, Culture & Society*, 25 (2003): 469–490.

remembering the

nation

part three

passing through

nightmares

cecil b. demille's *the plainsman* and epic

t e n

discourse in new deal america

p h i l   w a g n e r

*[T]he American cinema had the means to save its dream by
passing through nightmares.*[1]

This case study of Cecil B. DeMille's Americana epic of 1936, *The Plainsman,*
will illuminate the ways in which the epic film situates itself within
American culture as an authentic, monumental artistic form that endeavors to cultivate in its public a powerful (and politically advantageous) sense
of collective belonging, personal responsibility, and "spiritual" affinity with
venerable historical beings. I would like to argue that *The Plainsman* is not
only instructive of how the epic film *cinematically* conveys poignant themes
of historical continuity through visual metaphors of regeneration and
immersive spectacle that provokes strong empathy for historically representative characters. I would also like to show how the "historical eventfulness" of the Hollywood epic, those features of the epic film experience
that transcend "its already excessive screen boundaries," provides audiences with opportunities to *socially* perform continuity with the past, as

indicated by the Wild West fashion trends and schoolhouse reenactments that accompanied the film's theatrical run, and the eager participation in the film's production of alleged historical bona fides and modern-day servicemen.[2] The Plainsman is emblematic of how epic film discourse—as a conventionalized mode of public expression that implies a powerful existential bond between present-day spectators and represented pasts—both nurtures and restores what Gilles Deleuze sees as a reigning "consensus which allows [America] to develop illusions about itself, about its motives, its desires . . . values and its ideals."[3] As Jani Scandura reminds us, "the Depression shattered a national imaginary—perpetuated by big industry—that was grounded in progressive narratives of history and culture."[4] The Plainsman, and other Hollywood epics of the late 1930s, labored to resuscitate this dream.

"no cracked earth:" *the plainsman* and presentist address

Franklin Delano Roosevelt, in his Fireside Chat of September 6, 1936, recalled a haunting journey through America's Dustbowl. "I saw draught devastation in nine states," the President told his listeners, and then, in solemn, near-biblical language, proceeded to evoke the vast "fields of wheat so blasted by heat that they cannot be harvested," the "brown pastures which would not keep a cow on fifty acres," and the "families who had lost their . . . water in their well, lost their garden." But for FDR this scorched earth was not entirely fruitless. Roosevelt's affecting, ethnographic depiction of agrarian struggle not only provoked state sympathy for intensified governmental work relief but also produced a fertile symbol of American perseverance. The nation's wasteland became a canvas upon which Roosevelt projected an encouraging vision of human endurance. "I would not have you think for a single minute that there is permanent disaster in these drought regions," the President declared, "No cracked earth, no blistering sun, no burning wind . . . are a permanent match for the indomitable American farmers and stockmen and their wives and children who have carried on through desperate days, and inspire us with their self-reliance, their tenacity and their courage."[5]

The emotional tenor of Roosevelt's oratory—unflagging determination in the face of extraordinary disaster—informed the historical mythos of the Hollywood epic in New Deal America. Paramount screenwriter Jesse Lasky, Jr., recalled how, in the 1930s, American "audiences were ripe for sweeping vistas of continent-taming tribulations . . . We needed to regain a sense of purpose in the long hangover from Prohibition and the materialistic disestablishment of the Depression."[6] DeMille's tremendously successful western epic, The Plainsman, vividly demonstrates Lasky's observations on the contemporary cultural value of heroic tales of nation-building.[7] Consider, for example, the film's opening credit sequence.

The Plainsman begins as the Paramount logo dissolves to a shot of migrants' horses hauling a covered wagon toward a distant horizon. Composer George Antheil's exuberant orchestral march transforms this potentially somber scene of cultural dislocation into a commemorative image of national endurance. A second dissolve then leads to a static vista shot of an arid plain. The shot holds and the credits—which are not presented in a conventional top-to-bottom scroll but emerge from the frame's foreground and travel toward deep space—dissolve into the rolling hills that line the background of the shot. The opening credits come to a close, and the gleeful score is quickly replaced by a cacophony of foreboding horns and vertiginous strings. This orchestral digression reaches its climax, and a third dissolve segues to a murky image of tumbleweeds traveling through a dense cloud of dust. A wailing flute appears on the soundtrack, accentuating the violence of the storm.

The opening credits' progression toward the horizon mirrors the forward trajectory of the settlers in the first shot. This graphic comparison has rich implications. DeMille, by visually associating the A-list cast with the anonymous pioneers, suggests that his characters are not mere individuals, but, like so many epic characters, represent a collective "symbol of historical emergence."[8] In addition, the credits' eventual disappearance into the hills encourages spectators to imagine that they will soon rewitness a thrilling portion of the American past. The *names* Gary Cooper and Jean Arthur have disappeared into the landscape; but, according to the editorial logic of the sequence, these performers will reemerge from the earth as physical reincarnations of the film's protagonists, Wild Bill Hickok and Calamity Jane. DeMille once stated how "My idea in every picture I make is to duplicate historical figures as nearly as I can. Cooper, in general proportions and manner, might be *Hickok come to life* . . . Supporting players are also chosen to resemble extant photographs and sketches of the historical characters."[9] A *Life* profile on the film also highlighted the director's preoccupation with convincing historical personification: "DeMille read [and] re-read the story of Wild Bill Hickok and Calamity Jane. As a result, [the director's] newest production . . . has fan favorites Gary Cooper and Jean Arthur *re-living* the romance of those two hardbitten characters[.]"[10] Sobchack observes how stars "people the represented past with the present. . . . [They] serve to generalize historical specificity through their iconographic presence. Stars are cast not as characters, but in character—as 'types' who . . . signify universal general characteristics."[11] In this light, these symbolically loaded credits do not, as J. E. Smith argues, convey the deconstructive theme that "all history is based on recycled legends and elusive text," but instead graphically communicate the epic cinema's inveterate artistic goal of "authentic" historical embodiment, one of the definitive ways in which the genre makes its morally situated historiographic visions both legible and legitimate.[12]

But perhaps more important is the credit sequence's wasteland imagery, which can be taken as a graphic evocation of the Dust Bowl. The credits' desolate backdrop would have undoubtedly resonated with present-day audiences—especially those of the plains states, where DeMille premiered his film and where the public suffered the most from the agricultural catastrophe. Piers Brendon observes how "The Dust Bowl provided contemporaries with a potent symbol for the Depression decade . . . It was a metaphor of metamorphosis—the transformation of brave new world into wasteland, the turning of American dream into nightmare."[13] Likewise, Michael Denning, in his important *The Cultural Front,* notes that "the desiccated plains and violent dust storms of the Dust Bowl became the foremost natural analogue of the depression."[14] But DeMille, like Roosevelt in his moving address on the great drought, puts a positive spin on Dust Bowl imagery. As the opening sequence progresses, the dust cloud dissipates and the sequence dissolves to a vista shot of the plains on a fair day, over which the initial jubilance of the score has been restored and in front of which an epigraph introduces the film's principal characters: "Among the men who thrust forward America's frontier were Wild Bill Hickok and Buffalo Bill Cody. The story that follows compresses many years, many lives and widely separated events into one narrative—in an attempt to do justice to the courage of the plainsman of our west."

It is particularly telling that the dust storm—a metaphor for the nation's current ecological disaster and economic turmoil—clears once the film's historical protagonists are introduced. Here, DeMille situates the film's predominant message: the resilience and determination of America's frontiersmen, spiritually preserved in the present body politic, will steer the nation through the turbulence of the Depression.

"kindred fires"—the demillian epic as romantic historiography

Popular American storytelling of the 1930s was characterized, in large part, by a return of the repressed. Denning, for instance, has observed how a "gallery of allegorical icons of victimization, innocence, and resilience, ranging from Franklin Delano Roosevelt's 'forgotten man' to Steinbeck's Ma Joad, from Dorothea Lange's Migrant Mother to Frank Capra's Mr. Smith" *came to the surface* alongside Depression-bred sentiments such as vulnerability, rootlessness, and abandonment.[15] This representational tradition, defined by a taxing discovery of place and belonging, was a reflection of the "mainstream populism" of a New Deal state geared more toward bolstering faith in national endurance than fomenting desire for radical social change.[16] "Simply in being remembered the Forgotten Man seemed rescued," Scandura keenly observes.[17]

Newfound interest in the forgotten and the ordinary not only affected Hollywood's construction of fictional heroes but guided its selection of historical topics and characters as well. Indeed, this mass-mediated revision of American collective memory significantly inflected the DeMillian epic of the New Deal era. For instance, DeMille, on his popular *Lux Radio Theater* broadcast, described *The Plainsman* as the "first in the series of pictures based on the magnificent pageant of American history and its *unsung heroes*."[18] Months before, DeMille, also in reference to *The Plainsman,* noted how "It is the *unrecorded* episodes between events of history—the story between the lines—which have always fascinated me."[19] Around the same time, the director told the *New York Times* that *The Plainsman* is the first installment to "a series of American sketches . . . [on] some of the *obscurer,* less academic figures of history."[20] Alistair Cooke placed DeMille's frontier epic in context with the period's prevailing populist sentiments. Cooke noted how Frank Capra's *Mr. Deeds Goes to Town* (1936) was a timely success "because it glorified horse sense and canniness at the expense of subtlety, business acumen, sophistication."[21] "*The Plainsman* has exactly this quality," added Cooke.[22] DeMille's film, heralded as a commemorative portrait of the nation's pioneers and as a tribute to the enduring frontier ethos in contemporary America, was, on the surface, an exciting yarn set after the Civil War about old friends Wild Bill, Calamity Jane, and Buffalo Bill Cody and their valiant attempt to keep vengeful Indians from buying repeating rifles from venal governmental workers. "Not a plainsman in the group," observed Frank S. Nugent of the *New York Times.*[23] But Nugent overlooked the representative capacity of the film's heroes that profoundly resonated with audiences of the Depression.

David Levin, in his landmark book, *History as Romantic Art,* writes how "In order to understand the romantic historians' heroes . . . one must begin with what the heroes embodied . . . the People."[24] Here, Levin refers to a specific strand of historical thought—romantic history—practiced by nineteenth-century American writers such as Francis Parkman and William H. Prescott, who were influenced, first and foremost, by the historical novels of Sir Walter Scott. Despite Levin's period-specific frame of reference, his study can shed significant light on both DeMille's epic discourse and the general popular fiction of the New Deal state. Indeed, Levin's formulations offer revealing parallels with Deleuze's evaluation of the American epic through the critical lens of Nietzschean historiography. Levin argues that "The representative man was both a historical phenomenon and a literary device," and demonstrates how the pervading principles of a particular time and place can be gauged by the authorial orchestration of heroic action.[25] Deleuze, in a similar manner, maintains that "It is as representative of the collectivity that the hero becomes capable of an action which makes him equal to [an epic's unforgiving] milieu and re-establishes its accidentally or periodically endangered order."[26] Both critics' analytical subjects posit a morally charged, monumental vision of history as a perpetual duel between toxic and regenerative forces. As Levin writes, for the romantic historian,

> History was the unfolding of a vast Providential plan. . . . [with the] basic assumption [of] human progress. . . . [which] had proceeded westward, from the Middle East to North America. And all along the way, whether they knew it or not, the people had carried with them a new principle: Christianity in the 'German woods,' nationality in the Iberian peninsula, the Reformation in the Netherlands and England, Democracy (or Liberty) in the American colonies. . . . The historian studied the age, looked for the banner of progress in any conflict, and supported the side fighting under it.[27]

Likewise, Deleuze illustrates how the American epic film

> favors the analogies or parallels between the one civilization and another: great moments of humanity, however distant they are, are supposed to communicate via the peaks, and form a 'collection of effects in themselves' which can be more easily compared and act all the more strongly on the mind of the modern spectator.[28]

The Plainsman, therefore, as a romantic historical text, brings into focus both a chief artistic goal in New Deal America and a fundamental ambition of epic film discourse: the convincing and heartening communication of spiritual continuity between history's great men and present-day laypeople. This recurring theme of "the forgotten," which DeMille so visibly advocated in the late 1930s, calcified this emotional connection between the intrahistorical present and the collectively celebrated past. DeMille's epic of the Old West exemplifies romantic history's governing belief as conveyed by its most passionate spokesman, William Godwin: "It is the contemplation of illustrious men . . . that kindles into flame the hidden fire within us. . . . While we admire the poet and the hero, and sympathize with his generous ambition or his ardent expressions, we insensibly imbibe the same spirit, and burn with kindred fires."[29] In the end, DeMille's romantic history (characterized by a dramatic reliance on representative characters and an outspoken faith in both the affective power and didactic virtue of spectacle), reinforced the rhetorical platforms of the New Deal (the inevitably progressive flow of Western history, the everyman's ability to prevail through hard times) while it gave vivid expression to the epic cinema's bedrock theme of "the continuity of the nation."[30]

"take plenty of explosives to the location"—demille, frederic remington, historical participation

On November 1, 1935, Jeff Lazarus, a production supervisor at Paramount, contacted DeMille with concerns regarding *Buffalo Bill,* the director's western in its early developmental stages that would soon become *The Plainsman.* Lazarus feared that *Annie Oakley* (1935), an RKO production opening later that month, which depicted the sharpshooter's days on tour with the Buffalo Bill Wild West Show, might present legal hurdles before the DeMille project. DeMille assured the anxious Lazarus that there would be no creative conflict since "Buffalo Bill is a secondary character in *Annie Oakley,* and the entire picture deals with the show life of Annie Oakley," while our picture "is laid between the years 1865 and 1878, prior to the start of the Buffalo Bill Wild West Show." DeMille was not interested in "the ridiculous theatric adventures attributed to [Buffalo Bill] by so many authors," and recycled by RKO.[31] The director, who would repeatedly cite country-western stage shows, generic cowboy pictures, and apocryphal dime novels as artistic foils to his "super western," evoked a more dignified creative influence when discussing his film: "[*The Plainsman*] is a story of the West . . . a story of American character . . . pictured as Frederic Remington might have drawn it."[32] DeMille was so confident in the comparison that a "traveling collection of Frederic Remington's paintings . . . in theater lobbies in connection with premieres of the picture" was planned so his public could directly observe this estimable artistic resemblance.[33]

Both DeMille and Remington were native Easterners with boyish wonder for the American West. Though DeMille did not share Remington's elegiac outlook on the frontier's demise, he did share the painter's admiration for its stirring drama and sublime landscapes. DeMille's allusions to Remington implicitly guaranteed awe-inspiring spectacle and gripping action. But they also suggested meticulous attention to authentic details. It was well known that Remington frequently shadowed the nation's cavalry in order to witness at first hand the fading culture of the western frontier. The painter would sketch and photograph the behavior, customs, and dress of frontier life and, back in his studio in upstate New York, artistically render his observations. DeMille, on the other hand, found authentic inspiration in storied landscapes and primary documents.[34] "I have pursued verity from the Museum at Cairo to the smoking tepees of the Cheyenne at Lame Deer, Montana," DeMille once reminisced, "and a costly pursuit it has been. The charges of research alone on a major historical film are sixty thousand dollars."[35] Ultimately, however, in a DeMillian epic, authentic materials and locations did not acquire their greatest interest through the ability to corroborate, disprove, or even to educate, but through

213

their capacity to provide a liberating sense of "historical mobility," the thrilling sensation of "sitting invisible" at the table of the past.[36]

For DeMille, archival documents served as blueprints for exhilarating and morally instructive filmic scenarios. Like Theodore Roosevelt, the twentieth century's most vociferous advocate for the enduring social value of romantic history, DeMille believed that the "very accurate, very real and vivid presentation of the past can come only from one in whom the imaginative gift is strong."[37] Both men acknowledged that the "historian must of necessity be a master of the science of history, a man who has at his fingertips all the accumulated facts from the treasure-houses of the dead past."[38] But unless the historian possesses the "[imaginative] power to marshal what is dead so that before our eyes it lives again," the "accumulated facts from the treasure-houses of the dead past" fail to contribute to "the sum of man's wisdom, enjoyment and inspiration."[39] Unless imaginatively colored by the historian, accrued data remains, as William Godwin warned, "the mere chronicle of facts, places and dates" from which the "muscles, the articulations, everything in which the life emphatically resides, is absent."[40]

Remington—who illustrated Roosevelt's meditations on the beauty and hardships of the Plains, *Ranch Life and the Hunting Trail*, and later illustrated the Rough Riders' exploits in the Spanish–American War—served as DeMille's exemplar for the emotionally bracing and morally inspiring recreation of the past.[41] Though Remington's oeuvre is far from homogenous in topic, genre, or tone, he is mostly remembered—and emulated—for his dramatized renderings of frontier rituals and warfare.[42] David McCullough's description of *A Dash for the Timber*, Remington's vision of survival in the wilderness as personified by cowboys escaping rifle-wielding Apaches, captures nicely this popularly remembered side of the artist:

> The excitement is terrific. The missed riders charge pell-mell, nearly head on at the viewer. The horses are flying—hardly a hoof touches the ground—and the dead weight of one Indian soldier who has been hit makes the action of the other, and of the pursuing Indians, all the more alive. The dust flies . . . the guns blaze away, the wind whips the big hat brims . . . It is big action in big space.[43]

DeMille hoped to achieve this panoramic sense of peril in a scene in which a band of Cheyenne ambush Buffalo Bill and a brigade of cavalrymen. Though the scene was staged by Second-Unit Director Arthur Rosson, DeMille managed to leave his authorial stamp on the footage. In fact, the scene is particularly noteworthy since it forced the director to communicate to his auxiliary team his ideal vision of cinematic battle. DeMille's daily correspondences to his second unit illuminate the filmmaker's preference for sensorally combative techniques that elicit the impression of audience participation.

With DeMille's orders to "Take plenty of explosives to the location," the Second Unit ventured out into the snowcapped mountains of Birney, Montana.[44] DeMille was displeased with Rosson's early footage, mostly for its failure to leave a kinetic impression on the spectator. On June 20, 1936, an incensed DeMille wired Rosson, exclaiming how

> it is impossible to get a thrill from a charge coming directly
> at camera . . . we could not see any movement of either
> horse or man . . . the effect of this scene must be fast speed
> and thundering horses not little toy puppets two or three
> miles away . . . this must be the climax of an exciting
> sequence photographed as such.[45]

A later correspondence underscores the director's strong desire to provide spectators with a fully immersive sense of combat:

> the indians should come from the second or lower plat-
> form . . . they should start to fire immediately . . . fore-
> ground should always be full of indians . . . it is of the
> utmost importance that the audience sees firing at soldiers
> on island from all around . . . be certain that men are firing
> constantly from the trees in background of this shot and
> from other directions as well . . . any of your available help
> can do some of the firing . . . you can even use explosive
> bullets . . . puffs of smoke must be seen from trees all
> around especially trees in immediate background.[46]

The shots of the Indian war raid were to be returned to Hollywood and processed as transparencies—background scenes projected onto a screen in front of which a film's performers act.[47] The audience's sustained aware-ness of the Cheyenne war party, waiting in the background for the ideal moment to attack, was achieved by unceasing artillery fire. The puffs of smoke that span the frame and the relentless gunfire ricocheting on the soundtrack heighten this absorbing sense of battle sought by DeMille. The director's eye-level close-ups of Hickok and Buffalo Bill taking cover as bullets whiz by and over the shoulder shots of the cavalry picking off Cheyenne in the distance further enhance the spectator's illusion of par-taking in combat.[48] As Paul Ricoeur has demonstrated, the *experience* of an historical work is itself a form of "reenactment," for audiences imagina-tively "enter" a reconstructed past world as an attempt to grasp the feelings and decisions that instigate certain historical events.[49]

DeMille seemed inspired by Remington's 1897 painting, *Through the Smoke Sprang the Daring Solider,* a stirring vision of military sacrifice that anticipated these deliberate compositional arrangements provoking intimate viewer

215

involvement.[50] Art historian Doreen Bolger Burke has noted how "In works like *Through the Smoke Sprang the Daring Soldier* . . . [t]he viewer seems to participate in the battle: standing with the soldiers, who occupy the foreground, he faces an unseen enemy."[51] *The Plainsman*'s ambush scene also resonates with Alison Griffith's observations on nineteenth-century historical panoramas, how viewers of such colossal spectacles vicariously played the role of "historical witness or war reporter" and were thus able "to re-experience an event of enormous national significance [and] *step inside history*."[52] A Chicago exhibitor was similarly engrossed in *The Plainsman*: "The Indians were great. You have a feeling you're in the picture yourself."[53] DeMille's frontier epic reveals how the cinema amplifies this art-historical tradition of imaginary involvement in the represented past. Nineteenth-century visual media such as historical panoramas and Remington paintings not only "created expectations of verisimilitude and spectacle in the filmic treatment of battle," as Robert Burgoyne points out, but also highlight the symbiosis between the public's desire to viscerally experience the historical past and the lasting appeal of the Hollywood epic (see Figure 10.1).[54]

This sense of participation, so integral to the epic film experience, is firmly rooted in the romantic historical tradition. This is worth stressing because DeMille, like his romantic predecessors, believed that the human circumstances and moral lessons of the past are most affecting if presented in dramatic, immediate ways. Levin, for example, notes how Francis Parkman, in his picaresque rendering of exploration in the Americas, *France and England in North America,* repeatedly "tries to put the reader on the

Figure 10.1

Dan Sayre Groesbeck's sketch for *The Plainsman*'s Apache Raid. Source: With thanks to Brigham Young University.

scene—inside a small stockade attacked by Iroquois, bivouacking with a French and Indian war party, trying to sleep in a reeking Indian hut."[55] Incidentally, Remington, who shared Parkman's penchant for the direct presentation of tense moments, was commissioned to illustrate the fourth edition of Parkman's *The Oregon Trail*, much to the author's delight.[56] And like Parkman, Prescott, and Remington, DeMille repeatedly orchestrates narrative "point of view at moments of crisis" in order to furnish the illusion of participation and direct his audience's sympathies.[57] In *Conquest of Mexico*, Prescott's dehumanized vision of the Aztecs, relayed from "the Spanish point of view, from which they appear as a wild mass" structurally anticipates the grotesque close-ups and abstracted long shots of *The Plainsman*'s savages.[58]

Yet in the romantic historical epic it is not only crucial to "put the reader on the scene" of battle, but to convey as well the inner feelings of fighting men—the flesh and blood vessels of the work's moral principles. In *The Plainsman*, for instance, DeMille juxtaposes crowded wide shots of firing lines fending off Cheyenne with intimate close-ups of individual cavalrymen. The director repeatedly turns away from the battle at large and zeros in on, for example, a humorous exchange between fellow soldiers or a moving display of individual valor—like when an elderly soldier, blinded by shrapnel, struggles to load muskets for his able-bodied comrades. Here, DeMille successfully conveys the destructive scale of battle and the humanity caught in its grips. The sequences above, to be sure, mirror Godwin's choreographic preferences: "A scene incessantly floating cannot instruct us. . . . I would stop the flying figures, that I may mark them more clearly. There must be an exchange of real sentiments . . . There is a magnetical [sic] virtue in man, but there must be friction and heat before the virtue will operate."[59] DeMille's decoupage therefore not only enhances the audience's sense of danger but deepens its compassion for the imperiled soldiers. Empathy for these characters, in turn, engenders sympathy for the timely values which they embody—camaraderie, patriotism, and the good-natured perseverance through overwhelming odds.

the labors of authenticity, or: "who cares about historical correctness?"

As well as shedding light on the epic cinema's affective language and historical presentism, *The Plainsman* offers instructive examples of how the epic works to authenticate itself in order to acquire the attractive aura and persuasive power of historical documentation. The film's production history reveals an impressive assortment of tactics by which DeMille and company sought to bestow upon their film the cultural cachet of legitimate History.

The well-publicized involvement of eyewitnesses in the technical process gave *The Plainsman* an appealing truth value. During preproduction,

DeMille suggested to his associate producer, Bill Pine, how "We should get a great many old scouts, historians and old Westerners and everybody else to make statements that are to be published prior to the opening of [*The Plainsman*] relative to the historical accuracy of the picture."[60] DeMille's research team was later instructed to "to dig up outstanding people . . . and well-knowns of the Buffalo Bill days for a series of articles."[61] DeMille's researchers discovered Jim Moore, a veteran of Wounded Knee and the last surviving witness of Wild Bill's murder in Deadwood, South Dakota. Moore was summoned to *The Plainsman* set in order "to aid DeMille and see to it that the Bella Union saloon [where Wild Bill was slain] was reconstructed properly."[62] The participation of this elderly westerner was one step taken in DeMille's endeavor to silence critics who repeatedly questioned the veracity of his work. *The Oakland Tribune,* reporting from the set on the day of Moore's visit, emphasized the director's "perennial war with the critics on the matter of authenticity in his historical sequences," adding that Captain Moor's guidance would help guarantee that the reenactment of Wild Bill's death would be portrayed "with unimpeachable accuracy."[63] The *Los Angeles Times,* also on set that day, noted how the former Indian fighter helped Gary Cooper refine his authentic behavior by "teaching [him] all about six shooters."[64] DeMille hoped his epic would soak up the aura associated with Moor's lived experience.

In addition to publicizing Moor's authentic input, Paramount boasted DeMille's restaging "on the actual site of the original battle" of Custer's Last Stand.[65] The authentic historical scenery heightened the documentary value—the perceived referential bond between filmic representation and original historic event—of the action on screen. The authenticity of the filmed battle was accented as well by DeMille's recruitment of the National Guard Cavalry of Wyoming, which happily volunteered its entire regiment for the three-day shoot, and the director's casting of "real Indians" from nearby reservations.[66] In fact, DeMille was fortunate enough to find two elder Cheyenne who participated in the *real* Custer Massacre.[67] Cheyennes Louis Dog and Stump Horn, the *Los Angeles Times* reported, "were used as actors and technical advisers for the Custer scene and the other Indian sequences in 'The Plainsman.'"[68] Such impressive authentic ingredients helped elicit the sense that DeMille and company were not simply performing history but, as the studio proudly advertised, were actually "*re-fighting* the Custer Massacre."[69] *New York Times* critic Frank S. Nugent, typically dubious of DeMille's reconstructions, praised the film as "a picture in which small details are faithfully reproduced and established historical facts scrupulously rewritten."[70] Indeed, DeMille spoke of his epic as "an authentic record" of the opening of the frontier.[71] Welford Beaton of the *Hollywood Spectator* agreed, concluding that *The Plainsman* "is *a valuable historical document* to make future generations of Americans realize what they owe to a past generation of brave men and loyal women."[72]

DeMille was undoubtedly delighted when he read affirmations of the film's authenticity from people such as H. L. Hallett, a native plainsman in his late eighties. "I've seen everything you put in that picture," Hallet proclaimed, "It's a true life of the plains." Judge Dunker, a resident of the Black Hills since the early 1880s, echoed Hallet: "[The] picture is true to life."[73] Previewing the film in "towns and cities intimately associated" with the film's milieu was an effective publicity maneuver, as acclaim from *actual* plainsmen further embellished the film's historical value.[74] On December 1, 1936, DeMille left Hollywood for a "transcontinental preview tour" that targeted states connected to the film's historical background.[75] DeMille prefaced each screening with laudatory words on the nation's pioneers—some of whom were sitting in the audience. Preview cards were distributed so audience members could voice their opinions. Many trumpeted the praise DeMille wanted to hear—and publicize. O. L. Mills of Dallas wrote that *The Plainsman* was the "Finest picture I have witnessed depicting the Frontier."[76] Anonymous of Omaha who "has served many years on these same plains . . . thought it [was] the best portrayed of the customs of the ancient west we have ever seen."[77] Others admired the film's educational merits. The nation "needs more historical pictures like this one," a Dallas spectator proclaimed.[78] Mrs. J. J. McCarthur, also from Dallas, observed how "The historical background [was] quite correct," adding that the film "should go down in history as valuable educationally and in a class with [the great silent western] Covered Wagon."[79] Mrs. Grace Butler, a schoolteacher from Houston, saw the film as "a marvelous history lesson, even for elementary children."[80]

Not all plainsdwellers were so approving, however. Susan of Houston was unconvinced that DeMille significantly elevated the western genre: "Same Old Stuff Cecile Old Boy—Indians Vs. Cowboys + A Little Lovin.'"[81] Others weren't persuaded by the film's claims to authenticity. "As a biographical sketch it is rather faulty," wrote C. R. Lister of Dallas. John Conway, a gun enthusiast from Omaha, noted how the real "Wild Bill used [a] swivel holster, one only, not a 2-gun" like Cooper wears in the picture.[82] Furthermore, many would have preferred a less sanitized picture of the Old West. A Denver audience member felt that Jimmie Ellison, who played Buffalo Bill, showed "good acting [skill], but his face was too clean."[83] Mrs. M. J. Kahn of Denver also would have liked a less beautified Buffalo Bill: "the boy who played Bill Cody was . . . too feminine and weak."[84] Others objected to the glamour of Calamity Jane. Texan J. W. Buckett remarked how "Jean Arthur would be much more convincing as Calamity Jane if her hair were tousled some and if her face did not usually look like she had just left a beauty parlor."[85] Barney Oldfield of Nebraska's *Lincoln Sunday Journal and Star* wondered "how on earth any actress, especially one of Jean Arthur's smooth sophistication and unusual soft tongue, could re-enact with any faith the heavy holstered hoyden who chased Hickok wherever he went."[86]

For Houston's F. G. Shoemaker, Jean Arthur's charm diluted the film's historical value: "Calamity Jane was a trifle too nice to be historically correct."[87] Although the film's protagonists were said to personify "the strength, virtues and character" of both the nation's pioneers and present-day inhabitants of the Plains, for many they remained preternaturally beautiful creatures of Tinseltown.[88]

But authenticity, it should be said, had both its obvious and necessary limits. Smaller town audiences of the Depression era not only enjoyed the gratifying sense of historical continuity between legendary figures but also sought distraction from the general ugliness of 1930s America. For many, escapist urges outweighed appreciation for historical accuracy. Such an attitude was most pronounced in response to the film's tragic ending, when Wild Bill is shot in the back, as in history, by the craven glory-seeker Jack McCall. Ms. Alfred Jacoby of New Orleans pointed out how "the ending does not appeal to us *in these days and times* when there exists so much unhappiness and distress."[89] A Denver audience member opined, "I think it would be better to disregard History and make a happy ending."[90] A second Denver viewer rhetorically asked, "Why let the hero die? Who cares about historical correctness?"[91] Such sentiments spread throughout the New Orleans preview crowd, too. "A magnificent picture," admitted the Crescent City's Leo Hawks, "but I heard ladies all around . . . complain of the unhappy ending; they all think Gary [Cooper] should have lived for Calamity's sake."[92]

Ultimately, *The Plainsman* was a financial achievement precisely for its multifaceted appeal.[93] DeMille's historical work provided spectators with both the luring aura of historical authenticity and the soothing refuge of historical fantasy, both of which remain quintessential elements of epic film discourse. In the end, DeMille said it best: "The picture will be history to those who look for that . . . and a Western to those who don't."[94]

The Hollywood epic, seen by many as an unsettling reminder of America's conservative politics and material worship, was both framed and perceived rather contrarily in the late 1930s as an artistic reflection of core New Deal principles such as optimism, endurance, and public good will. Yet cultural friction between Hollywood and New Deal America remained evident. For one, DeMille touted the populist messages of *The Plainsman* while he scoffed at the prosaic traditions of the generic western, a beloved form of entertainment in the provincial regions the director was allegedly trying to win over. DeMille rejected an early draft of the script because it was merely "a straight Western."[95] He later assured the cultured readers of *Stage* that they should not hesitate to see *The Plainsman* because it starkly "differs from any Western we have ever seen," and then mockingly listed the generic trappings he made sure to avoid: "There is no half-breed . . . There is no snatching of the heroine off a runaway horse . . . There is no shooting out of the lights in the saloon . . . There isn't a single sheriff with a star badge."[96] DeMille's genteel airs clashed with the ostensibly populist character of his epic. Moreover, *The Plainsman's* status as tribute to the stoic residents of the devastated plains was weakened by the rise in admission fees that accompanied the film's "special release" in Omaha. The increased prices were met with anger and resistance and were quickly abandoned by the studio.[97] Apparently, Hammond Dale of the Omaha preview audience summarized the frustrations of many when he commented, "it cost too damn much to get into your 'theetah.'"[98] But nevertheless, Paramount's framing of the New Deal Hollywood epic as an encouraging symbol of American perseverance (predicated, of course, on big spending) reveals how epic form, by virtue of its baroque spectacle and patriotic zeal, can simultaneously represent studio prestige and social awareness.[99]

"into the depths of futurity:" allegory, regeneration, pedagogy

In *Projecting the Past: Ancient Rome, Cinema, and History,* Maria Wyke cogently demonstrates how the epic film, as "a selectively represented past," can provide a revealing window into cultural anxieties and political aspirations of the contemporary period of an epic's production. Through this presentist critical perspective, as Burgoyne points out, "the past in historical films becomes an allegory of the present; the milieu in which the film was produced stamps every frame."[100] *The Plainsman,* a film in concrete dialogue with the New Deal era, is especially revealing of how the epic genre lends historical expression to contemporary cultural energies.

In a letter addressed to DeMille dated January 27, 1937, N. A. Hickok, a distant relative of Wild Bill, explained to the director how he was offended by the media's consistent portrayal of his deceased ancestor "as a Desperado, stage robber, cutthroat and bad man in general."[101] DeMille quickly responded, assuring Hickok that Wild Bill will be depicted in *his* production as "a man of great patriotic fervor and not as a desperado," and then added how in the character of Wild Bill "I have attempted to summarize the strength and character of all the great scouts."[102] DeMille, of course, was making sure to preclude negative publicity that might arise from disgruntled relatives' protests against his film. DeMille's reply, however, has important structural implications that should not be overlooked. It is particularly telling that DeMille emphasizes in the above letter the emblematic nature of Wild Bill's character. This self-consciously representative quality of Wild Bill (and the film's other principal characters) guaranteed greater use-value for DeMille's epic as national tribute. In a letter to a New Mexico exhibitor, for instance, DeMille characterized *The Plainsman* as his personal contribution "to the commemorative program honoring the pioneers Deming and Luna County."[103] Likewise, in a correspondence to Buffalo Bill's nephew, Ernest W. Cody, DeMille expressed how he is "trying to make The Plainsman in which Colonel Cody is one of the central characters an everlasting tribute to him *and* other great plainsman of his time."[104]

This representative nature of *The Plainsman*'s protagonists—their metonymic relationship to a larger group—not only mitigated the creative burdens of biographical specificity but also facilitated the characters' allegorical significance for the present day. *The Plainsman* sheds considerable light on what might be seen as *the underlying politics of representativity in epic film discourse:* how remarkable feats of historical figures become both saleable spectacle and tacit celebrations of a contemporary people. Such allegorical implications are textually inscribed into *The Plainsman*'s structural design, perhaps most notably in the film's closing minutes, after Wild Bill is murdered.

In an intimate two-shot, Calamity Jane embraces the still body of Wild Bill and places a tender kiss on the dead man's lips. Jane, crying, lays her head down on her slain love's face. A slow dissolve then leads to a shot of an empty wheat field. The close-up of the sad embrace is briefly superimposed over the swaying stalks before the couple disappears into the harvest. Through Bill and Jane's "absorption" into the fertile land, the sequence metaphorically conveys the natural regeneration of the frontier spirit in American society. This intimation becomes explicit with the film's closing titles—"It shall be as it was in the past . . . Not with dreams, but with strength and courage, Shall a nation be molded to last"—which rest over a ghostly image of General Custer and Wild Bill on horseback, resolutely galloping toward the film's audience. The fallen characters' passage through this transcendental realm marks their triumphant emergence "into the depths of futurity."[105] *The Plainsman*'s slain heroes, in the end, become heartening symbols of "collective renewal" for American audiences of the Great Depression (see Figure 10.2).[106]

The Plainsman's allegorical implications—how the pioneer spirit can be channeled by the present for the sake of a brighter future—were crystallized by the film's role in the classroom. Paramount distributed a truncated 16-millimeter version of *The Plainsman*—renamed *The Valor of the Plains*—for exhibition in public schools nationwide. The didactic value of the scholastic adaptation—"the first educational film to be produced by a major studio for distribution to schools exclusively"—was explicit.[107] Ralph Jester, the Paramount Art Director who conceptualized and compiled the classroom version, told the *Los Angeles Times* how he "tried to show that courage is just as important today in battling floods, dust storms, and earthquakes as it was to pioneers 100 years ago."[108] An illustrated study guide was prepared as well so teachers could highlight the film's timely messages.[109]

Such pedagogic objectives were anticipated by the First Annual Buffalo Bill Essay Contest, sponsored by the Cody Club of Wyoming, an organization

Figure 10.2

Wild Bill's Death: Tragic romance as regeneration.

managed by Buffalo Bill's ancestors. The Essay Contest was part of the national commemoration of Buffalo Bill's ninetieth birthday, which took place just months before *The Plainsman*'s premiere. Schoolchildren through-out the USA were invited to partake in the contest and were instructed to write a brief essay honoring the life and achievements of the legendary westerner. The young author who could articulate best the good deeds and moral lessons available in the mythologized life of Buffalo Bill would receive from the Cody Club a $25 reward. The winning essay became prop-erty of the Cody Club and recirculated in a "nationwide entertainment and publicity" campaign dedicated to sparking interest in Buffalo Bill, "one of the most colorful figures in the history of the West."[110]

DeMille attributed to his protagonists a similarly didactic "idealization of American motives."[111] For DeMille, pedagogic virtue justified factual dis-tortion. DeMille, in a letter to a relative of Wild Bill Hickok, explained how "While Hickok actually lost his life in a casual poker game . . . I have found it necessary to imbue that poker game with a patriotic motive [in the film, Hickok is shot in the back while detaining gun smugglers]." DeMille then admitted that he has

223

> always found it necessary in picturizing [sic] the life of any actual character to make the motivations of their various acts a little more noble than they sometimes were . . . William Cody and Wild Bill Hickok are both heroes in the minds of the American people, and I believe it of impor-tance to build this heroism to a point beyond which it actu-ally ran *as an example for the youth of the country today.*[112]

Feeding idealized perceptions of historical figures meant preserving their mythic signification—which, in the case of *The Plainsman,* meant upholding faith in American manifest destiny. Ultimately, DeMille's didacticism worked to combat what Scandura calls the "depressive modernity" of the New Deal era, "an affective component of Americanism that exposes itself at those moments when the axioms of American culture and progressive modernity itself . . . [are] put into question."[113] *The Plainsman* remains a striking example of how the epic film, by way of its monumental iterations of national growth and assertive claims to historical accuracy, regional authenticity, and moral righteousness, can position itself within a particular moment in American history as a persuasive and inspirational didactic text.

conclusion: *the plainsman* and the performance of historical continuity

Yet *The Plainsman*'s youth objectives not only pointed to the inculcation of patriotic values. They also revealed how the epic cinema provokes the deeply rooted social desire to reenact the past.[114] Under Paramount's instruction, for instance, young Native Americans from nearby reservations were invited to act with schoolchildren of Western states in historical episodes adapted from *The Plainsman.*[115] Such schoolhouse spectacle presented children with the exciting opportunity to imitate both their ancestors and their idolized figures from the movie; for the adults in the audience, the youthful reenactment of Western expansion gestured in reassuring way toward the preservation of the pioneer spirit in New Deal America.[116] The public urge to perform history was demonstrated as well through Paramount's exploitation tie-up with the Boy Scouts of America— "the biggest tie-up ever effected on any picture!" (see Figure 10.3). Paramount encouraged Scouts to hold pageants and parades near theaters screening *The Plainsman* and "to scour surrounding territory for old relics having any relation to the picture" for use in theater lobbies displays.[117] Paramount was convinced that *The Plainsman*'s historical subject matter would appeal to the theatrical antimodernism of the Boys Scouts of America. The Boy Scout tradition—with its weekend escapades of adventure and self-reliance and ceremonial powwows in affiliate programs such as the Order of the Arrow—can indeed be seen as an ongoing reenactment of an idealized, preindustrial yesteryear. Street parades and artifact hunts gave scouts the opportunity to experience the past in a tangible, performative fashion. Although such tie-ups were motivated first and foremost by studio profit maximization (scouts' volunteer labor mitigated publicity costs, and eye-catching ads in *Boys' Life,* America's largest youth publication, significantly enhanced the film's visibility), it is just as important to recognize how *The Plainsman*'s external spectacle satisfied the desire to

Figure 10.3

The Plainsman and the Boy Scouts of America.

perform—and not just rewitness—the past.[118] The youth-oriented, extra-textual spectacle, in conjunction with *The Plainsman,* reveals how a collective sense of continuity with the past is realized, by and large, through a cyclical process of internalizing and then socially reciting the *available* historical narratives of a particular time and place. The DeMillean epic, through its ability to spiral beyond the screen and to engender a vast constellation of public historical imagery, stands as a powerful vehicle through which Americans have performatively situated themselves within an exemplary historical timeline.

Sumiko Higashi has cogently demonstrated how DeMille's historical imagery was a garish reflection of American consumerism of the early twentieth century. Higashi, writing on the similarities between civic pageantry of the early 1900s and DeMille's silent historical spectacles,

225

notes how the "selective and pragmatic approach to history in terms of its present usefulness had implications not only for an agenda of democratic reform but also for the commodification of the past as a form of commercial amusement."[119] DeMille—Hollywood's "architect of modern consumption"—proved that "even religious or spiritual uplift was subject to commodification" with his Orientalist biblical allegory, *The Ten Commandments* (1923).[120] The filmmaker's extravagant endorsement of material consumption persisted into the sound era, where DeMille "continued to reinforce consumer values by representing history . . . as a magnificent spectacle for visual appropriation" which was ripe for intriguing marketing tie-ups.[121] *The Plainsman* was no exception. For instance, the buckskin jacket worn by Jean Arthur in the film was entered into a fashion show at the Waldorf Astoria.[122] Photographs showing Arthur in that same costume were used at women's stores to promote the season's line of leather jackets. Paramount also planned a glove tie-up in which "any of the stills of Jean Arthur in which her gauntlets are prominently shown" were to be hung in department stores.[123] The studio devised male-targeted tie-ups as well. Stills of Gary Cooper seated in an antique barber's chair adorned the windows of local barbershops, and pictures of James Ellison as Buffalo Bill standing beside vintage suitcases decorated the walls of luggage vendors.[124]

Rather than see these marketing stunts as merely indicative of a mass culture's acquiescence to pseudo-needs invented by corporations, I would like to conclude by observing the social impulses that compelled Americans of the 1930s to, quite literally, step inside history's clothes. Like the Wyoming Cavalry's enthusiastic participation in DeMille's restaging of the Custer Massacre or the youthful pageantry in honor of *The Plainsman,* the social exhibition of frontier garb became a self-defining act that put on display one's perceived likeness to admirable historical figures. And like DeMille's western epic, this historical self-fashioning became a statement on the presence of the frontier ethos in present-day America. "Against its detractors," writes Theodor Adorno, "fashion's most powerful response is that it participates in the individual impulse, which is saturated with history."[125] Commercialized period dress provided the means to a far more powerful commodity: a tangible sense of historical groundedness. As John Don Passos wrote, looking back on the 1930s: "a sense of continuity with generations before can stretch like a lifeline across the scary present."[126]

Vivian Sobchack has argued how the epic film, through its self-conscious assertions of historical relevance by way of authoritative epigraphs and voice-overs and its expanded use of space and duration, "opens up a temporal field that creates the general possibility for re-cognizing oneself as a historical subject of a particular kind."[127] Indeed, the forms of public reenactment that accompanied *The Plainsman*'s release are social expressions of historical being, which can either be realized through or reaffirmed by the epic film experience. What begins as an affective response to the genre's artistic conventions—a spectator's perceived affinities with estimable representative figures; the illusion of participation elicited by immersive spectacle; the impression of here-and-nowness achieved through authentic locations and performances—becomes an existential reminder of one's place in historical time. The phenomenological plurality of DeMille's frontier epic—its ability to simultaneously stand as a hymn to the nation's pioneers, as an allegorical portrait of American resilience, and as a commemoration of Paramount's industrial fortitude, which, in turn, signified the perseverance of American capitalism—provided welcome diversion from the bleak realities of the Great Depression. *The Plainsman's* discursive narratives of national commemoration, triumph over adversity, and the enduring might of US industry, reflexively pointed to the downcast yet ultimately hopeful culture of New Deal America. History, as Godwin reminds us, "takes away the cause of our depression," a statement repeatedly emblazoned through the monumental fantasies of national regeneration at the heart of American epic cinema.[128]

notes

1. Gilles Deleuze, *Cinema 1: The Movement,* trans. Hugh Tomlinson and Barbara Habberjam (Minneapolis, Minn.: University of Minnesota Press, 1986), p. 145.
2. Vivian Sobchack, "Surge and Splendor: A Phenomenology of the Hollywood Historical Epic," *Representations,* 29 (1990): 9.
3. Deleuze, *Cinema 1,* p. 148.
4. Jani Scandura, *Down in the Dumps: Place, Modernity, American Depression* (Durham, Md.: Duke University Press, 2008), p. 17.
5. Franklin D. Roosevelt, Fireside Chat, September 6, 1936, available online at www.presidency.ucsb.edu/fireside.php (accessed September 1, 2008).
6. Jesse Lasky, Jr., *What Ever Happened to Hollywood* (New York: Funk & Wagnell, 1975), p. 150.
7. Timothy Corrigan and Patricia White provide an instructive definition of this hybrid genre: "the western epic concentrates on action and movement, developing a heroic character whose quests and battles serve to define the nation and its origins." *The Film Experience* (New York: Macmillan, 2004), p. 303.
8. Robert Burgoyne, *The Hollywood Historical Film* (Malden, Mass.: Blackwell, 2008), p. 94.
9. Cecil B. DeMille, "Why I Would Not Have Made 'The Plainsman' If I Had Not Been Able to Get Gary Cooper," September 8, 1936, Box 28/Folder 5, Cecil B. DeMille Archives, Harold B. Lee Library, Brigham Young University, Provo, Utah (hereafter DMA/BYU) (emphasis added).
10. "Movie of the Week: The Plainsman," *Life,* 4 January 1937, p. 69 (emphasis added).
11. Sobchack, "Surge and Splendor," p. 36.
12. J. E. Smith, *Reconstructing American Historical Cinema: From Cimarron to Citizen Kane* (Lexington, Ky.: University of Kentucky Press, 2006), p. 132.
13. Piers Brendon, *The Dark Valley: A Panorama of the 1930s* (New York: Vintage Books, 2002), p. 277.

14. Michael Denning, *The Cultural Front: The Laboring of American Culture in the Twentieth Century* (New York: Verso, 1996), p. 265.

15. Denning, *The Cultural Front*, p. 126.

16. See Robert S. McElvaine, *The Great Depression: America, 1929–1941* (New York: Random House, 1984), pp. 220–221: "The longing for an imagined golden age, for a feeling of security, for an identity, was evident in the thirties quest for a sense of place . . . [F]our of five top-selling novels of the Depression decade—*Gone With the Wind* (1936), *God's Little Acre* (1933), *The Good Earth* (1931), and *The Grapes of Wrath* (1939)—deal with the search for security in history or on the land."

17. Scandura, *Down in the Dumps*, p. 17.

18. *Lux Radio Theater*, May 31, 1937. Complete broadcast available at: www. archive.org/details/Lux02 (emphasis added) (accessed September 1, 2008).

19. Cecil B. DeMille, Galley Proof for January *Stage* article, December 7, 1936, Box 528/Folder 5, DMA/BYU (emphasis added). DeMille's article was published in the first 1937 issue of *Stage*.

20. B. R. Chrisler, "Gossip of the Films," *New York Times*, December 6, 1936, X8 (emphasis added).

21. Alistair Cooke, "The Cinema," transcript for radio broadcast of February 28, 1937, Box 526/Folder 16, DMA/BYU.

22. Cooke, "The Cinema."

23. Frank S. Nugent, "The Screen," *New York Times*, January 14, 1937, p. 16.

24. David Levin, *History as Romantic Art: Bancroft, Prescott, Motley, and Parkman* (New York: Harbinger, 1959), p. 49.

25. Levin, *History as Romantic Art*, p. 51.

26. Deleuze, *Cinema 1*, p. 146.

27. Levin, *History as Romantic Art*, pp. 26, 27, 29.

28. Deleuze, *Cinema 1*, p. 149.

29. William Godwin, "Of History and Romance," appendix IV in *Caleb Williams*, ed. Maurice Hindle (New York: Penguin, 1988), p. 362.

30. Deleuze, *Cinema 1*, p. 148.

31. Cecil B. DeMille to Mrs. Mary Jester Allen, Director, Buffalo Bill Museum, 14 November 1935, Box 521/Folder 14, DMA/BYU. See also Mary Jester Allen to Cecil B. DeMille, undated correspondence, Box 521/Folder 14, DMA/BYU. Allen lets DeMille know that the Buffalo Bill Memorial Association would appreciate "a very careful, historically correct motion picture of Buffalo Bill . . . Something as colorful as the last of the great scouts . . . With a real background of real pioneering America."

32. "Super-western" was one of many euphemisms used in the late 1930s in order to imply a prestigious variation on the traditional western. "Open-Air Epic," (Edwin Schallert, "Ridin' Buckaroos of Cinema Win New Triumphs at Box Office," *Los Angeles Times*, January 14, 1937, p. C1); "glorified western" (Edwin Schallert, "'The Plainsman' Dramatic Tale of Western Pioneers," *Los Angeles Times*, January 15, 1937, p. A18); "Historical Western" ("John Wayne in the Lonely Trail," *Film Daily*, November 3, 1936, p. 6); and "Outdoor Drama" ("Tom Keene in 'Rebellion,'" *Film Daily*, October 10, 1936, p. 7) were some of the other coded expressions for an elevated western. Such films stood in marked distinction to, say, the Buck Jones vehicle *Empty Saddles*, which was sold merely as a "hard-riding, straight-shooting western" ("Buck Jones in Empty Saddles," *Film Daily*, October 17, 1936, p. 3). DeMille to Jeff Lazarus, November 1, 1935, Box 526/Folder 16, DMA/BYU.

33. "Publicity-Advertising-Exploitation on 'The Plainsman,'" Box 528/Folder 5, DMA/BYU. DeMille's self-comparisons to Remington not only illuminate his affinities with romantic historiography but also indicate the director's tendency of enhancing his films' prestige through intertextual associations with the "finer" arts. For valuable discussions of DeMille and intertextuality, see Sumiko Higashi, *Cecil B. DeMille and American Culture: The Silent Era* (Berkeley, Calif.: University of California Press, 1994), pp. 20–25, and Lea Jacobs, "Belasco, DeMille and the Development of Lasky Lighting," *Film History,* 5 (5) (1993): 405–418. See also Cecil B. DeMille, *The Autobiography of Cecil B. DeMille* (Englewood Cliffs, NJ: Prentice-Hall, 1959), p. 115: DeMille recalls how after Lasky Co. producer Sam Goldfish (later Goldwyn) screened *The Warrens of Virginia* (1915), a civil-war drama in which DeMille experimented with theatrical low-key lighting effects, "a very disturbed Goldfish wired back to ask what we were doing. Didn't we know that if we showed only half an actor's face, the exhibitors would want to pay only half the usual price for the picture? Jesse [Lasky] and I wired back to Sam that if the exhibitors did not know Rembrandt lighting when they saw it, so much the worse for them. Sam's reply was jubilant with relief: for *Rembrandt lighting* the exhibitors would pay double!"

34. For a telling example of DeMille's preoccupation with authentic minor details, see "Uniforms and Equipments for Seventh Cavalry," Box 21/Folder 10, DMA/BYU. The document gives detailed descriptions of each piece of the cavalry uniform, from socks ("regulation issue was of gray wool or cotton"), to spurs ("the regulation was the brass, slightly curved one with small rowel"), to gauntlets "(the Officers wore what they pleased . . . the Men wore gauntlets of buff with about six inch cuff"), and so on.

35. Cecil B. DeMille, Galley Proof for *Stage* article, December 7, 1936, Box 528/Folder 5, DMA/BYU.

36. As Levin points out, the sense of "historical mobility" was a major factor in the public appeal of romantic history (*History as Romantic Art,* pp. 22–23): "Motley adds interest to his history [*Rise of the Dutch Republic*] by reminding that he is reading the 'secret never published correspondence of royalty'; Parkman insists repeatedly that he has actually studied the historic scenes, that he has painted his picture of Indians 'from life'; Prescott defends Ferdinand and Isabella as 'an honest record, from rare and authentic sources, of a period, rich in circumstance, of personages most remarkable in their character.'"

37. Theodore Roosevelt, *History as Literature and Other Essays* (New York: Charles Scribner's Sons, 1913) , p. 8.

38. Roosevelt, *History as Literature,* p. 10.

39. Roosevelt, *History as Literature,* p. 10.

40. Godwin, "Of History and Romance," p. 367.

41. James K. Ballinger, *Frederic Remington* (New York: Harry N. Abrams, Inc., 1989), pp. 37, 85–88.

42. For a lucid summary of Remington's stylistic evolution, see Doreen Bolger Burke, "Remington: In the Context of His Artistic Generation," in *Frederic Remington: The Masterworks,* eds. Michael E. Shapiro and Peter H. Hassrick, (New York: Henry N. Adams, Inc., 1991), p. 61: "[By 1908 the] exacting realism of [Remington's] earlier career—as well as the photographs, sketches, notes, and props and costumes he collected—had given way to a new romanticism. In his later work, particularly in his nocturnes, Remington was

trying to suggest mood. There is little action in works like *The Outlier,* for example. The mounted Indian is alone, lost in thought, illuminated by the full moon behind him."

43. David McCullough, "The Man," in Shapiro et al., *Frederic Remington: The Masterworks,* p. 20.

44. DeMille to Arthur Rosson and Gene Hornbustle, June 18, 1936, Box 527/ Folder 15, DMA/BYU.

45. DeMille, telegraph to Arthur Rosson, June 20, 1936, Box 527/Folder 15, DMA/BYU. See also Robert S. Birchard, *Cecil B. DeMille's Hollywood* (Lexington, Ky.: University Press of Kentucky, 2004), pp. 286–287. In his brief production history of *The Plainsman,* Birchard cites DeMille's telegram as indicative of the "direct and specific instructions the filmmaker would offer to those who worked with him."

46. Bill Pine, telegraph to Arthur Rosson, June 29, 1936, Box 527/Folder 15, DMA/BYU. Pine, DeMille's associate producer, was most likely passing on DeMille's directions.

47. "Transparency" was the industry's term for what is more commonly referred to as "rear projection." Farciot Edouart, a longtime collaborator of DeMille, was the transparency artist on *The Plainsman.* Edouart was also responsible for the stunning rear projection in *The Ten Commandments* (1956). Edouart's technical skills enhanced the brilliant artifice of Hitchcock, too, most notably in *To Catch a Thief* (1955) and *Vertigo* (1958). For more discussion on *The Plainsman*'s rear projection, see Birchard, *Cecil B. DeMille's Hollywood,* p. 297, and DeMille, *Autobiography,* p. 350.

48. DeMille's penchant for massive assemblies of extras also added to the sensorally immersive viewing experience. See Arthur Rosson, Description of Second Unit Shoot with Wyoming Mounted Militia, June 23, 1936, Box 527/ Folder 15, DMA/BYU: "The second unit will shoot . . . First: Custer's ride to the rescue of Beecher's Island . . . one hundred full costumes should cover the foreground."

49. Paul Ricoeur, *The Reality of the Historical Past* (Milwaukee, Wisc.: Marquette University Press, 1984), pp. 5–14.

50. See "'The Plainsman': List of Books Used in Research," Box 521/Folder 10, DMA/BYU, which includes Remington's *Crooked Trails* (New York: Harper & Brothers, 1898), in which an illustration of *Through the Smoke Sprang the Daring Soldier* appears on page 46.

51. Bolger Burke, "Remington," pp. 50–52.

52. Alison Griffiths, "'Shivers Down Your Spine': Panoramas and the Origins of the Cinematic Reenactment," *Screen,* 44 (1) (2003): 11, quoted in Burgoyne, *The Hollywood Historical Film,* p. 56 (emphasis added).

53. Gladys Rosson, Comments Re: Plainsman Preview Tour from Theater Managers and Exhibitors, December 7, 1936, Box 528/Folder 9, DMA/BYU.

54. Burgoyne, *The Hollywood Historical Film,* p. 57.

55. Levin, *History as Romantic Art,* p. 18.

56. James K. Ballinger, *Frederic Remington* (New York: Harry N. Abrams, Inc., 1989), p. 62. Parkman, after discovering that Remington had been commissioned to illustrate his volume, informed the painter that "I am very glad that you are to illustrate the 'Oregon Trail . . . [for] I have long admired your rendering of Western life, as superior to that of any other artist.'"

57. Levin, *History as Romantic Art,* p. 19.

58. Levin, *History as Romantic Art,* p. 168.

59. Godwin, "Of History and Romance," 363.

60. Office of Cecil B. DeMille, memo to Bill Pine Box, March 3, 1936, 527/Folder 6, DMA/BYU.

61. "Publicity-Advertising-Exploitation on 'The Plainsman,'" Box 528/Folder 5, DMA/BYU.

62. The Knave, "Wild Bill in Film," *Oakland Tribune,* November 1, 1936, unpaginated clipping, Box 527/Folder 22, DMA/BYU.

63. The Knave, "Wild Bill in Film."

64. "Learning How," August 15, 1936 *Los Angeles Times,* sec. 1, page 7.

65. "Paramount's Advertising Approach: The Plainsman," Box 528/Folder 5, DMA/BYU. The Art Department built "studio replicas of Hays City, Dodge City and St. Louis[.]" In addition, "A full-sized Mississippi river boat was constructed, manned by a full crew and jammed with passengers."

66. Gene Hornbostel to Mr. DeMille, June 22, 1936, Box 527/Folder 15, DMA/BYU. The guardsmen's desire to participate in the reenactment outweighed the demand for extras. Competitive drills were held in order to single out "the pick of the regiment."

67. "Indians Who Fought Custer Appear in Film," *Los Angeles Times,* January 19, 1937, p. 8: "The last two surviving Cheyenne who took part with the Sioux redskins in Custer's massacre in 1876, were hired by Cecil B. DeMille during the filming of 'The Plainsman'[.] . . . The two braves are Louis Dog, who claims to be 101 years old, and Stump Horn, a mere youngster of 87 years."

68. "Indians Who Fought Custer Appear in Film."

69. "Paramount's Advertising Approach: The Plainsman," Box 528/Folder 5, DMA/BYU (emphasis added).

70. Frank S. Nugent, "The Screen," *New York Times,* January 14, 1937, p. 16.

71. Cecil B. DeMille, telegraph to Mayor W. J. Evans, Deming, New Mexico, April 27, 1937, Box 528/Folder 5, DMA/BYU.

72. Welford Beaton, "DeMille on a Broad Canvas," *The Hollywood Spectator,* December 5, 1936, p. 10 (emphasis added).

73. Gladys Rosson, Re. *The Plainsman,* Misc. Comments Made in Lobbies after Showing of the Picture, December 7, 1936, Box 528/Folder 9, DMA/BYU.

74. "Publicity-Advertising-Exploitation on 'The Plainsman,'" Box 528/Folder 5, DMA/BYU.

75. "Coming and Going," *Film Daily,* December 3, 1936, p. 4: "Cecil B. DeMille left here yesterday for Chicago, Omaha, Denver [and then will return to] Hollywood." See also "Coming and Going," *Film Daily,* December 8, 1936, p. 2: "Cecil B. DeMille today returns to Hollywood from the transcontinental preview tour with 'The Plainsman.'" Though DeMille made live appearances only in the cities listed above, preview screenings were also held in Houston, New Orleans, and Dallas. For DeMille's travel itinerary, see "Plainsman Tour: December 1936," Box 528/Folder 10, DMA/BYU.

76. Dallas preview cards Box 528/Folder 7, DMA/BYU.

77. Omaha preview cards Box 528/Folder 7, DMA/BYU.

78. Dallas preview cards Box 528/Folder 7, DMA/BYU.

79. Dallas preview cards Box 528/Folder 7, DMA/BYU.

80. Houston preview cards Box 528/Folder 7, DMA/BYU.

81. Houston preview cards Box 528/Folder 7, DMA/BYU.

82. Omaha preview cards Box 528/Folder 7, DMA/BYU.

83. Denver preview cards Box 528/Folder 7, DMA/BYU.

84. Denver preview cards Box 528/Folder 7, DMA/BYU.
85. Houston preview cards Box 528/Folder 7, DMA/BYU.
86. Barney Oldfield, "Producer DeMille Shows 'The Plainsman' Depicting Cody, Hickok, to Nebraskans," *Lincoln Sunday Journal and Star,* December 6, 1936, p. 3.
87. Houston preview cards Box 528/Folder 7, DMA/BYU.
88. DeMille to Mrs. Agnes Robinson, November 18, 1936, Box 521/Folder 13, DMA/BYU.
89. New Orleans preview cards Box 528/Folder 7, DMA/BYU.
90. Denver preview cards Box 528/Folder 7, DMA/BYU.
91. Denver preview cards Box 528/Folder 7, DMA/BYU.
92. New Orleans preview cards Box 528/Folder 7, DMA/BYU.
93. Birchard, *Cecil B. DeMille's Hollywood,* p. 293. *The Plainsman* grossed $2,278,533.33, more than twice its production cost ($974,084.85), and returned DeMille to Paramount's good graces after losing money on his medieval epic, *The Crusades* (1936). See also, "Plainsman Will Hold Second Week," *Los Angeles Times,* January 21, 1937, p. A19, in which it's reported how *The Plainsman* is "Continuing its assault on Paramount box office records."
94. Edwal Jones, "Mr. DeMille Returns to the Plains," *New York Times,* January 10, 1937, p. X4.
95. Virginia Van Upp, script draft for "Buffalo Bill," March 4, 1936. Box 524/Folder 8, DMA/BYU. DeMille's comments are written in pencil in the document's margins.
96. Cecil B. DeMille, Galley Proof for *Stage* article, December 7, 1936, Box 528/Folder 5, DMA/BYU.
97. "Omaha Experiment with Higher Admish is Flop," *Film Daily,* December 7, 1936, p. 10.
98. Omaha preview cards, Box 528/Folder 7, DMA/BYU.
99. The Depression-era Hollywood epic not only allegorized the nation's prized values but also became in and of itself a sign of American economic recuperation. See "News of the Screen," *New York Times,* 15 February 1937, p. 12, in which it is related how *The Plainsman*'s enormous success had encouraged Paramount to prepare more large-scale historical pictures, including Frank Lloyd's recreation of the Salem witch trials *The Maid of Salem* and the slave trade drama *Souls at Sea.* See also Harold Hefferman, "Hollywood Digs More Gold," *New York Times,* 24 October 1937, p. X5, in which it is reported that "the greatest picture-spending orgy Hollywood has ever known rolls on unabated." For more on Hollywood's late-Depression discursive climate of industrial resilience, see "Para. Adds 12 Films to Zukor Jubilee Drive Schedule," *Film Daily,* 21 November 1936, pp. 1, 7; "Hollywood Confidence and Enthusiasm Highest in Years, Says Zukor," *Film Daily,* 5 September 1936; "New Season to Set Record in Outstanding Films, Says Will Hays," *Film Daily,* 21 August 1936, pp. 1, 13; and Jack Alicoate, "US Film Industry Sees 1937 Greatest Year," *Film Daily,* 23 December 1936, pp. 1, 8.
100. Burgoyne, *The Hollywood Historical Film,* p. 10.
101. N. A. Hickok to DeMille, January 27, 1937, Box 521/Folder 13, DMA/BYU.
102. DeMille to N. A. Hickok, February 4, 1937, Box 521/Folder 13, DMA/BYU. See also DeMille to Mrs. Agnes Robinson (granddaughter of Hickok's widow), November 18, 1936, Box 521/Folder 13, DMA/BYU, and DeMille to Ernest W. Cody, August 3, 1936, Box 521/Folder 14, DMA/BYU.

103. Cecil B. DeMille, telegraph to Mayor W. J. Evans, Deming, New Mexico, April 27, 1937, Box 528/Folder 5, DMA/BYU.

104. Cecil B. DeMille, telegraph to Ernest W. Cody, August 3, 1936, Box 521/Folder 14, DMA/BYU.

105. Here, William Godwin refers to the ability of historical characters to both inspire and represent future generations. This scene thematically antici-pates the ending of a much later epic film, Ridley Scott's *Gladiator* (2000), which, like *The Plainsman,* helped revitalize what seemed at the time to be a culturally degraded generic form. Robert Burgoyne's analysis of *Gladiator*'s conclusion brings the similarities between the two films into sharp focus: "After Maximus has been killed, Juba [the African gladiator whom Maximus has befriended] is viewed alone in the Colosseum. Here he buries Maximus' figurines of his family and ancestors in the dirt of the Colosseum floor . . . The planting of the figurines by the black gladiator, with its clear suggestion of an appeal to the future, can be read as a symbol of the planting of the seeds of a new nation, a new civilization" (Burgoyne, *The Hollywood Historical Film,* p. 97).

106. Burgoyne, *The Hollywood Historical Film,* p. 94.

107. "News of the Screen," *New York Times,* November 25, 1936, p. L19.

108. Andy Hamilton, "The Camera Moves into the Classroom," *Los Angeles Times Sunday Magazine,* p. 14.

109. Hamilton, "The Camera Moves into the Classroom." It should also be noted that the Schools Motion Picture Committee, "a voluntary organi-zation composed of parents and teachers," included *The Plainsman* on their list of films "For Young Audiences." See "Films of Week-End For Young Audiences," *New York Times,* February 25, 1937, p. L19.

110. "First Annual Buffalo Bill Essay Contest," Box 521/Folder 14, DMA/BYU. Unfortunately, the winning essay can not be found in the DeMille Archives at BYU.

111. Levin, *History as Romantic Art,* p. 53.

112. DeMille to Mrs. Agnes Robinson, November 18, 1936, Box 521/Folder 13, DMA/BYU (emphasis added).

113. Scandura, *Down in the Dumps,* p. 5.

114. For a discussion of reenactment as applied to cinematic historical repre-sentation, see Burgoyne, *The Hollywood Historical Film,* pp. 6–9: "the concept of reenactment [is an] act of imaginative re-creation that allows the spectator to imagine they are 'witnessing again' the events of the past . . . The historical film conveys its message about the world by reenacting the past[.]"

115. Publicity campaign manual for *The Plainsman,* pp. 13–14, Box 528/Folder 5, DMA/BYU.

116. I am indebted to David Glassberg's extraordinary *American Historical Pageantry: The Uses of Tradition in the Early Twentieth Century* (Chapel Hill, NC: University of North Carolina Press, 1990), which has influenced my thought on the public spectacle that surrounded *The Plainsman:* "Public historical imagery is an essential element of our culture, contributing to how we define our sense of identity and direction. It locates us in time, as we learn about our place in succession of past and future generations, as well as in space, as we learn the story of our locale . . . Ultimately, histori-cal imagery supplies orientation towards our future action" (Glassberg, *American Historical Pageantry,* p. 1).

117. Exhibitors booklet regarding *Plainsman*–Boy Scout tie-up, Box 528/Folder 1, DMA/BYU.

118. Bill Pine to DeMille, "Re Tie-Up with the Boy Scout Organization for THE PLAINSMAN," October 7, 1936, Box 538/Folder 1, DMA/BYU. "External spectacle" is Eric Schaefer's term for the intriguing advertising that surrounded the release of an exploitation film. Such "advertising, exploitation, and exhibition that was attached to the films were part and parcel of that [film's] spectacle," Schaefer observes. Though Schaefer is referring to low-budget films made outside the Hollywood studio system for exhibition in drive-ins and grind houses, "external spectacle" is nevertheless applicable to the ballyhoo and public spectacle that enriched and expanded the cinematic experience of a DeMille epic. See Eric Schaefer, *Bold! Daring! Shocking! True! A History of Exploitation Films, 1919–1959* (Durham, NC: Duke University Press, 1999), pp. 94–95.

119. Higashi, *Cecil B. DeMille and American Culture*, p. 120.

120. Higashi, *Cecil B. DeMille and American Culture*, pp. 6, 4.

121. Higashi, *Cecil B. DeMille and American Culture*, pp. 201–203.

122. C. J. Dunphy, to Bill Pine, August 27, 1936, Box 22/Folder 8, DMA/BYU.

123. Publicity campaign manual for *The Plainsman*, p. 12.

124. Publicity campaign manual for *The Plainsman*, pp. 16-17, Box 528/Folder 5, DMA/BYU.

125. Theodor W. Adorno, *Aesthetic Theory*, trans. Robert Hullot-Kentor (Minneapolis, Minn.: University of Minnesota Press, 1994), p. 316.

126. John Dos Passos, *The Ground We Stand On* (New York: Harcourt, Brace, 1941), quoted in Robert McElvaine, *The Great Depression: America, 1929–1941* (New York: Random House, 1984), p. 221. The need to situate oneself within a progressive historical genealogy is reflected as well by people's alleged personal ties to *The Plainsman*'s characters. DeMille, in a response to an alleged acquaintance to a friend of Buffalo Bill, gives a comical impression of the enormity of this public desire to be intimately connected to historical figures: "My desk is piled so high with letters from and about men who nursed Buffalo Bill in the cradle, carried him across the plains, rode in the Show with him, divorced him, shot him, etc. etc. etc., that I have come to the conclusion that more people were Buffalo Bill's pals than went on the crusades." See DeMille, letter to Mr. Milton E. Hoffman, November 18, 1935, Box 521/Folder 12, DMA/BYU.

127. Sobchack, "Surge and Splendor," p. 29.

128. Godwin, "Of History and Romance," p. 362.

epos indigenized

the new zealand wars films from

rudall hayward to vincent ward

e l e v e n

b r u c e   b a b i n g t o n

Though "epic film" applied to the New Zealand cinema may suggest only *The Lord of the Rings,* the focus here is four films spanning the history of New Zealand feature film production. Two of them are by the pioneer director Rudall Hayward (1900–1974): *The Te Kooti Trail* (1927) and *Rewi's Last Stand* (1940). The third, *Utu* (1983) was a key early film of the subsidized national film industry (1977–), while the fourth is *River Queen* (2006).[1] Each belongs to a highly differentiated moment of New Zealand film production—Hayward's to the preindustrial era, Murphy's to the early national industry period, and Ward's to the onset of global and "glocal" cinema. All four films dramatize historical conflicts centred on the years 1863–1872, variously known as the Maori Wars, Land Wars, and now the New Zealand Wars, between the new settler colony and substantial parts of the indigenous Maori population.[2] In doing so, "by means of characters who, in their psychology and destiny, always represent social trends and historical forces" they "engage . . . the issues, ideas, data and arguments of the ongoing discourse of history," as distinct from costume dramas which only "use the past as an exotic setting for romance and adventure."[3] While "epic" applied to modern literature or cinema is not transparent, and few films develop formal tropes imitating older epics—for example, the tableaux, choric elements, archaic dialogue, invocations to the nation, etc., of *Alexander Nevsky* (1938)—two defining characteristics outlined in this volume's introduction may be tested against these films. The first is the epic's celebration of national and cultural origins (e.g., *The Aeneid*, Camoens' *Os Lusiados, Cantar di mio Cid*, Eisenstein's *Alexander Nevsky*, Ford's westerns as collective text, and various biblical and Roman epics). The second is the epic film's investment in spectacle. New Zealand cinema's perennial low-budget constraints make this only fitful and relative. Hayward's films were made on miniscule budgets, while even *Utu*, in 1983 the most expensive film ever made in New Zealand, cost only NZ$3 million (about US$4.5 million), and the budget for Vincent Ward's *River Queen*, though very large by New Zealand standards at circa NZ$20 million, was only a third of the budget of his Hollywood film, *What Dreams May Come* (1998). Nevertheless, within the local context, these were major productions, with even Hayward's resources greater than for any of the few previous New Zealand-made fiction films. Further, all four subtextually announced optimistic possibilities for a national cinematic future—*The Te Kooti Trail's* title frame's design declaring "Produced in New Zealand for the World," unfulfillable then but a marker for the future. *Utu* demonstrated that the new industry could combine indigenous material with commercial and critical success; *River Queen* exhibited the new phenomenon of the successful expatriate director returning to make a New Zealand-based film, utilizing international coproduction and substantially greater budgets than ever before (if the huge, Hollywood-financed Peter Jackson productions are discounted). This chapter elucidates a series of continuities and differences within continuities over some eighty years, between films based on the same "national epic" material, with the later filmmakers rewriting the Hayward films, both unconsciously, as they approach the same historical material under different social and aesthetic pressures, and also very consciously as they allude to their cinematic predecessor's films and his primary source, the historian James Cowan.

the new zealand wars

This history may require a brief resumé for non-New Zealanders.[4] The Southern Pacific islands of New Zealand were the last habitable substantial land masses in the world to be humanly populated, by Polynesian voyagers c. 1300. These, who became the New Zealand Maori, numbered around 80,000, divided into tribal groups when the British Crown annexed the country in 1840. The Treaty of Waitangi (1840) signed by tribal chiefs, voluntarily ceded authority (though in ambiguous terms) to the British Crown in return for guarantees of protection, accelerating the immigration that soon altered the balance of the two populations, with the immigrants' need for land the primary source of conflict. As the State asserted dominance, the most serious conflicts took place from 1863 to 1872, at one point necessitating the presence of 12,000 imperial troops. The settler state's post-war ascendancy ensured its rapid consolidation, though having met enough resistance to prevent total Maori assimilation, resulting in the eventual unrest which peaked 100 years later and led to the State's commitment, via rereadings of the Treaty as the nation's founding covenant, to inflecting government interracial policies from an assimilationist–integrationist stance to a bicultural one, granting indigenous tribes large-scale compensation and restoration, and thus easing, if not completely removing, tensions.

Certain aspects of the wars need to be understood to view films based on them knowledgeably. First, Maori society's tribal structure meant that the war against the colonial state involved only certain Maori tribes, while others, called *kupapa,* fought with the colonists for their own advantage and against traditional tribal enemies. This lent a confused aspect to the wars, reflected in all the films. Second, the wars, though savagely fought, were small-scale. As James Cowan wrote, "As in the wars between British and French in Canadian forest, described by Parkman in *Montcalm and Woolf,* the problem was less how to fight the enemy than how to get at him."[5] Third, the Maori, a "powerful military race of indigenes," were formidable warriors and, though outnumbered, a match for the colonists and imperial troops in their own conditions.[6] They were proponents of a type of warfare, based on the *pa,* a fortified stockade, which, it has been persuasively argued, predated the trench warfare of World War I.[7]

rudall hayward: *the te kooti trail* and *rewi's last stand*

Distant though New Zealand was from Europe and North America, films were exhibited there by 1896 and made locally by 1898, the earliest, short "actualities" and "scenics." The first fiction filmmakers were largely visiting foreigners (the first was Gaston Méliès in 1912) who mostly exploited the country's double exoticism, its volcanic wonders and its Maori minority. The first local fiction feature, George Tarr's *Hinemoa,* was not made until 1914, by which time the neighboring Australian film industry, because of much larger urban populations, was thriving.

The central figure of early New Zealand filmmaking, Rudall Hayward (1900–1974), began in a film environment dominated by short "scenics," "actualities," government documentaries, and a few foreign features. As stressed by the American scholar Robert Sklar, who saw some of Hayward's films in New Zealand c. 1970, in an article important for placing a film-maker previously seen only in a local context within an international perspective, Hayward worked without any of the resources of early Hollywood filmmakers.[8] Overcoming obstacles to local feature production which persisted even into the 1970s—inferior technology, nonexistent industrial infrastructures, miniscule budgets, nonprofessional actors, small internal audiences, and a widespread conviction that features could not be made in New Zealand—he wrote, directed, photographed, and produced seven features, four silent and three sound, between 1921 and 1972. His central achievement was three New Zealand Wars films: the silent version of *Rewi's Last Stand* (1925, passed over here because only parts survive), its sound remake *Rewi's Last Stand* (1940), and the silent *The Te Kooti Trail* (1927) (see Figures 11.1 and 11.2). What immediately separated Hayward from early visiting American and British filmmakers was his refusal of the dominant mode of approaching the Maori by retreating into the realm of "Maoriland" in exotic fantasies played out in a pre-European New Zealand (Tarr's *Hinemoa* [1914], Pauli's *The Romance of Hine-Moa* [1927], Collins's *The Devil's Pit* [1930], and Markey's *Hei Tiki* [1935]). Rather than abolishing history, Hayward's narratives dramatized the more dynamic and difficult material

Figure 11.1

The Te Kooti Trail: Patiti Warbrick as Taranahi and Tina Hunt as Monika.

Figure 11.2

Rewi's Last Stand.

that Martin Blythe described as "the fall into history," the meeting and conflict of the races.[9]

Reminiscing about his artistic origins, Hayward said that his boyhood reading of *The Adventures of Kimble Bent,* the autobiography of an army deserter who lived very precariously with rebel Maori, convinced him "that in New Zealand . . . was material just as exciting and colourful as any Hollywood western."[10] Without significant local precedents, Hayward was profoundly influenced by D. W. Griffith, whose *The Birth of a Nation* (1915) was not only a template for family and nationalist melodrama, civil-war heroics, and pathos, but also for a racial paranoia that Hayward largely abjured.

239

His historical source (far removed from Dixon's *The Clansman*) was James Cowan's *The New Zealand Wars and the Pioneer Period,* published in 1923, just before the first *Rewi's Last Stand* and *The Te Kooti Trail.* To say that Cowan, and Hayward, who acknowledged him in *Rewi's Last Stand* (1940) with images of the turning pages of *The New Zealand Wars,* were of their time in producing stirring vindications of the pioneers, hopeful mythologies of interracial respect generated through combat, and premature sentimentalizing over the supposedly dying Maori race, is to repeat truisms that hardly do them justice, since every historian and filmmaker is of their time, and contemporary historians such as James Belich and Michael King themselves pursue updated agendas of national assertion quite as overt, though more in line with present ideologies.[11] Hayward's films, though acknowledged for their pioneering position, have often suffered from being viewed through a simplified version of their ideological parameters, thus ignoring the complexities that play within those limits.

Inspired by his twin mentors Cowan and Griffith, Hayward centered his historical films on two episodes of heroic siege resistance against overwhelming odds, one by hostile Maori and one by the colonial side, the celebrated siege of Orakau in which 300 Maori including women and children refused to surrender to 1,800 British soldiers (*Rewi's Last Stand*), and the smaller siege of the Te Poronu mill, in which the French manager and a few friendly Maori resisted before being overrun by overwhelming forces (*The Te Kooti Trail*). Cowan's sacramental response to both is characteristic of his and Hayward's desire for foundational images of patriotic nobility, whether colonial or rebel Maori. "The story of the last day in Orakau imperishably remains an inspiration to deeds of courage and fortitude. Nowhere in history does the spirit of pure patriotism blaze up more brightly than in that little earthwork redoubt."[12] And "No stone, no memorial of any kind marks the spot [at Te Poronu] defended by 'John the Frenchman' with such heroic valour. In a few years, but for this record, the memory of Jean Guerren's gallant stand would have perished. New Zealand should mark as one of its national monuments the ground made sacred by a brave son of France who defended his post to the death."[13]

If one major function of epic is narrating the nation's foundational events, Hayward's films obviously fit this pattern, restaging the recent past for the young dominion's later audience and gesturing toward a utopian future burned out of war's dystopia. This last is embodied in *The Te Kooti Trail*'s coda (Hayward's addition) where the now aged Lieutenant Gilbert Mair, the real-life settler hero, just before his death in 1923, writes to his old Arawa tribe allies, recalling both sides' sacrifices and envisioning a peaceful future, "the greatest nation, the English here side by side with the smallest race, the Maori, under one law and loving one another," with a final shift to the present of the film's making, as the camera dwells on a memorial to Mair as one "who loved the Maori race."

As such details indicate, Hayward interacted dynamically with his source, altering the historian for cinematic ends, something which should not have been alien to Cowan who advised Méliès on his 1912 filmmaking trip, left three short film scenarios of his own writing in his papers, and self-consciously gestured to future artistic uses of his Orakau account in details designed to aid some future painter (or, possibly, filmmaker).[14] His choice of painter over filmmaker, despite his connections with the newer art, was both because of New Zealand film's undeveloped state, with Hayward's first films not made till 1921–1922, and painting's higher artistic status. Hayward selected the most poignantly dramatic incidents from Cowan and then invented fictional characters (or in *The Te Kooti Trail* fleshed out minor real-life figures) to intersect with them, intuitively following the procedures analyzed by Lukács in Sir Walter Scott's historical fictions: with the major real-world historical figures placed in the margins, "medi-ocre" and "average" characters dominate, "bring[ing] the extremes whose struggle fills the novel . . . into contact with one another . . . as they enter into human contact with both camps."[15] In a definition that also under-lines the force of *The Birth of a Nation* and *Intolerance* (1916) for Hayward, Lukács noted that "the split of the nation into warring parties always runs through the centre of the closest human relationships. Parents and children, lover and beloved, old friends, etc, confront one another as oppo-nents or the inevitability of this confrontation carries the collision deep into their personal lives."[16] In view of later blanket critiques of the popular cinema's viewing political issues through individuals, Lukács's articulation of the personal as "world historical" throws positive light on Bob Beaumont's and Ariana's romance in *Rewi's Last Stand* and the splitting of the protagonists into opposite camps, Ariana with the Orakau defenders, her lover and father among the attackers. Despite such highly wrought situa-tions, Hayward's historical films are sometimes described unexcitingly as "docu-drama," for their use of actual sites for reconstructed events, looka-likes impersonating historical characters, screen footnotes derived from Griffith's epics testifying to the accuracy of reconstructions in the silent *Rewi's Last Stand,* and, in the later sound film, an occasional documentary voice-over, scene-setting intertitles, and a map representing military movements. These, though, should not occlude other more dramatic qualities. When the epigraph to *Rewi's Last Stand* states that the descendants of Te Awamutu's military settlers "filmed recently these pages from rough-hewn history, re-enacting on the actual locations the parts played by their pioneering forefathers," the trope is highly emotive, presenting the present generation as filially reenacting its fathers for posterity ("lest we forget").[17] For all his empathy with the defeated, it was impossible for Hayward to detach himself from the providential view of civilization's progress over savagery, which was so important to the settler self-image. But as with another ancestor of his fictions, the novelist James Fenimore

Cooper, the victory, while celebrated, is shadowed with regret and nostalgia, evident in the new white indigenes' attempts to transfer some essence of the Maori to themselves by appropriating Maori symbols and language (e.g., Bob Beaumont's use of Maori terms such as *mana, utu,* and *rangatira* and the use of the Maori *whare* for house in *The Te Kooti Trail*). Settler-centered as the epigraph is, it enacts a fugitive elision of the races like that which Cowan creates when claiming that:

> the passionate affection with which the Maori clung to his tribal lands is a quality which undeniably tinges the mind and outlook of the farm-bred, country-loving white New Zealander today. The native-born has unconsciously assimilated something of the peculiar patriotism that belongs to the soil: the genius loci of the old frontiers has not entirely vanished from the hills and streams.[18]

Hayward's filmic sensibilities find correlatives for this feeling. An example is his balancing of the moment in *The Te Kooti Trail* when Taranahi, dying in the arms of Lieutenant Mair, watches himself joining his dead lover, Monika, on Cape Reinga, the departure point of Maori souls, with the one where the Frenchman, Jules, dies in *The Te Kooti Trail,* and he becomes a New Zealander as his companions bury him in a bush grave. His interment is accompanied by an intertitle from Arthur H. Adams' poem "The Dwellings of Our Dead" with its thematic of the land claiming as its own, hungry for the graves that constitute tenancy, even those Pakeha (Maori word for whites, now common usage) war dead whose loyalties are still with their distant birthplaces:

> And till all time shall cease
> Our brooding bush shall fold them
> In its broad-bosomed peace.[19]

the te kooti trail

Watching *The Te Kooti Trail*'s successor, *Rewi's Last Stand,* on his visit to New Zealand in 1940, the documentarist John Grierson expressed surprise at "how near to producing a Cecil B. DeMille spectacle Mr Hayward has come with the resources at his disposal."[20] Even if slightly barbed, the comment points to Hayward's films' impressive battle scenes. However, while these are important to *The Te Kooti Trail,* Hayward's masterpiece's "epic" feel also depends on other aspects of an ambitious design. For instance, the Northumberland prologue, linking the old world to the new, stages New Zealand's British origins, while the Hadrian's Wall setting invokes a previous empire. In the legend of the disappearance of "The Lost Legion" while marching north against the Scots, the motif of forgotten soldiers enabling the new settler state is sounded, with intertitles from Kipling's poem "The Lost Legion" ("There's a legion that never was listed . . ."). When Eric Mantell is forced by false accusations to emigrate, he replays, in a melodramatic inflection, the history of early English settlement. Once arrived, and away from a regressive world of butlers, servants and "tennants" (*sic*), he enjoys frontier life so fully that when his fiancée Alice writes that he has been cleared, assuming that he will "come home to your own, my soldier boy," it is she who must journey out to him.

Balancing these Anglo-Scottish emphases, when Eric joins the colonial forces against Te Kooti's rebellion, one of his militia companions is Barney O'Halloran, representing Irish immigration to New Zealand, and the other is Jules Vialou, like Jean Guerren—the siege's hero—a Frenchman. Hayward inherited Guerren's nationality from Cowan's history, an unavoidable swerve from dominant settler Britishness, but, as if enamored of the idea of a more cosmopolitan local community, unexpectedly doubles him with the fictional Jules. Guerren's and Jules's Frenchness certainly plays on audience awareness that New Zealand might have become a French colony. As it is, both die heroically, leaving Eric and Barney to inherit the British/Irish future. Their role, however, is more than simply to sound an imperial last post, as they add to the small country's already variegated history, with Jules's "culinary genius" lending savoir faire to the yet-to-be-refined new society.

An intertitle preceding the narrative quotes the final verse of Arthur H. Adams's "The Dwellings of our Dead" (the poem in Jules's funerary intertitle), beginning "They came as lovers came, all else forsaking, / The bonds of home and kindred proudly breaking," announcing the film's concern with settler mythologies, with the filmic rendition of an emerging settler character and experience. This takes the form, however, of a proto-nationalism that sees the emerging New Zealander as a "better Briton" rather than an anti-Briton, and does not involve, as the later Murphy and Ward films do, assertion of the New Zealander against the mother country. Notable for its large cast of characters, historical and fictional, white and Maori (both friendly and hostile), the film is also ambitious in its many tones, moods, and rhythms, all established through Hayward's characteristic open-air location shooting, partly derived from lack of studio resources, but also reflecting commitment to the New Zealand terrain and the ethos of the outdoor life inherited from pioneer days. Comedy also features with the rough frontier humor of Barney's self-administered "bush dentistry" and the delicate charm of Monika kissing and playfully drilling Eric and his companions—"*Teihana!*" ("Attention!")—and asking if they'll fight for her (rather than, implicitly, for Queen and Country). Hayward's silent-film mastery of dynamic camera movement and montage was undoubtedly constrained by the formidable difficulties of early sound filming in New Zealand, which is a major reason why *The Te Kooti Trail* surpasses the later *Rewi's Last Stand.* Apart from the drama of the siege itself, *The Te Kooti Trail* is marked by exciting bush fighting skirmishes and vivid passages of parallel montage, developed from Griffith but with their own memorable specificities, where first Tarahini runs and swims for help, then Mair rides to raise his famous "Arawa Flying Column" and races with them to the mill. These are complexly intercut with the progress of the siege and feature exhilarating, sweeping traveling shots (intrinsic to Hayward's epic style) as Taranahi and Mair move across a terrain recalling western genre figures in landscape but subtly differentiated by native elements. Less action-dependent, and just as characteristic, are the interstitial subtleties of mood relating to landscape, suggested in off-duty moments when the soldiers relax, especially where Jules cooks for his companions on the beach, that most evocative of New Zealand sites, almost unknown to the western, the alfresco setting too of Mair's writing his letter to his Arawa "children."

There remains, however, inextricably entangled with such meanings, the question of the Maori. As Cowan wrote, distinguishing New Zealand's history from Australia's, the settlers' path was blocked by a "powerful warrior race of indigenes," and the Maori have a central role since pioneer self-definition is intimately bound up with interaction with them, both on and off the battlefield, physically and psychically. At one level this takes a Manichean form, radically dichotomizing the friendly from unfriendly Maori, with overtones of Cooper's virtuous Uncas and Chingachgook and the demonic Magua in *The Last of the Mohicans* (1992). On the one hand there is the tiny interracial utopia of the mill, with Guerren's family group (he, his wife Erihapeta [Elizabeth], her younger sister Monika and Monika's lover, Taranahi) and the friendly Ngati Pukeko tribe workers. Here, as in Lieutenant Gilbert Mair's loving homosocial relationship with Taranahi, exists a template for a golden age, with Monika's wearing both a tiki (a Maori charm) and a crucifix enacting a cross-fertilization of cultures and Peti's (Erihapeta's) Maori costume signifying that her native culture is unrepressed by marriage to a European. The film's sexual relationships offer a triad of possibilities of either mono-racial or bi-racial romance—the high white colonist love saga of Eric and Alice (more off screen than on); the pleasant, homely interracial marriage of Guerren and "Peti" (Erihapeta) and the "Maoriland"-like idyll of Peti's sister Monika ('Nika') and Taranahi, vying with Murnau's and Flaherty's *Tabu* in self-consciously prelapsarian beauty, as they float among the weeping willows on the river, before all but the absent white pair are destroyed by Te Kooti's attack.

On the other hand, Hayward's portrayal of Te Kooti, obviously problematic in the 2000s with their search for Maori motivations and justifications, also caused problems in 1927 when elders of Te Kooti's syncretic Ringatu church successfully pressured the government to remove intertitles describing the prophet as "resorting to fake miracles" and his lieutenant as his "torture master" and "stage manager" of miracles."[21] Though Hayward felt justified by the great Maori politician, Sir Apirana Ngata's view of Te Kooti as "the last and greatest representative of the worst side of the Maori character, its subtlety, cunning and treachery, and love of bloodshed—its immorality and its fanaticism," Ngata's denunciation effectively licensed Hayward's substitution of vivid demagoguery, impressive but unsubtle, for more complex enactments of his rebellion's appeal to his followers, as he preaches the word of his "atua" (God), huge mission bible in hand, with minatory gestures and looks, sometimes in "choker" close-up.[22] Shorn of context, his attack on the mill reads mainly as a malign assault on its idyllic interracial community. If in most respects *The Te Kooti Trail* is a more complexly realized work than *Rewi's Last Stand,* it is still the latter that manages to undemonize oppositional Maori characters such as Rewi Maniapoto, Ariana's uncle, and Tama, in a way that *The Te Kooti Trail* doesn't attempt, though in the context of the mutually congratulatory memory of the Orakau siege, this was easier to do. When the rescuers arrive too late, Guerren has been killed, Monika executed for not disclosing the whereabouts of hidden ammunition, and Peti forcibly remarried. Swearing revenge for Nika's death, the three soldiers, Taranahi, and Mair and his Arawa Flying Column pursue Te Kooti and his forces in the film's last phase, seeking besides Te Kooti, another historical figure, Peka Makarini (Maori version of Baker McLean), Te Kooti's lieutenant and bugler, whom Hayward, contradicting Cowan, makes more responsible for Nika's execution than Te Kooti, perhaps in anticipation of censorship, perhaps in artistic remorse for too simplistic a treatment of the rebel prophet. Peka (Baker), as his name indicates, was of mixed blood, bringing to mind the malign mulattos Silas Lynch and Lydia Brown in *The Birth of a Nation,* making it almost impossible not to feel the hovering presence of Hayward's great cinematic mentor and his vision of the disasters of interracial sexuality. In the pursuit, Peka is shot first by Mair and finished off by Taranahi, thus revenging Nika's death. But the film quickly retreats from Peka's mixed blood as the source of his "thirty murders," with no suggestion of the pale skin he was supposed to have, and keeps Griffith's mulatto mistresses and attempted rapes at a considerable distance, too paranoid for the New Zealand context.

In terms of the attempt to capture or kill Te Kooti, the narrative, moving into 1870, rather anticlimactically follows historical fact, with the rebel harried to the point where further war is impossible, but evading capture, and last seen on his white horse, being led by his men into Maori-dominated territories, bent low in disappointment and defeat, "The sun," an intertitle states, "sinking for ever on Te Kooti's dream of power." This ending is necessary for historical verisimilitude, but also means a less divisive closure with the 1927 audience's knowledge that Te Kooti (and the other most feared rebel, Titokowaru) died peacefully (1892 and 1888 respectively) and at relative peace with a changed world, giving more substance perhaps to the film's penultimate moments of symbolic reconciliation where Alice, Eric, Barney, and Mair take shelter in a friendly Maori *wharenui* (meeting house).

rewi's last stand

Despite surviving only in a drastically shortened print, the sound version of *Rewi's Last Stand* is the best known of Hayward's films, although his finest work was certainly in his silent epics and melodramas (*My Lady of the Cave* [1922], and *A Bush Cinderella* [1928]).[23] *Rewi's Last Stand*, unlike the archive-bound silents, has been relatively widely viewed. It dramatizes the perennial New Zealand legend of the famous "*ake, ake, ake*," ("[Fight you] for ever and ever and ever") Maori refusal of surrender at Orakau, in which the colonials are also ennobled by their cheering of the defenders' bravery. When Bob Beaumont, the Maori-speaking settler hero, translates the defenders' defiance, a look of pride crosses his face, as if to express the majority race's pleasure in the courage of the minority. The expression of a national legend of mutual respect, powerfully affective and in many ways socially progressive, also feeds into the oversimplified, even self-deceiving, view of the wars as chivalric that Belich criticizes.[24] The other element that has undoubtedly contributed to the film's popularity is its interracial romance, even if some later criticism has been suspicious of it as a means of bringing the Maori heroine under white patriarchal control.[25]

Set in the Waikato region as war breaks out (1863), its narrative couples a white colonial, Bob Beaumont, and a mixed-race Maori, Ariana (Ramai Te Miha), brought up by missionaries. The pair are presented as disposed to interracial union, Ariana, a *rangatira* (aristocrat), dressed like a colonial belle, speaking perfect English, and Bob as close to Maori as possible without his white identity sliding into the too fluid ambiguities of the "Pakeha Maori" gone native. As a figure taking on very conservatively aspects of Cooper's Natty Bumpo, Bob is a merchant, not a hunter, and much more at home in civilized society, friendly with the missionaries, and meeting Governor Grey in Auckland. Unlike Natty he does not adapt native elements into his dress (some readers will remember Baines's rudimentary facial tattoo in *The Piano* [1993]). But, in a milder cultural fusion, he is called Ropata (Maori for Robert), and, like Mair in *The Te Kooti Trail* (also known by a Maori name, "Tawa"), he speaks Maori—actually the first words he utters in the film, and translates for "Old Ben" the surrender negotiations at Orakau. He also tells the warrior, Tama, that he is a "blood brother" of tribal enemies of the Maniapoto, and is also skilled with *the taiaha* (the wooden weapon which Mr Bennett teaches Boogie to use in *Once Were Warriors* [1994]), as we see when he loses, but far from ignominiously, to Tama, the native expert. The film's most charming moment comes when the whites and Ariana, having evacuated the mission, set up camp, and the couple wander off into the bush where a teasing romantic encounter takes place with Ropata, claiming *utu* (payment) on behalf of "the tribe of Beaumont" for Ariana's playful mockery of him, then Ariana teasingly telling him that warriors take rather than ask, and running away provokingly. Here in the bush the close-ups of the two are fringed with ferns, and in the longer shots they are surrounded by indigenous bush, creating an idyllic native *locus amoenus* for the lovers, which balances the film's vision of the productive pastureland created by the colonists at the expense of native bush celebrated by the Reverend Morgan and Ropata as they ride through it.

In a movement that is a paradigm of the classic historical fiction's "split of the nation" "running through the centre of the closest human relationships," as Lukács says, the lovers are separated by the Ngati Maniapoto forcing all "half caste" children to return to the tribe. At first Ariana chooses to be with the whites, and her forced return is clearly against her will. But, when her uncle reminds her that his sons have been killed fighting Pakeha and insists that, as the daughter of her mother, her people need her, a close-up clearly articulates growing uncertainty. The classic love-versus-duty dilemma of eighteenth-century heroic drama, instead of being conventionally concentrated on the man, bears down on both parties, but more heavily on Ariana, with Bob's conscience apparently more malleable since he is willing to spy on the Maori under his trading persona, and, except for his dilemma as regards Ariana, shows little internal conflict over the war and killing her tribespeople, whereas she restricts her role in the siege to noncombatant nursing of wounded warriors and children, and, unlike the other Maori women, does not shoot at the whites. When Bob returns to the Waikato, he assumes that she will return to Auckland with him, but she answers him regretfully—"What would they think of me, a *rangatira* [if I failed to support them]? I cannot change what is in me." As these conflicts of duty and love climax with Bob in the sapper vanguard of the attack on the *pa,* within seeing distance of Ariana, the hermeneutic of the identity of Ariana's lost white father becomes dominant, with suspicions, later confirmed, that it is Bob's army companion, the scallywaggish "Old Ben" Horton. When the defenders break out of the *pa,* Hayward builds on details in Cowan's narrative, in particular the escape of a woman wounded in the thigh (which seems to be where Ariana's wound is), helped by a young Maori warrior who dies protecting her with an empty gun, who becomes the film's Tama, eulogized by the whites for his brave death.

As Ariana limps to the riverside for water, she is discovered by Bob and "Old Ben." The simultaneous reconciliation of the lovers and of father and daughter is staged ambiguously enough to have been read as clearly signifying her death (Old Ben's sorrowful headshake) but also as suggesting that she survives.[26] These antithetical interpretations of such a basic fact—though the former is more powerfully underwritten—may have been produced by the film's unfortunate shortening, but it is arguable that

Hayward may have deliberately created the ambiguity in order to avoid either a definitively affirmative (too optimistic?) or irrevocably negative (too pessimistic?) outcome, as either support for or counterweight to, the optimism of the epigraph at the other end of the film with its "slowly blending" race of New Zealanders. This would be in line with certain other ambiguities that block simple interpretation. The most prominent of these is the way in which the conservative ideological trope of the recovery of Ariana's paternity with its precedence of white patrilineal over Maori matrilineal and its fitting in with the rhetoric of the Maori as child (shared by both the Reverend Morgan and Gilbert Mair), is compromised by Stanley Knight's portrayal of "Old Ben." The scrawny, disheveled, alcoholic, possibly criminal, figure presented to the audience exposes the gap between the powerful ideal paternal function he may suggest in narrative and ideological outline and the ability of Hayward's films in their detail and subtlety to refine and sometimes trouble the ideological parameters within which they are constructed.

utu

Utu's director, Geoff Murphy, with Roger Donaldson, dominated the early post-1977 film industry before he followed Donaldson to Hollywood (1988), their exodus symptomatic of a small English-speaking cinema's difficulties in retaining talent. *Utu*, critically appreciated in Europe, Britain, and the USA, was extolled in Pauline Kael's laudatory *New Yorker* "horror comedy of colonialism" review (October 15, 1984), among other things for its "joshing" and "riffing," sometimes blackly comic take on the colonial race wars.[27] Received in the context of the "Vietnam westerns," it was also endorsed by current enthusiasms for post-colonial and new national cinemas, foreshadowing what later became a wide international response to the chief marker of New Zealand's cinematic "glocalism," its bicultural past and present—important in future widespread successes such as *Once Were Warriors* and *Whale Rider* (2003).

The local scene *Utu* derived from and spoke to in 1983 was very different from that addressed by Hayward's films in an era marked by fewer visible race-relations vicissitudes, with Pakeha and Maori unofficially separated by a rural—urban divide and New Zealand's sometimes self-congratulatory ethos of racial equality easily believed in because largely untested by proximity. By the time of *Utu*, postwar decades of Maori urban migration had brought into prominence previously distanced problems of cultural dislocation, social deprivation, and crime, with Auckland, much the largest city, the seedbed of protest movements. These, following the polarizing countrywide anti-apartheid disturbances attending the 1971 South African rugby tour, raised the specter of violent confrontation in a country with little experience of civil disorder and pushed governments into legislation emphasizing the biculturality of the state, making Maori an official language (1987) and giving the Waitangi Tribunal for Maori grievances (1975) retrospective powers back to 1840 (1985). *Utu* was made at the height of the unresolved situations that precipitated these actions. This context, which extended to Maori separatist rhetoric, pragmatically impossible but alarming, demonstrated the fragmentation of the "imagined community" the new film industry addressed, making the early 1980s a seemingly unpropitious time to return to national epic material, except as redefined in terms of contested and renegotiated foundational narratives. *Utu*'s impulse to represent national history, however ironized, with at least cautious optimism, is sonically signified in the film's two-minute orchestral overture, recalling those of the David Lean epics, *Lawrence of Arabia* (1962) and *Doctor Zhivago* (1965), of a slightly earlier time.[28] But as the action unfolds it is clear that the nostalgia and elegaicism which surrounded the Hayward epics, dependent to some degree, like Fenimore Cooper's novel-epics, on the ambiguously mourned vanishing indigene, can have no place in a later version, given the persistence of racial problems and the increasing Maori population.

Reminiscing the historical rebellions of Te Kooti and Titokowaru, *Utu* centres round Te Wheke (Anzac Wallace), a *kupapa* lance corporal, who, when soldiers massacre his home villagers, dedicates himself to *utu* (revenge), decapitating a reverend in front of his Maori congregation and preaching for an uprising. Subsequent narrative events follow the colonial army's pursuit of the elusive rebel and his small guerrilla band, as they carry out sporadic raids. Te Wheke is a much more developed presence than Hayward's shadowy Te Kooti (or indeed the stalwart Rewi Maniapoto in *Rewi's Last Stand*), but, like theirs, his rebellion is the catalyst for complex interactions among the various characters—white army personnel, settler civilians, *kupapa* soldiers tempted to transfer allegiance to Te Wheke, and other Maori in ambivalent situations—as they are plotted across a spectrum of politico-racial attitudes heightened by Te Wheke's actions, abstractable to the oppositions and relations (brown—white, monocultural—bicultural, colonial—imperialist) running across all four films. Apart from Te Wheke and Colonel Elliot, identified with unyielding mono-racist positions, *Utu*'s major characters are characteristically positioned with a foot in either camp. The settler Williamson (Bruno Lawrence), though committed to revenging Te Wheke's killing of his wife, is shown with a Maori friend, Horace, near the film's beginning, and at its end joins in the *kupapas' haka*. Captain Scott, though keen to try guerrilla tactics on the Maori, is friends with the *kupapa*, Henare, and sleeps with the Maori girl, Kura. The enigmatic *kupapa*, Wiremu (Wi Kuki Kaa), remaining with the army for reasons unstated but readable as his recognition of historical inevitability and the necessity of adapting to it, exhibits sympathies for and criticisms of both sides. Kura has two lovers, one white, one Maori, supports the Maori side, but makes sure that Scott is out of danger when Te Wheke attacks; and

249

Matu, though she has little apparent interest in the whites, is at least understanding when Scott risks attending his friend Henare's *tangi* (Maori funeral). Played on by opposing forces, many of the characters find negotiating positions between races and cultures, however desirable, difficult (some even fatal). Even Te Wheke shares something of this doubleness in his fascination with *Macbeth,* which he is twice seen reading, and several times quotes from, a fascination presumably based on his recognition of the parallels between the tragic criminal protagonist's situation and his own, making him even in his war to exterminate the whites paradoxically committed to aspects of their culture. And Colonel Elliot's racism is no bar to his sexual use of a young Maori servant boy which suggests that even he has an undertow of ambivalence. The third of the oppositions and relations (colonialist-imperialist) attempts to bind together old (Maori) and new (Pakeha) indigenes through the shared fact of birth in New Zealand, as when Scott asks Wiremu which side he is on, and Wiremu replies "The same as you, sir. I was born here too." This rapprochement demands a scapegoating of the reprehensible Englishman, Elliot, who looks down on Scott as a colonial and refuses to pronounce Te Wheke's name properly, and onto whom as the representative of imperial Britain the stain of settler racism is largely displaced, distorting historical fact (the imperial army was withdrawn in 1869) in its attempt to create paradoxical settler–Maori unities overriding the conflicts.

Utu, like the other films, pushes through violence toward a hoped-for racial reconciliation, but one harder to suggest with conviction in the divided climate of the 1980s, a reception context emphasized by the allusions to the 1980s present that accompany its nineteenth-century reconstructions. Te Wheke's hairstyle and clothing, like his followers', evoke 1980s street gang garb as much as the 1870s; Te Wheke's assumption of a facial *moko* (tattoo) in a painful ritual also suggests the growing use of tattoos by urban Maori gangs, with its quantum of contemporary threat; while Te Wheke's insinuation from the pulpit that 20,000 people could gather on the streets of Auckland in hours has obvious resonances in a time of mass demonstrations. Te Wheke's interest in *Macbeth* and his brother Wiremu's mastery of French and chess suggest the Maori university graduates of the time, much involved in the protest movements. More antically, in one sequence, the *kupapa* army drummers subversively embellish their drumming with slickly improvisatory drumstick actions recalling the popular Polynesian "showbands" of a later era, the "Quin Tikis" or the "Maori Volcanics." With a more obviously fractured audience than Hayward's, *Utu* emphasizes the difficulties attending the various interracial relationships, and even the ones between Maori, the latter (as when a pro-Te Wheke *kupapa* denounces Wiremu) reflecting the differences of the time among radicalized Maori as to the state's reformability. Accounts of the film's making, some preserved in Gaylene Preston's documentary,

The Making of Utu (1982), stress the degree of debate on location between Pakeha and Maori cast and crew, a sign of the volatility and contemporary meaningfulness of the historical subject matter.

Utu, while cultivating contemporary allusions, also displays a complex relation to cinematic tradition in its deconstruction and reconstruction of *The Te Kooti Trail* and *Rewi's Last Stand*. The army pursuit of Te Kooti is reworked, but with many more breakdowns of unity among the pursuers: the tensions between Elliot and Scott for instance, and the instability of the *kupapa* affiliations. While the army pursues Te Wheke for officially sanctioned justice, various characters also seek *utu* on personal grounds: Williamson, a settler (Bruno Lawrence), half maddened with grief, for Te Wheke's killing of his wife; Elliot out of racism and pride; while Scott, late in the film, wants it for Te Wheke's killing of his lover, the Maori girl Kura. Mair's closeness to Taranahi (who dies in his arms) in *The Te Kooti Trail* is reworked in the relationships between Scott and Henare and Scott and Wiremu, but in comparison these are low key and unfinished. Just as they suggest the difficulties of cultural interconnection, so the interracial romance between Kura and Scott falls short of providing a synecdoche for the resolving of cross-cultural difficulties, partly by its never assuming centrality as Bob and Ariana's love does in *Rewi's Last Stand*, and partly because the degree of Kura's commitment to Scott is unclear. If love is interpreted more diffusely, whereas *The Te Kooti Trail* ends with an encomium to Mair as the white man "who loved the Maori race," the end of *Utu*, placing Wiremu in the position occupied in the earlier texts by the cross-culturally sympathetic Pakeha, comes up with a reversal for the times, the Maori who loves, or at least understands and works with the Pakeha race. This reworking of the ancestral texts is particularly foregrounded in the screenwriters' revisiting of the less official works of Hayward's source, Cowan: *The Adventures of Kimble Bent* and *Tales of the Maori Bush*.[29] The first, adding to the prevalent grotesque, destabilizing comedy, surfaces in Henare's and Scott's discussion of the differences between Maori and Pakeha senses of humor, revolving around a Maori trick that substituted a barrel of minced soldiers' corpses for one of salted pork, thus turning the soldiers into unwitting cannibals as they eat it. The second is the source of the climactic scene of Te Wheke's execution.

The film's title, the Maori word *Utu*, has, in the narrative, the obvious meaning of "revenge." But it also possesses others—such as repayment, cost, price, compensation (as in the amorous "tribe of Beaumont demands *utu*" interchange in *Rewi's Last Stand*), and, most importantly, reciprocity, connected with the restoration of balance, harmony, and order.[30] Initially, when Te Wheke declares war, *utu* as revenge is totally dominant, and in Te Wheke's trial and execution, it threatens to remain so. The final episode is refashioned from Cowan's description of the "log court-martial" of Wi Heretaunga. There various of his Arawa captors claim the right to execute him, until his nephew argues that he alone, not being an Arawa, can shoot him without causing tribal fighting. *Utu* substitutes Te Wheke for Wi Heretaunga, and for the Arawa wishing to execute him the three characters demanding the right to shoot him in revenge: Lieutenant Scott, Matu (whose cousin and niece, Kura, Te Wheke has killed), and Williamson. The nephew's role as executioner is transferred to Wiremu, who, revealing himself as Te Wheke's brother, becomes the executioner in order to end the larger interracial conflict. Wiremu's shooting of his brother, though it carries out the court martial's sentence, is translated by its participants away from an impersonal legal act into an extraordinary ritual compact acted out semioperatically (with Maori chants) in both English and Maori, in which Te Wheke collaborates in his own death, not through guilt, but implicitly as a necessary sacrifice for the future. Wiremu, as the agent of the deaths of both Colonel Elliot (whom he has deliberately shot in a friendly fire incident) and his brother, removes the two characters who most stand in the way of reconciliation, and the various blood sacrifices, most importantly Te Wheke's, may nourish the future, some of the unspecific outlines of which are obliquely enacted, albeit in tragic mode, in the improvised dual culture ceremony of the film's end.[31]

As Kael emphasized, *Utu* cultivates unstable modes, creating dissonance on its epic base through grotesque comedy (the rebels defenestrating a grand piano, one of Te Wheke's men plastering his face with flour as if to experiment with a Pakeha persona). Not comic, but typical in their destabilizing ironies are two moments where John Charles's score moves into unadulterated epic-heroic-pastoral mode matching visuals of great sweeping vistas, different from the film's predominant winter rain and mist-wreathed landscapes, across which figures move, ironizing the visual-sonic presentation of the vistas—in one case soldiers, in the other the half-maddened lone-avenger figure, Williamson, both images playing idyllic landscape against human violence, in combinations that retain epic resonances while subjecting them to irony.

river queen

Vincent Ward, like Murphy, and others later, left the small New Zealand industry after early features, *Vigil* (1984) and *The Navigator: A Medieval Odyssey* (1987), which created his reputation. After the international coproduction *Map of the Human Heart* (1993) and the Hollywood-made *What Dreams May Come* (1998), he returned to make *River Queen* in troubled production circumstances that impacted negatively on the film's immediate reception. *The Navigator: A Medieval Odyssey*, with its title's Homeric epic allusion and its movement between different temporal and spatial worlds, defined his filmmaking's vertiginous ambitions, its medieval dream narrative linking thirteenth-century Cumbria and late-twentieth-century Auckland, and its through-a-glass-darkly voyage and quest motifs foreshadowing both *Map of the Human Heart* and *What Dreams May Come*. These two films (though situated outside Ward's homeland) enact heightened, extrapolated versions of traditional New Zealand motifs of solitude, geographical, and cultural isolation, journeyings between the different worlds of the Pacific, Britain, Europe and America (in *What Dreams May Come* extended to the metaphysical geographies of Heaven and Hell), and geographic and cultural double affiliations, obviously true of Maori, but also of Pakeha New Zealanders, poised between the Pacific and the mostly British and European places and cultures of origin. Within this perspective, certain aspects of *River Queen*'s replaying of the colonial wars are clarified: its constantly circulating thematics of home and exile, its sometimes unexpected intersection of cultures, as well as its central use of Te Kai Po's obscure dream vision, which provides a difficult, fragmented hermeneutic—the more art-film end of the crossing of mainstream commercial and art film cultivated by Ward's and his contemporary and compatriot Jane Campion's later films.

River Queen enacts a distinctly fabulous version of the wars, marked by Te Kai Po's obscure dream vision, by oneiric sequences where Boy (Rawiri Pene), like Puck in *A Midsummer Night's Dream* or Ariel in *The Tempest*, flits about the battlefield projecting voices to mislead the colonials, and by the Griffithian mixture of intense battlefield realism intersected by heightened coincidental encounters such as that of the Stoneman and Cameron boys at Petersburg in *The Birth of a Nation*, here with Sarah's friend, the Irish soldier Private Doyle, nearly shooting Boy, then letting him escape, Wiremu, misreading Doyle's actions, tragically shooting him, and Sarah nearly shooting her son when she sees him seemingly about to kill Doyle. But it also exhibits a deep interest in recent revisionist history, in particular Belich's reassessment of Titokowaru in *The New Zealand Wars* and his *Dictionary of New Zealand Biography* entry.[32] A written epilogue "acknowledg[es] with respect the extraordinary lives, words, and actions of not only Riwha Titokowaru," but also of "Caroline Perrett and Ann Evans," adding that "our story could not be as it is without theirs." Riwha Titokowaru was the most formidable Maori general of the wars, his memory repressed, Belich argues, by the majority culture, in favor of his contemporary Te Kooti, because as the greater military strategist, he inflicted major defeats on the colonial forces.[33] The tribute to Titokowaru whom the film figures (following the revisionist argument) both as war leader and peacemaker, signals the new foregrounding of Maori history. Those to Caroline Perrett and Ann Evans point to the recovery of "herstory" within "our story," the less written history of the New Zealand female in the context of dominant myths of pioneer masculinity. Caroline "Queenie" Perrett was the center of a New Zealand frontier "captivity narrative." Kidnapped by Maori as a child, probably as a retaliation for her father breaking a land *tapu* (taboo), she returned to white society in middle age, unharmed.[34] Ann Evans was an ex-Crimean nurse who—it is claimed in the grey area between legend and truth—was taken blindfolded by Maori to heal Titokowaru and then safely returned.[35] *River Queen*'s fictional heroine, Sarah O'Brien (Samantha Morton) combines aspects of both Perrett and Evans. Sarah's father, like Perrett's, breaks a land *tapu;* if not married to a Maori like Perrett, she has a child by one; and in a displacement that son, Boy, is kidnapped. Like Evans, Sarah has medical skills and is taken blindfolded to Te Kai Po (transparently Titokowaru) where she heals him. "Queenie," Perrett's nickname, is awarded to Sarah by Te Kai Po. Ward's phrase "Our story" (with its Haywardian echoes), suggests a less intensely fragmented audience than in the 1970s and 1980s, with this version including, in a role transcending the absolute "other," the Maori villain-hero and finding a more than honorific place for woman.

This foregrounding of the colonial female (following Ada in Campion's *The Piano* [1986]) is augmented by Sarah's possessing the film's narrative-framing overvoice, as she commits her journal to the sea. Her opening recall of her past immediately places her between the Pakeha and Maori worlds, through her love of a young Maori, Tommy Boy, who died of influenza. Their son, Boy, is kidnapped by his Maori uncle, Rangi the tattooist, initiating the quest narrative of Sarah's six-year search for him (with intricate allusions to John Ford's *The Searchers* [1956] running through the film), inverted from tradition by the quester being female, the quest's object not female but male, and mixed race rather than white, the latest version of the search for a more inclusive national identity which the four films share.[36] *River Queen*'s return to Griffithian family tropes (which *Utu* avoided, except for the Te Wheke brothers), may respond to a time where "national family" optimism is more widespread. However, since Boy, when Sarah finds him, has embraced the Maori tribal world over his mother's Irishnesss, the simpler quest turns into a more complex, more internalized and refined search for identity and "home," whether "downriver" or "upriver," to use the film's terms, and negotiating between Maori, Irish, and British identities. This last uses the surprising near-predominance of Irish soldiers in the British Army in the New Zealand campaign (40 percent according to Belich), exaggerated to the point where the only non-Irish Pakeha in the central actions seems to be the ruthless and racist Anglo-Scot Commander Baine. An unexpected bond between Maori and Irish is established when Private Doyle (Kiefer Sutherland) draws a parallel between Wiremu (Cliff Curtis), "one Maori that's more like us Irish," fighting first for the British Army and then against them, and the Irish soldiers' (parallel in reverse) experience, and again when he compares the ferocity with which the Maori fight the colonists to that of the Irish fighting Cromwell. The film's primarily Irish/Celtic-based music advances this thematic, especially the song "Danny Boy," that moving worldwide anthem of exilic (actual or metaphoric) Irishness, which is sung both in Maori and English by Boy and repeated chorically and in musical variations throughout. Presenting the Irish as subterraneanly related to the Maori even as they fight them, the stain of settler racism, as with Colonel Elliot in *Utu*, is deflected onto the Anglo-Scottish Baine. The question of whether Ward's use of "Danny Boy" recognizes the anachronism circa 1870, of its lyrics written in 1912, by an English lawyer, set to the "Londonderry Air," and popularized in the USA by a German singer's recording, is an interesting one, worth debate elsewhere, which might alter perceptions of the trope, underlining the self-conscious artificiality of its use.

When Sarah cures Te Kai Po (Temuera Morrison), this mystic bonding is given a further particular enactment as she symbiotically shares his vision (or part of it). Its content is relayed in compelling visual fragments, which, however, resist interpretation until late in the narrative. Limbs in the water, a Maori flag dipped in the river, blood in the water (underlined by verbal markers like "a river of blood" uttered by both Te Kai Po and Rangi), young women playing a skipping game in a bush clearing, Te Kai Po greeting a white-haired chief, a woman looking back enticingly at Te Kai Po, Te Kai Po having sex with a woman, his enigmatic statement that he will challenge death through woman—these fleeting oneiric fragments provide instances within the conventions of the action epic of the mixed popular and art-film mode Ward employs.

The ultimate revelation of their meaning involves still yet another reworking of Cowan. Historians agree that Titokowaru's Tauranga-ika *pa* was set to be the site of a major encounter between the colonial forces and Titokowaru and the allies rallying to him. Puzzlingly, it was suddenly abandoned. Cowan claimed (via Kimble Bent) that Titokowaru's liaison with a chief's wife and his subsequent loss of *mana* (charisma), provoked his allies' departure, and the *pa*'s abandonment, an explanation Belich cautiously accepts.[37] As some of the vision's fragmentary details are clarified, their full meaning is further deferred. The skipping girls are revealed as a honey trap distracting the soldiers, the blood in the river as presaging fighting, the elderly visitor as a chief bringing military support, the woman looking back, then entering Te Kai Po's dwelling, as the chief's wife. Historically, if his adultery did disintegrate Titokowaru's alliances, the consequences were accidental. But Ward, improvising on the revisionist view of Titokowaru's life as "always a dialectic between peace and war," develops the material remarkably.[38] When Te Kai Po ("He who devours the night"), asserts opaquely that he will challenge death through woman, the likely audience assumption is of some purely personal belief. But his meaning turns out to be wholly different, connected to a vision of peace, which is calculatingly, rather than accidentally, achieved through performing the adultery foreseen in his vision, which he knew would render further fighting impossible through the shattering of his alliances. Sarah later wonders, "Did his desire for the comfort of women get the better of him? Or did his dream warn him that he must provoke his people into retreat, and that way avoid a river of blood?" It is the second that is confirmed in Te Kai Po's words.

WIREMU: We could have won this day.

TE KAI PO: The battle yes, but winning the war? Never.

WIREMU: What now?

TE KAI PO: Let the people go . . . We adapt or die.

As in *Utu* a Maori figure assumes centrality, actually engineering the process of peacemaking, rather than having peace imposed on him.

River Queen's affirmative closure might provoke a brief meditation on all four films' endings. It locates the interracial couple Sarah and Wiremu living "upriver" in what appears to be a Maori community abutting on the Pakeha world, with the exchange of the great Whanganui river, so dominant in the film, for seashore, suggesting looking outwards rather than purely inwards. Sarah wears the chin *moko* she had Boy tattoo on her, though Wiremu has no facial *moko.* When the adult Boy, now a traveling tattooist, drops by, he also wears none, in spite of having sworn to his mother that he would, to define his Maoriness. Te Wheke's tattoo, which signified violent separatism in *Utu,* here has more variegated meanings. By her unlikely act of wearing it (because, she says, "we need to be a family"), Sarah draws closer to Maori culture, while by not doing so, Boy and Wiremu draw closer to the white world, with the film's image patterns drawing together in a single cross-cultural tradition different kinds of self-defining writing from Sarah's Victorian woman's journal to the tattoo's skinscript, all held within the pictorial "writing" of the photographic image. Deliberately or not, this ending has its share of ambivalent markers. For instance, is Sarah's and Wiremu's final interstitial position to be read positively or negatively? As independent or marginal? Does Boy's flamboyant Victorian gentleman's costume connote his ability to move easily in both worlds? Or parody or mimicry? Is his obviously peripatetic existence affirmative or negative? Is he in his art of graphic skin-writing a surrogate for the peripatetic film director who knows that the process of searching for home is endless?

Over eighty years, the four "New Zealand Wars epics" have played variations on the historical interpretations of their times, restaging past conflicts, reopening the lasting scars that are a reiterated motif in *River Queen,* in order to view the future optimistically. But in the end they can only hope that, to invoke again the particulars of *River Queen,* neither Baine's attitudes nor those of his Maori doppelgänger, Wiremu's cousin, Hone, whose cynicism and sadism balance the film's idealization of Titokowaru, will prevail. Patterns of hope crossed with ambivalence characterize all the films, whose problems of asserting unity in what (through various changing official ideologies of race relations—assimilation, integration, biculturalism, biculturalism/multiculturalism) is always seen as a civil war rather than a war against a foreign "other," are more complex than where the self is defined against external enemies, such as the Teutonic knights and their contemporary Nazi German parallels, in *Alexander Nevsky* or in those parts of *The Birth of a Nation* where Afro-Americans notoriously appear as "other," extra-familial, non-American. In every case, problematics potentially trouble conclusions that might be thought unreal without them, sometimes through details that call optimism into question, some-times by the strain of the conceits through which unity is attained—for instance the peace brought through Wiremu's double killing in *Utu,* the redemption of settler racism through the scapegoating of imperial English characters in *Utu* and *River Queen,* the ambiguities attending the close of *Rewi's Last Stand* suggested above, and the sudden transformation of Gilbert Mair from friend of the Arawa to lover of all Maori at the end of *The Te Kooti Trail.*

notes

1. Hayward's films are difficult to see outside New Zealand. *Rewi's Last Stand* is available on an American videotape, but the restored *The Te Kooti Trail* is only viewable through the New Zealand Film Archive. *Utu* is available on DVD and videotape, *River Queen* on DVD.
2. Conflict in the 1840s ended with a peaceful period lasting from 1847 to 1860, with the most serious fighting of the wars taking place in the 1860s.
3. Robert A. Rosenstone, "The Historical Film: Looking at the Past in a Postliterate Age," in Marcia Landy (ed.), *History and Memory in Film and Media* (New Brunswick, NJ: Rutgers University Press, 2000), p. 62.
4. The essential modern texts are Keith Sinclair, *The Origins of the Maori War* (Wellington: New Zealand University Press, 1957), and James Belich, *The New Zealand Wars and the Victorian Interpretation of Racial Conflict* (Auckland: Auckland University Press, 1986).
5. James Cowan, *The New Zealand Wars and The Pioneering Period,* 2 vols. (Wellington: R. E. Owen, Government Printer, 1956), vol. I, pp. 3–4.
6. Cowan, *The New Zealand Wars,* vol. I, p. 1.
7. Belich, *The New Zealand Wars,* pp. 291–298.
8. Robert Sklar, "Rudall Hayward: New Zealand Film Maker," *Landfall,* 25 (2) (1971): 147–153.
9. Martin Blythe, *Naming the Other: Images of the Maori in New Zealand Film and Television* (Metuchen, NJ: The Scarecrow Press, 1994).
10. Hayward's radio talk was printed in *The New Zealand Listener,* November 8, 1940. James Cowan, *The Adventures of Kimble Bent: A Story of Wild Life in the New Zealand Bush* (Christchurch: Capper Press, 1975).
11. James Belich, *A History of the New Zealanders,* 2 vols. (Auckland: Penguin, 2001); and Michael King, *The Penguin History of New Zealand* (Auckland: Penguin, 2003).
12. Cowan, *The New Zealand Wars,* vol. I, p. 359.
13. Cowan, *The New Zealand Wars,* vol. II, p. 319.
14. *Evening Post,* Wellington, September 17, 1912. Thanks to David Colquhoun of the Alexander Turnbull Library for copies of these manuscripts.

"The following is made for the guidance of artists who may essay some day to paint the historic scene at Orakau." Cowan quotes detailed descriptions of what Raureti Paiaka, who delivered Rewi's final reply, wore, from his son, and Tupothi's description of Rewi Maniapoto's war-dress, "an historical detail which also may be of use to our artists when the incidents of Orakau come to be painted." Cowan, *The New Zealand Wars,* vol. I, p. 394.

15. György Lukács, *The Historical Novel* (Harmondsworth: Penguin, 1969), pp. 32–37.

16. Lukács, *The Historical Novel,* p. 42.

17. Cowan has a short section titled "Lest We Forget" where he calls for action not only to commemorate battlefield sites but also to create burial places for the fallen of both sides, positively citing a mixed cemetery created by Maori at Ohaeawai (*The New Zealand Wars,* vol. II, p. 249).

18. Cowan, *The New Zealand Wars,* vol. I, p. 3.

19. "The Dwellings of Our Dead, " *Maoriland: And other Verses by Arthur H. Adams,* The Bulletin Newspaper Company, Sydney, 1899, pp. 5–7.

20. Robert Sklar, "Rudall Hayward, New Zealand Filmmaker," *Landfall,* 25 (2) (1971): 147–153; p. 151.

21. For example, Judith Binney, *Redemption Songs: A Life of Te Kooti Arikirangi Te Turuki* (Auckland: Auckland University Press with Bridget Williams Books, 1995). Internal Affairs censorship document, Hayward File, New Zealand Film Archive.

22. Kept by Hayward among his papers, Hayward File, New Zealand Film Archive.

23. When the film was sent to England, the only copy was used, and cut from about 112 minutes to 64 minutes by the English company who received it; cuts which were irrecoverable and are now part of the extant film.

24. Belich, *A History of the New Zealanders,* vol. II, pp. 241–242; Belich, *The New Zealand Wars,* p. 310.

25. See Russell Campbell, "In Order That They May Become Civilized: Pakeha Ideology in *Rewi's Last Stand, Broken Barrier,* and *Utu, " Illusions,* 1 (1986): 14.

26. Campbell, "In Order That They May Become Civilized."

27. Pauline Kael, *New Yorker,* October 15, 1984.

28. *Utu* exists in two basic versions: the original and a rearranged version in which Te Wheke's trial opens as well as closes the film. This discussion uses the original and the slightly extended "director's cut" (American videotape) version of the original.

29. Cowan, *The Adventures of Kimble Bent,* pp. 197–198; James Cowan, "A Bush Court Martial," *Tales of the Maori Bush,* 2nd edn (Wellington: A. H. & A. W Reed, 1966), pp. 55–59.

30. Te Aka Maori Dictionary, available online at www.maoridictionary.co.nz (accessed 16 May 2007).

31. Blythe puts the optimistic view with great force: "If the execution of one's own brother is the price to be paid for national reconciliation, what greater (self-)sacrifice can be expected of another? This implies a fraternal relationship between Maori and Pakeha which is sealed in blood, mana and utu" (*Naming the Other,* p. 248).

32. Belich, *The New Zealand Wars,* pp. 235–287; "Titokowaru, Rawhia," *Dictionary of New Zealand Bibliography* (updated June 22, 2007), available online at www. dnzb.govt.nz. (accessed August 12, 2007).

33. Belich, "Titokowaru, Rawhia."

34. Trevor Bentley, *Captured by Maori: White Female Captives, Sex and Racism on the Nineteenth Century New Zealand Frontier* (Auckland: Penguin, 2004), pp. 212–235.

35. Charlotte MacDonald, "Evans, Ann", *New Zealand Dictionary of Biography* (updated June 22, 2007), available online at www.dnzb.govt.nz (accessed August 12, 2007).

36. Bruce Babington, "What Streams May Come: Navigating Vincent Ward's *River Queen*," *Illusions,* 39 (2007): 10–11.

37. Cowan, *The New Zealand Wars,* vol. II, pp. 291–292. Belich, *The New Zealand Wars,* pp. 272–273.

38. Belich, "Titokowaru, Rawhia."

the family epic

part four

epic melodrama, or

cine-maps of the

global south

b h a s k a r   s a r k a r

Sometime in the mid-1990s, I "caught" two films from Mexico within a few days: *Miracle Alley* (1995), directed by Jorge Fons; and *Principio y Fin* (*The Beginning and the End*) (1993) directed by Arturo Ripstein. I was living in Los Angeles those days, so getting to watch two Mexican films in quick succession was not that remarkable an experience. *Miracle Alley*, touted at the time as "the most awarded film in Mexican history" (some forty-nine national and international accolades), and starring a young Salma Hayek, was released in theaters across the USA. Ripstein's film was screened at the University of Southern California's famed School of Cinema-Television, where the director and his partner Paz Alicia Garciadiego were teaching classes as visiting faculty. What was extraordinary, though, was that both films were based on the Egyptian writer Naguib Mahfouz's novels, *Midaq Alley* (1947) and *The Beginning and the End* (1950). This odd coincidence made me wonder: what was it about the Nobel Laureate's works that inspired these transcultural adaptations, transposing Cairo to Mexico City and converting an Islamic milieu into a Catholic one!

Some years later, I was to learn that the link was largely serendipitous: Alfredo Ripstein, the producer of the two films (and Arturo Ripstein's father), had obtained the film rights to the two novels simultaneously.[1] This piece of information, instructive as it is about the contingencies of film-producing, does not render superfluous my queries about the translation of the teeming Cairene world of the 1930s and 1940s to lower-middle-class life in Mexico City or about the strategies—and, perhaps, equivalences—that make such translation possible. This essay is an attempt to think through such questions of transcultural linkage and exchange in the face of seemingly insurmountable gaps. What resonances in material structures and phenomenological experiences might allow for congruent historical consciousnesses and aesthetic forms, in spite of all the differences of lifeworlds and habitus? What kind of translocal "reading strategy" might help us recognize, even consolidate, not an idealized register of "universal humanism" but the actually existing public intimacies and creative coalitions?

This line of enquiry leads me to a mode of cultural production, the *epic melodrama*, discernible in various cinemas across the world, but which seems to arise most regularly from the experiential maelstroms widely referred to as "transitional societies" of the global South. Here the epic form is conjoined to a melodramatic mode to produce a genre of representation that raises all the large-scale, transcendental questions of world-historical significance—social emancipation, human civilization, universal History—mainly to complicate these questions by staging their intrinsic contradictions. The epic melodrama counterpoises to the grandiose concerns the palpable messiness of local, quotidian struggles, thereby interrogating all those fictions that are offered as resolutions at both local and global levels—including the modernist teleologies of national development and progress. Marked by its sweeping preoccupations and its recurrence in various parts of the world, this aesthetic form invites a broad interpretive schema, a global reading perspective that is cognizant of its commonality-in-difference. In contrast to earlier elaborations of the epic melodrama—for instance, Ashish Rajadhyaksha's insightful analysis of the form's negotiation of modernity and nationhood in early and mid-twentieth-century Indian films associated first with studios such as Prabhat and New Theatres, and then with auteurs like Raj Kapoor and Mehboob Khan—I will focus on the translocal optic it affords us in its recursivity across multiple national sites (say, Egypt, India and Mexico).[2] A figuration with the capacity for simultaneous description, reflexion, and interrogation, the epic melodrama maps an entire material and intimate geography that allows us to divine otherwise opaque translocal structures, connections and processes.

In this chapter, I focus on two films: Bengali director Ritwik Ghatak's *Meghe Dhaka Tara* (*The Cloud-Capped Star*) (1960) and Ripstein's *The Beginning and the End,* films that, in spite of substantial disjunctions of time and space, reveal striking similarities in thematics and structure. Both films feature impoverished families with aspirations of social mobility; both focus on relations between parents and offsprings, brothers and sisters—relations that produce the most diabolical forms of sacrifice and abuse, until the family mutates beyond recognition into an exploitative apparatus. These narratives show up the emancipatory promises of Indian and Mexican nationalisms, and of global modernization, as largely structuring myths, constituting a prison house of ideology and ambitions.

One might productively add to this discussion Italian director Luchino Visconti's classic work, *Rocco and His Brothers* (1960), made just about the same time as the Ghatak film. While I do not draw on Visconti's film here, referencing *Rocco and His Brothers* in relation to *The Cloud-Capped Star* and *The Beginning and the End* (and Mahfouz's novel) helps explicate what I understand to be the global South: a geophysical configuration that is not beholden to archaic hemispheric cartographies but that derives from embodied experiences of comparable material conditions in far-flung locations such as Egypt, Italy, India, and Mexico. Needless to say, implicit in this mapping is a geopolitical extension of Antonio Gramsci's "south," a metaphysical space that animates the epic melodrama of *Rocco* in terms of its piquant regional traces, calling attention to the underlying relations of power.

A similar piquancy is at work in the Ghatak and Ripstein films, now realized by way of an exaggerated, highly politicized melodramatic mode. As I hope to demonstrate here, these films achieve their remarkable political acuity in terms of a virtuoso formalism whose address is at once deeply affective and incisively intellectual. Each film conjures up a cinematic sensorium that blurs the archaic mind/body polarity, engaging audiences in its complex, synesthetic modalities. The chapter ends with a critical interrogation of what remains one of the most interesting and useful cognitive-aesthetic articulations of a global consciousness informing cultural production: Fredric Jameson's identification of a "geopolitical aesthetic" in contemporary cinema as something of universal structure becoming legible in multiple locations—in effect, a modern epic imagination.

defining epic melodrama

What might constitute a modern epic consciousness, at best a paradoxical category? The *agon* of contemporary life, which points to fracture, dispersion, and drift as its constitutive conditions, makes an epic register appear precarious and outmoded. In our rational, post-sacral world, divine intervention and uncompromising heroes seem equally implausible. And yet, fundamental and pervasive concerns about the human condition and collective destiny persist: they present themselves in new guises, as questions of globality, ecology, history. Epic melodrama is being posited here as a form that enables contemporary cultural negotiations of persistent metaphysical questions, without shoring up the foundationalist fictions that pretend to be definitive answers. Neither of the two terms—epic, melodrama—is a mere qualification for the other, nor are they simply additive: their interaction produces a new aesthetic category. A comparison with the historical epic, and with melodrama, might help establish its formal and functional contours.

Cinema's historical epics are prereflective and transparent engagements with human experience: they work in terms of a broad, sweeping address to produce an ostentatious and reified sense of history that transcends the concreteness of experience—paradoxically, via the concreteness of cinematic form. As Vivian Sobchak has observed with respect to Hollywood historical epics, this type of "*conceptual* mimesis—that is, the representation or imitation of a general idea rather than a specific person, event or thing" usually "takes the most *literal* and *material* form of imitation," achieved in terms of a formal strategy that she calls "cinematic *onomatopoeia*."[3] This strategy of producing the epicness of History involves, among other things, sumptuous quantity and scale ("a cast of thousands"), big stars (Charlton Heston, Elizabeth Taylor), movement (chariot race, naval assembly on rough seas), expanded formats (70 millimeter, CinemaScope), extended duration (about twice the length of the average Hollywood film), excessive music, and spectacle. A kind of cinematic alchemy is operative here: in effect, the industry's "'production' of History" comes to coincide with "a stable and coherent narrative: History."[4]

This model of the historical epic is not exclusive to Hollywood; it is broadly applicable to other commercial cinemas, including Italian (*Cabiria* [1914]), Egyptian (*Saladin* [1963]) and Indian (*Mughal-e-Azam*, a.k.a. *The Emperor of the Mughals* [1960]). Local conventions shape the particular texts: thus, the legendary song-and-dance numbers of *The Emperor of the Mughals* (rendered in color in an otherwise black-and-white film) comprise a signature mark of Bombay cinema. Vernacular cosmologies inform the films, and they are driven by local ideological imperatives: for instance, the pan-Arab sense of pride that courses through *Saladin*. Nevertheless, what these films have in common is the fact that each proffers a particular cosmic vision marked by opulence and an intended unity. This is achieved in each case, as Sobchak suggests, through "the multileveled and isomorphic repetition" that produces a "sense of excess temporality and temporal significance"—in short, through an orchestrated production of History.[5]

A melodramatic mode already courses through historical epics. However, "epic melodrama" concedes a constitutive centrality to melodrama, recasting the very idea of the epic. The classical epic is in truck *not* with melodrama, but with tragedy: both the epic and the tragedy share a heroic horizon.[6] The individualist hero, who overreaches in terms of his aspirations, operates largely outside of social collectivities; it is only when his actions bring his downfall that he becomes aware of his hubris, but then it is already too late. Melodrama, for which this logic of the "too late" becomes even more fundamental, is a degenerate form of tragedy: it lacks the heroic scope of the latter; its protagonists are crucially structured by the social; and, in the end, it settles for decidedly unheroic compromises. The irruption of the melodramatic at the heart of the epic grounds the epic in contemporary networks of social interaction and conciliation: the focus shifts from the determinate to the performative, from preordained resolutions to the disorderly process of negotiation. In short, the epic melodrama updates the epic form, dragging it from its Olympian heights into the flux of contemporaneity.

What is at stake in inserting the epic back into the quotidian, in clipping its metaphysical wings? What is gained, and what is lost in such a move? I want to approach the experiential moorings of epic melodrama in terms of two distinct but related genealogies of materialist thinking: (1) twentieth-century Marxist theories that seek figurations of totality even as they foreground modernity's ruptures and shocks, and (2) phenomenological elaborations of materialism that cast embodied experience and consciousness not as transcendental essentialisms but as grounded in cultural and historical foment.

Marxist cultural theorists such as Mikhail Bakhtin, Bertolt Brecht, and György Lukács, who have been particularly attentive to the relationship between historical experience and aesthetic form, help us think through what might constitute the modern epic. But they focus more on a form's proximity and relevance to everyday struggles, its efficacy in figuring the totality of experience, and its transformative promises; in general, they remain suspicious of melodrama's emotional excess. Bakhtin, in theorizing the novel, sought to establish its connectedness to life by comparing it to the classical epic. If the novel was attuned to everyday textures and rhythms, its protagonists constantly evolving through their experiences, the epic remained lofty, remote, and beyond evaluation, with fully realized heroes. Stressing the novel's articulation of multiple perspectives and potentialities, its extra-linguistic intimations, and its adaptability—in short, its dialogism and its heteroglossic dimensions—Bakhtin privileged the novel over the epic because of the former's capacity for engagement and promise of transformation.[7] I will propose two elaborations that will be significant to this essay. First, Bakhtin's own insight that the novel is capable of transforming all other genres in the modern era opens up the possibility that the modern epic will get "novelized"—that it will take on some of the plastic attributes of the novel. Second, Bakhtin's presumed distance between the epic and quotidian life does not hold universally: for instance, in India, epics such as the *Ramayana* and the *Mahabharata* remain living cultural resources that provide people with cognitive frameworks and moral compasses to make sense of their daily lives.

Describing the novel as the epic for a godless world, Lukács championed works that represented an organic historical consciousness belonging to the progressive bourgeoisie of the nineteenth century. Therefore, as late as the 1930s and at a different stage of capitalism, he could still nostalgically hold onto the kind of seamless totality that was afforded by nineteenth-century realist authors such as Balzac and Tolstoy, to criticize forms of modernism that trained a more fragmented and, for him, alienating perspective on reality.[8] This stance prompted Lukács' detractors to claim that he had lost touch with the vanguard cultural impulses of his lifetime, initiatives that responded to a different phase of class antagonism and approached an increasingly complex and illegible totality in terms of a fractured optic. Primary among these critics was Bertolt Brecht, who countered Lukács' claims of modernist reification with the charge that it was Lukács who had held onto antiquated and reified forms that were no longer adequate in representing twentieth-century structures and experiences.

Brecht offers the most sustained elaboration of a modern epic form in his reflections on an "epic theater." Downplaying mimetic realism and entertainment, Brecht stresses a pedagogical motivation behind his drama-turgy: his primary aim is to engage audiences discursively, to inspire critical reflection, to mobilize consciousness.[9] The epic, for him, affords a detached and rational approach to the social-historical register, a portal to totality—however elusive or opaque. Central to his formulation is the category of the *gestus,* an articulation of "physical gesture" and the "gist" or "attitude" of a character: "The realm of attitudes adopted by the characters towards one another is what we call the realm of the gest."[10] It indexes a technique of acting that reveals a character's social embeddedness, relating all actions and emotions not to psychological motivations but to the social relations in which he or she is enmeshed. This technique also enables a capacious—*epic*—form of acting: while a character's mindset is projected from a particular political perspective that the actor chooses to adopt, he or she should not settle for the easy and obvious characterization but should "consider various other conceivable pronouncements" and "build into the character that element of 'Not-But'"—*not* simply content with the reproduction of things as they are *but* also allowing for the possibility of critical contemplation and even active transformation.[11] Brecht further states that the "expressions of a gest are usually highly complicated and contradictory, so that they cannot be rendered by any single word and the actor must take care that in giving his image the necessary emphasis he does not lose anything, but emphasizes the entire complex."[12]

This insistence on projecting "the entire complex," i.e. a social totality, points to a Marxist variant of an epic consciousness, closer to Walter Benjamin's allegorical mapping of an elusive totality from its fragments than to Lukács' idealized totality. This preoccupation is at the core of

Brecht's model of epic or dialectical theater, whose realism derives not from a timeless aesthetic mode but from a political and philosophical vision of the world that takes cognizance of its historical specificities and seeks to improve it.

But what of the decidedly more carnal materiality afforded by embodied modes of engagement, such as melodrama? Denouncing identificatory immersion in the narrative for its shaping of passive spectatorship, Brecht took melodrama to task for its manipulative modalities and bourgeois values, its consecration of the status quo as social inevitability. In spite of such polemics, many of his favored techniques, aimed at jolting spectators out of their habits of cultural consumption, worked in ways not that different from melodrama. His deliberate accent on specificities, including his citations of social and behavioral details and his staging of moments of great emotional intensity, was, for him, commensurate with his other presentational tactics (breaking the fourth wall, direct address and choral commentary, one actor playing multiple roles), all meant to engineer audience engagement through estrangement (what has come to be known as Brechtian alienation effect). Like Sergei Eisenstein, with whom he shared many theoretical and practical predilections, Brecht ultimately made a clear distinction between authentic and fake emotions, between progressive mobilization and tendentious manipulation—polarizations whose usefulness, not to mention validity, have been put to question in recent decades, with the focus of scholarship shifting to the overall apperceptions of reality and its representation.[13] As Thomas Elsaesser points out, Brechtian anti-illusionism, no longer tenable in the light of contemporary understandings of mediation, has now given way to a hyper-realism; we might even say that it now routinely inspires, and is folded into, a synesthetic spectacularism.[14]

Following the early work of Siegfried Kracauer and Walter Benjamin on cinema as a modernist medium, scholars such as Tom Gunning, Miriam Hansen, and Giuliana Bruno have stressed the sensate and immersive aspects of filmic representation.[15] In their view, cinema presents a sensorium in which various kinds of thrills and sensations, desires and emotions collide and intersect to produce an overall experience of knowing-feeling-understanding for its publics. At the heart of popular commercial cinema's enthralling and entertaining aspects, which raise charges of escapism in more orthodox circles, these scholars discern a deep engagement with contemporary structures of experience—an engagement that Hansen seeks to capture in her recognition of mainstream cinema's "vernacular" modernism.[16] Ben Singer extends this insight to argue that early cinematic melodrama comprises a novel form of cultural expression that mediates modernity's rapid social transformations and spectacular reworldings.[17]

Nevertheless, Vivian Sobchak—who, in her attempt to come to grips with the carnal dimensions of our apprehension of films, adopts a phenomenological approach associated with Merleau-Ponty—surmises that much of current "scholarly interest" in the bodily and sensate aspects of cinema

> has been focused less on *the capacity of films to physically arouse us to meaning* than on what such sensory cinematic appeal reveals about the rise and fall of classical narrative, or the contemporary transmedia structure of the entertainment industry, or the desires of our culture for the distractions of immediate sensory immersion in an age of pervasive mediation.[18]

In other words, even when film scholarship addresses popular film genres, it shies away from a headlong interrogation of "how cinematic intelligibility, meaning and value emerge carnally through our senses"—i.e. an embodied, incarnated understanding of cinema—instead deflecting attention to seemingly more serious-minded, reflective, and therefore "proper" topics such as narratology, convergence cultures and industrial organization, even pop-cultural amusements.[19] Indeed, as Linda Williams points out, the "excessive" elements of what she calls the "body genres"—pornography, horror, and, yes, melodrama—produce pleasures that are too readily described and dismissed as "gratuitous," even when these gratifications remain central to film viewing not necessarily limited to these genres.[20] Even feminist film theory, with its keen interest in gender construction and gendered address, sexuality, and the body, has all too often reduced the pleasures of film viewing to so many "perversions" ("fetishism, voyeurism, sadism and masochism").[21] Williams finds in much feminist scholarship on melodrama, including her own early work, a curious embarrassment: an "unwillingness to recognize the importance of melodramatic pathos—of being moved by a moving picture," as if to acknowledge it would be somehow to compromise one's critical acuity.[22] What was being overlooked in marking a properly critical feminist position was the complex nature of embodied engagement, which included a compelling, politically potent identification with "victimhood."

Sobchak cites Williams's work on the body genres as one of the few exceptional instances of film scholarship that does not simply objectify the body but recognizes it as a "sentient, sensual, and sensible ensemble of materialized capacities and agency," according incarnated aspects of spectatorship the serious attention they deserve.[23] Instead of being stymied by the sense of being manipulated ("jerked around") by melodramatic weepies, horror films, and pornography (widely referred to as, respectively, "tear-jerkers" and "fear-jerkers," or thought to induce an inclination to "jerk off"), or by the "apparent lack of proper esthetic distance, a sense of over-involvement in sensation and emotion," Williams seeks to understand the precise "success" of these lowly genres—"often measured by the degree to which the audience sensation mimics what is seen on the screen"—in terms of "form, function, and system of seemingly gratuitous excesses."[24] Interestingly, Williams suggests that it may even be reasonable "to consider all three of these genres under the extended rubric of melodrama," understood here "as a filmic mode of stylistic and/or emotional excess that stands in contrast to the more 'dominant' modes of realistic, goal-oriented narrative."[25]

Which brings us back to my point: recent scholarship on melodrama, in attending to carnal apprehension alongside critical reflection, embraces the multifarious, *actually operative* mechanisms of cinematic meaning-making. It is this complexity, this simultaneous attention to all aspects of consciousness across the archaic mind–body divide, which I want to emphasize in my elaboration of the epic melodrama. Amidst the oscillations between seemingly polarized positions—embodied response and deliberative reflection, enchantment and criticality, escapism and engagement, social reproduction and transformation, fractal consciousness and totality—the epic melodrama stakes out an aesthetic-analytical position that transcends these very polarities.

In sum, a modern epic imagination cannot aspire to a unified and omniscient perspective, nor can it claim a totalizing access to reality. It can no longer pretend to be transcendental: instead, it is implicated in the froth of daily life, rooted in incarnated subjectivities. This is where melodrama comes in: it recalibrates and transforms the epic form in terms of its emotions and bodily sensations, its hyperboles and coincidences, its overt repetitions and irrational excesses. Meanwhile, an epic sensibility expands melodrama beyond its narrow concerns, teleporting it onto broader horizons of signification. If the grand sweep of the epic is inflected with melodramatic qualifications, its heroic teleology interrupted by traces of subterranean contradictions, then the psychosexual dynamics of the melodramatic are now exteriorized and expanded into larger philosophical questions. The epic melodrama unfolds as a narrative that is at once timeless in its concerns and provisional in its solutions, universal in its scope and grounded in its insights. In other words, the epic melodrama is the aesthetic analog of a world-historical consciousness that is fractured, tentative, and situated. It is precisely such a tenuous global consciousness and a strained aesthetic that are in evidence in the work of Ritwik Ghatak or Arturo Ripstein.

271

two "southern" auteurs

Both Ghatak, who died in 1976 from chronic alcoholism, mental illness, and tuberculosis, and Ripstein, who continues to be a prolific filmmaker after four decades in the business, remain controversial figures. Ghatak was a Marxist intellectual expelled by the Communist Party of India for his renegade views and intemperate lifestyle; his trenchant films about the post-Partition sociocultural milieu (especially the so-called Partition trilogy: *The Cloud-Capped Star* [1960], *Komal Gandhar* [1961] and *Subarnarekha* [1962]) caused such a furor in the Bengali cultural establishment that he was unable to work in the Calcutta industry for the next decade. If Ripstein, the son of a prominent film producer, hails from an affluent family and has had the opportunity to collaborate from the very beginning with various cultural luminaries (including the director Luis Buñuel and the writers Carlos Fuentes and Gabriel García Márquez), he remains somewhat of an outsider: a Jewish artist in an inescapably Catholic society, he also does not fit easily into any of the contemporaneous film movements of Latin America. While both enjoy cult followings among sections of the global cine-cognoscenti, they also have their fair share of detractors. Even their avowed fans have, at times, been baffled by their extreme stylistics and unrelenting pessimism. Critic J. Hoberman calls Ripstein the "maestro of the feel-bad" film; Jorge Fons, director of the other Mexican film-adaptation of Mahfouz, *Miracle Alley,* differentiates his own work from the "pure acid that is Arturo's cinema."[26] George Sadoul, a champion of Ghatak's trail-blazing ecological work *Ajantrik* (1958), found the subsequent melodramatic excess of *Subarnarekha* so overbearing that he apparently urged the filmmaker to rethink certain sequences in the interest of making the film acceptable to the European festival circuit.[27]

The unease about Ghatak's melodramatic proclivities was not limited to his European audiences. At a time when Satyajit Ray's measured and modernist film language, inflected with the humanist objectivity of Italian neo-realism, sought a deliberate break with the maudlin sentimentalism of 1930s–1940s Bengali cinema associated with the New Theatres Studio, many considered Ghatak's passionate sensibility to constitute an anachronistic regression. With characteristic aplomb, Ghatak declared that "Melodrama is a birthright," defiantly defending it as "a form" that allowed him to bring out social contradictions.[28] In his films, this widely dismissed mode took on a remarkable critical charge: as self-conscious exaggerations revealed the narrative functions of clichéd melodramatic conventions, these components seemed to subvert their expected ideological operations. This reflexive dimension, far from attenuating the emotional, indeed haptic, intensity of these films, added to their potency and urgency.

Such deliberate politicization of the melodramatic characterizes the oeuvres of a select group of filmmakers, a group that includes Douglas Sirk, Rainer Warner Fassbinder, Pedro Almodóvar, and Ripstein. For Ripstein, the paradigm of Mexican melodrama established during the industry's "golden age" (mid-1930s to mid-1950s), provided a set of thematic concerns, formal conventions, and moral codes to draw on *and* to unsettle. These included the heroic perspectives and volumes of the films of Emilio "El Indio" Fernández and his cinematographer Gabriel Figueroa (films that were inspired simultaneously by the plot structures of classical Hollywood and Eisenstein's incorporation of Mexican folkloric idioms in *Que Viva Mexico* [1932]); the mythology of the innocent countryside and the duplicitous city; typical settings such as the family, the hacienda, chapels, dancehalls, and brothels; the hegemony of traditional moral values, temporarily threatened by adultery and excessive female sexuality, only to be reinstated in the final resolution.[29] In contrast, Ripstein refuses such reassuring resolution or redemption, reveling instead in the tortured and deeply troubling shenanigans of sinners, fools, and losers, and restricting his settings mainly to cramped, cluttered, and tawdry spaces. As Sergio de la Mora observes, Ripstein "runs a bulldozer right through" the "familiar territory of Mexican melodrama," exposing the "dark and disturbing underside of sacred icons, institutions, and sensibilities that are part of Mexican national identity."[30] Thus, in *La Mujer del Puerto* (1991), a remake of the 1933 classic, the incestuous sister does not succeed in her suicide attempt (as she does in the original) but goes on shockingly to live "happily ever after" married to her own brother. The audience is evicted from its moral comfort zone and forced to confront the "possibilities of life differently."[31]

Unraveling families, incestuous longings, and suicide also appear as core themes in Ghatak, enabling him to negotiate modernity's epic questions and imaginations—including national belonging and a community's place in the world. Where Ghatak differs from Ripstein is in his consistent and liberal invocation of ancient mythologies and the two great epics, *Ramayana* and *Mahabharata*—narratives that remain at the center of India's living traditions and continue to inflect the conduct of everyday life.[32]

As Ghatak asserted:

> We are an epic people. We like to sprawl, we are not much involved in story-intrigues, we like to be re-told the same myths and legends again and again. We, as a people, are not much sold on the "what" of the thing, but the "why" and "how" of it. This is the epic attitude.[33]

There are no comparable "civilizational" texts in mainstream Mexican culture: an epic imagination reaches back mainly to the nationalist novels of the nineteenth century, which consolidated the notion of a productive citizenry by articulating patriotism within the ambit of the heteropatriarchal family.[34] As Carlos Monsiváis points out, films of the "golden age" of Mexican cinema purveyed a similar dimension of normativity: "the public plagiarised the cinema" in "its way of speaking and gesturing, humour, respect of institutions and its typical perception of duties and pleasures," trusting its cinematic "idols" to "explain how to survive in a bewildering age of modernisation."[35]

The two films which this essay focuses on belong to different eras in world history: the late 1950s–early 1960s, the moment of high nationalism and rapid decolonization; and the early 1990s, when the expansion and acceleration of the processes of globalization appeared to put the nation form under erasure.[36] But the historicity of each film still matters in this anachronistic mapping. Ghatak produced his partition trilogy at a time when there was something like a willed cultural amnesia about India's political bifurcation and its attendant social upheaval.[37] While mainstream cinema participated in what Octavio Paz called India's "project of nationhood"—the enthusiastic building of an independent nation-state—Ghatak's melancholic investment in the ideal of a unified Bengal (one of the two provinces to be actually truncated, the eastern part becoming East Pakistan and the western part remaining in India) forced him to engage the trepidations of the post-Partition milieu.[38] Time and again, a deep sense of loss and longing irrupted in his films. In particular, the Partition trilogy marked an absolute refusal to overlook the laceration, to ignore its festering social traces, and to get on with the hegemonic program of capitalist development initiated by Jawaharlal Nehru's government. The epic melodrama form allowed Ghatak to trouble the certainties of nationalist fictions, to register the deep anxieties of the time, and to protest what he saw as social injustice. His artistic practice thus constituted a form of cultural mourning work—mourning both a lost nationalist unity and the emerging disillusionments of the postcolonial era with a remarkable critical potency.

In the early 1990s, in the wake of the NAFTA, Ripstein's long-term thematic and formal preoccupations coalesce into an authorial signature that serves him in terms of securing foreign coproduction and distribution, not to mention film-festival audiences.[39] As Marvin D'Lugo points out, Ripstein's films in the 1990s become "dialogical" in articulating national and global concerns: he focuses on a "critical debunking of the idols and icons of Mexican patriarchal society and cultural stereotypes, specifically those of motherhood and machismo, themes calculated to appeal to the transnational markets of auteur cinema."[40] In that respect, Ripstein emerges "as a deterritorialized *auteur* whose films" present "ever increasing critiques of Mexican film culture and society."[41] One might argue that Ghatak too was a "deterritorialized *auteur*," in the sense that his obsessive investment in a lost subnational ideal, a united Bengal, led him to launch a critique of the disavowal of heterogeneity and the illicit desires that motored a totalizing postcolonial nationalism. As he stated explicitly, "The engulfing uncertainty, the fracture that I see—the roots are in the splintering of Bengal."[42] Refusing to overlook the material and psychic traces of the partition, he focused on the social decay unleashed by it: the displacement of refugees, poverty and hunger, mounting unemployment, corruption, and indifference and cynicism. His melancholic introspection became the mark of his cultural-political dislocation, his troubled integrity.[43]

the mutant family

The Cloud-Capped Star focuses on a middle-class family displaced from East Bengal by the Partition of 1947 and now struggling in a refugee colony shack in the outskirts of Calcutta. As the traumatized father gradually loses his bearings, and the elder brother Shankar pursues a career in music, the onus of the entire family—including an embittered mother and two younger siblings, Geeta and Montu—falls on Neeta, the eldest daughter. As soon as Montu finds a factory job, he leaves home to lead his own life. Within the year, he loses a leg in a workplace accident and returns to the family fold as an invalid. As Neeta is consumed by work, Sanat, her beau, begins to wonder if she will ever be able to part with her family. Sensing his impatience, Geeta makes the moves on Sanat and marries him with her mother's blessing. Shankar, Neeta's main confidant, leaves in disgust at this turn of events. By the time he returns home, having achieved success as a singer, Neeta has succumbed to her exertions and contracted tuberculosis. While the mother excitedly plans a double-storey brick house, Shankar makes arrangements to transfer Neeta to a sanatorium in the mountains, the same mountains that she has always longed to visit, so she receives proper medical care during her last days.

The Ripstein–Garciadiego adaptation of Mahfouz's novel strikes an even bleaker note. The sudden death of the father leaves the low-income Botero family in economic disarray. Banking all her hopes of upward mobility on Gabriel, the smartest of her four offspring, the matriarch Ignacia throws out her first-born, the "bad-seed" Guama, leaving him to fend for himself. Following the mother's wishes, Mireya, the daughter, leaves school and becomes a seamstress; Nicolás, the other son, also abandons hopes of higher studies and takes on a job as school inspector in Veracruz. Gabi soon comes to believe that "his time is *now*," and that his siblings are making sacrifices in the hope that he will help them out once he becomes successful. Once in college, he needs more and more to keep up the pretense that he is from a "respectable" background (first good clothes, then a car); he assiduously keeps his college friends away from his downbeat family. When he gets Natalia—the daughter of a family friend, and once his cherished sweetheart—pregnant, he refuses to marry her, as she no longer fits into his grand ambitions; Ignacia convinces Nico to marry Natalia in the name of family honor. Guama becomes a pimp and bouncer in a local club and seems happy with his hooker-girlfriend; but he comes to a bad end when Ignacia, in a fit of moral rage, discards the stash of cocaine he had left in her safekeeping. César, the frisky local baker, seduces Mireya with false promises, and then casts her aside to marry a woman with resources. After a local mechanic takes advantage of her despondence and rapes her, an abject Mireya secretly turns to prostitution. When arrested by the police, she panics and gets Gabriel involved. Worried that the scandal would be disastrous for him and his powerful patron, the industrialist Luján, Gabi asks Mireya to end her miserable life. They go to the bathhouse where Mireya usually serves her clients, armed with razor blades; after she commits suicide, a shell-shocked Gabi slits his own wrists.

In both films, the family—the quintessential melodramatic *topos,* a microcosm of larger social formations—has mutated into a ruthless machine that wrings the life out of protagonists. Most of the characters are overwhelmed by the vagaries of modern life: the heartbroken father loses himself to dementia; the two careworn mothers turn harsh and manipulative; Nico, Mireya, and Neeta become martyrs, sacrificing their dreams in quiet desperation or giving in to compulsive desire. If Neeta incorporates the trace of a social wound in her consumptive lungs, Mireya and Gabi succumb under the crushing demands of bourgeois mobility. In an interview, Arturo Ripstein explicitly states that while families can "be a source of protection and serenity," these benefits come at "a very high price." For him, families are often "very demanding and very castrating," the "nucleus" of society-wide "destruction" and "horror." In his films, therefore, he has attempted to "demolish the basic values of certain bourgeoisie who believe that religion, family, and country are the most important factors one has." So he seeks "to tread on them and open up other possibilities," denormalizing the power of these normative institutions.[44] Likewise, for Ghatak, the family is the site from which he launches his critique of an unjust society, an indifferent nationalism. Speaking about a sequence in *Subarnarekha* (made two years after *The Cloud-Capped Star*) that his detractors describe as embarrassingly gratuitous melodrama—a drunk brother turning up as the very first client of his estranged sister, newly recruited into "entertaining" men—Ghatak places the forced coincidental structure in a social context: "If we keep in mind the narrative's thematic thrust, we realize that *any* prostitute the guy visited would *still* turn out to be his sister. Here that point has been expounded mechanically: the aim is to allude to the general through the particular."[45] Earlier in the same film, the siblings Ishwar and Seeta bicker affectionately as if they were a couple; Seeta finally elopes with their foster brother, Abhiram, upsetting her blood brother Ishwar.[46] The parents, missing from this narrative, possibly perished in the Partition riots; familial structures are on the verge of breakdown, and usually taboo desires threaten to take over—not unlike the illicit passions in a discordant, riot-ravaged society.[47]

Two related points deserve further explication. The first pertains to a certain "queering" of family ties that, in these films, become conduits for the expression of nonnormative desires. A distinctly Oedipal angle comes into play in certain exchanges between Ignacia and Guama (her first-born), or between Ignacia and Gabriel (her favorite). When Gabi convinces his mother that he and not Nico should pursue higher education, the scene unfolds like a seduction, mainly in medium close-up. As Ignacia steps out of the shower, Gabi hands her a bathrobe, rubs her neck and shoulders, and finally massages her legs with lotion. Ignacia tries to resist ("It is difficult to choose between one's children"), but in that fogged-up bathroom, Gabi's sensual overtures and persuasive rhetoric about the "best strategy" for the family cloud her reason (see Figure 12.1).

The entire family seems to be under the spell of Gabi's charm and promise. Mireya eagerly quizzes him about his classmates (how do they dress, act, and speak?), intent on living vicariously through Gabi's experiences. When she realizes that her arrest might jeopardize Gabi's prospects, she readily agrees to take her own life to establish her mental instability. Nicolás accepts his lot without remonstration, and keeps sending most of his salary for Gabi's education, prompting Julia—his landlady-turned-lover in Veracruz—to observe that there is something "queer" about his unquestioning love for his brother. When Nico agrees to marry Natalia, Gabi's pregnant fiancée, the latter becomes furious at his endless generosity. Confronting his brother in a haircutting salon, Gabi argues that Nico has it easy, for he does not have to live with the burden of everyone else's dreams. In a bid to rile Nico, he hisses in his face: "I have broken in and trained her for you." The proximity of the two brothers—caught here in a tight two-shot, their faces practically touching—accentuates a carnal intimacy between them, to be concretized through their imminent sharing of the same woman. Incensed by this dig at his masculinity, his prerogative as husband, Nico hits out at Gabi. But the insinuation plays out less as an affront than as a charged, homoerotic assertion of the close bond between the brothers, an impression that is reinforced when the scuffle ends in a tender embrace. Gabi says to him with quiet intensity: "See, it is

Figure 12.1
The Beginning and the End: Ignacia and Gabriel.

easier being a martyr: you get off easy. Me, I've made myself crazy with your dreams." As they lean against a mirrored wall, Nico kisses his brother's cheeks with febrile passion (see Figure 12.2). In consecrating Gabi as something of a super-ego, Nico has placed his own self under erasure: his brother is now the locus of his libidinal investments—indeed, of all his aspirations. In Ripstein's imploding scenario, bourgeois expectations appear to unsettle the bourgeois family. Or, perhaps more to the point, the tenuousness of bourgeois structures is the measure of an incomplete individuation: incomplete because a fixation on individualism has to contend with local, "southern" values that continue to privilege the family over the self. Hence Gabriel, the singular embodiment of bourgeois aspirations, feels trapped by the familial investments; his siblings, in placing all their hope in him, cease to be individualized subjects.

If Neeta, the female protagonist of *The Cloud-Capped Star,* also endures a similar attenuation of subjectivity, Ghatak deflects attention away from the psychosexual dimensions of the narrative to elicit—and mourn—an increasingly precarious sensuousness. For Ghatak, the tender and caring potentialities of the family have faded under the atomizing, alienating pressures of modern life. Neeta is undoubtedly closer to Shankar, her elder

Figure 12.2
The Beginning and the End: The passion of the Botero brothers.

brother, than to her beau, Sanat: here, this bond between siblings points to a fundamental human intimacy increasingly superceded by modern notions of romantic love between a conjugal couple.[48] When Shankar tells his bread-earning sister that he is ashamed of his (and the family's) continuing dependence on her, Neeta tells him: "I love you all madly." If this unconditional love seems pure and disinterested, it also indexes a sensuous, all-embracing abandon that appears thoroughly out of date and that pushes against modern social norms and kinship configurations. Within contemporary society's calculating ambit, this is an untenable form of love—a bit out of joint, a bit queer, even a bit disconcerting. To underscore the untimely nature of her affections, Ghatak places Neeta in a timeless, epic register drawn from Hindu mythology: she represents the archetype of the nurturing mother (we learn that she shares her birthday with Jagadhhatri, the avatar of the mother goddess that "holds" or preserves the universe). Her mother's cruel, embittered, and conniving disposition, as her sister's self-centered opportunism, brings out Neeta's tender benevolence.

Which leads us to the second point. While the "partition trilogy" abounds in epic and mythological allusions as shared horizons of sense-making and knowing, Ghatak also mobilizes a Brechtian epic frame, extending private emotions and dramas into an ever-widening intimation of the social. When Shankar announces to the family that Neeta is gravely sick, their senile father shouts out: "I accuse!" The camera frames him in the foreground, from the back of his head, his arm outstretched and fingers pointing ahead toward the rest of the family. Shankar, standing in the background of the frame with his face toward the father and the camera, anxiously asks, "Whom?" In response, the old man, now in frontal medium shot, manages only a feeble, "Nobody," as his face quivers and his arm comes trembling down. Neeta's suffering points beyond her exploitive family to an entire social system of indifference and injustice. Working under the sign of globalization, Ripstein connects the mutant family fold to even wider networks and hierarchies. With his excellent grades in college, Gabriel hopes to secure a Ford Foundation scholarship to study in the USA. But as his professor brusquely tells him, academic performance does not ensure an automatic passage to a transnational elite class: grades must be backed by recommendations from influential quarters. There are palpable structural constraints to the capacity to aspire and to succeed, marking the limits of modernity's egalitarian promises in the global South. His dreams dashed to the ground, Gabriel takes out his frustration on Natalia, his fiancée, at a party thrown by her parents to celebrate his expected scholarship. Following her into a bathroom, he forces himself on her, taking her virginity with his fingers in a grotesque play on her desire to remain "hand-holding sweethearts" until their marriage. Not only does Ripstein subject us to the visceral aspect of the violation in one long take—blood trickles down Gabi's arm as Natalia sobs in pain and mortification—but he also pushes his audience into a situation at once upsetting and iconically arousing: the shot ends with a close-up of an abject and simpering Natalia kneeling before Gabi's crotch as he opens his fly. Even as one recoils from the abusive situation, one is made to feel eerily complicit—not unlike Nicolás who, in the end, will have to assume responsibility for Gabi's transgressions.

melodrama: epic apertures

The unnervingly implicating address of Ripstein's and Ghatak's films arises from their overt melodramatic components. Primary among these is the figure of the tormented woman: Neeta, Mireya, and Natalia in the films that are the focus of this chapter, but also Seeta of *Subarnarekha* and La Manuela, the transvestite prostitute of *Place Without Limits* (1978). One might add to this list the conflicted and beleaguered mothers from *The Cloud-Capped Star* and *The Beginning and the End.* Together, they hold up the characterization of melodrama as the mise-en-scène of female suffering: the sheer performativity producing an embodied awareness of the social oppression of women, raising the possibility of the subversion of hetero-patriarchal structures. The patriarchs are either absent (Papa Botero dies at the beginning of the film, leaving the family penniless), or falling apart (Neeta's father breaks his leg and begins to lose his senses, leaving him unable to support his family); Shankar, Sanat, Montu, Guama, Nico, and Gabi are all men in crisis who depend on, or are regulated by, the women in their lives. More importantly, to track Mireya's gradual abjection or Neeta's slide toward a fatal disease is to become politicized through a kind of voyeuristic experiencing and enduring. Even if the resolution does not dislodge the status quo at the level of the narrative, one is left with a searing sense of loss, distress, even rage. It is not insignificant that Mireya, Seeta, and Manuela are prostitutes, women (or transvestites) forced by circumstance to sell their sexual services, thereby becoming commodities within a phallocentric exchange economy. (One might add to this list Guama's "woman," and Nadia from Visconti's *Rocco and His Brothers.*) While Neeta does not take to prostitution literally, she too sells her labor to support the family she loves so "madly," and comes to bear the mark of her toil on her consumptive body. Eventually Mireya and Seeta kill themselves, while La Manuela's macho lover murders her to "prove" his own masculinity. And yet, Ripstein and Ghatak's women do not fit the part of the silent victim. After César abandons her, Mireya does not wallow in her despondence; instead, she becomes a desiring subject without many internalized inhibitions. She figures out a way to assuage her carnal needs while earning a living: a remarkably practical "solution" to her situation. Toward the end of *The Cloud-Capped Star,* when Shankar visits Neeta at the sanatorium in the mountains and attempts to regale her with chitchat about the family's new-found affluence and their infant nephew's exploits, she suddenly cries out: "But I did want to live!" This sudden outburst from his soft-spoken sister takes Shankar by surprise. As the camera swirls around them, capturing the mountains in a 360-degree pan, Neeta's heart-rending cry reverberates in all directions. It is possible to read this defiant and melodramatic expression of her desire to live as Ghatak's protest against the national partition: just as tuberculosis has ravaged Neeta's body, communal rancor has eaten into the ideal of a unified nation-state. Filmmaker Kumar Shahani takes it even further, locating in this scene a critical impulse that engages not only the history that the truncation of 1947 launches, but targets all of Indian modernity for its capitulation to indigenous and Western structures of domination:

> In an atmosphere where our cultural attitudes and artifacts have been identified with the objectification of effete feudal Brahminism and European humanism inflicted on us by the colonials, Ritwikda's work is the *violent assertion of our identity*. It is the cry of the dying girl in *Meghe Dhaka Tara* [*The Cloud-Capped Star*] that echoes through the hills, our right to live.[49]

Here, in a decidedly "un-Brechtian" Brechtian move, melodrama is articulated with an epic lens, telescopically opening out a critical perspective from a rather contained family drama.

The Beginning and the End ends with a close-up freeze-frame of Mireya's high-heeled red shoes, a cinematic icon that has come to connote female sexuality and often an excess of it, with prostitution as its limit-case. Here Ripstein situates his work in relation to a common cinematic convention, inviting reflection on its global recurrence. He wants to focus beyond the image itself, to the transcultural reification of underlying circuits of exchange and power. The semantic charge of the red shoes derives from its status as the material trace of sexualized and commoditized social relations. Interestingly, in the last scene of *The Cloud-Capped Star,* Shankar looks on as a young woman tries to fix her torn sandal and then walks away with a self-conscious smile. She is a lower-middle-class woman, not unlike Neeta in her bearings, possibly forced to work long hours because of post-Partition economic deprivation. "Prostitution" hovers mainly as a figurative frame for the gendered overdetermination of labor (Ghatak himself renders the implicit connection explicit in *Subarnarekha*). We are reminded of a similar moment at the beginning of the film, when Neeta's sandal strap breaks and she drags her feet to work; and yet, instead of getting herself a new pair, she spends her hard-earned money on a sari for Geeta and a pair of soccer boots for Montu. Again, this recursive structure points to the many young women who work selflessly to support their families and then have to face moral injunctions from the very social structures that exploit them.[50] The shoe/sandal icon emerges as something of a Lacanian *point de capiton:* that which arrests the endless slide of signifiers and stops the narrative flow from conjuring up just yet another naturalized, seemingly inevitable "slice of real life" scenario. It is one of those hooks with which Ghatak and Ripstein compel their viewers to acknowledge the sociocultural production of anchoring values and institutions that trap and crush individuals with contradictory demands (Mireya and Natalia's chastity, prospects of Neeta's marriage and her mother's fears of losing the family bread-winner, Geeta's predatory moves on her sister's beau). And in one brief but piercing moment, when a distraught Gabriel begins to put on his dead sister's red shoes, any promise of immunity a gendered subjectivity might hold falls irrevocably apart: women and men alike are entangled in this epic psychosis.

Both filmmakers make the social contradictions palpable in terms of imaginative formalist mise-en-scènes, their bravura stylistic flourishes congealing into identifiable authorial signatures. Ghatak's refugee family lives in a squatter settlement known as Nabajiban (New Life) Colony: their rudimentary dwelling is made out of mud, bamboo, and straw. Depth of field photography, high- and low-angle shots, and use of wide-angle lens are complemented by ingenious perspective, framing, and editing to achieve an electrifying expressivity. Conflicts and tensions are innate to the individual shots: tensions between bodies caught in strange and continually shifting proxemic relations; between empty space and voluminous bodies; between crowded bodies and the space around them caught in deep focus; between what is visible and what is blocked from view; between shadow and light. In most indoor scenes, light falls directly on odd corners, surfaces and objects, leaving the more significant parts of the frame in a hallucinatory haze traversed by chiaroscuro lattices. This intense mise-en-scène marks a penumbra between the standard poles of objective reality and subjective interiority, mind and body, inviting a more sensuous awareness on the part of the spectators. The shots are then put together eschewing the typical master shot and dismissing any naturalized sense of spatial relation; juxtaposing deep focus, wide-angle shots, and crowded medium shots with extreme close-ups, producing disorientation and an unsettling sense of doom; music not only acting as a sound bridge across shots but carrying the shots on its melodic and rhythmic arc.[51]

To take a concrete example: when Shankar returns home having achieved success in Bombay, he enters Neeta's room to catch her concealing something under her pillow. Since she had tried to hide a love letter from him in an earlier scene, Shankar excitedly tussles with her to find out her secret: a bloodied handkerchief, the trace of her consumptive lungs, falls to the ground. As a male voice breaks into a plaintive melody on the soundtrack (since the nondiegetic music is quite like Shankar's own singing, it becomes a subjective cue to his state of mind), we see a close-up of the handkerchief on the floor; then a low-angle medium shot of Shankar, looking down (his face is in the shadow, while light falls on the thatched wall and roof behind him); then a remarkable close-up of Neeta's face in profile, taken from behind her, as she rises from the bed—her body moving across the frame from the lower left corner to the upper right corner (breaking the 180-degree rule in relation to the previous shot); another close-up of Neeta, this one also in profile but from the front, her face traversing the frame from lower right to upper left (clearly, the 180-degree rule has been broken again); finally, a close-up of Shankar's perturbed and sorrowful face looking down at her, as the singing gives way to contemplative strains on the *sarod* (the 180-degree rule having been broken yet again) (see Figure 12.3). Conventions of classical continuity editing are flouted repeatedly to produce an "impossible" location for the spectators in between the two characters, emplacing and embedding them corporeally in the unfolding drama. As the mobilization of conflict within and between shots would suggest, Ghatak counts Eisenstein as his main cinematic influence, invoking the greatest classical Sanskrit *litterateur* Kalidasa to salute the Russian filmmaker/theorist as "the Kalidasa of cinema."[52] In an essay titled "Dialectics in Film," Ghatak expresses his keen interest in the dialectical approach to reality and its representation.[53] He also aligns himself with the cultural politics of Brecht, two of whose plays—*Caucasian Chalk Circle* and

Figure 12.3

The Cloud-Capped Star: Shankar discovers Neeta's secret.

Galileo—he translated into Bengali. The Brechtian–Eisensteinian influences transform the loaded melodramatic moments in Ghatak's films: these moments mark his absolute refusal to resolve spatially, and thus to contain and domesticate, contradictions that have no easy solutions.

Ripstein works with similar formal strategies at the level of the mise-en-scène, but not at the level of editing: the main difference of his films from Ghatak's is the preponderance of very long takes. As Ripstein himself states in a 1999 interview: "I have found lately that my voice is clearer with very long takes. By breaking from the tradition of montage and eliminating point-of-view shots, long takes help develop my characters and create the atmosphere I want to convey."[54] The real-time denouement of these prolonged takes makes an entire sensorial universe accessible to the spectators: they are literally compelled to endure the action. The emplacement of spectators is now a function of their chronotopic immersion in a carefully orchestrated *plan séquence* or sequence shot, whose sheer durational and experiential integrity promotes such immersion. The haptic materiality of various spaces—the tawdry clutter of the Botero family's low-ceiling basement apartment (the crammed beds and couch; Mireya's sewing machine and work table covered with fabric; kitsch illuminated by the light coming through the small window: a jug, a crucifix, an old television), or the shabby ambience of the night club where Guama works (the gaudy carousel and lights, the cheap tables and chairs, the hard-boiled regulars and the overly made-up hookers)—are vivified in these long takes. Consider an extreme example: the nine-plus minutes shot at the end of *The Beginning and the End,* in the course of which both Mireya and Gabriel succumb to the confounding pressures of their déclassé lives and commit suicide. Much of the sequence takes place inside a bathhouse, where Mireya takes her clients. As the guy at the desk offers her the "usual" room, Gabi begins to fathom the extent of her involvement in prostitution. He follows his sister in bewilderment up two flights of stairs and a corridor to a tiny cubicle of a room with a narrow bed—one of many such rooms lining the corridor. The use of Steadicam keeps us close to the characters and lends a freewheeling mobility to the shot that becomes increasingly gestural as it progresses toward its cathartic end. Gabi sits down on the bed; Mireya begins to pull down her panties out of habit but stops as she catches her brother's shocked face. Next she starts slashing her wrist as he gets up and stands at the door, clutching onto her red shoes; she waves him goodbye; their labored breathing on the soundtrack; Gabi closes the door behind him, walks backwards into the closed door of another room, then walks away from the camera as it follows him down the corridor, glancing back with mounting terror on his face; walks back toward Mireya's room but then turns abruptly onto another corridor. He saunters into a large bathroom with adjoining sauna; a few men in towels lounge around in the steamed-up space and watch him in silence as he sits down on a bench;

in his state of panic, he takes off one of his boots and begins to put on Mireya's high heels; a man sits close to him, leaning forward in a not-so-veiled gesture of sexual solicitation. At this point, a percussive music begins, accompanied by a male chorus uttering a chant that sounds more like a syncopated collective exhalation: in the intensely homosocial space of the bathhouse, male desire transcends heteronormativity to find more primal expressions.[55] Gabi gets up, walks away from the guy and out of the bathroom; sees a custodian discover Mireya's body and run to get help; stands for a few seconds at the door, taking in his sister's dead body, a pool of blood on the floor. Closing the door obsessively, as if to shut out the horror, Gabi keeps walking around disconsolately, goes up to the next floor, stumbles around gasping and sobbing, then climbs another set of stairs to what looks like the roof of the building. He walks past brightly colored glass panes and corrugated walls into a laundry room with large water tanks and pipes; sits down, takes out a blade as camera closes in on him, then slashes his wrist—once, twice, as the camera pans down on Mireya's shoes on the floor. Cut to a blank screen, then a still close-up of the shoes.

The striking music during the last five minutes of this long take, which builds up to an inexorable crescendo underscoring Gabi's psychotic unraveling—his failure to hold onto his individualism in complete disregard of the catastrophic consequences of his ambitions—is a piece titled *La Valse des nuls* by the French industrial music group Tambours du Bronx. The genre of industrial music, at least in its original form, is inspired by the "found" ambient clang and drone of modern industrial centers: it seeks to capture a wider social atmospherics, the rhythms and textures of contemporary industrial life. Here, in the final sequence of *The Beginning and the End*, in the bare and labyrinthine bathhouse, it strikes a rather different tone from the mellifluous operatic music heard earlier, such as the excerpt from Delibes' *Lakmé* that the Botero patriarch used to play for his children. Gabriel's ability to identify the Delibes piece convinces the industrialist Luján of the former's cultured upbringing, his elite pedigree, prompting the latter to induct the young man into his *grupo clandestino* of opera aficionados and to become his benefactor. This conflation between cultural capital and economic class indexes one of the many ironies one might face in climbing the social ladder: ultimately, the refinement of opera cannot deliver Gabi from his petty-prole quagmire. Now, in the final moments of the film, the "dance of the deadbeats" provides the sonic matrix—hollow, eerie, and engulfing—in which our protagonist drowns along with all his aspirations.

In Ghatak, we encounter some of the most inspired instances of the use of acoustic elements for melodramatic accentuation. The famous Eisenstein–Pudovkin–Alexandrov manifesto on sound–image relations—"Only the contrapuntal use of sound vis-à-vis the visual fragment of montage will open up new possibilities for the development and perfection of montage"—gets elaborated to stunning effect.[56] In a scene much derided for its overt theatricality, Neeta senses the presence of another woman in Sanat's apartment, and walks out in quiet dismay. As she slowly comes down the stairs in medium close-up, we hear sounds of whiplash on the soundtrack. This acoustic emphasis is repeated twice—each time to convey a burgeoning sense of betrayal and disillusionment that engulfs the entire post-Partition milieu. Earlier, when Sanat visits Neeta's family, her mother comes out of the kitchen to greet him; we hear a crackling noise—ostensibly oil splattering in the wok, or water boiling over—energizing the off-screen space. Later, when Sanat and Neeta go for a walk, the mother anxiously looks on, worried that her breadwinning daughter is about to marry and to abandon the family: the same crackling noise is reproduced, now dissociated from the kitchen. Repeated yet again with the mother's face in close-up as Sanat chats with Neeta in her room, this recurring acoustic embellishment unifies the disparate scenes into one unfolding anxiety. The kitchen sound not only captures the ambience of a Bengali household but also serves as the acoustic approximation of an idiomatic vernacular expression that describes a soul ravaged by life's hardships as one "burnt to cinders" (here, the mother's self-interested acerbity).

The father, as played by Bijon Bhattacharya, is unmistakably a East Bengali refugee: his accented melodeclamatory enunciation and his bearing, while often dismissed as overacting, communicate not only regional speech patterns but also a world of suffering. Dislocated, disoriented, and increasingly helpless, his incantatory recitations of the romantic poets are his desperate attempts to hold onto a fast-receding sentience and life. Bhattacharya, who, like Ghatak, came from the Bengali stage associated with the Indian People's Theatre Association (the cultural wing of the Communist Party of India), developed an acting style that channels Brechtian *gestus*. In many ways, he incarnates the emotional core of Ghatak's Partition trilogy, essaying memorable refugee roles in all three films. In spite of the dementia, his character is allowed the most articulate position in *The Cloud-Capped Star*—evident in the sequence of Geeta's wedding to Sanat. As Neeta presides over the arrangements for her sister's wedding to her ex-beau, the father appears devastated by the underlying duplicity. With self-lacerating prescience, he observes that in the old days, young girls were married off to much older men; now that we have become "civilized" and "modern," we educate our daughters and then exploit them endlessly, wringing the life out of them.

This charged critical introspection about a putatively reformulated hetero-patriarchy follows another loaded scene between Neeta and her mother, a nondiegetic folk song providing the bridge *and* situating the father's reflection. The mother, who tacitly supports the nuptials in complete disregard of Neeta's desires, can barely look at her; all the same, she talks Neeta into giving up her share of the meager family jewels for her sister's benefit. An instrumental tune starts in the thick of this awkward transaction: a melancholy melody sung at weddings, when the young bride is about to leave her parents for her in-laws' house. Here, it becomes a searing comment on Neeta's unwed status and on the opportunistic abrogation of socially reinforced heteronormative expectations constitutive of her subjectivity. Later, the melody returns: a female chorus is heard on the soundtrack as the consumptive Neeta coughs up blood, and again when she is about to leave home in pouring rain. Ghatak's trilogy abounds in such quotations of folk songs and phrases connected to the material practices of Bengali life: much like the allusion to the Vedas, the two epics and the mythologies, these culturally specific citations set up an epic relay of exchanges, with the various fragments and levels commenting back on, and amplifying, each other. Ripstein, too, sets up a similar critical frame in *The Beginning and the End,* taking on local cultural institutions and obsessions. Parents keep telling their daughters that they must "marry in white," i.e. as virgins, but circumstances often thwart this dream. Mireya makes wedding dresses for others but has to give up her own hope of marriage. At one point, she puts on a white bridal veil and keeps looking at herself in the mirror. When she learns about Cesar's fiancée, Mireya angrily dips the white dress she has tailored for the fiancée in fish blood. Natalia marries Nico, but not before she loses her virginity to Gabi.

Both Ghatak and Ripstein take melodrama's logic of the "not yet" or the "too late" to an extreme. Neeta finally sees Shankar achieve success; as their father observes, she has enabled her family members to "stand on their feet." However, she can no longer enjoy the security and comfort that affluence brings. Just as Gabriel wins the support of an important industrialist, the kind of backing necessary for success in life, Mireya gets arrested for prostitution, compromising his and the family's prospects. These films offer no simple resolutions, no convenient closing off of social contradictions: the constitutive deferrals and delays of melodrama are now stretched out ad infinitum. In both films the melodramatic becomes an epic aperture, opening onto an entire social field beyond narrative peripeteia, beyond the characters' fortunes and despairs. The social here is a bit like off-screen space: a sensorium that is tangible even when not explicitly visible within the frame. Mobilizing critical acuity, haptic, and affective apprehension, the films intimate—make us sense and feel—their material and historical contexts. As Raymond Bellour observes of *The Cloud-Capped Star* (an observation that I think holds also for *The Beginning and the End*), it is a film that we have to "accompany."[57]

translocal intimations, historical difference

My central argument in this essay, that the epic melodrama is a figural form that, in its broad concerns and its recurrence across the global South, plots a translocal geography of material-sensate experiences, bears a certain resonance with Fredric Jameson's detection of a geopolitical aesthetic in post-1960s cinema. Jameson's 1992 book, *The Geopolitical Aesthetic,* begins with the sentence: "The films discussed here have been selected with a view towards an unsystematic mapping or scanning of the world system itself."[58] He moves from Hollywood conspiracy films to post-Nouvelle Vague Godard, from Soviet magical realism (Alexander Sokurov) to the Taiwanese New Cinema (Edward Yang) and the categorically reflexive work of Filipino filmmaker Kidlat Tahimik: the objective is to produce an "unsystematic"— fragmentary, imaginative, allegorical—plotting of "the underlying systemic reality" that remains largely opaque to cognition because of its scale, complexity, and dispersion.[59] Here, Jameson follows a Lukácsian–Brechtian–Benjaminian genealogy to develop an epic notion of allegory for the contemporary conjuncture, an allegorical approach he calls "cognitive mapping." What inspires such a move is the recognition of a "geopolitical unconscious" at the heart of cultural production in various parts of the globe. In a characteristically totalizing gesture, Jameson claims: "all thinking today is *also,* whatever else it is, an attempt to think the world system as such."[60]

Jameson's argument is convincing to a point. His insight that a geopolitical dimension now infiltrates and informs local consciousness, so that "national allegory" now gets "refashion[ed] . . . into a conceptual instrument for grasping our new being-in-world," is particularly illuminating (perhaps with the proviso that for the medium of cinema, a global sensibility was at work from its inception).[61] His methodology is provocative: articulating local, seemingly unrelated cultural impulses into a tentative mapping, thereby "allow[ing] the most random, minute, or isolated landscapes to function as a figurative machinery."[62] What distinguishes each of these "landscapes" from the earlier moment of national allegories is the remarkable "fluidity" with which "questions about the system and its control over the local ceaselessly rise and fall": in other words, these local cultural "landscapes" now become epic apertures onto global constellations.[63]

However, Jameson's investment in mapping a totality, signaled here in his repeated invocations of "the world system," leads to a bracketing of historical difference. I want to get to this point via an exegetical detour, a consideration of the curious position that melodrama occupies in his work. While the category is not listed in the index to *The Geopolitical Aesthetic,* it appears at least six times in the book. Each of these references makes sense in the context of the specific analysis; taken together, a certain pattern emerges, for each occurrence has to do with some kind of reinvention, diminution, or even overcoming of melodrama. For instance, "the recourse to the stock languages of older melodrama is an immediately identifiable sign of failure or of the admission of defeat."[64] Or, "the spectacle of a kind of chamber music in the realm of melodrama, a remarkable *Kammerspiel* from which a whole range of brassy instruments is excluded," producing "a remarkable diminution of effect, which dialectically transforms such limits into a whole new positive rather than privative type of representation."[65] Or, "the stuff of melodrama which can here exceptionally be reinvented, in a non-melodramatic way, on the occasion of multi-levelled textual reflexivity."[66] The epic optic that Jameson conjures up in his "geopolitical aesthetic" is predicated on the "sublimation" of "all the grossness of content" entailed in "garden variety melodrama" into a pure formalism of "sheer syntax."[67]

In Ghatak, as in Ripstein, "the stuff of melodrama" is what engenders reflexivity, "grossness of content" is married to form: one cannot be separated from the other. This inseparability is central to the epic melodrama. Jameson is able to unhinge one from the other since, for him, contemporary world history unfolds as a singular modernity.[68] Historical difference marks a temporary stage on the road to an eventually globalized consciousness: melodrama is the index of this transitional contingency, to be overcome in time by a modernist, reflexive formalism. Thus the "variety of forms and form-problems" that he sees from 1970s Hollywood to 1980s Taiwan or Philippines "is not a random variety" but, rather, a measure of uneven development.[69] This "developmental" or "uneven-developmental" rhetoric remains central to Jameson's understanding of a geopolitical aesthetic: he thus sees Edward Yang's film *Terrorizer* (1986) as a mark of the "belated emergence of a kind of modernism in the modernizing Third World, at a moment when the so-called advanced countries are themselves sinking into full postmodernity."[70] Postmodern Hollywood and at-long-last-modern Taiwanese "New" Cinema thus appear concurrently in this spatial schema. Notwithstanding his considered qualifications as in "so-called advanced countries," Jameson subjects his spatial mapping to a neo-Marxist periodizing imperative, reproducing an archaic distortion. As Dipesh Chakrabarty, among others, have pointed out, such cognitive acrobatics rehash a paradigm of world history in which "Third World" countries are forever consigned to "the waiting room of History."[71] I have argued elsewhere that this understanding of history is inherently melodramatic, since it turns certain populations into underdogs, who are always delayed on the road to advancement, always forced to play catch-up. Melodrama is thus structural to the narrative of world history, its constitutive condition.[72]

Jameson refers to the First World–Third World polarization, the "Cold War division," and the new "triumvirate of superstates (the US, Europe and Japan)" as the archaic categories that cannot capture the new world system. Even allowing for the passage of time (he missed out on the emergence of China, the so-called BRIC countries [Brazil, Russia, India, China], or the global Islamic alliance), his categories remain of "northern" origin and salience: he does not consider South–South collaborations or the Non-Aligned Movement (of which the Bandung Conference of 1955 remains only one, if iconic, moment). He thus overlooks the possibility of translocal imaginaries and cultural-political coalitions emerging from the global South: Yang and Tahimik matter only as far as they instantiate the penetration of the South by an already antiquated modernism. In contrast, the works of Ghatak and Ripstein (and Mahfouz and Visconti) constitute a geography of affinities and intimacies arising from certain experiential commonalities across decades. My point is not to disavow the historicity of their films but to complicate the "singular modernity" thesis in terms of their embodied *and* reflexive engagements with the differential, overlapping, even parallel experiences of modernity. They remind us that in spite of the universalized promises and aspirational horizons of modernity, the production and continuation of global inequities is necessary to global capital. The disjunctive spaces of modernity, such as the global South, index not so much the stages of a unitary process of capitalist development as concurrent and co-dependent spaces of capital. The epic melodrama is that contemporary figural form which purveys a cine-map of these spatialized historical differences.

acknowledgment

My thanks to Cesare Casarino, Bishnupriya Ghosh, and especially Cristina Venegas for their suggestions and insights.

notes

1. Conversation with Arturo Ripstein, Santa Barbara, 2002.
2. Ashish Rajadhyaksha, "The Epic Melodrama," *Journal of Arts and Ideas,* 25–26 (December 1993): 55–70.
3. Vivian Sobchak, "'Surge and Splendor': A Phenomenology of the Hollywood Historical Epic," *Representations,* 29 (winter, 1990): 24–49; p. 36; emphases in original.
4. Sobchak, "Surge and Splendor," p. 41.
5. Sobchak, "Surge and Splendor," p. 44.
6. See Louise Cowan, "The Epic as Cosmopoesis," in Larry Allums and Louise Cowan (eds.), *The Epic Cosmos* (Dallas, Tex.: The Dallas Institute of Humanities and Culture Publications, 2000), pp. 1–25.
7. Mikhail Bakhtin, "Epic and Novel," in *The Dialogic Imagination: Four Essays,* edited by Michael Holquist, translated by Caryl Emerson and Michael Holquist (Austin, Tex.: University of Texas Press, 1981), pp. 3–40.
8. György Lukács, "Realism in the Balance," in Theodor Adorno, Walter Benjamin, Ernst Bloch, Bertolt Brecht and Gyorg Lukács, *Aesthetics and Politics* (London: Verso, 2007), pp. 28–59.
9. See the various essays in *Screen,* 15 (2) (summer 1974), especially Colin MacCabe, "Realism and Cinema: Notes on Some Brechtian Theses" (pp. 7–27) and Stephen Heath, "Lessons from Brecht" (pp. 103–128).
10. Bertolt Brecht, "A Short Organum for the Theatre" (1949), in Terry Eagleton and Drew Milne (eds.), *Marxist Literary Theory* (Malden, Mass.: Blackwell), pp. 107–135; p. 128.

11. Brecht, "A Short Organum for the Theatre," pp. 126–127.

12. Brecht, "A Short Organum for the Theatre," p. 128.

13. To take just one example of Eisenstein's invocations of "genuine emotions" and "real compositions": "This is the secret of the genuinely emotional affect of real composition." Here, writing about the famous "Battle on the Ice" episode of *Alexander Nevsky*, Eisenstein goes on to stress the precise temporal correspondence between the "tangle of passions which originally designed the compositional scheme of the work" and the emotion of the spectator induced by the unfolding of the sequence: "Employing for source *the structure of human emotion, it unmistakably appeals to emotion*, unmistakably arouses the complex of those feelings that gave birth to the composition." Sergei Eisenstein, "The Structure of the Film," in *Film Form: Essays in Film Theory*, trans. Jay Leda (New York: Harcourt Brace & Company, 1949), pp. 150–178; p. 153, emphases in original. In contrast, Eisenstein is critical of the falsity of German Expressionism ("this combination of silent hysteria, parti-colored canvases, daubed flats, painted faces, and the unnatural broken gestures and actions of monstrous chimaeras"), which never appealed to a Soviet revolutionary consciousness: "our spirit urged us towards life, amidst the people—into the surging actuality of a regenerating country." Sergei Eisenstein, "Dickens, Griffith, and the Film Today," in *Film Form: Essays in Film Theory*, trans. Jay Leda (New York: Harcourt Brace & Company, 1949), pp. 195–255; p. 203. Eisenstein's position on embodied responses to cinema remained, at best, conflicted. Deleuze is correct in claiming that for the filmmaker-theorist, "'intellectual cinema' has as correlate 'sensory thought' or 'emotional intelligence,' and is worthless without it." Gilles Deleuze, *Cinema 2: The Time-Image*, trans. Hugh Tomlinson and Robert Galeta (Minneapolis, Minn.: University of Minnesota Press, 1997), p. 159. However, ultimately for Eisenstein, while the sensory priming achieved through Griffith's judicious parallel editing (say, switching between "the terror of the besieged" and the "ride of the rescuers") multiplied the emotional charge of a scene of dramatic rescue, the effect remained primarily a psychosomatic matter of "*quantitative accumulation.*" In contrast, "we sought for and found in juxtapositions more than that—*a qualitative leap*" that was, no doubt, achieved in the mind. Eisenstein, "Dickens, Griffith, and the Film Today," p. 239, emphases in original.

14. Thomas Elsaesser, "From Anti-illusionism to Hyper-realism: Bertolt Brecht and Contemporary Film," in Pia Kleber and Colin Visser (eds), *Re-interpreting Brecht: His Influence on Contemporary Drama and Film* (Cambridge: Cambridge University Press, 1990), pp. 170–185.

15. Tom Gunning, "An Aesthetic of Astonishment: Early Film and the [In] Credulous Spectator," *Art & Text*, 34 (spring 1989): 31–45; Miriam Hansen, "America, Paris and the Alps: Kracauer (and Benjamin) on Cinema and Modernity," in Leo Charney and Vanessa Schwartz (eds.), *Cinema and the Invention of Modern Life* (Berkeley, Calif.: University of California Press, 1995), pp. 362–402; Giuliana Bruno, *Atlas of Emotion: Journeys in Art, Architecture, and Film* (London: Verso, 2007).

16. Miriam Hansen, "The Mass Production of the Senses: Classical Cinema as Vernacular Modernism," *Modernism/Modernity*, 6 (2) (April 1999): 59–77.

17. Ben Singer, *Melodrama and Modernity* (New York: Columbia University Press, 2001).

18. Sobchak, "What My Fingers Knew," *Carnal Thoughts: Embodiment and Moving Image Culture* (Berkeley, Calif.: University of California Press, 2004), pp. 53–84;

p. 57, emphasis added. The phenomenology that Sobchak espouses is not the transcendental and idealist phenomenology of universal, "fixed essences" but Maurice Merleau-Ponty's existential phenomenology, a materialist paradigm that approaches experience and its meaning as "spatially and temporally embodied, lived, and valued by an objective subject" and, therefore, "always already qualified by the mutable specificities and constraints of history and culture." Vivian Sobchak, "Introduction," in *Carnal Thoughts: Embodiment and Moving Image Culture* (Berkeley, Calif.: University of California Press, 2004), pp. 1–10; p. 2. For Sobchak, then, embodiment is "a radically material condition of human being that necessarily entails both the body and consciousness, objectivity and subjectivity, in an *irreducible ensemble*. Thus we matter and we mean through processes and logics of sense-making that owe as much to our carnal existence as they do to our conscious thought" (*Carnal Thoughts*, p. 4).

19. Sobchak, "Introduction," p. 8.
20. Linda Williams, "Film Bodies: Gender, Genre, and Excess," *Film Quarterly*, 44 (4) (summer 1991): 2–13.
21. Williams, "Film Bodies," p. 6.
22. Linda Williams, "Melodrama Revised," in Nick Browne (ed.), *Refiguring American Film Genres: Theory and History* (Berkeley, Calif.: University of California Press, 1998), pp. 42–88; p. 47.
23. Sobchak, "Introduction," p. 2.
24. Williams, "Film Bodies," pp. 5, 4, 2.
25. Williams, "Film Bodies," p. 2.
26. See, for instance, J. Hoberman, "Mexico's Maestro of the Feel-Bad Pities His Monsters," *The Village Voice*, March 29, 2005, available online at http://radio.villagevoice.com/2005–03–29/screens/mexico-s-maestro-of-the-feel-bad-pities-his-monsters (accessed January 12, 2009). Jorge Fons quoted in Carl J. Mora, *Mexican Cinema: Reflections of a Society, 1896–2004* (London: McFarland & Company, 2005), p. 227.
27. Sadoul's letter from February 1965 is quoted in Bengali translation in Parthapratim Bandyopadhyay, "Filmey Melodrama: Ritwik Kumar Ghatak," in *Ritwik o Tar Chhobi*, edited by Rajat Roy (Calcutta: Annapurna Pustak Mandir, 1983), p. 81.
28. Quoted in Ashish Rajadhyaksha and Amrit Gangar (eds.), *Ritwik Ghatak: Arguments/Stories* (Bombay: Screen Unit, 1987), p. 103.
29. See the discussion of the Fernández–Figueroa style (comprising deep focus photography, high-contrast lighting, oblique perspective, low-angle shots and "Figueroa skies") in Charles Ramirez Berg, "The Cinematic Invention of Mexico: The Poetics and Politics of the Fernández-Figueroa Style," in Chon Noriega and Steven Ricci (eds), *The Mexican Cinema Project* (Los Angeles, Calif.: UCLA Film and Television Archive, 1994), pp. 13–24. Carlos Monsiváis, "Mythologies," in Paulo Antonio Paranagua (ed.), *Mexican Cinema* (London: British Film Institute, 1995), pp. 117–127.
30. Sergio de la Mora, *Cinemachismo: Masculinities and Sexuality in Mexican Film* (Austin, Tex.: University of Texas Press, 2006), p. 107.
31. Sergio de la Mora, "A Career in Perspective: An Interview with Arturo Ripstein," *Film Quarterly*, 52 (4) (summer, 1999): 2–11; p. 11. The filmmaker continues, "This is the most atrocious happy family ever depicted on film. [. . .] This is a perfect family and the ending is a comment on life, on my country, on reality, and on movies. My standpoint in this film is to destroy

our tradition and build another which can be seen from a different end and form a different perspective" (de la Mora, "A Career in Perspective," p. 11). See also the discussion of the 1933 original and Ripstein's remediation in Chapter 1 of Andrea Noble, *Mexican National Cinema* (London: Routledge, 2005), pp. 32–47.

32. Many Indians settle their dilemmas by asking, what would Seeta or Arjuna do in a similar situation? Perhaps the most salient instance of the epics being a part of contemporary lifeworlds is the way in which the *Bhagavadgita,* a segment of the *Mahabharata,* shape contemporary notions of duty and karma in India and beyond.

33. Ritwik Ghatak, "Music in Indian Cinema and the Epic Approach," in *Rows and Rows of Fences* (Calcutta: Seagull, 2000), p. 21. Originally published in *Artist,* 1 (1) (1963).

34. This "absence" is, no doubt, tied to the destructive nature of Spanish colonialism in Latin America. See Doris Somner's notion of an "erotics of politics" in her monograph, *Foundational Fictions: The National Romances of Latin America* (Berkeley, Calif.: University of Califronia Press, 1993).

35. Monsiváis, "Mythologies," p. 117.

36. Notwithstanding the shift from a primarily production-oriented, Fordist international economic system to a predominantly service-oriented paradigm of flexible accumulation, and the passage from a Cold War-era bipolar world order to a more unipolar geopolitical regime, the aspirations of both national publics remain circumscribed by the broad contours of a global bourgeois modernity. For our purposes, the main distinctions between India in 1960 and Mexico in 1993—besides obvious local cultural inflections—pertain to the expanded access of "Third World" populations to universalized lifestyles and expectations, and to the transformed nature of the national-global interpenetrations. Nevertheless, both changes are often exaggerated. In spite of strong transnational linkages and flows, the world is not rendered "flat": opportunities and even the "capacity to aspire" remain wildly incommensurate across the globe. As Néstor García Canclini has argued, "questions about identity and the national, the defense of sovereignty, and the unequal appropriation of knowledge and art do not disappear" with globalization; rather, they get "placed in a different regis-ter" where their mutual "autonomy" and interactions are "rethought." Néstor García Canclini, *Hybrid Cultures: Strategies for Entering and Leaving Modernity,* trans. Christopher Chiappari and Silvia López (Minneapolis, Minn.: University of Minnesota Press, 1995), pp. 240–241. My point is that Mexico of the 1990s and India of the 1960s evince enough material and felt similarities to be placed within a continually mutating global South. As we shall see presently, the intent of this topological tethering is not so much to discount historical shifts as to complicate a linear model of world history.

37. Over a million perished in the communal riots, at least 50,000 women were abducted and raped, and some 12 million people rendered homeless.

38. Octavio Paz, *In Light of India,* trans. Eliot Weinberger (New York: Harvest Books, 1998), pp. 73–75. In fact, mainstream cinema participated in such a project of nation-building with much ambivalence; even commercial films expressed displaced anxieties about the partition in allegorical form (index-ical traces of partition, such as documentary footage of refugees; narrative sublimations of the division, such as family feuds; two siblings getting

separated in their infancy, illegitimate pregnancy, disfigured or amnesiac protagonists). Bhaskar Sarkar, *Mourning the Nation: Indian Cinema in the Wake of Partition* (Durham, NC: Duke University Press, 2009).

39. *The Beginning and the End* appeared around the time that Canada, Mexico, and the USA signed the North American Free Trade Agreement (NAFTA), signaling an economic openness to trade and foreign investment that was about to become normative across the planet. Global interest in Mexican culture peaked around this time: Paz won the Nobel Prize for Literature in 1990; an exhibition of pre-Columbian art opened at the Metropolitan Museum of New York; the international art market was in thrall with Diego Riviera and Frida Kahlo; and the Centre George Pompidou in Paris organized the largest ever retrospective of Mexican cinema. Alfonso Arau's film *Like Water for Chocolate* (1992) became the biggest foreign hit in the lucrative US market. In 1993, responding in part to this global prominence of national culture, the Mexican Government awarded lifelong stipends to some sixty eminent intellectuals and artists: the group included Paz, Monsiváis, Fuentes, Márquez, and Ripstein. At the same time, the state under President Salinas inaugurated a period of rapid privatization, which saw the sale of state-owned film studios and production companies and the end of national public television. While this broad context is not explicitly thematized in *The Beginning and the End,* there are intimations of a worldview structured by US-centric global capital: the main protagonist longs for a Ford Foundation grant to go study in the USA; a powerful industrialist encourages his protégé to enter student politics to further the former's class interests; and an individualist calculus gradually supplants all considerations of family and community life.

40. Marvin D'Lugo, "Authorship, Globalization, and the New Identity of Latin American Cinema," in Anthony Guneratne and Wimal Dissanayake (eds.), *Rethinking Third Cinema* (New York: Routledge, 2003), pp. 103–125; p. 111.

41. D'Lugo, "Authorship, Globalization, and New Identity," p. 111.

42. Ritwik Ghatak, "Manabsamaj, Amder Aitihya, Chhabi-kora o Amar Pracheshta," in *Chalachchitra, Manush Ebang Aro Kichhu* (Calcutta: Sandhan Cooperative Publishing, 1975), pp. 3–10; p. 9 (my translation from the Bengali original).

43. See Sarkar, *Mourning the Nation,* Chapter 5, "Ghatak, Melodrama, and the Restitution of Experience," pp. 200–229.

44. De la Mora, "A Career in Perspective," p. 9.

45. Ritwik Ghatak, "*Subarnarekha:* Parichalaker Baktabya," in *Chalachchitra, Manush Ebang Aro Kichhu* (Calcutta: Sandhan Cooperative Publishing, 1975), pp. 38–43; p. 41 (my translation from Bengali, emphases added).

46. The incestuous underpinnings remain implicit in Ghatak, unlike in the films of Ripstein—especially his version of *La mujer del Puerto.* This dissimilarity has to do with cultural differences between Mexico and Bengal: one would be hard-pressed to find Bengali film that allude to—let alone explicitly represent—brother–sister incest.

47. See Moinak Biswas, "Her Mother's Son: Kinship and History in Ritwik Ghatak," *Rouge,* 3, available online at www.rouge.com.au/3/index.html accessed August 8, 2008).

48. This conjugality becomes the locus of a capitalist-consumerist transformation of the national citizenry in mainstream Bengali cinema of the 1950s and 1960s—for instance, in the immensely popular films starring Uttam

Kumar and Suchitra Sen. See Bhaskar Sarkar, "Bengali Cinema: A Spectral Subnationality," in *Mourning the Nation*, pp. 125–165.

49. Kumar Shahani, "Violence and Responsibility," in Ashish Rajadhyaksha and Amrit Gangar (eds), *Ritwik Ghatak: Arguments/Stories* (Bombay: Screen Unit, 1987), p. 59. Emphasis in original.

50. This gendered duplicity of social structures is subjected to scrutiny in several Bengali films in the 1960s and 1970s: most notably in Satyajit Ray's *The Big City* (1963) and *The Middleman* (1976), and in Mrinal Sen's *And Quiet Rolls the Dawn* (1979).

51. For a discussion of the linkages between women, landscape, and the soundtrack in Ghatak, see Erin O'Donnell, "'Woman' and 'Homeland' in Ritwik Ghatak's Films: Constructing Post-independence Bengali Cultural Identity," *Jump Cut*, available online at www.ejumpcut.org/archive/jc47.2005/ghatak/index.html (accessed February 1, 2009).

52. Interview in *Film Miscellany* (1976), reprinted in Shampa Banerjee (ed.), *Ritwik Ghatak* (New Delhi: Directorate of Film Festivals, National Film Development Corporation, 1982), p. 100.

53. Ritwik Ghatak, "Chhabitey Dialectics," in in *Chalachchitra, Manush Ebang Aro Kichhu* (Calcutta: Sandhan Cooperative Publishing, 1975), pp. 43–47.

54. De la Mora, "A Career in Perspective," p. 7.

55. This point is developed with respect to the homosocial environment of the brothel in *El lugar sin límites* by David William Foster, "Arturo Ripstein's *El lugar sin límites* and the Hell of Heteronormativity," in Arturo J. Aldama and Alfred Arteaga (eds), *Violence and the Body: Race, Gender and the State* (Bloomington, Ind.: Indiana University Press, 2003), pp. 375–387.

56. Sergei Eisenstein, Vsevolod Pudovkin, and Grigori Alexandrov, "Statement on Sound," in *S. M. Eisenstein: Selected Works, Volume 1: Writings, 1922–1934*, edited and translated by Richard Taylor (London: BFI, 1988), pp. 113–114.

57. Raymond Bellour, "The Film We Accompany," *Rouge*, 3 (2004), available online at www.rouge.com.au/3/film.html (accessed August 8, 2008).

58. Fredric Jameson, *The Geopolitical Aesthetic: Cinema and Space in the World System* (London: BFI, 1992), p. 1.

59. Jameson, *The Geopolitical Aesthetic*, p. 2.

60. Jameson, *The Geopolitical Aesthetic*, p. 4.

61. Jameson, *The Geopolitical Aesthetic*, p. 3.

62. Jameson, *The Geopolitical Aesthetic*, p. 5.

63. Jameson, *The Geopolitical Aesthetic*, p. 5.

64. Jameson, *The Geopolitical Aesthetic*, p. 64.

65. Jameson, *The Geopolitical Aesthetic*, p. 68.

66. Jameson, *The Geopolitical Aesthetic*, p. 133.

67. Jameson, *The Geopolitical Aesthetic*, p. 69.

68. It is this theme that is developed in his later work, *A Singular Modernity: Essay on the Ontology of the Present* (London: Verso, 2002).

69. Jameson, *The Geopolitical Aesthetic*, p. 1.

70. Jameson, *The Geopolitical Aesthetic*, p. 1.

71. Dipesh Chakrabarty, *Provincializing Europe: Postcolonial Thought and Historical Difference* (Princeton, NJ: Princeton University Press, 2000).

72. Bhaskar Sarkar, "The Melodramas of Globalization," *Cultural Dynamics*, 20 (1) (March 2008): 31–51.

295

"black blood"

there will be blood

thirteen

anne gjelsvik

> *Then the LORD said to Moses, "Say to Aaron, 'Take your*
> *staff and stretch out your hand over the waters of Egypt, over*
> *their rivers, over their streams, and over their pools, and over all*
> *their reservoirs of water, that they may become blood; and there*
> *will be blood throughout all the land of Egypt, both in vessels of*
> *wood and in vessels of stone.'"[1]*
>
> *Yea, go to now, make trial, that all these may see; forthwith*
> *thy dark blood shall gush about my spear.[2]*

The transformation of Upton Sinclair's book title *Oil!* to *There Will Be Blood*
prompts an allegorical reading of the depiction of oil in Paul Thomas
Anderson's 2007 epic. The phrase *There Will Be Blood* connotes both a threat
and a biblical prophecy, setting a dark and pessimistic chord, leading the
viewer to anticipate a story about blood-shedding even before the story
unfolds. In this chapter I will try to shed some light on the dark and different senses of these blood themes, which range from the promise of new life
to violent death.

Anderson's loose adaptation of Upton Sinclair's 1927 novel has also been dubbed "The Birth of an Oil Nation," placing it in the tradition of the American epic film going back to D. W. Griffith.[3] The American epic film can be said to replay a universal story, depicting, as Robert Burgoyne has formulated it: "a pattern of decadence, decline and the germs of new life."[4] As I intend to show, these elements are all present in *There Will Be Blood*: the film gives the viewer an experience of witnessing a beginning, the start of a new life, and the building of modern America. As Manohla Dargis foregrounds in her review in the *New York Times*:

> With a story of and for our times, "There Will Be Blood" can certainly be viewed through the smeary window that looks onto the larger world. It's timeless and topical, general and specific, abstract and as plain as the name of its fiery oilman. *It's an origin story of sorts.*[5]

Shadowing the film's depiction, however, are motifs of decay and degeneracy, symbolized through the violence that pervades the film, the accidents, the arson, the murders, and the public humiliations—*There Will Be Blood* depicts a story of emergence that is simultaneously a story of blood sacrifice, as if the biblical story of Abraham and Isaac were being told with a very different ending.

In what follows, I will discuss what kind of beginning the film could be said to depict, through what does indeed seem like a smeary window.

In his discussion of the epic genre, Burgoyne quotes Gilles Deleuze's description of American cinema as being one "single fundamental film, which is the birth of nation-civilization."[6] The movie offers an account, if not exactly of the birth of civilization, then of the transition from an agricultural to an industrial society, a dramatic change taking place over the course of a few years. By all accounts a well-researched historical movie, *There Will Be Blood* appears to give "an adequate empathetic reconstruction" of this historical transformation.[7] Set during the American oil boom of the late nineteenth and early twentieth century, *There Will Be Blood* depicts a historical period less spectacular and somewhat less mythical than the traditional epic film (like *Ben-Hur* [1959] or *Gladiator* [2000]) tends to do. It is therefore closer to our time and place in history than most epics are, and, accordingly, the movie also seems to be more realistic and less allegorical—but as I will argue, only at first glance.[8]

In bare outline, *There Will Be Blood* concerns the rise and fall of a self-made man in an industrial landscape, his rise to success, and his fall into the gutter. The movie follows the protagonist Daniel Plainview from his solitary search for silver in New Mexico in 1898, through his endeavors as an oil prospector and entrepreneur during the first years of the Californian oil industry, until old age, when he ends up rich but just as isolated as in the beginning.

I will begin my analysis by describing how the movie depicts the birth of an oil nation, and some of the central scenes and themes in it, following the traces of blood throughout the movie. I will take as a point of departure the importance of "building" in the film: the building (or digging) of an oil well, the building of the oil derrick (and what in the movie is called the "the rigging up"), the act of building a community, building a house (a church and a private residence), and, last but not least, the building of a home or a family. I will focus on the spectacular depictions, as well as the allegorical functions of these "building scenes." As I see it, the bleak buildings are closely connected to the dark blood, both in relation to optimistic beginnings depicted throughout the film, and the fatal and tragic end.

The movie could also be said to have elements of a jeremiad in its structure, theme, and tone, as well as in its prophecy of society's downfall.[9] Like the traditional sermons inspired by the book of Jeremiah, the movie is a narration both of covenants and conversion, although in a biblical sense the conversion of the protagonist must be considered a failure.[10] In what follows I will compare the movie's dark prophecy with elements from the American jeremiad and its critique of modern life, the tension between a public ideal and individual effort and between progress and failure.[11]

building, rebuilding or burning down the house

The movie's first picture, that of a barren landscape, is accompanied by an (almost) alarming musical soundscape; the music grows increasingly intense, until the alarm is replaced by the sound of one man digging in a dark silver mine deep under the ground.[12]

During the first fifteen minutes of the movie we follow the man in his physical struggle and pursuit for the hidden treasures of the soil. We track his progress from stubbornly crawling through the wilderness, wounded after falling into a hole after an explosion, to leading a team of workers digging an oil well some years later. This almost wordless sequence strikes the chord for the antagonistic storylines in the movie, between a solitary man doing things his own way, and the construction of a collective, whether this be a family or a community.[13] These themes are significantly condensed in a scene where one of the diggers climbs down into the dark, bubbling hole and releases the oil drill, with the whole team of men watching from above, standing in a circle of sunlight. And the protagonist celebrates the oil discovery by raising his oil-smeared hand as a sign of victory—the alarming sound now mixed with the sound of a crying child.

The title of the film suggests that "oil" can (and quite possibly should) be read as a metaphor for blood, and almost from the start its depiction of oil adds to that impression. Throughout the film, the extensive use of oil connotes to blood, and on several occasions the oil looks like some kind of bodily fluid (see, for instance, Figure 13.1).

As Pierre Sorlin has argued, the perception of the color of blood may have changed throughout the centuries.[14] While "red" is perhaps today the

Figure 13.1

There Will Be Blood: Daniel Plainview covered in oil, or is it blood?

immediate color term that springs to mind whenever the word "blood" is mentioned, this has not necessarily always been the case. In *The Iliad,* for one, Homer on several occasions describes blood as something black, dark or murky, all terms used to describe things that the sun never reaches.[15] Blood pouring from wounds, for example, is repeatedly described as black, and clotted black blood is washed away from spears and bodies.[16]

In *There Will Be Blood,* two deadly accidents in the wells are described with the use of the black oil, where the men are smeared in oil, and the bodies drenched in both blood and oil, more black than red. In the first fatal accident, in Daniel's first oil well, a part of the drilling rig falls down—from the clear sky—killing an anonymous man in a close-up of a mixture of blood and oil. The second deadly accident is depicted in the dark, without any daylight at all, as the men are working at night. The dead man "fished" up from the deep well is dragged from the even darker depths of the well and laid, dripping oil, on the floor of the newly built derrick.

The antagonism between success and accidents runs through the entire movie, starting with Daniel's own accident in the beginning, where he finds silver after falling down and injuring his leg. This contradiction is depicted, as already indicated above, through another, visual one, between black (oil) and light (sun or fire) (as seen in Figure 13.2).

The building of Eli Sunday's church and that of Daniel Plainview's well continue side by side, until the movie's most spectacular scene: a blow-out when the men finally strike oil, which was probably the scene Manohla Dargis had in mind when she characterized the film as "this expansively imagined period story with its pictorial and historical sweep, its raging fires, geysers of oil and inevitable blood."[17] The explosion knocks Daniel's son, H.W. (Dillon Freasier), off of his watching post at the roof and gives him a severe blow, which leaves him deaf. As the oil pours out like rain, Daniel runs, covered in black oil, with his son equally smeared with oil in his arms, carrying him into safety, while the other men are running toward

299

Figure 13.2
There Will Be Blood.

the uncontrolled well (see Figure 13.3). This scene gives perhaps the strongest indication for viewing oil as metaphor for blood. In Sinclair's novel the blow-out is depicted like this "there was a tower of flame, and the most amazing spectacle—the burning oil would hit the ground, and bounce up, and explode, and leap again and fall again, and great red masses of flame would unfold, and burst, and yield black masses of smoke, and these in turn red."[18]

When the derrick bursts into flames, Daniel has to choose between looking after his wounded son and saving the well. And he chooses the well, leaving as the boy cries, "Don't leave," with the (false) promise that he will be "Back in a minute." Watching his buildings being consumed by the flames, and the fire veiling the sky with thick, black smoke, Daniel asks his companion Fletcher Hamilton (Ciarán Hinds) why he looks so miserable, as he himself cheers: "There is a whole ocean of oil under our feet! No one can get at it except for me." When Hamilton asks "H.W. OK?," Daniel's black, oil-covered face does not give away any feelings, as he answers, "No, he isn't." Nevertheless, he stays the night watching the fire instead of

Figure 13.3
There Will Be Blood: Father and son.

tending to his son, until they can put out the fire with explosives in the light of the morning. Again, the depiction of the clash between misfortune and success is visualized as a clash between darkness and light, and the conflict between building an oil well or building a family is condensed in the image of Daniel's face covered in oil and its allusions to dark blood and blood shedding.

The way I see it, the figure of blood is associated with two separate yet related themes in this film. On one hand, we have the theme of origins (births, blood relations and blood ties), (both) on an overall or general level, as well as an actual fact in relation to the Daniel and Sunday families. On the other hand, we have the theme of bloodshed and death, which recurs throughout the movie, both in the form of the repeated accidents that kill and maim various characters and in the form of the two murders committed by the protagonist.

The film remains vague on the specific origins and consanguine relationships of its characters. For instance, the relationship between the two Sunday brothers is puzzling; it is not immediately clear to the spectator whether they are identical twins or in fact one and the same person, partly due to the fact that both characters are played by the same actor (Paul Dano).[19] And when one day a man, by the name of Henry Plainview (Kevin J. O'Connor), shows up out of nowhere claiming to be Daniel's unknown brother by a different mother, we are left in uncertainty about the truth of his origin for quite some time.

As for father and son Plainview, they also both seem to come from nowhere: Daniel is introduced just "out there," digging in the middle of nowhere, while his son H.W. also seems to have sprung from nowhere. I have thus far avoided mention of the fact that H.W. is not Daniel Plainview's biological son but his adopted child—or, to keep up with the dominant metaphor of the film, H.W. is not of his own blood. On the first viewing, this information is actually possible to overlook, although the death of H.W.'s real father—the worker who died in the accident in Daniel's first well—is the most dramatic event in the first part of the film. But the movie emphasizes neither who the (real) father is, nor the identity of the presumably orphaned child, apart from the father being an anonymous worker at Daniel's first well and the son a "bastard from a basket," as Daniel calls H.W. when, at the end of the film, he turns against him. Nor is any information about the mother provided, although we may well be inclined to think that she is dead, since the father brings his child to work.[20] When asked where H.W.'s mother is by someone who thinks Daniel is in fact the boy's actual father, he answers, "I don't want to talk about those things." Apart from the brief mention of Daniel's own mother and also the weak mother of the Sunday family and her little daughter Mary, women are almost invisible in the movie. This is a man's world, like in most traditional epics, but also a man's world where, to my mind, the role of the man—or rather of the father—is significantly new. As Daniel himself puts it: "I have a bond of family that very few oilmen understand."

Contrary to Sinclair's novel, the protagonist in the film is portrayed as a single parent; in the novel, the close-knit father–son relationship is a result of a far more complicated family setting, but Bunny is the actual son, by blood, of the book's "Dad," John Ross.[21] The "single-father plot" is an up-to-date transformation of the story, fitting nicely into contemporary American cinema's preoccupation with fatherhood.[22] Like other single fathers in contemporary cinema, Daniel is an unorthodox father, whose attitude toward fatherhood is highly ambiguous.[23] His adoption of H.W. could be merely an opportunistic act, characteristic of the way Daniel is always on the lookout for new resources to exploit. In this respect, his adoption of H.W. is no different from his drainage of the oil from under Mr. Bandy's land (which he obtained by drilling the land surrounding the farm).[24] Daniel uses whatever he can get his hands on in order to further his own interests, as he tells H.W. during their last confrontation: "You're an orphan from a basket in the middle of the desert. And I took you for no other reason than I needed a sweet face to buy land."[25]

Yet the viewer will have been discouraged from taking this angry statement at face value on the basis of several earlier scenes in the film, particularly when H.W. is growing up, where Daniel very much comes across as an affectionate father. For instance, the first time he puts the crying baby on his lap, despite his greasy clothes, the resulting smears of oil on the baby's light clothes can be seen as a manifestation of the bond being forged between the two. In keeping with oil symbolism running through the film, this scene could equally suggest that the relationship between father and son has been sealed in "blood." Daniel further appears as an anti-patriarchal father, for instance when he intervenes in Sunday's use of corporal punishment on his children. He himself never once hits H.W., not even when the boy, in an act of anger and jealousy, sets fire to his father's house, where both Daniel and Henry are sleeping, and very nearly burns them to death.

After this incident, Daniel decides to send the deaf boy away from home, echoing his untrustworthy promise from the fatal blow-out; "Stay here, I will be right back." Even though Daniel sends H.W. away to an institution for deaf children, this could be seen as an act of putting the child's needs first, or as a way to deal with a situation he is not up for. Daniel Plainview presents himself both as "I am an oil man" and as "I am a family man," but he separates the two. He can build an oil derrick and, in the end, even a beautiful house, but not a home. Still, the movie leaves one with the impression that this is in fact what men of the future should be able to do.

I will argue that the parental role is important to Daniel, and I see his actions as in part a nostalgic longing; the longing for a home.[26] Although

Daniel seems to be driven by an urge for development, progress and prosperity, the promise to rebuild the ideal home seems to be the core of his longings and can explain some of his actions, at least his most mysterious action—the adoption of a son.

Central to my reading here is the importance of his meeting with the man who claims to be his brother. Soon after the blow-out that leads to H.W.'s handicap, a man shows up at Daniel's doorstep, claiming to be his unknown half-brother. It is Henry who gains Daniel's confidence and to whom he soon confides that "I can't keep doing this on my own . . . with these . . . hem . . . people." In his desire for a family, he accepts Henry as his brother and pushes both his son and his companion and only friend Fletcher away, making the brother his new partner in work. After a journey that settles and secures the route for his oil pipeline to the coast, and the deal, which eventually makes him overwhelmingly rich, he tells his brother about a memory from the past that became his dream for the future:

DANIEL: There was that house in Fond du Lac that John Hollister built—do you remember?

HENRY: Mmm.

DANIEL: I thought as a boy that was the most beautiful house I'd ever seen and I wanted it. I wanted to live in it, and eat in it and clean it. And even as a boy, I wanted to have children to run around in it.

HENRY: You can have anything you like now, Daniel, and you should. Where are you going to build it?

DANIEL: Here, maybe. Near the ocean.

HENRY: Would you make it look like that house?

DANIEL: I'm sure if I saw that house now it'd make me sick.

After sharing this story, Daniel discovers that Henry is not who he claims to be, as he does not have any recollection of their mutual past, nor any memory of their hometown. When Henry confesses that he has stolen another (dead) man's identity, his story, and his diary, Daniel kills him in cold blood. Once again, he has to dig a hole in the ground, this time not to find something bringing new life, but to hide the dead. The sound of the alarm once again accompanies the sound of the man hacking away at the ground.

After the murder, Daniel reads the diary where his real brother has written about him: "my brother—a stranger to me." The strong and stern man, seemingly without any emotions or any close connection to his past, breaks down and cries when he finds a photograph of a little boy. (It is difficult to know whether the picture is of him as a child, or of his brother.) Since Daniel is a man without a home, both before the story begins and for a large part of the movie, this scene indicates a strong longing for the past or a home—in other words a nostalgic longing. And, as Linda Hutcheon has argued, the longing for a lost home is a male narrative, since the nostalgic narratives, starting with the Bible or with Odysseus, are the stories of men who "wander the world and risk getting homesick," or, as in Daniel's case, who "early left for Kansas."[27] The importance of this longing for home and family can be seen through the fact that trusting Henry's story is the only misjudgment the professional Daniel makes, and his disappointment with the fact that Henry is not of his own blood, and his failure to reveal this deception, change him from a stubborn and selfish man into a monstrous being. His longing for blood ties turns him into a shedder of blood.

In addition to giving allusions to both birth and death, the blood has one last function in *There Will Be Blood*—namely the blood as a figure of redemption, and this leads me to the biblical connotations in the movie.

beg for the blood

The title, *There Will Be Blood,* is a biblical allusion, to Exodus 7:19.[28] The prophecy of the blood is foretold in the following terms:

> And the LORD spoke to Moses, Say to Aaron, Take your rod,
>   and stretch
> out your hand on the waters of Egypt, on their streams,
>   on their rivers,
> and on their ponds, and on all their pools of water, that they
>   may become blood; and that there may be blood throughout
>   all the land of Egypt, both
> in vessels of wood, and in vessels of stone.[29]

The house Daniel has built himself could be said to contain blood throughout, and the bitter ending set in this beautiful house, sums up the dark side to the story of progress, as well as the overall ambiguity in the movie. Even darker than Exodus, is, of course, the apocalyptic prophecy from the Book of Revelations: "The first angel sounded, and there followed hail and fire mingled with blood, and they were cast on the earth: and the third part of trees was burnt up, and all green grass was burnt up."[30] As dark as this and the other prophecies for the final judgment may be, they also entail the possibility of a better world after the day of judgment. Krishna Kumar reminds us that utopianism is not only connected to modern Western society and its challenges, but also to Jewish messianism and Christian millenarianism.[31]

The relation between judgment and hope is also an element in the American jeremiad, and the movie can be read as an allegory of "The misfortunes of an era as a just penalty for great social and moral evils," but a jeremiad should also hold "out hope for changes that will bring a happier future."[32] According to the rhetorician Andrew Wood, the American jeremiad (as opposed to its European predecessors) has a dimension of progress as well as a paradoxical rhetoric of both hope and fear.[33] The jeremiad sermons are constructed around the tension between an ideal social life and its real manifestation, a contradiction similar to the incompatibility between what Daniel preaches in his speeches and how he lives. The conflicts between the public and the private and between the ideal and the real also call for a comparison between the movie and the jeremiad.

Daniel Plainview gives an almost monstrous first impression, but there are very few indications of how he has become this determined contractor willing to get blood on his hands in order to have his way with things. But Daniel is also a man full of contradictions: "He does not like to explain himself, he is full of hatred and of competition," as he confesses in a rare and contemplative moment in the movie. But, as an oilman of the new world, he *does* equal the hero in the traditional epic movie in one respect, as he truly shows the ability to "accomplish social change," or modern progress, at least this is the ideal image he wants to sell in public.[34] When persuading the farmers to sell him their land so that he can dig for oil, he argues in the name of progress:

> I like to think of myself as an oilman. As an oilman. . . . And I encourage my men to bring their families, as well. Of course it makes for an ever so much more rewarding life for them. Family means children. Children means education. So wherever we set up camp, education is a necessity, and we're just so happy to take care of that. So let's build a wonderful school in Little Boston. These children are the future that we strive for, so they should have the very best of things . . . We're going to dig water wells here. Water wells means irrigation, irrigation means cultivation. We're going to raise crops here where before it just simply was impossible. You're going to have more grain than you'll know what to do with. Bread will be coming right out of your ears, ma'am. New roads. Agriculture. Employment, education. These are just a few of the things we can offer you, and I assure you ladies and gentlemen, that if we do find oil here, and I think there's a very good chance that we will, this community of yours will not only survive, it will flourish.[35]

His speech could be seen to reflect "The American Dream," where every man can gain prosperity through hard work, as James Truslow Adams wrote in 1931: "that dream of a land in which life should be better and richer and fuller for every man, with opportunity for each according to his ability or achievement."[36] On the other hand, Daniel's behavior and actions seem for the most part to be motivated by his own benefit or simply by greed.[37]

Daniel does not seem to represent the strong pillar of society his speech suggests that he is. Whereas the epic hero traditionally stands up for the community, Daniel seems to fight against the others, most of the time. This raises the question: is his vision actually an ethical change for the community, or just an unethical and evil vision for subjective success? Is he in fact not building a community but digging a hole in the ground, underneath both the well, the church, and the home? In fact, the story could be said to have placed the villain as the protagonist, making it an epic in reverse, which, of course, makes him very much in need of conversion.

The name jeremiad has also been used in a pejorative sense, to imply that a piece of writing is overwrought and overblown, or as an angry harangue, and both these descriptions are also, in part, suitable for characterizing *There Will Be Blood*.[38] Sacvan Bercovitch describes the jeremiad as characterized by an internal tension and an effort to reconstruct personal and painful experiences, in an emotional but yet puritan narrative.[39] Today the term jeremiad is used to describe not only sermons but also prose and poetry, as a rhetorical formula that lament "recent and present ills, and crying out for a return to the original conduct and zeal."[40]

According to Wood, the invocation in the American jeremiad sermons involves a three-step structure: "(1) provide a biblical or spiritual standard for individual activity and public life, (2) outline the manners in which a people has fallen from that standard, (3) envision an ideal public life—with its concurrent individual benefits—that follows a return to the religious standard."[41] As such, the jeremiad is seeking a resolution that incorporates both a condemnation and a promise of something better. The structure of the jeremiad includes a *contrition* (where the sinner should examine his own life and look into the Law of God), *humiliation* (where the sinner realizes his sin), and *implantation* (where the sinner experiences true humiliation of the heart and fear and grief because of his sin).[42]

This structure can shed light on the relationship, or rather the conflict between Daniel and the preacher Eli. This conflict escalates when Daniel, in spite of his prior promise, does not allow Eli to say a blessing in front of the whole community on the day of the official opening of the well.[43] Instead he himself says a short blessing, and ignores the preacher: "You see, one man doesn't prospect from the ground. It takes a whole community of good people such as your selves and this is good. We stay together. We pray together. We work together. And if the Good Lord smiles kindly on our endeavor, we share the wealth together."

The conflict with the priest reaches its peak after the accident in which one of the workers dies and when Eli once again claims money for the church as payment for his father's land. Daniel, full of anger and guilt over his son's condition, punches the preacher to the ground. He drags the preacher into an oil pit, and, while he smears his white face with the black oil grease, he threatens the fallen man: "I am going to bury you under ground Eli, I am going to bury you under ground," and then walks away, leaving the preacher on the ground, gasping for air. Once again, the use of oil gives allusions to blood and bloodshed.

The elements from the jeremiad are in particular central in the sermons depicted in the movie, where Eli tries to convince and convert Daniel, and most directly in the important scene where Daniel agrees to be baptized in Eli's church, in order to gain control over the religious farmer Mr. Bandy's land. Or, as the farmer formulates it, he wants Daniel to be "Washed in the Blood of Jesus Christ." Eli describes Daniel as a sinner looking for salvation and as a man who has brought wealth and work to the community but also points to his bad habits as a "backslider," that is to say he has fallen below the standards of the community. Eli calls him to the front of his newly built church where a window, formed as a cross, sheds radiant lights on the congregation (see Figure 13.4). Eli forces him to declare: "I am a sinner," "I am sorry Lord!," "I want the blood," and, finally, "I have abandoned my child," on Eli's claim that he had failed to take care of H.W. when he was sick. But when Eli urges Daniel "To beg for the Blood!," he whispers, "Give me the Blood, Eli, and let me get out of here," before he calls out: "Give me the Blood, Lord, and let me get away," fully demonstrating that although he is humiliated, no implantation, salvation, redemption or true presence of faith is achieved. He achieved what he was coming for, a pipeline securing his oil source and his wealth. Accordingly, the six stages of conversion are not obtained in the case of Daniel Plainview,

Figure 13.4

There Will Be Blood: Eli Sunday forcing Daniel to beg for the blood.

in spite of the congregations' victorious chanting when Eli literally tries to drive the Devil out of Daniel by hitting him:

> Would you be free from the burden of sin?
> There's power in the blood
> Power in the blood
> Would you o'er evil or victory a win?
> There is wonderful power in the blood
> There is power, power, wonder-working power
> In the blood of the lamb.

The failure of conversion is fully demonstrated when the situation is reversed at the end of the movie, as Daniel humiliates Eli by forcing him to declare that he is "a false prophet and God a superstition."[44] Like the jeremiads, the movie could be said to in part account for "the misfortunes of an era as a just penalty for great social and moral evils," or in this case, the misfortunes of an era directed by greed, portrayed as individual egotism. As when it comes to the importance of holding out hope "for changes that will bring a happier future," neither Daniel nor his competitor Eli achieves redemption.[45] The purpose of the jeremiad is not accomplished.

Dark as *There Will Be Blood* may be, I also see an unveiling of a possible utopian notion in the movie, in particular related to the building themes. The utopia is a central dimension to the building of the well and the community, but above all or at least most obviously, the building of the Church of the Third Revelation. Several of the most optimistic and light scenes in the movie show men working together, building the church, the derrick, and the pipeline—perhaps echoing numerous scenes of church-building in John Ford's films. The film's focus on these elements gives the movie what reviewer David Denby described as follows: "'Blood' has the pulse of the future in its rhythms."[46] But building a future may cost more than sweat, and in this case ever so often the cost is, as the title indicates, blood, and the prospect depicted may be seen as more black than bright.

In contrast to many other epics, the movie seems to be less about a *nostalgic* longing for the past ("what has been, and what might have been") and more about a *utopian* longing for a possible future (of "what might be"), but mixed with strong elements of dystopia. In opposition to the traditional dystopian tale, the dystopian ending seems to be a result of our protagonist's acts, where his individualism is working against the community. Accordingly, Daniel is not a hero who brings salvation to a corrupted society, but he himself brings corruption to his society, and thus the jeremianic criticism in the movie is being directed more toward individualistic sin than institutional flaws.[47]

In the end, Daniel has built himself his beautiful house, and, as Eli declares when he comes to see him, "The house you built is a miracle."

But Daniel, like so many other moguls of the screen (Citizen Kane [1941], or Jett Rink in *Giant* [1956]), is left alone in his big empty house. There are no children running around. When the grown-up H.W. says that he will leave his father to "do my own drilling," Daniel tells him that "You are killing my image of you as a son." He tried to create a home and an image of a son, but as the son had none of his blood in him, the bonds were not strong enough to form a solid construction. His utopian dream of building a family did not come true because building a solid house needs a community, and Daniel failed to see the impossibility in building something beautiful that only covers a dark void.

He ends up killing Eli, although he has nothing to gain from it, and finally they both quite literally end up in the gutter of Daniel's private bowling lane; Eli, and the capitalist without a family, a home, or a future. A paradoxical tale about progress and hope in the new world ends in the dark, reflecting not so much an American dream as an American nightmare. The tragic tale of hope and fear ends, almost like a prophecy from the book of Jeremiah, with our hero in a forsaken place, and on his clothes "is found the lifeblood of the innocent poor."[48] "Because they have forsaken me, and have estranged this place, and have burned incense in it to other gods, whom neither they nor their fathers have known, nor the kings of Judah, and have filled this place with the blood of innocents."[49]

There Will Be Blood sheds light on both false prophets and false fathers, and draws a portrait of the man of progress, the oil man, in blood as dark as the oil in the soil. In this nightmare vision of the birth of an oil nation, oil is not the lifeblood of the new world but the dark stain on modern progress.[50]

notes

1. Exodus 7:19, in *The American King James Version,* available online at http://bible. cc/exodus/7–19.htm (accessed November 14, 2008).
2. *The Iliad,* 1.303.
3. Scott Foundas "Paul Thomas Anderson: Blood, Sweat and Tears," *LA Weekly,* January 6, 2008, available online at www.laweekly.com/film+tv/film/paul-thomas-anderson-blood-sweat-and-tears/18140 (accessed August 10, 2008) .
4. Robert Burgoyne, *The Hollywood Historical Film* (Malden, Mass.: Blackwell, 2008), p. 14.
5. Manhola Dargis, "There Will Be Blood," *The New York Times,* December 26, 2007, available online at http://movies.nytimes.com/2007/12/26/movies/26bloo.html (August 1, 2008). My italics.
6. Burgoyne, *The Hollywood Historical Film,* p. 75.
7. R. J. Raack, "Historiography as Cinematography: A Prolegomenon to Film Work for Historians," *Journal of Contemporary History,* 18 (1983): 411–438; p. 416. Quoted in Robert A. Rosenstone, *Visions of the Past* (Cambridge, Mass.: Harvard University Press, 1995), p. 26.

8. And far closer to our time than the traditional epic as it is described by Derek Elley in *The Epic Film: Myth and History* (London: Routledge & Kegan Paul, 1984).

9. Thanks to Robert Burgoyne for pointing me in this direction.

10. Donna M. Campbell, "Forms of Puritan Rhetoric: The Jeremiad and Conversion Narrative," *Literary Movements,* available online at www.wsu.edu~campbell/amlit/jeremiad.htm (accessed January 10, 2009).

11. Unlike the Biblical jeremiad, the American jeremiad includes not only sermons, but also prose and poetry. The intention of the sermons and texts was to create not only caution and anxiety but also hope in the congregation. In contrast to the European predecessors, the American jeremiad adds a dimension of hope related to progress. See first and foremost Sacvan Bercovitch, *The American Jeremiad* (Madison, Wisc.: University of Wisconsin Press, 1978), or Sacvan Bercovitch, "The Jeremiad," in Sacvan Bercovitch (ed.), *The Cambridge History of American Literature, Vol. I* (Cambridge: Cambridge University Press, 1994). More on this below.

12. The music and soundscape in the movie is composed by Johnny Greenwood, from the British rock band Radiohead.

13. The only words spoken are Daniel's to himself ("There she is") when he finds the silver ore.

14. Pierre Sorlin, "Did Cinema Change Our Perception of the World?," key note presentation at Network for European Cinema Studies, Budapest, June 21, 2008.

15. I owe Professor Steffan Wahlgren thanks for sorting this out for me, since both Norwegian and English translators use different terms. The translation by Samuel Butler uses red as a general rule. In Greek, "kelainos" (dark and murky), and sometimes the word "melas" (black) are used.

16. Different translators use different descriptions, but for instance in the version translated by Samuel Butler (available online at www.sacred-texts.com/cla/homer/ili), the blood is described as black on some occasions, for instance in Book XI: "He laid him at full length and cut out the sharp arrow from his thigh; he washed the black blood from the wound with warm water; he then crushed a bitter herb, rubbing it between his hands, and spread it upon the wound; this was a virtuous herb which killed all pain; so the wound presently dried and the blood left off flowing."

17. Dargis, "There Will Be Blood."

18. Upton Sinclair, *Oil!* (New York: Penguin, 2008), p. 161. The blow-out has a different function in the novel, and Bunny is not hurt in the accident.

19. In the book, the role of Paul is more prominent.

20. On one occasion when Daniel is asked where his wife is, he claims that she died in childbirth, and although this is a lie, it could still have been the destiny of H.W.'s mother.

21. In the novel, the protagonist lives together with his mother and his sister, a widow, while the son's mother lives somewhere else. Although they are still married, Mrs. M. has relations with several other men.

22. I discuss the different representations of fatherhood in contemporary American cinema in an ongoing book project with the working title "Nobody Told You to Play Dad!" I have borrowed the term "single-father plot" from Bjarne Markussen, *Rettshistorier: Foreldre og barn i litteratur, film og lovgivning* (Oslo: Unipub, 2008).

23. See, for instance, *Pursuit of Happyness* (2006) or *Martian Child* (2007).

24. In his review, Roger Ebert claims that Daniel, "needs him (H.W.) as a prop." "There Will Be Blood," January 4, 2008, available online at http://rogere-bert.suntimes.com/apps/pbcs.dll/article?AID=/20080103/REVIEWS/801030301/1023 (accessed August 10, 2009).

25. Paul Thomas Anderson's work has often included dark depictions of fathers, most notably in *Magnolia* (1999).

26. As Svetlana Boym has argued, a nostalgic longing can be seen as a part of a common ideological perspective today: "It is the promise to rebuild the ideal home that lies at the core of many powerful ideologies of today." Svetlana Boym, *The Future of Nostalgia* (New York: Basic Books, 2001), p. xvi.

27. Linda Hutcheon, "Irony, Nostalgia, and the Postmodern" (1998), available online at www.library.utoronto.ca/utel/criticism/hutchinp.html (accessed February 19, 2010).

28. Exodus is a book clearly favored by Anderson, who previously borrowed the motif of frogs raining from the sky in *Magnolia*. See Exodus 8:5: "And the LORD spoke to Moses, Say to Aaron, Stretch forth your hand with your rod over the streams, over the rivers, and over the ponds, and cause frogs to come up on the land of Egypt."

29. Exodus 7:19.

30. Revelation 8:7.

31. Krishan Kumar, *Utopianism* (Buckingham: Open University Press, 1991), p. 8.

32. Campbell, "Forms of Puritan Rhetoric."

33. Andrew Wood, "The American Jeremiad," available online at www.sjsu.edu/faculty/wooda/149/149syllabus5jeremiad.html (accessed January 10, 2009).

34. Burgoyne, *The Hollywood Historical Film*, p. 78.

35. This speech, together with a speech earlier in the movie, is one of the few parts of the movies taken directly from the novel. Sinclair, *Oil!* pp. 37–38. The points about building a community are added in the script.

36. James Truslow Adams, *The Epic of America* (Boston, Mass.: Little, Brown, & Company, 1994), p. 415.

37. Bob Mondello, "There Will Be Blood," *NPR*, December 26, 2007, available online at www.npr.org/templates/story/story.php?storyId=89182767 (accessed August 15, 2009).

38. See www.wisegeek.com/what-is-a-jeremiad.htm (accessed August 10, 2009). See, for instance, Roger Ebert's review, "There Will Be Blood": "Watching the movie is like viewing a natural disaster that you cannot turn away from. By that I do not mean that the movie is bad, any more than it is good. It is a force beyond categories. It has scenes of terror and poignancy, scenes of ruthless chicanery, scenes awesome for their scope, moments echoing with whispers and an ending that in some peculiar way this material demands, because it could not conclude on an appropriate note—there has been nothing appropriate about it."

39. Bercovitch, "The Jeremiad," p. 265.

40. Bercovitch, "The Jeremiad," p. 257.

41. Wood, "The American Jeremiad."

42. Campbell, "Forms of Puritan Rhetoric."

43. At least he gives Eli this impression with his response, "That's fine," and by concluding the conversation by settling a time for the official opening of the well but without actually giving him a promise.

44. From my point of view, this humiliation would make for a better ending than the end chosen where Daniel ends up killing Eli.

45. Campbell, "Forms of Puritan Rhetoric."

46. David Denby, "*Hard Life*," "*There Will Be Blood*," "*Juno*," "*The Kite Runner*," *The New Yorker*, December 17, 2007, available online at www.newyorker.com/arts/critics/cinema/2007/12/17/071217crci_cinema_denby (accessed August 1, 2008).

47. Campbell, "Forms of Puritan Rhetoric."

48. Jeremiah 2:34. In the *American King James Version*, the text goes as follows: "Also in your skirts is found the blood of the souls of the poor innocents: I have not found it by secret search, but on all these."

49. Jeremiah 19:4.

50. I would like to thank Robert Burgoyne, Rikke Schubart, and Nina Lager Vestberg for their comments on earlier drafts of this chapter.

the body

in the epic

part five

the monstrous epic

deciphering mel gibson's

the passion of the christ

f o u r t e e n

a l i s o n   g r i f f i t h s

This chapter investigates medieval Christian iconography and Mel Gibson's 2004 film *The Passion of the Christ* as distinct but related ways of experiencing the "monstrous epic." This term describes how the epic properties of the Passion narrative, especially ideas of visual spectacle, immersion, the grotesque, and the carnal, transform Christ's body into a monstrous image that is simultaneously divine and abject. Inspired by Timothy K. Beal's suggestion that "we can learn something about a religious tradition by getting to know its monsters, and that we can learn something about monsters by looking into their religious backgrounds," my goal is to consider how *The Passion of the Christ* not only drew heavily upon iconographic and discursive representations of the Crucifixion derived from medieval image-making but also transformed the figure of Christ into a metaphorically overdetermined "monster" for twenty-first-century audiences who could barely look at the screen for the second half of the film.[1] Following a discussion of the striking parallels between the devotional practices of believers from the Middle Ages and contemporary viewers of Gibson's film, I will examine the "monstrous dimensions" of *The Passion of the Christ*, drawing upon the work of medievalist theorists John Block Friedman, Jeffrey Jerome Cohen, and Timothy K. Beal.

Centered around a male hero who is transfigured and whose body is spectacularized, *The Passion of the Christ* is a de-facto epic story, its lineage in cinema taking us back to such epic spectacles as Cecil B. DeMille's *The King of Kings* (1927) on the one hand and more iconoclastic and idiosyncratic depictions such as Martin Scorsese's *The Last Temptation of Christ* (1998) on the other. Few would dispute the fact that the epic is the genre of choice for biblical narratives of all stripes, where male bodies can be displayed in what Robert Burgoyne calls "the fulfillment of a heroic destiny and in which the founding moment of a community, of a people, is staged with maximum dramatic intensity."[2] Mel Gibson's *The Passion of the Christ* evoked the epic on both textual and paratextual levels, generating a public outcry in the wake of its Holy Week 2004 release and, even before it opened, attracting the attention of the Anti-Defamation League, who, along with a group of Jewish and Catholic scholars, began calling for Gibson to purge the film of anti-Semitic representations.[3] The traditional link between the epic and the "imagined community" of the nation described by Benedict Anderson is in this instance imagined as the foundational community of the Christian church (emblematized by the Apostles). Gibson's film conforms to the generic rules of the epic film with unabashed deference, and the twelve hours leading up to Christ's crucifixion and resurrection incarnates the male sacrifice theme found in the epic genre, as Burgoyne puts it, "the spectacle of the male figure riding, fighting, or moving 'through history' is . . . the keystone of the epic cinema, along with the violent brutality that finds the male hero mutilated and then symbolically restored."[4] And spectacle, as Derek Elley writes in *The Epic Film: Myth and History,* is the genre's "most characteristic trademark," with the Gospels considered literary epics with enormous potential for adaptation into epic cinema."[5]

But if Gibson's *The Passion of the Christ* ups the ante in terms of heightened moments of melodrama, extreme violence, hysteria, and a form of masochistic spectatorship isomorphic with medieval models of divine viewing, the film also eschews some of the conventionalized features of the genre. These include the monumental mise-en-scène, which is largely absent, the embarrassed pleasures Vivian Sobchack associates with epic film spectatorship, and, I would argue, even the "prereflective, popular, and 'undisciplined'" qualities Sobchack associates with the popular epic.[6] What made Gibson's film both a superlative expression of the epic and, paradoxically, an unraveling of the discursive underlay of the Christ film, was the rhetorical fallout around the film which was unlike anything that had preceded it, easily overshadowing complaints directed at DeMille's *The King of Kings* and sparking even wider public debate than *The Last Temptation of Christ.* But other characteristics of the film, such as the Aramaic dialogue with English subtitles and the casting of relatively unknown actors (mitigating the fact that "stars people the represented historical past with the present," according to Sobchack) reference an art-cinema aesthetic that distanced the film from the overblown mise-en-scène of the traditional Hollywood epic.[7] At the same time, the film created such an excess of carnal *displeasures* that many audience members reported that they had been put through an emotional wringer by the time they reached the closing credits.

Moving beyond traditional readings of the epic as an expression of nationalist mythology and aspirations, it is possible to read *The Passion of the Christ* as symptomatic of a rhetorical praxis in which the genre, in Sobchack's words, "*allegorically* and *carnally* inscribes on the model spectator a sense and meaning of being in time and human events in a manner and at a magnitude exceeding any individual temporal construction or appropriation."[8] Thus, the closing shot of a resurrected Christ staring somewhat menacingly with retribution in his eyes, serves as an allegory of pumped-up US nationalism in the wake of the 2003 US invasion of Iraq, which, as several critics observed, informed the reception of the film at the time. This is, of course, not uncommon in the epic, an enunciation of a "reflexive and reflective mode . . . [that] *temporally extends* the emplotment of the story from the past to the present and confers significance on the story from the present to the past," in Sobchack's words.[9]

Common to the medium-specific and historically distinct renderings of the narrative of Christ's death and resurrection—medieval iconography versus twenty-first-century Hollywood filmmaking—is a notion of the "revered gaze," a way of understanding how the act of viewing religious images and iconography is uniquely shaped by a framework of piety, that, depending on the onlooker's faith, affects how he or she perceive the content. But, as a discursive construct, the "revered gaze" also signals the spectacular form and content of the imagery (stained-glass windows and religious statuary are just two examples), modes of representation that tend to generate religious reverence and even awe in some spectators. In the case of the Hollywood epic, the "revered gaze" takes on a double meaning insomuch as spectators are often expected to express reverence at the sheer extravagance of the production, its excessive will to visibility that Sobchack describes as a "spectatorial invitation to indulge in wantonly expansive, hyperbolic, even hysterical acts of cinema."[10] One of the issues this chapter addresses is what happens to the revered gaze when the act of viewing becomes so difficult or untenable for the spectator, when the grotesque and monstrous threaten to transform the experience from one of religious piety to abject disgust, as I would argue happened for two-thirds of the screen time of *The Passion of the Christ*.

By reading Gibson's film alongside visual representations of the Passion from the Middle Ages, I hope to parse their unique signifying properties as visual representations of epic themes of self-sacrifice, renewal, and displays of masculinity, producing in the process a more historically sensitive account of how ideas of spectacle and immersion, largely peripheral in critical discussions of Gibson's controversial film, come to define the viewing experience of this epic narrative. But I want to move beyond prevalent discussions of Gibson's film in order to begin a more phenomenologically informed consideration of historical precedents for *The Passion of the Christ*'s textual forms and ideologies, since it is only by doing this that we can begin to understand how it constructs the idea of the "monstrous epic."[11] Writing about *The Passion of the Christ* is by no means an unproblematic task, however, and for this reason I will eschew the protocols of scholarly writing for a moment and admit that there is much I vehemently oppose in Gibson's hagiography. It is therefore impossible to write about Mel Gibson's *The Passion of the Christ* without passion; but this will not be vitriolic passion, razor-sharp polemic that slices through the film's weaknesses without considering why so many viewers were left speechless and with tears running down their cheeks when they walked out of the movie theater. My views on the film are neither suppressed nor the driving force here; *The Passion of the Christ* cries out for an interdisciplinary—as opposed to an incendiary—approach, and to that end I move freely between medieval, cinema, visual, and cultural studies.

My intervention also builds upon the increasing appropriation of postmodern theory within medieval studies, in particular work on monster theory much of which was inspired by John Block Friedman's seminal book *Monstrous Races in the Middle Ages.*[12] This chapter is also a response to medievalist Pamela Sheingorn's call for scholars to continually keep the Common Era in mind when conducting research, to excavate the "sedimentation of the Medieval" in contemporary discourse rather than simply view the Middle Ages as darkly "Other."[13] Addressing the late medievalist Michael Camille's criticisms of studies of the history of visuality for lumping together medieval ways of seeing into an "Edenic, free-floating era before the 'Fall' into the 'real world' of Renaissance perspectival vision," this essay is keenly aware of the "period eye" but also of its reverberations in contemporary image-making and representational practice.[14] While distinct media clearly present unique possibilities for representing the Passion narrative as an epic story of self-sacrifice in the service of a divinely plotted greater good that will redeem mankind, and there are obvious differences in how these themes play out in religious paintings, artifacts, illuminated manuscripts, Books of Hours (illustrated private prayer books), statuary, stained glass, architecture, furniture, and cinema, there are nevertheless remarkable consistencies in the aesthetics and practices of the crucifixion as an epic story that delivers the triple whammy of "violent spectacle, physical punishment and a contemplation of the male body."[15]

Given it is impossible, as art historian David Freedberg has argued, to know whether modern spectators responded in the same ways to religious artifacts as their thirteenth-century contemporaries, we can explore, in Freedberg's words, "why images elicit, provoke, or arouse the responses they do . . . and why behavior that reveals itself in such apparently similar and recurrent ways is awakened by dead form."[16] If conjecture is the only tool available to the analyst of such historically distant and ephemeral practices as medieval spectatorship, in the case of critical and popular responses to Gibson's *The Passion of the Christ,* we can, as Michel de Certeau reminds us, "tentatively analyze the function of discourses which can throw light on [our] question" since these discourses, "written after or beside many others of the same order" speak both *"of* history" while inescapably "already situated *in* history."[17] Our understanding of spectators' reactions to the monstrous transformation of Jesus in Gibson's film must acknowledge the fact that the very idea of the monstrous (and its etymological meanings) are inflected by a religious discourse, as Beal points out: "monster derives from the Latin *monstrum,* which is related to the verbs *monstrare* ('show' or 'reveal') and *monere* ('warn' or 'portend') which sometimes refers to a divine portend that reveals the will or judgment of the gods."[18]

More specifically, I argue that historical spectators were as intrigued and frequently moved by two- and three-dimensional representations of the crucifixion encountered in medieval cathedrals as were contemporary viewers of Mel Gibson's *The Passion of the Christ.* While Christian studies scholar Amy Hollywood's argument that film is a "radically different genre from the stories, prayers, and relatively static devotional images produced during the Middle Ages," is reasonable at first blush, it fails to acknowledge the echoes of a medieval aesthetic across time, and her claim that Gibson's film produces an "intensely corporeal meditative reenactment of the Passion" insinuates that nonfilmic media cannot deliver such a response.[19] Hollywood also admits elsewhere in her essay that as *The Passion of the Christ* draws to a close, the images become increasingly static, resembling "medieval and early modern religious paintings, sculptures, woodcuts, and manuscript illuminations derived from and often used as pictorial aids to the meditation on Christ's Passion."[20]

Thus, the space between the religious spectacle and the spectator— ways in which worshippers are invited to project themselves into the image or the breakdown of distinctions between witness and image—will be closely examined, especially the sensory appeal of religious iconography from the medieval period to the present. Of course, in pursuing this goal, I will be mindful of the way in which spectators across ages are able to maintain what W. J. T. Mitchell calls a "'double consciousness' toward images, pictures, and representations in a variety of media, vacillating between magical beliefs and skeptical doubts, naïve animism and hard-headed materialism, mystical and critical attitudes."[21] I will also consider the converse, the possibility that audiences fail to connect with the images due to Christ's mutation into the monstrous, which paradoxically sabotages audience identification with Christ or any of the other historical actors in the film. I conclude by arguing that the resurrection serves as a useful metaphor for making sense of the cathedral, motion picture, and even the epic, which in their own distinct ways (Bazinian in the case of cinema), all bring back the dead. The epic film achieves this though rematerializing the past, hefting History onto the screen in visually spectacular stories of male struggle and sacrifice. Ironically, the resurrection receives short shrift in Gibson's *The Passion of the Christ,* which should come as no surprise when we consider that medieval mystery plays, which also marginalized the Resurrection, serve as the film's hypertexts. The Passion play tradition of the Oberammergau is another potent iconographic influence in the film. According to theological historian John W. O'Malley, when Passion plays became popular from the end of the thirteenth century through the sixteenth century, a "common feature was the practical neglect of the Resurrection. The Stations of the Cross . . . were precisely that. They ended with the placing of Christ in the tomb."[22]

witnessing faith gibson style: revisiting the epic hagiopic

Mel Gibson's *The Passion of the Christ* opened on Ash Wednesday 2004 with Hollywood's highest-ever February weekend, making over $84 million in over 3,000 theaters (including $20 million on its opening day). By the end of the month, US box-office receipts reached the $300 million mark, and, according to Timothy K. Beal and Tod Linafelt, authors of *Mel Gibson's Bible,* one of several scholarly anthologies published in response to the film, by mid-June, the film had grossed $370 million, almost as much as *The Lord of the Rings: Return of the King*'s $377 million. Within a month of *The Passion of the Christ*'s Holy Week opening in Italy it had made $25 million, and the film broke box-office records in Latin America, Europe, and the Middle East. Two months after its opening, Gibson's film could claim the honor of being the year's highest-grossing film worldwide, having earned a remarkable $608 million.[23] Made with $25 million of Gibson's money (and by his own production company Icon Distribution Inc.), *The Passion of the Christ* was a lot more than a drama that, in Gibson's words, "unfolds rapidly and with searing realism."[24] It was a box-office goliath.

According to epic film scholars Bruce Babington and Peter William Evans, there are three main subgroups of the classic "Hollywood Biblical Epic": the Old Testament epic films, the Christ film, and the Roman/ Christian epic. On several levels, Gibson's film conforms to Babington's and Evans's topoi of the epic Christ film, which is narratively obligated to accept Christ's divinity either by "actively expressing belief" or at minimum "not actively expressing disbelief." What *The Passion of the Christ,* did, however, was take Babington and Evans's maxim that the Christ film "must mean most things to most men [sic]: literal belief for the believer, a metaphor of human aspiration for the unbeliever" and skew it to such an extent that constituents from both camps found it incredibly difficult to grasp the bigger picture of God's redemptive grand plan (believers and nonbelievers alike were freaked out by the human brutality and carnage taking up so much screen time).[25] Critics of *The Passion of the Christ* immediately seized upon what was perceived to be its ecumenical shortcomings, in particular the film's virulent anti-Semitic agenda, which reached a frenzy of the visible in the Sanhedrin scenes and the stomach-churning flagellation as seen in this still from the film (see Figure 14.1), delivering a graphic realism unsurpassed in previous cinematic renditions of the Passion narrative such as De Mille's *The King of Kings* (1927), Nicholas Ray's *King of Kings* (1961), George Stevens's *The Greatest Story Ever Told* (1965), and *The Last Temptation of Christ* (1998).

Babington and Evans's claim that the Hollywood Christian film is "bound into many specific conventions . . . of music, casting, acting styles, language, etc" was also turned on its head in *The Passion of the Christ,* a film that circumvented the star system Christ-impersonator Catch-22 by casting

Figure 14.1

The Passion of the Christ: The monstrous body of Jesus after the flagellation scene.

the unknown actor Jim Caviezel; by having the actors speak Latin (anachronistically) and Aramaic, instead of English; by appropriating the look and feel of a darker, arthouse film rather than the Technicolor gloss of the stereotypical widescreen epic; and finally by taking the image of the "Man of Sorrows," in which Christ's physical crucifixion wounds and suffering are graphically represented, to an entirely new level.[26]

Gibson was careful, however, not to throw the baby out with the bathwater in terms of resignifying the biblical epic for twenty-first-century audiences. What's interesting, though, is that very few critics talked about *The Passion of the Christ* as an epic film per se, focusing instead on the charges of anti-Semitism and R-rated violence. Thus, for many audience members and film critics, *The Passion of the Christ* most resembled a Gothic horror film hyperbolized for a violence-numbed contemporary audience, its meanings overdetermined by the larger geopolitical instability triggered by the US occupation in Iraq and the Bush Administration's crusade to remake the Middle East. Indeed, Camille's claim that medieval images were "so much more powerful, moving, and instrumental, as well as disturbing and dangerous than later works of art" has an ominous link to Gibson's film.[27]

But this is also an idiosyncratically *Gibson* film—part of his action-adventure oeuvre and apotropaic efforts to be a good Catholic; viewed this way, the film invites us to see it not only as a personal penance for a "crowd of modern moviegoing sinners in need of a dose of shock and awe," in *Entertainment Weekly*'s Lisa Schwartzbaum's words, but to exorcise Gibson's obsessions and demons.[28] Gibson's "identity," as media scholar Toby Miller has pointed out, is an extremely complex social sign, a combination of the nineteenth-century Irish larrikin (a white, male, uneducated, anti-authoritarian "lad") and its antithesis, the educated frat boy. Also part of Gibson's on-screen and off-screen personae are the "avengeful father/ Messiah figure, the right wing real estate magnate, and oleaginous businessman," in Miller's words.[29]

But *The Passion of the Christ*'s reverent pilgrims to the "multiplex shrine" only dimly echo the twelfth-century epoch of pilgrimages and the Crusades, when individuals undertook long, hazardous journeys across, in von Simson's words "the threshold that separates the known from the unknown, the customary from the wonderful."[30] The Franciscan practice of *via crucis*, observing the fourteen stages of the cross while on a pilgrimage, "amounted to the perfecting of a saint's imitation of Christ."[31] Marked as a devotee by dint of being on a pilgrimage, the reenactment of the Stations of the Cross during the journey invests the pilgrimage experience with another layer of spirituality; upon reaching the journey's end, pilgrims and crusaders alike crossed the border from the terrestrial into the holy, a sacred space where relics, such as pieces of the cross, replicas of the Veronica (the cloth given to Jesus on his way to Golgotha and also known as the *vernicle* or the *sudarium,* meaning cloth for wiping sweat), or even relics purporting to be the baby Jesus's foreskin became objects of veneration.[32]

We should also not lose sight of the larger cultural context in which ideas about performance in the Middle Ages circulated, since representations of the Passion have *always* provoked the ire of religious leaders, especially thirteenth-century iconophobes such as John Wycliffe and his successors, the Lollards, who wanted to see the church return to a more primitive (pure) state. Not only was there a "degree of medieval theoretical self-consciousness about performance," as Glending Olson argues, but medieval culture itself was "not monolithic in its views of performance," and representations of the Passion were seen as especially problematic in terms of performers bringing the role of Christ to life.[33] According to Olson, "a basic Christian distinction between wicked, human, and spiritual play obtained widespread cultural currency during the time," and that while "much significant thought . . . was concerned with mimesis, even more is concerned with questions of purpose and social role, the kinds of questions that one asks particularly about performance, where the relationship between presentations, response, and context are so immediate and perceptible."[34]

Even the act of pilgrimage, as the case of the medieval mystic extraordinaire and "autohagiographer" Margery Kempe so vividly illustrates, could be a performative—albeit dangerous—experience, where constructions of self are determined (or possibly overdetermined) by the outward display of religious fervor (in Kempe's case, uncontrollable crying and erotic envisioning of the body of Christ), a masquerade of sorts where one "becomes" a pilgrim, in part, through pilgrimesque behavior and the purchase of relics on the journey.[35] If the sacred reality medieval men and women sought in their encounter with religious emblems was ineffable, it could nevertheless be made present in the veneration of saints and their relics.[36] As David Morgan argues in his analysis of the history of visual piety, "just looking upon relics afforded the forgiveness of sin."[37] In an era where commodity fetishism and the accumulation of material wealth and products promising to radically enhance our lifestyles have largely replaced the worship of relics, it is striking to note the return of the relic in the religious merchandising spawned by *The Passion of the Christ,* including pewter crucifixion nail necklaces, replicas of the ones used in Gibson's film, offered for $16.99.[38] In addition, a total of 50,000 promotional DVDs were sent to clergy around the country asking that they be played for the congregations; a website supplied churches with hundreds of posters and postcards, and some 15,000 religious leaders were invited to advance screenings and 300 Passion summit meetings.[39]

What the medieval icon and motion picture share, on a phenomenological level at least, is their power to transform abstract ideas and representations of the world into a decipherable visual language that can be decoded by the spectator within an enclosed space (church or auditorium). Furthermore, over the centuries, audiences witnessing spectacular religious iconography didn't simply catch on to the notion of the affective power of religious iconography but had been exposed to the *idea* of images standing in for something absent (i.e. God) and thus being capable of eliciting powerful reactions (the Eucharist is a classic example of this) for a very long time. Thus, while it would be naive to equate Christian Metz's cinematic imaginary signifier to an act of faith, there are, nevertheless, similar kinds of psychic investments spectators of religious iconography and cinema are invited to make. A common feature of spectacular image-making is the idea of the whole exceeding the sum of its parts, offering the spectator an experience that hovers between real and unreal, now and then, natural and supernatural. These acts of viewing also take place in liminal spaces that hover between past and future, sacred and profane. During a medieval Passion play (or Gibson's film) awareness of the performance as staged while simultaneously "real," defines the experience as one of constant oscillation between two states of being.

I am thus arguing that the suspension of disbelief requisite for understanding films such as Gibson's *The Passion of the Christ* was also necessary for religious believers walking into a medieval cathedral in the thirteenth century; for some people at least, while in these architectural spaces, seeing is *believing.* The organization of vision in a cathedral shares something in common with the ways of seeing in cinema. For example, the organization of key iconic moments depicting the events surrounding Christ's crucifixion into narrativized scenes—the Stations of the Cross—refers to a series of fourteen crosses, usually accompanied by images, representing the Passion and its aftermath that developed in the Middle Ages as a devotional substitute for actually following the Via Dolorosa (Christ's route from Jerusalem to Calvary). In addition to representing an event, each station signifies the actual site where it took place and was usually placed along the walls of a church or chapel, outdoors such as on a pilgrimage site, or wayside shrine, or in a freestanding group.[40] The Stations of the Cross require spectators have a tacit understanding of the principles of editing, a series of tableaux standing in for a linear narrative. Taddeo Gaddi's paintings in the basilica of the Baroncelli Chapel in Sante Croce, Florence, for example, a richly decorated private space where wealthy merchant families were commemorated, are comprised of rectangular images organized around a central window that resemble the edited scenes one might find in a film of the Nativity. Besides representing emblematic moments from the Nativity, the images painted around the lancet windows are also concerned with light: the Annunciation of the Virgin, the flash of light awakening the shepherds, and the Magi kneeling before a vision point to the association of light with revelation and serve as a visual complement to the light streaming through the actual window.[41]

The Gothic cathedral and motion-picture auditorium all employ technologies for "engaging beholders in certain visual forms" and with a propensity toward epic spectacle, whether in the form of brilliant stained-glass windows, sculptural art, intricately carved ceiling bosses, misericords, frescoes, etc. These are images that ask a great deal of us, as W. J. T. Mitchell argues in his book *What Do Images Want?* According to Mitchell, "magical attitudes toward images are just as powerful in the modern world as they were in so-called ages of faith."[42] These images are all concerned with a suprareality, a reality beyond the experiential grasp of the average person (according to von Simson, "cathedral architecture was designed and experienced as a representation of an *ultimate* reality").[43] There is, however, an important difference in how each form functions as a signifying practice; as Simson notes, "the tie that connects the great order of Gothic architecture with a transcendental truth is not that of optical illusion" (how can an architectural space be read as an "image" of Christ?) but rather Christian symbolism, or more accurately, the concept of analogy (the degree to which God can be discerned in an object).[44] As an architectural "language," the Gothic style developed local dialects, all of which strove to capture the ultimate reality of Christian faith, the "symbol of the kingdom of God on earth."[45]

Elaborating objects and architecture into a visual style that bespoke a coherent sacred experience was the function of much Gothic art, a point underscoring the centrality of sight and vision in medieval cosmology. These technologies of wonder foreground the act of looking as an intrinsic part of the experience; for medieval spectators, the icon engendered a corporeal gaze and a haptic quality, "a look that touches" and that offers a stimulus for an identification with the suffering Christ, through the *imitatio Christi* in which the body "participated in an integrated devotional practice of imitating Christ, of imagining him in one's own body."[46] But how were spectators invited to take up certain stances (both literally, in terms of prostrations, and figuratively) within the scopic regimes of medieval visuality? What were the defining features of the spectacle that greeted audiences upon entering their respective exhibition sites? It is to the representation of the Crucifixion and its shifting iconography that we now turn.

the revered gaze: epic spectatorship as witnessing

> "*A torture film of singular blood and brutality.*"[47]
> "*A profoundly medieval movie . . .*"[48]

Medieval art was a highly codified way of representing terra firma and the celestial heavens; the rules governing the representation of angels, devils, saints, and the natural world, that a circular nimbus placed vertically behind the head expressed sanctity, for example, were tacitly understood by medieval spectators.[49] The *varietas* or pictorial richness of images incorporating flowers, animals, and architectural structures left an imprint on beholders, who, with varying degrees of sophistication, mined images for their symbolic value. Palimpsests were the order of the day; even time was multilayered, with past, present, and future at Chartres, for example, coexisting "simultaneously in the visual integration of the three doorways," the movement of time organized vertically as one's gaze follows the columns upwards.[50] The rules and pleasures elicited by medieval art were by no means simple, however; according to art historian Frank Kendon, "Medieval art had humor, horror, the grotesque, and a quaint expressive ugliness," all of which made it a highly expressive art form.[51] Few would disagree with Kendon's summoning of horror and the grotesque as fitting adjectives; indeed, "medieval" is widely used as a synonym to characterize an experience that is gruesome, brutalizing, or at the very least unpleasant.

If one accepts Morgan's argument that "the act of looking" is itself inextricably bound to one's religious identity and "constitutes a powerful practice of belief," it is possible to see how submitting one's gaze to an image of Jesus nailed to the cross can be read as an act of visual piety. But when was the crucifixion first represented in the visual arts and what impact did the gradual introduction of more graphic realism have on the spectator's reactions to the image of suffering? It is in the Carolingian period, c. ad 600—1000, that we first see a desire on the part of Christians for a visualization of the crucifixion, and it was during this period that the image of the dead Christ on the cross first made its appearance in the West; indeed, as Hahn points out, "although the contemplation of the cross was a much-recommended visual exercise, its promise was limited."[52] However, representations of the crucifixion during this period were not in the least bit concerned with realism or narrative; as Kendon notes, Christ's death was represented from a doctrinal and passive point of view with "no attempt at expressing anguish." Fully robed and lying, as opposed to being nailed, to the cross, the crucified Christ is shown alone and in no apparent discomfort.

However, the thirteenth and fourteenth centuries usher in two new developments: first, a desire to represent the crucifixion with heightened verisimilitude via the "Man of Sorrows" trope, including, as religious art historian Gertrud Schiller points out in her study of Christian iconography, a shift toward extending the realism to the reactions and emotions of those who witnessed the event, and second, an interest in giving expression to Mary's suffering as she becomes a second object of meditation on the Passion.[53] Schiller sees this as a pivotal moment in the history of Christian art: "Biblical events are no longer interpreted; they are brought home to the spectator in a personal, visual confrontation. This relationship, in which the believer, in his [sic] meditations, follows Christ's way to the Cross, is reflected in pictorial realism."[54] Christ's body is no longer fully robed, his genitals are covered only by a loincloth, and bleeding wounds inflicted by the crown of thorns and sword insertions are increasingly depicted. The representation of blood and greater emphasis on physical pain is connected not only to the veneration of holy blood, as Schiller points out, but part of a larger shift toward more realistic depictions of the crucifixion; as Kendon argues, "The denuding of the body of Jesus proceeds: men began to study the anatomy of agony. . . . His head droops; blood issues from the five wounds; his body sags under its own weight; the crown of thorns is added; and the abdominal muscles reveal the intensity of his suffering."[55] But as Camille notes (echoing medievalist Mary Carruthers), this shift must be understood not simply as part of the move toward heightened verisimilitude in the Middle Ages but inextricably bound to the notion of memory as affect; thus, "it was not so much that the image of Christ as the 'Man of Sorrows' was 'realistic' that made this striking new image such a resonant one, but the fact that the emaciated body, the blood, the gaze of the suffering man/God carried them physically into the mind."[56] But representing Christ realistically is also, as Steinberg argues, justified in the faith itself: "the rendering of the incarnate Christ ever more unmistakenly flesh and blood [which began in the Renaissance] is a religious enterprise because it testifies to God's greatest achievement. . . . The pivotal moment in the history of the race was God's alliance with the human condition."[57] One cannot help think that this desire to imprint the image of Christ on the cross as an indelible sign of ultimate sacrifice and suffering was also an important goal for Mel Gibson's *The Passion of the Christ* beyond the hyperrealism of the brutalized body; for many Christian viewers of the film the emblematic imagery certainly heightened the devotional quality of the experience.

Notwithstanding this epistemic shift in visualizing the crucifixion, two other major influences have shaped the history of imaging Jesus Christ up to *The Passion of the Christ:* on the one hand, a Eurocentric bias in the suppression of Jesus's ethnicity as a first-century Palestinian Jew; and second, what Morgan sees as a "dense intericonic space" that can be traced to the fourth or fifth centuries. Morgan's argument that every representation of Christ is part of an "interpretation of an ongoing tradition of imaging Jesus" seems especially relevant in the case of Gibson's *The Passion of the Christ,* since Gibson eschews contemporary conventional constructions of Jesus à la Warner Sallman, whose 1940 *Head of Christ* and *Sacred Heart of Jesus* have become "powerful symbols in American Protestant and Catholic piety," and instead reaches back to the medieval period.[58]

Furthermore, Morgan's observation that each image is "tailored to the situation of an image maker, the market that manufactures and disseminates the image, and the public that beholds it" suggests both Gibson's exploitation of the *Braveheart*-inspired, pumped-up masculinity that is a defining feature of *The Passion of the Christ* and his own brand of orthodox Catholicism.

Figure 14.2

The Passion of the Christ: Christ on his way to be crucified.

That Gibson was drawing upon a medieval sensibility in depicting the final twelve hours of Christ's life goes without saying and became something of a leitmotif in the film's critical discourse. For example, for British critic Deborah Orr, Gibson's "dubious achievement" was to have "married the aesthetics of medieval obsession with the unflinching shock values of popular culture," while Jeff Simon of the *Buffalo News* felt as if Gibson "wanted to take his audience back before the Renaissance to the gore of artistic medievalism."[59] Jonathan Romney, writing in the British *Independent*, went the furthest in making the medieval connection when he argued that "With its punishing sensibility, the film does nothing for cinema . . . except to help us imagine how things might have been if the *art form had been invented in the eleventh century*."[60] Peter Steinfels offered a more nuanced reading when he argued that "the Passion-centered spirituality [that] arose in the Middle Ages and is therefore all too easily dismissed as medieval . . . was kept alive in the hymns and devotions of some strands of Protestantism but especially in the mystical fervor and visual imagery of Counter-Reformation Catholicism."[61]

Transformed into "live-action tableaux," the ritualized Stations of the Cross serve as the film's dramatic architecture, especially for Catholic viewers who may be more responsive to the emblematic, reenactment formula used by Gibson. *World Magazine* critic Andrée Seu, who analogized the experience of watching the film to Gibson taking us "by the hand along the church nave walls to pause between each stained glass eye and bow before Twelve Stations of the Cross, as once we children did on many a Good Friday" grasped both the narrative and coercive underpinnings of the film.[62] Moreover, Steinfels's argument that the "movie reignites religious embers that may have cooled over the years" is a reference both to Gibson's resignification of the Passion as an inexorably violent event, a "chamber of horrors gore . . . unique in the history of Bible movies" in the words of MSNBC film critic John Hartl, and to the film's anti-Semitism and ecumenically suspect history.[63] While it is impossible to extrapolate responses to graphic depictions of Christ's suffering from the historical archive, in part because we are haunted, in Michel de Certeau's words, "by presuppositions . . . by 'models' of interpretation that are invariably linked to a contemporary situation of Christianity," we can nevertheless still draw some tentative conclusions on the nature of historical Passion spectating from the representations themselves;[64] in other words, how artists chose to represent the Passion betrays a good deal about popular perceptions of such notions as realism, torture, suffering, spectacle, and the interpellation of the spectator into the scene.

enfleshed sensations: blood, more blood, and the figure of the monstrous

There is no denying the fact that Christ becomes "monstrous" in Gibson's *The Passion of the Christ,* especially after the flagellation when so much of his skin peels from his body. A number of reviewers singled out Gibson's representation of Christ's flagellation as an extreme and especially sadistic act of brutalization. For some viewers, the violence made it extremely hard to connect with the movie, since Christ was reduced, in the words of one viewer, to "this bloody creature."[65] First appearing in the twelfth century in sculpture, by the thirteenth century the flagellation was represented in stained glass, wall paintings, and, most commonly, on Passion altars.[66] By the baroque period, relatively private meditations on Christ's suffering that had been the norm in the late Middle Ages moved out of the realm of the contemplative and into the public sphere of the church. If for some viewers of Gibson's *The Passion of the Christ,* the "gobbets of flesh dislodged from Christ's back by the flagellators (that) stain the flagstones" pushed them over the edge, forcing them to reject the film as little more than a "sacramental splatter movie," then it was obviously a form of visual piety that broke with normative significatory practice by representing Christ's suffering as heightened expressionist drama rather than naturalism.[67] Gibson showed little restraint in tempering the realism of the brutality, using cinema's mimeticism to "crucify every viewer," in the words of one critic, and with a love of carnage that even outdid Matthias Grünewald's extremely graphic 1515 Isenheim altarpiece of the crucifixion.[68] Indeed, Grünewald is just one of several hypertextual/intertextual referents in the film that journalist Jack Miles identifies, in this case, the image of Christ's hand contracting into a claw the moment the nail pierces it, which is eerily similar to Christ's hand in the Isenheim crucifixion painting.[69]

Gibson credits some of his influences in the preface to the book accompanying the film—Caravaggio, Mantegna, Masaccio, Piero della Fransesca—artists whose paintings, Gibson informs us, "were as true to their inspiration as I wanted the film to be of mine." However, as Gibson acknowledges, "it is one thing to paint one moment of The Passion and be true to it; it is quite another to dramatize the entire mysterious event."[70] Once again, we see Gibson, whether consciously or not, playing into a tradition that dates back at least to the Renaissance of venerating realism in painterly style as coterminous with faith, the idea, in Steinberg's words, that "realism, the more penetrating the better, was consecrated a form of worship."[71]

The representation of Christ's torturers as sadistically enjoying their work, a trope that Gibson exploits to the hilt, goes back to early images of the flagellation scene (which from the early fifteenth century onward show Christ completely naked) and crucifixion; indeed, Olson refers to a medieval "sermon exemplum" uncovered by Siegfried Wenzel suggesting that "performers taking on the role of Christ's torturers in a passion play enjoyed what they were acting out on stage, perhaps to the point that their revelry came to obscure or interfere with the presumably religious goals of the presentation."[72] Gibson's torturers come from a long lineage of gruesome, sadistic soldiers. In Arnoul Gréban's *The Mystery of the Passion: The Third Day,* the miniature image of the flagellation shows the soldiers energetically engaged in their work, almost appearing as if they are dancing upon the elaborate black and white tile pattern on the floor. Halfway down the folio, the stage direction, "They spit in his face" appears, proffering evidence that while the manuscript is primarily aimed at the reader, there are nevertheless ample indications of performative elements, the text not so much recording as *evoking* the idea of performance. Another stage direction reads, "here they beat him for a while without speaking."[73] Clearly we have no idea how long this beating might have ensued.

What the close-ups of Christ's grotesque body in *The Passion of the Christ* suggest, therefore, is that, as medievalist Joyce Tally Lionarons argues, "the boundary between human and monster has been shown to be permeable, and the [viewer] necessarily remains conscious of how easy it would be, in the absence of direct textual pointers to the contrary, to mistake the saint for the monster and the monster for the saint."[74] Christ is also doubly Othered in this film, never fully human thanks to the Holy Trinity, and barely human by the end of the film due to his physical deformity. Working with Cohen's construction of the monster as a dangerous hybrid that refuses to "participate in the classificatory 'order of things'" gives us a provocative, if controversial handle on how some spectators may have responded to Gibson's representation of Christ as a brutalized sign, virtually emptied of meaning beyond that of symbolizing hatred and man's inhumanity to man.[75] The relentless violence reminiscent of the slasher horror genre, along with the Devil carrying the deformed baby seem to legitimize Beal's contention that there are "cases where the monstrous-chaotic is *identified with* the divine" and that monsters are never stable signifiers but "conglomerations of many different forms of otherness—cosmological, political, psychological and religious otherness."[76]

Gibson's fascination with the monstrous in *The Passion of the Christ* has disturbing corollaries to ways of seeing the monstrous Other from the Middle Ages, speaking to medievalist Mary B. Campbell's argument that the "grotesque is a mode of vision we invoke for the purposes of entertainment: it is expressive, symbolic, shocking, but never mimetic."[77] Moreover, despite the recency of the term "grotesque" as an aesthetic judgment, the idea of the grotesque as a representational mode is far older, "its effects accessible to an eleventh century reader as well as to our ourselves" in Campbell's words.[78] Margaret M. Miles contends that Gibson drew inspiration for his grotesque rendition of Christ's last twelve hours from "grotesquely suffering Crucifixion images of the Spanish-influenced southwestern United States. Contorted bodies, blood, and anguished expressions are featured in this art, for which the suffering of oppressed and marginalized people provides the context."[79]

However, in order to fully understand the impact of representational shifts in crucifixion iconography and to gain better traction on the Christ film as a cinematic epic, we must contextualize the Passion within a larger epistemological framework and consider the role of violence as a whole in medieval and early Renaissance culture. Medievalist Jody Enders points out that while violence has been a consistent feature of cultures going back at least to the first century, the question of "how audiences were to discern which violent, bloody struggles it was acceptable to enjoy is a question to which writers keep returning."[80] Thus, in the US at least, we find ourselves in a culture riddled with contradictions vis-à-vis the kinds of representations of violence considered acceptable versus those considered taboo, with the Christian right pressuring public officials to morally legislate the entertainment industry. While avoiding the claim that violent medieval dramatizations of the Passion are identical to contemporary performances or rituals of self-mutilation (such as the 1995 Easter celebrations that took place in the Philippines, where believers were crucified with thin nails that had been dipped in alcohol), Enders does not deny that they both engender a "pleasure, obsession, or fascination eternally aroused in audiences."[81]

This troubling surplus of dangerous pleasure was one of the reasons why the performance of miracle plays came under attack in the classic antitheatrical manifesto *A Tretise of Miraclis Pleyinge* (written sometime between 1380 and 1425) and characterized by Clifford Davidson as the "longest and most significant piece of dramatic criticism in Middle English."[82] While the term "miraclis" in the document seems to refer to a broad range of dramatic activity and representation, religious drama, especially performances of the Passion are singled out as "utterly reprehensible."[83]

Medievalist Garth Epp goes so far as to argue that it is concern with "lustis of the fleyssh," mentioned innumerable times in the *Tretise,* that really rubs the authors the wrong way; as Epp explains, the *Tretise*

> treats theatrical performance and spectatorship as themselves inherently sexual activities, most dangerously so when they are centered on a representation of the actions and body of Christ . . . [which], unlike any other, must be seen as utterly antithetical to lechery; its theatrical representation cannot be seen to provoke erotic desire.[84]

And yet, as Leo Steinberg magisterially demonstrates in his book-length essay on the sexuality of Christ, this touchy subject demands careful scrutiny, not only because it is closely connected to complex issues of realism in representation, but because it functions as a demonstrative sign, bespeaking an "aboriginal innocence which in Adam was lost."[85] The countless Renaissance paintings in which the infant Christ's penis is not only exposed but touched, prodded, tweaked, fondled, shielded, and stared at in moments that range from the sublimely tender to the unsettlingly bizarre was a risqué interlude indeed, a phase of "exceptional daring" for Christianity, "when the full implications of Incarnational faith were put forth in icons that recoiled not even from the God-man's assumption of sexuality" in Steinberg's words.[86]

Gibson's *The Passion of the Christ* ironically brings us full circle with regards to an *imperative* element underlining both medieval *mystères* (mystery plays) and Gibson's film: just as medieval religious theater saw no alternative to portraying physical suffering, since torture, rhetoric, and law were complicit in the construction of a medieval truth system that was as violent as it was theatrical, so too did Gibson, in an ostensive act to "profoundly change people," see no other option than to "push viewers over the edge."[87] Philosopher Mark Wrathall puts it this way: "Gibson's depiction makes perfect sense if the point is precisely to show that Christ's suffering is not rationalizable, and that one's response to the absurdity of his suffering must be put at the center of one's faith."[88] Consistent with his onscreen portrayals of avenging, sadomasochistic heroes, Gibson was probably acutely aware of the Janus-faced nature of violence and torture; as Enders argues, "whether the representations are dramatic, cinematic, literary, or juridico-political, nothing reviles the imagination more than torture. Yet nothing titillates it more."[89] But can we really compare the Catholic bornagain self-aggrandizing Gibson to a medieval dramatist staging the Passion for a community performance? Or, more to the point, what does it mean in terms of furthering our understanding of the history of the epic and visual spectacle, to compare the special effects Gibson employs in order to represent Christ's suffering (dramatic music and slow motion) with the theatrical effects of the medieval mystery play?

In the 1547 Passion play staged at Valenciennes, special stage effects were used to create the illusion of flowing blood from the bodies of the Innocents when they are massacred and from Christ's wounds in the crucifixion scene.[90] These illusions, as French medieval-theater scholar Darwin Smith points out, would have been the responsibility of a prop master trained in special effects, including the flash of light created with mirrors that appears on Christ's face after the transfiguration.[91] The appearance of blood loss was created via a mixture of vermilion and water added to a hydraulic system that moved the liquids from a barrel into pipes hidden behind the body of the actor playing Christ (the addition of different liquids would alter the pressure in the pipes and create the illusion of oozing bodily fluids). With blood seeping from every pore, "spattering upon the earth, such that the entire set 'glistens with blood,'" in the words of Enders, special-effects masters in the Middle Ages performed

> all manner of technological miracles . . . flesh-suits with pre-imprinted gash marks, unpeeled layer by layer and with great slight of hand as the scourging progresses. The brutality is so overwhelming that viewers feel they must turn away, yet they are compelled to watch this piece of instructional entertainment that has been provided by their culture, by their community, and by their church.[92]

Gibson was clearly not the first producer of a Passion play to rely upon special effects to deliver not only conventions of the epic genre but also to generate shock, empathy, anger, and a twinge of pleasure in the spectator. He was most certainly not the first to promote the idea that "bloodshed and belief went hand in hand (or hand in fist) with graphic, spectacular violence."[93] The profusion of blood in *The Passion of the Christ* would therefore have not been at all out of place in the *Mistère de la Sainte Hostie* held in Metz, France, in 1513, during which, as one contemporaneous spectator tells us, "there emerged a great deal of blood . . . until the whole center stage glistened with blood and the whole place was full of blood . . . And all this was accomplished by devices and hidden places."[94] And yet one crucial difference must be noted: sometimes the violence in Middle Ages performances was actually happening on stage with stage directions for the Sainte Geneviève *Passion* specifying that "blows upon the body of Jesus must be genuine, not imitated." There is also uncorroborated mention of the possibility of condemned criminals substituting for actors so that they could be burned alive on stage.[95]

Expectation thus plays a huge role in the encounter between spectator and religious spectacle and never more so than in the epic. When viewing religious spectacle, one *expects* a somatic engagement that could be as extreme as the *imitatio Christi* or as innocuous as possessing an image of Christ that returns one's gaze. Each of these spectacular modes of representing the Crucifixion foregrounds an immersive and interactive gaze, the idea that the act of looking not only demands more of the spectator—a bodily engagement in the case of *imitatio Christi*—but somehow delivers more.[96] But there is an important difference here in theatrical stagings of Passion plays and versions rendered on film, differences that speak to the representation and consumption of flesh (and other modalities that I won't focus on here); according to Epp, "in medieval English passion plays, Christ repeatedly, even insistently, offers his flesh for the gaze of others, both on and off the stage."[97] In the cinema, that flesh is transposed onto the screen via the magic of light, and the looking relations, while similar in terms of the construction of the gaze, are by no means identical. The "all-too-human body" of the medieval passion-play actor on display "invites our collective gaze, and the meditative tradition of *imitatio Christi* invites our identification with that body's suffering," although in the case of the complete performances of the York plays, this would have resulted in no fewer than twenty-four actors playing the adult Christ in successive pageants, each in multiple performances, "one God in many persons," as Epp puts it.[98] "Seeing" Christ was neither a predictable nor consistent experience for either mystery-cycles audiences or for those viewers of James Caviezel (voted one of the fifty most beautiful people in the world by *People* magazine in 2004).[99] Desiring Christ's body as an ecumenical sign told only half the story; identification with Christ's body, especially when that body was played by a large number of the town's young men, might have been based upon any number of variables including how one's version of Christ matched up to the various body types, visages, homoerotic or heterosexual desire, or nondescript notions of "Christness." But when that body becomes so extremely monstrous, as it does in Gibson's *The Passion of the Christ,* then we are reminded of medievalist Jeffrey Jerome Cohen's idea of the monster as a "category that is itself a kind of limit case, an extreme version of marginalization."[100] Cohen's definition of the monster could in fact be an adequate description of Jesus insofar as his Holy Trinity identity and ability to perform miracles is, as Cohen argues, an "embodiment of difference, a breaker of category, and a resistant Other known only through process and movement, never through dissection-table analysis."[101] Gibson's Jesus, perhaps more than any other representation in the history of the hagiopic, comes closest I feel to Cohen's definition of the monster.

334 In the discourse surrounding *The Passion of the Christ,* the conventional protocol of viewing was often replaced by the idea of experiencing the film, a characteristic, one could argue, of epic spectatorship in general; for example, film critic David Reinhardt said that "experienced would probably be a better word" than "saw" to describe his encounter with a film that came across as "more of a meditation than a movie."[102] A pastor quoted in the *Milwaukee Journal Sentinel* offered a similar response when he opined, "I think what is very important to understand, having seen the film, is it is

an *experience.* Like powerful art does, it moves you, it demands a response from you."[103] According to some press accounts, audiences purportedly did not leave the theatre until the final credit had rolled, and the only sound that punctured the eerie silence reported in many screenings was that of quiet sobbing (the other three women at the sparsely attended matinee I went to were visibly crying as they left the auditorium). The sobbing by Christian audiences during the brutal scenes was a response to "images deeply embedded in a collective religious imagination," in the words of religion-studies scholar Karen Jo Torjesen, the source for such imagery originating "not with the early Christian martyrs but in the Irish monastic roots of medieval penitentiary piety."[104]

Audience responses to the intense emotional experience of watching Christ being crucified reminds us not only of some of the traditional messages embedded in the epic genre, in this case the idea of the birth of Christianity through the sacrifice of God's son on earth, but is also evocative of the magical implications of images which Nicolas Calas writes about in his book *Transfigurations,* namely the illusion of communication that stems from the "magical belief that two similar objects, such as the portrait and the model, are identical."[105] In this respect, a "portrait [or film] can be worshipped like an idol . . . and expected to hearken to our prayer."[106] Responses from viewers of *The Passion of the Christ* confirm these comparisons: "It was like being at the foot of the cross," said one spectator from Ohio, while another viewer from Salem, North Carolina, compared watching the film to viewing television news footage of the burning Twin Towers in lower Manhattan.[107] By exploiting the religious iconography and aesthetic tenor of medieval Passion plays, Gibson addresses us as self-doubters whose faith will be reaffirmed by this conversion film, although, as Susannah Heschel argues, the idea of the film converting nonbelievers is superceded by a quite different goal, namely, "to reveal those in its audience who are saved and those who are not."[108] Not all spectators, however, experienced *The Passion of the Christ* in the same way, just as medieval spectators would have responded to Passion plays with their own sense of pathos, shock, horror, disbelief (or none of the above). What extant commentaries on medieval performance such as the *Tretise* reveal is that "medieval audiences were clearly aware of varied dimensions of the dramatic activity they saw" and that performances were complex enough in tone that they engendered harsh critiques, including the attacks on stagings of Christ's Passion singled out in the *Tretise.*[109]

But there is one fundamental flaw in Gibson's "vision" that Gibson himself acknowledged was heavily influenced by Anne Catherine Emmerich's book *The Dolorous Passion of Our Lord Jesus Christ,* which documents with excruciatingly gruesome detail her proto-cinematic "visions" of the Passion. As Jody Enders points out in her essay "Seeing is Not Believing," "the very truths that violence holds to be self-evident by dint of its so-called realism are not evident simply because they are seen."[110] If we accept Enders' basic premise that "religious faith is based on what people *cannot* see, unless they happen to bear witness to a miracle," equating verisimilitude with historical truth or fact is fundamentally misguided.[111] Our interpellation into the roles of eyewitnesses to a gruesome event—spectators of French Passion plays were actually called *témoins oculaires*—does not guarantee or authenticate the realism of the violence. When a viewer's "authentically powerful emotions feel like historical fact," and when the unfamiliar languages spoken in the film deliver a second dose of purported realism, chances are we will most likely get sucked into mistaking representation for reality; as Enders bluntly puts it: "not all the Latin or Aramaic in the world can transmute verisimilitude into truth or perspective into dogma. Contemporary audiences are in no better position to judge the alleged accuracy of these languages than were their medieval forebears."[112] What the Aramaic and fifth-century ecclesiastical Latin dialogue does accomplish in the film (the Roman soldiers, sociolinguists inform us, would have actually spoken Greek) is to privilege the film's image track, and, coupled with the assertive editing, slow motion, digitally produced demons, melodramatic score, and repeated close-ups of Jesus's face, helps hone our attention to a heavily corporealized Christ (rather than a spiritually Incarnated God) that substitutes for his lack of interiority and psychological depth. A relatively small detail such as Jesus's lips, which, by the end of the film, are grotesquely chapped, assumes a metonymic relationship to the representation of suffering as a whole. This also relates to William G. Little's reservations about the "matter of Incarnation" in the film, the way in which the "only aspects of the person with which the viewer is permitted familiarity are the body's surfaces and extremities: a swollen eye, matted tips of hair, gouged-out chunks of flesh, crucified hands and feet."[113]

That *The Passion of the Christ* offered viewers an experience that somehow transcended the protocols and pleasures of ordinary moviegoing should come as no surprise. Gibson's eschewal of point-of-view shots and his disavowal of identification with any specific character throughout the film means that, as Mark D. Jordan and Kent L. Brintnall argue, "the point of view is always slightly different from that of the disciples, Jesus, or Satan."[114] There is also something familiar in the references in the critical discourse surrounding Gibson's film to feeling immersed in the image or virtually present at the crucifixion. One only has to look at the history of crucifixion iconology to see that religious onlookers have long assumed the role of virtual witnesses to the event, identifying with the crying crowd at Golgotha, for example, or in the case of a painting of the Madonna and child, deeply moved by the sensation of Mary coming "toward us out of the picture."[115] Not only did Mary feel compassion for Jesus's suffering on the cross, but also *co*-passion, experiencing the event as if in her actual body.[116] Maia Morgenstern's performance as Mary in Gibson's *The Passion of* the *Christ* corresponds closely to that of the twelfth-century Passion play *Ludud de Passione* from The Benediktbeuren Passion Play, in which Mary delivers such lines as "Was there ever such torment / And such terrible anguish? / Now perceive the torment, agony, and death / And the entire body red with blood" (the accompanying stage direction reads "Again the Mother of the Lord, with every sort of lamentation, bewailing greatly, cries out to the weeping women, complaining vehemently").[117]

Countless accounts of how mystics, saints, and sometimes ordinary citizens communicated the passion through their bodies attest to the performative nature of the Passion as an epic narrative, subject to diverse appropriations, including extension to the Last Judgment, and elision, to represent only the last twelve hours of Jesus's life as in Gibson's film. As R. N. Swanson observes, "Passion narrative structure allows individual events to be highlighted, or the isolation of particular sequences," although "different depictions, manifestations, manipulations, produce different responses, especially if further complicated by regional variations."[118] This point suggests that, while correspondences can be traced over time, the Passion story as an *epic* story is an especially open text, not so much a blueprint for performance but a series of emblematic tableaux. The performance of the Passion narrative, especially in the case of devotional images involving representations of the instruments of the Passion (the *arm Christi*) including the hosts, chalice, and a pelican in piety, allows the devotee to "transport the Christ-who-suffered into the present, to become the Christ-who-suffers," so that the man of sorrows context shifts from that of the Passion to that of the Eucharist, from a past event to one which may be both present and future.[119]

the spectrality of devotional imagery: is seeing really believing?

The striking correspondences among medieval iconography and *The Passion of the Christ* do not evoke a consistent theological message or ideology so much as a suggestion of how the epic signifies over time and has very little connection with its original meaning—the term derives from the Greek *epos* (word), which in its plural form, *epea,* the Greeks used to describe heroic songs of Homer[120]—and how vision, spectacle, and, above all, affect are discursively constructed and manipulated in each medium, how vision can engender a feeling of copresence so that "people feel themselves to be in a more direct relationship with the living God because of the imaginative power of newly animated images."[121] How else can we explain why so many spectators were deeply moved by *The Passion of the Christ?* And while there is validity in Swanson's argument about the role of context as a key determination in Passion experiences ("The response evoked by a triptych publicly displayed in a church will not match that by a miniature in a private Book of Hours. . . . A play watched and enjoyed will not produce the same mental state as a text meditated on . . . [and] the domestic setting of a tapestry, the decorative function of a piece of jewelry, will likewise produce different responses, may lose all connotations of devotion, and pass into furniture"[122]), it runs the risk of eliding points of similarity across devotional speech acts whose utterances, while context-bound, are never completely overdetermined by that context. Shock, horror, the monstrous, pathos, anger, and peace all might be engendered by any one of the examples Swanson cites; as Gibson's film reminds us, we may have come full circle to the visceral reactions elicited by medieval Passion plays that, like Gibson's film, transform their hero into a monstrous vision by the end of the play.

I have argued in this chapter that these historically distinct ways of representing epic religious spectacle share one feature: they all offer spectators access to things beyond ordinary ways of seeing. For the devout, the knowledge to be gained from medieval art, a crucifixion panorama, or a film about the Passion, is knowledge that, despite being familiar (almost everyone knows the story of the Passion), is "expressed in the language of enfleshed sensations," a feeling that for some spectators at least, is that of being copresent with a higher being or force, of feeling empathy, but most of all, of encountering spectacle unlike anything else one might come across in daily life.[123] What unites these ways of seeing the Passion as an epic narrative is that they attempt to transform theology into emotions and sensations (including pain, disgust, nausea, guilt, and exaltation) that are meant to bring us into closer communion with a Christian God.

And yet even the act of seeing is subject to historically specific connotative meanings, as Clifford Davidson reminds us: "According to the understanding of vision prevalent in both learned and popular circles [in the middle ages], *seeing* meant coming into direct visual contact with the object, which if it were idolatrous would contaminate the viewer."[124] Seeing was no less potent in the testimonies of viewers leaving Mel Gibson's *The Passion of the Christ* who saw flesh torn asunder and, if Gibson's aims were achieved, had their faith reaffirmed. When the steam has evaporated from the boiling pot of journalistic and scholarly rhetoric surrounding Gibson's *The Passion of the Christ*, what we are left with, I believe, is a residue of anxiety over mimesis itself and the burden of representing Christ's life. Unlike biblical epics that rely heavily on set-pieces requiring a widescreen format to fully appreciate the overpowering format of the epic (hardly a problem today for the large number of flat-screen HDTV owners), *The Passion of the Christ*'s temporal circumscription to the last twelve hours of Jesus's life delimits the film spatially given its reliance in the last third on shot sizes paradoxically associated far more with television than film, namely, the medium and close-up shots of Christ's suffering body and face.

Not only is Mel Gibson's *The Passion of the Christ* one of the most controversial films in the history of cinema, even outdoing the hoopla surrounding

Scorcese's *The Last Temptation of Christ* though clearly leveraging meaning from the controversy generated by that film—an almost obligatory process it would now seem with the release of any hagiopic—the film is also exemplary of one of the oldest genres in world cinema, plumbing the mythic depths of the epic in skillful if unsettling and politically inflammatory ways. The question remains, however, whether Gibson tipped the scales when he turned Caviezel into a slasher-film victim à la Carrie in the closing sequence of the eponymous film, undermining perhaps the doctrine of the Incarnation which, as Steinberg argues, requires "that everything done to Christ be attracted, so that passive and active concur in unison with Christ, that it be suffered and at the same time elicited or commanded, so that passive and active concur in unison with Christ's concurrent natures."[125] Although the closing shot of the resurrected Christ claws back a semblance of agency, the scales tip heavily in favor of passivity for the simple reason that Christ's body is so brutalized. While the film eschews few of the hallmark generic features of the epic film (technical virtuosity, grandiose narrative, and themes), its transformation of Christ into a monstrous figure who repels to an extent that even believers found it hard to look, brings an interesting (if disturbing) new dimension to the epic, demanding an optic that turns to the history of medieval image-making and spectatorship for explanation as well as a history of the religious hagiopic.[126]

acknowledgment

This chapter is a significantly reworked version of my essay "The Revered Gaze: The Medieval Imaginary of Mel Gibson's *The Passion of the Christ*," published in *Cinema Journal*, 47 (4) (winter 2006–2007): 3–39. Sections that discuss the "revered gaze" (but not Mel Gibson's *Passion of the Christ*) also appear in Chapter 1 of my book *Shivers Down Your Spine: Cinema, Museums, and the Immersive View* (New York: Columbia University Press, 2008), pp. 15–36. Both are reproduced with permission from the publishers. The material on the monstrous and the epic is new. My thanks to Robert Burgoyne and William Boddy for editorial feedback on earlier drafts.

notes

1. Timothy K. Beal, *Religion and Its Monsters* (New York: Routledge, 2002), p. 4.
2. Robert Burgoyne, *The Hollywood Historical Film* (Oxford: Blackwell, 2008), p. 38. For more on masculinity and the epic, see Leon Hunt, "What Are Big Boys Made Of? *Spartacus, El Cid* and the Male Epic," in Pat Kirkham and Janet Thumin (eds), *You Tarzan: Masculinity, Movies and Men* (London: St. Martin's Press, 1993), pp. 65–83.
3. Jolyon Mitchell and S. Brent Plate, "Viewing and Writing on *The Passion of the Christ*," in Jolyon Mitchell and S. Brent Plate, *The Religion and Film Reader* (New York: Routledge, 2007), p. 343 (pp. 343–47).

4. See, for the initial formulation of this idea, Paul Willeman, "Anthony Mann: Looking at the Male," *Framework,* 15–17 (summer 1981): 18. Quoted in Burgoyne, *The Hollywood Historical Film,* p. 84.

5. Derek Elley, *The Epic Film: Myth and History* (London: Routledge & Kegan Paul, 1984), pp. 1, 43.

6. Vivian Sobchack, "'Surge and Splendor': A Phenomenology of the Hollywood Historical Epic," *Representations,* 29 (winter 1990): 26 (pp. 24–49).

7. Sobchack, "Surge and Splendor," p. 36.

8. Sobchack, "Surge and Splendor," p. 29.

9. Sobchack, "Surge and Splendor," p. 34.

10. Sobchack, "Surge and Splendor," p. 24.

11. This chapter does not compare the representation of Christ in Gibson's *The Passion of the Christ* with other cinematic versions, since the history of Christ on screen has already been covered in several monographs, anthologies, and articles. Readers interested in that history could start with the following: R. C. Stern, C. N. Jefford, and G. DeBona, *Savior on the Silver Screen* (New York: Paulist Press, 1999); L. Baugh, *Imagining the Divine: Jesus and Christ-Like Figures in Film* (Kansas City, Miss.: Sheed, 1997); W. B. Tatum, *Jesus at the Movies: A Guide to the First Hundred Years* (Santa Rosa, Calif.: Polebridge Press, 1997); J. W. Martin and C. E. Ostwalt, Jr. (eds), R. Kinnard and T. Davis, *Divine Images: A History of Jesus on the Screen* (New York: Citadel Press, 1992); F. A. Eigo (ed.), *Imaging Christ: Politics, Art, Spirituality* (Villanova, Pa.: Villanova University Press, 1991); and P. O. Brunstad, "Jesus in Hollywood: The Cinematic Jesus in a Christological and Contemporary Perspective," *Studies Theologica,* 55 (2001): 145–156.

12. John Block Friedman, *The Monstrous Races in Medieval Art and Thought* (New York: Syracuse University Press, 2000).

13. Pamela Sheingorn, "Gender, Performance, Visual Culture: Medieval Studies in the 21st Century," lecture delivered at Columbia University, February 15, 2006. I am grateful to Pam Sheingorn for exposing me to so much of the medieval primary and secondary literature incorporated into this essay.

14. Michael Camille, "Before the Gaze: The Internal Senses and Late Medieval Practices of Seeing," in Robert S. Nelson (ed.), *Visuality Before and Beyond the Renaissance* (Cambridge: Cambridge University Press, 2000), p. 198. (pp. 197-223).

15. Hunt, "What Are Big Boys Made Of?" p. 69.

16. David Freedberg, *The Power of Images: Studies in the History and Theory of Response* (Chicago, Ill.: University of Chicago Press, 1989), pp. 1, 19.

17. Michel de Certeau, *The Writing of History,* trans. Tom Conley (New York: Columbia University Press, 1988), p. 20.

18. Beal, *Religion and its Monsters,* p. 6.

19. Amy Hollywood, "Kill Jesus," in Timothy K. Beal and Tod Linafelt, *Mel Gibson's Bible* (Chicago, Ill.: University of Chicago Press, 2006), pp. 159–67; p. 164.

20. Hollywood, "Kill Jesus," p. 166.

21. W. J. T. Mitchell, *What Do Images Want? The Lives and Loves of Images* (Chicago, Ill.: University of Chicago Press, 2005), p. 7.

22. John W. O'Malley, "A Movie, a Mystic, a Spiritual Tradition," *America,* 190 (9) (March 15, 2004), p. 13.

23. Timothy K. Beal and Tod Linafelt, *Mel Gibson's Bible* (Chicago, Ill.: University of Chicago Press, 2006), p. 2.

24. Frontispiece, *The Passion: Photography from the Movie The Passion of the Christ* (Icon Distribution, Inc., 2004). The film's soundtrack, which was released by Integrity Music to the Christian market and Sony Music to the general market, went gold (reaching 500,000 sales) within two months of its opening and is expected to reach platinum. The score was composed by John Debney, who produced soundtracks for such hits as *Elf, Spy Kids, The Emperor's New Groove,* and *The Scorpion King.* For more on the marketing of the film, including the extremely lucrative ancillary markets, see Peter A. Maresco, "Mel Gibson's *The Passion of the Christ:* Market Segmentation, Mass Marketing and Promotion, and the Internet," *Journal of Religion and Popular Culture,* 8 (fall 2004), available online at http://www.usask.ca/relst/jrpc/art8-melgibson-marketing.html (accessed March 13, 2010).

25. Bruce Babington and Peter William Evans, *Biblical Epics: Sacred Narrative in the Hollywood Cinema* (Manchester: Manchester University Press, 1993), p. 99.

26. Babington and Evans, *Biblical Epics,* p. 100.

27. Michael Camille, "Before the Gaze: The Internal Senses and Late Medieval Practices of Seeing," in Nelson, ed., *Visuality,* p. 217.

28. Lisa Schwartzbaum, "Faith Healer?" *Entertainment Weekly,* March 5, 2004, p. 47

29. Toby Miller, "Who Owns the Passion?" Symposium, organized by the Center for Religion and Media, New York University, March 12, 2004.

30. Otto von Simpson, *The Gothic Cathedral: Origins of Gothic Architecture and the Medieval Concept of Order* (New York: Pantheon Books, 1956), p. 79

31. David Morgan, *Visual Piety: A History and Theory of Popular Religious Images* (Berkeley: University of California Press, 1998), p. 63.

32. Gabriele Finaldi, *The Image of Christ* (London and New Haven, Conn.: National Gallery Company Limited and Yale University Press, 2000), pp. 58, 75.

33. Glending Olson, "Plays as Play: A Medieval Ethical Theory of Performance and the Intellectual Context of the Tretise of Miraclis Pleyinge," *Viator,* 26 (1995): 195, 200.

34. Olson, "Plays as Play," pp. 205, 207.

35. The term "autohagiographer" is Richard Kieckhefer's from his book *Unquiet Souls: Fourteenth Century Saints and their Religious Milieu* (Chicago, Ill.: University of Chicago Press, 1984), p. 6; cited in Sarah Salih, "Staging Conversion: The Digby Saint Plays and *The Book of Margery Kemp,*" in Samantha J. E. Riches and Sarah Salih (eds), *Gender and Holiness: Men, Women, and Saints in Late Medieval Europe* (New York: Routledge, 2002), p. 122 (pp. 121-43). For more on Margery Kempe, a "master performance artist" who cast herself as star of her visionary work *The Book of Margery Kempe,* see Nanda Hopenwasser, "A Performance Artist and Her Performance Text: Margery Kempe on Tour," in Mary A. Suydam and Joanna E. Zeigler, *Performance and Transformation: New Approaches to Late Medieval Spirituality* (New York: St. Martin's Press, 1999), pp. 97–131. Hopenwasser's bibliography is a wonderful resource for students of Kempe.

36. von Simson, *The Gothic Cathedral,* p. 164.

37. Morgan, *Visual Piety,* p. 60.

38. Barbara Amiel, "Mel Gibson's 'Passion of Christ' Is an Act of Faith, Not Hatred," *The Daily Telegraph,* February 23, 2004, p. 18.

39. The website is www.passionmaterials.com. Katy Kelly, "Scourging and Buzz," *US News & World Report,* March 8, 2004, p. 45.

341

40. The fourteen stations are: The Condemnation of Jesus by Pilate; Jesus's Acceptance of the Cross; His First Fall; The Encounter with His Mother Mary; Simon of Cyrene Helping Jesus; Vernonica Wiping Jesus's Face; His Second Fall; the Encounter with the Women of Jerusalem; His Third Fall; Jesus Being Stripped of His Garments; The Crucifixion; Jesus's Death; Jesus's Removal from the Cross; and the Burial of Jesus.

41. Michael Camille, *Gothic Art: Visions and Revelations of the Medieval World* (London: Everyman Art Library, 1996), p. 51.

42. Camille, *Gothic Art,* p. 14. Mitchell, *What Do Images Want?* p. 8.

43. Simson, *The Gothic,* p. xxi.

44. Simson, *The Gothic,* p. 54.

45. Simson, *The Gothic,* p. xix.

46. Simson, *The Gothic,* p. xix.

47. Jeff Simon, "Gibson's Gospel: A Religious Zealot's 'The Passion of the Christ' Is Not Sacred, Just Sadistic," *Buffalo News,* February 25, 2004, p. D1.

48. Ty Burr, "'The Passion of the Christ," *The Boston Globe,* February 24, 2004, p. D1.

49. Ken Hillis makes a connection between a medieval understanding of emblems and the "contemporary implosion of image, reality, and discourse" in simulated, virtual technologies. Ken Hillis, *Digital Sensations: Space, Identity, and Embodiment in Virtual Reality* (Minneapolis, Minn.: University of Minnesota Press, 1999), p. 67.

50. Camille, *Gothic Art,* p. 72.

51. Frank Kendon, *Mural Paintings in English Churches during the Middle Ages: An Introductory Essay on the Folk Influence in Religious Art* (London: John Lane, The Bodley Head Limited, 1923), pp. 118–119.

52. Gertrud Schiller, *Iconography of Christian Art,* trans. Janet Seligman (Greenwich, Conn.: New York Graphic Society, 1972), vol. II, p. 10; Cynthia Hahn, "Vision Dei: Changes in Medieval Visuality," in Nelson, ed., *Visuality* p. 182 (pp. 169–96).

53. Schiller, *Iconography,* p. 11.

54. Schiller, *Iconography,* p. 11.

55. Kendon, *Mural Paintings,* p. 88.

56. Camille, "Before the Gaze," p. 214.

57. Steinberg, "The Sexuality of Christ in Renaissance Art and Modern Oblivion," *October,* 25 (Summer 1983): 10–11.

58. Morgan, *Visual Piety,* p. 1.

59. Simon, "Gibson's Gospel," p. D1.

60. Jonathan Romney, "Pulp Crucifixion: Medieval Horror on a Biblical Scale," *Independent on Sunday* (London), March 28, 2004, pp. 16–17.

61. Peter Steinfels, "Beliefs: In the End, Does 'The Passion of the Christ' Point to Christian Truths or Obscure Them?" *New York Times,* Feb. 28, 2004, p. A13.

62. Andrée Seu, "After the Movie," *World Magazine,* 19 (11), March 20, 2004.

63. Steinfels, "Belief," p. 13 and Hartl, "'Passion of the Christ' Creates Passionate Divide," *The Houston Chronicle,* February 25, 2004, p. 8.

64. de Certeau, *The Writing of History,* p. 23.

65. C. W. Nevius and Joshunda Sanders, "'The Passion of the Christ,'" *The San Francisco Chronicle,* February 26, 2004, p. A13.

66. Schiller, *Iconography of Christian Art,* pp. 66–68.

67. Peter Conrad, "The Art of Pain," *The Observer* (London), April 4, 2004, p. 6.

68. The rise of Passion plays in twelfth-century Europe—religious dramatizations drawn from the Gospels that played a prominent role in furthering anti-Semitism—sculptural Stations of the Cross, and the development of certain groups of devotional images, including the veneration of Passion relics, would all contribute to what Schiller sees as an important tension that emerged throughout this period, between, on the one hand, a desire to enlarge the image of the crucifixion by including related popular scenes, and on the other to remain faithful to the devotional image and to represent Jesus in "gestures of ostentation" such as the Virgin and Child, the Man of Sorrows, and the Crucifixion. Schiller, *Iconography of Christian Art*, p. 76. Morgan, *Visual Piety*, p. 63.

69. Jack Miles, "The Art of *The Passion*," in Beal and Linafelt, *Mel Gibson's Bible*, p. 18. Other references Miles identifies include Georges de la Tour, during candlelit interiors; Rembrandt's famous head of Christ during the Last Supper; and Bellini's Pietà in the cut and color of Mary's veils ("The Art of *The Passion*").

70. Mel Gibson, "Forward," *The Passion: Photography from the Movie* The Passion of the Christ (Los Angeles: Icon Distribution, 2004).

71. Steinberg, "The Sexuality of Christ," p. 12.

72. Steinberg, "The Sexuality of Christ," p. 132; Siegfried Wenzel, "'Somer Game' and Sermon Reference to a Corpus Christi Play," *Modern Philology*, 86 (1988–1989): 274–283; cited in Olson, "Plays as Play," p. 213.

73. Arnoul Gréban, *The Mystery of the Passion: The Third Day*, trans. Paula Guiliano (Asheville, NC: Pegasus Press, 1996).

74. Joyce Tally Lionarons, "From Monster to Martyr: The Old English Legend of Saint Christopher," in Timothy S. Joes and David A. Spruger (eds), *Marvels, Monsters, and Miracles: Studies in the Medieval and Early Modern Imaginations* (Kalamazoo, Mich.: Western Michigan University, 2002), p. 181.

75. Jeffrey Jerome Cohen, "Monster Culture (Seven Theses)," in Cohen, "Preface: In a Time of Monsters," in *Monster Theory: Reading Culture* (Minneapolis, Minn.: University of Minnesota Press, 1996), p. 6.

76. Beal, *Religion and Its Monsters*, pp. 10 (emphasis in original) and 103.

77. Mary Bayne Campbell, *The Witness and the World: Exotic European Travel Writing, 400-1600* (Ithica: Cornell University Press, 1988), p. 80.

78. Campbell, *The Witness and the World: Exotic European Travel Writing*, pp. 80, 73.

79. Margaret R. Miles, "The Passion for Social Justice and *The Passion of the Christ*," in Timothy K. Beal and Tod Linafelt, *Mel Gibson's Bible* (Chicago, Ill.: University of Chicago Press, 2006), p. 123.

80. Jody Enders, *The Medieval Theater of Cruelty: Rhetoric, Memory, Violence* (Ithaca, NY: Cornell University Press, 1999), p. 13.

81. Enders, *The Medieval Theater of Cruelty*, p. 13.

82. Clifford Davidson, "Introduction," *A Tretise of Miralis Pleyinge*, Early Drama, Art and Music Monograph Series 19 (Kalamazoo, Mich.: Medieval Institute 1993), p. 1.

83. Clifford Davidson, "Introduction," *A Tretise of Miraclis Pleyinge*, Early Drama, Art, and Music Monograph Series 19 (Kalamazoo, Mich.: Medieval Institute Publications, 1993), p. 1. For an insightful interpretation of the *Miraclis*, see Erick Kelemen, "Drama in Sermons: Quotation, Performativity, and Conversion in a Middle English Sermon on the Prodigal Son and in *A Tretise of Miraclis Pleyinge*," *ELH*, 69 (2002): 1–19. Kelemen makes a compelling argument about the anxiety surrounding mimesis and conversion in

the *Tretise* using semiotics to make his point: "the mimetic performance of God's word strays too far from the word and causes the audience to be caught up in the spatial lure of dramatic activity and spectacle, caught up in the world of the signifier and missing entirely the world of the signified" ("Drama in Sermons," p. 16).

84. Garrett P. Epp, "Ecce Homo," in Glen Berger and Steven F. Kruger (eds), *Queering the Middle Ages* (Minneapolis, Minn.: University of Minnesota Press, 2001), pp. 237–238.

85. Steinberg, "The Sexuality of Christ," p. 23

86. Ibid., p. 45.

87. Anon., "The Passion of the Christ at Easter," *Sydney Morning Herald,* April 9, 2004, p. 28; Steinfels, "Belief," p. 13.

88. Mark A. Wrathall, "Seeing the World Made New: Depictions of the Passion and Christian Life," in Jorge J. E. Gracia, ed., *Mel Gibson's Passion and Philosophy: The Cross, the Questions, the Controversy* (Chicago: Open Court, 2004), p. 16.

89. Enders, *The Medieval Theater of Cruelty,* p. 6.

90. Enders, *The Medieval Theater of Cruelty,* p. 193.

91. Darwin Smith, "The Role of Christ in Medieval French Passions: What Can We Know?" Doctoral Program in Theater Studies lecture given at the CUNY Graduate Center, October 14, 2004.

92. Jody Enders, "Seeing Is Not Believing," in Timothy K. Beal and Tod Linafelt, *Mel Gibson's Bible* (Chicago, Ill.: University of Chicago Press, 2006), p. 187 (pp. 187-93). Despite wearing both full-body and facial prostheses, there were accounts of Jim Caviezel sustaining injuries while the film was in production.

93. Enders, "Seeing Is Not Believing," p. 190.

94. Philippe de Vigneulles, cited in Heinrich Michelant's edition of the *Gedenkbuch des Metzer BÜrgers Philippe von Vigneulles,* pp. 244–245 quoted and translated in Enders, *The Medieval Theater of Cruelty,* pp. 194–195.

95. Enders, *The Medieval Theater of Cruelty,* pp. 197, 201.

96. See Camille's discussion of *imitation Christi* in relation to nuns being surrounded by images, *Gothic Art,* p. 24.

97. For more on the representation of the Passion narrative in the early cinema period, see Roland Cosandey, Andre Gaudreault, and Tom Gunning (eds), *An Invention of the Devil* (Sainte-Foy and Lausanne: Les Presses de l'Université Laval and éditions Payot, 1993). Epp, "Ecce Homo," p. 241.

98. Epp, "Ecco Homo," p. 241.

99. This factoid appeared in William G. Little's essay, "Jesus's Extreme Makeover," in Beal and Linafelt, *Mel Gibson's Bible,* p. 176 (pp. 169–78).

100. Jeffrey Jerome Cohen, "Preface: In a Time of Monsters," in *Monster Theory: Reading Culture* (Minneapolis, Minn.: University of Minnesota Press, 1996), pp. ix (pp. vii–3).

101. Jeffrey Jerome Cohen, "Preface," p. x.

102. David Reinhard, "What I Saw at 'The Passion of the Christ," *The Oregonian,* February 29, 2004, p. E04.

103. Tom Heinen, "'Who Do You Say That I Am?'; 'The Passion of the Christ' Could Shape Our Image of Jesus for Decades," *Milwaukee Journal Sentinel,* February 24, 2004, p. 01A. Emphasis added.

104. Karen Jo Torjesen, "The Journey of the Passion Play from Medieval Piety to Contemporary Spirituality," in J. Shawn Landres and Michael Berenbaum (eds), *After the Passion Is Gone: American Religious Consequences* (Walnut Creek, Calif.: Altamira Press, 2004), pp. 94, 97 (pp. 93–104).

105. Nicolas Calas, *Transfigurations: Art Critical Essays on the Modern Period* (Ann Arbor, Mich.: UMI Research Press, 1985), p. 46.

106. Calas, *Transfigurations,* p. 46.

107. Liz Szabo, "*Passion of Christ* Moves Film's Early Viewers," *USA Today,* February 18, 2004, p. 1D.

108. Susannah Heschel, "Christ's Passion: Homoeroticism and the Origins of Christianity," in Beal and Linafelt, eds., *Mel Gibson's Bible,* p. 107 (pp. 99–107).

109. Olson, "Plays as Play," p. 213.

110. According to Mark D. Jordan and Kent L. Brintnall, "gesture, facial expression, costumes, hair styles, décor, even color temperature are registered [by Emmerich] with precision and exactitude," in "Mel Gibson, Bride of Christ," in Timothy K. Beal and Tod Linafelt, *Mel Gibson's Bible* (Chicago, Ill.: University of Chicago Press, 2006), p. 82 (pp. 81–87).

111. Jody Enders, "Seeing is Not Believing," in Beal and Linafelt, *Mel Gibson's Bible,* p. 189.

112. Enders, "Seeing is Not Believing," p. 191.

113. William G. Little, "Jesus's Extreme Makeover," in Beal and Linafelt, *Mel Gibson's Bible,* p. 174 (pp. 169–76).

114. Jordan and Brintnall, "Mel Gibson, Bride of Christ," p. 82.

115. John Drury, *Painting the Word: Christian Pictures and Their Meanings* (New Haven, Conn.: Yale University Press in Association with National Gallery Publications Ltd., 1999), p. 35.

116. This observation was made by Pamela Sheingorn in a lecture on theatrical stagings of the Passion as part of her "Medieval Performance" class at the CUNY Graduate Center, March 13, 2006.

117. David Bevington, *Medieval Drama* (Boston, Mass.: Houghton Mifflin, 1975), p. 220.

118. R. N. Swanson, "Passion and Practice: The Social and Ecclesiastical Implications of Passion Devotion in the Late Middle Ages," in A. A. MacDonald and H. N. B. Ridderbos and R. M. Schlusemann (eds), *The Broken Body: Passion Devotion in Late Medieval Culture* (Groningen: Ebgert Forste, 1996), p. 6 (pp. 1–30).

119. Swanson, "Passion and Practice," pp. 6, 8.

120. Elley, *The Epic Film,* p. 10.

121. Camille, *Gothic Art,* p. 104.

122. Swanson, "Passion and Practice," p. 11.

123. Morgan, *Visual Piety,* p. 66.

124. Davidson, "Introduction," p. 96; cited in Epp, "Ecce Homo," p. 245.

125. Steinberg, "The Sexuality of Christ," p. 190.

126. For more on the hagiopic, see Pamela Grace, "Blockbuster Jesus: The Hagiopic, Fundamentalism, and Religious Violence," New York University PhD Dissertation, 2004.

diegetic masculinities

reading the black body

in epic cinema

saër maty bâ

The aim of this chapter is to demonstrate ways in which an analysis of black bodies in epic cinema communicates the idea of multiple times, histories, and cultures. His or her role is to initiate and channel the "dream" and struggle of the future while embodying at the same time an ancient history and a discrete perspective of history. In this line of thinking, black characters analyzed in this chapter—slave gladiators Draba (*Spartacus* [1960]) and Juba (*Gladiator* [2000]), and African captive Cinqué (*Amistad* [1997])— signify this dream and embodiment while urging one to question earlier portrayals of black characters in epic films (Sobuza, Shaka, and Dingaan in *Winning a Continent* [*De Voortrekkers,* 1916]) and of blackface actors (Silas Lynch, Lydia, and Gus in *The Birth of a Nation* [1915]), two films that can be described as mythologized history of (white) conquest films.

The chapter is divided into five parts. "Critical Contexts: Gilroy's Planetary Conviviality, Petty's Contact Zone" explains the theoretical framework by providing critical contexts, in particular the work of Paul Gilroy, Sheila Petty, and Andrei Tarkovsky. The following four parts each look at specific aspects of black bodies in epic cinema. "The Black Body as

Past Future (Im)perfect: A Stoic Theme" focuses on Draba the gladiator in *Spartacus;* "The Black Body as Future Past (Im)perfect: A Planetary-Convivial Theme" focuses on Juba from *Gladiator;* "The Black Body as 'Recombinant Exchange': A Mende Theme" concentrates on Cinqué and, to some extent, on his relation to black characters James Covey and Theodore Joadson from *Amistad;* "Transcending the Black Body as White 'Nation' Myth: A Zulu/Swazi-Blackface Theme" focuses on Silas Lynch, Lydia, and Gus from *The Birth of a Nation,* and, to a lesser extent, on the figure of the Zulu King from *Winning a Continent* (using Chaka Zulu and Dingaan as examples). The chapter's conclusion returns to Gilroy, Petty, and Tarkovsky in order to suggest that characters such as Draba, Juba, Cinqué, and Sobuza can "converse" with each other, creating a kind of dialogical interplay and, in so doing, allow us to look toward an idea of a planetary-convivial, diasporic black body in epic cinema.

critical contexts: gilroy's planetary conviviality, petty's contact zone

Paul Gilroy's ideas of "Planetarity" and "Conviviality" can help one see more clearly issues around "race," black bodies, and time in epic cinema.[1] Planetarity is a transnational and transcontinental form of solidarity: "The planetary suggests both contingency and movement. It specifies a smaller scale than the global, which transmits all the triumphalism and complacency of ever-expanding imperial universals."[2] "The concept of space . . . is transformed when it is seen less through outmoded notions of fixity and place and more in terms of the ex-centric communicative circuitry that has enabled dispersed populations to converse, interact and even synchronize."[3] The point of using Gilroy's planetarity is not to exaggerate reach or to deny the flow, fluidity, and cross-fertilization at play between those who control the production of and representation in epic cinema; nor is it to ignore that epic films can potentially suppress the complexities of blackness by perverting, freezing or imposing *stasis* upon time. Rather, the logic of planetarity argues the importance of the idea of flowing multiple times, of fate and memory. As we shall see, in order to survive and be free—with no pretension to imperial triumphalism or global reach within, as well as between, nations and continents, slave ships, the Middle Passage, slavery, migrancy, and exile—black bodies have been in motion, dependent on each other and noncomplacent. Furthermore, black bodies incarnate conviviality, a term that

> introduces a measure of distance from the pivotal term "identity," which has proved to be such an ambiguous resource in the analysis of race, ethnicity, and politics. The radical openness that brings conviviality alive makes a nonsense of closed, fixed, and reified identity and turns

attention toward the always-unpredictable mechanisms of identification.[4]

In this line of thinking, black bodies are complex planetary-convivial processes, open, fluid and changing entities; bodies that may problematize a film's diegesis when there is evidence that they are being reduced to the local, e.g., the national. Gilroy's planetarity and conviviality speak to empire-building and the aftermath of empire; we know also, thanks to Gilroy, that black bodies can be convivial after "empire." Due to black bodies having been routed and rerouted, displaced and reterritorialized by traumas such as the Middle Passage, slavery, migrancy, exile, imperialism, colonization, and voluntary journeys, black perspectives (on theory) have been overwhelmingly less about discreet nations and cultures than about diaspora. Stated differently, black bodies (literal and metaphorical) always already speak at once to many nations while at the same time being central to the construction of nations that, in turn, might deny, pervert or subvert these bodies' existence—the theoretical substance of Gilroy's Black Atlantic and Sheila Petty's (borrowed) idea of contact zones comes in large part from this contradictory state of affairs.[5]

black atlantic, contact zones

Black Atlantic theory is important for this chapter because it unfixes and routes space toward an "ex-centric communicative circuitry" and "does not privilege the modern nation-state and its institutional order over the sub-national and supra-national networks and patterns of power, communication and conflict that they work to discipline, regulate and govern."[6] Black Atlantic theory is particularly relevant if one agrees with philosopher Jonathan Rée that "individual nations arise within a field of general internationality; or in other words . . . the logic of internationality preceded the formation of [individual] nations."[7] Thus, I read earlier notions of contact zones, such as Gilroy's contested contact zones between cultures and histories, as, first and foremost, a reiteration of Rée's line of reasoning; in so doing Gilroy argues usefully for the need to perceive both the "intercultural positionality" of black thinking and the emergence of "intermediate concepts lodged between the local and the global" (e.g., "diaspora") as breakers of the "dogmatic focus on discrete *national* dynamics."[8] Of course, Rée's argument makes Gilroy's "outernational, transcultural reconceptualisation" move beyond a mere "alternative to the nationalist focus" in order to actively disable and displace the national.[9] Gilroy is aware of the "tragic popularity of ideas about the integrity and purity of cultures, [particularly] the relationship between nationality and ethnicity," of ethnicity as "an infinite process of identity construction," and that the main raison d'être for the Black Atlantic (theory and book) is to recognize black people as "agents . . . people with cognitive capacities and even with an intellectual

348

history—attributes denied by modern racism."[10] This is because demonstrating such an appreciation accents further how useful and needed Rée's logic of internationality is. Thus, when discussing epic cinema in general, one may want to take seriously the useful point that "memories of history and nation are called forth and reconfigured as they are adapted to a new context."[11]

Reconfiguration and adaptation to new places, contact zones, are recurring phenomena in black history and memory. Petty's recent black diasporic contact-zones theory reflects this state of affairs while extending possibilities for black bodies that Rée, Gilroy, and, as we shall see, Tarkovsky and others have already set forth. In effect, contact-zones theory reaccents the need for more comprehensive, multiple cross-diaporic links and experiences between black diasporic bodies:

> encapsulation of the black diaspora is futile . . . The plethora of theory may seem daunting, or even impenetrable, but rather than viewing it as a competition in which the validity of one stance should triumph over another, one can find it worthwhile to recognize that the multiplicity of theories generated by and within the black diaspora is emblematic of its vitality and diversity.[12]

Ultimately, then, the Black Atlantic and contact-zones theories are means of breaking binaries that are or that might be at play in depictions of blackness in epic cinema, or ways of recomplexifying black bodies and their relations to multiple temporalities, histories and cultural inscriptions. In effect, be it Imperial Rome, Africa, America, or between these and other places of memory, I would follow Anthony W. Marx in saying that the complexity of black "identity" and protest precedes and outlives narrow state determinism and policies (e.g., slavery in Ancient Rome, apartheid in South Africa, or Jim Crow in America) and that blacks have repeatedly followed their own interests "by migrating."[13] Therefore, as we shall see, black bodies can embody transcontinental uprooting, connote intra-African migration and belong to African kingdoms that cover a massive landmass: somehow, these dispersed bodies communicate, interrelate, and even, in Gilroy's word, synchronize. Moreover, Black Atlantic and contact-zones theories argue that black bodies are not mere "response[s] to actions from above": "Blacks have . . . often forc[ed] a reconfiguration of rule imposed upon them."[14]

mirror, time

Andrei Tarkovsky has very often challenged actions from the Soviet state; his work rises against any form of dictatorship, brings past and future into the present, and foregrounds the all-so-important question of time and its relation to the making of the cinematic image.[15] Tarkovsky believed "firmly, almost literally" in the fact that if a person's life exists "at all profoundly" it does so "in the continuity of one generation to the next."[16] It is from this belief that one can best understand his thinking about "mirror" and "time" as both nonstatic and able to flow in multiple directions. I would suggest that using this thinking to read black bodies in epic cinema is a way of crafting a new and different approach. There are two main interconnected reasons for this. First, epic films seem to create versions of black history and portrayals of blackness that become central to these films' meaning, whether or not such centrality is acknowledged. Second, although full of dates, processes, and time frames, epic films have not yet been looked at through a Tarkovskyan mirror. As we shall see, looking at epic films through such a mirror highlights them at once as embodiments of multiple times (a "time" that may flow in any direction), metaphors of fate and memory, and a means of looking to a future that had not (or has not) yet come. In following this line of thinking, a new perspective can be opened on epic cinema. Furthermore, I will argue that black bodies are crucial to how epic films can be read through a Tarkovskyan mirror.

If Tarkovsky's film *The Mirror* (1975) is taken literally, its mirrors and polished or shiny surfaces (objects imbued with memory) may reflect "a connection of *stasis*" between past and present, while "nothing of importance" seems to ever change.[17] However, as pointed out above, Tarkovsky believed that a person's life can only exist deeply through the connection of one generation to the next. And I am convinced, like Tarkovsky, that "We exist as moral beings in so far as we possess, love and imitate the ancestors" and that "Our past is our fortune."[18] This conviction opens epic films to a number of possible readings that could be summarized collectively as follows: the relation between past and present can be set in motion so that the affirmation of life's continuity, and our existence as moral beings, can exist and continue to exist. This in turn means that the gaze of the epic film's viewer/reader is directed toward both past and future.

It might be worth reiterating at this juncture that I am interested in extracting the idea of flowing multiple times, fate, and memory from the *diegesis* of epic films discussed here (and not so much in considering extradiegetic issues), hence my recourse to Tarkovsky whose work on time's relation to the making of the cinematic image is a posture against the primacy and dictatorship of editing. It is to examining Tarkovsky's view on time and the cinematic image that I will now turn before addressing succinctly how it helps effect a new look at black bodies in epic cinema.

If the process of shooting a film gives birth to the "cinema image," an image that exists "*within* the frame," then it makes sense for the director to focus on "the course of time in the frame, in order to reproduce and record it"; for Tarkovsky, the selective, collating, and adjusting technique called editing deals with "shots that are already filled with time" and organizes "the unified, living structure inherent in the film."[19] Thus, conceiving cinema might not be possible without the notion of "time passing through the shots," but time dictates also the use of a particular editing principle.[20] Stated differently, the importance of editing should not be overstated to the detriment of time. Moreover, "the pieces that 'won't edit'—that can't be properly joined—are those which record a radically different kind of time. One cannot, for instance, put *actual time* together with *conceptual time,* any more than one can join water pipes of different diameter."[21] Last but not least, as we shall see, Tarkovsky's ideas are useful to this chapter because they make us see epic cinema's willingness to demonstrate that a bridge exists between "those [artists] who create their own inner world, and those who recreate reality," namely in matters of black bodies, race and time in epic films.[22]

the black body as past future (im)perfect: a stoic theme

Spartacus tells the tale of slave gladiator Spartacus (Kirk Douglas) who leads an army of former slaves to take on the power of Rome, embodied by General Crassus (Laurence Olivier). The film is about love, commitment, and a fight for freedom and features a black African character crucial to its narrative of freedom, Draba (Woody Strode).

Issues of race and freedom permeate black presence in epic films. The scene where slave gladiator Draba fights to the death against Spartacus for Crassus and his wedding party's pleasures has been the subject of very useful readings (e.g., Burgoyne in *The Hollywood Historical Film*) and will be looked at below. However, I would suggest that in order to read black bodies' relation to multiple temporalities, histories, and cultural inscriptions, one needs also to consider the preceding scene where Draba and Spartacus await their fight, for it can provide complex points of entry into the character of Draba and thus lead to a new approach able to problematize, challenge, and transcend current readings of Draba's body.

This scene has been read through a 1960s lens as a moment of mute racial tension between a black man and a white man who are "not really enemies" but rather "victims" of a deeply rooted degrading system they must overcome; both gladiators are slaves "in chains to the power of Rome" who illustrate "the dilemma of modern [American] race relations" to be defeated.[23] Martin Winkler goes on to argue that "Draba and Spartacus do not succeed, but . . . fight the good fight and point the way for others."[24]

As the fight preceding Draba and Spartacus's own contest begins, a close-up shows the latter looking at Draba. When Kubrick cuts to a medium close-up of Draba, he is not looking at Spartacus but focuses straight ahead, head slightly down, as if mentally rehearsing his forthcoming fight or picturing techniques being used in the fight under way; Draba's gaze is so

Figure 15.1

Spartacus: Draba's gaze penetrates the limits of the wooden box; his smile shows contentment, confidence, and experience as an African gladiator.

penetrating that it seemingly allows him to see through the limits of the wooden box in which he and Spartacus are sitting. As Draba finally turns his head toward the arena, he maintains the same penetrating gaze, which, in this instance, seems to go beyond the fighting space of the arena itself and toward the gallery in which Crassus and his party are sitting (see Figure 15.1). Draba is now smiling—an expression showing his contentment, confidence, and experience as a gladiator—while he still does not look at Spartacus. Meanwhile, Spartacus has focused nervously on the fight underway before turning toward Draba again with an anxious, piercing, hatred- and fear-filled gaze that leaves Draba unperturbed.

Therefore, if one concentrates on Draba, this scene seems devoid of tension in that his face, lit softly around the cheekbone and eyes, shows someone at peace with himself and with the impending deadly contest. Draba's smile signifies a decision already made, although the viewer will only know the decision's nature once the fight with Spartacus takes place. Furthermore, a crucial point worth reiterating is that Draba never looks at Spartacus. It is as if the latter is insignificant in relation to Draba's aims and objectives or as if these aims and objectives are bigger than the imminent contest: in both scenarios, Spartacus is out of the picture. The point I am making is that, if one wishes to find one's way into the complexity of diegetic black bodies in epic cinema, one needs to consider these bodies in their own right, with the understanding that "black" does not always need "white" in order to make sense.[25] I shall illustrate this point through Draba's profile offered below.

The meaning of the Draba-versus-Spartacus fight scene should not be contained within an American national framework, although race and Hollywood cinema's usually problematic depictions of black characters make this tempting.[26] Similarly, pondering what would have happened had Draba lived longer, or had he been allowed to kill Spartacus, would be pure conjecture. Thus, it seems futile to argue that "the outcome of Spartacus' and Draba's fight is unavoidable" while everything in the diegesis of *Spartacus* tends to indicate that Draba's significance lies in life through death.[27]

Draba's death is not a sacrifice, at least not for the character of Spartacus, beyond whom, as we have seen, Draba looks (literally and metaphorically). Nor can the fact that Draba's dead body is hung upside down and left to rot in the slave gladiators' quarter as a deterrent allow one to construe his death as sacrifice. Granted, Draba's living body is defined to a large extent by corporeal beauty and the concomitant "amount of erotic stimulation" and "languorous gazings" it can provide white women: Helena's (Joanna Barnes) "I want the most beautiful . . . give me the big black one" when she and Claudia (Nina Foch) choose two gladiators to fight to the death is a case in point.[28] It follows that even if, as Ina Rae Hark incisively points out, "Draba made no statement about watching men kill; he vowed not to kill on another's command," her subsequent thoughts on Draba, based on psychoanalysis, frame his death and body within two perspectives of history and culture that appear too narrow to be able to contain Draba's meaning:

> Yet he could not maintain his choice to renounce phallic aggression; he could only direct that aggression towards his masters, a move that brought his death at Crassus's hands, precisely the trajectory that the gladiators' revolt itself traces. To be truly free, the slaves must both liberate themselves from spectacularization and gain the option to forswear the sword. Neither Rome nor Hollywood is ready for that.[29]

Hark echoes Winkler's problematic "unavoidability" argument and therefore prompts a reading of Draba's death as a long, planned suicide and of his living body and actions as processes or means of achieving such a death. Draba's death, body, and actions perceived as such free him from obsolescence and narrowcasting not least because, as we shall see, the Black Atlantic and Greek and Roman philosophies combine to influence both this reading and the Hollywood filmic text it targets, i.e. *Spartacus*.

In life and death, the character of Draba is in motion within a Gilroyian disputed contact zone, between cultures and histories where his ethnicity goes through an endless process of construction. Draba demands that his agency as a person with cognitive abilities and intellectual history are recognized. Through his body, as Burgoyne writes, "memories of history and nation are called forth and reconfigured as they are adapted to a new context."[30] In this instance, the black body fuses with epic cinema while Draba becomes an epic hero who controls his destiny through a Stoic's death.

The three main features of Stoicism come across in *Spartacus,* and the second and third aspects are especially useful to a reading of Draba: life should be ruled by, and death accepted in keeping with, "reason, nature, and political action"; "slavery and any slavish attitudes to death are morally unacceptable"; and "the ready acceptance that all life ends in death, irrespective of the type of death that one suffers."[31] Francisco Javier Tovaz Paz makes a similar point, but I disagree with his reading in significant ways. Although Draba's refusal to kill Spartacus is "political," I do not agree that the meaning of his death should be construed as "dying in [Spartacus's] place" after Draba's supposed "discovery of Spartacus's rebellious spirit and his potential as a liberator."[32] This is because Draba cannot possibly see Spartacus's rebellious spirit without, simultaneously, grasping that "being a slave is akin to being dead" and that such understanding happens over a period of time—not "in a moment of moral outrage and rebelliousness."[33] Thus, Draba's death points toward a Stoic's suicide, for Stoics lead a noble existence until "reason, nature, or political circumstances" make such a life impossible. At such stage, suicide, which embodies "the fundamental [ethical] question of how to lead one's life appropriately," becomes comprehensible.[34] Draba's acceptance that all life ends in death demonstrates as well that his major concern is with life—whenever he appears in *Spartacus,* Draba is focused on managing his life under Roman slavery with particular attention to developing his spiritual freedom "and without excessive concern for death."[35] Thus, Draba embodies Stoicism's vital ideals of asserting freedom, rebelling against oppression, and being fatalistic when faced with the unavoidability of death. These "philosophical attitudes" may be present in the character Spartacus, but they cannot make sense if he is read without Draba in the frame of analysis.[36] Conversely, Draba embodies the same philosophical attitudes irrespective of Spartacus; the latter always looks up to Draba, and this is neither accidental nor gratuitous: the scene where Draba and Spartacus first make contact is a case in point.

Bought from the mines of Libya, a scruffy Spartacus arrives at Batiatus's gladiatorial school in Capua with other captives, seated on ox-driven carts. Once in the courtyard, from the top of the gallery where Crassus and his wedding party will watch Draba and Spartacus fight, Batiatus explains what their new life means while Kubrick cross-cuts between Batiatus, a seated Spartacus, and the slave gladiators' gated training area: "Approximately half of our graduates live for five, ten, ten years! Some of them even attain freedom and become trainers themselves." A right-to-left panning shot from Spartacus's point of view reveals gladiators standing behind the gate, erect like soldiers, facing the courtyard and gallery. Spartacus's gaze stops at and lingers on Draba, whose magnificent body, closest to Spartacus and framed neatly between the vertical iron bars of the gate, seems to epitomize gladiatorial perfection. Draba turns his head left toward Spartacus, returns the gaze by looking downward with the confident smile I have already mentioned above in another context.

This arrival scene emphasizes the fact that Draba's poise and, again, Stoic's control of his destiny is a long process, not a sudden occurrence. The iron bars separating him from Spartacus will remain, symbolically, throughout the film as Draba refuses to relate to Spartacus in any other way than as a gladiator. Committed to life, Draba's attitude connotes a desire to graduate and attain freedom like a true Stoic. Draba seems to never include Spartacus in his worldview; their fight to the death in Batiatus's school accelerates Draba's attainment of freedom in view of the speedy decadence of Roman reason, nature, and political circumstances, while not denying Draba control over his own destiny. The fight does not even work well as a narrative twist, for its aftermath exposes a fundamental narrative flaw in how the character Spartacus mobilizes Draba's death in order to forge a concept of post-slavery masculinity distanced from Roman decadent visual pleasure: "I swore that if I ever got out of this place [i.e. Batiatus's gladiatorial school], I'd die before I watched two men fight to the death again. Draba made that promise, too. He kept it. So will I." In fact, Draba made no such statement; "he vowed not to kill [anymore] on another's command."[37] In short, Draba dies a Stoic epic hero's death.

the black body as future past (im)perfect: a planetary-convivial theme

Gladiator tells the story of Maximus (Russell Crowe), the Roman general who became a slave gladiator and challenged the power and corruption of the Roman Empire incarnated by Commodus (Joaquin Phoenix). Like *Spartacus*, the film features a black African character crucial to its narrative of freedom: Juba, the Nubian slave gladiator (Djimon Hounsou). However, while Draba chooses solitude and a Stoic's principles and death, Juba opts for conviviality and a staunch commitment to staying alive. The scene where he and Maximus are chained together when fighting other gladiators illustrates how matters of race and freedom permeate black presence in *Gladiator*; it has been pertinently analyzed by scholars such as Burgoyne in *The Hollywood Historical Film* and will be considered below. As with *Spartacus*, I would suggest vis-à-vis *Gladiator* that in order to read black bodies' relationship to multiple temporalities, histories, and cultural inscriptions, one needs to consider scenes taking place apart from the fight where Juba and Maximus are chained together—in this instance, after the fight. This is because, similar to the function of scenes located prior to the Draba–Spartacus fight in *Spartacus*, the ones situated after the Juba–Maximus chained fight provide complex points of entry into the character of Juba that are also conducive to problematizing, challenging, and transcending current readings of this body.

355

One such scene is the final one in the film, where, following Maximus's death, Juba is seen in close-up burying Maximus's small figurines in the soil of the Colosseum, a form of gladiators temple and "cache," with "Now we are free. And we'll meet again. But not yet; not yet!" thus denoting Juba's vow to fight on.[38] The figurines are memory objects representing Maximus's family and ancestors through which he prayed to his gods. The burial of the figurines is symbolic because Maximus's desire to meet his wife and son again when he died was already fulfilled in the film's narrative: they had been massacred by Emperor Commodus's men following Maximus's demotion from the Roman Army and subsequent failed execution. Through Juba's words, the burial communicates Juba's embodiment of multiple times, histories, and cultures. Non-Roman, ancient forces seem to give his leitmotif in *Gladiator*—meeting with loved ones again after death but "Not yet!"—ancient historical and prophetic status.[39]

Indeed, when the viewer first meets Juba with Maximus in North Africa, Juba's off-screen, "voice of God" is heard saying to a sick and confused Maximus, "Don't die . . . You'll meet them again. Not yet!"[40] The viewer can infer from the dark-blue images and sound effects, interspersed with diegetic contemporary footage in quick succession, that Maximus seems to have had visions of and mumbled words about his house, fields, horse, wife, and son waiting for him. It is uncertain whether or not he utters these words, or does so clearly enough, because he drifts in and out of consciousness. This idea of uncertain utterance, combined with Juba's prophetic status, is compounded by a later conversation Juba and Maximus have about their respective families and homes, and about death, on the eve of their departure from the Roman province of Zucchabar to Rome to fight other gladiators in the Colosseum:

JUBA: It's somewhere out there, my country, my home. My wife is preparing food; my daughter is carrying water from the river. Will I ever see them again? I think no.

MAXIMUS: Do you believe you'll see them again when you die?

JUBA: I think so. But then, I will die soon. They will not die for many years. I have to wait.

MAXIMUS: But you would wait?

JUBA: Of course.

MAXIMUS: You see, my wife and my son are already waiting for me.

JUBA: You'll meet them again, but not yet. Not yet! Yes?

MAXIMUS: Yes, not yet.

Only after this exchange does the full meaning of Juba's firm belief in meeting loved ones again after death "but not yet. Not yet!" emerge. This conviction derives from his Nubian history and culture, and he uses it to install a strong desire for survival and perpetual struggle toward freedom within an emotionally drained, albeit physically strong Maximus. Juba knows that an imminent death would make him wait a long time before meeting his wife and daughter again, hence his refusal to die just yet. On the other hand, Maximus, who can meet his wife and son anytime, for they are already dead, has to be motivated to stay alive and to free himself from slavery. This is significant because Rome's history and culture of military conquest had inordinately dominated General Maximus's core worldview, a view at the periphery of which lurked his constant wishful thought of returning to his land and family. Stated differently, whether or not Maximus had visions and mumbled words when he and Juba are first seen together bears not much diegetic impact on the origin and significance of Juba's leitmotif. Thus, to return to *Gladiator*'s ultimate scene, "The planting of the figurines by the black slave gladiator, with its clear suggestion of an appeal to the future, can be read as a symbol of the planting of the seeds of a new nation, a new civilization."[41] The scene is filmed at night, while Juba is alone and looks up to the skies in order to speak to Maximus's soul. Together, mise-en-scène and acting signify a literal and metaphorical breaking up of a slave chain that had also become a symbol of friendship between Juba and Maximus. The friends will meet again, but not before the seeds of a new nation and a new civilization being planted germinate. However, what or whose new nation and civilization is to rise from these seeds? An answer can be found in Juba if he is considered independently from Maximus, just like Draba has been vis-à-vis Spartacus (because "black" does not always need "white" in order to make sense) a point to which I will now turn.

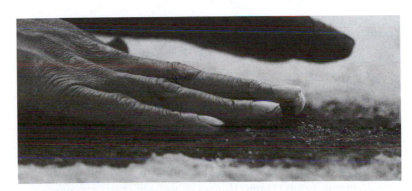

Figure 15.2

Gladiator: Juba burying Maximus's figurines in the sand of the Colosseum.

Seemingly very different from Draba, Juba represents a type of "antira-
cist screen persona" whose distinct story is interwoven with Maximus's. As
Burgoyne explains, "in the black—white pairing of Maximus and Juba, the
traditional epic themes—the emergence of a people, the birth of a nation,
the fulfillment of a heroic destiny—are here rewritten to express a story of
emergence in which black and white are connected by a central thread."[42]
Of course, Juba's Nubian African culture problematizes if not transcends
"nation," and, as mentioned above, the question is, when he is considered
on his own, what nation and civilization Juba represents. There is no denying the friendship between black Juba and white Maximus. Once chained
together in the arena, Juba and Maximus fight for survival "as one" and
create "a new weapon from the chain that binds them."[43] As we know, by
the time they reach Rome's Colosseum, the chain is broken, leaving Juba
and Maximus to fight as two distinct individuals who equally need to relate
as such. At this point in the film, as a gladiator, Juba no longer needs
Maximus in order to make sense and thus can be understood further
through Gilroy's notion of "radical openness that brings conviviality alive."
Indeed, like Draba, Juba is from Africa, the place of his general internationality or logic of internationality. Thus, Juba's outer-national history and
culture (vis-à-vis Imperial Rome) should, at least, shift the way he is perceived as follows: from a so-called "naively obedient" or "subordinate and
obedient" character to someone who is a physical and "spiritual healer"
whose Nubian African's knowledge precedes and transcends Maximus's
needs.[44] As a case in point, Juba's burial of the statuettes in the Colosseum/
temple/cache is as much about his culture, history, and beliefs as it is about
Maximus. Similarly, Maximus dies, while Juba survives and renews his
commitment to winning battles in order to avoid reaching the afterlife earlier than his wife and daughter. As we shall see, *Amistad*'s African captive
Cinqué displays a similar commitment to winning battles in a foreign land
but one located more squarely (than Draba's and Juba's) at the interstice of
individual agency and collective purpose.

the black body as "recombinant exchange': a *mende* theme

Amistad asserts "the power of dialogue within the ideals of the [American]
Declaration of Independence," "while undermining the official discourse to
lay bare the horrors of slavery."[45] Indeed, in 1839, Cinqué led a rebellion of
forty-nine men and women aboard the slave ship *La Amistad* during which
many of the Spanish crew members, and some captives, were killed. Captured
and tried in America (Connecticut) for murder and piracy, the Africans were
eventually found not guilty and allowed to return home following a successful Supreme Court hearing: Human rights triumphed over color.

If, as Burgoyne suggests, the display of a male slave's body on screen
generates complex messages not yet considered in analyses of masculinity

in epic films, then his subsequent thought on the issue applies most pointedly to Cinqué and *Amistad:* "the body of the male slave becomes a kind of document, on which questions of ownership, authorship, and history are traced and retraced, and in which the familiar narratives of honor, emotion, and sacrifice become fraught and complicated by questions of agency and collective purpose."[46]

Notions of ownership and authorship of the *La Amistad* Africans come across clearly in the film's very first courtroom scene, where, almost simultaneously, a district attorney brings charges of piracy and murder; an abolitionist, Mr. Tappan, presents a petition writ; US Secretary of State John Forsyth, "on behalf of the President of the United States [Martin Van Buren] representing the claims of Her Majesty Queen Isabella of Spain," argues that "these slaves are by right . . . the property of Spain, and as such are to be returned post-haste"; two commissioned US naval officers, who had "salvaged" *La Amistad* from the high seas and stand in front of the court as "private citizens," claim the ship "and all her cargo"; while yet another attorney acting on behalf of the two surviving captors José Ruiz and Pedro Montès and in possession of a receipt for purchase "executed in Havana, Cuba, June 18 1839," asks the court to "immediately release these goods, and the ship over there to my clients!" The hearing ends in chaos, and the case unresolved. Throughout, Cinqué and his fellow captives display puzzlement at how disorganized court proceedings are, followed by sheer fear combined with loud vocal protest upon seeing Ruiz and Montès again.

As subsequent courtroom proceedings would illustrate further, the African captives' bodies are traced and retraced constantly not only by issues of ownership and authorship but also by their own African origins, histories, and cultures—which eventually make the Supreme Court acquit and give them the choice of returning to Africa—while honor, emotion, and sacrifice premise and sustain Cinqué's and his fellow African captives' journey on the Atlantic Ocean and into the American judicial system. Such complex processes are accented by what Paul Gilroy has called "always-unpredictable mechanisms of identification," for, were it not for the African captives' agency and collective purpose, attorneys, abolitionists, politicians, naval officers, and slave traders speaking to, at, for, or against the African captives could have easily acquired the latter's black bodies (dead or alive). Thus, the fact that Cinqué is an agent with intellectual history, who is motivated by the collective needs of his fellow African captives, urges one not to read displays of his body, or *Amistad's* diegesis per se, as a progression from apparent monstrosity to discovered humanity. Rather, Cinqué affirms strongly how black bodies are active receptacles of coalescing multiple times, histories, and cultures, a collective illustration of which can be found in the following sections of *Amistad:* the rebellion on *La Amistad;* the flashback of Cinqué's life and capture in Africa and the horrors of the Middle Passage; and Cinqué's conversation with John Quincy

Adams at the ex-American President's home—facilitated by *Mende*-speaking ex-slave-turned-sailor James Covey translating—its impact on both Adams's subsequent speech at the Supreme Court and the outcome of the *La Amistad* case. These parts of *Amistad* need to be considered as a single narrative or statement for their collective illustration of Cinqué's above-mentioned characteristics to emerge. It is to this new reading of black bodies in *Amistad* that I will now turn.

The opening sequence of *Amistad,* where Cinqué frees himself and leads the rebellion, illustrates problems that may arise when black or African subjectivity is subsumed into or bears an indexical connection to what might be perceived as a filmmaker's praxis. Additionally, this opening sequence seems to set up in the viewer's or critic's mind a thought process whereby the film's flashback sequence might be read as a way to "better understand [Cinqué's] actions [in the opening sequence] and future events": "we have no idea who [Cinqué] is, or anything about him beyond his desperate fight for freedom, [and] remain initially confused during the ensuing battle between whites and Blacks [*sic*], uncertain if these are captured slaves or dangerous criminals."[47]

In this line of thinking, it may make sense as well to point out that Spielberg had just finished *The Lost World: Jurassic Park* (1997), and then draw attention to visual similarities between his dinosaur films and the opening sequence of *Amistad.*[48]

However, problems arise regarding both race and how the remainder of *Amistad*'s narrative might be read when one perceives Cinqué's black body in connection to visual creations in Spielberg's dinosaur movies. I would argue that what follows *Amistad*'s opening sequence is not Cinqué's redemption and humanization. Similarly, that the close-up on Cinqué's eyes may recall one of the tyrannosaurs in *Jurassic Park* does not mean that the parallel must be made: descriptions such as "savage," "striking instinctively," "The comparison, however offensive, is apt. His initial depiction is truly monstrous by means of similar cinematography" leveled at Cinqué seem to miss the point.[49] This is because *Amistad*'s opening sequence embodies signs inviting the attentive and perceptive viewer into black agency, intellect, and collective purpose. Cinqué is dressed in no more than a nappy-shaped fabric to hide his genitals; within the belly of a ship, he frees himself and others—all black—from shackles, and they rise to fight and kill an all-white crew—denotations and connotations of slavery and the need for collective insurrection to punish slave traders are unambiguous. Thus, the fragmentary representation of Cinqué's sweat, quick breathing, jet-black body sleeked occasionally by lightning and the storm raging on the film's visual and sound tracks, as well as Cinqué's grunts, shouts, and roars, mark him as an anxious human being unsure of the outcome of his planned insurrection. At the same time, Cinqué's corporeal blackness and his actions on behalf of the African collective show his adherence to "universal principles of justice."[50] Moreover, by appropriating the crew's sword, Cinqué disrupts the process of tracing and retracing ownership on and over his body. In short, the seeming confusion and uncertainty conveyed through film style and film technique is in fact the crystal clarity that should allow the viewer to see that, like Draba, for example, Cinqué believes in freedom as obliteration of the root and branch of an oppressive system. His exact motivation may not be fully known at the opening-sequence stage but this incentive is strong enough, justified, and worth risking everything for. The point about this opening sequence then is that it does not make anything that follows it in *Amistad*'s narrative untrue, or need correction. Rather, it affirms a necessary universal human need that the remainder of the film—such as the flashback on Cinqué's African life, capture, and the horrors of the Middle Passage—reinforces, corroborates, and puts into sharp focus.

It is not coincidental that when Cinqué learns that President Van Buren appealed the court decision that had ruled in favor of their release and return to Africa, he strips off of all his Western clothes, throws them in the burning fire and, therefore, reverts to what he had brought from Africa, to the "document" with which he had ended white subjugation on *La Amistad* and which carried him throughout his mental and physical journey to and within America: his corporeality. In this unclothing scene, Cinqué reclaims ownership of his body for purification from a land "where you *almost* mean what you say . . . laws *almost* work," without, I hasten to add, failing to see that the American legal system can succeed in addressing the situation of African abductees dumped on a strange land. Cinqué's cognitive capacity and intellect allow him to interconnect and process multiple time, historical and cultural frameworks in a contested contact zone—nineteenth-century America—where his and the other African captives' subjectivities are still being forged at the intersection of history, power, and politics, to paraphrase Sheila Petty.

Thus, Cinqué is like a black cultural historian and theoretician, whom, by the time he meets ex-President Adams at his home, had already been "urged on in [his] labour by the brutal absurdity of racial classification that derives from and also celebrates racially exclusive conceptions of national identity from which blacks were excluded as either non-humans or non-citizens."[51] We have seen Cinqué shout, roar, and wield weapons with dexterity to bring death to his captors. Yet, at his meeting with Adams, Cinqué is soft-spoken, quiet, deferential, and gentle. The camera always pans slowly to and from him; lighting softens Cinqué's relaxed face from which his intelligence and confidence that he will not be going "in" the Supreme Court "alone" unambiguously come through (see Figure 15.3).[52]

ADAMS: Listen Cinqué, we're about to bring your case
before the highest court in our land. We're about
to do battle with a lion that is threatening to rip

Figure 15.3

Amistad: Cinqué as African cultural historian and Tarkovskyan moral calling on his ancestors.

> our country in two, and all we have on our side is a rock. [. . .] Listen Cinqué, I am being honest with you; anything less would be disrespectful. I am telling you, I am preparing you . . . I am explaining to you that the test in front of us is an exceptionally difficult one.
>
> CINQUÉ: We won't be going in there alone.
>
> ADAMS: Alone? Indeed not. We have right on our side, we have righteousness on our side, we have [Defense Attorney] Mr. Baldwin over there.
>
> CINQUÉ: I meant my ancestors. I will call into the past, far back to the beginning of time, and beg them to come and help me at the judgment. I will reach back and *draw them into me,* and *they must come* for at this moment I am the whole reason they have existed at all.[53]

Indeed, Cinqué is a Tarkovskyan moral being who possesses, loves, and imitates his ancestors with a firm belief that his past is his fortune. In fact, it can be argued that Cinqué had called on and drawn his ancestors into him several times before his meeting with Adams. From the opening scene of *Amistad* onwards, these ancestors have been into him, e.g., during his revolutionary suicidal insurrection on *La Amistad,* when coming to terms with the American judicial system's betrayal (Van Buren's appeal), and throughout the whole of the *La Amistad* affair. Once Adams gets involved in the African captives' defense, Cinqué summons the same ancestors to empower Adams through him, not least because Adams speaks for the Africans but does not pretend to own them or to author the speech he delivers at the Supreme Court. Adams is literally and metaphorically a vessel through which Cinqué's ancestors speak while at the same time observing Adams from the vantage point of Cinqué's body. This is a form of convivial spirit-possession whereby Cinqué's ancestors (male and female), having spoken to the "Founding Fathers" (one can imagine a very heated debate!), channel their agreements into Adams.[54] Cinqué's ancestors do not only free "the whole reason they have existed at all," i.e. Cinqué himself, but they also liberate Adams, 1839 America—a "dysfunctional family ripped apart by bitter disputes about slavery"[55]—and James Covey, who returns to Africa with Cinqué. (The ancestors must have reached out for Covey as well to make this possible.) Furthermore, Cinqué, an African, can be credited with helping change the meaning and perception of the Founding Fathers' American Creed, alongside Americans who care about the African captives (for example, Mr. Baldwin, black abolitionist Theodore Joadson, and translator Covey) and other Americans concerned only with the state of the American nation (for example, Adams). In effect, "We hold these Truths to be self-evident, that all Men are created equal, that they are endowed by their creator with certain unalienable Rights, that among these are Life, Liberty and the pursuit of Happiness" had brought about America's independence but was exclusive as well. The Creed is a myth "for in [it] we find the primal meaning of the [American] nation"; "[w]hen [Thomas] Jefferson used the phrase 'all men,' he meant all white men of property. [W]e have enlarged the meaning of that story to include . . . women, and . . . people of every race on the face of the earth."[56] Cinqué is crucial to this collective endeavor.

At the Supreme Court, a freed Cinqué gives Joadson the tooth of a lion he had killed in Africa as a token of his gratitude. It is clear that the act of giving, the object given, and the acceptance of the object create an explicit link between Joadson (an ex-slave from Georgia) and an idea(l) of Africa. This Africa is one of bravery, defiance, and humbleness, where a man would defend his village against a lion, armed with nothing but a rock, as Cinqué had done. Thus, the triangle Cinqué—lion's tooth—Joadson is yet another corroboration of *Amistad*'s opening sequence: slave traders, slavery, and anti-abolitionists represent the lion threatening the village, and to fight this beast can hardly be construed as criminal, savage, monstrous, and instinctive.

transcending the black body as white "nation" myth: a zulu/swazi-blackface

As suggested in the chapter's introduction, analyses of Draba, Juba, and Cinqué compel one to ask how these characters cast the portrayal of black characters Sobuza (my main focus), Shaka Zulu, and Dingaan in films such as "the first South African epic film" *Winning a Continent* and of black characters played in blackface by white actors (Silas Lynch, Lydia, and Gus) in films such as *The Birth of a Nation.*[57] What do these two films try to achieve, and does it work? What can one take from their portrayal of black African characters and blackface actors that would allow one to pose—with Draba, Juba, and Cinqué in mind—a theory of conversation and synchronization between black bodies in epic cinema?

Produced by South African Cinema, *Winning a Continent* was directed by an American from Kentucky to whom "the colonial always appeals," Harold Shaw, from a screenplay by Gustav Preller, an anti-Zulu, Boer-Afrikaner nationalist and South African oral historian.[58] Set in nineteenth-century South Africa, *Winning a Continent* details how the white settler Boers-Afrikaners, of Dutch origin, migrated northward from the British-controlled Cape Colony to Natal—also known as the Great Trek, started in 1836—where they aimed to establish a "Free Dutch Republic." The year in which it was released, 1916, was also the year in which *The Birth of a Nation,* the first of a series of "'Old South' [of America] epics" was distributed abroad and screened in South Africa, where it continued to be seen until the early 1930s at least.[59]

Winning a Continent narrates the Boers' intention, under the leadership of "farmer" Piet Retief, to purchase land from Zulu leader Dingaan on which to establish their Dutch Free Republic. Betrayed by Portuguese traders and massacred altogether by Dingaan as a result, after a treaty legally giving them Natal had been signed, the stage was set for revenge. A general named Pretorius hurried to the scene of the massacre, defeating the Zulus at the (in)famous battle of Blood/Ncome river on September 16, 1838. *Winning a Continent*'s diegesis accents the Boers' dramatic battles against the native black Zulus—in which the former were victorious, killing black warriors en masse—but also their subsequent assassination of Dingaan through Sobuza, as we shall see.

Winning a Continent is thus a text about the idea and myth of "nation," and how native black African bodies can be eliminated from the process of shaping a white settlers' "nation" in Africa, unless construed as "massive blood sacrifice," "Faithful Servant" or "Savage Other": Zulus disappear from the diegetic "nation" taking shape. Through the "grandiose misnomer," *Winning a Continent,* "suggesting more than the Boers ever achieved, or sought to achieve," Shaw and Preller construct a myth of a white South African nation, one which transformed *Winning a Continent* into a "cultural icon for the celebration of the Afrikaner 'nation.'"[60]

The Birth of a Nation's narrative thrust and crux come from two rape attempts by black men on white women, the American Civil War, and the slaying of President Abraham Lincoln, as well as the birth of a so-called new American nation thanks to the White Knights of the Ku Klux Klan. The film's plot revolves around the Stonemans (from the North) and the

Camerons (their cousins from the South), and on romance between the two families. *The Birth of a Nation* "reflects the combined work and ideas of three white male Southerners living in the North at the end of the nineteenth century": Thomas Dixon, Woodrow Wilson, and D. W. Griffith.[61] Last but not least, three salient facts about *The Birth of a Nation* cannot be overlooked: first, it is built on a black erasure—white solidarity paradigm; second, the film links race, myth, and nation at the same time as it capitalizes on perverting the myth of "nation" upon which it is built; and third, naming a "black" character Silas Lynch turns the victim into a perpetrator of violence.[62]

While not disputing the merit of tendencies in past and current studies and approaches of *Winning a Continent* and *The Birth of a Nation*, I would argue for the need to craft a new and different approach for two interconnected reasons.[63] First, both epic films' diegesis were central to versions of "nation" they helped create. Second, although pregnant with dates, nation-building processes and time frames, paradoxically, *Winning a Continent* and *The Birth of a Nation* have not yet been looked at through a Tarkovskyan mirror, i.e. simultaneously as embodiments of multiple times, with "time" having the capacity to flow in any direction, metaphors of fate and memory, and a way of looking to a future that had not (or has not) yet come.

Winning a Continent and *The Birth of a Nation* seem to craft and maintain a static relationship between past and present and not look to the future, while disallowing black bodies any form of connections. Nonetheless, I would argue that black bodies are crucial to how these texts can be read through a Tarkovskyan mirror. Like Tarkovsky, I am convinced that Draba, Juba, and Cinqué, for example, are moral beings in synchrony with their ancestors and whose bodies do value and carry the past.

Instead of considering events and issues beyond the diegesis of *Winning a Continent* and *The Birth of a Nation*, I am extracting the idea of flowing multiple times and of fate and memory from the diegesis itself. This explains my recourse to Tarkovsky, whose work brings past and future into the present and, as shown earlier, foregrounds the question of time and its connection to the cinematic image: "actual time" cannot be put together with "conceptual time" any further than water pipes of different diameter can be joined.

First, Griffith perverts actual time by ignoring the fact that, five decades after the American Civil War, Southern separatism became obsolete and Southern nationhood impossible. Second, and as a result of Griffith imagining an "'invisible" nation," in *The Birth of a Nation* conceptual time is based on a nonexistent actual time; Griffith crafts (artistically, aesthetically, and politically) a conceptual time of "*a nation that never was.*"[64] Moreover, with *The Birth of a Nation*, Griffith seems willing to demonstrate that there is a bridge between what Tarkovsky called artists who create their own inner world and those who recreate reality but, as evidenced in the above-mentioned problems about race, black bodies, and time, Griffith does not succeed.

The Birth of a Nation's conceptual time and actual time are unable to show black bodies' embodiment of multiple times, and how these bodies' fate and memory allow them a look to the future, as opposed to being stuck in the past and the present. By exposing time-arrangement problems, I suggest a new analysis of *Winning a Continent* and *The Birth of a Nation*, based on the Tarkovskyan mirror that makes diegetic black bodies converse, interact, and synchronize at the interstice of nation-building, nostalgia, and myth on the one hand, and of presence/absence on the other hand. Thus freed from conscription within the film's diegesis, these black bodies will be ready for a (wider) relation with Draba, Juba, and Cinqué—as we shall see in the chapter's conclusion.

nation building?

South Africa and America share some strikingly similar national myths lived by and perpetuated through nostalgia. Diegetic nation-building links up with the wider processes of nondiegetic nation-building that *Winning a Continent, The Birth of a Nation,* and their makers belong to, something which, in turn, is associated with the myths that had helped build the actual (South African or American) nation.[65] Myths are real because the wish-fulfilled, diegetic, and wider-real nation lives them. The fact that myths are "real" in a nation's psyche means that they concern both insiders and outsiders involved with that nation's ideals and real and imagined borders. For example, we have seen how Cinqué, an African captive transplanted to Connecticut, became crucial to the collective (Americans' and Africans') effort that changed the meaning of the American nation for Americans.

Winning a Continent constructs and exaggerates a myth of Boer achievement.[66] This exaggeration connotes the fact that *Winning a Continent*'s diegesis is constructed by collapsing conceptual time. In addition to *Winning a Continent*'s scriptwriter Preller being a Trek Boer descendant and director Shaw's Southern US cultural-national point of enunciation and attraction to the colonial, the transnational if not transcontinental solidarity among those who controlled the production of *Winning a Continent*—the film's British production company (African Film Productions Ltd.) and the film's British target audience in terms of profit expectations—this transnational and transcontinental amplified solidarity can be seen as an early and perverse form of Gilroy's idea of planetarity.[67] *Winning a Continent* suppresses the complexity of black bodies by freezing and perverting time. As a result, *Winning a Continent* negates the idea of flowing multiple times and of fate and memory in connection to black bodies.

christianity, cruelty: sobuza

In connection to the Zulu/Swazi warrior Sobuza and *Winning a Continent*, it helps to know that Zulu King Dingaan is the so-called cruel and barbaric half-brother of Zulu King Shaka; not only had Dingaan come to power by taking part in Shaka's murder, he would go on to instruct that his own baby son be murdered as well. This is shown clearly in a scene where the baby dangles dangerously upside down, by one leg, in Dingaan's hand before being taken away by Sobuza and other warriors.[68] The baby murder is also the culmination of a litany of diegetic Zulu cruel acts used in *Winning a Continent* to justify Sobuza's conversion to Christianity. Not only are black Zulu/Swazi bodies one-dimensional (cruel and barbaric) in the film, their sole chance of redemption must come also through what is in effect a non-African religion. Additionally, *Winning a Continent* demands that these black bodies be predisposed to possess, like Sobuza, "an internalisation of 'Thou shalt not kill.'"[69] As a result, the Zulu time(s) is (or are) stopped and black loyalty pledged to Trek Boers as the film shows an infantilized and emasculated Sobuza—a far cry from Draba, Juba, and Cinqué—defecting to Piet Retief in order to fight the Zulus: "Henceforth thou [i.e. Retief] art my Father and my Chief / And Thy people shall be my people" (film intertitle).[70] Furthermore, if Sobuza seeks refuge in "Thou shalt not kill" because he had been offended and repulsed by Zulu cruelty and barbarism, he is made to kill Dingaan nonetheless. Even if Sobuza's conversion could be read as logical in view of his so-called natural Christian emotional response to Zulu cruelty, I would still argue that *Winning a Continent* sets Sobuza an impossible task: i.e. to be both a tabula rasa-meets-Christian enlightenment and an incarnation of cruelty because Sobuza kills Dingaan.[71] One can only make sense of such "unreconciled strivings . . . warring ideals" by pointing out that Sobuza epitomizes "a glorification that turns immediately to denigration," a trademark of how Boers such as Preller included Zulu history into their own.[72]

seeds of (dis)union, myths-nostalgia: beyond lynch, gus, and lydia

The Birth of a Nation's treatment of black bodies is different from *Winning a Continent*'s but is equally extreme. *The Birth of a Nation* sustains its diegesis by subverting and exaggerating nation-building, something it achieves by blaming blacks for the Southern violent threat at the core of the North–South solidarity to which the film objects. *The Birth of a Nation*'s strategy is signaled early with the intertitle/title card, "The bringing of the African to America planted the first seed of disunion"; through omission, this statement embodies the fact that the film's whole title-card narrative clashes with the footage it presents. Indeed, Africans seem to have landed mysteriously in America since no slave trading or slavery of the kind seen in *Spartacus, Gladiator,* and *Amistad* seem to be responsible for their presence. As James Snead puts it, "While blacks happily picking cotton seeds in the fields are represented as the pride of a lost Golden Age (their labor being the 'seed' of what made Southern aristocratic life . . . possible), they themselves are called the 'seed of disunion.' Somehow, they cannot be both."[73] *The Birth* of a Nation overlooks such a problem in order to argue that "America is 'born' in the 1880s" and that "the harmonious bonds of this newborn nation" needed loyal blacks as one of its emblems.[74] Such an argument then clears the space for *The Birth of a Nation*'s depiction of blacks as naturally cruel or barbaric, expendable, and unredeemable.

The fact of living by myths implies moving from the unconscious to consciousness and realizing that a myth is not fictitious or imaginary. This dual process makes myths visible, and it is such emergence from invisibility that allows one to investigate the function of myths, past, present, and future. Indeed, myths "must remain invisible unless we name them"; a myth is "a story that speaks of meaning and purpose . . . speaks truth to those who take it seriously . . . a story that conveys commonly shared convictions on the purposes and the meaning of the nation."[75] Thus, the American Creed, through which Americans assert what "nation" means, is a myth in the same way that the so-called Great Trek is one for Boer nationalism. These two myths are glued to *The Birth of a Nation*'s and *Winning a Continent*'s diegesis through these texts' retrospective fixation on a questionable idea of "nation" that in turn determines the type of nostalgia they both embrace. As a case in point, *The Birth of a Nation* is nostalgic for an outdated way of life while decreeing that American history began in the 1880s: "'nostalgia' as 'history'"; similarly, *Winning a Continent* is "enamoured" with the so-called "expression of pioneer courage that justified the Boers' entitlement to land and consequently their imagination of nation."[76] At this juncture then, the question is no longer why *Winning a Continent*'s and *The Birth of a Nation*'s myths are based on black exclusion, suppression, and conscription. Rather, the issue is what does this reveal about myths in relation to black presence in or absence from the films? If, as suggested above, the makers of *Winning a Continent* and *The Birth of a Nation* could not control or handle the diegetic planetary-convivial, open, fluid, and changing black bodies, what does this mean for the presence–absence paradigm?

Myths are absolutized when those living by them deliberately overlook what is wrong with their "nation" and avoid engagement in "national self-examination."[77] The outer-national American Creed and the inflated Great Trek myths are absolutized in *Winning a Continent* and in *The Birth of a Nation*. Having seen through Draba, Juba, Cinqué, and Sobuza, but also through the Tarkovskyan mirror, how problematic *Winning a Continent*'s and *The Birth of a Nation*'s treatment of time is, the films' context of absolutized myths can help us understand further their respective attempts to silence black bodies. Black bodies are present in, and yet absent from, these films' voices: in *Winning a Continent*, black absence is partial because black representation is oversimplified, while in *The Birth of a Nation* black absence is total for Lynch and Gus were played by white actors in blackface in the same way that black characters in minor roles were played by the white actors who portrayed the Ku Klux Klan riders.[78] In summary then, black bodies are silenced in or disappear from *Winning a Continent* and *The Birth of a Nation*. However, this silence is precisely the site of black presence, black speech, and black voice, as we shall see in the conclusion to this chapter through black bodies' ability to break binaries.

conclusion: relate, converse and synchronize—toward a planetary-convivial-diasporic black body in epic cinema

Earlier, I asked if one could not draw on planetarity and other theories in order to free black bodies from *Winning a Continent*'s and *The Birth of a Nation*'s diegetic straitjackets before proceeding to offer beginnings of an answer through Paul Gilroy's planetarity and conviviality, theories speaking to empire-building and the aftermath of empire. If, as I have argued, black bodies can be convivial after "empire," and black perspectives on theory are less about discrete nations and cultures than about the idea of the diasporic, then, black bodies (literal and metaphorical) embody a myriad of national myths at the same time.

Thus, Black Atlantic theory has been important for this chapter because it unfixes and ex-centers space while accenting challenges to the ontology of the modern nation-state. I have demonstrated that this is philosopher Jonathan Rée's logic of internationality in effect and is useful for intercultural and transcultural locations of diegetic black bodies at the interstice of the local and the global. Such an active disabling, displacement or questioning of the national in analyses of diegetic black bodies in *Spartacus*, *Gladiator*, *Amistad*, *Winning a Continent*, and *The Birth of a Nation* offered in this chapter has demonstrated an appreciation of attributes Gilroy identifies as black agency, cognition, and intellectual history.

Consequently this chapter has suggested readings of *Spartacus*, *Gladiator*, *Amistad*, *Winning a Continent*, and *The Birth of a Nation* that take into account the implications of internationality, reconfiguration, and adaptation to new contested contact zones vis-à-vis the representation of black bodies in epic cinema—in different ways, Draba, Juba, Cinqué, and Sobuza have been cases in point. Contact-zones theory, in particular, has allowed the unpicking of *Winning a Continent*'s and *The Birth of a Nation*'s inability to see black bodies' shared histories, politics, and diasporic subjectivities, such as those at play in *Spartacus*, *Gladiator*, and *Amistad*. Additionally, contact-zones theory reaccents the need to establish, between black bodies in epic cinema, further multiple, cross-diaporic links and experiences unpicked from this chapter's corpus—although such inquiry is beyond the scope of the present chapter.

Nonetheless, through the lens of Black Atlantic and contact-zones theories, Draba, Juba, and Cinqué have cast the portrayals of Sobuza, Chaka, and Dingaan (*Winning a Continent*) and of white actors in blackface (*The Birth of a Nation*) in such a way as to break binaries evident in both films' depiction of black bodies. These bodies have been reproblematized by rereading standard epic films set in Imperial Rome, Africa, and America and between these spaces. Therefore, being aware of the following becomes essential: if Sobuza is Swazi (i.e. from Swaziland), he connotes intra-African migration (the Zulu kingdom under Chaka and Dingaan covered a massive landmass), and, if Griffith used black actors, Lynch, Lydia and Gus would have embodied transcontinental uprooting. These dispersed bodies should be, and can be, allowed to communicate, interrelate, and even synchronize, not least because of their shared histories. The intersecting flows where Sobuza, Chaka, Dingaan, Draba, Juba, Cinqué, and (the absent blacks present through) Lynch, Lydia, and Gus are shaped is also the location where they must communicate, interrelate, and synchronize. This intersection-place allows black bodies to challenge the status quo and to force a rethinking of their so-called subaltern positions. Draba dies a Stoic's death, Juba vows to fight on, Cinqué changes American perspectives on race and slavery: each one's motives and actions cannot be reduced to the nation or the local. Similarly, with *Winning a Continent*'s Chaka, Dingaan, and, in particular, Sobuza in mind, reading the ultimate scene of *Winning a Continent* as follows makes little sense: "the image of the black servant [to a white Treker family] Sobuza seated outside the church, acts as a reference point for a 'nation' that is very specifically and exclusively positioned . . . Without Sobuza's position as servant, the white 'nation' and its hegemony cannot survive."[79]

Indeed, one has to ask several questions of such a reading: what way out for Sobuza, whom it extracts from black, Zulu, and Swazi culture, converts to Christianity, leads to fight his own people and kill Zulu ruler Dingaan, and then reduces him to serving a family that symbolizes the future of a Boer "nation"? What of Sobuza's right to an excentric space, mainly when the diegetic "nation" Maingard discusses is based on exaggeration and a questionable view of history? The Zulus' enduring (diegetic) position as "Faithful Servant" has never been more than an illusion from above that masqueraded as reality through a repressive state apparatus. Similarly, the so-called binding between black and white identities can never rise beyond historical wish-fulfillment, unless black history, agency, cognitive capacities, and black purpose are acknowledged as distinct, and taken seriously.

notes

1. I understand race "as an analytical concept referring to the social construction of ideas related to different ethnic and cultural groups and formations. I recognize that race in general, and Blackness in particular, exists and is represented through a range of variables such as class, religion, gender and sexuality." For further details, see Sarita Malik, *Representing Black Britain: Black and Asian Images on Television* (London: Sage Publications, 2002), p. 3.
2. Paul Gilroy, *After Empire: Melancholia or Convivial Culture?* (London: Routledge, 2004), p. xii. This solidarity aspect of the planetarity can be perverse.

Perversity happens when one tries to render worldly "angles of vision" parochial (see Gilroy, *After Empire*, p. xi). On the subject of the global as a "threat," see, for example, the special issue of *Race & Class*, 40 (2/3) (October 1998–November 1999) titled "The Threat of Globalism," especially John Berger's "Against the Defeat of the World" (pp. 1–4) and James Davis and Cheryl Bishop's "The MAI: Multiculturalism from Above" (pp. 159–170).

3. Paul Gilroy, "Route Work: The Black Atlantic and the Politics of Exile," in Ian Chambers and Lidia Curti (eds.), *The Post-Colonial Question: Common Skies, Divided Horizons* (London and New York: Routledge, 2008) pp. 17–29; p. 22.

4. Gilroy, *After Empire*, p. xi.

5. Petty borrows "the term *contact zones* from James Clifford as a means of describing the way in which different experiences of the black diaspora are constituted in transcultural contexts." See Sheila Petty, *Contact Zones: Memory, Origin, and Discourses in Black Diasporic Cinema* (Detroit, Mich.: Wayne State University Press, 2008), p. 259, footnote 1.

6. Gilroy, "Route Work: The Black Atlantic and the Politics of Exile," p. 22

7. Jonathan Rée, "Internationality," *Radical Philosophy*, 60 (1992): pp. 3–11; p. 9.

8. Paul Gilroy, *The Black Atlantic: Modernity and Double-Consciousness* (London: Verso), p. 6.

9. Gilroy, *The Black Atlantic*, pp. 17, 6.

10. Gilroy, *The Black Atlantic*, pp. 7, 6.

11. Robert Burgoyne, *The Hollywood Historical Film* (Malden, Mass.: Blackwell, 2008), pp. 74–75. Burgoyne makes this point when discussing the interconnections between *Spartacus*, *Gladiator*, and American national identity.

12. Petty, *Contact Zones*, p. 6.

13. Anthony W. Marx, *Making Race and Nation: A Comparison of the United States, South Africa and Brazil* (Cambridge: Cambridge University Press, 1998), p. 18.

14. Marx, *Making Race and Nation*, p. 18.

15. See, for example, George Faraday, *Revolt of the Filmmakers: The Struggle for Artistic Autonomy and the Fall of the Soviet Film Industry* (Pennsylvania, Pa.: Pennsylvania State University Press, 2000), pp. 88–109, especially; Anna Lawton (ed.), *The Red Screen: Politics, Society, Art in Soviet Cinema* (London and New York: Routledge, 1992); and Herbert Marshall, *Masters of the Soviet Cinema: Crippled Creative Biographies* (London: Routledge & Kegan Paul, 1983).

16. Mark Le Fanu, *The Cinema of Andrei Tarkovsky* (London: BFI, 1987), p. 73.

17. Le Fanu, *The Cinema of Andrei Tarkovsky*, p. 73.

18. Le Fanu, *The Cinema of Andrei Tarkovsky*, p. 73.

19. Andrei Tarkovsky, *Sculpting in Time: Reflections on the Cinema*, trans. Kitty Hunter-Blair (London: Faber & Faber, 1989), p. 114.

20. Tarkovsky, *Sculpting in Time*, p. 113.

21. Tarkovsky, *Sculpting in Time*, p. 117. (My emphasis.)

22. Tarkovsky, *Sculpting in Time*, p. 118.

23. Martin M. Winkler, "The Holy Cause of Freedom: American Ideals in *Spartacus*," in Martin M. Winkler (ed.), *Spartacus: Film and History* (Oxford: Blackwell Publishing), pp. 154–188; p. 174.

24. Winkler, "The Holy Cause of Freedom: American Ideals in *Spartacus*," p. 175.

25. I have argued this point elsewhere as follows: "Not only can the opposition black–white be transcended, it can certainly be avoided or ignored as well: black does not (always) need white in order to make sense. If black (always) needed white in this regard, the notion of black alternative experience and tradition, central to black cinema, would never have made sense, or carry

any conceptual weight." See Saër Maty Bâ, "*Voix noires:* Black Documentary Theory, 'The Black Moving Cube,'" in D. A. Bailey (ed.), *The Black Moving Cube: Black Figuration and the Moving Image* (Berlin: The Green Box), pp. 31–54; p. 32.

26. On the topic of Hollywood's depiction of blackness, see, for example, Thomas Cripps, *Slow Fade to Black: The Negro in American Film, 1900–1942* (Oxford: Oxford University Press, 1977); Ed Guerrero, *Framing Blackness: The African-American Image in Film* (Philadelphia, Pa.: Temple University Press, 1993); and Donald Bogle, *Toms, Coons, Mammies, & Bucks: An Interpretive History of Blacks in American Films* (Oxford: Roundhouse, 1994).

27. Winkler, "The Holy Cause of Freedom", p. 173.

28. Ina Rae Hark, "Animals or Romans: Looking at Masculinity in *Spartacus,*" in Steve Cohan and Ina Rae Hark (eds), *Screening the Male: Exploring Masculinities in Hollywood Cinema* (London and New York: Routledge, 1993), pp. 151–172; p. 154.

29. Hark, "Animals or Romans," p. 154.

30. Robert Burgoyne, *The Hollywood Historical Film* (Malden, Mass.: Blackwell), pp. 74-75.

31. Francisco Javier Tovaz Paz, "*Spartacus* and the Stoic Ideal of Death," in Martin M. Winkler (ed.), *Spartacus: Film and History* (Oxford: Blackwell Publishing), pp. 189–197; pp. 195–196.

32. Paz, "*Spartacus* and the Stoic Ideal of Death," p. 191.

33. Paz, "*Spartacus* and the Stoic Ideal of Death," p. 191.

34. Paz, "*Spartacus* and the Stoic Ideal of Death," p. 195.

35. Paz, "*Spartacus* and the Stoic Ideal of Death," p. 196.

36. Paz, "*Spartacus* and the Stoic Ideal of Death," p. 196.

37. Hark, "Animals and Romans," p. 160. Of course, Draba's death ties in well with suicides during the Middle Passage and slavery in general. For example, in the film *Amistad,* analyzed below, a woman quietly throwing herself overboard *La Amistad* with a baby in her arms, and Cinqué leads a potentially suicidal slave rebellion.

38. For Ancient Nubians, "[a] "cache" is a sacred store for precious objects that deserved respect and protection . . . the location of the caches is not random, since they are found in or very near the temples." See Charles Bonnet and Dominique Valbelle, *The Nubian Pharaohs: Black Kings on the Nile* (Cairo and New York: American University in Cairo Press, 2006), p. 174.

39. "During excavations such as those conducted at Kerma [in 2003], archaeologists are often amazed at the profusion of statues. Usually . . . they are small-scale statuettes." See Bonnet and Valbelle, *The Nubian Pharaohs,* p. 174. Additionally, when discussing the above-mentioned archaeological discovery, Jean Clelant argues: "We now have a much better idea of the long-underestimated originality of Nubian culture and its deep roots in an extremely distant past. The weight of this Nubian past did not . . . rule out openness to other cultural models, particularly Egyptian. Certainly, many . . . will be delighted to find here unexpectedly concrete evidence of negritude. We are thus a long way from the purely theoretical speculation that once animated conversations about Kushite civilization." See Jean Clelant, "Foreword," in Bonnet and Valbelle, *The Nubian Pharaohs,* pp. 7–9; p. 11.

40. The phrase "voice of God" is adapted from documentary film theory which defines it, among other things, as emanating from a commentator "with a deep, male voice [who] informs us about some aspect of the world in an

impersonal but authoritative manner." See Bill Nichols, *Introduction to Documentary* (Bloomington, Ind.: Indiana University Press, 2001), p. 17. Juba has a deep, male voice, is authoritative but not impersonal.

41. Burgoyne, *The Hollywood Historical Film*, p. 97.

42. Burgoyne, *The Hollywood Historical Film*, p. 90.

43. Burgoyne, *The Hollywood Historical Film*, p. 90.

44. P. W. Rose, "The Politics of *Gladiator*," in Martin M. Winkler (ed.), *Gladiator: Film and History* (Oxford: Blackwell, 2005), pp. 151–172; p. 163. Burgoyne, *The Hollywood Historical Film*, p. 90.

45. Nigel Morris, *The Cinema of Steven Spielberg: Empire of Light* (London and New York: Wallflower Press 2007), p. 252.

46. Burgoyne, *The Hollywood Historical Film*, p. 86. See also Note 3 above.

47. Lester D. Friedman, *Citizen Spielberg* (Urbana, Ill.: University of Illinois Press, 2006), pp. 281, 280–281.

48. Friedman, *Citizen Spielberg*, p. 259.

49. Morris, *The Cinema of Steven Spielberg*, p. 259.

50. Please note Morris's different use of the phrase, i.e. to describe the legal process which "accords Cinqué a voice." See *The Cinema of Steven Spielberg*, p. 260.

51. Gilroy, *The Black Atlantic*, p. 6.

52. In contrast, ex-President Adams appears nervous and stressed, if not ashamed of the risks America had been taking by not purging firmly slave trading and slavery out of its system.

53. My emphasis.

54. By "spirit-possession," I understand a dialectics of strong and compelling history and ethnography turning into spirits that possess their human host while allowing the possessed to remain or to become a subject in her or his own right. For further details, see Heike Behrend and Ute Luig (eds.), *Spirit Possession: Modernity and Power in Africa* (Oxford: James Currey, 1999) from which I have drawn this particular idea of spirit-possession.

55. Friedman, *Citizen Spielberg*, p. 276.

56. Robert T. Hughes, *Myths America Lives By* (Urbana, Ill.: University of Illinois Press, 2003), p. 3.

57. Peter Davis, *In Darkest Hollywood: Exploring the Jungles of Cinema's South Africa* (Athens, Ohio: Ohio University Press. 1996), p. 128.

58. Jacqueline Maingard, *South African National Cinema* (London and New York: Routledge, 2007), p. 24; Davis, *In Darkest Hollywood*, p. 129.

59. On *The Birth of a Nation* as an Old South epic, see Guerrero, *Framing Blackness*, p. 10; for details of the film's screening and reception in South Africa, see Maingard, *South African National Cinema*, p. 19.

60. Davis, *In Darkest Hollywood*, pp. 128, 132, 134. Maingard, *South African National Cinema*, p. 21.

61. Guerrero, *Framing Blackness*, p. 11.

62. M. Rogin "'The Sword Became a Flashing Vision': D. W. Griffith's *The Birth of a Nation*," in R. Lang (ed.), *The Birth of a Nation: D. W. Griffith, Director* (New Brunswick, NJ: Rutgers University Press, 1994), pp. 250–293; p. 268.

63. Studies of and approaches, comparative or not, tend to gravitate around the following key aspects: rape and the threat of rape (black man on young white woman), the emphasis on the woman's menstruating age and whiteness, as well as the excessive racism outlined above. See, for example, Rogin "'The Sword," and Jane M. Gaines, "Birthing Nations," in Mette Hjort

and Scott Mackenzie (eds.), *Cinema and Nation* (London and New York: Routledge, 2000).

64. Gaines "Birthing Nations," p. 299.

65. Even when actively suppressed, as in *De Voortrekkers,* the connection remains: "The impetus for [the Great Trek] migration was a desire to escape from British rule, which threatened the Boers' slave economy. However, this historical background is suppressed in the film." See Davis, *In Darkest Hollywood,* p. 129.

66. Boers were supposed to be "Winning a Continent," and the very top of the film's original 1916 poster reads "South Africa's national film."

67. For details, see Note 10 of this chapter or Gilroy, *After Empire,* p. xi.

68. Sobuza disobeys Dingaan's order to kill the baby. As a result, he is humiliated and expulsed from the Zulus.

69. Gaines, "Birthing Nations," p. 310.

70. "Sobuza becomes part of the voortrekker family . . . as a servant of a particular kind. Soon after his arrival at [Piet Retief's] camp, he is preparing to cook an evening meal—something normally done by women . . . Not only has the warrior Sobuza been domesticated, he has been emasculated—turned into a nanny." See Davis, *In Darkest Hollywood,* p. 134.

71. Following the Zulu Army's defeat, Sobuza hunts Dingaan down and kills him "in personal combat." See Davis, *In Darkest Hollywood,* p. 134.

72. These strivings and ideals are described as such in W. E. B. DuBois, *The Souls of Black Folk* (New York: Dover, 1994), p. 2. For the Boers' problematic inclusion of Zulus into Boer history, see Gaines, "Birthing Nations," p. 311.

73. James Snead, *White Screens, Black Images: Hollywood from the Dark Side* (New York and London: Routledge 1989), p. 43.

74. Snead, *White Screens, Black Images,* pp. 43, 39.

75. Hughes, *Myths America Lives By,* pp. 8, 2.

76. For nostalgia as history see Snead, *White Screens, Black Images,* p. 43; and, regarding the connection between *De Voortrekkers* and the Boers' imagination of nation, Gaines, "Birthing Nations," p. 301.

77. Hughes, *Myths America Lives By,* p. 4.

78. Additionally, as already mentioned, there were no black actors employed in major roles and no black actor's name appears in the film credits. "Griffith would not use blacks because he thought they could not act" (Davis, *In Darkest Hollywood,* p. 8). Davis makes this comment in relation to a seven-minute melodrama Griffith made for Biograph Studio in 1908 entitled *A Zulu's Heart.* Having acquired a copy of this film when researching this project, I would echo Davis's following comments, made in *In Darkest Hollywood,* pp. 9, 8: "Griffith's Zulus either threaten whites, or serve them. The Zulu chief, who does both in turn, is a Noble Savage . . . Shot in New Jersey, across the Hudson River from Biograph's New York headquarters, with white actors playing the Zulu roles . . . this primitive film demands a considerable suspension of belief." When seen in relation to *The Birth of a Nation, The Zulu's Heart* illustrates Griffith's perversion of planetarity—what should have been worldly angles of vision were simply rendered perversely parochial.

79. Maingard, *South African National Cinema,* p. 22.

contributors

Dr. Saër Maty Bâ holds an MA in English and Wolof (Cheikh Anta Diop University, Senegal), an M.Phil. in American Cultural Studies (2002), and a Ph.D. in Film Studies (Documentary) (2006) from the University of Exeter. His research interests blur boundaries between black diaspora, film, media, and cultural studies and include visual and sonic cultures of the "Black Atlantic," cinema history, "intertexts" (across cultures and "national" cinemas), and the theory and practice of film representation. Prior to joining St Andrews in 2008, he held research fellowships in media film studies at the University of East London (2006–2007) and the National Institute for Excellence in the Creative Industries, Bangor University (2007–2008). His past and recent publications include "Visualising Rhythm, Transforming Relationship: Jazz and *Seven Songs for Malcolm X* (1993)," and "Gathering Dust in the Wind: Memory and the 'Real' in Rithy Panh's *S21* (France: INA, Arté France, 2002)".

Bruce Babington is Emeritus Professor of Film at Newcastle University. He has written extensively on the Hollywood, British, European and New Zealand cinemas. His latest books are the co-authored *Carmen on Film: A*

Cultural History (2007) and *A History of the New Zealand Fiction Feature Film* (2007). He is at present writing a book on the sports film.

Dr. Bettina Bildhauer is a lecturer in German at the University of St Andrews in Scotland. She studied medieval culture, art history, and film in Cologne and Cambridge. She is the editor of *Medieval Film* (2009, with Anke Bernau), of *The Monstrous Middle Ages* (2004, with Robert Mills) and author of *Medieval Blood* (2006). She is currently working on a medieval history of film.

Robert Burgoyne is Professor and Chair of Film Studies at the University of St Andrews. His research and publications focus on historical representation and film, narrative theory, and the relation of film to digital media. His recent work includes *Film Nation: Hollywood Looks at U.S. History*, revised edition (2010), and *The Hollywood Historical Film* (2008).

Ruby Cheung is Research Associate at the Centre for Film Studies at the University of St Andrews, Scotland. She holds a Ph.D. in Film Studies from the University of St Andrews and works on the Leverhulme Trust-funded project, Dynamics of World Cinema. Of third-generation Chinese immigrant origin, she was born and educated in Hong Kong before commencing university studies in the USA, followed by a decade in communications management for Hong Kong-based media, finance, and property corporations. Over the past twenty years she has lived and worked in Hong Kong, the USA, and the UK. She currently resides in Scotland. Cheung's research interests include East Asian cinemas, Asian film industries, diasporic film distribution, regional and national film policy, Chinese diasporic online fandom, and issues of film promotion. She is the editor of *Cinemas, Identities and Beyond* (2009) and the co-editor of *Film Festival Yearbook 2: Film Festivals and Imagined Communities* (2010). Her latest work includes investigations of diasporic online fandom of epic cinema, different funding models of specialized film festivals, as well as an anthology on Asian film festivals.

Tom Conley is Abbott Lawrence Lowell Professor in the Departments of Romance Languages and Visual/Environmental Studies at Harvard University. Author of *Cartographic Cinema* (2007), he has recently translated Marc Augé, *Casablanca: Movies and Memory* (2009). His *Errant Eye: Topography and Poetry in Renaissance France* is forthcoming (2010). Other works include *Film Hieroglyphs* and *The Graphic Unconscious* (2006 reeditions) and translations of Michel de Certeau, Gilles Deleuze, and others.

Monica S. Cyrino is Professor of Classics at the University of New Mexico. Her research focuses on the intersection of the ancient world and popular culture. She is the author of *Big Screen Rome* (2005) and *Aphrodite* (2010), and the editor of *Rome, Season One: History Makes Television* (2008). She has appeared as an academic consultant on the show *History vs. Hollywood* on the History Channel.

Anne Gjelsvik is a Professor at the Department of Art and Media Studies, Faculty of Arts, Norwegian University of Science and Technology, Norway. She has worked on popular cinema, film and violence and ethics, and the representation of gender in the media over a period of ten years. She has written extensively in Norwegian, her most central books being her latest publication on film and violence, *Bad and Beautiful*, and her book on film reviewing, *Eyes of Darkness: Film Reviewing, Analysis and Judgments* (*Mørkets Øyne: Filmkritikk, analyse og vurdering*, 2002). She has co-edited several books, among them *Femme Fatalities: Representations of Strong Women in the Media* (with Rikke Schubart, 2004). She is presently working on a book on representations of fatherhood in contemporary American and co-editing (together with Rikke Schubart) *Eastwood's Iwo Jima: A Critical Engagement with* Flags of Our Fathers *and* Letters from Iwo Jima (forthcoming 2010). She was also Chief Editor for the Norwegian media journal *Norsk Medietidsskrift* between 2002 and 2006.

Alison Griffiths is a Professor in the Department of Communication Studies at Baruch College, the City University of New York and a member of the doctoral faculty in Theater at the CUNY Graduate Center. She is the author of the award-winning *Wondrous Difference: Cinema, Anthropology, and Turn-of-the-Century Visual Culture* (2002), *Shivers Down Your Spine: Cinema, Museums, and the Immersive View* (2008) and numerous essays on precinema, museums, and visual culture. Her new book project examines nontheatrical film exhibition in museums, prisons, and hospitals from 1899 to 1930.

Leon Hunt is Senior Lecturer in Screen Media at Brunel University. He is the author of *British Low Culture: From Safari Suits to Sexploitation; Kung Fu Cult Masters: From Bruce Lee to Crouching Tiger;* and the BFI TV Classics volume on *The League of Gentlemen*, and co-editor of *East Asian Cinemas: Exploring Transnational Connections on Film*.

Dina Iordanova founded the Film Studies programme at Scotland's oldest University at St Andrews. She is Director of the Centre for Film Studies and runs the Leverhulme-funded project on Dynamics of World Cinema. Her publications address matters of international and peripheral cinema, particularly focusing on Eastern Europe and the Balkans. Her current work is concentrated on the international film industry and the festival circuit. She is the publisher of a series dedicated to various aspects of film festivals.

Mark Jancovich is Professor of Film and Television Studies at the University of East Anglia. He is the author of several books: *Horror* (1992), *The Cultural Politics of the New Criticism* (1993), *Rational Fears: American Horror in the 1950s* (1996), and *The Place of the Audience: Cultural Geographies of Film Consumption* (with Lucy Faire and Sarah Stubbings, BFI, 2003). He is also the editor of several collections: *Approaches to Popular Film* (with Joanne Hollows, 1995); *The Film Studies Reader* (with Joanne Hollows and Peter Hutchings, 2000); *Horror, The Film*

Reader (2001); *Quality Popular Television: Cult TV, the Industry and Fans* (with James Lyons, 2003); *Defining Cult Movies: The Cultural Politics of Oppositional Taste* (with Antonio Lazaro-Reboll, Julian Stringer and Andrew Willis, 2003); *Film Histories: An Introduction and Reader* (with Paul Grainge and Sharon Monteith, 2006); *Film and Comic Books* (with Ian Gordon and Matt McAllister, 2007); and *The Shifting Definitions of Genre: Essays on Labeling Films, Television Shows and Media* (with Lincoln Geraghty, 2008) . He was also the founder of *Scope: An Online Journal of Film Studies* and is the series editor (with Eric Schaefer) of the series Inside Popular Film, and (with Charles Acland) of the series Introductions to Film Genre. He is currently writing a history of horror in the 1940s.

Bhaskar Sarkar teaches in the Department of Film and Media at the University of California, Santa Barbara. He is the author of *Mourning the Nation: Indian Cinema in the Wake of Partition* (2009) and co-editor of the collection *Documentary Testimonies: Global Archives of Suffering* (2009). He is currently working on a monograph about plastic nationalisms in the era of the global.

Dr. Kirsten Moana Thompson is an Associate Professor and Director of the Film Studies Program in the Department of English at Wayne State University in Detroit, Michigan. She is the author of *Apocalyptic Dread: American Film at the Turn of the Millennium* (2007) and *Crime Films; Investigating the Scene* (2007) as well as essays on special effects, animation, and New Zealand cinema.

Phil Wagner is a doctoral student in the Department of Cinema and Media Studies at the University of California, Los Angeles. His most recent articles, "John Ford Made . . . Monsters?" and "Visionary Video: The Archive and the National Center for Experiments in Television," can be found in *Senses of Cinema* and *Afterimage*. He is currently elaborating his thought on aesthetic politics and social reenactment in a critical survey of DeMille's historical films.

filmography

The films are listed alphabetically, with the English language title listed first.

1900 (*Novecento*) (1976), dir. Bernardo Bertolucci. Italy, France, West Germany.

300 (2006), dir. Zack Snyder. USA.

300 Spartans, The (1962), dir. Rudolph Maté. USA.

Ajantrik (1958), dir. Ritwik Ghatak. India.

Alexander (2004), dir. Oliver Stone. Germany, USA, Netherlands, France, UK, Italy.

Alexander Nevsky (1938), dir. Sergei M. Eisenstein. Soviet Union.

Alexander the Great (1956), dir. Robert Rossen. USA, Spain.

Amistad (1997), dir. Steven Spielberg. USA.

Annie Oakley (1935), dir. George Stevens. USA.

Apocalypse Now (1979), dir. Francis Ford Coppola. USA.

Artificial Intelligence: AI (2001), dir. Steven Spielberg. USA.

Asoka (2001), dir. Santosh Sivan. India.

Attila (1954), dir. Pietro Francisci. Italy, France.

Aucassin and Nicolette (1975), dir. Lotte Reiniger. Canada.

Banquet, The (*Ye Yan*) (2006), dir. Xiaogang Feng. China.

Barabbas (1961), dir. Richard Fleischer. Italy.

Battleship Potemkin (*Bronenosets Potyomkin*) (1925), dir. Sergei M. Eisenstein. Soviet Union.

Beauty and the Beast (*La Belle et la bête*) (1946), dir. Jean Cocteau. France.

Beginning and the End, The (*Principio y fin*) (1993), dir. Arturo Ripstein. Mexico.

Bend of the River (1952), dir. Anthony Mann. USA.

Ben-Hur (1959), dir. William Wyler. USA.

Beowulf (1999), dir. Graham Baker. USA.

Best of Youth, The (*La meglio gioventù*) (2003), dir. Marco Tullio Giordana. Italy.

Better Tomorrow, A (*Ying hung boon sik*), dir. John Woo. Hong Kong.

Bible, The (1966), dir. John Huston. USA, Italy.

Birth of a Nation, The (1915), dir. D.W. Griffith. USA.

Black Shield of Falsworth, The (1954), dir. Rudolph Maté. USA.

Blade Runner (1982), dir. Ridley Scott. USA, Hong Kong.

Blood Brothers (*Gong wu*) (2004), dir. Ching-Po Wong. Hong Kong.

Border Incident (1959), dir. Anthony Mann. USA.

Bourne Supremacy, The (2004), dir. Paul Greengrass. USA, Germany.

Braveheart (1995), dir. Mel Gibson. USA.

Buffalo Bill (1994), dir. William A. Wellman. USA.

Bullet in the Head (*Die xue jie tou*) (1990), dir. John Woo. Hong Kong.

Bush Cinderella, The (1928), dir. Rudall Hayward. New Zealand.

Cabinet of Dr. Caligari, The (*Das Cabinet des Dr. Caligari*) (1920), dir. Robert Wiene. Germany.

Cabiria (1914), dir. Giovanni Pastrone. Italy.

Chronicle History of King Henry the Fifth with His Battell Fought at Agincourt in France, The (*Henry V*) (1944), dir. Laurence Olivier. UK.

Cimarron (1960), dir. Anthony Mann. USA.

Citizen Kane (1941), dir. Orson Welles. USA.

Cleopatra (1963), dir. Joseph L. Mankiewicz. UK, USA, Switzerland.

Cloud-Capped Star, The (*Meghe Dhaka Tara*) (1960), dir. Ritwik Ghatak. India.

Cloverfield (2008), dir. Matt Reeves. USA.

Colossus of Rhodes (*Il colosso di Rodi*) (1961), dir. Sergio Leone. Spain, Italy, France.

Conqueror, The (1956), dir. Dick Powell. USA.

Crouching Tiger, Hidden Dragon (*Wo hu cang long*) (2000), dir. Ang Lee. Taiwan, Hong Kong, USA, China.

Curse of the Golden Flower, The (*Man cheng jin dai huang jin jia*) (2006), dir. Zhang Yimou. Hong Kong, China.

Dawn of the Dead (2004), dir. Zack Snyder. USA, Canada, Japan, France.

Demetrius and the Gladiators (1954), Delmer Daves. USA.

Destiny (*Al-Massir*) (1997), dir. Youssef Chahine. France, Egypt.

Devil's Pit, The (1929), dir. Lewis D. Collins. USA.

Die Hard with a Vengeance (1995), dir. John McTiernan. USA.

Doctor Zhivago (1965), dir. David Lean. USA, Italy.

Earth (1998), dir. Deepa Mehta. India, Canada.

El Cid (1961), dir. Anthony Mann. Italy, USA, UK.

Emperor and the Assassin, The (*Jing ke ci qin wang*) (1998), dir. Kaige Chen. France, Japan, China.

Fall of the Roman Empire, The (1964), dir. Anthony Mann. USA.

Farewell My Concubine (*Ba wang bie ji*) (1993), dir. Kaige Chen. China, Hong Kong.

Fearless (*Huo yuan jia*) (2006), dir. Ronny Yu. China, Hong Kong, USA.

Fight Club (1999), dir. David Fincher. USA, Germany.

Fist of Fury (*Jing wu men*) (1972), dir. Wei Lo. Hong Kong.

Giant (1956), dir. George Stevens. USA.

Gladiator (2000), dir. Ridley Scott. UK, USA.

Golden Compass, The (2007), dir. Chris Weitz. USA, UK.

Golden Swallow (*Gam yin ji*) (1988), dir. Sing-Pui O. Hong Kong.

Golden Thread, The (*Subarnarekha*) (1965), dir. Ritwik Ghatak. India.

Gospel According to St. Matthew, The (*Il vangelo secondo Matteo*) (1964), dir. Pier Paolo Pasolini. Italy, France.

Great Mughal, The (*Mughal-E-Azam*) (1960), dir. K. Asif. India.

Greatest Story Ever Told, The (1965), dir. George Stevens. USA.

He Walked by Night (1948), dir. Alfred L. Werker. USA.

Hei Tiki (1935), dir. Alexander Markey.

Helen of Troy (1956), dir. Robert Wise. USA, Italy.

Hellboy (2004), dir. Guillermo del Toro. USA.

Hercules (*Le fatiche di Ercole*) (1958), dir. Pietro Francisci. Italy, Spain.

Hero (*Ying xiong*) (2002), dir. Zhang Yimou. Hong Kong, China.

Hinemoa (1913), dir. Gaston Méliès. USA.

House of Flying Daggers (*Shi mian mai fu*) (2004), dir. Zhang Yimou. China, Hong Kong.

I, Robot (2004), dir. Alex Proyas. USA, Germany.

Incredible Hulk, The (2008), dir. Louis Leterrier. USA.

Intolerance: Love's Struggle throughout the Ages (1916), dir. D. W. Griffith. USA.

Ivanhoe (1952), dir. Richard Thorpe. USA.

Jinnah (1998), dir. Jamil Dehlavi. UK, Pakistan.

Joan of Arc (1948), dir. Victor Fleming. USA.

Jodhaa Akbar (2008), dir. Ashutosh Gowariker. India.

Killer, The (*Dip huet seung hung*) (1989), dir. John Woo. Hong Kong.

King of Kings (1961), dir. Nicholas Ray. USA.

King of Kings, The (1927), dir. Cecil B. DeMille. USA.

King Richard and the Crusaders (1954), dir. David Butler. USA.

Kingdom of Heaven (2005), dir. Ridley Scott. UK, Spain, USA, Germany.

Knights of the Round Table (1953), dir. Richard Thorpe. USA.

Komal Gandhar (1961), dir. Ritwik Ghatak. India.

La Mujer del puerto (1991), dir. Arturo Ripstein. Mexico.

Lagaan: Once Upon a Time in India (2001), dir. Ashutosh Gowariker. India.

Last Hurrah for Chivalry (*Hao xia*), dir. John Woo. Hong Kong.

Last of the Mohicans, The (1992), dir. Michael Mann. USA.

Last Temptation of Christ, The (1998), dir. Martin Scorsese. USA.

Lawrence of Arabia (1962), dir. David Lean. UK.

Legend of Bhagat Singh, The (2002), dir. Rajkumar Santoshi. India.

Legend of King Naresuan: Hostage of Hongsawadi, The (*Naresuan*) (2006), dir. Chatrichalerm Yukol. Thailand.

Legend of Naresuan: Declaration in Independence, The (*Tamnaan somdet phra Naresuan maharat: Phaak prakaat itsaraphaap*) (2007), dir. Chatrichalerm Yukol. Thailand.

Legend of Suriyothai, The (*Suriyothai*) (2001), dir. Chatrichalerm Yukol. Thailand.

Leopard, The (*Il gattopardo*) (1963), dir. Luchino Visconti. Italy, France.

Lord of the Rings: The Return of the King, The (2003), dir. Peter Jackson. USA, Germany, New Zealand.

Lost World: Jurassic Park, The (1997), dir. Steven Spielberg. USA.

Magic Blade, The (*Tien ya ming yue dao*) (1976), dir. Yuen Chor. Hong Kong.

Magnificent Obsession (1954), dir. Douglas Sirk. USA.

Man of the West (1958), dir. Anthony Mann. USA.

Map of the Human Heart (1993), dir. Vincent Ward. Australia, UK, Canada, France.

Martial Club, The (*Wu guan*) (1981), dir. Chia-Liang Liu. Hong Kong.

Matrix, The (1999), dirs. Andy Wachowski and Larry Wachowski. USA, Australia.

Meet the Spartans (2008), dirs. Jason Friedberg and Aaron Seltzer. USA.

Michael the Brave (*Mihai Viteazul*) (1970), dir. Sergiu Nicolaescu. Romania.

Minority Report (2002), dir. Steven Spielberg. USA.

Miracle Alley (*El callejón de los milagros*) (1995), dir. Jorge Fons. Mexico.

Mirror, The (*Zerkalo*) (1975), dir. Andrei Tarkovsky. Soviet Union.

Mongol (2007), dir. Sergei Bodrov. Kazakhstan, Mongolia, Russia, Germany.

Mother India (*Bharat Mata*) (1957), dir. Mehboob Khan.

Moulin Rouge (2001), dir. Baz Luhrmann. USA, Australia.

Mr. Deeds Goes to Town (1936), dir. Frank Capra. USA.

My Lady of the Cave (1922), dir. Rudall Hayward. New Zealand.

Navigator: A Medieval Odyssey, The (1988), dir. Vincent Ward. Australia, New Zealand.

Nomad (2005), dirs. Sergei Bodrov and Ivan Passer. France, Kazakhstan.

O Brother, Where Art Thou? (2000), dir. Joel Coen. UK, France, USA.

October: Ten Days that Shook the World (*Oktyabr*) (1928), dirs. Grigori Aleksandrov and Sergei M. Eisenstein. Soviet Union.

Olympia: Part One: Festival of the Nations (*Olympia 1. Teil - Fest der Völker*) (1938), dir. Leni Reifenstahl. Germany.

Once a Thief (*Zong heng si hai*) (1991), dir. John Woo. Hong Kong.

Once Upon a Time in China II (*Wong Fei Hung II: Nam yi dong ji keung*) (1992), dir. Hark Tsui. Hong Kong.

Once Were Warriors (1994), dir. Lee Tamahori. New Zealand.

Oregon Trail, The (1959), dir. Gene Fowler Jr. USA.

Paint It Yellow (*Rang De Basanti*) (2006), dir. Rakesh Omprakash Mehra. India.

Passion of the Christ, The (2004), dir. Mel Gibson. USA.

Phantom of the Opera, The (2004), dir. Joel Schumacher. USA, UK.

Piano, The (1993), dir. Jane Campion. Australia, New Zealand, France.

Place without Limits (*El lugar sin límites*) (1978), dir. Arturo Ripstein.

Plainsman, The (1936), dir. Cecil B. DeMille. USA.

Polar Express, The (2004), dir. Robert Zemeckis. USA.

Poseidon (2006), dir. Wolfgang Petersen. USA.

Prayer for Hetman Mazepa, A (*Molitva za getmana Mazepu*) (2002), dir. Yuri Ilienko. Ukraine.

Prince Valiant (1954), dir. Henry Hathaway. USA.

Promise, The (*Wu ji*) (2005), dir. Kaige Chen. China, USA, South Korea.

Quo Vadis (1925), dir. Gabriellino D'Annunzio and Georg Jacoby. Italy.

Rabia Balkhi (1965), dir. Abdullah Shadaan. Afghanistan.

Ran (1985), dir. Akira Kurosawa. France, Japan.

Rashômon (1950), dir. Akira Kurosawa. Japan.

Ratatouille (2007), dirs. Brad Bird and Jan Pinkava. France.

Raw Deal (1948), dir. Anthony Mann. USA.

Red Cliff (Chi bi) (2008), John Woo. China.

Reign of Terror (The Black Book) (1948), dir. Anthony Mann. USA.

Rewi's Last Stand (1925), dir. Rudall Hayward. New Zealand.

Rising: Ballad of Mangal Pandey, The (2005), dir. Ketan Mehta. India.

River Queen (2005), dir. Vincent Ward. New Zealand, UK.

Rocco and His Brothers (Rocco e i suoi fratelli) (1960), dir. Luchino Visconti. Italy, France.

Romance of Hine-Moa, The (1927), dir. Gustav Pauli. New Zealand, UK.

Saladin (El Naser Salah el Dine) (1963), dir. Youssef Chahine. Egypt.

Saving Private Ryan (1998), dir. Steven Spielberg. USA.

Searchers, The (1956), dir. John Ford. USA.

Seven Swords (Chat gim) (2005), dir. Hark Tsui. South Korea, Hong Kong, China.

Shrek (2001), dir. Andrew Adamson and Vicky Jenson.USA.

Sign of the Cross, The (1932), dir. Cecil B. DeMille. USA.

Sign of the Pagan (1954), dir. Douglas Sirk. USA.

Sin City (2005), dirs. Frank Miller and Robert Rodriguez. USA.

Sodom and Gomorrah (1962), dir. Robert Aldrich. USA, Italy, France.

Soft Note on a Sharp Scale, A (Komal Gandhar), dir. Ritwik Ghatak. India.

Solomon and Sheba (1959), dir. King Vidor. USA.

Spartacus (1960), dir. Stanley Kubrick. USA.

Spirit, The (2008), dir. Frank Miller. USA.

Stardust (2007), dir. Matthew Vaughn. UK, USA.

Subarnarekha (1962), dir. Ritwik Ghatak. India.

Te Kooti Trail, The (1927), dir. Rudall Hayward. New Zealand.

Ten Commandments, The (1923), dir. Cecil B. DeMille. USA.

Ten Commandments, The (1956), dir. Cecil B. DeMille. USA.

Terrorizer (Kong bu fen zi) (1986), dir. Edward Yang. Taiwan, Hong Kong.

The Man from Laramie (1955), dir. Anthony Mann. USA.

The Naked Spur (1953), dir. Anthony Mann. USA.

The Robe (1953), dir. Henry Koster. USA.

There Will Be Blood (2007), dir. Paul Thomas Anderson. USA.

Three Kingdoms: Resurrection of the Dragon (Saam gwok dzi gin lung se gap) (2008), dir. Daniel Lee. China, South Korea, Hong Kong.

Time to Love and a Time to Die, A (1958), dir. Douglas Sirk. USA.

To Live (*Huozhe*) (1994), dir. Zhang Yimou. China, Hong Kong.

Triumph of the Will (*Triumph des Willens*) (1935), dir. Leni Riefenstahl. Germany.

Troy (2004), dir. Wolfgang Petersen. USA, Malta, UK.

Utu (1983), dir. Geoff Murphy. New Zealand.

Vigil (1984), dir. Vincent Ward. New Zealand.

Vikings, The (1958), dir. Richard Fleischer. USA.

Wall-E (2008), dir. Andrew Stanton. USA.

Warlords, The (*Tau ming chong*) (2007), dirs. Peter Chan and Wai Man Yip. China, Hong Kong.

Whale Rider (2002), dir. Niki Caro. New Zealand, Germany.

What Dreams May Come (1998), dir. Vincent Ward. USA, New Zealand.

Who Killed the Shadows? (*Hacivat Karagöz neden öldürüldü?*) (2006), dir. Ezel Akay, Turkey.

Winchester '73 (1950), dir. Anthony Mann. USA.

Winning a Continent (*Die Voortrekkers*) (1916), dir. Harold M. Shaw. USA.

World Trade Center (2006), dir. Oliver Stone, USA.

X-Men (2000), dir. Bryan Singer. USA.

index